CENTER FOR JEWISH STUDIES

HARVARD JUDAICA TEXTS AND STUDIES

II

HARVARD UNIVERSITY
CENTER FOR JEWISH STUDIES

Jewish Thought in the Sixteenth Century

Edited by
BERNARD DOV COOPERMAN

Distributed by
HARVARD UNIVERSITY PRESS
Cambridge, Massachusetts and London, England
1983

Printed in the United States of America

Main entry under title:

Jewish thought in the sixteenth century.

(Texts and studies / Harvard University Center for Jewish Studies ; 2)

1. Judaism—History—Medieval and early modern period, 425–1789—Addresses, essays, lectures.

2. Jews—Intellectual life—History—16th century—Addresses, essays, lectures. I. Cooperman, Bernard Dov, 1946- . II. Series: Texts and studies ; 2.

BM193.J48 1983 296'.09'031 83-13006
ISBN 0-674-47461-9
ISBN 0-674-47462-7 (pbk.)

ISBN (cloth) 0-674-47461-9
ISBN (paper) 0-674-47462-7

Publication of this book was made possible by funds from the William Landau Lecture and Publication Fund, Harvard University Center for Jewish Studies.

Printed by
Harvard University Printing Office

Contents

Preface

The international colloquium on "Jewish Thought in the Sixteenth Century" was funded in part by a generous grant from the National Endowment for the Humanities to the Harvard University Center for Jewish Studies. The Center would like to express its thanks for this support.

Income from the William Landau Lecture and Publication Fund established at the Harvard University Center for Jewish Studies by the family of the late William Landau helped make the publication of this volume possible.

Thanks are due to Ms Shirley Siroka and Ms Carol Cross for their help in typing and re-typing parts of the manuscript, and to the staff of the Harvard University Printing Office, particularly Mr. Peter Imrie and Ms Joni Rosenblatt, for their patient and careful attention to a long task.

In preparing this volume for publication, the editor has striven for a degree of uniformity between papers, recognizing however that variations in form, style and presentation inevitably remain. Hebrew characters have been transcribed in a fashion as close as possible to common Israeli pronunciation.

Bernard Dov Cooperman

Cambridge, Mass.,
Autumn, 1982.

INTRODUCTION

Jewish Thought in the Sixteenth Century: Problems and Perspectives

I

This large volume, distinguished by original analyses, authoritative syntheses, and sophisticated suggestions for revisionist approaches to certain problems, contains most of the papers prepared for the international colloquium on "Jewish Thought in the Sixteenth Century" which was held at Harvard University under the auspices of the Center for Jewish Studies. Our ambitious goal was to assimilate the substantial advances of scholarly research of recent decades, to deal with topics which have not received sufficient attention, to emphasize unperceived connections, to make available unknown literary or archival materials, and to reflect new perspectives gained from shifts in thought, sensibility and information or interpretation. There would also be an unavoidable increment, both substantive and theoretical. Inasmuch as any period may serve as a microcosm of the total Jewish historical process and experience, we knew that certain overarching methodological and conceptual questions would inevitably be of great concern as well. This was particularly true in our case because of the fact that the sixteenth century has long been recognized as a crucial period in Jewish history—what Selma Stern labeled a "fateful turn in history"—a period of synthesis and innovation, expulsion and relocation, decline of old centers and burgeoning of new ones, intellectual turmoil and resourcefulness, cultural decline and transformation together with creativity and versatility, religious restlessness and resurgence, spiritual challenge and response. This characterization is valid regardless of what one prefers to see at the core of the century: the sunset of Spanish-Jewish history, the dynamism of east-European Jewry, the creativity and diversity of

Italian Jewry, or the vitality of the centers in Turkey and the Land of Israel (particularly Safed). It was, moreover, a century which left its mark on subsequent developments in Judaism and Jewish history: authoritative codification of Halakhah and a practically unbroken chain of commentaries, supercommentaries, glosses and animadversions all relating to this authoritative code (the *Shulḥan Arukh*); liturgical creativity and the final formation of the *sidur* (e.g., *kabalat shabat*, insertion of relevant Zoharic passages, directives [*kavanot*] for proper contemplation during the recitation of various benedictions); kabbalistic and ethical sources of Hasidism (e.g., Lurianic thought, such big popular works as Sefer *Ḥaredim* and *Reshit Ḥokhma*, writings of the MaHaRaL); the emergence of eastern Europe as the dominant center of Jewish life until the Holocaust; the intermittent but intense attachment to the Land of Israel (the romantic attempt to rebuild Tiberias, the kabbalistic activity in Safed, the movement to re-introduce ordination in the so-called "*smikha* controversy" and the migration or visits by individuals and groups all attest to this); and finally the long-range negative consequences of the dormancy of the philosophic tradition, particularly in eastern Europe, at the very time that the general Enlightenment begins to influence Judaism. It was, in sum, a period of continuities and discontinuities—an obvious feature of any historical epoch — with its special paradoxes, acute problems and, consequently, unique features. We aimed to produce a carefully circumscribed work of analysis and synthesis of major intellectual-spiritual developments for which, *mutatis mutandis*, we might appropriate the title of Henry Osborn Taylor's work: *Thought and Expression in the Sixteenth Century*.

The topic presented many stimuli and problems. We had certain ideas and expectations, elaborated some guidelines, emphasized the a priori importance of certain themes and genres as well as places, but also allowed for a measure of flexibility which would be shaped by the contributors and their divergent approaches to the diversified sources and interlocking themes.

II

While we tried to minimize exclusively biographical presentations, we knew that certain key figures would obviously and appropriately occupy important roles in many papers. Such figures—

the list is representative, not exhaustive—as Solomon Alkabetz, Yoḥanan Alemanno, Moses Alsheikh, Eliezer Ashkenazi, Saul Cohen Ashkenazi, Eliezer Azikri, Elijah Baḥur, Jacob Berav, Elijah Capsali, Moses Cordovero, Elijah Del Medigo, Azriel Diena, Leone Ebreo (Judah Abravanel), Menaḥem Azariah da Fano, Abraham Farissol, Azariah Figo, David Gans, Jacob ibn Gabbai, Jacob ibn Ḥabib, Abraham Isaac ha-Levi, Isaiah Horowitz, Moses Isserles, Mordekhai Jaffe, Isaac Campanton and his many disciples, Joseph Karo, Judah Messer Leon and his son David, Ephraim Luntshitz, Isaac Luria, Solomon Luria, Abraham ibn Migash, Leone da Modena, Judah Moscato, Judah Loeb of Prague (MaHaRaL), Abraham Portaleone, Azariah de Rossi, Abraham Saba, Abraham Shalom, Obadiah Sforno, Joseph Taytatzak and his disciples, Elijah de Vidas, Yeḥiel of Pisa, Joseph Yavetz and David ben Solomon ibn Zimra—all of these figures concerned many of the authors at different points. Careful, co-ordinated study of the papers would thus yield a significant biographical dividend. Talmudists, biblical exegetes, philosophers, kabbalists, ethicists, homilists, chroniclers—they all, with a sharp perception of contemporary realities and needs as related to eternal verities and ideals, embody the charming heterogeneity and colorful creativity, the tensions and turmoil of the time. While contributing to the cultural macrocosm of the sixteenth century, each one in the galaxy is intrinsically important and deserves comprehensive analysis as a micro-unit. In any event, the "biographical approach" to history, which we did not adopt, may be quite instructive and illuminating; the field of Jewish biography is not very well cultivated—witness the state of research concerning the names on this list. Any advances, however slight, and even if unintentional, are therefore welcome.

We also expected that certain topics would recur with some frequency, examined and assessed from different vantage points: e.g., change and continuity; the influence of non-Jewish thought (particularly in the Renaissance—was there only surface contact or was there a genuine impact of one on the other?—and the question is applicable not only to Italy but to Germany and even Poland); the role of the Counter-Reformation; Jewish-Christian polemics; the attack on, and defense of, the Oral Law; popular genres (e.g., homilies, commentaries) as vehicles of Jewish thought; the relation of literary form to content; unity and diversity within various Jewish centers; the impact and repercussions of Lurianic Kabbalah and the fate of pre-Lurianic Kabbalah; historical periodization from the point of view of Jewish thought; the re-emergence of "orthodox" Aristotelianism; the confrontation, co-existence, or intermingling of philosophy and Kabbalah; eclecticism and/or originality, especially in a period when the authority and appeal of classical works were widely recognized; wide-ranging, often passionate, interpretations of *galut* (the diaspora) and the Jewish historical experience; the impact of the Spanish expulsion—trauma together with a quickened pace of creativity; and the relation of systematic thought (as in philosophy and Halakhah) to popular religion. Here again the overlapping would be fruitful and zeroing in on the same theme from different angles would produce vivid, revealing insights, a stereoscopic view not otherwise available. The presumed role of the Renaissance as a stimulus for Jewish historical writing and thinking or the assumed role of the Counter-Reformation in the accelerated decline of philosophy are good examples. These assumptions are critically assessed and related to other perspectives. The relation between the metaphysical (cosmological, philosophical, theosophical) and ethical components of the various systems of thought and the greater influence of the ethical teachings—this is the heyday of kabbalistic ethics and pietistic writing in the form of monographs, wills, commentaries, *hanhagot*, or moral-halakhic manuals—is still another. Awareness of this far-reaching principle helps us understand the role of philosophic and/or mystical speculation in Jewish history.

Within this topical array, it was clear that some phenomena would actually deserve to occupy center stage: the apparent waning of philosophy, its remarkable recrudescence in certain forms, and the variety of motives (intellectual, apologetic, spiritualistic) for its study; the ascendancy of Kabbalah, the magnificent *summa, Pardes Rimonim*, of R. Moses Cordovero, and the dramatic appearance of the all-embracing Lurianic system recorded and elaborated by R. Ḥayyim Vital and his disciples as well as by other authors such as R. Israel Sarug and R. Joseph ibn Tabul; the jostling of rationalism and anti-rationalism; the continued, ramified halakhic creativity with its special achievements in codification, manuals of methodology and commentaries on Maimonides' *Mishne Tora* as well as heated debates concerning the proper methods of Talmud study; the centrality of ethical teachings (particularly kabbalistic ones) and their rapid, intensive dissemination; the relative but not enduring efflorescence of historical writing and historical thinking; the fusion of historical and philosophical interests—associated, for example, with Ibn Khaldun in an earlier period (fourteenth century) and Vico in a later period (seventeenth century)—as represented here by Azariah de Rossi and continued by Leone da Modena; a colorful spectrum of exegesis, particularly of the *Ketuvim*, a fact which has yet to be appreciated and, if possible, explained; intense introspection and self-criticism. The problem of external influences and/or internal developments is of intrinsic importance, but also impinges on most of the other issues mentioned here. All of these topics and problems of interpretation are the very substance of the history of Jewish thought.

Furthermore, from a literary point of view, there would be great generic variability in two ways. Most literary genres would be of intrinsic interest and would invite study in their own right: halakhic, philosophic, kabbalistic, ethical, homiletical, poetic, rhetorical, exegetical, polemical, historiographical. In addition, there would be a hybridization or cross-fertilization in the use of various genres for the purpose of conceptual analysis or total re-construction of ideas: systematic books on philosophy and mysticism would be effectively supplemented by material embedded in exegetical and homiletical works. The latter, of course, are fraught with difficulties for the researcher—repetitiousness, inconsistency, allusiveness and the constraints as well as the inducements to interpretive tours de force implicit in textual exegesis—and the attempt to systematize non-systematic writings, to extrapolate rigorously structured concepts from soft, pliable molds, is always problematic. The scholar must attempt to provide a central focus for interpreting and systematizing unsystematic writings, but needs to be careful not to impose rigid forms or fully-etched blueprints that are incongruous or unreal. This is true not only for the history of ideas—following a specific theme through the works of Del Medigo and Yeḥiel of Pisa together with the commentaries of Almosnino or the homilies of Moscato—but even with regard to individual authors who contributed to, and expressed themselves through, many genres—e.g., Arama, MaHaRaL, Sforno or Yavetz. These difficulties undoubtedly contributed to the fact that most thinkers who used the discursive, homiletical or exegetical media have not made their way as yet into the standard surveys. (There is, of course, some progress with regard to this deficiency, as a hurried glance at the works of Isaac Husik, Julius Guttmann, and Colette Sirat reveals.) We are receiving, and may expect, an increasing number of monographs on these very important figures: Abraham Saba, Abraham Farissol, David Messer Leon, Moses Almosnino, MaHaRaL and Obadiah Sforno.

III

All this is tantamount to saying that the conference aim—which is *eo ipso* the aim of this volume—was rather bold, aggressive and expansive. It did not focus on one major achievement or pivotal phenomenon—comparable, for instance, to the Renaissance, Reformation, the Copernican Revolution, the typographic revolution, etc., in general history. Our aim was integrative-holistic, an investigation of Jewish thought in its many facets, expressed in diverse genres and media in order to confront its centrifugal and centripetal tendencies, its tensions and harmonies, commonplaces and innovations. This turned out to be both exhilarating and problematic—and inevitably a bit frustrating, for obviously not all topics, genres, authors or ideas could be encompassed. Genuine comprehensiveness was beyond our reach. However, the panoramic conception illumined most areas and crevices, even those which remained unexplored. The clear realization of the lacunae was itself instructive and turned out to be a stimulant rather than an irritant. Lurianic Kabbalah was discussed, directly and allusively: perceptive, probing questions about its assumed relation to, or actual rootedness in, the Expulsion from Spain were raised, although there was no session—or even one full paper—devoted to it. Thus, paradoxically, the omission reflected full awareness of its overarching importance and of the fact that, while much had been done to present its complex, repercussive teachings, much still awaited detailed, perceptive study. The theoretical systems, ethical instructions, and ritual practices of R. Isaac Luria, R. Ḥayyim Vital and others stand in need of careful analysis. These systems were of such magnitude, of such great originality, provocativeness and enduring influence, that they demanded undiluted attention. Similarly, halakhic literature per se was not a topic and modalities, compels us to raise searching questions about the nature of the Jewish historical experience.

When we, for example, approach sixteenth century *darshanim*—Rabbis Isaac Adarbi, Moshe Almosnino, Moshe Alsheikh, Moshe Galanti, Shlomo le-Bet ha-Levi, Ephraim Luntshitz, MaHaRaL and his brother Ḥayyim b. Betzalel—irrespective of geographic boundaries and apparent socio-historical forces, we must be mindful of the basic questions of unity and continuity, local influences and common methodologies, special historical stimuli and ideational topoi. Similarly, when we pursue philosophic problems across political-geographic borders (e.g., in the writings of R. Eliezer Ashkenazi, R. Moses Isserles, R. Mordekhai Jaffe, Judah Messer Leon, Judah Abravanel, Moses Almosnino, or Obadiah Sforno or in the autobiographical or personal comments of Abraham Portaleone, Azariah Figo, Abraham ibn Migash, or when we discuss as a unit Jewish historiography in Italy, Bohemia and Turkey (e.g., Azariah de Rossi, Solomon ibn Verga, David Gans, Elijah Capsali, Samuel Usque, Joseph ha-Cohen) we implicitly or explicitly advance ideas or defend propositions concerning the essence and dynamism of Jewish history. Many years ago, in a different context, I tried to understand the emergence of the *Shulḥan Arukh* in the sixteenth century primarily in terms of immanent literary traditions, competing genres, and basic halakhic attitudes rather than contemporary contingencies and historical influences. I noted, inter alia, that

> this whole story is important because it expands the historical background against which the *Shulḥan Arukh* is to be seen and cautions against excessive preoccupation with purely sociological data, with contemporary stimuli and contingencies. It makes the *Shulḥan Arukh* understandable in terms of the general history of halakhic literature and its major trends. It provides an obvious vertical perspective—i.e., literary categories seen as part of an ongoing halakhic enterprise—to be used alongside of an, at best, implicit horizontal perspective—i.e., historical pressures and eschatological hopes—for an explanation of the emergence of the *Shulḥan Arukh*. This is strengthened by the striking parallelism between the literary careers of R. Moses Isserles and R. Joseph Karo; their historical situations, environmental influences, social contexts (in a phrase of contemporary jargon, their *Sitz-im-Leben*) are so different, but their aspirations and attainments are so similar.

The question hovering over all this is: by virtue of what do we posit an organic entity and speak of an essentially unified Jewish history rather than merely the history of Jews in Spain, Italy, Poland, or Turkey? What is the interplay between local factors and national-geographic determinants on one hand, and universal features and tendencies on the other? Does increased or lessened mobility of ideas play a role? This pivotal problem demands detailed, judicious deliberation. Students of Judaism and of Jewish history are for the most part convinced that the very essence of Jewish history combines apparently different dimensions of reality—geographic, cultural, spiritual, literary, demographic, ethnic—into a single, continuous landscape. Polarity and diversity do not negate an underlying unity. This is not merely a methaphysical mold for Jewish history but its actual substance: its operative categories and its empirical constructs.

As a component and corollary of the problem of periodization as well as that of methodology, it became clearer than ever that one must allow horizontal and vertical perspectives to intersect if cultural-spiritual developments are to be properly understood. This is automatically underscored in any general treatment of philosophy or of exegesis—and its validity is not diminished even when we find explicit declarations concerning innovative intent (as, e.g., in the *Ma'ase ha-Shem* of R. Eliezer Ashkenazi); it is also clearly discernible in specific analyses of MaHaRaL or David Ganz, Leone Ebreo or Abraham Saba, Abraham Shalom or Judah Moscato. Should one characterize MaHaRaL as modern or as traditional or should one see the apparent modernity emerging from a re-alignment of traditional motifs? "Modern" is never intelligible outside of a specific context. The emergence of the *Shulḥan Arukh*, as we have noted, is also a case in point.

The interaction of these two perspectives is important also for the prospective gesture of the scholar, for his inquiry into what remained alive, influential, repercussive as the century waned. Just as he analyzes the maturation or atrophy of certain earlier developments he may also pay attention to the sowing of seeds of future developments. As noted, the avoidance of precursorism does not mean insensitivity to ongoing influences or to the recognition of the beginnings of movements and tendencies which will flourish in future eras. It means only avoiding a skewed view of history, a subjective selection of facts and phenomena leading "inexorably" to modernity and modernization.

V

Louis B. Wright begins his article on "The Modern Relevance of the Renaissance" (*Medieval and Renaissance Studies* 1 [1966]) by asking the reader to suspend rigid definitions and exclusions and use the Renaissance to refer to that "long period of ferment." We may say the same for the sixteenth century in Jewish history. Of course, even the ferment is understandable only in terms of the interaction of "old" and "new," continuity and innovation. The penchant for the "modern," the varieties of precursorism with their patent foibles and fallacies, the writing of history in light of the features of modernity—such approaches are untenable and unproductive. Only the awareness of the dialectical interlacing of old and new, traditional and critical, will guide one to perceptive analysis and substantive synthesis.

ISADORE TWERSKY

Cambridge, Mass.,
Autumn, 1982

Ars Rhetorica as Reflected in Some Jewish Figures of the Italian Renaissance

ALEXANDER ALTMANN

Jews living in Renaissance Italy had access to two different philosophical traditions: (1) the Arabic and Judeo-Arabic one, which was inherited from the Middle Ages, and (2) the Latin one, which was being enriched by the discoveries of fresh texts, Latin and Greek, and was being infused with a new spirit, that of humanism. The two traditions did not necessarily converge toward a unified pattern. Their respective attitudes toward the art of rhetoric is a case in point. The Latin sphere of philosophical culture had been able to draw, throughout the medieval period, upon a rich classical legacy that included the writings of Aristotle, Cicero, and Quintilian,[1] while Arabic philosophy had known only Aristotle.[2] The translations of Arabic texts into Latin produced from the twelfth century onward had reinforced the Aristotelian perspective of rhetoric in Latin culture but had hardly changed the overall picture. Rhetoric in the Latin West remained more or less under the dominance of the Ciceronian tradition, no matter how arid and formalistic in its application. The revival of a broader concept of classical rhetoric in the Renaissance was due, to a large extent, to the rediscovery of Quintilian's complete text and of Cicero's *De oratore* in 1416 and 1421 respectively. The Italian Jews of the Renaissance were therefore confronted with two somewhat divergent legacies and, as could have been expected, they were by no means unanimous in the choice of options presented to them. Elijah del Medigo, for example, seems to have decided to adhere to the medieval orientation,[3] while other prominent figures like Judah ben Yeḥiel Messer Leon, Azariah de Rossi, and Judah Moscato clearly reflect the impact of Renaissance thinking.

What was the role and place of rhetorical art in the Arabic and Judeo-Arabic tradition? Aristotle had defined rhetoric as "the faculty of discovering the possible means of persuasion in reference to any subject whatever" (*Rhetorica*, I.ii.1). Proofs common to all branches of rhetoric were said by him to be of two kinds, example and enthymeme, and to correspond to the use of induction and syllogism in the art of dialectical argumentation, rhetoric being as it were "an offshoot of dialectic" (I.ii.7-8; II.xx.1). As a parallel to the possible "topics" of the dialectical syllogism discussed in *Topica*, Aristotle deals with the specifically rhetorical topics (II.xxiii). The *Rhetorica* does not contrast the art of persuasion and dialectic with the science of demonstration. Aristotle's view concerning the relationship between these three types of argument is spelled out in his logical writings and it may be summed up as follows: The dialectic syllogism and the rhetorical enthymeme proceed from probable premises and arrive at conclusions that are merely probable, whereas strict demonstration or scientific proof is based on incontrovertibly true, i.e., self-evident, premises and reaches equally true conclusions (*Anal. Prior*, II.xxiii, xxvii; *Topica*, I.1). It was this suggestion of a descending scale of logical validity that was seized upon by the Arabic philosophers in determining the place of the *Rhetorica* (and *Poetica*) as the last treaties in the *Organon*, thus highlighting the art of rhetoric as inferior in logical terms to both scientific and dialectical proofs, the difference between dialectic and rhetoric consisting in the kind of probable premises from which they proceed: dialectical probable premises being generally accepted by well-informed people, whereas rhetorical probable premises were accepted by the common people.

This relegation of rhetoric to a logically inferior position, though in accord with Aristotle's stated opinion, tended to ignore the important function that the *Rhetorica* assigns to the art of persuasion in the context of political life and, more precisely, in relation to ethics (*Rhetorica*, I.ii.7). It also failed to attach due prominence to the three kinds of rhetoric (deliberative, forensic, and epideictic), by the careful delineation of which (I.iii.1–6 and passim) Aristotle illuminated the significant role rhetoric exercised in society. By fastening upon the *logical* status of the art, the Arabic philosophers succeeded in downplaying the orator in contrast to the philosopher, and by stressing the close proximity of orator and dialectician, if not their essential identity, they deliberately sought to equate theology and rhetoric. While Aristotle considered oratory the legitimate province of political reality and projected a thoroughly approved use of it in the three kinds of rhetorical activity spelled out in rich detail, the *falāsifa* narrowed down this field of applicability by focusing upon the theologians or preachers of religion as the representatives of a logically faulty rhetoric. To be sure, they did not deny the politically useful role of this particular form of rhetoric, but whereas for Aristotle politics and rhetoric were organically connected, these two elements were now linked in a somewhat artificial manner: For the sake of the common people's happiness — which is the goal of politics — the philosophical truth can be communicated only in the disguise of rhetoric, that is, by procceding from premises accepted by the common people.

This reading of Aristotle in the light of changed religious and social conditions was initiated by Alfarabi, continued by Avicenna and perfected by Averroes. Alfarabi's *Kitāb al-Khaṭāba* ("Book of Rhetoric") was part of the lost *Mukhtaṣar al-Manṭiq* ("Abridgment of Logic"), and it has been described by its editor (Jacques Langhade) as a work in which "le pointe de vue logique prédomine tout au long de l'oeuvre. C'est par des définitions logiques qu'Al-Fārābī commence, et c'est en logicien qu'il continue à envisager et à expliquer la Rhétorique" (p. 26). Alfarabi's lost commentary on the *Rhetorica* seems to have been on a grand scale, but the introduction to it (which is known from Hermann the German's *Didascalia in Rhetoricam Aristotelis ex Glosa Alpharabii*, a simple translation of the introduction and folio 1 of the text) is again heavily weighted on the side of logic. In the words of its editor (Mario Grignaschi), "L'idée maitresse d'Al-Fārābī" was "que la rhétorique et la poétique font partie de la logique" (p. 139). It is in complete agreement with this idea that Alfarabi's *Iḥṣā' al-'ulūm* ("Enumeration of Sciences") lists rhetoric and poetics as the last topics (nos. 7 and 8) under the rubric of logic (*'ilm al-manṭiq*). Avicenna followed this trend. The very first chapter of his rhetoric in *Al-Shifā'* (I.8) is related to Alfarabi's *Kitāb al-Khaṭāba*, as Grignaschi suggested (p. 132). As for Averroes, he wrote a *Middle Commentary (Talkhīṣ)* as well as a *Short Commentary (Jāmi')* on Aristotle's *Rhetorica*, and, according to the incisive analysis of the former by its editor and translator (Charles E. Butterworth), he included rhetoric and poetics in the *Organon* in order to alert the reader to the inferior status of rhetorical and poetical arguments compared with demonstrative and even dialectical proofs. Averroes is said to have indicated the advisability of the use of rhetoric rather than dialectic by the theologians, which tallies with the stance he took in his *Faṣl al-Maqāl* ("The Decisive Treatise"): For every Muslim the Law has offered a specific way to truth according to his nature, through demonstrative, dialectical, or rhetorical methods. In Scripture, dialectical and rhetorical arguments are preferred because it is the purpose of Scripture to teach and guide the majority of men.[4]

Medieval Jewish philosophy adopted this assessment of rhetoric. Moses ibn Ezra's *Poetics (Kitāb al-Muḥāḍara wal-Mudhākara)* opens its chapter on "Rhetoric and Rhetoricians"[5] by defining the art, in the name of Aristotle, as "persuasive speech" but, significantly, adds the qualification "below firm opinion" and further explains that there are five logical arts in all: demonstrative, dialectical, poetical, rhetorical, and sophistical. Maimonides briefly discusses the difference between demonstrative, dialectical, rhetorical, sophistical, and poetical syllogisms in his *Maqāla fī Sana'at al-Mantiq (Milot ha-Higayon)*, ch. VIII. He describes the difference between dialectical and rhetorical proofs as proceeding from generally accepted and traditionally received opinions respectively. Rhetoric is thereby closely associated with religious revealed doctrine. In the *Guide of the Perplexed* there is only a single reference to Aristotle's *Rhetorica* (III, 49), but it must be assumed that his famous interpretation of Rabbi Ishmael's dictum, *dibra tora ki-leshon bney adam* expresses a distinctly rhetorical device. "The meaning of this is," says Maimonides (I.26), "that everything that all men are capable of understanding and representing to themselves at first thought (*bi-awwal fikrihi; bi-teḥilat ha-maḥshava*) has been ascribed to Him." The term "at first thought" has a rhetorical connotation. Alfarabi used its equivalent when describing the condition under which the enthymeme (the rhetorical syllogism) becomes persuasive "for the immediate common view" (*fī bādī al-ra'y al-mushtarak*; Langhade, p. 62; s. note), and Averroes in his *Short Commentary on the Rhetorica* did likewise when defining the enthymeme as a syllogism leading to a conclusion that "corresponds to the immediate view (Butterworth: 'unnexamined opinion') previously existing among all or most people" (*bi-ḥasabi bādī al-ra'y* . . . ; Butterworth, pp. 63, 170). The "first" or "immediate" (unexaṃined) view of the multitude has to be addressed and persuaded by rhetoric, and this is why Maimonides' defense of anthropomorphic language in Scripture amounts to a vindication of rhetoric. Yet the fact remains that for him (and Averroes) scriptural language, however necessary, is *only* rhetoric. Strangely enough, he has little or no use for the artistic element of rhetoric. Aristotle's elaborate discussion of the various elements of style and arrangement evokes no response. He does not refer to this aspect of rhetoric when dealing with the "figurative expressions and rhetorical speeches" of the prophets in *Guide*, II, 29, where the hyperbolic language of eschatological passages might have invited some reference to the persuasiveness achieved by certain rhetorical devices. All he mentions in this repect is the fact that "every prophet has a kind of speech peculiar to him," as noted already in the Talmud (*Sanh.* 89a). Rhetoric somehow dwindles down to the comparative evaluation of its place in the hierarchy of logical syllogisms, and its low rank is determined by its function to persuade the multitude, a view that persisted throughout the medieval period and can still be discerned in Elijah del Medigo's *Beḥinat ha-Dat.*[6]

A radically new attitude to the art of rhetoric is manifested in Judah ben Yeḥi'el Messer Leon's *Nofet Tzufim*, which was written some time between 1454 and 1474 and appeared in print shortly afterwards (Mantua, 1476–80 ?) as one of the first Hebrew incunabula. Adolf Jellinek, who republished it (Vienna, 1863), correctly described it on the German title page as a "Rhetorik nach Aristoteles, Cicero und Quintilian, mit besonderer Beziehung auf die Heilige Schrift." In other words, it is a full-fledged treatise on rhetoric, not a manual designed for the benefit of pulpit oratory, as Moritz Steinschneider (*Hebr. Übers.*, 78) suggested. As such, it takes its place alongside some of the major works on the subject that were produced in the fifteenth and sixteenth centuries in response to the Ciceronianism that pervaded the age. Thus, prior to the *Nofet Tzufim* the Greek émigré George of Trebizond known as Trapezuntius (1395–1486), having studied Cicero with Guarino Veronese, wrote his *Rhetoricorum libri quinque* in 1436 or 1437. To the following century belong Philipp Melanchthon's *Institutiones rhetoricae*, Leonard Cox's *Rhetorike* (London, c. 1530) and, perhaps the closest analogue to Messer Leon's work, Thomsas Wilson's *The Arte of Rhetorique* (London, 1585).

Messer Leon's openness to Ciceronian humanism is all the more noteworthy in light of the fact that he also continued the medieval tradition of studying, presenting, and commenting upon Aristotle. In 1453/54 he wrote a compendium of Aristotelian logic (*Mikhlal Yofi*) which, significantly, does not comprise the *Rhetorica* and *Poetica*, a departure from the medieval pattern that may be said to point to the more independent status of these two arts about to emerge. The rhetorical concern is evident already in this early work, for the introduction states the purpose of presenting "old and new subject matters in excellent order (*be-sidur nifla*) and in the utmost degree of elegance and beauty attainable (*be-takhlit ma she-efshar be-erki min ha-hidur ve-ha-yofi*)" so as to duly impress the reader and facilitate his understanding. He wrote, in addition, a commentary on Averroes' *Middle Commentary* to the first five books of the *Organon*, which Jacob Anatoli had translated into Hebrew in 1232. According to his son's report, he also commented on other Aristotelian works.

Messer Leon's *Nofet Tzufim* may be characterized as a judiciously performed synthesis or amalgam of most of the classical texts on rhetoric, selecting from each one what seemed to be the clearest and most felicitous passages dealing with the manifold issues discussed. The following sources are used in the compilation:

1. Aristotle's *Rhetorica (halatza)* as quoted and discussed in Averroes' *Middle Commentary* known to Leon in the Hebrew version by Todros ben Meshullam (1337), the text edited by Jacob Goldenthal (Leipzig, 1842). Leon's use of this version is attested by the terminology he employed; e.g., the term *haspaka* for "persuasion" was obviously taken from Todros' Hebrew version, which renders Arabic *quanā'a* and/or *iqnā'*. Likewise, *siman* (pp. 135, 137) in the sense of "enthymeme" is borrowed from Todros' version, where it translates Arabic *ḍamīr*. Steinschneider already noted that Leon consulted Averroes' *Middle Commentary* rather than the original Aristotle. Yet it is possible that he knew also the Latin version of the *Rhetorica*.

2. The (pseudo-Aristotelian) *Rhetorica ad Alexandrum (ha-halatza asher asa le-Aleksander)*, the genuineness of which was first doubted by Erasmus of Rotterdam, is but rarely quoted. It is referred to also as an "abridgment" of the *Rhetorica* (*Kitzuro she-shalaḥ le-Aleksander*; s. p. 16).

3. Cicero's *De inventione*, known also as the *Rhetorica vetus*, is referred to by Leon as *Tullio ba-halatza ha-yeshana.*

4. (Pseudo-) Cicero's *Rhetorica ad Herrenium*, known also as the *Rhetorica nova*, is referred to by Leon as *Tullio ba-halatza ha-ḥadasha.* It was, again, Erasmus who questioned first the genuineness of the work.

5. Fabius Laurentius Victorinus' *Explanationes in Rhetoricam M. Tulli Ciceronis* is referred to by Leon as *Vittorio ha-mefaresh.* The author is a fourth-century rhetorician who is mentioned by St. Augustine (*Confessio* VII.ix), and the work quoted is a commentary on Cicero's *De inventione.*[7]

6. Quintilian's *Institutio oratoria*, the most elaborate and accomplished work in rhetorical literature, is referred to by Leon simply as *Quintiliano ba-perek . . . me-ha-ḥelek ha- . . . (min ha-ma'amar ha- . . .).* It was the impact of the rediscovery of the complete text by Poggio Bracciolini in 1416 that helped to rekindle the enthusiasm for the rhetorical art as a potent element in education. Leon's fulsome quotations from this work in all its parts show the remarkable extent of his familiarity with it.[8]

A major work not quoted by Messer Leon is Cicero's *De oratore*, the complete text of which had been rediscovered by Bishop Gerardo Landriani five years after the find of Quintilian's opus.[9] He probably did not come accross this work in either its mutilated form (which had been used by Petrarch) or in its completeness. Otherwise he would have used it, since the image of the orator drawn therein would have suited his purposes.

What motivated Messer Leon to write the *Nofet Tzufim*? It is obvious from the scholarship he invested in this work as well as from the lofty style he employed that he was fascinated by the new look at rhetoric that dominated the era and by the classical texts themselves that he had studied. He could not have failed to notice that the ancient authors (Aristotle, Cicero, Quintilian) were able to illustrate the rhetorical rules by an abundance of quotations from their own literature, and he must therefore have felt the urge to discover the rhetorical dimension also in the Hebrew Bible. It seems that it was the prospect of finding the rhetorical principles embodied in biblical speech that gave wings to his efforts. For this is how he summed up, at the opening of the fourth and last part of his work, what he had so far accomplished (p. 147):

> After the foregoing account of the subject-matters of this book and having entered into their domains by searching every section of the

writings of the ancient and modern rhetoricians for precious material [*divrey ḥefetz*], it now remains for us to treat the various categories of rhetorical embellishment . . . and most of what we shall have to say thereon will be taken from Cicero's *Rhetorica* [*ad Herrenium*] and from part III of Aristotle's *Rhetorica*. Yet the illustrations [*ha-meshalim lahem*] I shall adduce from our own glorious sanctuary, from the words of the prophets and from the biblical narratives that "sit first in the kingdom" [Esther 1:14] of rhetorical perfection [*ha-arevut ve-ha-tzaḥut*] and which "cannot be gotten for gold, neither shall the exchange thereof be vessels of fine gold" [Job 28:15, 17].

The assertion that biblical oratory occupied the highest rank in the "kingdom of rhetoric" has to be understood not merely as an expression of piety, but, more particularly, as an attempt to cope with the awareness so characteristic for the Renasissance that there was a common human element, a universal law as it were that ruled rhetoric, the art of communication, everywhere. The universalism that was all-pervasive in the syncretistic culture of the period made it psychologically imperative for a Jewish traditionalist like Messer Leon to stress the superiority of the Jewish heritage within the commonality of mankind. He was sophisticated enough to realize that the enthusiastic manner in which he applied, to the Hebrew Bible, the rules of rhetoric formulated by the ancient pagans presented some problems. To obviate any misunderstanding he made his position clear at the end of the introduction to *Nofet Tzŭfim*: Addressing the reader, he emphatically warned him against assuming that it was the conformity of the prophets' speeches to the rhetorical rules of the Gentiles that constituted, in his view, their claim to greatness. One who were to interpret him in this fashion would be utterly wrong. He continued: "Yet if it occurred to you that I turned to those writings because they approximate to the words of the prophets and form a close link with them, you would guess my intent correctly." Classical rhetoric is thus described not as a yardstick for biblical oratory but as an intriguing parallel that caught his fancy. The true facts of the case are not so clear-cut, however. Messer Leon was obviously first drawn to the classical works on the subject, found them highly illuminating, and then sought to discover their rules and devices in the biblical texts. In so doing he brought a hitherto untried method to bear on the comprehension of the Bible. Whereas Maimonides and those following him saw in biblical rhetoric a mere concession to the need of addressing the multitude in terms compatible with their mental capacity, rhetoric now took on the character of a noble art indispensable for effective communication on all levels of public life. It was, above all, the figure of the orator that now commanded a new respect.

The heightened importance attached to oratory and orator is clearly reflected in the *Nofet Tzufim.* Quintilian (II.xv) had passed in review the various definitions of the art of rhetoric previously advanced. They had apparently all taken their cue from the role of the art in sophistry. Hence the tendency to equate rhetoric with persuasiveness, which was adopted also in Aristotle's definition. By contrast, Quintilian professed to have undertaken the task of molding the perfect orator who had to be a good man, and he therefore proposed the definition of rhetoric as "the science of speaking well" (*bene dicendi scientiam*). This definition was meant to imply that "no man could speak well unless he was good himself." The corollary of this definition was the view that the orator and his art were independent of results (II.xvii). Indeed, the speaker aimed at victory, but if he spoke well, he had lived up to the ideals of his art, even if he was defeated. Like Quintilian, Messer Leon (I.1) reviewed the possible definitions of rhetoric but, unlike Quintilian, he suggested that they all amounted to the same thing and could be squared with Aristotle's. He did not mention the famous definition that Cicero gave in *De optimo genere oratorum* (I.3–4): "The supreme orator, then, is the one whose speech instructs, delights, and moves the minds of his audience," a definition not referred to in Quintilian's discussion either. He quoted instead Cicero's statement in *De inventione* (I.v.6) that the function of eloquence was to persuade by speech. In the end he suggested that one might distinguish between the inner and outer purpose of oratory, the one being the inner quality of the speech ("speaking well"), the other the outer effect ("persuasion"). He saw the inner purpose alluded to in Isa. 50:4, "The Lord hath given me the tongue of them that are taught" (*leshon limudim*), and the outer purpose indicated by Prov. 10:32, "The lips of the righteous know what is acceptable" (*siftey tzadik yed'un ratzon*), persuasion being *hafakat ha-ratzon be-ma'amar (persuadere dictione).* The orator is tacitly identified with the *tzadik* (Quintilian's *vir bonus*, a view that is not just coincidental but will be pursued later.

Messer Leon is not unmindful of the havoc and misery that may be effected by eloquent speech and, like Cicero (*De inv.* I.i.1) and Quintilian (II.xvi.1–4), he dwells at some length upon the ruin wrought by the wicked whose "tongue walketh through the earth" (Ps.73:9). This gloomy picture serves, however, only as a counterpoint to the brightness of the portrait he draws of the immense benefit that a nation derives from its great orators. In answer to the question "What is the orator?" (*mahu ha-melitz*), he now completely identifies himself with Quintilian's idealistic image, which he finds also supported by the commentators: It is impossible for the perfect orator (*ha-melitz ha-shalem*) not to be "good and righteous man" (*adam tov ve-tzadik*) (I.2, p. 9). How could he be a leader of men wielding full power of persuasion unless he was utterly sincere (*piv ve-libo shalem*)? Moverover, he had to master the three branches of sciences, viz., the natural, political, and linguistic fields of knowledge, into which Quintilian had divided philosophy. The last-mentioned science (comprising the *artes sermocinales*) included logic, rhetoric and grammar, while natural science embraced the divine science (metaphysics), as Victorinus had pointed out. To be sure, the orator was not supposed to discuss philosophical subjects in all their technical details and in great depth, for persuasion was achieved only if things were presented to the audience in a manner easily comprehensible to all. It is clear, however, that Messer Leon wished to depict the orator as a figure of considerable philosophic erudition, whose words were both eloquent and weighty.

The image of the orator drawn by Messer Leon corresponds to the humanist aspirations which, following Cicero's vision, sought to combine philosophy and rhetoric, a trend that had been initiated by Petrarch and was continued by men like Coluccio Salutati, Leonardo Bruni and, in a way, also by Lorenzo Valla, who would subordinate philosophy to rhetoric.[10] The *Nofet Tzufim* was written prior to the revolution of the "New Logic" that was started by Rudolph Agricola (1444–1485) and was brought to fruition by Peter Ramus (1515–1572). The meaning of that revolt was the creation of a unified field of logic by breaking down the barriers between the *topoi* of dialectic and rhetoric established by Aristotle. It thereby signified the relegation of rhetoric to pure eloquence. It expressed, at its deepest level, a protest against the intrusion of person-to-person communication into the realm of intellectual life, and thus it marked the transition from dialogue to the scientific age of reason.[11] Messer Leon belonged to the "dialogical" humanism of the Renaissance, and to him the nontechnical orator-philosopher represents the ideal figure because of the role he is destined to play in the nation.

This favorable evaluation is articulated in striking fashion by the equation of the orator with the *tzadik*, brief mention of which has already been made. We have here an interpretation of the *tzadik* figure poles apart from the understanding of that term in contemporary Kabbalah. Leon quotes Prov. 10:20, "The tongue of the *tzadik* is as choice silver," and he understands it as a characterization of the orator as a man "perfect in his character and philosophical notions" (*shalem ha-midot ve-ha-de'ot*). There were numerous biblical verses testifying to the same view of the orator, and he concludes the chapter (I.2) by describing the prophets of Israel as the most illustrious representatives of this type. All this, he points out, supported Quintilian's definition of oratory.

The following are a few selected examples of the way in which Messer Leon projected rhetorical rules upon biblical material. In Deut. 32:2, the opening of Moses' farewell song, he (I.4) discovers an affirmation, in poetic language, of the five operations in which, according to Cicero (*De inv.* I.vii.9; see also *Ad Herr.* I.ii.3) and Quintilian (III.iii.1ff.), the art of rhetoric consists: invention (*inventio, hamtza'a*); arrangement (*dispositio, seder*); style (*elocutio, tzaḥut*); memory (*memoria, zekhira*); and delivery (*pronunciatio, remiza*). Invention and style are said to be alluded to by the term *lekaḥ* (*likḥi*), which denotes a "taking hold" of the subject-matter as well as the "winning" power achieved by beauty of language. Arrangement and memory are hinted at in the metaphors "dropping as the rain" and "distilling as the dew" respectively. The metaphors "as the small rain upon the tender grass" and "as the showers upon the herb" are interpreted as the persuasive power of the oration, which is attuned to all levels of the audience's understanding. They are also applied to the successful delivery, i.e., the appropriate manner of tone and gesticulation. Moses invoked the testimony of heaven and earth (32:1) for his intention of delivering a speech in which none of the five operations constituting a perfect oration shall be missing. The constrained and artificial manner of Messer Leon's exegesis illustrates his keen desire to find some biblical *locus probandi* for so prominent a rule as the one concerning the five elements of oratory.

Judah's oration before Joseph (Gen. 44:18–34) is seen by Messer Leon as structured according to the sixpartite division of forensic (*'itzumi*) speech advocated by Cicero (*De inv.* I.xiv.19; *Ad Herr.* I.iii.7): introduction (*exordium, petiḥa*); statement of fact (*narratio, sipur*); partition (*partitio, ḥiluk*); confirmation (*confirmatio, kiyum*); refutation (*reprehensio* or *confutatio, hatara*); and peroration (*conclusio, ḥatima*). Leon inaccurately attributed the same division also to Aristotle and Cicero, who prescribe, however, only four and five parts respectively (*Rhet.* III.xiii; *Inst. or.* III.ix). In I.7 (p. 24) he does refer, though, to Aristotle's statement (*Rhet.* III.xiii) that in speeches of an epideictic (*mekayem*) or deliberative (*'atzati*) kind — as distinct from forensic oratory—only two parts are required: the statement of subject and the proof. He also quotes Cicero's counsel against counterproductive introductions (*De inv.* I.xviii.26) and mentions Quintilian's similar caveat (IV.i.72–73), it being the purpose of the exordium to make the audience attentive (*attentum, makshiv*), well-disposed (*benevolum, meḥabev*), and ready to receive instruction (*docilem, mitlamed*) (I.5; *Ad Alex.* XXIX 1436a; *Inst. or.* IV.i.5). The conclusion Messer Leon draws from these various points of view is the realization of the need for a certain flexibility, which he finds confirmed by biblical testimony: "If you consider the Holy Scriptures, you will find that what Aristotle and Quintilian said is undoubtedly true." Only in rare cases, he points out, did biblical speeches contain all six parts. Abigail's oration (1 Sam. 25:24–31), he tries to show, was structured in the following way: statement of fact (24a); exordium (24b); confirmation (25a); refutation (25b); conclusion (26). The rest is amplification and rhetorical embellishment. Messer Leon regards this speech as a model of oration hardly matched by any other (p. 26).

Of particular significance is Messer Leon's attention to the style peculiar to biblical oratory. From the *Rhetorica ad Herrenium* (IV.viii.11) he probably took the distinction between three kinds of style called "types" (*figuras, tzurot*): the grand (*gravem, nisa'*), the middle (*mediocrem, beynoni*) and the simple (*extenuatam, shafel*). He (I.14) characterizes the grand style as one employing special or figurative words of utmost elegance or as one of speeches that include amplification (*amplificatio, harḥava*)—see II.11; *Ad Herr.*

II.xxix.48ff.—and pathetic form (*conquestio, raḥmanut*; see *Ad Herr.* III.xiii.24; *De inv.* I.lv.106) or a combination of rhetorical embellishments (*yipuyim halatziyim*). He considers most of the speeches of Isaiah and some of the narrations of Ezekiel the very epitome of the grand style.

These specimens of Messer Leon's recourse to biblical rhetoric unmistakably show how profoundly he was impressed by the elaborate structure of the rhetorical art as manifested in the sources at his disposal, and how strongly he felt the need to project those rules upon the biblical material. An almost autobiographical note to this effect occurs in I.13 (pp. 47–48), where he pleads for the study of the secular sciences as help toward an increased awareness of the riches contained in the Holy Scriptures. The "science of rhetoric" (*ḥokhmat ha-halatza*), he says, is particularly useful in this regard.

> For when I had studied the Torah in the habitual way, I had not been able to fathom that it embraced the science [of rhetoric] or part of it. Only after I had learned, searched and mastered it [rhetoric] in all its depth from the writings of the Gentiles, could I visualize, when returning to the Holy Scriptures, what they were like. Now the eyes of my understanding were opened and I saw that there was, in fact, a vast difference [*hevdel muflag*] between the pleasantness and elegance of their speeches [*'arevut amareha ve-tzaḥiyuteha*] . . . and all that is found in this [genre] among the rest of the nations, the difference resembling that between "the hyssop out of the wall" and "the cedar that is in Lebanon" [1 Kings 5:13].

Yet for all its emphasis on the uniqueness of the Bible, the aesthetic viewpoint, which Leon pushed to the foreground, contained the seed of secularism, for it saw the Scriptures as great "literature." This approach had been anticipated, under the influence of Aristotle's *Poetica*, in Moses ibn Ezra's *Kitāb al-Muḥāḍara wal-Mudhākara* and in Abu'l-Barakāt's *Kitāb al-Mu'tabar* in the twelfth century,[12] but the Middle Ages had not been hospitable to the idea. It was different now in the intellectual climate of Renaissance thought. From Judah Messer Leon's *Nofet Tzufim* the road leads to Azariah de Rossi in the sixteenth century and thence to Robert Lowth and Moses Mendelssohn in the eighteenth.

While Messer Leon applied the classical rules of rhetorical art to the Hebrew Scriptures, Azariah de Rossi took the novel step of referring to them, albeit in limited degree, when dealing with rabbinic Aggadah. In so doing he consciously followed in Messer

Leon's footsteps. He quoted him twice in *Imrey Bina* and once in *Matzref la-Kesef.* The first passage[13] draws attention to "the book *Nofet Tzufim* of the great scholar R. Judah known as Messer Leon of Mantua," in particular to the statement at the end of I.13 (cited above), which he sums up in these words: "From the indications of the rhetorical embellishments to which the Gentile scholars alert us we come to recognize how superbly beautiful and pleasant are the Holy Scriptures." He then literally reproduces Messer Leon's concluding remark in which he deprecates the unwillingness of many rabbis to accept the truth from foreign sources. The second passage is more specific. It occurs in a context (*I.B.*, 234–239) discussing the rabbinic use of hyperbole as a rhetorical device and makes corroborative reference to the acknowledgment of the same device by the Gentile rhetoricians as a praiseworthy one, "as you find it stated by their leading writers, Cicero (*Tullio*) in *Topica* IV [should read: X, 44–45] and Quintilian in *Insitutio oratoria (be-ha-latzato)* VIII.vi [67–76], from whom the Jewish rhetorician (*ha-melitz ha-yehudi*), author of the *Nofet Tzufim*, borrowed in IV.43 (*Perek ha-Guzma*)" (p. 236).

Interestingly enough, de Rossi considers it necessary to refer to Gentile support for an oratorical form of expression which, as his Talmudic references show, was fully recognized within the Jewish tradition. He was obviously motivated by the desire to legitimize the use of this kind of interpretation also concerning matters that *prima facie* are asserted as historical facts. For he uses it subsequently in an effort to show that R. Yoḥanan's statement (*Yoma* 19a) about the number (over 300) of high priests during the Second Temple period was not historical but hyperbolic (ibid.). Quintilian's phrase describing the hyperbole as "an elegant straining of the truth" must have appealed to him. He might have quoted other sources such as Aristotle, *Rhetorica* III.X.15–16 and the *Ad Herrenium* IV.xxxiii. The third passage is similar in intent to the second. It is found in *Matzref la-Kesef* II.13 (p. 107, note) and relates to a rabbinic statement (*Ned.* 37b) about the Sinaitic origin of certain masoretic elements. De Rossi considers it a purely rhetorical assertion, "for in all languages do we find essential embellishments (*yipuyim atzmiyim*) and all the more so in this holy and primeval language, as has been shown by the scholarly author of *Nofet Tzufim* who adduced scriptural examples for every form of rhetorical embellishment found therein." It appears from these statements by de Rossi that he valued rhetorical theory as an aid to historical scholarship.

In similar fashion oratorical technique is resorted to as the explanation of the Talmudic-midrashic legend about the strange punishment God decreed upon Titus (*Gittin* 56b; *Pirqey R. Eliezer* 49), which seemed unbelievable to de Rossi as an historical account (*I.B.* 214–219). He quoted "the mellifluous speaker of theirs"—a reference to Cicero—and "our truly wise sages" (*ḥakhamenu ha-meḥukamim be-emet*) who would purposely invent stories of this kind in order to impress people by their fancifulness and thereby drive home certain moral or intellectual verities (p. 217). Oratory as seen from this perspective comes close to poetry, and de Rossi, in a mood of poetic inspiration, felicitously likens the *aggadot* of the rabbis to those groups of angels that are said to arise from the "fiery stream" (*nehar di-nur*), deliver their song, and, having fulfilled their purpose, return to that element not to be seen again. He takes great pains to collect the numerous rabbinic dicta in which the fluidity of Aggadah is contrasted with the exactness of Halakhah and the rule is laid down that in aggadic matters contentious debate is out of place (*eyn makshin be-aggada*) (*I.B.* 210–212). He has a whole section on poetic theory in which he quotes, among others, Moses ibn Ḥabib's *Darkhey No'am* (*I.B.* 477–484). In *Matzref la-Kesef* he refers to Horace's *De arte poetica* (p. 121). He was clearly groping for a rabbinic rhetoric and poetic and he was well equipped to undertake such a task. Yet he remained content to use certain aspects of both in the service of historical research.

Judah Moscato (1530–c. 1593), a contemporary of de Rossi (b. 1513) and his friend and supporter, represented the Hebrew version of the Renaissance in the most accomplished manner. His erudition was steeped in classical, medieval, and Renaissance literature, and his superb Hebrew style exemplified, and did not merely discourse upon, the humanist concern for *ars rhetorica*. Yet there is no lack of direct references to oratorical theory in both his published works, the sermonic collection *Nefutzot Yehuda*[14] and the commentary on Judah ha-Levi's *Sefer ha-Kuzari* called *Kol Yehuda.*[15] With de Rossi, he shared, among other things, a sense of indebtedness to Messer Leon's pioneering work in Hebrew rhetoric. In Sermon V (fol. 19d) he quoted, *in extenso*, the concluding passage of the introduction to *Nofet Tzufim*[16] in which Messer Leon had sought to define his priorities. Moscato obviously wished to identify himself with the sentiments expressed. He was not, however, an uncritical follower of Messer Leon's outline of rhetoric. He used additional sources such as Cicero's *De partitione oratoria* (19d) and Rudolph Agricola's *De inventione dialectica* (20a), which had been published in 1538 in Paris, and he reached partly different conclusions. He acknowledged five operations of rhetoric instead of six (*Kol Yehuda* on II.72, p. 161f.) and four parts of speech instead of six (*Nefutzot* 19d–20a). He somewhat changed the terminology. The term *haspaka* ("persuasion"), which was an imitation of Arab. *qinā'a*, he replaced by the more idiomatic Hebrew phrase *hafakat ratzon* (20a), which Leon had used only occasionally. Instead of *sipur*, he used *hatza'a* to denote the *narratio* (statement of fact; 19d); and in designating the rhetorical operations by their Italian terms, he referred to *elocutio* (style; *tzaḥut*) as *enunciatione*.

The strong impression that classical rhetoric made upon Moscato's mind is strikingly attested by his attempt to rediscover some of its features in rabbinic sources. Like de Rossi, he applied the urge for projections of this kind to rabbinic literature, seeing that Messer Leon had focused his attention on biblical material. There are two rather bizzare examples of this procedure. The first concerns the aggadic story told in *Sanhedrin* 44b: The angel (Rashi: Gabriel) appointed for the defense of Israel before the heavenly court protests, in exceedingly bold language, against the harsh words uttered by God to Ezekiel (16:3) about the patriarchs. The question is asked whether the angel did not overstep his authority in using such language before God. The answer given is to the effect that he was within his rights, for he bore three names spelling out his legitimate functions: *piskon*, i.e., the one who lays down things before God; *itmon*, i.e., the one who suppresses the sins of Israel; and *sigron*, i.e., he who, having closed the case, does not reopen it. Moscato finds in these three names of the celestial forensic advocate of Israel a reference to three of the four parts of forensic oratory mentioned in Cicero's *De partitione*: statement of fact; proof and refutation; and peroration. What is missing is the exordium, but Moscato is delighted to discover this missing part in the list of four names attributed to the angel (*Metatron*) in *Tikuney ha-Zohar* (no. 57): *piskon, piṭhon, sigron, itmon. Piṭhon* stands, of course, for the exordium. The fact that this part is omitted in the Talmudic passage is not disturbing to Moscato, for, as he points out, the introductory part is but a "preparation" to what follows and, besides, may be dispensed with in certain circumstances, as had been stated by Agricola in his *De inventione dialectia* (II.22). To be sure, the Talmudic story could not be taken literally, but it was appropriate to depict, metaphorically, the proceedings in the celestial court in analogy to the rules obtaining in the terrestrial court (*Nefutzot* 19b–20a).

The other example refers to a discussion in *Sanhedrin* 100a where the phrase *ve-'alehu li-terufa* ("and the leaf thereof for healing," Ezek. 47:12) is anagrammatically explained in various ways: 1. The leaf has the power *le-hatir pe shel ma'la*, i.e., to confer eloquence on the dumb; 2. *le-hatir pe shel mata*, i.e., to open the womb of the sterile; 3. *le-to'ar panim shel ba'aley lashon*, i.e., to enliven the facial expression of the speaker. Moscato sees in these three terms an allusion to the five operations of rhetorical art as prescribed by Cicero: the opening of the womb means three of these (*inventione, dispositione*, and *memoria*) for they entail creative activity; the conferment of eloquence denotes the faculty of *enunciatione* (*elocutio*, delivery); and the improvement of facial expression points to *pronunciation*, which includes gesticulation, a subject discussed at length, as Moscato recalls, in the eleventh book of Quintilian's *Institutio oratoria* (*Kol Yehuda* on II.72, pp. 161f.). We may say that it is precisely the far-fetched nature of these cases of eisegesis that illustrates the degree to which Moscato was preoccupied with classical rhetoric.

Indigenous rabbinic oratory comes into its own in Sermon XII, where Moscato elaborates on *Canticles Rabba* IV:11, 1. The passage chosen by him offers five different views of the verse "Thy lips . . . drop honey—Honey and milk are under thy tongue . . . ," all of which do agree on the application of its praises to the public orator delivering words of Torah, and all of which declare that "If one discourses on the Torah in public and his words are not tasteful (*arevim*) to his hearers . . . , it were better that he had not spoken." Here we have a genuinely rabbinic stress on the elements of persuasive rhetoric, and all Moscato does is to conceptualize the various poetic descriptions of pleasantness presented by the rabbis. They amount, in his view, (1) to the clarity ("sifting") of the material that forms the subject-matter of the oration; (2) to the quality of the disposition ("as honey from the comb"); (3) to the combination of (1) and (2) ("as honey with milk"); (4) to the element of beauty ("as a bride to her husband"). The upshot of his discussion is a summary portrayal of what a public orator discoursing on the Torah should be like: "He must be of pleasant speech, presenting matters in proper order and in conformity to intellectual speculation, being also a man of excellent character." The last condition is best expressed by the rabbinic phrase "*na'e doresh ve-na'e mekayem*" (36c–37b). This image, though authentically rabbinic, conforms, at the same time, to the concept of the ideal orator drawn by Quintilian and eagerly adopted by Messer Leon.

The perfect orator, according to humanist sentiment, is also the perfect man, and this larger perspective was not absent from Moscato's consciousness. In Sermon IX (22d) he permitted himself to quote a lengthy passage from another of his writings—he gave no hint as to its whereabouts—in which he described "the speech of perfect men." There was no "tasteless word" (*mila tefela*) on their lips, he said, and a certain "fragrance and beauty" (*reaḥ tov ve-yofi*) radiated from their faces, for beauty was but the fragrance of goodness (*reaḥ ha-toviut*), as the Platonists (*ba'aley brit Aflaton*) would say.[17] Moscato linked eloquence of rhetoric also to the dignity of man, another celebrated *topos* of humanist thought, on which Gianozzo Manetti and Pico della Mirandola had written in the fifteenth century.[18] In *Kol Yehuda* (II.68, p. 157), he pointed out that the faculty of speech was the special prerogative of man and that its quality had to be considered the criterion of the rank of a nation. Hence, given the unique character of the Jewish people, its language had to be of the utmost perfection. Moscato shared the belief predominantly held by Jewish scholars (see de Rossi, *Imrey Bina*, 453) that Hebrew was the primeval language, the *lingua Adamica*. In his *Kol Yehuda* (II.67, p. 153ff.), Moscato quoted Abraham ibn Ezra's *Safa Brura* in support of his critique of *Genesis Rabba* 18.6, which led him to a new interpretation of this midrashic passage. In his view the burden of the proof that "the Torah was given in the holy tongue" had to be placed upon the fact that the etymologies of proper names offered in the Torah (e.g., Adam: *adama*; Kayin: *kaniti*) could not possibly be regarded as translations from another, earlier tongue because translations invariably left *nomina propria* in their original form. De Rossi, who recalled Isaac Arama's skepticism about the midrashic argument from the consonance of the nouns *ish* ("man") and *isha* ("woman") allegedly peculiar to Hebrew and who adopted Moscato's proof, relates yet another argument which, he says, Moscato had "taught" him: Hebrew is the primeval language, for God, who is perfect, can bestow only perfection. He, who bestowed circularity, the most perfect form (Aristotle, *De coelo* II.iv), upon matter when creating the heaven, could have endowed Adam with but the most perfect language. The argument entails two assumptions: (1) that Hebrew is the most perfect tongue, a view corroborated by de Rossi from a variety of sources; and (2) that the language of the first man was not his own invention but a divine gift. Moscato clearly affirms this view in *Kol Yehuda* when commenting on *Kuzari* II.72 (p. 162): The Hebrew language is not conventional (*muskemet mi-bney adam*) but a *creatio ex nihilo (me'ayin timatze)*, as Ha-Levi's phrase *ha-notzeret ha-beru'a* (Judah ibn Tibbon's rendition of *al-makhlūqa al-mukhtara'a*) means to indicate. The revealed character of Hebrew had been stressed also in *Kuzari* IV.25 and in a passage from Profiat Duran's *Ma'ase Efod* (ch. 3) quoted approvingly by Moscato earlier on (p. 155). From Gen. 2:20, Maimonides (*Guide*, II.30) had inferred that languages, including Hebrew, are conventional, and Naḥmanides (*Commentary on the Torah*, Ex. 30:13) had opposed this doctrine from a mystically inspired position. Moscato explicitly noted (p. 162) that Gen. 2:20 did not disprove the view held by Ha-Levi. As for all other languages, they were conventional.[19] Moscato's position on this issue is clear: The Hebrew language is both *lingua Adamica* and God-given.

What introduces a Renaissance flavor into the medieval texture of this position is Moscato's fondness of syncretistic etymologies. Since Hebrew was the original language of the human race, he found it quite natural that, as he believed, many Hebrew words survived in the other tongues. This belief helped to restore a sense of universal human kinship that the consciousness of Hebrew singularity might have been apt to undermine. Hence the search for words common to many languages, while assuming the primacy of Hebrew, tended, at the same time, to create a bridge between the cultures. It was the counterpart to the intellectual syncretism that permitted Christian Renaissance philosophers to defer, in all innocence, to the pagan deities, and that made it inoffensive in Moscato's eyes to follow the Platonists and Pico in calling the first hypostasis in the process of emanations by the name of the "Son of God" (*Nefutzot* 23c; see Pico, *Discourse on Love* I.iii). It seems that Moscato's excursions into the nebulous region of etymology owed some stimulus to the treatise *Dor ha-Pelaga* written by his friend David Provençal, one of the three Provençal brothers whom de Rossi described as the "upholders of Torah" (*tofsey ha-tora*) in Mantua (*Imrey Bina*, p. 146). In this well-intentioned work, more than two thousand Hebrew words had been collected that were said to be found also in Greek, Latin, Italian and/or other tongues. Examples recorded by de Rossi (*I.B.*, p. 456f.) include the following: *ezer—uxor; pilegesh—paelex, pallakis; osef dalim—hospidale; kol yafe—Kalliope; bet eked—academia.* A list of etymologies found in Moscato's writings has been compiled by Abba Apfelbaum in his valuable monograph on Moscato.[20] Among others, we meet here again *Kalliope*, the first of the nine Muses and protectress of music, as bearing a name derived from Hebrew *kol yafe* (*Nefutzot* 1c). "Music" is said to be a word identical with Hebrew *mezeg* in the sense of a "well-proportioned" arrangement of voices (1b). "Simile" is identical with *mashal* (88c); etc. The most striking etymology concerns the name Moshe (Moses), which is said to be akin (*karov*) to *Musa*, from which name the noun "music" is derived (3c). Moscato adds that, according to some writers, the word music comes from Egyptian *moys*, denoting water, for the art originated near the water (where reeds grow?). This, he says, agrees with Exod. 2:10 ("Moses . . . Because I drew him out of the water"). The same derivation occurs also in the famous encyclopaedia of the sciences written by the monk and imperial father confessor Gregorius Reisch and known as the *Margarita philosophica,*[21] where also Greek *Musa* is mentioned as a possible derivation. Moscato knew and made use of this work, which he described as "well-known among the Gentiles" (*sefer mefursam etzlam*; 2d), and it is most likely that his etymology is indebted to it. The knowledge of the Egyptian word for water was probably obtained from Philo's *Moses* I.17: "Since he had been taken up from the water, the princess gave him a name derived from this, and called him Moses, for Möu is the Egyptian word for water."

These playful theories as well as the concern for establishing the precise character and origin of the Hebrew language are all part of the larger preoccupation with language as the vehicle of human communication and with the *ars rhetorica* as the ultimate consummation of man's faculty of speech. As we have seen, the three writers whom we have analyzed made a determined effort, each in his own way, to adapt the understanding of the Scriptures and of rabbinic literature to the spirit of Renaissance humanism.

NOTES

1. See Richard McKeon, "Rhetoric in the Middle Ages," *Speculum* 17(1942), 1–32; James J. Murphy, *Rhetoric in the Middle Ages* (Berkeley, Los Angeles, London, 1974).

2. See J. Langhade and M. Grignaschi, *Al-Fārābī, Deux ouvrages inédits sur la rhétorique* (Beyrouth, 1971); Charles E. Butterworth (ed. and tr.), *Averroës' Three Short Commentaries on Aristotle's "Topics," "Rhetoric," and "Poetics,"* (Albany, 1977).

3. See below and n. 6.

4. See George F. Hourani, *Averroes on the Harmony of Religion and Philosophy* (London, 1961), pp. 45, 49, 63. The logical orientation of the *falāsifa*'s approach to the *Rhetoric* (and *Poetics*) was well perceived by Hermann the German. In his Prologue to the "Rhetoric," he wrote: Quod autem hi duo libri logicales sint, nemo dubitat qui libros perspexerit arabum famosorum, Alfarabii videlicet et Avicennae et Avenrosdi et quorundam aliorum. See William F. Boggess, "Hermannus Alemanus's Rhetorical Translations," *Viator* 2 (1971), 249–250. For a discussion of the Averroes Latinus on Poetics, see H. A. Kelly, "Aristotle on Tragedy: The Influence of the 'Poetics' on the Latin Middle Ages," *Viator* 10 (1979), 161–209.

5. See A. S. Halkin, *Moshe ben Yaakov ibn Ezra, Kitāb al-Muḥāḍara wal-Mudhākara—Liber Discussionis et Commemorationis (Poetica Hebraica)* (Jerusalem, 1975), p. 13.

6. See Elijah del Medigo, *Sefer Beḥinat ha-Dat,* ed. by Isaac Reggio (Vienna, 1833), p. 5.

7. For the text, see Charles Halm, *Rhetores latini minores* (Leipzig, 1863), pp. 155–304. Another commentator (on Cicero?) referred to by Leon (pp. 6, 9) as *ha-mefaresh Alano* could not be identified with certainty. Steinschneider (*Hebr. Übers.,* p. 79) suggested that Alano was the Italianized form of Aelianus. He obviously had in mind Claudius Aelianus (c. 170–235), the Roman author and teacher of rhetoric, but I have been unable to trace a reference to, let alone a manuscript or printed edition of, a commentary by him on Cicero. No reference to such a commentary occurs in Halm's *Rhetores latini minores.*

8. For the story of the recovery of the text, see James J. Murphy, *Rhetoric,* pp. 357–363.

9. See ibid, 360f.

10. See Hannah Holborn Gray, "Renaissance Humanism: The Pursuit of Eloquence," *Journal of the History of Ideas* 24 (1963); Jerrold E. Seigel, *Rhetoric and Philosophy in Renaissance Humanism* (Princeton, N.J., 1968); Eckhard Kessler, *Petrarca und die Geschichte* (Munich, 1978); Jan Lindhardt, *Rhetor. Poeta, Historicus* (Leiden, 1979). Edward E. Hale, Jr., "Ideas on Rhetoric in the Sixteenth Century," *Publications of the Modern Language Association of America,* 17 (1903), 424–444 deals only with sixteenth-century England.

11. See Walter J. Ong, *Ramus, Method and the Decay of Dialogue* (Cambridge, Mass., 1959), p. 288f.

12. See Shlomo Pines, "Studies in Abu'l-Barakāt al-Baghādī's Poetics and Metaphysics," *The Collected Works of Shlomo Pines, Vol. I: Studies in Abu'l-Barakāt al-Baghdādī Physics and Metaphysics* (Jerusalem-Leiden, 1979), pp. 259–334.

13. Azarya min ha-Adumim, *Sefer Me'or Enayim,* ed. by David Cassel (Vilna, 1866), part III *Imrey Bina* [*I.B.*], p. 89.

14. Venice, 1589; quoted here from the Lemberg, 1850 edition.

15. Venice, 1594; quoted here from the Warsaw, 1880 edition.

16. See above, p. 104.

17. See Plotinus, *Enneads,* V.i.6; Pico della Mirandola's *Discourse on Love,* II.i: "Love is a species of desire; beauty of good"; Pico's *Discourse* is quoted in *Nefutzot,* 23c.

18. See Paul Oskar Kristeller, *Humanism and Renaissance,* II (Munich, 1976), pp. 110, 120–123.

19. For the theories of language in medieval Islam, see Bernard G. Weiss's article on the subject in *ZDMG,* 124.1 (1974), 33–41.

20. Abba Apfelbaum, *Sefer Toldot Ha-Gaon Rabbi Yehuda Moscato* (Drohobicz, 1900), p. 12.

21. The first edition probably appeared in 1496; the work is quoted here from the 1504 edition, V.i.2.

Some Reflections on the Place of Azariah de Rossi's *Meor Enayim* in the Cultural Milieu of Italian Renaissance Jewry*

ROBERT BONFIL

I

Habent sua fata libelli. Azariah de Rossi's *Meor Enayim* had a very peculiar fate. The vociferous opposition expressed by de Rossi's contemporaries stimulated the polemical ardor of nineteenth-century scholars who praised the book for apparently the very same reasons the former had condemned it. Both contemporary criticism and retrospective praise contributed jointly to conferring an aura of uniqueness upon the work and its author, that seems hardly to have been dissipated by the penetrating analysis of Salo W. Baron's revisionary essays on the subject.[1]

We may differ concerning the extent of innovation versus medieval continuity in the *Meor Enayim*[2] and in this matter we may extend to Jewish history the widely debated question of the "real" achievements of the Renaissance. Be that as it may, the vociferous opposition encountered by the *Meor Enayim* among sixteenth-century Italian Jews clearly indicates that it could at least seem extraordinary within the cultural milieu in which it appeared. In other words, a close connection between opposition to the book and the opponents' perception of the book as extraordinary might be assumed. More precisely, it might seem that the exceptionality of the book would stand in direct proportion to the intensity of opposition, and that the nature of this exceptionality would be defined negatively by the nature of the opposition. Needless to

*This study was aided by a grant from the Research Committee of the Ben-Gurion University of the Negev. It is both a duty and pleasure for me to acknowledge my friend, Elliot Horowitz, for having dedicated much of his time to making the text of this paper readable in Shakespeare's idiom.

say, the way in which we define these two complex variables profoundly influences not only our understanding of the *Meor Enayim* controversy, but also our general grasp of the cultural atmosphere of Italian Jewry in the seventies of the sixteenth century.

For example, if we combine the assumption that the Jewish establishment's opposition (as represented by the opinion of the rabbis who signed the manifesto against the book) was largely consolidated,[3] with Baron's assertion that the *Meor Enayim* was not very original if set in its *locus naturalis* (that is, in the framework of Renaissance historiography and the particular Italian Jewish thought of that period), we would conclude that in de Rossi's days there occurred a cultural involution among Italian Jewry, possibly as a result of the Counter-Reformation climate, and that the signatories of the manifesto gave expression to this involution.[4] Even if we were to assume that position, the involution still should not be defined in linear terms. Were de Rossi's secular learning and heavy reliance upon gentile authors together with his rationalistic interpretation of *Aggadot* the focus of the controversy, thus marking his opponents as anti-rationalist adherents of intellectual isolationism? Or was the controversy focused on de Rossi's critical-historical approach and his "sense of the past" (as Peter Burke would put it),[5] and were de Rossi's opponents, then, merely unaffected by the "Renaissance sense of the past," and therefore opposed to the critical-historical method? In either case, why were de Rossi's opponents silent on the subject?[6]

On the other hand, let us here consider whether it be correct to assume that the opposition to the *Meor Enayim* was consolidated and representative of the Jewish establishment. After all, even if de Rossi's method of interpreting *Aggadot* was unacceptable to a few hypersensitive kabbalists,[7] it was, at worst, a disputable position on an already controversial issue, and thus, not likely to upset the entire Jewish leadership.[8] It seems even less likely that such vociferous opposition could have been engendered by de Rossi's heavy reliance upon gentile authors, or by his method, "common among gentiles," of writing apparently disconnected essays.[9]

True, there was the chronological issue.[10] This might seem to have been the main problem. Even de Rossi's friends raised objections to his position on this matter, on both practical and theoretical grounds. On practical grounds they questioned whether a difference in calculations of some twenty years justified planting seeds of doubt concerning the veracity of Talmudic statements.[11]

On theoretical grounds they wondered whether the critical-historical approach utilized by de Rossi could really yield reliable results.[12] Objections of this sort, however, could easily have been restricted within the bounds of academic discussion, and this, indeed, seems to have been the case so far as the prominent Italian Jewish rabbis who raised them were concerned. It does not seem likely that Italian Jewry could have coalesced in consolidated opposition to such issues as those discussed above.

What does seem considerably more probable, however, is that de Rossi's views could upset the religious sensibilities of a marginal group among Italian Jewry. These men instinctively feared that the chronological issue might have harmful practical consequences and were suspicious of the intentions that lay behind de Rossi's motley erudition.[13]

I venture to argue that the opposition to the *Meor Enayim* was rooted in the uproar of a vociferous minority who themselves did not have a very precise idea of what heresies they suspected the book to contain. This is not to suggest that the entire affair was merely a tempest in a teapot. The idiosyncratic fears of a handful of shaken men, living in anxious times, could cause much trouble—and did. But, on the other hand, it was not quite the cyclone described by later historiography, not entirely for disinterested reasons. I maintain that a close, if not detailed re-examination of the extant evidence, both printed and manuscript,[14] can justify this argument fully, and would, moreover, shed new light on the place of the *Meor Enayim* in the cultural atmosphere of Italian Jewry in the late sixteenth century.

II

The printing of the *Meor Enayim* was completed in Mantua on November 18, 1573. It would be interesting to know if de Rossi ever took pains to obtain "the approbation of three rabbis ordained by three rabbis" and that of the leaders of the Mantuan Community, as required by the Ferrara ordinance of 1554. If he did, he did not feel compelled, as others did not, to publish "the names of the rabbis and the community leaders in the introduction of the book." Was it, perhaps, as some maintain, because the ordinance fell into disuse soon after 1554, thereby freeing de Rossi from the necessity of requesting an approbation?[15] Whatever the case, we know that R. Moses Proventzalo had the opportunity, before November 1573, to read the problematic chapters dealing with chronology, possibly in proof. He raised then in concise form the objection developed in extenso after the book's publication: that de Rossi's chronological thesis would revolutionize the Jewish calendar.[16] Writing several days before *Rosh ha-Shana* he offered the following example:

> . . . The new moon for the coming *Tishrei* 5334 A.M. [is to occur] on Thursday night, at four [= ten p.m.] and 1004/1080 hours and *Rosh ha-Shana* is set for the following Saturday. . . . With, however, the additional twenty years of the first Temple period which have been reckoned, the new moon of *Tishrei* 5334 would occur on Saturday, at nineteen [=1 p.m.] and 28/1080 hours . . . thus requiring *Rosh ha-Shana* to be set for the following Monday.

R. Proventzalo added:

> And if one were to claim that the calculation evens out, and that he who adds in one place subtracts in another, then the entire inquiry deals with pointless calculations, for whatever happened, happened.

At this point de Rossi could feel sure that R. Proventzalo's objections were based on a radical misunderstanding of his argument and could feel confident in his ability to rebut this or similar objections, were they to enter, as they indeed would, the public domain. He had, in the book itself, anticipated certain objections of this sort and provided replies to them, so that he could reasonably claim that his opponents had not done their homework.[17]

De Rossi's real problem began once R. Isaac Foa of Reggio read the book. The old rabbi, whose intellectual energies seem to have been devoted entirely to Talmudic studies interspersed with mystical speculation,[18] appears to have been shocked at the nonchalance with which de Rossi dealt with certain *Aggadot* believed by kabbalists to have great theosophical implications. For the likes of R. Foa, this was unthinkable. He dispatched an alarmed letter to Venice, where his son-in-law, R. Menaḥem Azariah da Fano, had been residing for some months.[19] The letter has not been preserved, so we do not know exactly what alarmed R. Foa. We do know, however, that the letter left a deep impression upon R. Samuel Judah Katzenellenbogen. This scholar, though a competent Talmudist, does not seem to have been distinguished either by his intellectual sensitivity or by his realism,[20] and was, moreover, rather young at the time. He acted impulsively, apparently before he had even had a chance to read the *Meor Enayim*.[21] In a circular letter addressed to the Italian Jewish communities, he summarized the warnings of R. Foa and appended to it the text of a manifesto against the book that he proposed for signature. The letter itself has not been preserved, and therefore we do not know whether R. Katzenellenbogen was any more specific in it than in his manifesto, where his charge against the book was rather vague, to say the least: "And there were some chapters," he wrote, "of that third section, called *Days of the World*, full of new issues never dreamed of by our fathers."[22]

R. Katzenellenbogen did not claim any position of leadership for himself in the crusade he called for. Perhaps he thought, or hoped, that "the very excellent scholars of each and every city" would agree to sign the manifesto, especially since it merely sought to require that every Jew who wanted to read or own the book "obtain written permission from the rabbis of his city."[23] This was not a particularly exacting request, especially since the rabbis could regard it as an indirect means of strengthening their own authority, regardless of the real impact of the book.

Nonetheless, R. Katzenellenbogen's initiative seems to have come as a major surprise. Those who heeded his call and signed with him in Venice were not outstanding scholars. Most of them were leaders of the Levantine community, recently settled in Venice; some are unfamiliar to us, and may have also been so to their contemporaries.[24] A typical expression of the surprised response to R. Katzenellenbogen's initiative may be seen in the puzzled and excited letter addressed by R. Abraham Manaḥem Porto ha-Cohen to R. Menaḥem Azariah da Fano in Venice.[25] He reported that he had received "an epistle containing the decree of the excellent scholars [*ge'onim*] and leaders of the holy community of Venice."[26] From that letter he had learned "the important steps that had been taken in this matter on the part of that excellent scholar and leader, his [i.e., R. da Fano's] father-in-law . . . who was the first to take holy action in this matter." R. Porto, however, was certain that de Rossi (whom he had known in Mantua) would have answers to all objections. He was perplexed and did not want to commit a blunder. R. Porto's situation was further complicated by his having heard that R. Eliezer Ashkenazi, who was not then in Cremona and whose opinion was always of great concern to him "had spoken positively of the book."[27] R. Porto had not read the book, but testified rather that "through hearsay I heard of him [de Rossi] having treated lightly the words of the Sages." He had, moreover, heard from de Rossi himself about his dangerously novel chronological theory. What then should he do? R. Porto delivered before his flock a standard sermon on the prohibition of reading *sfarim ḥitzoniyim,* warned them of the potential harmful consequences of a practical nature that could result from de Rossi's chronological reckonings,[28] posted the manifesto in the synagogue *without signing it*, and stood by for clarifications.

We do not know if R. Porto ever received a reply from R. da Fano. We do know, however, that from the information reaching him he could conclude that, notwithstanding his prudence, he had been thrust unintentionally onto the first line of attack, overtly exposed and with no real protection. With the exception of the two rabbis from Verona, a community then subordinate to Venice,[29] and of the leaders of Padua, where there was no appointed rabbi and probably no rabbi at all,[30] almost none of the "excellent scholars of each and every city of the nearby communities in Italy"[31] saw fit to join R. Katzenellenbogen's campaign.

It must be admitted that R. Katzenellenbogen's appeal did not fall solely on deaf ears. The rabbis of the two remaining communities in the Papal States—Rome and Ancona—joined him. The rabbis of Pesaro, some rabbis of Ferrara, and R. Isaac Cohen da Viterbo in Siena, signed as well. It is difficult to characterize these signatories as a group or to understand their motivation. One feels tempted to minimize the weight they carried as representatives of the Italian rabbinic establishment, even if not all of them were "*obscuri viri*." Of the Roman rabbis we know very little, but it is difficult to regard them as outstanding scholars, since contemporary rabbis hinted that they were not.[32] It is also impossible to evaluate the extent to which inquisitional fear in the Papal States during the post-Tridentine period might have played a role in the decision-making process of those rabbis. Some thought might also be given to the possible role of familial ties in bringing some of the signatories together,[33] and to the possible impact on Italian kabbalists[34] of the fact that the appeal originated in a leading kabbalistic center.[35]

All of these considerations, however, proceed on questionable grounds. What is undeniable is that *the majority and senior part of the outstanding Italian scholars never joined R. Katzenellenbogen's campaign*. It was not only such "friends" of de Rossi as R. Moses Proventzalo and R. Judah Moscato (both of whom were among the few who *did* object to de Rossi's arguments) whose names did not appear on the manifesto. Others who did not sign included: R. Raphael Joseph Treves, R. Ḥizkiya (Cesare) Finzi, R. Samuel del Vecchio and R. Abraham Proventzalo of Ferrara; R. Eliezer Ashkenazi, R. Aaron David Norlinghen and R. Isaac Seligman Ḥefetz (Gentili) of Cremona; R. Zangwil Pescarol of Alessandria; and R. David Proventzalo of Mantua. This without mentioning such minor personalities as R. Peretz Trabot, R. Avtalion Modena and R. Solomon Modena in Ferrara; R. Samuel Archivolti, still in Venice at that time; R. Ezra Fano (the teacher of R. Menaḥem Azariah da Fano) and R. Moses Norzi in Mantua.

We must consider that by 1574 the vast majority of Italian Jewry was concentrated in northern Italy, particularly in the duchies of Ferrara, Mantua (including Monferrato) and Milan and in the Venetian Republic. Hence the absence of the above mentioned rabbis, the leading figures of the north Italian rabbinate, from the anti-de Rossi campaign appears all the more significant. In fact, it seems that beyond abstaining, they even supported de Rossi by appending their signature to a document which, unfortunately, has not reached us.[36] In any case, de Rossi had good reason to believe that he could bring the entire affair to an end with minimal effort—by publicizing the signatures of the rabbis who supported him on the one hand, and by printing R. Proventzalo's objections together with his own answers, as well as by making some editorial changes in the troublesome sections of the *Meor Enayim*, on the other.

With that aim in mind he travelled to Venice, where he indeed struck such an agreement. It should be emphasized that *this agreement did not obligate him to retract his statements on the chronological issue*, nor to remove the relevant chapters from the book. This having been achieved, he returned to Mantua, fulfilled his part of the agreement, and could, so far as he was concerned, regard the affair as closed.[37]

De Rossi was now in a position to demand of his opponents to recant. Indeed, once R. Porto saw with his own eyes "bundles of signed testimonies acquitting him and his book, especially those of the two excellent Mantuan scholars" and noted that "the excellent scholars here with us removed the painful thorn from chapter twenty," he fully recanted and removed any restrictions from owning or reading the book. R. Porto signed a document to this effect,[38] and there can be little doubt that his recantation was directly related to the agreement reached by de Rossi in Venice.

In contrast to R. Porto's explicit and public recantation, the signatories of the manifesto simply confined themselves to silence. Anyhow, during the following year some academic discussion of the chronological issue continued,[39] but in other respects, the storm had passed and the book sold.[40] It is even possible that de Rossi benefited from the publicity aroused by the storm, despite the continued reluctance of the more bigoted elements of Italian Jewry to deal with such delicate issues.

The printed manifesto, however, diffused by R. Katzenellenbogen and his acolytes, continued to be preserved. This should not be disregarded. *Verba volant, scripta manent.* Even after the *dramatis personae* had passed away, the printed sheet was capable of triggering the hypersensitive consciences of religious minds whose authoritarian orientation demanded that all controversies be settled in the most stringent manner, so as to satisfy all opinions. With little difficulty one's conscience could be calmed by obtaining formal permission to own and read the book. Doing so could involve other psychological benefits as well: one could pride oneself on having been considered sufficiently mature and sophisticated to read a dangerous book without fear of harm; and the rabbis granting such recognition could see their spiritual authority strengthened as a result of their being empowered to do so.

It seems to me that this psychological dimension helps to explain the survival of statements of permission to read the *Meor Enayim* which were preserved mostly in copies of the book. The earliest of them was issued twenty years after the affair[41] and the others are considerably later.[42] We can reasonably assume that with the passage of time anathemas launched from abroad, such as that of the MaHaRaL, strengthened the impact of the manifesto.

It is possible to adduce indirect testimony concerning the inhibitory powers of the printed edict upon persons who sincerely considered it foreign to their own reality. R. Ḥananel (Graziadio) Neppi (1759–1863), for example, stated that "from his youth" he had heard "that it is prohibited for any student to read this book without first obtaining permission from his master." Upon discovering, however, that there was not to be found in the book "a morsel of heresy or unbelief," he was forced to conclude that

> all this flurry stirred up by those excellent scholars and foundations of the world was probably a result of their apprehension that the book might perhaps come into the hands of some unworthy student, who could drink from the noxious waters of various opinions of certain authors in these matters, and be influenced by them, causing him to stray from the opinions of the Sages and to deny the principles of our holy Torah.[43]

To the original condemnation, itself uncritical and rooted in the idiosyncratic fears of contemporaries, was now added the standard and uncritical assumption that the printed manifesto, despite its perceivable inconsistencies, contained, beneath its surface, certain wise and noble intentions. The ideological exploitation of the past by later scholars did the rest. Thus the *Meor Enayim* came to be presented as a revolutionary and open-minded intellectual system, a precursor of modern Jewish thought, which had confronted the consolidated resistance of a fundamentalist and bigoted rabbinical establishment unwilling to tolerate novelty in such proportions. The later reduction of de Rossi's innovativeness to more modest dimensions only accentuated the apparent bigotry and narrow-mindedness of his rabbinic contemporaries and served to illustrate more clearly the supposed cultural involution which then affected Italian Jewry.

In summation, the *Meor Enayim* controversy can really be seen as little more than a tempest in a teapot, rooted in the misunderstanding of some, the uncritical bigotry of others, most of whom were rather insignificant and by no means representative of either Italian Jewry or its rabbinic establishment.

III

If the preceding reconstruction is correct, regardless of the revolutionary implications of the *Meor Enayim* for later generations, the fact that the contemporary established leadership did not, by and large, disqualify the book, and to some extent even supported it, would seem to indicate that the *Meor Enayim* should be considered an integral part of, and not an exception to, the

Italian Jewish cultural milieu of its time. Perhaps such a presentation of the *Meor Enayim* removes some of the lustre and exotic charm traditionally associated with it. Nonetheless, it is not an excessive price to pay for a more balanced evaluation of the book, *sine ira et studio*, in its proper context, as one type of Jewish response to the intellectual challenges and existential struggles of the Counter-Reformation climate. With this purpose in mind, let us review the basic outlines of the framework of Jewish life in Italy during the early seventies of the sixteenth century.

We may feel inclined to free ourselves from "lachrymose conceptions" of Jewish history, but fashionable and commendable as this inclination might be, it should not induce us to minimize the oppressiveness of the situation in which Jews found themselves. Jews had long been expelled from Sicily and the areas under the sovereignty of Naples. They had, in 1569, been expelled from all Papal territories except Rome and Ancona (an expulsion of which de Rossi himself had been a victim). The Duchy of Tuscany refused shelter to refugees from the Papal States and even hardened its policies towards the Jews.[44] The Venetian attitude too, worsened daily and reached its climax in the late sixties and early seventies.[45] The thousand or so Jews who then lived in the Duchy of Milan were constantly menaced by the fear that *el rey prudente* would finally actualize the thought he had expressed to Milan's governor since 1560, when he wrote from Toledo "*tenemos pensado che seria bien desterrarles desse stado y prohibir que no habiten mas en ello.*"[46] The toleration of a few remaining Jews in some imperial feuds of Liguria and beyond the boundaries of the Genoan Republic, and the aleatory prospects of a pro-Jewish policy expected from the Duke of Savoy[47] did not contribute much to altering the overall picture. Only within the boundaries of the Este and Gonzaga dominions (including Monferrato) was the situation less oppressive.

The dominant anti-Jewish tendency was well suited to the strategic goals and tactics of the Church's policymakers in the Counter-Reformation period. Among the available means of strengthening Catholic orthodoxy, turning the screws on the Jews could surely have appeared as salutary. Destitute as they were of political shelter, the Jews must have been a tempting target. A strike against them would have had immediately visible effects (e.g. the Jewish badge, enforcement of a ghetto policy, the public burning of books), and intensive preoccupation with the "Jewish question" could deflect some of the evangelic energies of perplexed Catholics from the more problematic and delicate issues which faced the Roman Curia. For example, the frenetic missionary activity focused on the "domus cathecumenorum"[48] could have been intended to absorb some of the enthusiastic ardor of the Jesuits. Their "fourth vow" allowed them to regard themselves as the most adept weapon in reformatory issues, and precisely because of this they may have engaged the thoughts of papal policy-makers. It was not a secret that even Paul IV considered their sainted founder a fraud and a tyrant.[49]

In addition to the possibility of tactical considerations of this sort, we must not underestimate the impact of genuine Christian missionary sentiment. In fact, the atmosphere of fundamentalist revival which pervaded Europe at this time contributed to the militant aggressiveness in this sphere. Holiness was linked to ideological war and persecutions, and many were ready to suffer privation and even death for the sake of a single convert.[50] It is understandable that in such a period conversionary pressure increased.

At least one modern scholar has come to the conclusion, based primarily upon changes apparently occurring in official papal documents, that conversion was not only the focus of papal policy toward the Jews in the later sixteenth century, but the core of all papal policy during that period.[51] The deeper we delve into Italian Jewish history of the late sixteenth century, the more numerous become the expressions of the pervading conversionary obsession.[52] Perhaps only one who has had some experience with the pious conversionary aggressiveness of merciful nuns in our own day, or with the ardent militance of missionaries working among poor and infirm non-Christians, can appreciate the oppressive realities of Jewish life in that period.

In an atmosphere of such conversionary enthusiasm, nearly every Christian would regard it as his sacred duty to contribute to the missionary effort. It seems that the first goal was to undermine the Jews' sense of ideological security, although there was some disagreement on how this should be accomplished. Some would argue for a massive attack upon the foundations of Jewish cultural life and for the destruction of their books, particularly the Talmud. After the first edict calling for the burning of the

Talmud (1553), many Italian Catholics had more than one occasion to warm themselves at a "good fire" kindled with Hebrew books.[53] Others would propose to intensify Jewish obligatory attendance at catechismal sermons.[54] Still others would prefer violent pressure upon Jewish scholars,[55] convinced that the conversion of a Jewish leader would not be without consequences among his fellow Jews.

Such repressive steps, however, often provoke counter-productive effects. Despite the burning of the Talmud, for example, many Jews managed to study it clandestinely.[56] The recent experience of Russian Jewry is surely illustrative of what can be done by those who refuse to abandon their peculiar intellectual activity. This is only one step removed from the development of a spirit of martyrdom.[57]

A Jewish defensive response to the pressures exerted upon them could certainly rely heavily upon the apologetic cliché of Jewish superiority that pervaded much of Jewish literature in the fifteenth and sixteenth centuries.[58] Apologetics of this sort, however, can be of different varieties. Sometimes they can represent a creative revival of dormant forces, expressing renewed vigor and self-confidence. At other times, however, the assertion of superiority can be a sign of weakness and decline. It seems to me that between the mid-fifteenth and late sixteenth centuries, with the fundamental change of existential and cultural realities, Italian Jewry moved from one apologetic posture to the other. An illustrative example would be the contrast between the vigorous assertion of Jewish rhetorical supremacy by Messer Leon,[59] and R. Judah Moscato's somewhat stale and artificial comments on Jewish supremacy in music.[60] The former was the expression of an intellectually secure Jewish physician, heir to a rich and proud medieval heritage, which he perpetuated within an enlarged horizon. The latter was a symptomatic expression of the general collapse of the medieval philosophical edifice, hardly bolstered by the newly popular mystical fideism.

I have tried elsewhere to schematically sketch this intellectual crisis in which the ruins of authoritarian medieval thought, mystical fideism, eclecticism and, especially, many interrogatives coexisted in a hodge-podge manner.[61] The practical consequence of this crisis in the realm of Judeo-Christian relations was that the concentrated conversionary effort in the post-Tridentine era caught the Jews in a moment of weakness. Under such circumstances, traditional apologetics would obviously have been less effective. The Jewish response to Christian ideological attack at this time shows signs of perplexity and doubt.[62] Jewish apostates, familiar with the situation in the Jewish camp, directed their Christian patrons in the intensified effort to plant seeds of doubt among Jews by encouraging them to cultivate a previously marginal aspect of Judeo-Christian disputation—the attack upon those aspects of Jewish tradition hardly defensible on logical grounds. This was a radical change of approach from that used when Jews felt ideologically confident and intellectually secure. Earlier in the history of Judeo-Christian disputations, allegations had been made concerning theological inconsistencies and immoral teachings contained in rabbinic literature.[63] The basic arguments of Christians, however, had always centered on christological dogmas (e.g., the Trinity, the divinity of Jesus, etc.) which the Jews had been able to refute on both logical and scriptural grounds. As a result of the general intellectual crisis affecting Italian Jewry, however, Christians began to discover that Jews were no less vulnerable than they when confronted with their own *fabulae et inanes superstitiones* of which there seemed to be no shortage in rabbinic literature. Consequently, this weapon became a regular part of the arsenal of anti-Jewish argumentation.

It should be emphasized that this tactic served both the repressive tendency and the disputational one. On the one hand, Jewish books were burned; on the other, Jews were constrained to answer the questions about these books put to them by Christians. The logical inconsistency of using rabbinic literature both for christological purposes and for demonstrating its own faults never bothered Christian polemicists in their attacks upon Judaism. These Christians could be confident that if they persisted long enough, their efforts would bear fruit. Propaganda, to be effective, must be vociferous, hard-hitting, and persistent; consistency is of little importance. *Calomniez, calomniez, il en restera toujours quelque chose*!

From the Jewish point of view, this inconsistency did not exist. Anything appearing in the rabbinic literature was for most Jews an expression of divine revelation, so that any *inanitas* found there would create serious problems of interpretation. Sixteenth-century Jews were confronted with many such *inanitates* and inconsistencies. Pamphlets in Hebrew, Italian and Latin were published placing particular emphasis upon this problematic aspect of Judaism, and Jews were obliged, therefore, to reflect upon it at every instance of Judeo-Christian debate.[64] Some three hundred years previously, in a climate of relative intellectual security, Naḥmanides could assert nonchalantly that he was not bound to accept the veracity of *Aggadot*. In the sixteenth-century atmosphere of intellectual crisis, a Jew could no longer bypass so easily the apparent challenge presented before him by his faith. He had to wonder honestly whether the writings of the Rabbis really were theologically inconsistent, idolatrous, irrational, and immoral. In addition, with the Renaissance "revival of the sense of the past" and the consequent efforts made by many to reconcile chronological inconsistencies by amassing and critically evaluating erudite evidence from classical authors, Jews were puzzled as to how to respond to Christian arguments claiming that the appearance of Jesus coincided chronologically with the eschatological end predicted by Daniel.[65]

The various Jewish responses to this intellectual challenge were colored, as might be expected, by the individual psychological characteristics of the *dramatis personae*. Some sought shelter through the compilation of handbooks containing traditional Jewish responses to Christian arguments. These felt that originality was less valuable than tested cogency for the practical purposes of daily polemical encounter.[66] Others concentrated on intricate attempts to explain satisfactorily some of the Talmudic passages used in anti-Jewish polemic. Perhaps it was their hope that even if the Christians were not quieted as a result, Jewish ideological self-confidence would be strengthened by the belief that everything in rabbinic literature had profound meaning on both esoteric and exoteric levels, and was deserving therefore of both veneration and defense.[67] The resort to kabbalistic interpretation of some of these problematic passages certainly contributed to fortifying the isolationist component of the Jewish response. It is difficult to determine, however, to what extent this approach stemmed from tactical considerations and to what extent it was a function of sincere conviction rooted in a specific mental framework.

In contrast to these, however, others could reasonably maintain that the refusal to meet the intellectual challenge head-on would have dangerous and self-destructive consequences—among them, the isolation of Jews from organic contact with the surrounding environment. After all, many problems posed by Christian polemic were real ones for every believing Jew, and had to be confronted sooner or later.

I venture to argue that de Rossi's main purpose in the *Meor Enayim* was to formulate a confidently straightforward and intellectually tenable position within the framework of the above described problematic. De Rossi, as I understand him, was of the conviction that Judaism could not be defended without bringing truth to light, because "truth is God's seal."[68] If Naḥmanides asserted disingenuously that he did not feel bound to accept the veracity of *Aggadot*, de Rossi said the same in earnest and made his opinion known to his coreligionists. He could not identify with the efforts of those rabbis who continually pursued any dialectical contortion that would free them from confronting the real problem. Rather, he sought to determine the limits of rabbinic authority and concluded that rabbinic statements were binding only insofar as they affected the normative structure of Judaism.

The distinction between normative and non-normative issues dealt with in rabbinic literature had important consequences. On a practical level, and of particular relevance to the Judeo-Christian confrontation, it meant that one could accept the presence of inconsistencies, and even *inanitates*, in the Talmud without having to reject its basic authority. Even further, one could freely examine rabbinic chronology and deduce the impossibility of certainty in such matters without weakening rabbinic authority on normative issues. The practical consequence of this claim was that all chronological theories were subject to doubt, and hence, all messianic speculations based upon them of dubious value. This would obviously weaken the demonstrative edge of Christian messianic calculations in addition to eliminating the traumatic frustrations which always accompanied messianic expectation—frustrations which de Rossi seems to have suffered from in his youth.[69] In sum, it appears that de Rossi regarded the critical approach to rabbinic literature, in non-normative matters, as the most effective means of defending Judaism.

IV

In presenting the above argument, let me defend myself in the manner of de Rossi. There is no originality in the argument itself. Baron already noted the apologetic thread connecting the essays in the *Meor Enayim*. Baron, however, saw in it a dogmatic restraint imposed upon de Rossi by his religious *habitus mentalis*, which had a restraining impact upon his critical approach. The apologetic spirit present in the *Meor Enayim* seemed to Baron a vestige of an anti-rationalistic tendency from which de Rossi did not succeed in freeing himself completely.[70] I suggest that the apologetic trend is the principal and essential force behind de Rossi's intellectual effort, and that this trend determined both the scope and direction of his research. There were, to be sure, other goals of great importance for Jewish posterity which were achieved as by-products. With regard to these, however, I fully support Baron's assertion that de Rossi "unconsciously and rather blindly and timidly" stumbled into celebrity.[71]

Indeed, it would be difficult to deny the pervading presence of apologetic enthusiams in the *Meor Enayim*. Cicero would surely praise de Rossi for his acting as *exornator rerum* in reporting the laudable conduct of the Jews during the Ferrara earthquake.[72] Any Renaissance Jew would certainly have been grateful to de Rossi for having made known Ptolemy's testimony in the letter of Aristeas concerning the superior political achievements of the Jews; de Rossi devoted much space to the subject (all of *Hadrat Zkenim* as well as chapters 8–9), so that Jews could learn that Alexander's admiration of Jewish wisdom, known to them from rabbinic literature, was no isolated phenomenon. De Rossi's "sense of the past" seems to have been oriented also to discovering what recent efforts of a similar nature have called *The Jewish Contribution*: the Jewish contribution to linguistics, poetry, etc. (chapters 56–60). More generally, de Rossi sought to marshal every testimony from the past that would bring honor to Judaism. Philo's testimony might well, in his opinion, have served as a *pendant* to the testimony of Aristeas; he devoted four chapters to him. The six chapters devoted to the priestly garments and the splendors of the Temple of Jerusalem may also have been intended to serve the same purpose. In my opinion de Rossi is presenting here his own response to the claim of "whatever happened, happened" as far as sacerdotal garments are considered.[73]

The same apologetic tendency can be discerned in his special interest in converts to Judaism (chapters 45, 52). De Rossi himself openly declared that his major aim in consulting gentile literature was to find whatever evidence would be useful "in supporting any part of our Torah."[74] And there is, of course, no need to stress the apologetic thrust of the chapter demonstrating the obligation of Jews to pray for the safety of the ruling authorities.[75]

De Rossi, in addition, openly stated that his search for truth was subordinate to his desire to understand Scripture or to clarify certain messianic problems. I see no reason to doubt the sincerity of his three-fold justification for historical research:

> First, for the sake of truth itself, which is sought also by thousands of scholars through investigations more irrelevant than this one. It is like a divine seal; [it is] the virtue of a beautiful soul; [it is] worthy of being sought after by all. Second, *and more important*, is that in the process of this inquiry we shall have occasion to understand certain scriptural passages better. . . . And the third reason, not to be dismissed, is that from this discussion will be truly clarified issues relevant to the time of the Messiah [*hilkheta li-meshiḥa*], whose coming, according to many reliable sources, is imminent, and who will remove the obstacles in the path of our people.[76]

I venture to propose that these words express not only a rather modern motivation for historical research,[77] but also a programmatic exposition of de Rossi's own intentions in writing the book. True, we are informed that beyond the aesthetic pleasure it can provide, research into truth itself is history's "raison d'être." However, such a justification is insufficient. History must be of actual concern to the historian himself, otherwise it lacks relevance—"whatever happened, happened". The search for historical truth must be integrally rooted in the existential interests of the seeker. One of the primary existential concerns of de Rossi and his contemporaries was the defense of Judaism. This involved meeting the challenge of interpreting Scripture in a manner consonant with both reason and experience, defending rabbinic literature from the attacks of Christians and Jewish apostates, as well as seeking to discredit messianic calculations, especially Christian ones of the "historical" sort. As a result, beyond the general and panegyric tendencies discussed previously, we notice de Rossi confronting the specific aspects of the above-mentioned problematic.

De Rossi sought to formulate a proper method for dealing with these problems—a method based on the courage to accept whatever *ratio* and experience decreed to be self-evident, even at the cost of slaughtering several holy cows. His strategy was simple: unveil the truth. He was firmly convinced that this was sufficient to wage the battle successfully.

Without taking this into consideration, it would be difficult to explain the lengthy exegetical digressions and tedious cosmogonic excursus that constitute the bulk of de Rossi's description of the Ferrara earthquake, even if we generously recognize that he was one of the more attentive observers of the event.[78] It would be even more difficult to understand how a writer who could demand of his readers that they follow his dull reckonings concerning the impossibility of determining whether or not some years must be added to the number of years elapsed since creation, could reply nonchalantly on a similar issue that "in truth, as far as antiquity is concerned . . . we can say that whatever happened, happened."[79] We must conclude that for de Rossi, more important than the calculations themselves was the importance of showing that there existed no reliable chronology, so that all messianic speculations based on chronology were of no value.

In my opinion, even the sequence of chapters dealing with this problematic issue, which constitute, in fact, the bulk of the book, can be shown to support this conclusion. After chapter forty, which closes the chronological section, comes a chapter in which de Rossi presents his own interpretation of the "seventy weeks" in Daniel's prophecy (Daniel 9). Then follows a chapter dealing with general chronological principles which closes with a discussion concerning the advisability of raising doubts on such issues among the masses, in light of the potentially dangerous consequences. De Rossi states here that his book is not intended for the masses, but rather, for their spiritual leaders, since, in his opinion, "the masses are merely the trumpet of the learned whose sound depends upon how much they blow into it."[80] As for himself, de Rossi believed that the three-fold advantage to be gained from the search after truth justified every risk it involved. These were, to repeat, the clarification of truth for its own sake, clarification of the meaning of Scripture, and achieving a better understanding of messianic issues. After this discussion there follows a chapter dealing with the messianic expectations of the Jews for the year 1575, and then one which investigates the rabbinic dictum, "The world is to exist for six thousand years and to be destroyed for one thousand."

Does not this sequence suggest an internal thread connecting these apparently disconnected essays and does the thread not seem to be related to the messianic issue in the context of Judeo-Christian debates? In my opinion, this conclusion is fully consistent with my prior assertion that de Rossi's heavy reliance upon gentile authors was essentially an expression of his conviction that Judaism could be defended more effectively by using non-Jewish sources. There seems no reason to doubt his sincerity. Modern anti-defamation tactics have naturally followed a similar direction.[81] Even his textual criticism, which, in my opinion, does not differ substantially from the editorial work of preparing texts for print, and was surely then a common feature of learned study,[82] has an apologetic edge, for it suggests the possibility that embarrassing passages may have resulted from corruptions or falsifications.[83]

This conclusion harmonizes with still another one—that de Rossi's particular method of dealing with *Aggadot* was formulated principally for the purpose of defending rabbinic literature from slurs concerning its contents. I see no reason not to accept de Rossi's programmatic statement at face value: "Our Sages in their *midrashim* interpreted many verses in a variety of ways, not because they believed these interpretations to be [literally] correct. . . . Hence, anyone who questions the *midrash* on the basis of *pshat* or who understands the *midrash* to be *pshat* attributes to them [i.e., the Rabbis] what they never imagined."[84] In this case too there is a thread connecting the apparently disconnected essays of the second part of *Meor Enayim*—the underlying notion that rabbinic statements need not be accepted at face value, and even that the Rabbis could err in their discussions of non-normative issues. To cite de Rossi's own words, he was acting here also "in the manner of a good physician who widens the wound for the purpose of administering the proper cure."[85] The entire second part of *Meor Enayim* is devoted to widening the wound, coming progressively to the conclusion that if rabbinic statements can be questioned, there is *a fortiori* nothing wrong with applying critical method to a chronological tradition demonstrably post-Talmudic. Neither *Aggadot* nor chronological traditions were of normative significance and therefore one could confidently maintain that the Rabbis could err in these spheres. There was no reason to infer from errors of this sort, however, that rabbinic tradition itself was to be rejected. De Rossi explicitly states in the closing sections of Part II that his primary aiṃ is to present "an apology for our Sages"[86] in such issues, allowing for errors on their part. I see no reason to doubt him.

In summary, then, with the exception of some marginal chapters, basically academic excursus regarding problems discussed earlier (e.g. chapters 53, 54), the gist of the book, as well as the message conveyed by the structure of the chapters was: Jews need not be perplexed by errors, inconsistencies or even, *inanitates* to be found in rabbinic literature nor need they be confused by chronological reckonings bolstering Christian arguments, but neither should these problems be avoided by means of intricate and insincere dialectics. Rather, Jews should apply critical methods based on *ratio* and experience to the search for pure and inviolate truth. Such an approach would cause them to admit that there were indeed unreliable and problematic passages in rabbinic literature, but there was nothing wrong or dangerous in that admission. On the contrary, the search for truth would provide formidable weapons for defending Judaism in times of intellectual crisis.[87]

It may well be that the *Meor Enayim* was not very original so far as method, critical approach to texts, or comparative use of sources was concerned. De Rossi himself made some effort to help us perceive his ties to medieval Jewish predecessors as well as to the learned gentile milieu of the Renaissance. There is no denying his originality, however, in the manner in which he sought to meet the intellectual challenge facing the Jews of this time.[88]

The book did not achieve its goal. De Rossi's message reached neither his fellow Jews nor the gentiles. The latter thought in the same terms as de Rossi's rabbinic antagonists—they caught in de Rossi's critical treatment of traditional texts a hint of subversionary tendencies, inferring that he was distancing himself from Judaism and approaching conversion to Christianity.[89] Rabbi Judah Moscato was indeed correct—the reaction to doubt is difficult to control. But it seems to me that de Rossi was also correct; it is impossible to defend Judaism in times of crisis by taking shelter in a fortress built upon false foundations. The tragedy of the situation was that, as always, the clash of ideologies in a climate of fervent hatred prevented truth from finding its way to quiet the storm. De Rossi remained alone in his time, not because of his revolutionary breakthroughs in scientific criticism and research, but because such is the fate of men who persevere in battle during troubled times armed only with the weapon of truth.

NOTES

1. See Salo W. Baron's three articles: "Azariah de' Rossi's Attitude to Life," *Jewish Studies in Memory of Israel Abrahams* (New York, 1927), pp. 12–52; "Azariah de' Rossi—A Biographical Sketch," (revised translation of the Hebrew published in Eshkol, *Hebrew Encyclopedia* [Berlin, 1929], coll. 689–693); and "Azariah de' Rossi's Historical Method," (revised translation of "La méthode historique d'Azaria de Rossi," *REJ* 86 [1928] 157–175; 87 [1929], 43–78); all reprinted in Baron's *History and Jewish Historians* (Philadelphia, 1964), pp. 167–239 and 405–442. The essential literature up to the dates of Baron's publications is listed in the notes. Some additional pertinent literature will be given below.

2. See Baron, "A Biographical Sketch," and idem, "Historical Method," and cf. also Isaac E. Barzilay, "The Italian and Berlin Haskalah: Parallels and Differences," *PAAJR* 29 (1960–61), p. 30.

3. A bird's-eye survey of the literature on this particular point would prove instructive concerning the conditioning effects of scholars' cultural backgrounds on the one hand, and of the inertial dynamic inherent in the cumulative force of repetition on the other. To early scholarship it seemed that the opposition was focused, naturally enough, in Safed, due to the fact that Safed's rabbis were ignorant of the peculiar cultural atmosphere of Renaissance Italian Jewry. Consequently it was suggested that Italian rabbis aligned themselves behind the injunction upon the members of their community that none under the age of twenty-five read the *Meor Enayim* without rabbinic authorization. Y. L. Zunz, "R. Azariah de Rossi" [Hebrew], *Kerem Ḥemed* 5 (5601), 131–158; 7(5603), 119–124 (reprinted at the end of *Sefer Meor Enayim*, ed. Ben-Ya'akov [Vilna, 5623–5626]). This position proved untenable upon publication of evidence discovered by David Kaufmann, "Contributions à l'histoire des luttes d'Azaria de Rossi," *REJ* 33 (1896), 77–87 (reprinted as "Geschichte der Kämpfe Azarja dei Rossis," *Gesammelte Schriften*, III [Frankfurt a. M., 1915], pp. 83–95) and by S. Z. H. Halberstamm, "Three Letters Concerning the *Meor Enayim* and a Letter Concerning Its Author R. Azariah de Rossi as well as Another Letter about Him" [Hebrew], in *Tehila le-Moshe: Kvutzat Ma'amarim li-Khvod Moshe Shteinshneider* (Leipzig, 5656), pp. 1–8. Now some bigoted and fundamentalist Italian rabbis seemed to be allied with Safed's rabbis in condemning de Rossi's excessively progressive spirit. From this point it was only a short step to presenting de Rossi as "this free investigator and founder of scientific historical criticism" who "was too far in advance of his generation" (Israel Zinberg, *A History of Jewish Literature*, tr. and ed. by Bernard Martin [New York, 1974], IV, p. 107). Thus, according to Zinberg's account, "the report of dei Rossi's heretical work agitated *all* the Italian rabbis and Talmudic scholars (ibid., p. 111). "Immediately after the Venetian rabbis, those of other cities (Rome, Ferrara, Padua, Pesaro, Verona, Ancona *and others*) also came out against *Meor Enayim*" (ibid., p. 112; cf. the list of signatories of the manifesto reproduced in Kaufmann, "Contributions," pp. 83–85, and see infra). The only exception was registered in Mantua: "In Mantua where *Meor Enayim* was published and where such a prominent role was played by dei Rossi's old and intimate friends Jehudah Moscato and Moses Provinciali [*sic*] the Rabbis forbade anyone who was not yet twenty-five to read the work without special permission" (ibid., p. 113; see also Israel Mehlmann, "Concerning the Book *Meor Enayim* of R. Azariah de Rossi" [Hebrew], *Sefer Zer li-Gvurot: Sefer ShaZaR* [Jerusalem, 5733], pp. 638–57, reprinted in Mehlmann's *Genuzot Sfarim: Ma'amarim Bibliografiyim* [Jerusalem, 5736], pp. 21–39). Even Baron who quite rightly wrote that "some Italian rabbis

and elders . . . decided to proclaim a mild ban" ("A Biographical Sketch," p. 171), referred immediately after that to the "attitude of the Italian leaders" in general (p. 172). To be sure, it is not difficult to find more balanced and shaded presentations. Due to the importance that Hebrew scholarship has, since the last century, attributed to de Rossi, reference to him and to his book is to be found in almost every study of the intellectual history of the Jews. In most cases, however, one receives the impression that balance and gradation are really the expression of not more than precaution adopted by skilled historians compelled to rely on the results of others' research. See, e.g., Shlomo Simonsohn, *History of the Jews in the Duchy of Mantua* (Jerusalem, 1977), pp. 634ff.

4. Such a conclusion, drawn from this particular issue, would be consistent with an apparently general tendency of Jewish historiography with regard to sixteenth-century Italian Jewry. In the last chapter of my general study on *The Rabbinate in Renaissance Italy* (in Hebrew: *Ha-Rabanut be-Italya bi-Tkufat ha-Renesans* [Jerusalem, 5739]), pp. 173ff., I set forward some reservations regarding this tendency. As shall be easily seen, the position suggested in this article is consistent with the general line adopted there.

5. Peter Burke, *The Renaissance Sense of the Past* (New York, 1969).

6. As far as I can see, the opposition to de Rossi's work did not insist upon any of these arguments; see infra my schematic reconstruction of the controversy.

7. On the kabbalistic component of the opposition to de Rossi's work, see infra.

8. It would be superfluous to mention here the terms of the debate upon this issue starting with Maimonides who formulated the question clearly in his introduction to *Perek Ḥelek*. The evidence adduced by de Rossi himself (chapters 14–16) is sufficient.

9. See Baron, "De Rossi's Historical Method." Baron is surely correct in pointing to figures such as Panvinio as possible models for de Rossi. De Rossi's motley essays are indeed very similar to the erudite notes composed by Panvinio on similar subjects. See, e.g., Panvinio's notes to Platina's "Delle vite dei Pontefici," passim. But how much *historiography* is to be found there?

10. As is well known, the core of de Rossi's argument was that, due to a complex of chronological inconsistencies in traditional biblical exegesis as well as in the historical evidence borrowed from both Jewish and gentile sources, it was impossible to maintain with certainty that the number of years that had elapsed since the creation of the world was identical with the number retained by tradition. As a corollary to this point de Rossi stated that the traditional view, according to which in the year of creation the new moon appeared on Monday at five o'clock and 204/1080 of an hour (בהר״ד), was pure convention, useful for calendrical calculations but not true in itself.

11. In formulating this phrase I had in mind the semi-polemical letter of R. Judah Moscato (see Halberstamm, "Three Letters") and the argument of R. Moses Proventzalo (see infra), where reference is made to the First Temple only. *Cela va sans dire* that if we add the difference relating to the Second Temple, the reckoning turns out quite differently. As shall be seen, augmentation of the discrepancy would sharpen proportionally the message of the book within the particular atmosphere in which, I believe, it was conceived. I am grateful to Professor David Berger who very opportunely noted the necessity of making it clear that "some twenty years" is not to be taken literally.

12. For the first objection see R. Moscato's letter in Kaufmann, "Contributions à l'histoire des luttes," pp. 81–83. For the second, see R. Proventzalo's formulation in his letter printed at the end of the *Meor Enayim* (Cassel's edition, pp. 491ff.; all future references will be to that edition). It may be interesting to note that this was not simply the uncritical argument of a bigoted rabbi, but one of the main issues debated by theoreticians of historiography in de Rossi's days; see Eckhard Kessler, *Theoretiker humanistischer Geschichtsschreibung* (Munich, 1971).

13. E.g., would not the chronological findings cause the annulment of all bills of divorce? See R. Abraham Menaḥem Porto ha-Cohen's letter to R. Menaḥem Azariah da Fano (Kaufmann, "Contributions à l'histoire des luttes," pp. 85–86). Or, as all calendrical calculations begin with בהר״ד (see supra, n. 10) and are based upon the principle that between two new-moons is a fixed interval, would not de Rossi's assumption that בהר״ד was not true in itself revolutionize all future calendrical calculations? This objection was raised by R. Proventzalo in his above-mentioned letter, and was clearly refuted by de

Rossi, but his opponents do not seem to have been convinced. Cf. Rabbi Isaac Finzi's questions as summarized in *Matzref le-Kesef*.

14. As far as I know the only evidence still in manuscript concerning the *Meor Enayim* affair are paragraphs 65–68 in R. Proventzalo's still unpublished responsa. See my "The Commentary of R. Moses Proventzalo to Maimonides' Twenty-Five Axioms" [Hebrew], *Kiryat Sefer* 50 (5735), pp. 164–65. These responsa were well known to Kaufmann who only published paragraph 69. Kaufmann surely held the opinion that the remaining paragraphs did not add useful information, and he seems to have been quite correct in that regard.

15. See Meir Benayahu, *Haskama u-Reshut bi-Dfusei Venetziya* [Copyright, Authorization and Imprimatur for Hebrew Books Printed in Venice] (Jerusalem, 1971), p. 92.

16. R. Proventzalo's letter is dated Elul, 5333 (August, 1573) and is in paragraph 68 of his responsa (above, n. 14). Kaufmann did not publish it because the main argument it contained was included in the longer letter, dated 24 Ḥeshvan (21 October) 1573, that was published by de Rossi himself at the end of *Meor Enayim* together with his own comments (and see infra).

17. See de Rossi's answer to R. Proventzalo's second letter, as appended to the *Meor Enayim*.

18. Reggio seems to have been a center of kabbalistic studies even before Menaḥem Azariah da Fano settled there. This may be inferred from an anonymous letter sent from Venice to the Jewish leaders of Reggio, stating that these were the leading figures in the kabbalistic field of the day. The letter states: "For you are the leaders of the holy nation, the sons of Reggio, and we depend upon your words in the wisdom of Kabbalah." It was written around the year 1580 (MS Alliance Israélite Universelle H2 A, f. 162r). I am grateful to Professor Meir Benayahu who brought it to my attention. The style of this statement seems to exclude the possibility that it alludes *sic et simpliciter* to R. Menaḥem Azariah da Fano who moved from Venice to Reggio only in 1580 as can be demonstrated with a quite high degree of precision. See my Hebrew article, "New Information on the Life and Times of R. Menaḥem Azariah da Fano," in *Sefer ha-Yovel li-Khvod Ya'akov Katz* (Jerusalem, 5740), pp. 98–134.

19. Bonfil, "Information on da Fano." On R. Foa's letter see the one written by R. Abraham Manaḥem Porto ha-Cohen to R. Manaḥem Azariah da Fano (Kaufmann, "Contributions à l'histoire des luttes," pp. 85–86).

20. Bonfil, *Ha-Rabanut be-Italya*, pp. 143, 197–199.

21. It may be inferred from the opening passage of the manifesto that R. Katzenellenbogen took the initiative to disseminate "upon hearing of the book written and newly printed by R. Azariah de Rossi." The words "newly printed" (*hidpis me-ḥadash*) seem to allude to the text of the above-mentioned Ferrara ordinance "that publishers may not print any book never before printed." From that and other possible allusions it seems that the ordinance not only did not fall into disuse but even was, in R. Katzenellenbogen's eyes, the juridical basis of the opposition. If so, R. Katzenellenbogen may have seen himself as defending the honor of his father who was the first signatory of the Ferrara ordinances. But see Benayahu, *Haskama u-Reshut*, loc. cit. above n. 15.

22. See Kaufmann, "Contributions à l'histoire des luttes," p. 83.

23. Ibid., idem.

24. See their names apud Kaufmann, ibid. According to Sh. Simonsohn in the "Introduction" to his edition of R. Judah Arye da Modena's *She'elot u-Tshuvot Ziknei Yehuda* [Responsa] (Jerusalem, 5715), p. 43, R. Abraham Barukh Katz "was among the signatories of the ban published against Rabbi Azariah de Rossi." I was not able to check this assertion. Needless to say, among the signatories do not appear the names of the other "excellent leaders" (*ge'onim rashiyim*) who frequently signed after R. Katzenellenbogen: R. Avigdor Cividal, R. Ben-Zion Zarfatti, R. Yehuda Leib Saraval. Perhaps they had not yet settled in Venice in 1574.

25. See above, note 19. On Rabbi Porto and his position in Cremona, see Bonfil, *Ha-Rabanut be-Italya*, pp. 88–92.

26. As previously stated, no "ge'onim" of Venice joined Rabbi Katzelellenbogen's manifesto. R. Porto is simply, but diplomatically, borrowing the expression from the text of

the manifesto. It seems to me that the personality of Rabbi Porto, his peculiar position in Cremona and the fact that the letter was addressed to R. da Fano, make it improbable that he is being ironic.

27. See Bonfil, *Ha-Rabanut be-Italya*, pp. 88–92 for how weighty such an argument could be in R. Porto's considerations.

28. See above, n. 13

29. See Bonfil, *Ha-Rabanut be-Italya*, pp. 76–80.

30. Ibid., pp. 81–88.

31. Kaufmann, "Contributions à l'histoire des luttes."

32. See H.-M. Merḥavya, "An Anti-Talmudic Pamphlet from the Period of the Burning of the Talmud in Italy" [Hebrew], *Tarbitz* 37 (5728), p. 82 and n. 9.

33. In Ferrara two of the six signatories were brothers (Moses and Aaron Finzi); in Pesaro two of the five were brothers-in-law (Yeḥiel Trabot and Mahalalel Yedidya ben Barukh). See Eric Zimmer, "Biographical Data on Italian Jewry from the Pen of Abraham Graziadio" [Hebrew], *Kiryat Sefer* 49 (5734), p. 444 and n. 24.

34. In particular, two of the Pesaro signatories were rather famous kabbalists: Emanuel ben Gavriel and Isaac Finzi.

35. See above, n. 18.

36. See below.

37. See de Rossi's own statement at the end of the pages he revised and printed in fulfillment of the agreement, as reproduced by Mehlmann, "Concerning the *Meor Enayim*." It may be of interest to note, en passant, that the revised chapter 20 with the exclusion of the paragraphs that shocked his opponents, differs not at all from the original, so far as its main thesis is concerned. One can reasonably suggest that in its new form that thesis is even more effectively stated.

38. See Halberstamm, "Three Letters," pp. 1–3.

39. R. Moses Proventzalo corresponded with R. Zangwill Pescarol and R. Eliezer Ashkenazi concerning certain calendrical problems related to issues raised by de Rossi. See R. Proventzalo's *Responsa*, paragraphs 65–67. R. Isaac Finzi wrote a pamphlet which elicited de Rossi's response in *Matzref le-Kesef*.

40. It is unnecessary to emphasize that commercial considerations surely were among the prominent factors which encouraged de Rossi to compromise and to accept the abovementioned agreement. He had invested several hundred ducats (possibly some two thousand) in the book and was not so wealthy that he could accept such a loss easily.

41. See David Tamar, "The Messianic Expectations in Italy for the Year 1575," *Sefunot* 2 (1958), p. 66, n. 34.

42. In a copy in the library of Professor Meir Benayahu, there are two such permissions: one signed in 1650 by R. Jacob Ḥagiz and R. Joshua Fermi, and another signed in Ancona in 1705 by R. Shabbetai Panzieri and R. Joseph Fiammetta. I am indebted to Professor Benayahu for having made this information available to me.

43. See Halberstamm, "Three Letters." This document was reproduced by Joseph Jarè, "Fragments from the Writings of R. Ḥananel Neppi," in *Zikaron le-Avraham Eliyahu Harkavi* (St. Petersburg, 5769).

44. See Umberto Cassuto, *Gli ebrei a Firenze nell'età del Rinascimento* (Florence, 1918; reprint 1965), pp. 98–117.

45. See Brian Pullan, *Rich and Poor in Renaissance Venice* (Cambridge, MA, 1971), pp. 510–537.

46. See Renata Segre, *Gli ebrei lombardi nell'età spagnola. Storia di un'espulsione* (Turin, 1973). The citation of Philip's words is on p. 37.

47. See Ḥayim Beinart, "The Settlement of the Jews in the Duchy of Savoy as a result of the 1572 Privilege" [Hebrew], *Sefer Zikaron le-Arye Leone Carpi* (Milan and Jerusalem, 1967), Hebrew section, pp. 72–118.

48. On the *domus catechumenorum* see Kenneth R. Stow, *Catholic Thought and Papal Jewry 1555–1593* (New York, 1977), pp. 52ff. and the literature listed there. See also Attilio Milano, "Battesimi di ebrei a Roma dal cinquecento all'ottocento," *Scritti in memoria di Enzo Sereni* (Milan and Jerusalem, 1970), pp. 101–167, and Joseph B. Sermonetta, "Tredici

giorni nella casa dei conversi dal diario di una giovane ebrea del 18° secolo," *Michael* 1 (1972), pp. 261–315.

49. Marvin R. O'Connell, *The Counter-Reformation 1559–1610* (New York, 1974).

50. Ibid., p. 31.

51. Stow, *Catholic Thought*, p. 5.

52. See Renata Segre, "Neophytes during the Italian Counter-Reformation: Identities and Biographies," *Proceedings of the Sixth World Congress of Jewish Studies* (Jerusalem, 1975), II, pp. 131–142; Stow, *Catholic Thought*, pp. 3–59; Milano, "Battesimi di ebrei a Roma"; Salo W. Baron, *A Social and Religious History of the Jews*, 2nd ed., XIV (New York, 1969), pp. 71–146; and the literature cited by these authors.

53. See on this subject the recent contributions of Kenneth R. Stow, "The Burning of the Talmud in 1553 in the Light of Sixteenth-Century Catholic Attitudes toward the Talmud," *Bibliothèque d'Humanisme et Renaissance* 34 (1972), pp. 435–459; Paul Grendler, "The Destruction of Hebrew Books in Venice, 1568," *PAAJR* 45 (1978), pp. 103–130, and the bibliographical references listed by them.

54. See Stow, *Catholic Thought*, pp. 19–21 and the literature cited there.

55. See the description of R. Ishmael da Valmontone upon his encounter with the inquisition in Bologna published in *Ha-Shaḥar* 2 (5631), pp. 17–23. On the traumatic experience of a stay in the *domus cathecumenorum* see the 17th-century (!) diary of a young lady published by Sermonetta (above, n. 48).

56. See Bonfil, *Ha-Rabanut be-Italya*, pp. 22–23.

57. See R. Ishmael da Valmontone's account (above, n. 55) and my article, "One of R. Mordekhai Dato's Italian Sermons" [Hebrew], *Italia* 1 (1976), pp. 1–32 of the Hebrew section.

58. See Bonfil, "Expressions of the Unity of the People of Israel in Italy during the Renaissance," *Sinai* 76 (5735), 36–46.

59. See my forthcoming introduction to *Sefer Nofet Tzufim*, reprint of the *editio princeps* by the Jewish National and University Library.

60. Israel Adler, *Hebrew Writings Concerning Music in Manuscripts and Printed Books from Geonic Times up to 1800* (Munich, 1975), pp. 221–239.

61. Bonfil, *Ha-Rabanut be-Italya*, pp. 173ff.

62. See Rabbi Obadiah Sforno's introduction to *Sefer Or Amim*, and cf. Bonfil, "Theories of the Soul and of Sanctity in the Teachings of R. Obadiah Sforno" [Hebrew], *Eshel Be'er Sheva* 1 (5736), 200–257.

63. See Amos Funkenstein, "Changes in the Religious Debate between Christians and Jews in the Twelfth Century" (Hebrew), *Zion* 37 (5728), pp. 125–144.

64. See Merḥavya, "An Anti-Talmudic Pamphlet"; Gerard Vultuyck, *Shvilei Tohu, Itinera deserti* (Venice, 1539) passim. On the daily obsessive meetings on these issues see Shlomo Simonsohn, "I banchieri Da Rieti in Toscana," *RMI* 38 (1972), 406–423, 487–499, documents 6–7.

65. See, e.g., F. Fioghi, *Dialogo fra il Cathecumeno e il padre Cathechizante* (Rome, 1582), f. 199–206. In all Fioghi's reckonings the duration of the Second Temple is understood to have been 420 years.

66. See, e.g., Ya'ir da Correggio, *Ḥerev Pifiyot*, ed. Judah Rosenthal (Jerusalem, 5718).

67. See R. Jacob Israel ben Raphael Finzi's responsum in MS Montefiore 113, paragraph 132 (the responsum is also found in JNUL MS 8° 1992, f. 6^{v}–9^{v}). Rabbi Jacob Israel ben Raphael Finzi was the great-uncle of Rabbi Isaac Finzi, the opponent of de Rossi. I hope to publish this responsum in the future.

68. *Meor Enayim*, chapter 29, p. 276.

69. This can be inferred from the fact that he copied extensively from messianic literature when he was nearly seventeen. See Malakhi Bet-Arye, "A Letter concerning the Ten Tribes by the Kabbalist R. Abraham ben Eliezer ha-Levi from the Year [5]288" [Hebrew], *Kovetz al Yad*, n.s., 6 [=16] (5726), pp. 369–378.

70. See Baron, "De Rossi's Historical Method," and cf. Barzilay, "Italian and Berlin Haskalah," p. 30.

71. See Baron, "De Rossi's Attitude to Life," p. 174.

72. It may be interesting to compare de Rossi's narrative with Elia Levita's description of Venetian Jews' behavior in similarly adverse circumstances. See Ḥ. Shmeruk, "Elijah Baḥur's Poem About the Burning of Venice" [Hebrew], *Kovetz al Yad*, n.s., 6 [=16] (5726), pp. 343–368.

73. Cf. BT, *Yoma*, 6b.

74. *Meor Enayim*, p. 101; and cf. Bonfil, "Expressions of Unity".

75. Chap. 45. It may be interesting to note that R. Jacob Israel Finzi endeavored to do the same in his previously mentioned responsum (above, n. 67).

76. I am well aware that the literal meaning of 'hilkheta li-meshiḥa' is not as broad as the one I propose here. I hope, however, that my remarks below will lend support to my translation.

77. Cf. Eliezer Schweid, *Toldot he-Hagut ha-Yehudit ba-Et ha-Ḥadasha* [History of Jewish Thought in Modern Times] (Jerusalem, 5738), p. 88. In my opinion, Schweid is right in seeing here one of the outstanding contributions of de Rossi to modern Jewish thought. Cf. Croce's definition of all history as contemporary history; Benedetto Croce, *Il concetto della storia* (Bari, 1954), pp. 124–127.

78. See N. Shalem, "Una fonte ebraica poco nota sul terremoto di Ferrara del 1570," *Rivista geografica italiana* (1938), pp. 66–76.

79. *Meor Enayim*, p. 501.

80. Ibid., p. 365.

81. See above, n. 78 and de Rossi's statements in *Meor Enayim*, chap. 2.

82. See e.g., de Rossi's own testimony, ibid., p. 233.

83. Chap. 19 seems to have been devoted to this purpose.

84. Ibid., p. 201.

85. Ibid., end of chap. 14, p. 201.

86. See, e.g., the titles of chap. 27 and 28: "An Apology for our Sages, even if it be assumed that in narrating certain events which are not relevant to the laws of the Torah, they did not penetrate to their truth and did not relate it to us," and "A Second Apology regarding any error which might be found in their incidental remarks [*mili de-alma*] from which, however, one may on no account infer or state that they erred, God forbid, one whit, in a matter of Law [*divrei tora*].

87. In such a position one is tempted to see the roots of some of S. D. Luzzatto's positions. Cf. Barzilay, "Italian and Berlin Haskalah," p. 20.

88. It was a pleasant surprise for me to discover that Professor Bezalel Safran's reading of the *Meor Enayim* points in the same direction I suggest here. See his "Azariah de Rossi's *Meor Enayim*," doctoral dissertation, Harvard University, 1979. The "intelligent reader" (this being *my* interpretation of de Rossi's term *kore maskil*) will find there additional textual support for the central argument presented here. Professor Safran and I carried on, within the warm hospitality of his home, several long and friendly discussions on this matter. Just as he did not succeed in convincing me of the comprehensively esoteric character of the *Meor Enayim* affair, so I was unsuccessful in my attempt to convince him that pushing the argument *ad limitem* is at the same time pushing it *ad absurdum*. In any case it should be stressed that our having pointed in the same direction independently would seem to corroborate its general correctness.

In the meantime I have had the opportunity to discuss these topics with Miss Joanna Weinberg who has for some time been working on the *Meor Enayim*. She kindly brought to my attention the recent master's dissertation presented by Elizabeth Neylan to the University of Leeds (1975–76; to date *non vidi*) in which were formulated some other ideas in this direction. Miss Weinberg was also kind enough to inform me of some of her own findings concerning de Rossi's use of his sources. (The necessity of a detailed inquiry in this direction was already noted by Baron, "De Rossi's Historical Method," p. 152, n. 1, although he unfortunately did not accomplish this task.) I received the impression that the argument here presented is confirmed by these findings and I strongly encourage her, if only for this reason, to make them public knowledge soon.

89. See Joanna Weinberg, "Azariah dei Rossi; Towards a Reappraisal of the Last Years of His Life," *Annali della Scuola Normale Superiore di Pisa*, ser. 3, 8, 2 (1978), pp. 493–511.

Modernism and Traditionalism in Sixteenth-Century Jewish Historiography: A Study of David Gans' *Tzemaḥ David.*

MORDECHAI BREUER

The sudden flowering of Jewish historiography in the sixteenth century has often been attributed to the impact of the expulsion of the Jews from Spain upon European Jewry. Jews, becoming increasingly preoccupied with the problem of their fate and survival, turned to the annals of Jewish history, and particularly to the history of Jewish martyrology, to seek comfort and reassurance in the heroism of their ancestors and in the evidence of God's special relationship with His chosen people even amidst its most acute sufferings. Their tragic experiences estranged the Jews from the contemporary non-Jewish scene and society. They became, if one may borrow a psychological term, introvert. Faced with a seemingly hopeless and senseless present they turned for consolation to the glories of the past and the expectations of a future redemption. Jewish historiography and Lurianic Kabbalah thus appear to stem from the same state of mind, facing the same political and social situation. Seen in this light, the two phenomena seem to confirm the commonly held view that the sixteenth century and most of the seventeenth century in Jewish history are still essentially part of the Jewish Middle Ages, though they may be singled out as a closing phase or perhaps as a period of transition from medieval to modern Jewish history.[1]

A study in depth of one of the least renowned chronicles of the sixteenth century might contribute towards a revision of this interpretation. Demonstrably, this chronicle, *Tzemaḥ David* by David Gans, bears no special relationship to the Spanish expulsion and systematically plays down Jewish martyrology. In writing this book the author was stimulated by external impulses coming from the European scene and society no less than by intrinsically Jewish interests. These external impulses, if analyzed and taken as a whole, seem to present what can only be designated as the genuine impact of the Renaissance upon sections of the contemporary Ashkenazic Jewish society. The number, quality and prominence of phenomena which the book shares with typical Renaissance and humanist attitudes in Germany must be considered as truly remarkable. What marks the book as part of a modernist trend is not so much Gans' conscious aims *qua* chronicler (though, as will be seen, Gans was conscious of living in an age of change and progress) as it is the book's style, structure and subject matter. If the history of historiography is the history of changing world outlooks,[2] then the emergence of this book should be rated as one of the events ushering in a new period in Jewish intellectual history that should appropriately be called Early Modern Times.[3]

Gans' contribution to Jewish historiography must first of all be seen against the background of the Jewish society in which he lived and the gentile society with which he maintained many links. He was born in 1541 in Westphalia, north-western Germany. As a youth he studied the Talmud at Bonn and Frankfurt, and later he travelled to Cracow where he became a pupil of R. Moses Isserles. After his return to Germany he married and spent some time in the house of his father-in-law. About the year 1564 he settled in Prague and engaged in business. On his many business trips he revisited his country of birth several times. In Prague he used to listen to the lessons and sermons given by the famous R. Loew, the MaHaRaL, and by his brother R. Sinai. At an advanced age Gans was supported by his brother Joshua and devoted his time to study and to writing. He died in 1613 and was buried in Prague.[4]

In those years Prague had become the metropolis of all German-speaking lands. In 1526 the kingdom of Bohemia had passed from the Polish crown to the House of Hapsburg, and from 1556 the head of the Holy Roman Empire was also crowned king of Bohemia. The emperor Rudolph II (1576–1612) made Prague his capital city and permanent residence. His reign was marked by peace, economic prosperity and flourishing cultural activity. The imperial court attracted officials, diplomats and businessmen from many countries, and Rudolph's scientific and artistic inclinations, as well as his preoccupation with collecting exotic objects, opened the palace gates to scholars, writers and artists, especially from Italy. The city acquired a cosmopolitan character. Although the emperor was considered the chief protector of the Catholic Church against the challenge of the Reformation and despite the fact that those were the prime years of the Counter-Reformation, there prevailed an atmosphere of comparative religious tolerance in Prague and all over Bohemia where the Catholics were a minority group within the population.[5]

Under these circumstances the Jews of the ancient community of Prague enjoyed some relief from the excessive hardships entailed by their medieval status as social outcasts. The expulsion order of 1559 was finally rescinded in 1564, and in 1567 Maximilian II confirmed the ancient privileges of the Jews of Prague. In matters of communal concern the leaders of the Prague community appealed directly to the imperial administration, and personal contact was established with members of the imperial court. The visit by the emperor with his wife in the Prague ghetto in 1571 was considered by the Jews as an indication of imperial grace and benevolence towards them. The MaHaRaL's audience with the emperor in 1592 caused a sensation in the ghetto and was considered a confirmation of the Jews' hopes for a speedy reconciliation between Christians and Jews with subsequent further improvements in their economic and social position. Mordekhai Maysel's dealings with the court were also taken as a token of the changed times. This rich Prague *parnas* had attained the position of permanent financial agent to the imperial treasury and was acting as a beneficent Maecenas to the Prague community, erecting new and splendidly built synagogues and paving the narrow alleys of the ghetto with stones, thereby giving it a more respectable appearance.

The Jews of Prague inhabited two quarters in the city, surrounded by walls. The larger and more ancient of the two was called the "Jews' city" (*Judenstadt*). At the end of the sixteenth century 150 Jewish houses were counted in Prague out of a total population of about 50,000. The community was not homogeneous. A number of families were considered as being wealthy, while the majority were poor, supporting themselves on scanty livelihoods. Frequently the social contrasts gave rise to communal controversies, particularly when rabbis and communal officers were being elected. The leaders of the Prague community often interceded with the Imperial Chamber on behalf of Prague Jewry, as well as other communities scattered over the Empire, and they naturally considered themselves the spokesmen of the Jewish people in Central Europe.[6]

Prague was also a center of Jewish study and learning, outstanding among the leading European communities, and the panegyric by one of her rabbis, Ephraim of Luntshitz, was none too extravagant: "A great city before God, full of sages, writers and wealthy men who are famous for their learning, religious practice and fear of God. For a long time there has not been seen such a saintly gathering." There was a tradition among local rabbis and learned men, dating back to the fourteenth century, to expand their studies well beyond the "four ells of Halakhah," and thus we find among them students of philosophy, liturgical poets, grammarians and students of natural science. In the second half of the sixteenth century the preoccupation of the Prague Jewish intelligentsia with "extraneous" studies became increasingly intensified and was thereupon challenged by adherents of extreme traditionalism who wished to uphold the ancient Ashkenazic ideal of exclusive Talmud study. The famous "Maimonidean controversy" in Prague and Posen, as well as later references in contemporary writings by Prague Jewish authors, clearly attest to a rift between the friends and opponents of secular erudition.[7]

Foremost among the causes which may have contributed to this growth of secular interests stands the improved political situation of the Prague community under Rudolph II. It is a well-known phenomenon in Jewish history that diminishing manifestations of gentile hatred of the Jews have often been coincident with a corresponding increase of Jewish sympathy and open-mindedness towards gentile philosophy and science. However, we must beware of confusing coincidence with causal nexus, for while some correlation between these two transformations is evident, gentile tolerance has never been the sole cause of Jewish-Christian intellectual rapprochement. A more potent factor seems to have been the general cultural climate of renaissance and humanism which did indeed exercise a powerful influence over those Jewish intellectuals who maintained some links with the non-Jewish scene. These links were not limited to Prague's cosmopolitan intelligentsia alone. Prague Jews also maintained close connections with the Jewish communities of Northern Italy, Venice in particular, as well as with the community of Cracow. These were two centers of active Jewish participation in the pursuit of science and research, arising out of a sense of involvement with the epoch-making events then occurring in the gentile world of learning.[8]

Moreover, since the fourteenth century, a number of Jews of non-Ashkenazic origin who had been reared in the Sephardic Jewish culture had settled in Prague and, following the expulsion from Spain, this population element increased and became more influential. Towards the end of the century there lived in Prague two famous scholars with Sephardic cultural backgrounds, Rabbi Eliezer Ashkenazi and Rabbi Isaac Ḥayyot, and the latter even served for some time as Prague's communal rabbi. A strong intellectual impulse came from the writings and personality of R. Loew, the MaHaRaL, who was considered *spiritus rector* by all members of the Prague intelligentsia, including those who had not studied in his *yeshiva*.[9]

The Prague elite of Jewish men of letters included, in this period, a plethora of well-known figures: Abraham Horowitz (in his youth) and other members of his prominent family; Mordekhai Tzemaḥ the printer and his sons; Sinai, brother of the MaHaRaL; Joseph Yekutiel Wahl, the secretary to the community; Mordekhai Jaffe, the famous author of the *Levushim* series who was elected rabbi of Prague in 1592; Yomtov Lipman Heller who served as *dayyan* in Prague for twenty-eight years as well as David Gans the chronicler and astronomer. The outstanding characteristic common to all these men was that they were rabbinical scholars, some of them among the greatest sages of their time, who devoted a considerable part of their studies to *ḥakira* and *ḥokhma*, that is, they went beyond the study of Torah in the narrow sense current in Ashkenaz. Only a few of them engaged in philosophy as did the MaHaRaL. Several, such as Horowitz, Gans and Yaffe, had studied in Cracow with R. Moses Isserles who was known for his inclination towards philosophy and the sciences. All of them were lovers of books and showed some interest in publishing. The printing-house of the Tzemaḥ-Katz family served them as a focus and meeting place. This printing house, the first in Central Europe to be established by Jews (1512), increased its activity during the last quarter of the century after going through difficult times in the '50s and '60s, and its proprietors enjoyed great prestige in the community.[10]

David Gans himself, as far as we know, held no official position in the community, either in the rabbinate and rabbinical courts or within the communal leadership. He seems to have been active in certain public matters, but he did not publicize it. That he was a rabbinical scholar we see from his tombstone on which is engraved the rabbinical title of *morenu ha-rav*. Still, he did not try to distinguish himself in the mastery of Halakhah and in Talmudic disputation. Nearly all quotations from the Talmud in his books were taken from secondary sources, though he complemented them here and there from his own store of knowledge. In the view of his contemporaries his outstanding personal qualities were his piety, modesty and moral perfection; hence they added the epithet *ḥasid* to his name on the tombstone. He was very well versed in the Bible which he read and studied a great deal, sometimes making use of a concordance. He was attracted by the study of the Hebrew language and tried to get hold of all the works of Elijah Baḥur the linguist and grammarian, as well as of other writers in this field. He also tried his hand at composing Hebrew poems and quasi-liturgical pieces. His special field in Jewish studies, however, was Jewish chronology and the mathematics of the Jewish calendar. It is from this field that he set out on his literary exploits and came into contact with the European world of science and learning, making the acquaintance of world-famous scientists of the stature of Tycho Brahe and Johannes Kepler.[11]

Gans' desire to gain entry into the learned world outside the secluded Ashkenazic-Jewish house of study is noticeable throughout his life and in all his intellectual and literary pursuits. This desire may have been awakened at the *yeshiva* of his teacher Isserles who occupied himself with the study of natural science and history and was aware of the advantage of a wide general education for a better understanding of Jewish sources. "From the days of my youth," wrote Gans in an autobiographical note, "I felt a strong longing for the knowledge and study of history." Elsewhere he referred to himself as one of "the lovers of the science of numbers and measures." After returning from Cracow to his native land he settled down to the study of Euclid, a manuscript copy of whose book he seems to have found in the home of his father-in-law. There he also discovered some additional old manuscripts on non-halakhic subjects, a fact which bears witness to the unflagging interest some Ashkenazic Jews were taking in subjects outside the realm of Halakhah even in the generation preceding the period of humanism. All his life Gans was absorbed with essentially secular branches of learning and to these he devoted his literary endeavors. If he had any pupils he did not teach them Torah and Halakhah but astronomy and cosmology. In these fields he proved himself an excellent pedagogue, as every reader of *Neḥmad ve-Na'im* can see for himself.[12]

Whence did Gans acquire his broad erudition? At his time scientists and men of learning wrote their books in Latin. Can we deduce from this that Gans was able to read Latin? Some scholars, such as D. Cassel and A. Berliner, assumed that this in fact was the case. However, our examination of this question has shown that all the books used by Gans as sources for his chronicle were composed either in Hebrew or in German. He apparently knew some Latin words, such as members of his circle were familiar with and such as were mentioned in some of his Hebrew sources, and so he may have been able to construe some of the Latin words used here and there in his German texts, yet this was not enough for him to understand a Latin text. Many Roman and latinized German names in the second part of the *Tzemaḥ David* are transcribed into Hebrew in such a manner as to prove that he was ignorant of elementary Latin grammar. Even his reading of German was not faultless and there are many spelling errors which were obviously caused by confusing letters or by misunderstanding words. Factual errors occur even in some fields of knowledge that were familiar to him. Here and there his reading of figures or his calculation of dates is inaccurate, and surprisingly he was unaware of the fundamental character of the Muslim calendar.[13]

The amazing thing about Gans is not, of course, his faulty writing and his lack of education, but his success in spite of his limitations and failings. He exploited to the full one of the characteristic innovations in the science and history books which were beginning to appear in Germany during the Reformation period, namely, the publication of books in the national tongue intended not for academics but for the lay, middle-class, reading public. Had Gans been born at the beginning of the century, he would not have been able to acquire even the measure of erudition which he actually did. He was a child of his time in acquiring knowledge by means of those tools which his time was the first to put at the disposal of people lacking formal academic education. However, tools were not enough. What is even more impressive about Gans is the quality of his literary achievement, his acute sense of form and structure regarding subject matter from the world of science and research, and especially his associative capacity for compiling and relating to each other details and scraps of information culled from the most diverse and dispersed sources.[14]

Gans' most remarkable trait is his high susceptibility. This stands out particularly in those passages in his book where he relates with enthusiasm his own immediate experiences, such as his eulogy of the land of Bohemia, the marvelous story of the secret courts of Westphalia, the exuberant praise of the invention of printing and many others. Gans' susceptibility arises from an acute sensibility which contains also some marks of naiveté. He represents the converse type of a man of learning replete with knowledge and doctrine, theories and principles, who observes the universe from the pinnacle of his erudition through the prism of his preconceived ideas about the past and the future. Not so Gans. Although he is preoccupied with history he is essentially a man of the present and of reality, a man who never tires of learning and perfecting his knowledge and who views everything human with the immediacy of personal involvement. To a certain degree he spontaneously lives up to the revolutionary maxim that self-reliant man ought to stop collecting his knowledge from "books" and base it on experience and reason alone.[15]

This as well as his strong sense of contemporaneity, shows Gans as a man who, while deeply rooted in Jewish traditional society, exemplified some of the typical traits of the men of the Renaissance. In his important paper on "The Self-awareness of the Renaissance as a Criterion of the Renaissance" H. Weisinger writes:

> The men of the Renaissance were acutely aware of the fact that they were participating in activities which set them apart from the men of the preceding centuries . . . . They were cognizant that in some way their age was different, and they tried to account for the difference. . . . The writers of the Renaissance were describing contemporary phenomena; there is a strong feeling of contemporaneity which [shows] that [to these writers] the Renaissance was a real thing which actually happened to them, for they centered their attention on activities which they themselves had either engaged in or observed.[16]

Weisinger further tells us that he had

> collected some fifty datings of the Renaissance made in the Renaissance

from 1395 to 1599. In these datings the Renaissance is said to be taking place 'in our times,' and . . . this phrase . . . refers to a set of events taking place contemporaneously, that is, at the time of writing.[17]

Now one of the most frequently recurring phrases used by Gans is *bi-zmanenu ze*, the exact counterpart of "in our times," and although Gans' sense of the changed conditions of his time was not identical with that of the humanists, we still find in him the same acute awareness that amazing and unprecedented things were happening in his lifetime. The following additional statement by Weisinger can be applied in its entirety to David Gans:

In the estimation of [the men of the Renaissance] who looked forward rather than back, what distinguished the modern period from all those which had preceded it was the rise of science, which to them meant the discoveries and the new information revealed through them, the invention of instruments the ancients had not known, the effects of these inventions and, finally, the application of science toward more discoveries and inventions, so that the outlook for the future was not one of sameness . . . but one of continuous change for the better. . . . Men became aware of their era . . . because it was different from any other era on the basis of its own distinguishing accomplishments.[18]

The greatest event of Gans' life was undoubtedly his series of visits to the great astronomer Tycho Brahe at his palace not far from Prague, eight years after the publication of *Tzemaḥ David.* Gans' stay there brought him into the first and only personal contact in his life with some outstanding men of learning, the University of Prague being closed to the Jews. Tycho and Kepler received him with kindness, talked with him about some scientific subjects which were of common interest to them, and obtained Gans' cooperation in translating from Hebrew into German the Alphonsine astronomical tables.[19] Thus there came about a meeting of the bearers of European humanism and of the scholasticism which had preceded it, with the Jewish man of learning who came from the world of Torah and tried to catch up in one leap, as it were, with the new technology and science of the sixteenth century, unburdened with academic or Latin education. This leap may explain the naive "modernism" which singled Gans out from his contemporaries. Among these we must make specific mention of Azariah de Rossi, the author of *Me'or Enayim*, and of Gedalyah ibn Yaḥya, the author of *Shalshelet ha-Kabbala*, since Gans relied heavily upon their works.

De Rossi's "modernism" is not naive but deliberate, the fruit of his wide Jewish and general knowledge combined with a keen critical sense. Contrary to Gans, de Rossi's personal experience in itself is secondary to its academic implications. Where Gans expresses amazement and leaves his questions unanswered, de Rossi writes with the absolute assurance of a judge passing judgment. Where de Rossi sounds a little blasé, Gans disarms us by his naiveté. In fact, a comparison between the two many conjure up in the mind those two old and rather questionable concepts of *Bildungserlebnis* and *Urerlebnis*.[20] The reader of *Me'or Enayim* gets the impression that the author sometimes knew more than he wrote, disclosing only part of his thoughts, whereas Gans sometimes appears not to have been fully conscious of the theological and philosophical implications of certain topics he touched upon.

This may explain the conciliatory and accomodating position taken by Gans in the MaHaRaL's controversy against de Rossi. The MaHaRaL attacked de Rossi with an indignation and a pungency nowhere else to be found in his copious writings:

> This man has not comprehended the words of the Sages, neither their minor sayings nor even less their major pronouncements . . . . All his words are completely vain and void, unworthy of any reply . . . . Therefore this book belongs to the type of extraneous books which are forbidden to read, and every man who adheres to the religion and law of Moses and believes in the Written and Oral Law should keep this book out of his home and should not look into it, either mentally or physically.

The MaHaRaL's position was known to Gans even before it was made public, yet he did not refrain from quoting *Me'or Enayim* many times and discussing *sine ira et studio* the points de Rossi had made. De Rossi had stated his doubts and questions about the traditional chronology of the biblical and Second Temple periods, and these Gans quoted by accurately summarizing de Rossi's theses and giving full details of his arguments and proofs. Gans recoiled only from taking the logical last step and repudiating the customary reckoning of years from the time of creation. Short of this he defended de Rossi by adopting his assertion that no change in reckoning the number of years would necessarily entail a change that might effect any of the Jewish laws. Gans was not prepared to deny the inner logic of de Rossi's argumentation. He was also more lenient than the MaHaRaL in his attitude toward gentile scholars and regarding the question of whether one might quote from them alongside citations from the Jewish Sages. Still, Gans did not enter deeply into the controversy. Rather he presented the two conflicting viewpoints to the reader and left it to him to pronounce judgment and to decide whether he would take sides with the more exacting MaHaRaL or with the more lenient de Rossi. At all events he Gans the "hasid," would opt for stringency.[21]

Tzemaḥ David's "modernism" is even more striking when compared to *Shalshelet ha-Kabbala.* Ibn Yaḥya came from an enlightened, Spanish-Portuguese family of noble descent. He was born in Italy less than one generation before Gans and lived there nearly all his life. Unlike his treatment in the *Tzemaḥ David*, de Rossi is not mentioned even once in *Shalshelet ha-Kabbala*, although Ibn Yaḥya recorded many details he found in *Me'or Enayim.* The reason for this may have been the opposition with which *Me'or Enayim* was met in some rabbinical circles in Italy. Against the transparent and orderly structure of *Tzemaḥ David* the unsystematic arrangement of topics in *Shalshelet ha-Kabbala* stands out unfavorably. But the principal feature which makes Ibn Yaḥya's book appear much more "medieval" is the fact that he devoted a number of lengthy chapters to such branches of speculative and scholastic science as astrology, quasi-embryology (*yetzirat ha-vlad*), necromancy, transmigration, demonology, angelology, and doctrines concerning paradise and hell. Of all these there is almost nothing in the *Tzemaḥ David*, apart from astrology and prognostication, and even in these fields there is very little in the way of fundamental exposition. Gans emphasized the portentous significance of celestial and terrestial phenomena such as eclipses of the sun and the moon, the appearance of comets, and the occurrence of earthquakes. Like all his contemporaries, including such scientists as Brahe and Kepler, Gans firmly believed that divine providence made these occurrences come to pass so as to signify an imminent emergency and call upon mortals to mend their ways and thereby avert disaster. However, in a way similar to his treatment of traditional chronology Gans put forward the religious and theological problem involved with this belief, i.e., the relationship between *zekhut* and *mazal* ("merit" and "fortune"), without attempting to present a substantive philosophical solution. Here again his lack of profound scholarship in all but his favorite fields of interest allowed him to assume a more "modern" attitude than that of his teachers and of Ibn Yaḥya who were completely steeped in a world of metaphysics — a world which a more modern scientist would consider a world of unrealities.[22]

Tzemaḥ David was the last in a series of historiographical works which were composed by Jewish authors in the sixteenth century and whose publication was highly characteristic of this period in Jewish history. It was also the first written by an Ashkenazic Jew. Contrary to the best among the authors who preceded him, Gans wrote his book, save for a number of isolated passages, in the form of a chronicle without any pretense at a causal analysis of historical contexts. He made this plain in the introduction to the first part where he announced that his book was but "a register covering the books of the ancients in chronological order." The main achievement of his work was presented by him as the first attempt ever made to arrange the entire chain of events in Jewish and universal history "according to the years of creation." "Wherever I found occasion for making an original contribution of my own," he declared, "there was only very little I could add." Gans consistently adhered to this procedure throughout the two parts of his book, preferring chronology and annalistic presentation to historical interpretation and consistently exploiting every chronological hint and each bit of contextual evidence in his sources in order to discover and determine the location of men and events in the sequence of time. This commitment to chronology was not only rooted in the author's passion for order and numbers and in his lifelong attachment to astronomy. It also served an outspoken dialectic and apologetical purpose: "to dispel any doubts in the minds of the multitude about the years of creation." Evidently these doubts, disseminated by de Rossi's daring and unprecedented research, had created a sensation among Prague's Jewish intelligentsia and were being discussed in homes and synagogues. Hence Gans was aroused to embark upon an apologia for the Jewish chronology sanctioned by ancient tradition.[23]

The traditionalist tendency of the book, along with its annalistic structure, have combined to give it a certain reputation for backwardness and inferiority as measured against the standard of Renaissance historiography at its best. Graetz wrote: "One cannot call Gans' historical work great. He introduced among Jews the dry, bare form of historical narrative formerly employed by [dull] monks, which at that time had already given place to a more artistic method." For Graetz, therefore, the Jews, at least the German Jews, lagged behind the educated world by several centuries. This critical evaluation, justifiable as it is from the point of view of the history of universal historiography, is not valid if we allow for the quality of the contemporary German works which Gans studied and which served him as models. The bulk of the historical writings that were published in German during the sixteenth century have been justly censured for their deficiencies both as history books and as literary works. German humanism, as distinct from Italian, remained for a long time embedded in late-medieval philosophy and theology. Incipient attempts at a secularized view of history which had been made at the beginning of the century were arrested and suffocated for the rest of the century under the impact of the Reformation. Following the lead of Melanchthon, the first professorships of history were indeed installed at the Protestant universities, but it was precisely Melanchthon who fixed Protestant historiography on a firm basis of religious ethics and theological concepts regarding the evolution and meaning of history. Thus Protestant historiography was harnessed to the literary struggle of the Reformation against the Roman establishment. On the other hand, the Catholic hierarchy throughout the sixteenth century suppressed all attempts at creating a Catholic model of historiographical literature, and even the leaders of the Counter-Reformation considered historical research in itself a danger to simple faith that might jeopardize the reader's loyalty to the Roman Church. Hence practically all German chronicles and historical works which appeared in the second half of the sixteenth century were written by authors who hated the pope and worshiped Luther. Several among the chroniclers whose books were used by Gans were Protestant theologians, and all of them lacked the capacity of distinguishing between significant and trivial events in history, were wanting in critical sense, and overemphasized their ethico-religious historiosophy.[24]

It is against this literary background that we must judge Gans' work, taking into consideration that he lacked the tools required in order to be able to recognize the scientific and literary deficiencies of the books he was reading. In comparing *Tzemaḥ David* to the German chronicles one is struck by Gans' universalism and present-mindedness as against the antiquarianism and narrow territorial interests of most German authors. These latter usually concentrated on local history, glorifying the antiquity and hence the dignity and importance of a certain region and referring to the present only when an occasion arose for hitting out at the Roman Church. The *Tzemaḥ David*, on the other hand, is a world chronicle whose author's interest was largely focused on present actuality and on what was going on in front of his readers' eyes at the time of writing. Gans' insistence on the chronology of creation was no more dogmatic than that of the German chroniclers, many of whom, headed by Melanchthon himself, refused as yet to recognize any sources for biblical chronology other than the Bible itself. Gans' cautious gropings towards a new way for himself in the field of chronological and historical research occasionally lent his book a more progressive character than is discernible in most of his sources. The "very little" he contributed out of his own was in fact not so little at all. He did not stop even at refuting interpretations offered by RaSHI, rejecting them without much hesitation. Of one legendary story which he found among the miscellaneous dicta attributed to the MaHaRIL and which was neither to his taste nor based on any Talmudic source he could find, Gans wrote that it was a "gross exaggeration" and historically worthless.[25]

Gans' scientific approach, historical sense, and critical capacity were far more developed than Ibn Yaḥya's. Contrary to Ibn Yaḥya and following some of his German models, he usually stated the sources from which he had taken his information. This he did with comparative accuracy with regard to both Jewish and gentile literature, and in this respect he could claim to be a pioneer in Jewish and Hebrew literature. He devoted much time to examining his sources, collating different editions for textual criticism and venturing, occasionally with surprising success, to offer some chronological and biographical conjectures based on scientific data. He fixed dates and corrected misprints in his sources proffering scientific arguments to justify his preference. He was aware of the danger that historians might mar their work with excessive subjectivity and that authors and printers might lower the trustworthiness of books through linguistic inaccuracy and general untidiness. He adopted certain objective criteria for judging the reliability of historians. Foremost among these was general agreement among different sources and authors, followed by scientific consensus as to some writer's authority. A statement agreed upon by a majority of sources was also to be considered as authoritative.[26]

This principle of making decisions, as it were, by majority vote was of course a universal rule in Halakhah and as such very familiar to Gans. But he did not always resolve difficulties and conflicting opinions according to this rule, especially when the conflict was between two authors who were both regarded as sages. In such a case he would apply another halakhic maxim which aimed at a harmonizing compromise rather than a clear, unequivocal decision: *elu va-elu divrei elokim ḥayyim* ("both opinions are the words of the living God") or, in other words several times quoted by Gans: *me-ro'e eḥad nitnu* ("[both opinions] were handed down from one shepherd [i.e., Moses]"). Sometimes he would apply an eclectic method, announcing that since the varying opinions of authoritative authors were of equal weight he was going to "pluck a flower here and a rose there," this being a method common in the study and application of Aggadah. In order to explain an ostensibly unreasonable statement by a famous scholar he would sometimes resort to casuistry. In resolving contradictions between different sources by inventing two persons with identical names at different periods or two identical events at different dates he followed well-known precedents in Jewish and general historiography. It could also happen that he utterly failed to identify an outstanding personality in Jewish history, a somewhat surprising lapse, in particular when occurring with reference to Ashkenazic scholars. Again, considering the paucity of the tools he had at his disposal one should rather wonder that he did not go wrong more frequently, particularly if one compares him to Ibn Yaḥya.[27]

Thus we see that Gans typifies, even if only in miniature, the co-existence of the old and the new which was so common among the men of learning of his generation. They were constantly wavering between their devotion to tradition and their inclination to criticism, between germinating scientific attitudes and age-old religious beliefs and concepts, between scholasticism and humanism. Gans was an inveterate lover of novelties and he filled his book with them, but he felt completely free and uninhibited only in the field of technological innovation and in those branches of learning, including astronomy, which to him did not involve a confrontation between scientific investigation and religious belief. As soon as his research brought him to the verge of such a confrontation, compelling him to choose between an express opinion of the ancients and a logical conclusion of his own reasoning, he recoiled and declared:

> Let us not seek novel things, for we have only what our ancestors bequeathed to us, and the tradition and custom of our forefathers shall be as a law to us and shall not depart from our mouths and from the mouths of our children and from the mouths of our children's children to all eternity.

Veneration of the ancients, a common feature of the period, is prominent in Gans. The words of the ancients, he wrote, "do not need to be rectified," and antiquity is a test of reliability. Nevertheless he was fully conscious of living in an epoch when things were discovered and devised of which the ancients had not dreamed and so his modesty is tinged with self-confidence, a feeling which he shared with many scholars of his day. Along with generations of humanists he likened himself to the proverbial dwarf riding on the shoulders of a giant, and while this metaphor did contain an element of humility, Gans used it distinctly to assert the originality of his contribution.[28]

Tzemaḥ David, whether the work of a traditionalist or that of a critical investigator and innovator, is pervaded by one outstanding purpose: the pursuit of truth. It is this purpose which stamped the book, despite its shortcomings, with the character of science in the modern sense of the word. Notwithstanding his conservative approach to questions of religious doctrine he offered his readers pending doubts, conflicting arguments and controversial opinions with the maximum of impartiality of which he was capable. In several passages he struck a downright pluralistic note, telling the reader, as it were: These are the different views; there is an element of truth in each of them; let the reader decide the issue for himself. Information was more important to him than edification and inculcation. He wished to enlighten his readers, not to educate them. This scientific approach freed his book from the heavy burden of controversy and ideology, and seen from this angle the *Tzemaḥ David* should be included among the pacemakers of modern Jewish historiography. Gans never turned his mind away from his central historiographic design and, unlike his predecessors, he refrained from any significant deviation, evidently not always an easy task for him. Despite its lean, annalistic structure, the *Tzemaḥ David*, through its exclusive focus on matters relevant to history, made an important contribution to the emergence of Jewish historiography as an autonomous, scholarly and literary discipline. Leopold Zunz sensed this correctly when in his early days he found himself attracted by this book to what he later expounded as the Science of Judaism.[29]

Lean, annalistic structure indeed, yet it is precisely this structure that requires us to find out by painstaking research the criteria by which Gans was guided in selecting from his many sources the historical events and figures to be included in his annals, in devoting more space to some and less to others, and in totally ignoring some while enlarging upon others by drawing on his own knowledge and imagination. In so doing we will discover that chronology was not his sole concern.

In his introduction to *Tzemaḥ David*, and particularly to the second part, Gans stated explicitly that his book was intended for laymen—*ba'alei batim*—and not for men of learning:

> I have written this part of my book for a generation tired of *galut* with a view to gladden the somber hearts of breadwinners who earn their livelihood by strenuous exertion, so that coming home from their toil and drudgery they might rest and take comfort in reading if many new and old things.

The book was thus designed to be read by merchants, shopkeepers, peddlars and craftsmen for their diversion and amusement in their hours of leisure after an exhausting working day. Among this working sector of Central European Jewry there were also men of letters whom Gans apostrophized as *maskilim*, but for lack of free time even they wished "to learn the whole Torah while standing on one foot." Like the rest of their contemporaries, both Christians and Jews, Gans' readers had a great craving for sensational news. Catering to this craving—a craving which in a subsequent generation was attested by Leone da Modena's dictum "everything novel is deeply desired"—was Gans' chief motivation for filling his book with a variety of news items, a detailed analysis of which enables us to appraise his view of readers' tastes and interests.[30]

Foremost among these news items were the natural disasters and portents referred to above, including all kinds of unusual and monstrous occurrences which were capable of arousing sensations of fear, amazement, terror and compassion. Another type of detailed information is the long list of wars, rebellions, outbreaks of violence and crimes filling the pages of *Tzemaḥ David.* The common feature which stands out in all these objects of the readers' curiosity is an excessive accumulation of bloodshed, the number of victims, both human and animal, mounting to such fantastic figures that the author, and with him the reader, becomes positively drunk with them. Events of a less sanguinary nature that suited the readers' inclination were associated with the world of technology and the geography of distant lands, including particularly the new discoveries. In passing it should be noted that the main types of technological innovations repeatedly mentioned by Gans coincide with the three inventions which according to Francis Bacon (1561–1626) "transformed the appearance and state of the world," viz., printing, gunpowder and the compass. All these topics, teeming with the spirit of excitement and novelty, projected the contemporary European scene of inter-religious warfare and persecution, as well as the feverish activity in the realms of technology and science into the homes of Jewish readers who were presumably isolated from the outside world. It would thus appear to be a legitimate conclusion from Gans' selection and presentation of the subject-matter of the second part of *Tzemaḥ David* that the average *ba'al bayit* in Central Europe followed the events taking place in the Christian world with keen interest.[31]

Among the *to'aliyot* ("lessons") he enumerated in his introduction to the second part, Gans emphasized the ethical value of historical events as examples of human behavior either to be emulated or to be avoided. The predominantly ethical purpose of historiography had distinguished Melanchthon from the German compilators of world history who had preceded him. According to his conception the purpose of the study of history should be to provide examples for all situations of life: "History is recorded for the sake of example and it should be read for the sake of example." But while in Melanchthon's historical writings every item is divided into a factual report and a moral lesson derived from it, this ethico-pedagogical emphasis stands out much less in the *Tzemaḥ David*, despite Gans' introductory declaration of intent. To many reports of alarming and monstrous events he did indeed append an appeal for moral improvement as the only means of modifying fate, but one may be permitted to doubt whether thereby his book became a *musar* book in the opinion of its readers. The deeds of righteous and wicked men related in the book were evidently selected for their own sake, i.e., for their "news value," so to speak, and not just for their moral significance. It seems that Gans' friend, the one who undertook the publication of the book, was aware of this, for in his prefatory remarks he found it necessary to emphasize that in addition to the "lessons" enumerated by the author himself his book would serve as a guide book to distinguish between good and evil. In actual fact, even the moral "lessons" extolled by Gans stressed the physical and material benefits entailed in virtuous living rather than their intrinsic religious and ethical merit. Let the man of success beware lest he be precipitated from fortune to utter failure; let him therefore take care not to quarrel with one who is more powerful than he and who is favored by fate; anyhow man cannot escape just retribution and in the long run the wicked shall not live in peace, not even in this world. These maxims, expounded and illustrated in the *Tzemaḥ David*, have an unmistakable pedestrian, secular and utilitarian touch, with a flavor of Italian Renaissance ideas on the one hand and Protestant ethics on the other. Incidentally, this secular touch is reinforced by the surprisingly large number of spicy stories centering upon outstanding women and featuring sexual crimes. Gans repeatedly lingered upon accounts of feminine beauty, women acting as rulers and warriors, details of marital life, and incidents of rape, adultery and prostitution.[32]

Unlike his Hebrew and German models whose religious and theological bias was conspicuous both in their texts and in their introductions, Gans preferred the cognitive value of historical knowledge and the benefit which his readers would derive from it for their active and professional life. This, too, gave the second part of the book a decidedly secular tinge. Far less than the only other Ashkenazic chronicler of the period, Josel of Rosheim, did Gans stress the theological link between the fate of the Jews and their moral and religious behavior. Although he included many items from Jewish history in the part devoted to universal history, he refrained from commenting on the Jewish-religious significance of events even where it would seem to be most called for. Two examples will suffice. Gans devoted many extended, laudatory paragraphs to his favorite lands and cities, such as Westphalia,

Bohemia, Prague, Rome, Venice; yet in none of them did he even so much as hint at the contributions of their Jewish communities and men of learning to the survival of the Jewish people and the study of Torah.[33]

Still more surprising in this respect is the passage which Gans dedicated to the invention of printing. It is well-known that this invention was not acclaimed as an unmixed blessing by the learned circles of either Jews or Christians. Although the printed book was speedily put into the service of Torah study and dissemination, some halakhists were rather reluctant to accept printing as an equivalent for writing and copying by hand for any religious purposes. Among the reasons they put forward was the typically traditionalist argument that since Moses and Solomon had not invented the art of printing it must be inferior to writing. Christian antagonism to printing was not confined to the monasteries. An eminent lay humanist like Sebastian Franck expressed his horror at the debasement of morals which in his opinion was being caused by such technological achievements as the printing press. Gans shared neither the misgivings of the halakhists nor the anxiety of Sebastian Franck. His profuse praise of Gutenberg's invention was not qualified by moral or religious considerations. His attitude was eminently practical and remarkably secular. Other Jewish men of learning had indeed praised the invention of printing, but while they emphasized its potentialities for the dissemination of Torah, Gans made only a passing reference to its usefulness for "the divine disciplines of wisdom," devoting the major part of that passage to the benefits accruing from printing to the vocational training of craftsmen. This direct and pragmatic approach which, so far as I could ascertain, had no parallel in contemporary German literature, contrasts not only with the opinions voiced by other Jewish writers but with those of Christian writers as well.[34]

Tzemaḥ David is replete with information relevant to economic and political geography, jurisprudence, commerce, diplomacy and other spheres of interest to readers engaged in business and trade. Many of these details are not to be found in Gans' German sources but were drawn from his own knowledge and experience; hence our surmise that he was engaged in business. This utilitarian emphasis in Gans' study of history may have been of some practical social importance, for the acquisition of the knowledge he offered his readers was relevant to broadening their capacity for social mobility. It also seems that he was favorably inclined toward the class of artisans, and here and there he even displayed an understanding attitude to the needs of the economically deprived. Thus when writing of the German Peasants' Revolt of 1525 he pointed out that the demands made by the peasants were "good and fair things." A sympathetic appreciation such as this is not to be found in any of Gans' German sources, and it should be remembered, moreover, that German Reformation circles shared with the humanists a deep-seated contempt for the masses and for mass movements.[35]

Gans presents himself as the spokespman of a new class of comparatively open-minded and enlightened laymen whose value scales and ideals were different from those that had been traditional in Ashkenazic Jewry. This can be clearly seen in his obvious preference for those Jewish men of learning who distinguished themselves not only in the knowledge of Torah but in the secular branches of knowledge as well. He never omitted to mention any Jewish sage of whom his sources reported that he "excelled in all branches of wisdom." He actually embraced the Sephardic ideal of the universally learned *ḥakham*, and in his note on the Barcelona ban of 1305 on secular studies he stressed the fact that it had been intended to be enforced only with regard to persons below the age of twenty-five. Conversely, he was plainly critical of the typical Ashkenazic rabbi of his time. Following his master, the MaHaRaL, he deprecated the excessive use of the pilpulistic method of Talmud study that had become dominant in rabbinical circles. We may safely assume that if Gans had attempeted to emulate the MaHaRaL's critique of traditional Jewish education he would have advocated the inclusion of vocational training and elementary instruction in general knowledge for a new generation of young people many of whom could be expected to devote a larger proportion of their time to their occupations and a lesser one to religious studies and exercises than had been customary in previous generations.[36]

Gans also attacked the "Ashkenazic *semikha*", or mode of rabbinical ordination, which had become the universal criterion of rabbinical and social status, and he quoted at length Abravanel's diatribe against this usage. In the second half of the sixteenth century it had become customary for the rabbis and communal leaders in Prague and elsewhere to confer the title of *morenu* on *yeshiva* graduates irrespective of their academic achievements. Gans opposed this practice not only because it went counter to his ideal of a Jewish sage but because he was evidently inclined to support a shifting of the balance between rabbinical and enlightened lay authority in communal leadership in favor of the latter. This shift had in fact been in process since the fifteenth century, culminating in the evolution of the Ashkenazic Court Jews of whom Mordecai Maisel in Prague, so profusely eulogized in the *Tzemaḥ David*, was an early prototype. In his low opinion of the rabbinical titularies and hierarchy Gans may have been influenced by the elevation of the lay element in the congregation effected by the Lutheran Reformation, and more particularly by the egalitarianism practiced by the Bohemian Brothers who required their priests to make their living through the work of their own hands.[37]

Furthermore, unlike many contemporary men of learning, both Ashkenazic and Sephardic, including Josel of Rosheim, Gans evidently did not think much of Kabbalah and of those engaged in the study and practice of Jewish mysticism. Although some of his teachers were known for their deep involvement with Kabbalah Gans systematically omitted the kabbalistic discipline from lists of the fields of study and expertise by which Jewish sages had been characterized in his sources, in particular the *Shalshelet ha-Kabbala*. Moreover, unlike the author of that work, Gans never quoted from the Zohar. From among the mystics of Safed mentioned by Ibn Yaḥyah he suppressed all but those sages whom he did not find designated as "learned in the wisdom of Kabbalah." Studying the *Tzemaḥ David* leaves one with the clear impression that its author did not consider mysticism and asceticism as significant accomplishments for the ideal Jewish scholar. This attitude is striking, especially when we consider the fact that in those years when the book was being written and just before Lurianic Kabbalah was beginning to spread in Eastern Europe, the debate on the status of Kabbalah in Jewish study and life was still going on in scholarly circles.[38]

Gans' ideal of the man of wisdom is significant not only for enabling us to evaluate his own individuality. It must also be seen in the context of Jewish-Christian relations. In the ninth "lesson" among those enumerated in the introduction to the second part Gans recommended his book as a useful guide to those of his readers who had occasion to converse with non-Jews. A study of his book would enable them to participate in intelligent conversation and thereby "to find grace and respect" in the eyes of their Christian partners. Gans and his readers evidently attached great importance to what educated Christians thought about them, not only as Jews but as individual persons. Many items of information recorded in the *Tzemaḥ David* were intended as intellecutal equipment for its readers' social intercourse with their non-Jewish neighbors and customers. It was considered as a matter of importance that Jews coming into contact with Christians should create a favorable impression, and Gans was among those who thought that talmudic erudition alone was not enough for this purpose and possibly even detrimental to it.[39]

If this analysis is not mere conjecture it seems to be of special relevance to the scholarly debate about the measure of Jewish indifference or involvement vis-à-vis the Christian world in that period. Evidently Gans and his readers were greatly concerned about their image in Christian circles with whom they maintained lively contacts. Their attitude to their non-Jewish acquaintances was marked by comparative open-mindedness and tolerance and by a disposition to relate to their personal and intellectual standards with comparative objectivity. They must have sensed something of the change in the attitude of European society towards the Jews as human beings which resulted from the new individualism, a readiness to judge persons as individuals and not as members of a religious or national group. It was to this changed relationship that Gans responded, though probably not fully consciously, with his ideal of the man of wisdom.[40]

To a certain degree Gans' attitude to the gentile world seems to be free from the heaviness and bitterness of the *galut* experiences of previous generations. His view of the gentile attitude to the Jews is notably optimistic. The reign of Rudolph II had brought a period of relative tranquility to the Jews of Prague who began to believe that the horrors of the times of persecution and slaughter were gone for ever. This confidence was reinforced by the traditional conception that Jew-baiting had always sprung from the vulgar masses while the rulers and men of culture were supposedly exerting themselves to protect the Jews. With the incipient rise of absolutist regimes headed by powerful rulers there was increasing hope in the hearts of Bohemian Jewry that those in authority would no longer yield to the pressure of the masses.

Furthermore, the ideal ruler pictured in contemporary literature was the philosopher-king, and the highest praise which Gans could find for some outstanding sovereign was that he "loved wise men" and "was a patron of the arts and sciences." Conversely, the most severe censure of a depraved ruler was that he "hated wise men." It was unthinkable that a wise ruler should hate the people of Israel, "the nation of wisdom and reason." Thus not only the emperor Augustus was a "lover of Israel" but even Titus was "excellent in all branches of wisdom" and "governed his nation with justice and righteousness," and therefore Gans, who found these traits in his sources, made a point of telling his readers that Titus "was reported to have regretted the vast bloodshed which he had caused." Such gentile rulers might be held up as models to be emulated even by Jewish readers; hence the sixth of Gans' "lessons": "Moral teachings have more power on the masses when they are said to have been proclaimed by a monarch." And if all good kings were presumably filled with "loving kindness" towards the Jews, this surely was true of the sovereigns ruling the lands where Gans was born and where he lived. At this point the admiration for the ruler was reinforced by the strong sense of civic loyalty and the considerable measure of identification with the non-Jewish enviroment which are such remarkable features of the *Tzemaḥ David*.[41]

Gans was the spokesman of a generation of *ye'efei ha-galut*, of men who were tired of the hardships of exile and trusted that the time had come for a favorable turn in the history of Jewish martyrology. This sense led him to a very specific and peculiar treatment of the disastrous experiences of the Jewish people in the past. Unlike Ibn Verga, the author of *Shevet Yehuda*, and in striking contrast to Ibn Yaḥyah, Gans did not mention the enumeration of persecutions among the aims and "lessons" of his book. Where the other chroniclers dwelt at length upon the horrors of these murderous events, Gans has only curt notes, and several among those events he failed to mention altogether. Only one persecution, that which occurred during the First Crusade in 1096, he described in some detail, concluding with the following sentence: "And as to the rest of the detailed accounts of persecutions and slaughters that came over the holy nation, these I did not wish to record in my book for some special reason." The nature of this "special reason" has already become clear to us: The persecutions and slaughters belong to the past, and at the present time it is more relevant to retell the events signifying Israel's survival and deliverance than its misfortunes. This follows plainly from the words Gans inscribed on the title page of the second part. His Jewish historiography was definitely not "lachrymose," to use Professor Baron's well-known phrase. To him the time was not appropriate for Jews to become absorbed in the unhappy fate of their ancestors. Again the contrast with Josel of Rosheim is striking, for about him it has correctly been said that he was as powerfully filled with the saga of *kidush ha-shem* as all Ashkenazic Jews in the previous generations.

An additional aspect of his attitude to martyrology was given prominence by Gans in the opening passage of his list of aims and "lessons":

> At a time when Christians are fighting among themselves and "more than a million Christians have been killed and slaughtered in our time during the past fifty years, the children of Israel have remained unscathed, and blessed be the Lord who has bestowed his loving kindness upon us.

The apocalyptic events which Gans and his generation were witnessing and which shook the Christian world to its very foundations made it pointless for him to enlarge upon the sufferings of Jewish martyrs. So he did something that was without precedent in Jewish historiography—he made the history of Christian martyrology one of the major themes of his book. With great care and accuracy he copied from the German chronicles all that he could find of the persecutions of Christians by Romans, pagans, Muslims and warring Christian sects. In excessive detail he recounted the stories telling of the stubborn refusal of the ancient European races to yield to their conquerors' religion of the cross, resulting in the death of unnumbered victims. Any reader of the *Tzemaḥ David* may get the impression that all the accounts of cruelties which Gans omitted from the history of Jewish suffering he projected into Christian martyrology, using the very terms and idioms which had since ancient times been set aside for tales about Jews enduring the pains inflicted upon them for clinging to their faith. This stands out most conspicuously when we compare the *Tzemaḥ David* with its sources. In many places Gans added much of his own imagination, changed or omitted words to drive home the point he wished to make, and took pains to register any atrocities and acts of desecration and torture that had been perpetrated upon ministers of the Christian church.[42]

Gans laid much stress on the fact that most of the troubles and sufferings of the Christian people had been caused by their own coreligionists. He registered dozens of clashes between different Christian sects, giving particulars about some heresies which denied the Trinity and the divinity of Jesus. In general he was alive to Chrisitan rituals and customs, especially to those that were controversial or that pointed, in his opinion, to the inferiority of Christianity compared to Judaism. It was clearly one of Gans' purposes in that period of religious wars to hold up to his readers the lack of unity and peace among the Christians and the transience and instability of their beliefs, customs and institutions. By contrast, he minimized or omitted altogether such internal Jewish struggles as the Karaite schism and the Maimonidean controversy. On the other hand, he dwelt at length on any event which was likely to enhance the prestige of the Jewish people among the gentiles, like the meeting between Alexander the Great and the elders of Israel, the Greek translation of the Bible by Jewish sages at the invitation of King Ptolemy, and the conversion of the royal house of Adiabene. While giving only short summaries of the Jews' suffering under Antiochus Epiphanes and the prayers and fasts held by Judah Maccabee, he wrote lengthy passages on the heroic deeds of the Hasmoneans and of the Jewish fighters in the war with the Romans and in the Bar-Kokhba rebellion. His characterization of Antipater and Herod contains more praise than censure, even more, be it noted, than he had found in the *Book of Yosifon.* Incidentally it should be noted that among all the Jewish historiographers in the sixteenth century, excluding de Rossi who was mainly engaged in chronological research, Gans was the only one who devoted a substantial part of his book to the Second Temple period and to the Hasmonean monarchy.[43]

As a citizen of Prague, the capital and residence of the emperor, Gans may have wished to demonstrate to his readers that royalty had been a concrete historical reality in Israel which might again become concrete reality with the coming of the Messiah. There is in fact a clearly discernible messianic trend in the *Tzemaḥ David.* This is not only expressly set forth in the tenth "lesson" which says that by learning about the gentile kings and emperors the reader will be aroused to pray for the restoration of the Davidic monarchy.

Nor is it merely hinted at in the double meaning of the name Gans chose for his book, however significant this may be, especially when compared to the more somber ambiguity of Ibn Verga's *Shevet Yehuda.* The messianic motive in the *Tzemaḥ David* emerges in many passages that point to the proximity of the Messiah's coming and bear testimony to alert messianic expectations.[44]

The entire historical world picture presented by Gans was structured upon the concept of the Four Monarchies which was an intrinsically eschatological concept, for, as the MaHaRaL wrote: "The reign of the Messiah will not begin before the reign of the Four Monarchies will have come to an end." Moreover, "When the Fourth Monarchy ceases to exist the Messiah must of necessity make his appearance." The question about the identity of the Fourth Monarchy was frequently debated in medieval literature, particularly in view of the rise of an additional monarchy, the realm of Ishmael, which could only with difficulty be explained as being included within the fourfold vision of Daniel. Gans followed the MaHaRaL in identifying the Fourth Monarchy with the totality of Christian kingdoms throughout their multifarious medieval history. The "fall of the Christians," after a long succession of alternating kingdoms and dynasties, was thus tantamount to the fall of the Fourth Monarchy.[45]

The Four-Monarchy scheme was taken over by Gans from his German models which followed the lead of Protestant historiographers. Ever since Melanchthon had adopted this scheme, which served his conception of the Reformation as the last stage of *historia sacra*, it had been copied by most other Protestant writers and Sleidan's *De quatuor summis imperiis* had gone through a number of editions. Gans was aware that in those writings it was implied that the imminent downfall of the pope signified the fall of the Fourth Monarchy. This may partly account for the fact that while the MaHaRaL discussed the fall of the Fourth Monarchy as an event of mainly spiritual significance, Gans was filled with its political implications and potentialities for the forthcoming redemption of the Jewish people. We will better understand his characteristically direct approach to events of eschatological significance if we remember again that Lurianic Kabbalah with its spiritualizing impact on Jewish messiansim had not yet reached Eastern Europe when Gans wrote his book. Following Professor Scholem's evaluation of Lurianic Kabbalah as a step towards introducing a national, secular dimension into Jewish messianism, we can see how in this respect the naive modernism of Gans caused his book to become out of date almost on the day of its publication.[46]

Many events which Gans emphasized for their messianic import he found in Heinrich Buenting's *Itinerarium Sacra Scripturae*, a book which he presumably acquired for this purpose. From there he took his information about the recurring conquests of Jerusalem by invading armies. Outstanding among other events is the rise of the Ottoman Empire and its successful wars against Christendom and its efforts to be "a stumbling block to the [Holy] Roman Empire." It should be remembered that during the reign of Rudolph II the Turks were encamped less than a hundred miles from Vienna. This may be the reason that Gans did not dare mention Don Joseph Nasi and Dona Gracia and their achievements on behalf of their people, if he knew about them. He did twice refer to Sultan Suleiman whom "God aroused . . . to rebuild the walls of the holy city of Jerusalem." His account of the Ten Tribes and their whereabouts is charged with highly messianic tension and like many others living in those times, both Jews and non-Jews, he followed the geographical discoveries of the period with a mixture of eager scientific interest, passionate craving for news, and messianic yearnings. While there is no indication that he tried to calculate the year of redemption, it is not impossible that his defense of the traditional chronology against de Rossi's challenge was also prompted by eschatological considerations. By reconfirming the traditional chronology Gans actually gave a new lease on life to the persistent endeavors to predict the year of the Messiah. In this respect, as in so many others, he stands out in contrast to Josel of Rosheim who systematically suppressed all messianic allusions in his writings. The well-known story told by Gans about his grandfather who made feverish preparations for travelling to the Holy Land in the wake of Asher Lemlein's messianic movement is convincing proof of the dynamic alertness to the historic changes of the period which prevailed in Ashkenazic Jewry throughout the century.[47]

This messianic dimension of Gans' work thus opens up an additional aspect of his unprecedented undertaking in writing a full chronicle not only of Jewish history but of universal history as well. In doing so he was confronted with the alternative of either presenting the two histories in one single chronological sequence or in two separate sequences. Unlike Joseph ha-Cohen who, in his *Divrei ha-Yamim le-Malkhei Tzarfat u-Malkhei Bet Otoman ha-Tugar* had integrated items of Jewish history into his partial and regional treatment of medieval history, Gans adopted a procedure which was in principle based upon a full-length division between the two spheres. We may assume that this was done in deference to the MaHaRaL who denounced de Rossi specifically for quoting Jewish and non-Jewish sources in one and the same context. In his introduction Gans gave the following reasons for his procedure: The history of the gentile nations is of a secular nature and "one must keep the holy apart from the profane"; the history of the nations has been recorded by non-Jewish authors without divine inspiration, and while it is permissible to quote them, yet they must not be intermingled with "the words of the living God"; the authority of the Jewish historical sources is beyond doubt, whereas the authenticity of non-Jewish sources is questionable.

In several of the German chronicles which he studied Gans also read about the obligation of the religiously oriented historian to distinguish between "religious" and "profane" history. This goes back to Luther and Melanchthon who insisted upon the fundamental difference between *sacrae historiae* and *historiae gentiles.* But precisely this separation of spiritual and worldly history led Protestant historiography to recognize the intrinsic importance of worldly history. Medieval historiography had subordinated it to church history; humanist Italian historiography had monopolized it. Luther assigned to each of the two histories its appropriate sphere in the affairs of mankind. In his message "To the City Councillors" of 1524 he advised them to stock their libraries with "the chronicles and histories, in whatever language they may be had, for they are of wondrous value for understanding and controlling the course of this world and especially for noting the wonderful works of God."[48]

Gans, too, by emancipating, as it were, the history of the world for his Jewish readers greatly enhanced its value and significance. Characteristically, he did not keep strictly to his preconceived pattern but intermingled the two histories in various ways. When it came to verifying dates and events, and in pursuance of Isserles' dictum that "from the gentile sages we can furnish proof for our sages," he repeatedly noted agreement and correspondence of Jewish and non-Jewish sources in both parts of his book, and thus considerably bridged the alleged gulf between them. In a number of cases he interpolated events from world history in the first part, events which he regarded as being of special significance for Jewish history. In the second part he mentioned many items from Jewish history just as he found them in his German sources. Thus, in his actual writing Gans was less concerned with separating Jewish and non-Jewish history than with distinguishing Jewish from non-Jewish sources. In truth he valued universal history as being secular only so far as its sources and documentation were secular. Universal history in itself, being the sphere of divine providence and justice and the stage of messianic enactment, was to him indistinguishable from Jewish history.[49]

In conclusion, there seems to be a firm basis for considering David Gans as the spokesman of a generation of sixteenth-century Ashkenazic Jewry which shared many characteristics with men of the Renaissance. Above all it was their awareness of living in a new period of history that distinguished them from the men of the Middle Ages and by this standard Gans and his work must be regarded as typical of early modern times in Jewish history. Some of his attitudes seem to correspond strikingly to those that in his lifetime were becoming the political and spiritual foundations for religious tolerance in European society. The progress of secularization; the growing influence of the lay element in the cultural and political spheres; the regard for the economic usefulness of the Jews to the state; the renewed appreciation of Christians for Jewish culture—all these have their counterparts in the challenges with which Gans confronted his readers and which he regarded himself to be confronted with. One could almost say that his response to these challenges foreshadows the apologetical tactics which marked the Jewish struggle for emanicpation in the nineteenth century.[50]

On the surface it is hard to detect any continuity between the early modernism of Gans and his circle and the men of the Jewish enlightenment in the eighteenth century. The *Tzemaḥ David* did indeed go through many editions, but the second edition appeared only one hundred years after the first. The invention of printing which had been acclaimed so enthusiastically by Gans became an important factor in spreading the Lurianic Kabbalah which cut short any modernist development that may have been set in motion by Gans and his friends. Thus their movement, if indeed it may be called one, was no more than an episode. However it should be considered as one of the first signs of the changing character of Ashkenazic Jewry in modern times.

NOTES

(For full references to works quoted in the notes see bibliography.

1. For the concept summarized here see, in particular, Baer, p. 59; idem, *Zion* 7, p. 60; Katz, p. 3; H.H. Ben-Sasson in *Encyclopaedia Judaica* (1972), Vol. 8, col. 692.

2. Menke-Glueckert, p. 1.

3. The term *Fruehneuzeit* for the sixteenth and seventeenth centuries was coined by Kamlah, passim.

4. It is unlikely that Gans settled in Prague in 1559, as assumed by Neher, p. 32. In that year the imperial expulsion order was carried out. For several reasons 1564 seems to be the most likely year.

5. On Prague at the time of Rudolph II see Evans, especially pp. 74f., 123; Moryson, p. 282. On the Jewish situation see Heřman, p. 48.

6. Muneles, *Prague*, pp. 27, 60; Moryson, pp. 275, 281; Evans, p. 27; Bondy-Dworsky, pp. 732, 578f. (Nr. 776). On communal strife in Prague see Judah b. Betzalel (MaHaRaL), *Netzaḥ Yisra'el* (1599), ch. 25. On the election of communal leaders see Ben-Sasson, p. 271; Muneles, p. 106. On Prague Jews' interventions on behalf of other communities see *TzD*, 5352, s.v. Heinrich and cf. Bondy-Dworsky, pp. 727-730 (Nr. 939).

7. The quotation from Ephraim of Luntshitz is from his preface to *Amudei Esh* (Prague, 1618). On Jewish men of learning in Prague from the fourteenth century on, see E. Kupfer, *Tarbitz* 42 (1973), pp. 113–147. On controversies in Prague and Posen see *NvN*, p. 9b; Ph. Bloch, *Der Streit* etc., *MGWJ* 47 (1903); G. Scholem, *Tarbitz* 28 (1959), pp. 59–89.

8. The wide intellectual interests prevailing among rabbinical scholars in Poland is attested by such writings as Manoaḥ Hendel's *Manoaḥ Levavot* (Lublin, 1596), and Joseph b. Isaac ha-Levi's *Giv'at ha-More* (Prague, 1612), Cf. also Ḥ. Shmeruk, *Tarbitz* 46 (1977), pp. 258–314. For humanist and Renaissance literature in Poland see the article by S. Kot in *Bibliothèque d'humanisme et renaissance* 14 (1952), pp. 348f.; ibid., 15 (1953), pp. 233f. For the close relations between Prague, Cracow and Venice see Breuer, *Bar-Ilan*, p. 113; *Judaica Bohemiae* 4 (1968), p. 41.

9. On Sephardi Jews in Prague see Muneles, *Prague*, p. 35. On the encouragement given by the MaHaRaL to those engaged in general science see, e.g., *Netivot Olam* (1595), *Netiv ha-Tora*, ch. 14.

10. For details on the members of the Prague élite see Breuer, *Bar-Ilan*, pp. 97–103. On the Jewish printing presses see Muneles, p. 115; Lieben B'nai B'rith, note 17. Cf. also the list of Y.L. Heller's writings which was compiled by I. Heilprin, *Kiryat Sefer* 7 (1930/31), pp. 140f.

11. In the circles opposed to *ḥokhma* the use of a concordance for Bible study was also condemned; see Scholem, op. cit., p. 78. Eliyahu Baḥur is mentioned six times in *TzD*.

12. For Gans' autobiographical note see *TzD*, 5030; Part Two, 1; Introduction to Part One, beginning and conclusion. On his various fields of research see Breuer, *Bar-Ilan*, pp. 105–118. For his interest in pathology and medicine see *TzD*, Part Two, 3446, 1494, 1529. That Gans engaged in teaching astronomy and cosmology is hinted in *NvN*, #69, 270.

13. Cf. D. Cassel, in *Ersch-Gruber*, Section 1, Vol. 2c; Berliner, p. 21; Breuer, *Bar-Ilan*, p. 105 note 47. Gans' erroneous concept of the Muslim calendar emerges from many of his datings in the sections dealing with events in the history of the Ottoman Empire.

14. Cf. McLuhan, p. 208. In the introduction to his German translation of Bernau's *Chronica*, one of Gans' sources, Jacob Eysenberg wrote that his endeavor was aimed at laymen thirsty for knowledge yet ignorant of Latin.

15. Gans' naiveté has been pointed out by Neher, pp. 268–269. On his preoccupation with reality see also Kohn, pp. 10–14. On the preference for reason and experience to

book knowledge see Kamlah, p. 329; however, cf. K. Joel, *Der Ursprung der Naturphilosophie aus dem Geiste der Mystik* (Jena, 1906), pp. 19–21.

16. Weisinger's paper was published in *Papers of the Michigan Academy* 29 (1943), pp. 561–567. The quotation is on p. 562. See also Menke-Glueckert, p. 71, on the German historiographer Sleiden.

17. Weisinger, p. 563.

18. Ibid., p. 566.

19. *NvN*, f. 9a-b; 82d. It is noteworthy that Prague University is mentioned twice in *TzD*: 1351 and 1408.

20. Cf. Baron, p. 413 note 58; Neher, p. 58; Neher, *L'exégèse*, p. 191. With Gans the distinction between *Bildungserlebnis* and *Urerlebnis* becomes so blurred as to be almost meaningless. See, e.g., *TzD*, 140, where he writes about his fascination with the coins of the Roman emperors as if he had seen actual specimens of them, while in reality he had only seen engravings of them in Eysenberg's book.

21. MaHaRaL attacked *Me'or Enayim* in *Be'er ha-Gola* (1600), conclusion of ch. 6; *Netzaḥ Yisrael*, ch. 5; and alluded to it in *Netivot Olam, Netiv Ha-Tora*, ch. 8. Cf. Neher, *Le puits*, pp. 103–105; Breuer, *Shema'tin*, p. 58. For Gans' attitude see *TzD*, Introduction to Part One; 3100; 3448. He also quoted de Rossi in *NvN* (which he prepared for publication after MaHaRaL's death), ch. 89, although he mentioned the sixth chapter of *Be'er ha-Gola* in the introduction. Undoubtedly he was aware that other rabbis had also taken exception to *Me'or Enayim*; see I. Mehlman, *Genuzot Sfarim* (Jerusalem, 1976), pp. 21–39. For other rabbinical scholars, including Y.L. Heller, who quoted *Me'or Enayim* without any reservations, see L. Zunz, *Kerem Ḥemed* 5 (1841), pp. 145–146.

22. On Ibn Yaḥya's attitude to *Me'or Enayim* see David, pp. 65 and 290, note 8. On Gans' attitude to astrology and related subjects see Breuer, *Bar-Ilan*, pp. 109–114; Neher, pp. 93f. On de Rossi's treatment of earthquakes and the theological problems raised by them see Baron, p. 176. Gans mentions approximately seventy cases of earthquakes and similar portents in *TzD*. For Isserles' concept of *zekhut* and *mazal* see Ben-Sasson, *Hagut*, pp. 78–79. Gans' treatment of this subject in his introduction to Part Two, eighth "lesson," and in the passage on the year 1590, differs strikingly from that of his master. Gans returned to this problem in *NvN*, chs. 297–298, where he dealt with it in terms recalling the MaHaRaL's discussion in *Be'er ha-Gola*, ch. 4, s.v. *Be-ferek ha-ro'e*.

23. See *TzD*, 3448 s.v. *Al ken*; 2964, 3100, 3008 (Part Two). Gans enumerated all the Persian kings (Part Two, 3393) whose names and years are wanting in the traditional chronology, yet deliberately omitted the years of their reigns which he found in his non-Jewish sources (see also below, note 25). He also changed some dates mentioned in the chronicles so as to make them correspond with the traditional chronology he followed in Part One.

24. Graetz, 4th German edition, Vol. 9, p. 423. The bracketed words were wisely omitted in the English edition, Vol. 4 (Philadelphia, 1894), p. 638, but were retained in subsequent German editions. Baron, p. 196, detected elements of medievalism even in de Rossi's approach to history, something that was overlooked by Graetz, op. cit., pp. 383, 386. On German historiography in the sixteenth century there is an abundance of literature; see, in particular, Fueter, pp. 181f.; Srbik, p. 54; Thompson, pp. 527f.; Klempt, pp. 11, 17–19; Ulsamer, pp. 11–13, 25, 34, 47; Clemen, pp. 32–33; Borchardt, p. 424; Menke-Glueckert, passim. To show how gans was misled by his sources one example will do. Although several humanists had already discredited Berosus' stories as mere legends, Sprangenberg, one of Gans' chief models, relied on him, taking pains to prove his credibility. De Rossi also quoted Berosus several times. Gans followed their lead. Melanchthon rejected Berosus, yet following the Talmud fixed the duration of the world at 6000 years; see Menke-Glueckert, pp. 30, 44.

25. On the territorial interest of early humanist historiography see Kamlah, p. 328. On the rise of a critical approach to biblical chronology in German historiography see Grafton, pp. 167f.; Klempt, p. 84. Gans' basic readiness for far-reaching critcism, though stopping short of clear-cut conclusions, stands out in his list of the Achaemenid dynasty of Persian kings (see above, note 23). Every king in addition to the four mentioned in the Bible and in *Seder Olam* aggravated the chronological problem, yet instead of limiting himself to the

ten kings he found in Faustus, Gans followed Eusebius' record of fourteen which he read in *Me'or Enayim.* He also showed considerable independence in correcting the chronology of the Geonim. In rejecting RaSHI's interpretations (*TzD*, 2764, 3098) he followed the MaHaRaL; see *Netivot Olam, Netiv ha-Tora*, ch. 15; *Netiv Ahavat Re'a*, ch. 1. For the legend reported by MaHaRIL see *TzD*, 3448 s.v. *Yeshu'a.* In *NvN*, f. 7d–8a, Gans cited "many well-known men of learning," including Maimonides and Isaac Arama, who held that the sayings of the Sages contained things "which are not [authoritative] like their other pronouncements which they made on the authority of tradition." However, he himself adopted the practice of Isserles and MaHaRaL who "went to great lengths . . . in interpreting the words of the Sages in such a manner that they should not clash with well-known truths."

26. On Ibn Yaḥya see David, p. 215. On Spangenberg's lack of source criticism and historical sense see Ulsamer, pp. 22–34. For Gans' more advanced method see, e.g., *TzD*, 3042, 3442, 3668, 3978, 4234, 4881, 4900, 4934, Introduction to Part Two, 3008 (Part Two), 490, 1162, 1187.

27. *TzD*, 3100, 3448 s.v. *Gam ha-mevukha*, 3646, 3829, 3840 (on Onkelos), 3880, 4500, 4810 (cf. 4866), 4830 (cf. 4863, 4865, 4910), 4900, 4977, 5070 (cf. 5046), 5089, 5108 (cf. 5160). On harmonizing tendencies in Isserles' and de Rossi's writings see Neher, pp. 55, 303; Baron, p. 176. Tyco Brahe's world picture was harmonistic in that it involved the traditional geocentric conception with Copernican heliocentrism. The phrase "a flower here and a rose there" echoes a similar phrase in *Me'or Enayim*, p. 78. On the invention of two persons with identical names or titles by de Rossi see Baron, p. 238.

28. The literature on the co-existence of the old and the new in Renaissance and humanism, especially in Germany, is profuse. For the aspects dealt with here see, in particular, Rice, p. 213; Rabb, p. 110; Baron, p. 410 note 37; and cf. Breuer, *Bar-Ilan*, p. 102 note 28. On the simile of the dwarf and the giant, mentioned by Gans in the Introduction to Part One, see Merton. An instance of this half humble and half self-confident dwarf-giant relationship can also be found in Mordekhai Yaffe's *Levush* on *Oraḥ Ḥayyim* #267, where he wrote that the rabbinical scholars of the fourteenth century did not study astronomy and for this reason misconstrued certain dicta of the Sages. On Gans' positive attitude to Copernicus' "new astronomy," especially after his visit with Brahe and Kepler, and unlike MaHaRaL's reserved attitude, see Neher, especially pp. 91–92; Neher, *Le puits*, p. 15; Neher, *L'exégèse*. Cf. also Jones, pp. 10, 276 note 19.

29. See *TzD*, 3448 s.v. *Amar ha-meḥaber*; and cf. Neher, pp. 43, 64, 81. Passages like the one about "the men of learning who contested many words of the Torah and are called Bnei Asher and Bnei Naftali" reveal Gans' informative purpose, even when it came to topics subject to dogmatic controversy. His quest for truth may also be discerned in those places where he left the discussion of some point undecided and open to further study, e.g., *TzD*, 3460, 3757, 4060. Cf. Menke-Glueckert, p. 77, on Sleiden.

30. A phrase similar to Gans' "tired of *galut*" appears in *Sefer ha-Ḥayyim* by MaHaRaL's brother Hayyim (Cracow, 1593), Part Three, ch. 6. There was weariness of *galut* in Gans' circle but no despair of redemption as was widespread among the Spanish exiles at the beginning of the century. See Y. Hacker, in *Tarbitz* 39 (1970), p. 195. Gans' statement the he composed his book for the diversion of *ba'alei batim* in their hours of leisure strikingly echoes a very similar statement by Tam ibn Yaḥya in his introduction to his edition of *Yosifon* (Constantinople, 1510). See Houminer's edition (Jerusalem, 1956), p. 43. I am indebted to Prof. Y. H. Yerushalmi for drawing my attention to this fact. Gans' *maskil* (*TzD*, 3448 s.v. *Al ken*) was supposed to be interested in the arithmetics of the Jewish calendar (*TzD*, 4003), or to have among his books a copy of Sebastian Muenster's translation of the Book of Tobias (Part Two, 3209), possibly having some knowledge of the Trojan War (Part Two, 2758) and Homer (3090). The thirst for news in the sixteenth century became more intensified as travel abroad became more frequent and as popular curiosity was aroused by the discoveries and inventions; see, e.g., Schottenloher, p. 153; Elliott, p. 30.

31. The thirst of Prague Jews for news of an extraordinary and monstrous nature may have been reinforced by Rudolph's taste for eccentricities and exotic objects which fashioned the life style of his palace at Prague; see Evans, p. 251. On the three outstanding inventions see Elliott, pp. 9–10; Weisinger, p. 421; Jones, p. 34. Spangenberg, too, emphasized technological progress and Ulsamer, p. 66, thinks that in this he anticipated his time.

32. Gans' eminently pragmatic ethics, centering upon material success, seem to be at the back of his lengthy discourse, the only one of its kind in *TzD*, on divine retribution in this world, *TzD*, 3460. Cf. Abravanel's discussion of the subject in *Naḥalat Avot* (Venice, 1545), ff. 26–29, which Gans quoted in his discourse; MaHaRaL, *Netivot Olam*, *Netiv ha-Osher*, ch. 2; Ben-Sasson, chs. 5–7. Spangenberg emphasized in his introduction the element of divine providence and retribution in history, while Faustus pointed out that one of the chief purposes of his book was to show that readers could learn from the history of rulers how to avoid disasters in their own lives. For Melanchthon see Menke-Glueckert, pp. 10–11, 32 and passim.

33. A detailed comparison between *TzD* and its German sources shows that Gans often omitted the authors' remarks of a theological and historiosophical character, and not only with specifically Christian undertones. On the secularizing trend in sixteenth-century German historiography see Klempt, p. 17; Buck, p. 15; *TzD* on Westphalia etc. Part Two, 2455, 3700, 476.

34. *TzD* on printing: 1440. Cf. A. Berliner in *Jahresbericht des Berliner Rabbinerseminars, 5653–4* (Frankfurt a.M., 1896), *Beilage*, pp. 5f.; Breuer, *Bar-Ilan*, p. 102 note 26; I.Z. Kahana, *Meḥkarim* (Jerusalem, 1973), p. 273; R. Stadelmann, *Vom Geist des ausgehenden Mittelalters* (Halle/S., 1929), p. 120. Gans' praise of printing is more "secular" in tone than his chief source, Goltzius, who emphasized the potentialities of the printed book for preserving the cultural achievements of mankind. It is far more secular than the relevant remarks of the German humanist Wimpheling who wrote that the invention of printing had made the Germans into the bearers of Chritianity, since innumerable prayers and supplications rose to heaven from printed prayer books; see Clemen, p. 2. See also d'Ester and cf. Eisenstein, *Advent*, pp. 56, 67–68.

35. Cf. Breuer, *Bar-Ilan*, pp. 114–115. To the passages cited there from *TzD* the following should be added: Part One: 5300, 5346, 5352 s.v. *Mordekhai Maysel*; Part Two: 60, 140, 412, 451, 1230, 1366, 1490. On arts and crafts see Part One: 3840, 4881; Part Two: 1440. Ben-Sasson's statement (Ben-Sasson, p. 56) that manual labor did not stand in high regard in leading Jewish circles needs qualification, at any rate with reference to Prague where men engaged in printing occupied high positions in the community. Cf. Eisenstein, *Advent*, pp. 63, 68. On the attitude of the leaders of the Reformation to the masses see Menke-Glueckert, p. 53.

36. *TzD*, 5065 (see also register, Part One, for this year); 3500, 3768, 4118, 4727, 5290; cf. Breuer, *Ha-Ma'ayan*, pp. 24–25; Neuman, p. 619. On the admiration for men of learning in humanist historiography see Horawitz, p. 619; Menke-Glueckert, p. 83. On the secularization of the ideal of wisdom see Rice and Archambault. On a similar process in Jewish society see Ben-Sasson, p. 195. On the impact of the new occupations on Torah study see ibid., p. 55.

37. *TzD*, 5187; cf. Breuer, in *Zion* 41 (1968), pp. 29f.; Muneles, p. 94. On the rise of lay leadership in the German communities see Breuer in *Zion* 41 (1976), pp. 47–67. On Luther's campaign against the traditional privileges of the clergy see H. Lieberg, *Amt und Ordination bei Luther und Melanchthon* (Goettingen, 1962); Menke-Glueckert, pp. 2–3.

38. See Breuer, *Ha-Ma'ayan*, pp. 25–26. On de Rossi's appreciative references to Kabbalah see Baron, pp. 197, 198, 224. However, contrary to Baron's opinion this had nothing to do with the spread of Lurianic Kabbalah since this occurred only at the end of the sixteenth century, as was shown by G. Scholem, in *Zion* 5 (1940), p. 236. On the debate on the status of Kabbalah see Bloch, op. cit.; I. Heilprin, *Yehudim ve-Yahadut* (Jerusalem, 1969), p. 82; Solomon Luria, *Responsa* (Lublin, 1574), Nr. 98. On Josel of Rosheim's strong Kabbalistic leanings see Fraenkel-Goldschmidt, pp. 72–73.

39. At the conclusion of the ninth "lesson" Gans added a remark raising some doubt as to its practical value. However, at the end of his introduction to *NvN* he emphatically repeated the same "lesson" without any reservation. Similar consideration for gentile attitudes to the Jews can be found in MaHaRaL, *Be'er ha-Gola*, ch. 4; Ḥayyim b. Betzalel, *Etz Ḥayyim* (London, 1973), preface; Bloch, op. cit.

40. For the well-known debate between J. Katz and H.H. Ben-Sasson see *Tarbitz* 29 (1960), pp. 297–312; ibid., 30 (1960), pp. 62–72; see also S. Ettinger, *Kiryat Sefer* 35 (1960), p. 16. On Gans' tolerance and the frequency of Jewish-Gentile contracts at his time see

Breuer, *Ha-Ma'ayan*, pp. 21–22; idem, Bar-Ilan, pp. 103–104. See also Neher, *Hagut*, pp. 112–113, for MaHaRaL's attitude to the contemporary gentile world and cf. Y. Emanuel in *Ha-Ma'ayan* (Tevet, 5724), pp. 50f., on Y.L. Heller. On the changing attitude of European society towards the Jews see S.W. Baron, *A Social and Religious History of the Jews*², XIII (1969), pp. 159–160, 204–205; S. Ettinger, *Scripta Hierosolymitana* 7 (1961), p. 219.

41. Cf. Breuer, *Ha-Ma'ayan*, pp. 21–25; Ben-Sasson, *Jews*, pp. 374–375. The widespread opinion that the masses and not the kings were responsible for outbreaks of violence against the Jews stands out in Ibn Verga's *Shevet Yehuda* and S. Usque's *Consolaçam* etc.; cf. Y. Hacker, Zion 34 (1969), pp. 71–74; Y. H. Yerushalmi, *The Lisbon Massacre of 1506 and the Royal Image in the* Shebet Yehudah (Cincinnati, 1976), pp. 42–44, 49. On the ideal of the philosopher-king in contemporary literature see Rice, p. 75; Hall, p. 4. On the influence of admonitions attributed to monarchs see also the quotation from Abravanel, *TzD*, Part Two, 3718, and cf. E. Capsali, *Seder Eliyahu Zuta* (Jerusalem, 1976), p. 10. Gans' strong attachment to his homelands emerges also from *TzD*, Part Two, 887, 1349, 1458, 1516. It should also be noted that the Katz printing house in Prague used to adorn the front pages of some of their books with the crests of Bohemia and Prague; see Muneles, p. 115.

42. On martyrology in *TzD* see Breuer, *Ha-Ma'ayan*, pp. 19–20, where only a partial list of incidents of Christian martyrdom is given. Ibn Verga indeed wrote that "there are things which are not fit to write" regarding the "persecutions and exiles suffered by Israel" (49th persecution), yet his motive is precisely the opposite of Gans' "special reason": "Already [the biblical prophecy] 'Ye shall be lost among the nations' has been fulfilled upon us." On Josel of Rosheim's strong attachment to *kidush ha-shem* see Fraenkel-Goldschmidt, p. 71. Gans' optimism stands out not only against the general preoccupation of contemporary Jewish historiography with martyrology but also against the pessimism prevailing in Christian intellectual circles in Prague; see Evans, p. 278.

43. On Christian sects in *TzD* see Breuer, *Ha-Ma'ayan*, pp. 18–19; Ben-Sasson, *Jews*, pp. 375–377. Gans' vivid interest in the introduction of the Gregorian calendar (1583) was not merely aroused through his general involvement with astronomy and calendar calculation. The calendar change stood, in his eyes, for a general lack of stability in the Christian world against which the Jewish calendar stood out in permanent inflexibility; see also *NvN*, f. 7d. On Gans' summary treatment of inter-Jewish conflicts see Breuer, *Bar-Ilan*, p. 98; cf. also *TzD*, 4515, 3697 (Part One and Two). On his attitude to Herod see Breuer, *Ha-Ma'ayan*, p. 24; cf. Flusser pp. 217–219; H.H. Ben-Sasson, *Perakim*, II (1971), p. 214.

44. Gans used every opportunity that presented itself to drive home the fact that Israel had once been ruled by kings. Following Talmudical precedent he referred to the heads of the Sanhedrin and to leading rabbis in each generation as "kings"; cf. Breuer, *Ha-Ma'ayan*, p. 24 note 62. All the more surprising it therefore seems that he never mentioned Josel of Rosheim, although Josel has been a famous *shtadlan* who had been regarded as the "king" of the Jews in his time; cf. MaHaRaL, *Netzaḥ Yisrael*, ch. 10; J. Katz, in *Zion* 10 (1945), p. 32 note 71; Neher, p. 36 note 1. Was it Gans' desire to avoid offending Prague Jewish sensibilities? See Josel's diary, *REJ* 16 (1888), pp. 91–92, n. 20.

45. See Breuer, *Ha-Ma'ayan*, p. 18. The four beasts symbolizing the Four Monarchies are displayed on the front pages of *TzD*, Parts One and Two surrounding the images of David and Solomon. In both introductions the Four Monarchies are mentioned prominently. For MaHaRaL's view on the fourth monarchy see *Netzaḥ Yisrael*, chs. 16, 17, 21, 28.

46. On the Four-Monarchy scheme in sixteenth-century historiography see Eisenstein, *Clio*, p. 44 note 22; Srbik, pp. 53–57; Manuel. pp. 17–18; Buck, p. 12; Klempt. pp. 26, 34, 50, 54; Menke-Glueckert, pp. 46, 56, 65, 85; Kamlah, p. 328. On the fall of the pope as being synonymous with the fall of the Fourth Monarchy Gans read in Faustus, the introduction to his chronicle.

47. On the danger of the Turkish invasion and its impact on public opinion see Evans, pp. 22, 75; Schottenloher, p. 168; idem, *Bibliographie*, IV, pp. 677–687. On the Ten Tribes and geographical discoveries see Ruderman, pp. 175–176; Neher, pp. 183f. On the calculation of the messianic year in the sixteenth century see David, pp. 176–179. On MaHaRaL's aversion to messianic speculation see Gross, pp. 217-221, and on his general

approach to messianism see Neher, *Le puits*, pp. 79–87. On the Star of David, a symbol of messianic significance, engraved on Gans' tombstone, see G. Scholem, in *Encyclopaedia Judaica* (1972), 11, col. 695; Neher, *Tarbitz*, p. 141 note 8. On Josel of Rosheim's silence on matters connected with messianism see Fraenkel-Goldschmidt, pp. 40, 67f. For Asher Lemlein see *TzD*, 5260.

48. M. Luther, *Works* (Philadelphia, 1931), Vol. 4, pp. 128–129; Menke-Glueckert, pp. 4–5, 28, 124 (*historia divina* and *historia naturalis* [1594]), 125 (*historia divina* and *historia humana* [1600]); Klempt, p. 20.

49. In Spangenberg and Faustus Gans found many cross-references between the two histories; cf. *TzD*, 3910, 5046 and their counterparts in Part Two. There are also double entries: 4946–1186, 4958–1198.

50. Isserles' dictum is quoted in Gans' introduction to Part Two. Cf. W. A. Nitze, "The So-called Twelfth Century Renaissance," *Speculum* 23 (1948), pp. 464f.; S.W. Baron, loc. cit.; S. Ettinger, op. cit., pp. 195–196.

BIBLIOGRAPHY

Primary Sources

Me'or Enayim – Azariah de Rossi, *Me'or Enayim*. Vilna: 5626 (1865/66).

NvN – David Gans, *Neḥmad ve-Na'im*. Jasnitz, 5503 (1742/43).

TzD – David Gans, *Tzemaḥ David*. Prague: 5352 (1591/92).

German Chronicles Used by Gans:

Buenting – Heinrich Buenting, *Itinerarium Sacrae Scripturae, das ist ein Reisebuch*. Leipzig, 1585.

Eysenberg – Praetorius (Paulus) von Bernau, *Chronica, darinnen der Roemischen Keiser historien verdeutscht durch Jacobum Eysenberg*. Wittenberg, 1561.

Faustus – Laurentius Faustus, *Chronologia auch Anatomia . . . von den vier Monarchien*. Leipzig, 1586.

Goltzius Hubert Goltz(ius), *Keyserliche Chronik*. Frankfurt a. M., 1588.

Spangenberg – Cyriak Spangenberg, *Saechsische Chronica*. Frankfurt a. M., 1585.

Secondary Sources

Archambault – P. Archambault, "Commynes' Saigesse and the Renaissance Idea of Wisdom," *Bibliothèque d'Humanisme et Renaissance* 29 (1967), pp. 613–632.

Baron – S. W. Baron, *History and Jewish Historians*. Philadelphia, 1964.

Baer – Y. Baer, "On the Periodization of History" [Hebrew], *Proceedings of the Fourth World Congress for Jewish Studies*. Jerusalem, 1967.

Ben-Sasson – H. H. Ben-Sasson, *Toldot Am Yisrael bi-Ymei ha-Beynayim*. Tel Aviv, 1969.

---, *Hagut* – Idem, *Hagut ve-Hanhaga*. Tel Aviv, 1959.

---, *Jews* – Idem, "Jews and Christian Sectarians: Existential Similarity and Dialectical Tensions in 16th-Century Moravia and Poland-Lithuania," *Viator* 4 (1973), pp. 369–385.

Berliner – A. Berliner, *Persoenliche Beziehungen zwischen Christen und Juden im Mittelalter*. Halberstadt, 1882.

Bondy-Dworský – G. Bondy and F. Dworský, *Zur Geschichte der Juden in Boehmen, Maehren und Schlesien*. Prague, 1906.

Borchardt – F. Borchardt, "Etymology in Tradition and in the Northern Renaissance," *Journal of the History of Ideas* 29 (1968), pp. 415–429.

Breuer, *Bar-Ilan* – M. Breuer, "Rabbi David Gans, Author of the *Tzemaḥ David* – An Outline" [Hebrew], *Bar-Ilan* 11 (1972/73), pp. 97–118.

---, *Ha-Ma'ayan* – Idem, "The Aims of *Tzemaḥ David* by Rabbi David Gans" [Hebrew], *Ha-Ma'ayan* 5, no. 2 (Tevet, 5725 [1964]), pp. 15–27.

---, *Shema'tin* – Idem, "The Teaching of History and the Beliefs of the Sages" [Hebrew], *Shema'tin* 36/37 (1973/74), pp. 52–62.

Buck – A. Buck, *Das Geschichtsedenken der Renaissance*. Krefeld, 1957.

David – A. David, "The Historiographic Accomplishment of Gedaliah ibn Yaḥya, Author of *Shalshelet ha-Kabbala*." Dissertation, Hebrew University, 1976.

d'Ester – K. d'Ester, "Das Werk Gutenbergs und seine Auswirkungen im Urteil der Philosophen," *Gutenberg Jahrbuch* (1959), pp. 45–53.

Eisenstein, *Advent* – E. L. Eisenstein, "The Advent of Printing and the Problem of the Renaissance," *Past and Present* 45, pp. 19–89.

---, Clio – Idem, "Clio and Chronos: Aspects of History-Book Time," *History and Theory* 6 (1966), pp. 36–65.

Elliott – J. E. Elliott, *The Old World and the New*. Cambridge, 1970.

Ersch-Gruber – J. S. Ersch and J. G. Gruber, *Allgemeine Encyclopaedie der Wissenschaften und Kuenste*: Leipzig, 1818–89.

Evans – R. J. W. Evans, *Rudolf II and His World*. Oxford, 1973.

Fueter – E. Fueter, *Geschichte der neueren Historiographie*. Muenchen, 1925.

Flusser – D. Flusser, "The Author of the *Sefer Yosifon* as a Historian" [Hebrew], *Hartza'ot be-Kinsei ha-Iyun be-Historiya*, Israeli Historical Society, Jerusalem, 1972/73. Pp. 302–26.

Fraenkel-Goldschmidt – H. Fraenkel-Goldschmidt, "Introduction to *Sefer ha-Makne* of Joseph ben Gershom of Rossheim" [Hebrew]. Dissertation, Hebrew University, 1969/70.

Grafton – A. T. Grafton, "Joseph Scaliger and Historical Chronology," *History and Theory* 14 (1975), pp. 156–185.

Gross – B. Gross, *'Netzaḥ Yisrael'-Hashkafato ha-Meshiḥit shel ha-MaHaRaL mi-Prag al ha-Galut ve-ha-Geulah*. Tel-Aviv, 1973/74.

Heřman, – J. Heřman, "La communauté juive de Prague et sa structure au commencement des temps modernes," *Judaica Bohemiae* 5 (1969), pp. 31–71.

Jones – R. F. Jones, *Ancients and Moderns*. St. Louis, 1961.

Kamlah – W. Kamlah, "'Zeitalter' ueberhaupt, 'Neuzeit' und 'Fruehzeit'," *Saeculum* 8 (1957), pp. 313–332.

Katz – J. Katz, *Masoret u-Mashber*. Jerusalem, 1958.

Klempt – A. Klempt, *Die Saekularisierung der universalhistorischen Auffassung im 16. und 17. Jahrhundert*. Goettingen, 1960.

Kohn – J. Kohn, "Soziologische Einfuehrungsskizze," *Jahrbuch der*

Gesellschaft fuer Geschichte der Juden in der CSR 2 (1930), pp. 1–16.

Lieben, Bnai Brith – S. H. Lieben, "Der hebraeische Buchdruck in Prag," *Juden in Prag*, Bnai Brith. Prague, 1927.

McLuhan – M. McLuhan, *The Gutenberg Galaxy*. Toronto, 1962.

Manuel – F. E. Manuel, *Shapes of Philosophical History*. Stanford, 1965.

Menke-Glueckert – Menke-Glueckert, *Die Geschichtschreibung der Reformation und Gegenreformation*. Leipzig, 1912.

Merton – R. K. Merton, *On the Shoulder of Giants*. New York, 1965.

Moryson – Fynes Moryson, *Shakespeare's Europe*. London, 1903.

Muneles – O. Muneles, "Die Rabbiner der Altneuschul," *Judaica Bohemiae* 5 (1969), pp. 92–107.

Muneles, Prague – Idem, *The Prague Ghetto in the Renaissance Period*. Prague, 1965.

Neher – A. Neher, *David Gans*. Paris, 1974.

---, *Hagut* – Idem, "The MaHaRaL of Prague as Humanist" [Hebrew], *Hagut Ivrit be-Eyropa*. Tel Aviv, 1969. Pp. 107–117.

---, *L'exégèse* – Idem, "L'exégèse biblique juive face à Copernic," *Studies presented to M. A. Beek*. Amsterdam, 1974, pp. 190–196.

---, *Le puits* – Idem, *Le puits de l'exile*. Paris, 1966.

---, *Tarbitz* – Idem, "New Material on David Gans as Astronomer" [Hebrew], *Tarbitz* 45 (1976), pp. 138–147.

Neuman – A. A. Neuman, "Abraham Zacuto, Historiographer," *H. A Wolfson Jubilee Volume*, II. Jerusalem, 1965. Pp. 597–629.

Rabb – T. K. Rabb, *The Struggle for Stability in Early Modern Europe*. New York, 1975.

Rice – E. F. Rice, Jr. *The Renaissance Idea of Wisdom.* Cambridge, MA, 1958.

Ruderman – D. Ruderman, "The *'Igeret Orḥot Olam'* by Abraham Farissol in its Historical Context" [Hebrew], *Proceedings of the Sixth*

World Congress for Jewish Studies. Jerusalem, 1976. Pp. 169–178.

Schottenloher – K. Schottenloher, *Flugblatt und Zeitung.* Berlin, 1922.

---, *Bibliographie* – Idem, *Bibliographie zur Deutschen Geschichte im Zeitalter der Glaubenspaltung 1517–1585.* Stuttgart, 1957.

Srbik – H. v. Srbik, *Geist und Geschichte.* Muenchen, 1950.

Thompson – J. W. Thompson, *A History of Historical Writing*, Vol. I. New York, 1942.

Ulsamer – H. Ulsamer, "Curiacus Spangenberg als Geschichtsschreiber des deutschen Adels im 16. Jahrhundert," Dissertation, Munich, 1921.

Weisinger H. Weisinger, "Ideas of History during the Renaissance," *Journal of the History of Ideas* 6 (1945), pp. 415–435.

“No Evil Descends from Heaven” Sixteenth-Century Jewish Concepts of Evil

JOSEPH DAN

I

Very few of the main ideas formulated by Jewish thinkers in the sixteenth century in the atmosphere of the Jewish Renaissance had any important impact on seventeenth- and eighteenth-century Jewish thought. Many ideological trends which began in this period either died out or had to wait two centuries and more until the period of the Enlightenment, in order to be reborn in new historical and cultural circumstances and then take root. Some of them, like the idea of a Jewish university, had to wait till the twentieth century.

The one school of thought which flourished in sixteenth-century Judaism as well as in previous and subsequent periods was the Kabbalah. The history of kabbalistic literature marks an uninterrupted creative effort which began late in the twelfth century and continued steadily till the nineteenth century at least. The Renaissance period in Jewish culture is one link in the long chain of kabbalistic literature which, from the beginning of the sixteenth century till the nineteenth, was gaining in impact and cultural influence, until it became the dominant popular Jewish ideology and served as a basis for the development of particular trends, sects and movements.

It is therefore of some scholarly interest to examine sixteenth-century Kabbalah in comparison with other Renaissance cultural phenomena, and to check whether there is some common element of historical development even though Kabbalah continued its steady development while many other sixteenth-century literary and cultural trends, like Jewish historiography or the classically-influenced Jewish homily, were discontinued. Did the kabbalists ignore, in the sixteenth century, contemporary events and trends, and thus succeed in being prepared for the changes brought by the reaction of the seventeenth century, or did they participate in the major innovative trends of the Renaissance, and still remain ready to adapt to the completely different cultural values of seventeenth-century East-European Judaism?

It is our intention in this paper to show, even though limiting ourselves to only one example, that the Kabbalah did fully participate in, reflect and express the major ideological trends of the Jewish Renaissance, but that at the same time the Kabbalah had the spiritual resources to introduce a drastic change at the end of that century, which enabled it to present the subsequent century with an ideology suited to, and expressing, the new cultural demands.

When speaking about sixteenth-century Kabbalah as compared to that of the seventeenth, one really deals with the relationship between two great kabbalists—probably the greatest after the thirteenth century, who lived together in Safed in the second half of the sixteenth century and shared the same disciples to some extent, namely Rabbi Moses Cordovero and Rabbi Isaac Luria.[1] It is the purpose of this paper to present the relationship between their differing mystical systems against the background of the conflicting cultural trends of the sixteenth and seventeenth centuries, and to describe Cordovero as the great spokesman for the sixteenth. We contend that Luria, on the other hand, paved the way for a revolution within the Kabbalah, a revolution which made it possible for Jewish mysticism to become the dominant spiritual force in seventeenth-century Judaism.

II

Lurianic Kabbalah differed from earlier Jewish mystical systems first and foremost in its insistence on describing the beginning of divine history long before the creation.[2] In the Lurianic drama, the creation of the world comes in the third act, while the previous two decide to a very large extent the character and potentialities of all occurrences after the creation. The myths of the *tzimtzum* and the *shevira* are the decisive events,[3] while all the history of the created worlds—including the divine *Sefirot*—serves only to enhance the *tikun*, putting to right what went wrong in the first two acts. Therefore, there can be no doubt that the main antagonists in the divine drama described by Luria preceded Creation and Man, who are nothing but latecomers participating in the last act of a mythical struggle. The most extreme and strange theological idea to be presented by Luria in his mythical symbolism is that the roots of evil are an integral part of the eternal God; they did not emerge within the framework of cosmogony or history, but were present even before the divine *Sefirot* were emanated; they are as ancient and eternal as the Godhead, *Ein-Sof*, itself.[4] According to Lurianic theology, the source of evil is completely independent of human action; its future will be decided by the behavior of human beings, but originally evil is one of the basic potentialities of the eternal Godhead.

The concept of evil in the extensive works of Rabbi Moses Cordovero is completely different. It seems to me that it is impossible to harmonize the various references to this problem in Cordovero's works into one systematic, coherent philosophical system;[5] it is better to analyze the conflicting descriptions separately, and then to attempt to discover what are the basic drives, basic intuitions and major motives which are common to these various answers to the problem of the source of evil. Only thus will it be possible to evaluate correctly the relationship between Luria's myth of the source of evil and Cordovero's treatment of the same subject.

In Cordovero's magnum opus of systematic Kabbalah, *Pardes Rimonim*,[6] the "Sha'ar ha-Temurot" (Chapter on Opposites)[7] is dedicated to the nature of evil. Most of this chapter is devoted (like many other parts of that book) to a systematic elucidation of the various traditions in the Zohar and other early sources concerning this subject; very little space is alloted to discussion of the basic problem of the source and nature of evil. It is quite evident that Cordovero was much more comfortable when describing the manifestations of evil in the world than when he was treating the fundamental questions of the origins of evil and its purpose. The first sub-chapter in this discussion is dedicated, however, to the basic problem.

The key statement concerning our problem is made when Cordovero presents the conclusion of a detailed parable equating the creation with human endeavor. He says: "The truth is that above, in the world of the divine emanations, no evil thing descends from heaven, for up there everything is absolutely spiritual."[8] While this statement is presented as an answer, obviously it is nothing but a formulation of a question: Evil cannot be produced by the divine world, because this world is completely spiritual. Where, then, is the source of evil?

The parable presented by Cordovero is an attempt to answer this question. Cordovero begins by stating that God created everything in a system of harmony between opposites; therefore every good thing must have its evil counterpart, every holy thing its sinful parallel. But if so, a similar harmony should exist also at the source, and evil should have a divine manifestation. Cordovero recognizes that the harmony of opposites on earth does not reflect a similar harmony in the divine realm, and asks:

If so, where did the evil powers come from, where were the sinful things before they were created? This seems to be a penetrating and difficult question which could confuse the wise, but we have received from our teachers a very good answer to it. This is like the pure wheat, which had been cleaned from every impure element, but still, when a man eats it and the food has been digested in his stomach, a great deal of dirt and excrement will remain there. Now, can we say that when he ate that food he ate that dirt and excrement? Of course not, for before it was eaten, the food was clean and pure as it could be, completely separated from dirt and excrement. But after it was eaten, the best part is separated from the food, and the excrement remains, even though it did not exist till then.[9]

In the conclusion of this parable Cordovero presents the statement that no evil descends from heaven, and continues with a Neoplatonic description of the materialization of spiritual things. As they descend downwards they are removed from their source, and then "there is no way but that the good [=food, *okhel*] is separated from good [=food] and dirt is created there." Another, similar parable follows:

Like human semen, which is from the best part of the human body, it is created within the body and originates in the brain, and them comes out from the testicles to the penis. Now, from that very same drop will the embryo be created in the full belly, and other dirty things besides the embryo. Is it conceivable that in the human brain, which is the best part of the body, all that dirt will be created? Of course not, for if it were so, the person would die that instant. But that dirt is created by the descent of that drop from stage to stage, when the best part of it is the origin of the infant and the rest is turned into that dirt. It is the same with the process of divine emanation: In its place of origin, there is no element of evil, but when it is being drawn downwards, the most sacred and pure elements will be separated, and the dirt will remain." [10]

It seems that these parables should not be interpreted too meticulously—for instance, by asking whether the separation of evil from good in the process of emanation and descent does not prove that evil was, at least potentially, part of the divine world. Parables point out the most important element in a thinker's concept, but often obscure secondary points. Cordovero's thesis is quite clear: First, it is imperative for him to state conclusively that no divine evil power exists; second, in answer to the problem of the actual existence of evil, he presents a modification of the Neoplatonic conception of the degradation and materialization of all things as they are being emanated away from their divine source.

Cordovero's attitude is not new in the history of Jewish thought. One of the earliest—and most popular—presentations of this concept is to be found in the thirteenth-century anonymous ethical work, *Sefer ha-Yashar*, which explains the existence of the wicked and wrong-doers in the world as the result of a natural process, like that which causes thorns to be created together with the rose, and dirt together with the fruitful seed of wheat.[11] The author describes the natural force which compels creation to develop in this way as *koaḥ teva ha-beriya*, "the force of the nature of creation." A somewhat similar attitude is to be found in the early-thirteenth-century *Sefer ha-Ḥayim*, which described a power called *reyaḥ ha-avir ha-ḥay*, "the smell [or: spirit] of the living air," which brings into existence dirt, excrement and unclean beings.[12] Throughout the history of Jewish thought, mystical and non-mystical alike, we find various echoes of these ideas in the works of many scholars. Cordovero, therefore, followed here a clear tendency inherent in the history of Jewish thought.

The fact that this answer to the problem of the origin of evil was given often before does not make it more satisfactory from a theological point of view. Indeed, it is even more difficult within the framework of a mystical system. There is no answer in these parables to the question of the necessity of evil and its purpose. On the contrary, these parables seem to point out that God could not create a good world without an evil element being produced in the process even if He wanted to. The emergence of evil and dirt in the process of creation seems to be a natural law which binds even God Himself. If that is so, evil need not necessarily fulfill a positive function in the world, for it exists because of basic, independent laws of creation. Of course every thinker who presented such a system continued to explain how evil benefits the world, for instance by offering the possibility of religious and ethical free choice. Cordovero does so as well. The question of whether God would have created evil in this world were it not necessary according to the natural laws of creation is not answered.

Cordovero did not base his treatment of all the theological and exegetical problems connected with the question of the origin of evil on these parables; they are hardly mentioned elsewhere in his voluminous works, and in other contexts he adopts different attitudes. It is important, therefore, to try to discover the underlying, common motifs in his different treatments of the various aspects of the problem.

III

Cordovero's attitude towards the problem of the pre-existence of evil is best exemplified by his treatment of the medieval Jewish myth of the ancient evil worlds which were destroyed before the creation of this world. This subject in Cordovero's thought was studied in some detail by I. Tishby[13] and J. Ben-Shlomo;[14] it is our intention here to combine it with the general picture of the problem of the origin of evil.

Discussion of the status of the concept of evil in a mystical system should differentiate between explanations of the role of evil in the created world, often (and certainly in Cordovero's thought) a theodicy, and the problem of the source of evil. Theodicy attempts to explain the necessity of an evil element within the created system, and stipulates that its existence is needed in order that the divine creation produce maximum good. Thus theodicy cleanses the Divinity from any suspicion of containing an evil element. The divine purpose is completely good, even though some of its means necessitate some evil. Evil as such is hated by God and has no place in the divine world, nor in the ideal state of affairs which will prevail when God's purpose in the creation is ultimately achieved. Evil, therefore, is clearly confined in time and place; it can exist only in the material world, and only as long as the world has not achieved perfection.

Such a theodicy cannot sustain the conception of a pre-existent evil power having a place in the divine realm before the creation. Evil is not needed in the pre-existent period, and therefore it cannot fulfill any function. If it existed then, it would mean that it was independent, unbound by the confines of time and place needed for it to fulfill its function of helping Man make his moral and religious choices. Its existence then would denote its divine character, and reflect upon the nature of the Godhead itself. Every mystic whose purpose is to show the complete unity of the divine world and its absolute goodness must, therefore, confine evil to the material world as long as it is imperfect. Any hint at the pre-existence of evil would reveal a tendency towards a more mythical, dualistic attitude in the conception of the Godhead.

The key group of symbols used by the kabbalists to denote the pre-existence of evil is based on the midrashic cryptic reference to worlds created and destroyed before the present world came into being.[15] This tradition was used by thirteenth-century mystics to create a myth of evil worlds which came into being and then were destroyed because of their complete satanic nature, giving way to the creation of a more harmonious world, in which good and evil were in balance. It seems that the *Ḥasidei Ashkenaz* and especially Rabbi Eleazar of Worms,[16] contributed to the creation of this myth, but it was crystallized in the "Tractate on the Left Emanation," written by Rabbi Isaac ha-Kohen in Spain between 1260 and 1270.[17] When I. Tishby presented a brief survey of the development of the mythical element in the Kabbalah he correctly chose this group of symbols as an indicator of the attitudes of every circle of kabbalists and every generation of Jewish mystics towards mythological symbolism when describing the divine worlds.[18] These symbols are central to the Zoharic concept of evil,[19] as well as to the Lurianic.[20] For Cordovero, however, they pose a very difficult problem.

When Cordovero attempts to confine the realm of evil to the created world within the framework of a monistic theodicy, the Zoharic sections dealing with the destroyed evil worlds (whose remnants feed evil in the present world) present enormous difficulties. Cordovero saw himself as—and to a very large extent he really was—an interpreter of the Zohar. His *Pardes Rimonim* is an Herculean effort to present Zoharic mysticism in a systematic, non-mythical, somewhat logical form. His major work, *Or Yakar*, is a voluminous, extensive commentary on the Zohar. He could not dismiss Zoharic ideas and symbols as irrelevant or wrong. All his discussions are closely based on Zoharic quotations, even when he clearly departs from ancient ideas and presents new ones.

In several places in his systematic works[21] (analyzed by J. Ben-Shlomo[22]), Cordovero interpreted the Zoharic story of the destroyed evil worlds and the kings of Edom (who ruled before the kings of Israel according to Genesis 36, and were homiletically identified by the Zohar with the evil worlds). According to Cordovero's interpretation, these worlds were not evil. The story of their destruction is a veiled symbol for internal divine processes which were going on within the divine realm before the actual creation. In one of his several discussions of the subject, Cordovero states: "The matter of the kings who reigned, this is the secret of the roots of the *Sefirot* in the *ḥokhma* of *Keter*, which vanished. These same roots were emanated stage after stage and existence after existence until the existing things became revealed."[23] Later he explains that their revelation in existence is to be found also in the realm of *din*, which, according to the Zohar, is the source of earthly evil. In this brief description Cordovero summed up a lenghty, detailed study of the subject which he presented in the chapters of the first *tamar* of the section "Eyn ha-Bedolaḥ" in his theological work, *Sefer Elima*.[24]

While the details are many, and often discrepancies and even conflicting statements are to be found in these descriptions (especially when the texts of *Sefer Elima* are compared with the treatment of the subject in his *Shiur Koma*,[25] the dominant elements of the Cordoverian thesis can be clearly stated. The process referred to in previous kabbalistic texts, and especially in the Zohar, as the destruction of the evil worlds or the death of the early kings of Edom, is not a certain occurrence in a mythical past, but a constant, on-going process in a most hidden and remote part of the Godhead, in the first *Sefira, Keter*, which is the divine will. This supreme part of the Godhead is in itself divided into ten aspects, corresponding to the ten *Sefirot.* The process of the "death of the kings" occurs between the aspects called *Ḥokhma* and *Bina*, the second and third highest aspects within the divine will. In this sublime, hidden part of the Godhead every thought of existence or creation is still unformed and unclear; it wavers, appears and vanishes in a constant rhythm. It is as if neither the wish to create nor the plan of creation crystallized in the divine mind. This process of the appearance of the thought and its immediate disappearance is the one referred to by the more mythically inclined Zohar as the destruction of the worlds or the death of the Idumean kings.

These roots, or fleeting thoughts, deep in the Godhead and completely remote from even divine existence, become, by a slow and gradual process of emanation, the roots of all existence—including earthly evil, but are not specifically concerned with this particular aspect of the creation. Again and again Cordovero stresses that nothing in the divine realm can be called, even symbolically, "a source of evil."

Cordovero's repeated treatments of this subject are in clear contradiction to the descriptions of the Zohar, which are relatively clear and emphatic. The term "Edom" itself is indicative of evil, because of its association with Esau and Rome, and therefore with Christianity. Cordovero disregards all these associations, as well as the mythical statements of the Zohar,[26] thus revealing his insistent aim to cleanse the divine world from any element of evil. The myth of the destroyed worlds is the clearest indication in early Kabbalah of the conception of pre-existent evil. Cordovero reveals in his treatment of the subject that for him evil is an earthly, temporary phenomenon, without any possibility of a counterpart or source in the divine realm.

IV

As a systematic thinker, Cordovero could not avoid the problem which naturally arises from his insistence on negating any divine or independent source for evil, and that problem is: how evil really is evil? If God did not create it, and it did not create itself (as in a dualistic system of thought), what is its nature? Like all kabbalists, Cordovero based his mystical attitude on the premise that everything that occurs on earth has a counterpart in heaven. What, then, is the divine counterpart to earthy evil?

It seems that Cordovero faced these problems and offered his answer in a quite radical manner in his short, popular ethical work, *Tomer Devora* (*The Palm Tree of Deborah*).[27] This short treatise attempts to lay a kabbalistic foundation for ethical behavior, and is the first of many such kabbalistic works written in the sixteenth-century and later. While this book itself did not gain a very large audience, it was incorporated in other books, like *Reshit Ḥokhma* by Rabbi Elijah de Vidas[28] and *Shney Luḥot ha-Brit* (*SHeLaH*) by Isaiah ha-Levi Horowitz,[29] which became one of the most widely read works on Jewish ethics from the seventeenth century onward.

The thesis of this book is that every human action reflects a divine process on the one hand, while it influences divine processes in either a positive or negative way, on the other. There is nothing new to Zoharic kabbalists in this idea, but Cordovero's formulation in this brief treatise is a radical and clear one, which had through the works which used it, an enormous impact.

The problem of evil is treated by Cordovero when he deals with the subject of repentance, *teshuva*, in the fourth chapter of the book. It is obvious that during the process of repentance good and evil come into very close contact, and the relationship between them has to be clarified. Cordovero does not choose the easy, conventional way of explaining to the reader that repentance means withdrawing from evil and forsaking it while embracing good ways. He follows the Zoharic concept of evil as an emanation from the power of *Din* when it leaves the *Sefira Bina*, but goes further than the Zohar does in his description of the power of repentance.

The process of earthly repentance resembles, according to Cordovero's explanation, the divine process of *sod ha-yovel* (the mystical process of the jubilee): the lower *Sefirot*, like all spiritual beings, return to their source as a part of a cosmic cycle of descent and ascent from the Godhead. That source is the third *Sefira, Bina*, symbolized in the Kabbalah by all the relevant terms: Jubilee, the number fifty, and especially *teshuva* (which of course means "the returning"). The orgin of earthly evil is the point at which the various divine emanations leave the *Bina* and assume their particular characteristics; this point-of-departure is reversed during the process of the Jubliee, and at the place where things had become differentiated they now lose their specific attributes and become part of the divine unity, completely good and completely merciful. The power of *Din* participates in this cyclical process, and it, together with all its derivatives, including evil, are united again within the Godhead, losing all traces of evil. In the next cycle, the same divine elements may return to the revealed world as powers of good.

This mystical cycle, which Cordovero adopted from the Zohar to a large extent, makes it possible for him to raise a question not usually discussed in repentance literature: Does *teshuva* affect only the good part of a human being, or does it also affect his evil part? Cordovero's discussion of this problem seems to be somewhat out of character as far as the tone of his argument is concerned; he is more vehement and emphatic than usual in his works.[30] He states clearly: "You should not say that *teshuva* helps only the holy part in man; rather [it] also [helps] his evil part, which becomes sweetened [i.e. turns into good]." Cordovero then goes on to discuss in some detail a specific example. That example is none other than Cain himself, who, according to kabbalistic myth based on some midrashic homilies, was the son of the snake, that is, of Satan. Cordovero repeats, with his own interpretation, God's words to Cain:[31] "Do not think that because you are from the evil side [that is, the *sitra aḥra*] there is no remedy for you; *this is a lie* [*ze sheker*], for if you will attach yourself to the supreme mystery of *teshuva* and then return from there in the mystery of the good which is rooted there," you will become completely good.

Relying on some Zoharic symbols and some radical rabbinic sayings,[32] Cordovero concludes this brief discussion by making it absolutely clear that every evil element in existence, within man and outside, and even the sins themselves, can be turned into good by the process of the Jubilee. The more sins a person had before repenting, the more righteous deeds he is credited with when completing his repentance, for the evil deeds themselves become righteous elements. He even states that if Cain had repented, he would have corrected not only his own sins, but also those of Adam, thus freeing the human race from the curse of the original sin.

The implications of these statements for the history of Jewish mystical thought in the seventeenth and eighteenth centuries are considerable,[33] but they also serve to clarify Cordovero's attitude towards evil in the best way. According to this, evil is not really evil from a divine point of view. The powers of evil are such only temporarily, in their present place in the cycle of the Jubilee. When the time comes—or when repentance is done—they will return to their source in *Bina* and will re-assume their original good selves. Its appearance as earthly evil is but a stage in the history of a divine particle, which does not affect its inherent, potential goodness. Spiritual power cannot be lost, even the spiritual power used to commit the worst crimes, like murder; it waits till it can return to the root of everything in *Bina* and then will be transformed into goodness equivalent in its degree to its former degree in the realm of evil.[34]

In a mystical way Cordovero revives here the philsosophical attitude which denied the very existence of evil and explained it away as a lack of goodness or as "in the eye of the beholder," that is, man alone. But Cordovero is even more radical: he does not deny the actual existence, or even the ferocity, of earthly evil; he just denies that it is really, constantly bad. Evil is ephemeral, while good is eternal. Therefore good is dominant even among the characteristics of the most starkly evil elements; when the Jubilee cycle is completed, it will be evident that evil was just a temporary mask on the face of divine goodness.

The three examples discussed here, even though different in their detailed theological implications, do form a whole as far as Cordovero's intuitive attitude towards evil is concerned: God had no intention of creating evil; some dirt and excrement are to be expected naturally when some good process is going on. Traditional myths concerning pre-existent evil should be re-interpreted to prove that they denote perfectly good processes within the highest realms of the Godhead; and even human evil and sins are but a transitory phase in the cosmic divine cycle, and they reveal their truly good selves when they return to their divine source. All three theses are united by the basic axiom: No evil descends from heaven.

V

Cordovero is a unique figure in the history of Jewish thought in many respects, but not in his attitude towards evil. While many of his formulations and theological theses are his own, in his basic attitude he represents cultural and ideological processes both within the Kabbalah and in the general Jewish culture. Tishby has already pointed out that Cordovero represents the culmination of a process begun in the fourteenth century of withdrawing from the mythological symbolism of the Zohar and adopting a more philosophical symbolism.[35] As far as the history of the conception of evil in Kabbalah is concerned, even the Zohar itself is less radical than its source, the writings of Rabbi Isaac ha-Kohen. It is quite clear, however, that in denying the pre-existence and divinity of evil Cordovero gives expression to the prevailing attitude among the kabbalists of his age and in previous generations. Many kabbalists avoided the problem completely, dealt with it in Neoplatonic terms like Rabbi Yoḥanan Alemanno,[36] or obscured it, like Rabbi Meir Ibn Gabai in his popular summary of the Kabbalah, *Avodat ha-Kodesh*.[37]

This process within the Kabbalah coincided with a similar one in nonkabbalistic circles. It is impossible to review all the many facets of Jewish sixteenth-century thought, but it seems quite clear that the dominant atmosphere concerning the origin and nature of evil is exactly the one reflected in Cordovero's discussions, though the symbolism and terminology are completely different. Rabbi Judah Moscato, one of the most typical of Jewish thinkers of the period and one whose writings reflect the impact of the Italian Renaissance upon Judaism more clearly than many others, can serve as an example.[38] Moscato dedicated a special sermon to the problem, one which was included in his book, *Nefutzot Yehuda*.[39] This sermon is entitled appropriately: "No evil descends from heaven." Using rabbinic and philosophical sources Moscato explains that all evil originates in man, and that the abolition of evil is dependent upon human ethical and religious behavior. Moscato was not a kabbalist,[40] even though he quoted kabbalistic sources occasionally. In this sermon he did not quote the Zohar, but relied on other sources to make his point. The homily does not reveal any polemical motives, as do some other parts of this book, so that it seems that Moscato did not expect anyone to hold different views than the ones expressed by him. Moscato's example may indicate that Cordovero's basic views were the common ones found in Jewish intellectual circles in the sixteenth century.

Another example which should be briefly mentioned is the sixteenth-century attitude towards witchcraft and demonology. Jewish thinkers, like the non-Jewish ones, were almost unanimous in this period in their complete belief in the veracity of demonic phenomena, and one cannot find any significant difference between kabbalists and non-kabbalists in their acceptance of witchcraft and demonology as integral parts of natural and human laws. The Zohar, three centuries earlier, emphasized the link between Satan and demonic forces (an idea almost completely absent from pre-thirteenth-century Jewish thought), and some later kabbalists developed this theme.[41] In the sixteenth century, however, we find kabbalists discussing demonic forces in great detail, without ever linking them with any supreme principle,[43] and certainly without identifying witches as the servants of Satan (at the time that the witch-hunts in Europe were in full force). This fact seems to indicate that Jewish thinkers did not find any evidence in this realm for the power, or even the existence, of a principle of evil which had emissaries throughout creation. Their basic disbelief in the divinity of the source of evil prevented them from seeking such evidence. Thus we find both sixteenth-century and seventeenth-century thinkers, most notably Rabbi Menasseh ben Israel in his *Nishmat Ḥayim*,[43] who could use evidence derived from the realms of witchcraft and demonology to prove, for instance, the eternity of the soul, without for a moment doubting that these phenomena might have a source which is not the same one as the Creator of all natural existence. In this they were returning, in a completely different way, to views held by the theologians of the Ashkenazi Ḥasidic movement in the twelfth and early thirteenth centuries,[44] in pre-Zoharic times. If no evil can descend from heaven, all worldly phenomena should be explained as the workings of the one and good God.

The clearest example of this prevailing attitude among sixteenth-century thinkers is to be found in their treatment of historical occurrences in their own times. One might expect people who have witnessed, or even suffered, the tortures of the period of the expulsion from Spain and Portugal and the undisturbed rule of the Inquisition, to express some doubt as to whether all these misfortunes were caused by God himself, or whether an evil power had anything to do with them. I have been unable to find such themes in that period. It seems that the belief that God himself instigated all these tortures, for one reason or another, is almost universal. The post-expulsion thinkers, beginning with Rabbi Joseph Yavetz and Rabbi Isaac Abravanel, were building their theodical systems, counting human sins which had caused the destruction of Spanish Jewry and revealing in the suffering a divine promise for an imminent messianic redemption.[45] The minority who did not adopt a clearly theodical attitude tried to formulate socio-economic explanations for the misfortunes of exilic Judaism, like the views expressed in Solomon Ibn Verga's *Shevet Yehuda*.[46] Again, no worldly evidence could shake Jewish thinkers in the sixteenth century from their deep conviction that no evil descends from heaven.

This background might help us understand the force of the Lurianic revolution in Jewish thought. When explaining the rapid spread of Lurianic concepts in the late sixteenth and early seventeenth centuries, G. Scholem pointed out that Luria put the desired emphasis upon the exilic state of the Jewish people by making the exile of the Godhead the cornerstone of his mythological system.[47] It seems that our analysis might add another element to that picture. One may wonder whether Jews could really be happy with an ideology which was going farther and farther away from the concept of an independent, pre-existent evil power, when history developing all around them was proving time after time the rule of evil in this world. It seemed as if Satan was constantly advancing in his role in history, while he was receding from the ideological systems presented by Jewish thinkers.

When Lurianic mysticism began to spread, putting forward the concepts that evil is the ruler of this world, and that evil was in a constant—and often winning—struggle against God, reality seemed to prove the veracity of this most mythological of all Jewish theologies. When Luria explained the power of the gentiles as derived from the power of Satan, his ideas were much more easily accepted than theories explaining that the tortures inflicted by the gentiles on the Jews sprang from God's eternal love for the people of Israel.

One may surmise that the fierce revolutionary process by which the Jewish Renaissance-influenced theology of the sixteenth century was replaced by Lurianism in the first half of the seventeenth was enhanced by the enormous gap created by thinkers like Cordovero and Moscato between theology and national and private experience. Lurianic myth became the dominant Jewish ideology because it succeeded in creating a harmony between its symbols and Jewish reality, while destroying the harmony in the divine worlds and postulating that evil did indeed descend from heaven.

NOTES

1. See G. Scholem, *Major Trends in Jewish Mysticism*[2] (New York, 1954), pp. 252–258; on the spiritual atmosphere in which these two kabbalists created their systems see S. Schechter, *Studies in Judaism* (New York, 1970), 231–297; R.J. Zwi Werblowsky, *Joseph Karo, Lawyer and Mystic*[2] (Philadelphia, 1977), pp. 38–83.

2. G. Scholem's descriptions of Lurianic Kabbalah are presented both in his *Major Trends*, pp. 258–286, and in his *Sabbatai Sevi, The Mystical Messiah* (Princeton, 1973), pp. 22–26.

3. The myth of the *tzimtzum* is a description of God's withdrawal from a certain part of the universe in which the world was subsequently created; the *shevira* is the myth of God's first attempt to emanate the *Sefirot* into the empty space created by the *tzimtzum* and the catastrophic breaking of the vessels that contained the divine light. Evil elements were responsible for both processes.

4. According to Luria, roots of potential evil which were present in the eternal Godhead remained in the empty space after God's withdrawal in the *tzimtzum*. They were called *reshimu*, impression or remnants. These elements became actually evil during the *shevira*. See I. Tishby, *Torat ha-Ra ve-ha-Klipa be-Kabalat ha-Ari* (Jerusalem, 1942; reprinted 1963), pp. 39–61.

5. J. Ben-Shlomo, *The Mystical Theology of Moses Cordovero* [Hebrew] (Jerusalem, 1965), pp. 290–291.

6. The book was completed by the young Cordovero (born in 1522) in 1548, and printed in Cracow in 1592.

7. This is the 25th chapter in the book, divided into 7 sub-chapters. Chapter 26 deals with the palaces of the evil powers.

8. *Sha'ar ha-Temurot*, first sub-chapter (vol. II, 53c, in the Jerusalem, 1962 edition). Concerning the history of this expression see M. Ḥalamish, "A Gnomic Collection" [Hebrew], *Sinai* 80 (1977), p. 278.

9. *Pardes*, 53c.

10. Ibid., idem.

11. (Venice, 1544), chapter 1.

12. British Museum MS 756, f. 149r. *Sefer ha-Ḥayyim* (Jerusalem, 1977), p. 14.

13. Tishby, *Netivey Emuna u-Minut* (Ramat Gan, 1964), pp. 26–27.

14. Ben-Shlomo, *The Mystical Theology of Cordovero*, pp. 231–238.

15. *Genesis Rabba* 9:2, and compare *Ecclesiastes Rabba* 3:11.

16. See *Ḥokhmat ha-Nefesh* (Lvov, 1876), 12c–d.

17. The text was published by G. Scholem in *Mada'ey ha-Yahadut* II (Jerusalem, 1927), pp. 244–266. A comparison between the Ashkenazi Ḥasidic treatment of the subject and that of Rabbi Isaac ha-Kohen is included in my paper: "Samuel, Lilith and the Concept of Evil," to be published in vol. V of the *AJS Review*.

18. I. Tishby, *Netivey Emuna u-Minut*, pp. 25–29.

19. G Scholem, "Kabbalot Rabbi Jacob and Rabbi Isaac", *Mada'ey ha-Yahadut* II (1927), pp. 193–196; I. Tishby, *Mishnat ha-Zohar* I (Jerusalem, 1949), pp. 183–184, 296.

20. See I. Tishby, *Torat ha-Ra ve-ha-Klipa*, pp. 28–34.

21. *Shiur Koma* (Jerusalem, 1966), pp. 130–135; *Elimah Rabati* (Jerusalem, 1966), 57a–59a; *Pardes Rimonim* I, 25 c–d (*Shaar Seder ha-Atzilut*, chapter 4).

22. J. Ben-Shlomo dedicated special discussions to Cordovero's interpretation of each of these sources because of these differences (pp. 232–234, 235–238).

23. *Elimah Rabati, Ein Roi, Tamar* VI, chapter 20 (87d).

24. *Elimah Rabbati, Ein ha-Bedolaḥ, Tamar* I, chapters 16–21.

25. This book is mainly dedicated to the re-interpretation of the anthropomorphic symbols concerning the body of God, which Cordovero tried to demythologize.

26. Cordovero even wrote a special homiletical exegesis on the names of the kings of Edom in order to show that even their names denoted divine, good processes within the Godhead. See *Elimah Rabati, Ein ha-Bedolaḥ, Tamar* I, ch. 17 (57c–58c).

27. Venice, 1589. An English translation by L. Jacobs *The Palm Tree of Deborah*, was published in London, 1960.
28. Venice, 1579. The author was one of Cordovero's disciples, and used his teachings in many of the book's chapters.
29. Amsterdam, 1653. The whole text of Cordovero's book was included in this work.
30. The contemporary problem of the attitude towards the repentant converts to Catholicism in Spain and Portugal could have had some influence on Cordovero's tone here.
31. This is a part of Cordovero's interpretation of the verse in Genesis 4:7 (see also L. Jacobs' edition, 86–89).
32. *Yoma* 86b (sins will become merits after repentance).
33. M. Piekarz has recently raised the possibility that ideas of the use of sins in order to enhance the redemption could develop in rabbinic, non-Sabbatian ethical literature. See his *The Beginning of Ḥasidism* [Hebrew] (Jerusalem, 1978), pp. 175–268.
34. Cain, for instance, was regarded as the source of the soul of the Messiah, even by Rabbi Ḥayim Vital, the great disciple of Luria, who regarded himself as possessing a part of the messiah's soul. See his *Sefer ha-Ḥezyonot*, ed. A.Z. Eshkoli (Jerusalem, 1954), pp. 204–205 and passim.
35. I. Tishby, *Netivey Emuna u-Minut*, 23–26.
36. Thanks are due to Dr. M. Idel, who studied Alemanno's works and discussed his results with me.
37. Mantua, 1545.
38. See J. Dan, *Hebrew Ethical and Homiletical Literature* [Hebrew] (Jerusalem, 1975), pp. 188–197; I. Bettan, *Studies in Jewish Preaching* (Cincinnati, 1939), pp. 192–226.
39. *Nefutzot Yehuda* was first printed in Venice, 1589. This homily is the 48th chapter in the book (Warsaw, 1871 edition, pp. 124–128).
40. Moscato's attitude towards the Kabbalah and the structure of one of his homiles are discussed in my paper in *Sinai* 76 (1975), pp. 209–232.
41. A clear example is Rabbi Menaḥem Tziyoni's treatise on evil, *Tzfunei Tziyoni*, MS Oxford 1651. See J. Dan, *The Esoteric Theology of the Ashkenazi Ḥasidim* (Jerusalem, 1968), pp. 259–260.
42. Johanan Alemanno is a perfect example. Demonology and witchcraft play a major role in his works, yet they are not connected with any divine power antagonistic to God.
43. Amsterdam, 1652. This seems to be the book which includes the most detailed discussions concerning witchcraft and demonology in that period, yet the only theological implications from the vast material are those relating to the eternity of the soul.
44. See *The Esoteric Theology of the Ashkenazi Ḥasidim*, pp. 184–202.
45. H.H. Ben-Sasson, "Dor Goley Sefarad al Atzmo," *Zion* 26 (1961), pp. 23–64.
46. I. Baer, "Yediot Ḥadashot al Sefer Shevet Yehuda," *Tarbitz* 6 (1935), pp. 152–179; J. Dan, *Ethical and Homiletical Literature*, pp. 184–188.
47. G. Scholem, *Major Trends*, pp. 248–251.

Medieval Jewish Philosophy in the Sixteenth Century

HERBERT DAVIDSON

The first section of my paper sketches the character of medieval Jewish philosophy in the fifteenth century. The second section shows philosophic activity in the sixteenth century to be fundamentally the same as in the fifteenth. The third section examines cosmological passages from Leone Ebreo (Judah Abravanel), Judah Moscato, R. Moses Isserles, and Judah Loeb of Prague. I employ the term *philosophy* throughout in what I take to be the strict, academic sense. Without essaying a complete definition, I would suggest that philosophy in the strict sense satisfies the following conditions: It undertakes to elucidate existence or a segment or aspect of existence in a reasoned and systematic fashion. It is conscious of its own instrument, the human reason, and its utilization of the human reason. Excluded from its purview are universally accepted knowledge and what at any particular period is expected eventually to enter the domain of universally accepted knowledge. The last condition explains how the natural sciences—although not their underpinnings—can be distinct from philosophy in the modern period, yet form part of ancient and medieval philosophy.

1. *Medieval Jewish philosophy in the fifteenth century.* It is a commonplace that the accommodation between revelation and reason lies at the heart of medieval philosophy. The medieval philosopher saw himself in possession of two valid and reliable sources of knowledge. He was confident that the human reason is a valid source of knowledge and truth, that human reason is capable of proving certain propositions incontrovertibly. And he was equally confident that divine revelation is a valid source of knowledge and truth. The situation of the medieval philosopher—whether Moslem, Jewish, or Christian, with the possible exception of later Chris-

tian nominalists and empiricists—was further complicated; for he supposed that each source of knowledge and truth had been exercised fully in the past and that each had deposited its teachings in an authoritative corpus. Knowledge through revelation had been embodied in Scripture, and knowledge attained through the exercise of human reason had been embodied in a corpus of philosophic and scientific writings. Whenever the two bodies of knowledge agreed, the medieval philosopher enjoyed an enviable *embarras de richesse;* he could be doubly confident of his conclusions. When the two bodies of knowledge disagreed, he found himself simply in a state of embarrassment.

Different religious groups naturally delimited the repository of divinely revealed knowledge differently. Rabbinite Jews delimited it as the Written Law together with the Oral Law. Different schools of philosophy also delimited the second authoritative body of knowledge, knowledge attained through human reason, differently; and each school of Jewish philosophy was dependent upon a corresponding school of Islamic philosophy. The most prominent school of Islamic philosophy was the Kalam, a school distinguished by the theory that physical existence consists of durable *atoms* and transient *accidents* inhering in the atoms. The atoms in themselves, the theory went, are totally devoid of quality; and qualities are imparted to them by the accidents. The roots of Kalam atomism presumably go back to either ancient Greece or India.[1] But no system of ancient philosophy can be identified as the specific system that the Kalam school adopted. Consequently, although the Kalam, no less than the other schools of Islamic philosophy, saw itself in possession of a fixed authoritative body of human knowledge, it was not to the same extent burdened by a sense of dependence on an ancient, secular system of thought.

The other schools of Islamic philosophy were cognizant of their dependence on ancient Greek philosophy. In one instance, the authoritative body of rational knowledge was a more or less pure Neoplatonism.[2] The distinctive constituent here was the theory that the first cause of the universe brings a cosmic intellect into existence through a process of emanation; the cosmic intellect emanates a cosmic soul; and the cosmic soul emanates the physical world.[3] The remaining school of Islamic philosophy had as its authoritative body of rational knowledge a more or less pure Aristotelianism. The distinctive constituent now was a picture of the universe in which the stars and planets are embedded in translucent spheres; each sphere is moved by an incorporeal being, a so-called *intelligence*; and the rotation of the spheres around the earth gives rise to the apparent motions of the stars and planets. Medieval Islamic Aristotelianism usually is less, rather than more, pure, inasmuch as it usually contains a strong Neoplatonic admixture. The added feature is the linking of the several levels of existence through emanation. The intelligences are understood to be brought into existence by the first cause of the universe through a process of emanation, and the spheres and the lower region are understood to be emanated by the intelligences.[4]

The Neoplatonic and Aristotelian strands of medieval Islamic philosophy are, to repeat, oriented entirely towards the ancient past, the rational source of knowledge having, as they assumed, deposited its findings centuries ago in the writings of the Greeks, and the divinely revealed source of knowledge having deposited its teachings centuries ago in Scripture. Neoplatonism and Aristotelianism are the only schools of importance for medieval Jewish philosophy. And by the fifteenth century, Aristotelianism, with the Neoplatonic admixture, had become dominant.

It is another commonplace that medieval philosophers attached varying weights to the two sources, and the two bodies, of knowledge at their disposal; some attached greater weight to reason, and some, greater weight to revelation. The divergent positions adopted by Moslem and Jewish philosophers[5] on the issue of reason and revelation, or the issue of philosophy and Scripture, may be conceived[6] as forming a spectrum, with thinkers who give greater weight to reason and philosophy on the left, and those who give greater weight to revelation and Scripture on the right. No philosopher, it has to be stressed, moves so far to the left that he disputes the validity of revelation as a source of knowledge or the reliability of Scripture as a repository thereof. When Islamic and Jewish philosophers on the left perceive discordances between Scripture and philosophy, they assume that the two sources, and the two bodies, of knowledge differ not in accuracy but in levels of expression: Scripture and philosophy address dissimilar audiences, and Scripture expresses in a rhetorical and figurative language to its audience, the very propositions that philosophy expresses in technical language to its.[7] The prime illustration is creation. Islamic and Jewish philosophers on the left read the scriptural account of creation as a rhetorical and figurative mode of stating a proposition that ordinary people could not comprehend if stated precisely and technically. The precise and technical statement is that God is the eternal cause of the world, that God has indeed brought the world into existence, but that He has done so from all eternity and not merely for a finite time.

Philosophers who stand towards the right on the issue of reason and revelation are, by contrast to those at the left extreme, quite willing to admit that one of the authoritative bodies of knowledge—the body of knowledge generated by reason—can err. And the further to the right a philosopher stands, the more willing, and even eager, he is to voice misgivings regarding the accuracy of human reason as a source, and the accuracy of philosophy as a repository, of knowledge. A philosopher standing on the extreme right would be one who, while recognizing philosophy as a legitimate form of human activity, voices maximum reservations about its accuracy. Anyone going further than that and rejecting the study of philosophy outright would place himself beyond the reason–revelation spectrum and could no longer be designated a philosopher. As turns out, the position at the extreme right is occupied by philosophers who deem the science of mathematics[8] alone to be incontrovertible and who question all branches of the science of physics as well as the science of metaphysics.

Medieval Jewish philosophers who do adopt a position on the extreme left, who accept a corpus of philosophic knowledge unreservedly and maintain that Scripture expresses the same propositions as philosophy in a rhetorical, non-technical fashion, are Albalag,[9] Kaspi,[10] and Narboni.[11] Jewish philosophers who stand on the extreme right are Ha-Levi[12] and, as I would interpret him, Ḥasdai Crescas.[13] Other Jewish philosophers distribute themselves between the two extremes. Maimonides, for example, accepts most branches of Aristotelian physics but has reservations regarding Aristotle's pronouncements on the subject of astronomy, which is a branch of physics, and also regarding some Aristotelian pronouncements on the nature of God, which is a subject belonging to the science of metaphysics.[14] Standing beyond the spectrum on the right side and condemning the philosophic enterprise outright, are authors such as Moses Taku, R. Asher, and R. Isaac b. Sheshet.[15] No medieval philosopher, as already mentioned, places himself beyond the spectrum on the left side. No one, that is, rejects the phenomenon of divine revelation or denies the veracity of Scripture as Spinoza was to do.

If medieval Jewish philosophy is taken to be the form of thought which rests on two authoritative bodies of knowledge, the Written together with the Oral Law, on the one hand, and a system of philosophy whose roots go back to the ancient period, on the other, a considerable number of fifteenth-century texts meet the description. A larger number of medieval Jewish philosophic works has, in fact, survived from the fifteenth century than from any comparable period. They include works of Simon Duran, Joseph Albo, Isaac ibn Shem Tov, Joseph ibn Shem Tov, Shem Tov b. Joseph ibn Shem Tov, Abraham Shalom, Elijah Del Medigo, Abraham Bibago, Isaac Arama, Isaac Abravanel, and Saul ha-Cohen. Several literary genres are represented, namely philosophic treatises, philosophic commentaries, works of a homiletic cast, and in one instance an exchange of letters. And diverse positions on the issue of reason and revelation are in evidence.

The fifteenth-century writer furthest to the left on the issue of reason and revelation is plainly Del Medigo, but Del Medigo was not above dissimulating, and his exact views remain open to interpretation. In a book devoted entirely to the subject of reason and revelation, he states that Scripture and philosophy are designed for different audiences and consequently employ different levels of expression. Scripture expresses itself in "rhetorical and dialectic" language, although intimating all the while what the precise truth is; and philosophy expresses itself in "demonstrative" language.[16] These remarks would appear to place Del Medigo solidly at the left extreme. But he immediately turns round and declares that if perchance "there should exist" disagreements between Scripture and philosophy, every Jew has the obligation of following the former.[17] In another of his works Del Medigo indulges in equivocal statements of a similar sort. He tells of a plan he had for a piece refuting theories of the "philosophers . . . which seem . . . to contradict the Law"; he planned the essay, strangely enough, "even though" his "opinion is that when the Law and science are viewed correctly, no dispute exists between them."[18] And in yet another work, Del Medigo writes that philosophers need not be troubled in the least if they arrive at conclusions "contrary to the Law"; for the "way of the Law, which is more strictly a matter of faith, is different from the philosophic way."[19] Only a single contruction is capable of harmonizing the various statements. If Del Medigo is writing what he does advisedly, he can only be construed as believing that no conflict does "exist" between Scripture and philosophy, although sometimes a conflict may "seem" to be present. His position would be that Scripture teaches, through means of a rhetorical mode of expression, propositions completely in accord with philosophy; and he would after all stand at the extreme left on the issue of revelation and reason.[20]

Other writers in the fifteenth century take a position on the extreme right. Joseph ibn Shem Tov maintains: "Philosophy, that is to say, [knowledge] of existing things . . . through demonstrative speculation, is necessary for human theoretical perfection insofar as a man is a man"; "but . . . it is not necessary . . . for a Jew . . . . . . insofar as he is a Jew," the perfection proper to a Jew being attainable exclusively through the "divine Torah." After having said this much, Ibn Shem Tov concedes that knowledge of the philosophic sciences, although not "necessary," does nonetheless "contribute" to the perfection of a Jew. The study of "mathematics, . . . physics, . . . and metaphysics" is hence permissible and desirable.[21] Here, however, an additional qualification is introduced. Permissible science, Joseph ibn Shem Tov writes, is "science in the true sense" and not "science and philosophy" as found in "the books of the Greeks"; for science and philosophy in the latter sense comprises "corrupt conjectures, destructive of religion."[22] As happens, Ibn Shem Tov knows of no access to scientific knowledge except through the Greeks, and the best practical recommendation he can offer is that the study of Greek philosophy be sanctioned solely for persons of maturity and discretion.[23] His considered opinion, then, is that the study of philosophy is legitimate, but students must constantly be on their guard against errors—errors occurring, we may suppose, in the science of physics and the science of metaphysics, mathematics presumably being free of error. Ibn Shem Tov thereby places himself at the extreme right on the issue of reason and revelation.

A position similar to Joseph ibn Shem Tov's is taken by Isaac Arama, a writer who quite literally sanctions "good" philosophy and condemns "bad" philosophy.[24] One other notable fifteenth-century figure, Shem Tov ibn Shem Tov, is usually portrayed as an implacable opponent of philosophy in all its aspects, but a case might be made for locating him as well at the conservative extreme on the reason-revelation spectrum, and not beyond.[25] The remaining fifteenth-century figures whom I have identified as philosophic writers and whose positions can be determined stand between the two extremes.[26] A full spectrum on the issue is thus exhibited.

Several traits can be set down as the general characteristics of fifteenth-century Jewish philosophic writers.

(a) The majority, even such as do not stand at the right extreme on the issue of reason and revelation, gravitate towards the right.[27] They insist, for example, that the phenomenon of revelation and prophecy is radically unlike the phenomenon of rational human thought; and the superiority of revealed knowledge to rational knowledge—given the legitimacy of the latter—is beyond doubt for them.[28] In conjunction with, or as a corollary of, their position on reason and revelation, they dissociate human perfection from purely intellectual development and tie it instead to the performance of religious acts and the study of the Law.[29] And they subscribe to a doctrine of divine recompense and individual providence, whereby every person—or at least every Jew—is rewarded and punished specifically in accordance with his moral and religious accomplishments.[30] In each of these respects—in regarding prophecy as a phenomenon unlike, and superior to, rational knowledge; and in associating human perfection and providence with religious, rather than with scientific, attainments—fifteenth-century writers assume a more conservative stance than the thinker whom they all looked upon as the pre-eminent Jewish philosopher, to wit Maimonides.[31]

(b) The majority of the fifteenth-century philosophic writers adduce the Kabbalah as an authoritative source of religious knowledge.[32] The favorable disposition towards the Kabbalah is undoubtedly in harmony with the conservative attitude of mind [33] evidenced by the writers in question, but it nowise symptomizes unphilosophical, mystical, or obscurantist proclivities on their part. The majority of the fifteenth-century philosophic writers simply consider the Zohar to be a genuine midrashic text and treat the Zohar and other kabbalistic books—taking the *kabbalah* at its word—as authentic tradition. In the accommodation of philosophy and Scripture, the scriptural component had, from the beginning of philosophic speculation among Jews, comprised the Oral Law together with the Written Law; and the fifteenth-century writers are pleased to have at their disposal an additional branch of the Oral Law, the Kabbalah.

(c) All the fifteenth-century philosophic writers, from one end of the spectrum to the other, work with a common picture of the universe, the picture propagated by the Neoplatonic version of medieval Aristotelianism. The universe is represented as having three realms: a sublunar realm, located in the center of the corporeal universe; the surrounding realm, comprising the celestial spheres, the rational souls of the spheres, and the stars and planets imbedded in the spheres; and the realm of the intelligences which keep the celestial spheres in circular motion.[34] Physical objects in the sublunar region are understood to be composed of matter and form and to be subject to constant change; the celestial spheres, the stars, and the planets, are understood to consist in a corporeal substance unique to themselves and immune from change; and the intelligences, which move the spheres, are understood to consist in pure thought with no material side whatsoever. The three realms are moreover, understood to be linked with each other and with the deity through a process of emanation: The first cause of the universe, the deity, emanates the intelligences, and they in turn emanate the celestial and sublunar regions. Sometimes a fifteenth-century author hesitates over the picture of the universe outlined here, but in doing so he is consciously struggling against what he recognizes as authoritative philosophic doctrine. The degree to which the medieval Aristotelian picture of the universe penetrated fifteenth-century Jewish thought is illustrated particularly well in two writers, Shem Tov ibn Shem Tov and Isaac Arama, who were harsh critics of Greek philosophy. Shem Tov is reputedly the arch-traditionalist and sworn opponent of philosophy. Yet he presupposes a universe in which the beings "closest" to God are "incorporeal intelligences," in which "the world of the spheres and all the host of the heavens" stand "below" the intelligences in the hierarchy of existence, and in which the heavens are living beings endowed with "intellect." [35] Arama likewise presupposes the common division of the universe into three realms, but he wrestles with doubts concerning an important component in the scheme. He is not easily convinced that the intelligences must be construed as the movers of the spheres, for the celestial spheres might possibly be such that their motion is due to their "nature" and not to an external agent.[36] In the end, however, Arama lacks the courage of his doubts. He discovers that "the traditional Jewish scholars *(ha-ḥakhamim ha-toraniyim)*"—with a single exception—embrace the "philosophic view." They assume that "the spheres are emanated from the incorporeal intelligences" and that the "[incorporeal intelligences], or angels, are the movers of the spheres." In addition, Arama discovers, Scripture itself apparently alludes to the thesis that the intelligences emanate the spheres and maintain them in motion. Out of just deference to the Jewish authorities, he accordingly withdraws his hesitations and accepts the Aristotelian theory of intelligences and spheres in its entirety.[37]

(d) If we choose to judge honestly, though it be cruelly, a further trait of the fifteenth-century philosophic writers must be recorded: Not one of them, and for that matter no known medieval Jewish writer on philosophy after Ḥasdai Crescas, displays the slightest originality. None deserves to be called a 'philosopher' in a true sense; [38] and therefore I have allowed myself an awakard appellation and have called them 'philosophic writers' rather than 'philosophers.'

2. *Medieval Jewish philosophy in the sixteenth century.* When we turn from the fifteenth to the sixteenth century, we cannot help expecting changes in Jewish philosophy. We do realize at some level of awareness that European chronology is a mere accident of history, and that the conventional partitioning out of the centuries is arbitrary as regards Christian Europe,[39] not to speak of groups like the medieval Jews, who took no notice of European dates. Nevertheless we are so conditioned by the convention, the reification of the centuries is so enslaving, that we expect each century to evince an inner coherence of its own and a distinctiveness over against the other centuries.[40] In the passage from the fifteenth to the sixteenth century, another, stronger convention is also at work, since the end of the fifteenth century is the most widely accepted division between the medieval and modern periods. We know that as regards the Jews at least, the periodization of European history has a most limited pertinence. Yet we are so conditioned by this convention too that we cannot help awaiting momentous changes as the Jews emerge from the Middle Ages and enter modern times. The end of the fifteenth century happens in addition to coincide with one of the disastrous events of Jewish history; the Spanish Jewish community, precisely the community where philosophy

found its most congenial home, disappeared. That was a true event, not a convention, and surely it would alter the course of Jewish philosophy.

The new circumstances—a fresh century, a fresh period of history, the destruction of the chief habitat of medieval Jewish philosophy—might conceivably have led Jewish thinkers in either of two directions. A radical reaction might well have been elicited. Jewish thinkers in the sixteenth century might finally have allowed themselves a measure of skepticism concerning Scripture; and they might, furthermore, have embraced, as their rational body of knowledge, a modern brand of philosophy in place of medieval Aristotelianism. Alternatively, a conservative reaction might have been elicited. The opponents of philosophy might now have won the day, and the community of Jewish thinkers might have dismissed rational knowledge altogether, retreating entirely into traditional studies. Or again, both reactions might have occurred simultaneously. A segment, let us say the Italian Jews, might have pursued one path, while another segment, perhaps the Polish Jews, pursued the other.

As far as can be seen from preserved texts, neither reaction was elicited. If medieval Jewish philosophy is taken to be the form of thought which rests on two authoritative bodies of knowledge, the Written and Oral Law and a system of philosophy whose roots go back to the ancient authors, sixteenth-century texts meeting the description are almost as numerous as those from the fifteenth century. And Jewish philosophy in the sixteenth century barely differs from Jewish philosophy in the fifteenth. Its affinity with Jewish philosophy in the fifteenth century is greater than the affinity of Jewish philosophy in the fifteenth century with that in the fourteenth century, or of Jewish philosophy in any comparable period with that in the preceding or succeeding period.

The sixteenth-century thinkers who can be identified as writers of philosophy are Leone Ebreo (Judah Abravanel), Obadiah Sforno, Yeḥi'el b. Samuel of Pisa, Moses Almosnino, Abraham Ibn Migas, Judah Moscato, Moses Isserles, Mordekhai Jaffe, Joseph ben Isaac ha-Levi, and perhaps Judah Loeb of Prague.[41] They are by no means men of a single stamp; included are physicians, communal rabbis of the Spanish or Italian type, Polish legists, and a wealthy man of affairs. Some of the sixteenth-century philosophic writers had broad secular knowledge; some probably never opened a non-Jewish book.[42] They convey philosophic notions through a variety of genres, in philosophic treatises (Sforno, Ibn Migas, Joseph ben Isaac), dialogue (Leone Ebreo), polemic (Yeḥi'el of Pisa), homiletic compositions (Almosnino, Moscato, Isserles, Judah Loeb of Prague), and philosophic commentaries (Moscato, Jaffe). And on the issue of reason and revelation, they take diverse positions, although not all the positions that are possible. Yeḥi'el of Pisa and Moscato stand at the right extreme; Leone Ebreo and Almosnino lean to the right; Sforno, Ibn Migas, Isserles, Joseph ben Isaac and Judah Loeb of Prague, occupy positions near the center of the spectrum.

Yeḥi'el of Pisa proclaims the superiority of Scripture over philosophy repeatedly and unambiguously. "The science of philosophy" and even the "science of logic," he asserts, proceed "in accordance with demonstrations that are drawn from sense perceptions and that reduce each object to the object's nature"; [43] whereas Scripture is a body of supernatural knowledge. "How, then, might speculative science stand on the same level as the Law, considering that the Law is superior to all syllogism and to the human intellect?" [44] At times, Yeḥi'el uses still harsher language, language that not merely underlines the inferiority of philosophy to Scripture, but that would seem to disclose an unmitigated opposition to the study of philosophy. He writes: To "equate the two sciences [i.e., Scripture and philosophy] is to do injustice; for they are adversaries." [45] Again: "The study of philosophy" and the application of "demonstrations and syllogisms" to "the beliefs of the Law can afford us no benefit" and, moreover, "may lead to great damage." [46] A careful reading of Yeḥi'el nonetheless shows that his intent is not to reject Greek philosophy and science without qualification. "My complaint," he confesses, "is not against the searching out of the secrets of science; for science qua science, science insofar as it makes known the . . . natural causes of things, . . . deserves to be studied and pursued." [47] Astronomy in particular—which is one of the mathematical sciences—is an indispensable tool of the traditional scholar.[48] What Yeḥi'el fears is the infringement of Greek philosophy upon the study of the Law. Infringement on the study of the Law may manifest itself through the supposition that the science of metaphysics has a role in matters of doctrine; through the supposition that Greek logic might play a role in Talmudic dialectics; or through the attitude of mind which suspends judgment whenever demonstrations are not forthcoming. Any trespass of the sort is deprecated by Yeḥi'el. The domain of the Law, he insists, must remain inviolate, and the Law must be allowed to conduct its affairs in conformity with its own methods.[49] But outside the domain of the Law, and in one instance, that of astronomy, even within the domain of the Law, the study of the philosophic sciences does have value. Especially when a person has already mastered the Law and only afterwards ventures to "peruse the words of speculative scholars, no harm will befall him; in fact he will learn the difference between the two [i.e., between Scripture and philosophy]." [50] Yeḥi'el's posture is akin to Joseph ibn Shem Tov's. Ibn Shem Tov, it will be recalled, maintained that knowledge of the philosophic sciences is "not necessary" for the perfection of a Jew insofar as he is a Jew, but does "contribute" to the perfection of a Jew; and he too wished to restrict the study of philosophy to persons who have mastered the Written and Oral Law.[51] Neither Yeḥi'el's recommendation of the study of philosophy, nor Ibn Shem Tov's, is very warm. Yet Yeḥi'el, like Ibn Shem Tov, does recognize that the study of philosophy has legitimacy; that with caution, benefit can be gained from it. He thereby locates himself on the reason–revelation spectrum, at the right extreme.

A position similar to Yeḥi'el's, although stated somewhat more moderately, is adopted by Moscato. The "investigation of intellectual matters in a speculative fashion . . . to the extent of one's ability" is, Moscato writes, not merely legitimate. It is "obligatory," with the critical proviso, however, that when the limits of human understanding are reached, "faith" be deferred to.[52] And the limits of human understanding are quickly reached. The philosophic sciences, Moscato explains, are reliable only at the elementary levels, only up to the level of mathematics. At higher levels, in the "science of ethics, the science of physics, and a fortiori in the science of metaphysics, philosophy fails to furnish irrefutable demonstration" and "error is present." [53] Given the obligation to engage in speculation, on the one hand, and the inability of philosophy to satisfy man's speculative needs, on the other, the body of knowledge which will supply man's needs is easily surmised. All sciences are contained "in the Law . . either explicitly or implicitly"; [54] and the Greek sciences were themselves not engendered by the unaided human intellect, but consist in material "borrowed" from the Jews and subsequently "distorted" by the ungrateful borrowers.[55] Moscato's stand is thus that while Jews should study science, Greek science cannot be relied on beyond the level of mathematics, and guidance must thenceforth be sought from Scripture. Moscato has hereby also located himself at the extreme right on the issue of reason and revelation.

Other sixteenth-century philosophic writers plainly lean towards the right, but fail to set forth their thinking rigorously enough to permit an exact determination of their position. Leone Ebreo, for example, presupposes, as does every medieval Jewish philosopher, that nothing demonstrably false can be a subject of belief. He accordingly requires that "reason does not disprove" what is to be believed. That is a negative stipulation; and its positive counterpart, the stipulation that whatever is to be believed must be "demonstrated," is expressly renounced by Leone, because belief based on a demonstration would "be science . . . and not faith." Pure faith, he holds, is "sufficient" for men's needs.[56] By preferring faith to demonstrative science, while never questioning the legitimacy of the latter, Leone situates himself somewhere towards the right on the issue of reason and revelation.

Moses Almosnino does the same. "The Law" and "the other sciences," Almosnino maintains, are not "separate," or "distinct" enterprises (*leḥod . . . leḥod*). They cover a similar territory, and Scripture is of higher rank. Scripture subsumes all science, "there being no science in the world which one cannot find in it." [57] Furthermore, Scripture is "superlatively perfect," accomplishing everything philosophy attempts to accomplish, in a more direct and more correct fashion.[58] And Scripture has precedence over philosophy in an additional respect. Even when one does "study the other sciences," one's "object should be to bring what one studies into agreement with what is written in the Law." [59] Almosnino's view is that the philosophic sciences have legitimacy but must remain wholly subservient to Scripture. He therefore has also located himself towards the right on the issue of reason and revelation.

Other sixteenth-century writers take various intermediate positions. Judah Loeb of Prague does so in at least some passages. On occasion, Judah Loeb delights in dwelling upon the total inferiority of philosophy to Scripture. He belittles "physical science and mathematical science" because they treat topics that are petty in comparison with the topics treated by Scripture,[60] and he belittles the human science of physics on the added ground that it can at most elucidate a mere fragment of the myriad natural phenomena it undertakes to examine.[61] But there are occasions when Judah Loeb finds he cannot avoid certifying the legitimacy of the philosophical sciences. The "science [*ḥokhma*] of the gentiles," he acknowledges, comes "from God," no less than does the Law; it is no less an offshoot of "God's wisdom [*ḥokhma*]." [62] The Law itself, though chiefly concerned with exalted matters, "embraces all forms of knowledge and omits nothing," [63] thus subsuming all the secular sciences. Greek science is described by Judah Loeb as "a ladder to the science of the Law." And in a still stronger statement, Judah Loeb lays down the requirement that "a person should, nay must, study . . . every subject . . . which might enable him to comprehend the world . . . and through the world its Creator." Explicitly included herein are "the science of physics" and "the science of the paths of the stars and planets." [64] Judah Loeb's considered position would seem to be that studying the philosophic sciences of physics and astronomy is not merely legitimate, but obligatory; yet human science will ever remain inferior to Scripture.

R. Moses Isserles is another sixteenth-century writer who takes an intermediate position. Isserles voices the catchword that "the Law is above human speculation." It nonetheless is, he understands, commonly "recognized that man has the obligation both to believe and to know, to believe through tradition and to know through speculation." [65] When assessing the three philosophic sciences, Isserles, unlike philosophers on the right, restricts his reservations to the science of metaphysics, while expressly endorsing the science of physics.[66] And he goes as far as to incorporate an endorsement of philosophic studies—albeit gingerly—into an official code of Jewish law.[67]

A peculiar intermediate position is adopted by Sforno. Sforno rejects the proposition, which was embraced by his countryman Moscato, that human reason is quickly beyond its depth and must defer to faith. Nor does he, like Isserles, regard reason and faith as parallel mandatory routes to a single end. His contention is, on the contrary, that for "the fundamental doctrines of religion," blind faith cannot imaginably be obligatory. "A man is not able to believe merely by willing. . . . And a man is surely not able to believe as he is commanded to believe, although he may open his mouth . . . and recite with his lips because commanded to do so."[68] It follows that the doctrines of religion must be founded upon rational demonstration and not accepted on mere faith. The conclusion might appear to derogate from Scripture. But Scripture performs as indispensable a function for Sforno as it does for the firmest fideist. A series of Jewish thinkers had held that all scientific knowledge is comprehended within the Law either *explicitly* or *implicitly*,[69] and Sforno carries the notion a step farther. He explains that Scripture's proper function is not to serve as a credo, but to provide scientific guidance. Scripture "furnishes knowledge," setting down scientific principles and intimating solutions to scientific problems, among which are problems that the greatest philosophers could not solve definitively.[70] Sforno himself applies the method he prescribes to the central problems of theology. He reviews what Aristotelian philosophers had to say on each problem and proceeds to develop a solution with the aid of guideposts uncovered by him in Scripture.[71]

A more liberal position, the position furthest to the left which I could find in the sixteenth century, is that of Abraham ibn Migas. In contrast to his countryman, Almosnino, who asserted that Scripture and science are not "distinct,"[72] Ibn Migas proves from Scripture itself that the two are genuinely "distinct" (*leḥod . . . leḥod*).[73] And in contrast to Moscato, Isserles, Judah Loeb of Prague and Sforno, he does not delineate an area where reason must defer to faith; he does not judge belief in Scripture to be equally mandatory with, and indeed a higher road than, scientific knowledge; he never belittles the accomplishments of Greek science; nor does he, while assigning primacy to rational knowledge over faith, construe Scripture as the ultimate scientific guide. In Ibn Migas' view, "the simple faith written in the Book of the Law" is intended by God for persons—notably "women, the unintelligent," and the young[74]—who are incapable of arriving at truth through reason. But anyone who is blessed by God with "wisdom, understanding, and intellect" has an "obligation," a religious obligation imposed repeatedly by Scripture, to rely exclusively upon knowledge through "proof and demonstration."[75] Although Ibn Migas ranks knowledge through demonstration above faith, he is free of the notion that Scripture, throughout, expresses philosophic notions in figurative language; and on the pivotal question of creation, he accepts the Scriptural account literally—and undertakes to demonstrate it philosophically.[76] His position is therefore something less than the position at the extreme left.

Of the remaining sixteenth-century philosophic writers, Joseph ben Isaac ha-Levi indicates an intermediary position on the issue of reason and revelation; [77] and Mordekhai Jaffe, as far as I could detect, does not state a position.[78]

Sixteenth-century Jewish philosophic literature, to recapitulate, discloses no position at the extreme left on the issue of reason and revelation, but does know a diversity ranging from positions in the middle zone to the extreme right. The sixteenth century, like previous centuries, also knows authors who place themselves beyond the spectrum on the right by totally rejecting philosophy and science. Joseph Yavetz apparently is such a writer. Jews, Yavetz avers, are "commanded not to follow speculative syllogisms"; for the human intellect is nothing other than a guise of the "evil inclination," which "constantly lies in wait for man," hoping to destroy him.[79] The prohibition of studying the works of the philosophers remains in force, Yavetz adds, even for scholars who have mastered the Written and Oral Law, and even in instances where philosophers "say the truth." [80] Thus far he is wholly uncompromising; but, it should be recorded, Yavetz can speak less uncompromisingly as well. He concedes that the science of mathematics has value.[81] And he would, in one passage, sanction access to the works of the philosophers for "great scholars who possess a pure intellect, a fine soul, and a sharp knife." [82]

Another author who declares his outright opposition to philosophy is Solomon Luria. Luria berates Moses Isserles for having decided a halakhic question with the aid of the findings of secular science. The rabbis, Luria points out, directed all Jews to "remove [themselves] far" from "the door" of "heresy" (*minut*); [83] and no "heresy" he contends, is the equal of "their [i.e., the Greeks'] science." [84] It is nevertheless worth noting here too that Luria besprinkles his letter to Isserles with philosophic terms; and that he claims to be as familiar with "their science" as Isserles, although he is proud to have exercised forbearance and to have renounced philosophic science in conformity with the rabbis' injunction.[85]

The recognition of two sources of knowledge and two authoritative bodies of knowledge is not a sufficient justification for designating an author as a writer of medieval philosophy. First, and most obviously, the mere statement that the study of philosophy is legitimate does not in itself constitute philosophy; a composition can be considered a work of philosophy only if it contains something of philosophic substance. Secondly, if an author is to be designated a writer specifically of medieval philosophy, the authoritative body of rational knowledge which he recognized must be a form of, or have its roots in, ancient philosophy. All the authors whom I have classified as sixteenth-century philosophic writers did produce works containing, in lesser or greater measure, something of philosophic substance. And all of them do recognize a form of ancient philosophy as their authoritative body of rational knowledge. In fact, with a few exceptions[86] they all recognize the same body of rational knowledge, the Neoplatonic version of medieval Aristotelianism. They visualize the universe outside of God as divided into three realms: the realm of the incorporeal intelligences; the realm of the celestial spheres, which rotate around the earth, and in which the stars and planets are imbedded; and the realm of the lower world, located at the center of the universe. And they understand that the intelligences are brought into existence by the deity through a process of emanation; the intelligences in turn emanate the spheres and the lower world; and the intelligences fulfill the additional function of sustaining the spheres in continual motion.

Yeḥi'el of Pisa can serve as one illustration, other illustrations being provided in the next section. Yeḥi'el's position on the issue of reason and revelation was the position furthest to the right which a philosopher can take. He brands philosophic science an "adversary" of Scripture, and he warns that the study of philosophy "may lead to great damage." Yet he is as convinced as any Aristotelian that the "incorporeal" intelligences, which he prefers to describe as "created" by God rather than emanated, keep the celestial spheres in continual motion; and his account of the mechanism through which the intelligences perform that function is wholly Aristotelian. Aristotle had explained that since the intelligences are incorporeal and immovable, they cannot act through contact. They must act indirectly and move the spheres by presenting themselves as objects of desire, thereby inducing the spheres to perform circular motion.[87] In total agreement with the Aristotelian explanation, Yeḥi'el, for his part, observes that the incorporeal intelligences bring about motion inasmuch as they are "objects of desire for the spheres and the souls of the spheres." [88]

Nine or ten sixteenth-century Jewish authors, in sum, wrote medieval philosophy. No known sixteenth-century Jewish text reveals any other kind of philosophy.

Sixteenth-century medieval Jewish philosophy is soon seen to have the characteristics of fifteenth-century philosophy. The majority of sixteenth-century philosophic writers, like their immediate predecessors, recognize the Neoplantonic version of medieval Aristotelianism as their authoritative body of rational knowledge. The conservative orientation of the fifteenth-century writers likewise carries over into the sixteenth century. With the sole exception of Ibn Migas, every sixteenth-century writer ranks the scriptural body of knowledge above the philosophic; and usually—the added exception here being Sforno, for whom the superiority of Scripture lies in the guidance it provides the human reason—the superiority of Scripture is found in the possibility of accepting it implicitly, on faith. The conservative orientation of the sixteenth century is similarly in evidence in the recurring statement that human perfection and immortality are achieved through study of the Law and observance of the religious commands, not through the study of philosophy. Even Ibn Migas, who ranks perfection through philosophy above perfection through Scripture, knows of a "peculiar property" in the religious commands which brings salvation to persons incapable of attaining perfection and immortality by the preferable route, through reason.[89]

The sixteenth-century philosophic writers employ the Kabbalah as an authoritative source of knowledge, and indeed do so more extensively than did philosophic writers in the preceding century. The use of the Kabbalah undoubtedly accords with the conservative bent of the sixteenth-century authors. It is not, however, by any means incompatible with philosophy as philosophy was pursued in the Middle Ages, and it nowise symptomizes a mystical or obscurantist spirit. The Kabbalah represented itself as an authentic component of the Oral Law, hence as a branch of the Scriptural body of knowledge, and to the extent that the sixteenth-century writers employ the Kabbalah, they acquiesce in the claim.

To take one example of the attitude of sixteenth-century writers towards the Kabbalah, Leone Ebreo reports a kabbalistic doctrine bearing on the problem of creation,[90] a doctrine ascribed by him to "theologians" who are "called *cabalisti*." The name *cabalisti*, Leone remarks, reflects the contention by the theologians who bear the name that they possess an "oral tradition," a "*caballá*," going back through Noah to Enoch and Adam. Leone hesitates to accept the kabbalistic doctrine in question, and the grounds for his hesitancy are purely formal. The texts [91] where the doctrine is recorded are "not clear, but figurative," and therefore their meaning is uncertain.[92] R. Moses Isserles, to take another example, quotes from the "Kabbalah" and from a number of "kabbalists" [93] yet he also hesitates to embrace the teachings of the Kabbalah. His hesitation is due to the circumstance that he has no "transmitted (*mekubelet*) knowledge" of kabbalistic teachings and is acquainted with no contemporary who has that knowledge. Without a sound chain of transmission, the Kabbalah lacks legitimacy, since "transmitted knowledge . . . is the basis of divine belief and the peg on which everything depends." [94] The kabbalistic doctrine that most perturbs Isserles is the theory of the *Sefirot*; and when he eventually succeeds in harmonizing the theory of the *Sefirot* with Maimonides' philosophic theory of divine attributes,[95] his reservations concerning the Kabbalah are suddenly dispelled. Isserles thereupon announces that the Kabbalah is what it represents itself to be. It is a "tradition" going back to Sinai, whereby propositions that the philosophers learn with great effort are made available to the Sages of Israel effortlessly.[96] To take one more example, Abraham ibn Migas, the philosophic writer furthest to the left in the sixteenth century, cities kabbalistic texts with no qualms whatsoever. But Ibn Migas does challenge reputed "kabbalists (*mekubalim*)" of his day who "are wise in their own eyes." Those self proclaimed kabbalists do not merit the name; for "they are not in possession of a tradition (*lo kiblu*) . . . [which has come] to each recipient (*mekubal*) [in the chain] from the mouth of another recipient, and which ultimately goes back to the Source of Life [i.e., to the theophany at Sinai]." [97] Alleged but inauthentic Kabbalah is, in other words, exposed by the absence of a sound chain of transmission. In all three sixteenth-century writers quoted here, it will have been noted, senses of Kabbalah which we suppose to be distinct—Kabbalah in the sense of a specific theosophic system and Kabbalah in the broad sense of tradition—are permitted to merge.

The remaining characteristic of fifteenth-century philosophic activity also carries into the sixteenth century. The sixteenth-century philosophic writers exhibit no originality, and none of them properly deserves to be termed a 'philosopher.' Yet the sixteenth-century writers do partake of the medieval philosophic outlook and they handle philosophic notions in the way fifteenth-century writers do. They may therefore be granted an appelation more modest than 'philosopher' and, like their fifteenth-century predecessors, may be called medieval philosophic writers.

3. *Leone Ebreo, Moscato, Isserles, Judah Loeb of Prague.* The label "Renaissance" is often affixed to Leone Ebreo's philosophic activity. Although perhaps applicable to Leone when considered as a litterateur, the label is highly doubtful where the strictly philosophic sections of his work are concerned; and for that matter, it is debatable whether the label "Renaissance" has any legitimate application at all for the history of European philosophy, whether anything in fifteenth- and sixteenth-century European thought deserves to be singled out as distinctively "Renaissance" philosophy.[98] No more than two non-medieval philosophic threads are, as far as I could see, present in Leone, and he might accordingly be designated a Renasissance, rather than a medieval, philosophic writer, only if the presence of those two threads warrants the new designation. One of the two threads is a sympathy for the Platonic theory of Ideas, a theory never taken seriously by medieval Islamic and Jewish philosophers. The other is the attribution to Plato of what are in fact Neoplatonic doctrines. The attribution of Neoplatonic doctrines to Plato is a peculiarity of the fifteenth-century Italian writers Ficino [99] and Giovanni Pico,[100] whereas the medieval Islamic and Jewish Neoplatonists did not connect their brand of philosophy with the name of Plato and knew nothing of the expression *Neoplatonic.* Like the character in literature who spoke prose without realizing it, they were not aware that they were neoplatonizing.

When Leone first treats the subject of the dependence of the universe on its cause, his discussion is wholly circumscribed by what he had learnt from Avicenna and Averroes. Medieval Aristotelianism in its Neoplatonic version had to explain how the plurality and complexity of the universe can have emerged from the unity and simplicity of the first cause. How, the question went, might an undifferentiated cause give rise to a complex effect? A recurring answer ran: The first cause, which consists in pure thought, emanates its effect by the mere act of thinking. Since the first cause has only a single object of thought, namely itself, only a single effect is emanated; and the effect, flowing as it does from an entity that consists in pure thought, is likewise incorporeal and consists in pure thought. This is the first of the incorporeal intelligences. The first intelligence differs now from its cause in a critical respect, since although it too is incorporeal and consists in pure thought, its thought is directed to more than one object. In Avicenna's formulation, the first celestial intelligence has three separate objects of thought, namely its cause and two distinct aspects of itself; [101] and by the mere act of thinking, it brings forth three separate effects. Its thought of its cause gives rise to a second incorporeal intelligence, its thought of one aspect of itself gives rise to the first, outermost celestial sphere, and its thought of the other aspect of itself gives rise to the rational soul of the sphere. The second intelligence similarly has three objects of thought and, through them, brings forth an additional intelligence—the third, an additional celestial sphere—the second, and the rational soul of that sphere. The process repeats itself over and over again until there emerge the full complement of nine incorporeal intelligences, nine celestial spheres together with their souls, and finally a tenth incorporeal intelligent being—the so-called active intellect—and the sublunar world. The relationship of the active intellect to the sublunar world is analogous to the relationship of the several celestial intelligences to their respective spheres.[102]

Avicenna's theory of the origin and structure of the universe, outlined here, reappears in Ghazali's summary of Avicenna's philosophy and in Maimonides' account of what he calls the cosmology of "Aristotle." But Ghazali, in his summary of Avicenna's philosophy,[103] and Maimonides simplify the theory. They omit the nuance that enabled Avicenna to distinguish three separate objects of thought in the incorporeal intelligences and instead state merely that each intelligence has two thoughts; [104] through one of the two thoughts, the intelligence brings forth a further intelligence, and through the other it brings forth a celestial sphere together with the rational soul of the sphere.[105] A more radical departure from Avicenna was made by Averroes, who rejected Neoplatonic elements in Avicenna's philosophy in the name of a purer Aristotelianism. Averroes did agree that the intelligent beings responsible for the motion of the celestial spheres, the spheres themselves, and the sublunar world, are somehow dependent on the first cause of the universe; but his conception of their dependence on the first cause is not easily deciphered.[106]

In Leone Ebreo's main treatment of the subject of cosmology, his horizon is defined by the theories of Avicenna and Averroes. Leone writes: "Avicenna, Ghazali, and our rabbi Moses [ben Maimon], maintain that the first cause . . . brings forth the first intelligence . . . from itself." And there the seed is sown from which the complexity of the universe evolves. For the intelligence has "two thoughts (*contemplazioni*)," one of them, "of the beauty of its cause, . . . and the second, . . . of its own beauty." "By virtue and love [of the former]," the first intelligence "brings forth . . . the second intelligence"; "by virtue and love of the latter, it produces the first sphere," a sphere "composed of an indestructible body . . . and intellectual soul." The phrase "by virtue and love [of the former]" and the phrase "by virtue and love of the latter" are, it may be noted, ambiguous and awkward. Had Leone been working in a purely medieval philosophic context, he would, as a matter of course, have written: 'by virtue of the former *thought*,' that is, by virtue of the intelligence's thought of the cause of the universe, the intelligence brings forth a new intelligence, and 'by virtue of the latter *thought*,' by virtue of its thought of itself, it brings forth a celestial sphere together with the soul of the sphere. But Leone happens to be interpolating a philosophic discussion into a dialogue on love and consequently feels called upon to pay obeisance to the concepts of love and beauty. What he seems to be saying is that 'by virtue and love of its thought of the former *beauty*'—by virtue and by love of the thought the intelligence has of the beauty of the first cause—the intelligence brings forth an intelligence, and 'by virtue and love of its thought of the latter beauty'—by virtue and by love of the thought it has of its own beauty—it brings forth a sphere.

The second incorporeal intelligence, Leone continues, likewise has "two thoughts," and by virtue of them brings forth the third intelligence and the second celestial sphere. The process is thereupon repeated again and again until all the celestial spheres,[107] the incorporeal intelligences governing them, the sublunar world, and the "active intellect," have been brought into existence. In a slight augmentation of the medieval material, Leone comments that Avicenna and the others regarded the active intellect as a repository of the "Forms" known from Plato's philosophy.[108]

Such is Leone's restatement of Avicenna's cosmology, a restatement clearly based on the simplified formulation of Ghazali and Maimonides. Avicenna's cosmology, Leone knows, did not remain unchallenged: "Averroes . . . endeavored" at every opportunity "to refute . . . what he did not find in Aristotle," and since none of the authentic works of Aristotle speaks of successive stages of emanation, Averroes, so Leone reports, "rejected [the theory of] his Arabic predecessors." Averroes' position was that "all the intelligences, . . . their several spheres, and . . . [everything in] the lower world, . . . derive directly" from God.[109] Leone refuses, in the passage being considered, to adjudicate between the cosmologies of Avicenna and Averroes; he judges them equally plausible.[110] He would seem to recognize, then that the universe consists of intelligences, rotating celestial spheres, and the lower world, all of which in some way go back to a first cause, but he is unwilling to express an opinion as to whether or not the universe is emanated from the first cause in successive stages.

In a later passage, Leone briefly returns, however, to the subject of the emanation of the universe from the first cause, and he performs something of a *volte face.* He recommends the position of "Plato," according to which the cosmic "intellect"—comprising "all the essence and Forms" or "Ideas"— is "emanated" from God and "dependent . . . on Him, . . . just as the light from the sun." Leone explicitly prefers Plato's position to that of "Avicenna, Ghazali, and our rabbi Moses," the "opinion" of the latter now being described as a "composite" of the systems of Plato and Aristotle and "inferior . . . to each." [111] What Leone calls Plato's position is unmistakably the standard Neoplatonic emanation scheme. In the present passage, therefore, Leone in effect indicates a preference for the genuine Neoplatonic scheme, wherein the first cause emanates a cosmic intellect and it in turn emanates a cosmic soul, over the Neoplatonic version of medieval Aristotelianism, wherein a series of intelligences is emanated from the first cause and each intelligence emanates a celestial sphere.[112]

Avicenna and Averroes, in addition to their differing stands on the emanation of the universe from the first cause, had also differed on another, related issue. They were led by divergent interpretations of Aristotle and divergent interpretations of the phenomena to divergent theories regarding the factors producing celestial motion. In Avicenna's system, the outermost celestial sphere is moved by the first emanated intelligence, in other words, by the intelligence that brings the sphere into existence; and the first cause of the universe, the deity, stands above, and apart from, the movers of the spheres.[113] In Averroes' system, the first cause does not stand above the movers of the spheres, but is itself the mover of the outermost sphere; in other words, it is itself the first intelligence.[114] Avicenna further explained that each intelligence effects the motion of its celestial sphere indirectly, through an interaction between the intelligence and the rational soul of the sphere. The sphere is kept in circular motion by the desire that its rational soul has to mirror the self-contained nature of the corresponding incorporeal intelligence.[115] Averroes, as Jewish commentators read certain of his works, again disagreed. He rejected—so the interpretation went—the distinction between a rational soul joined to the sphere and an incorporeal intelligence paralleling, but unconnected with, the sphere; and he explained that each celestial sphere possesses a single intellectual aspect, which sustains the sphere in constant circular motion.[116]

In a discussion of the subject of celestial motion, as in the main passage where he discussed the subject of emanation, Leone's horizon is defined by the theories of Avicenna and Averroes. "Alfarabi, Avicenna, Ghazali, and our rabbi Moses [ben Maimon]," he writes, maintain that "the first mover," the mover of the outermost sphere, "is not the most high God," but rather "the first intelligence." "Averroes and other, later . . . commentators on Aristotle," by contrast, "maintain . . that the most high God is the first mover." The school of Alfarabi, Avicenna, and their followers, supposes moreover that each sphere has not one, but "two intelligences." The sphere has an "intellectual, motive soul," which "moves it as an efficient [cause]," and an incorporeal intelligence, "which moves it as a final [cause]." Motion results from the incorporeal intelligence's being "loved" by the intellectual soul of the sphere; the soul of the sphere, "desiring to be united with what it loves, moves its heaven eternally." [117] Here too Averroes demurred, his grounds being that the distinction between an intellectual soul of the sphere and an incorporeal intelligence multiplies entities unnecessarily. "It is unphilosophical, Averroes said, to posit more intelligences than the force of philosophical reasoning requires," and he therefore recognized "as many intelligences as spheres and not more." [118] Leone, although he was unwilling to judge between the theories of Avicenna and Averroes on the subject of emanation, does disclose a preference for the theory of Averroes in the question of celestial motion. Each sphere he tentatively proposes, has a single intelligent mover that sustains its motion, not through love and desire of a corresponding intelligence but through love and desire of God. And he proposes still more tentatively that God, the intelligent mover of the outermost sphere, moves His sphere through love of Himself.[119] Leone does not, as far as I could discover, bring his preference for Averroes' position on the mover of the outermost sphere into harmony with his recommendation of the standard Neoplatonic emanation scheme. He thus leaves us with a careful statement of the positions held by medieval Arabic Aristotelians on the subject of the emanation of the universe and on the subject of celestial motion; and he subsequently appends thereto a brief recommendation of the standard Neoplatonic cosmological scheme. The Neoplatonic scheme was known to Leone from the medieval Jewish Neoplatonists,[120] but he does add a non-medieval feature when he attaches Plato's name to it.

Judah Moscato works with similar materials, but his handling of them is more superficial and more eclectic. Moscato writes: "Those who follow in the footsteps of Plato believe that at the initial stage the Creator emanated a most perfect intellect . . . and He placed within it traces of the models of all things." "The emanated intellect," which is "the first caused being, . . . brings into existence the soul of the world, which is the first of the souls." And the soul of the world "brings into existence, and emanates, the bodies of the celestial spheres and [the bodies] of other objects." [121] What Moscato has set forth so far is, once again, the standard Neoplatonic scheme, wherein the first cause emanates a cosmic intellect, the cosmic intellect emanates a cosmic soul, and the cosmic soul emanates the physical universe.[122] The scheme itself would have been known to Moscato from the medieval Jewish Neoplatonists. The sole non-medieval threads are, as in Leone, the linking of Plato's name to a Neoplatonic cosmology, and the allusion—in the phrase "traces of the models of all things"—to the Platonic Ideas. A reference by Moscato to Giovanni Pico [123] suggests that it was Pico who led him to link Neoplatonic doctrines to Plato.

A few lines after the statements already quoted, Moscato undertakes to summarize what he calls the system of "Plato" for the purpose of rendering his own account of "their views [presumably: the views of the followers of Plato] complete." In the Platonic hierarchy, he reports, "the Forms, . . . which Plato calls Ideas," stand at "the initial level"; and of the Forms or Ideas, one transcends the rest, inasmuch as "from one single Idea [124] the form and model of all else is emanated and derived." At the next level in the ladder of existence, "after" the Forms, there stand "the incorporeal intelligences. The souls [are] at the third level; and after [come] the several kinds of matter." [125] This second cosmological scheme recorded by Moscato would appear to be quite different from the previous one. The previous scheme portrayed a typical Neoplatonic hierarchy, in which the cosmic intellect comes immediately after the first cause; and Moscato construed the cosmic intellect as a repository of Platonic Ideas. The new scheme introduces an independent realm of Ideas which is distinct from, and superior to, intellect. And Moscato no longer speaks of a single cosmic intellect (*sekhel*) and cosmic soul, but rather of "incorporeal intelligences (*sekhalim nivdalim*)" and "souls." Despite the apparent variance, Moscato ascribes the new cosmology to the same philosophers to whom he ascribed the earlier one, and he nowise reveals that he saw any difference between the two. Of the two cosmological schemes, at least the earlier is—despite his strictures in respect to Greek philosophy [126]—endorsed by Moscato, for he utilizes it when expounding a traditional text.[127] Where Moscato might have found the second scheme is not known to me.

In a completely separate context, Moscato employs still another picture of the universe, the cosmology of the medieval Aristotelians. He takes for granted that existence outside of God is divided into "three worlds," the highest of which is "the world of the angels." The term "angel" is glossed by him as equivalent to "intelligible (*sikhli*)" [128]—in other words, the "angels" are the celestial intelligences. After the angels, or intelligences, come "the world of the spheres, and the lower world." [129]

Moscato operates, then, with three schemes: the standard Neoplatonic cosmology, in which the deity emanates a cosmic intellect, the intellect emanates a cosmic soul, and the soul emanates the physical world; the medieval Aristotelian cosmology, in which the universe outside the deity is divided into intelligences, spheres, and the sublunar world; and an eclectic Platonic cosmology, in which the realm of Ideas stands at the highest level, the intelligences at the second level, souls at the third, and "the several kinds of matter" at the bottom. If Moscato envisaged an identification of the cosmic intellect and cosmic soul of genuine Neoplatonic philosophy with the incorporeal intelligences and celestial souls of medieval Aristotelianism, he had precedents in the Middle Ages. Avicenna, when reading the Arabic paraphrases of Plotinus, had assumed that the cosmic intellect referred to there was nothing but a collective name for the incorporeal intelligences; and that the cosmic soul was a collective name for the souls of the spheres.[130] The identification of the cosmic intellect and cosmic soul with the celestial intelligences and the souls of the spheres is also suggested by Abraham Ibn Ezra,[131] and Moscato might easily have presupposed it. Clearly non-medieval, by contrast, is the introduction of a separate realm of Platonic Ideas. Moscato's picture of the universe would, in fine, seem to consist in a loose harmonization of three cosmologies, with most, though not all, of the elements being available from medieval Jewish philosophy. He would seem to picture the universe as comprising: the realm of Ideas, wherein one Idea—possibly, but not definitely, to be identified with the deity—is supreme; the cosmic intellect, which contains the "traces" of everything below it and which is identified with the realm of the intelligences, or movers of the spheres; the cosmic soul, which is identified with the souls of the spheres; the spheres; and the sublunar world.

R. Moses Isserles was familiar with only a single cosmological scheme, the cosmology of the medieval Aristotelians, and he is certain that it represents the actual structure of the universe. He is certain that the universe outside of God is divided into three realms: the realm of the incorporeal intelligences, the realm of the celestial spheres, and the sublunar region.[132] Isserles concurs as well with "all the early scholars," who believed "the spheres" to be "living beings that exercise thought." [133] He understands that the incorporeal intelligences induce motion in the heavens by presenting themselves as objects of "desire." [134] He knows of the theory of "Avicenna," according to which God emanates the first incorporeal intelligence, whereupon the first intelligence emanates a second "incorporeal intelligence . . . through its thought of its cause" and "a sphere through its thought of itself," and so on.[135] He likewise knows of "Averroes' " position, which dispenses with successive emanations and views all the intelligences as "equally" dependent on the first cause.[136] And sometimes, but not always, he subscribes specifically to Avicenna's theory.[137]

Isserles is not satisfied merely to accept the medieval Aristotelian picture of the universe. He offers an elaborate exegesis designed to show that that picture of the universe is mirrored in the most sacred Jewish cultic object, the Holy Temple. The conceit is hardly original, since several medieval Jewish Bible commentators had found the biblical tabernacle and its appurtenances to be symbols of the universe.[138] Isserles goes beyond his predecessors, however. Pre-eminent student of the Oral Law that he was, he directs his attention to the Jerusalem Temple described, or prescribed, in the Mishna[139] rather than to the Tabernacle described in Exodus; and he contends that not only the overall plan of the Temple, but the very dimensions, reflect the structure of the universe.

In Isserles' exegesis, the inner sanctum of the Temple symbolizes the deity, and the sanctum's width of twenty cubits is an intimation of the same. The numerical value of the letters in the Hebrew word for *twenty* totals 620, and 620 turns out to be the numerical value of the letters in the Hebrew word for *crown.* God alone, of course, is worthy of the "crown of royalty." Hence the width of the inner sanctum, Isserles avers, alludes to God in His capacity of King.[140] The second chamber of the Temple symbolizes, in Isserles' exegesis, the realm of the "incorporeal intelligences," and he struggles to uncover allusions to the intelligences in the chamber's forty-cubit width. The vestibule of the Temple symbolizes "the active intellect, . . . the giver of forms." [141] And the main courtyard symbolizes the realm of celestial spheres. The distance from the Temple entrance to the altar standing in the main courtyard was twenty-two cubits, the altar itself had a width of thirty-two cubits, and the numbers twenty-two and thirty-two, Isserles endeavors to prove, are integral to the courtyard's symbolism.

Nine primary celestial spheres had been recognized in medieval Islamic and Jewish astronomy, but additional, subordinate spheres had to be posited as well. The hypothesis of celestial spheres had the function of explaining the apparent motions of the stars and planets; and locating each star and planet in a single sphere that rotates around the earth could not suffice, since no star or planet does travel around the earth in a simple circle. In order to reduce the apparent movements of stars and planets to circular motion, the assumption was made that secondary spheres rotate at the surface of the primary spheres, and that, in some instances, still other spheres rotate at the surface of the secondary spheres. By supposing that each star or planet is fixed to a subordinate sphere and by supposing that the subordinate sphere rotates at the surface of another sphere, which in turn perhaps rotates at the surface of still another, and it at the surface of yet another—which is, finally, the primary sphere—the complicated, apparent motion of the given star or planet around the earth could be accounted for. Some systems of astronomy hypothesized a total of fifty or more spheres, that is, primary spheres together with subordinate spheres. But Maimonides had remarked that the absolute minimum number of spheres which has to be assumed is eighteen.[142] Maimonides had also remarked that four separate factors contribute to the motion of each sphere.[143] And he once wrote that the spheres can be thought of as the "heart" of the physical universe inasmuch as their motion imparts motion and life to the universe.[144] Isserles adduces all these passages in Maimonides and asserts, in seemingly complete seriousness, that the distance of twenty-two cubits from the Temple entrance to the altar is an allusion to the sum of the minimum number of spheres which has to be recognized—eighteen—and the number of separate factors—four—contributing to each sphere's motion. The width of the altar signifies the sphere's role as the "heart" of the universe, for the figure thirty-two, the width of the altar in cubits, is identical with the numerical value of the letters in the Hebrew word for *heart.*[145]

Accessories of the main courtyard are shown by Isserles to symbolize aspects of the celestial spheres. The outer courtyard, the so-called "women's court," and its accessories are taken by him to symbolize the active intellect insofar as it operates within the sublunar world. The sublunar world is, he supposes, symbolized by the terraces leading down from the Temple precincts.[146]

One question concerning the mechanism of celestial motion did exercise Isserles. Medieval astronomy had portrayed the stars and planets as imbedded in spheres and borne in circular motion by the rotation of their spheres. The path each star or planet traces through the heavens would be the product of the motions of the several subordinate spheres and the primary sphere that underlie the particular star or planet. Now, the ancient rabbis too had recognized the existence of celestial spheres, but they conceived the function of the spheres differently. In contrast to the non-Jewish astronomers who believed, as the Talmud put it, that "the sphere rotates and the planets are stationary," the rabbis believed that the "sphere is stationary and the planets rotate," [147] in other words, that the planets move along the surface of stationary spheres. Maimonides resolved the disagreement between philosophic, and traditional Jewish, astronomy by granting that here "the non-Jewish scholars had prevailed over the Jewish scholars." [148] Isserles is not willing to take the same course; for if science can demonstrate that the stars and planets have no motion of their own and move only insofar as they are carried by their spheres, the rabbis, in Isserles' opinion, cannot possibly have affirmed the contrary. How "could the people of God and their prophets [149] . . . have believed something refuted by rational demonstration?" [150] Isserles accordingly seeks an alternative resolution of the disagreement between the rabbis and non-Jewish scientists. And he finds what he seeks in a passage in which Maimonides had evaluated the science of astronomy.

The principal task of astronomical science, Maimonides had written, is to formulate the simplest hypothesis that will cover the phenomena, irrespective of whether the hypothesis is objectively true.[151] If such is the function of astronomy, Isserles reasons, more than one hypothesis might conceivably answer the purpose. The rabbinic hypothesis to the effect "that the sphere is stationary and the planet rotates" could therefore "very likely" be more "true," even though the philosophic hypothesis is more serviceable in the present state of human knowledge; the rabbinic hypothesis surely has the stronger claim seeing that it was promulgated by the progenitors of the Jewish nation and is rooted in prophecy, "which is superior to speculation." If the prophets and early rabbis were "with us today, they could spell out their astronomy" and exhibit its "agreement with appearances." They are not with us. And unfortunately, "with the passage of time, and in consequence of our sins, the wisdom of our people has been lost," [152] so that Jewish scholars no longer comprehend how their ancestral hypothesis "agrees with the apparent motions of the heavens." The non-Jewish hypothesis alone remains fully developed and it has, as a result, won the day by default.[153]

Besides the foregoing defense of rabbinic astronomy, Isserles proposes a further, bolder defense of the rabbinic dictum that "the sphere is stationary and the planets rotate," a defense again growing out of statements in Maimonides. Philosophers, Maimonides had argued, cannot tell us why, in the celestial region, given portions of matter and given forms are wedded to each other permanently. It is of the nature of matter, he noted, continually to divest itself of one form and to assume another. The matter of the celestial spheres, of the stars, and of the planets, should be expected to behave as the nature of matter requires and continually to change form. Yet the unvarying paths of the celestial bodies and the unvarying quality of their light discloses that in the heavens matter acts anomalously and is permanently wedded to the same form. Such was Maimonides' reasoning concerning matter in the celestial region; [154] and it furnishes Isserles with a rationale for defending the rabbis' thesis that the spheres are stationary and the planets move. Perhaps, Isserles ventures, the matter of the heavens does in fact constantly change its forms. Perhaps the stars and planets do not exist as stable bodies and the following occurs: Portions of matter lying in a circular band around the sphere successively receive and lose the form of a star and of a planet—just as, to take a modern illustration, lights arranged in a row on an electric sign go on and off *seriatim*. The star's ceasing to exist at one spot and immediately coming into existence at the next spot would occasion what the earthly observer perceives as the rotation of a stable star or planet around the earth. The dictum that the "sphere is stationary and the planet rotates" would thus be confirmed. For the sphere would be stationary, and each planet—that is, the continual coming into existence of a planet at successive spots—would travel in a circle around the sphere.[155]

Judah Loeb of Prague constantly strove to be independent, but the division of the universe into three realms is a doctrine he was incapable of doubting. The lowest of the three realms is defined by him as the region "up to the world of the spheres," and he characterizes it, in conformity with the tenets of Aristotelian philosophy, as "the world of generation and destruction." The "middle realm, . . . the world of the spheres," is characterized, again in conformity with Aristotelian tenets, as "not subject to generation" and as "containing no contrary qualities whatsoever." The "highest realm" is the realm of intellect, . . . which is called [by philosophers] the realm of incorporeal intelligences." [156] The division of the universe into three realms is not, for Judah Loeb, specifically philosophic. He understands that the same division of existence is presupposed by the rabbis, and indeed that the philosophers erred, and have to be corrected, on two scores. They erred in their supposition that the spheres are "living, thinking" entities, the accurate, and the traditional Jewish, position being in his view that the spheres are inanimate objects. The philosophers also erred in their supposition that the intelligences are wholly "incorporeal." If the intelligences were wholly incorporeal, they would, Judah Loeb expostulates, equal the deity in rank, which is inadmissible; and the intelligences must accordingly be presumed to have a material aspect.[157]

Judah Loeb of Prague, like Moses Isserles, was troubled by the rabbinic dictum stating that "the sphere is stationary, and the planets rotate." He refuses to accept the dictum at face value, because, he writes, it is "absolutely impossible to affirm" that the "star should rotate by itself" along the surface of a stationary sphere. "The intellect cannot possibly countenance," and the rabbis could not have put forward, such a proposition; the rabbis, no less than the Greek philosophers, must have realized that each planet is imbedded in, and rotates together with, a sphere. Judah Loeb is as a consequence drawn to harmonize the rabbinic dictum that the "sphere is stationary" with the unquestioned truth that the planet rotates together with the sphere it is imbedded in. To accomplish the harmonization, he offers his own ingenious interpretation of the rabbinic dictum.

When the rabbis stated that the sphere is stationary, they can, he submits, be read in only one way: They must have meant that the sphere does not itself furnish the motive power whereby the complex of sphere and planet is sustained in motion. And when the rabbis continued that the planet does rotate, they must have meant that the source of motive power is the planet. Philosophic and rabbinic astronomy would therefore concur in recognizing that neither stars and planets nor spheres are stationary, that the stars and planets are imbedded in spheres and rotate together with them. The two astronomies would differ in that the philosophers located the power moving the complex of sphere and planet in the sphere, whereas the rabbis located the motive power in the planet. On the former conception, the planet or star is "moved together with" the spherical body to which it is attached "like a nail attached to a boat." On the latter, "the sphere moves thanks to the star, . . . like a carriage . . . which is moved thanks to the horse pulling [it]." [158] Judah Loeb does not quite brand the philosophic conception as mistaken, but he does find the rabbis' conception to be "more plausible." His grounds therefor are, unhappily, not very substantial or even perfectly clear. He comments merely: "That the cause of motion should be the planet" is "more likely," since the planet "is more actual [or: active, *p'l yoter*] than the sphere." [159]

Moses Isserles and Judah Loeb of Prague plainly treat the topic of celestial motion less as a scientific problem than as a problem of harmonization, less as a problem in fathoming natural phenomena than as a problem in accomodating authoritative bodies of knowledge. In doing that, they of course do nothing unmedieval. Perhaps, though, they have moved further away from the philosophic spirit than their predecessors, in the degree to which they forget the underlying scientific issue. Neither Isserles' interpretation—or interpretations—of the dictum that "the planets rotate" nor Judah Loeb's interpretation explains the force responsible for celestial motion in accord with any philosophic system or any set of natural laws. Neither, moreover, keeps sight of the purpose for which the scientific hypothesis of celestial spheres had been designed, namely, the elucidation of the actual non-circular motion of the heavenly bodies; their interpretations could at best account for a simple circular motion of the planets around the earth, not for the motions of the planets as actually seen by an earthly observer. It may be fair to say that Isserles and Judah Loeb are not after all engaged so much in accomodating disparate bodies of authoritative knowledge as in doing what Eastern European Talmudists did masterfully, to wit, harmonizing disparate texts.

4. *Conclusion.* Changes can be discerned in sixteenth-century Jewish philosophic writing, changes both traceable to non-Jewish models and attributable to indigenous evolution. Leone Ebreo, for example, incorporates his philosophic discussions into a dialogue on love,[160] and he has no scruples in citing Greek mythology,

whereas citations from mythology by a Jewish author would have been unthinkable in earlier centuries.[161] Moscato quotes sixteenth-century Christian works and also ancient works that were unknown to the medieval Jews.[162] The philosophic discussions in Leone and Moscato incorporate Platonic elements, which are borrowed from Italian philosophic writers. Isserles and Judah Loeb of Prague transform philosophic and scientific issues into problems of text harmonization to a greater extent than did authors in the previous century. The changes are minor, however, and are clearly outweighed by the essential affinity of sixteenth-century, to fifteenth-century, philosophic writing.

NOTES

1. See S. Pines, *Beitraege zur islamischen Atomenlehre* (Berlin, 1936), pp. 94-124; H. Wolfson, *Philosophy of the Kalam* (Cambridge, 1976), pp. 466-469.
2. The Islamic Neoplantonists did not, however, realize that they were 'Neoplantonists.'
3. In Plotinus himself, the emanation of the physical world from the cosmic soul is problematical. See E. Zeller, *Die Philosophie der Griechen*, III, 2, fifth edition (Leipzig, 1923), pp. 603-605.
4. See below at nn. 101-105.
5. The spectrum notion is applicable, as far as my knowledge extends, to the Christian philosophers as well.
6. It should go without saying—and I state the obvious only becuse the present paragraph in my paper, strangely, generated controversy in the session where the paper was discussed—that the classifications, schemata, and diverse theories formulated by historians are no more than a matter of convenience. They are true solely in a pragmatic sense—in the sense, and to the degree, that the historian or the historian's reader feels they help him understand phenomena.
7. Cf. Averroes, *K. al-Kashf*, edited as *Philosophie und Theologie von Averroes*, ed. M. Mueller (Munich, 1859), p. 27; German translation: *Philosophie und Theologie von Averroes . . . uebersetzt*, transl. M. Mueller (Munich, 1875), pp. 26-27; Averroes, *K. Faṣl al-Maqāl*, ed. G. Hourani (Leiden, 1959), p. 30; English translation: *Averroes on the Harmony of Religion and Philosophy*, transl. G. Hourani (London, 1961), pp. 63-64.
8. The most common division of sciences among medieval Islamic and Jewish philosophers was the Aristotelian, according to which the theoretical sciences fall into three classes: mathematical sciences, physical sciences, and metaphysics. See H. Wolfson, "The Classification of Sciences in Mediaeval Jewish Philosophy," reprinted in his *Studies in the History of Philosophy and Religion*, I (Cambridge, 1973), pp. 494-496; 511-513.
9. I. Albalag, *S. Tikkun ha-De'ot* (a commentary of Ghazali's *Maqāṣid*), ed. G. Vajda (Jerusalem, 1973), pp. 2-3, 47; French translation: G. Vajda, *Isaac Albalag averroïste juif* (Paris, 1960), pp. 16-17, 159-160. Albalag seems to state another doctrine on pp. 37-38, 43-44; French translation, pp. 144-145, 153-155. See Vajda's remarks in the French volume, pp. 251-266.
10. J. Kaspi, *Maskiyot Kesef* (Frankfort, 1848), pp. 8, 45, 100-101. Kaspi goes as far as to say that the prophets sometimes have to speak falsely for pedagogical purposes. See ibid., pp. 38-39; I. Twersky, "Joseph ibn Kaspi," *Studies in Medieval Jewish History and Literature*, ed. I. Twersky (Cambridge, 1979), p. 239.
11. Moses Narboni, *Commentary on the Guide*, ed. J. Goldenthal (Vienna, 1852), 1a.

12. Ha-Levi, *Kuzari*, V, §14. Cf. Ghazali, *Al-Munqidh min al-Ḍalāl*, ed. and transl. F. Jabre (Beirut, 1959), text, pp. 20-27; French translation, pp. 72-84. English translation: M. Watt, *The Faith and Practice of al-Ghazālī* (London, 1953), pp. 32-43.

13. Cf. Ḥ. Crescas, *Or ha-Shem* (Vienna, 1859), Introduction, p. 2b.

14. Maimonides, *Guide*, II, 22 (end).

15. M. Taku, *Ketav Tamin*, published in *Otzar Neḥmad*, III (1860), pp. 58-99; Asher b. Yeḥi'el, *Responsa*, §55.9; Isaac b. Sheshet, *Responsa*, §45.

16. Elijah Del Medigo, *Beḥinat ha-Dat* (Vienna, 1833), pp. 5-6; cf. p. 52. Del Medigo is echoing the passage in Averroes' *K. Faṣl al-Maqāl*, cited above, n.7.

17. *Ibid.*, p. 8; cf. pp. 11, 18.

18. Quoted by M. Steinschneider, "Miscellen," *MGWJ*, XXXVII (1893), pp. 187-188.

19. Quoted by J. Perles, *Beitraege zur Geschichte der hebraeischen und aramaeischen Studien* (Munich, 1884), p. 197. The passage seems to echo Albalag, op. cit., p. 43; French translation, p. 153.

20. Julius Guttmann interprets Del Medigo as advocating the 'Double Truth' theory, the paradoxical theory of certain Christian Averroists who held that philosophy and religion state incompatible propositions, both of which are true. See J. Guttmann, "Elia del Medigos Verhaeltnis zu Averroes in seinem Bechinat ha-Dat," *Jewish Studies in Memory of Israel Abrahams* (New York, 1927), pp. 196, 208. Passages in Albalag might be read in the same way unless he too is—as is probable—dissimulating; see Vajda, *Isaac Albalag*, pp. 251-266. Also cf. A. Huebsch, "Elia Delmedigo's Bechinath ha-Dath und Ibn Roschd's Façl ul-Maqâl," *MGWJ*, XXXII (1883), p. 33.

21. Joseph ibn Shem Tov, *Kevod Elokim* (Ferrara, 1555), pp. 24 a-b. (I am following the pagination of the reprint, where the page beginning *"Kol ha-nikra bi-shemi"* is numbered as leaf 1.)

22. Ibid., pp. 25a-26a; cf. p. 23a.

23. Ibid., p. 26b; cf. p. 27a. In support of his position, Ibn Shem Tov cites R. Asher b. Yeḥi'el (see above n. 15), R. Solomon b. Adret, and Abba Mari's *Minḥat Kena'ot.*

24. I. Arama, *Ḥazut Kasha*, in *Akedat Yitzḥak* (Pressburg, 1849), V, p. 21b. See also *Akedat Yitzḥak*, I, 11a-b; *Ḥazut Kasha*, pp. 6b, 10a-b, 13b; *Yad Avshalom* (Leipzig, 1859), pp. 44b-45a, 74b; S. Heller-Wilensky, *R. Yitzḥak Arama u-Mishnato* (Jerusalem-Tel Aviv, 1956), pp. 65-69.

25. See below at n. 35.

26. S. Duran, *Magen Avot* (Livorno, 1785), pp. 1a-2a; Shem Tov b. Joseph ibn Shem Tov, Introduction to *Commentary on Guide*; Abraham Shalom, *Neveh Shalom* (Venice, 1575), V, 7, 77a; X, 2, 173a-b; XII, i, 3, 201a; A. Bibago, *Derekh Emuna* (Constantinople, 1521), pp. 11a, 46a, 47a, 60b.

27. The exceptions are Del Medigo, Shem Tov b. Joseph ibn Shem Tov and possibly Saul ha-Cohen, a student of Del Medigo.

28. S. Duran, *Magen Avot*, pp. 2a, 76b; Jac. Guttmann, "Die Stellung des Simon ben Zemach Duran. . . ," *MGWJ*, LII (1908), p. 656; J. Albo, *Ikkarim*, III, chaps. 8, 10, 11; Jos. ibn Shem Tov, *Kevod Elokim*, p. 16b; A. Shalom, *Neveh Shalom*, VI, 4, 92a; VIII, 8, 141a; VIII, 10, 148a; H. Davidson, *The Philosophy of Abraham Shalom* (Berkeley-Los Angeles, 1964), pp. 8-9, 85; A. Bibago, *Derekh Emuna*, 11a; I. Arama, *Akedat Yitzḥak*, II, 11a; *Ḥazut Kasha*, pp. 10a-b, 21b; I. Abravanel, *Commentary to Guide*, II, 36.

29. Duran, *Magen Avot*, 90a; Albo *Ikkarim*, III, chap. 5; Joseph ibn Shem Tov, *Kevod Elokim*, pp. 2a, 19a-21b; Davidson, *The Philosophy of Abraham Shalom*, p. 87; Bibago, *Derekh Emuna*, pp. 17a, 53a-54a; Arama, *Akedat Yitzḥak*, I, 261b-262a; Heller-Wilensky, *R. Yitzḥak Arama*, p. 188-190; I. Abravanel , *Ateret Zekenim* (Sabbionetta, 1557), chap. 12, *shoresh* 5; *Correspondence with Saul ha-Cohen* (Venice, 1574), pp. 21a-21b; *Commentary* on I Samuel, chap. 25, *shoresh* 3.

30. Duran, *Magen Avot*, pp. 33b, 89b-91a; Albo, *Ikkarim*, I, chap. 21; IV, chaps. 11-13; Joseph ibn Shem Tov, *Kevod Elokim*, 19b; Davidson, *The Philosophy of Abraham Shalom*, pp. 75-76; Bibago, *Derekh Emuna*, p. 59b; Heller-Wilensky, *R. Yitzḥak Arama*, pp. 215-216; 218-221.

31. Cf. Maimonides, *Guide*, II, 37; III, 18 (end); 51.

32. Citations from kabbalistic literature are to be found in Duran, Albo, Shalom, Bibago, Arama, and Abravanel.

33. That is to say, conservative in regard to this issue of reason and revelation. In a certain sense, the Kabbalah may be regarded as highly revolutionary.

34. Duran, *Magen Avot*, pp. 14a-b, 21b; Albo, *Ikkarim*, IV, chap. 50; Joseph ibn Shem Tov, *Kevod Elokim*, p. 22b; Davidson, *The Philosophy of Abraham Shalom*, pp. 43-48; Bibago, *Derekh Emuna*, pp. 10a, 13b, 28a; Abravanel, *Mif'alot Elokim* (Venice, 1592), III, chaps. 8, 9. For Arama, see below, n. 37.

35. Shem Tov ibn Shem Tov, *Sefer ha-Emunot* (Ferrara, 1556), p. 2a. On p. 22a, Shem Tov remarks that philosophers failed to prove the dependence of the celestial spheres on movers outside themselves.

36. Cf. Ghazali, *Tahāfut al-Falāsifa* (Beirut, 1927), XIV, §11; English translation: *Averroes' Tahafut al-Tahafut*, transl. S. van den Bergh (London, 1954), p. 290; Crescas, *Or ha-Shem*, I, i, 6; ii, 15; H. Wolfson, *Crescas' Critique of Aristotle* (Cambridge, 1929), pp. 236-237.

37. *Akedat Yitzḥak*, I, 16a-17b. The exception mentioned by Arama is Isaac ibn Latif, but Arama could have found additional exceptions; see Heller-Wilensky, *R. Yitzḥak Arama*, p. 115.

38. For a similar judgment, see G. Vajda, *Introduction à la pensée juive du moyen âge* (Paris, 1947), p. 183.

39. The dividing of years into 'centuries' is apparently post-medieval. The medieval Latin dictionaries do not record the usage.

40. The popular press, of course, no longer limits itself to centuries. It expects each decade to evince an inner coherence.

41. The following might possibly be added: Abraham Horowitz, the author of a commentary on Maimonides' *Eight Chapters* — cf. G. Scholem, "*Yedi'ot Ḥadashot . . .*," *Tarbiẓ*, XXVIII (1959-1960), pp. 64-65; Moses Provençal, author of a commentary on *Guide*, II, Introduction — cf. R. Bonfil, "Perush R. Moshe Proventzalo . . . ," *Kirjath Sepher* 50 (1975), pp. 157-176; David Gans, by reason of his cosmological discussions. My hesitation regarding Judah Loeb is due to his habit of using philosophical terms in idiosyncratic senses.

42. See M. Isserles, *Responsa*, ed. A. Siev (Jerusalem, 1970), §7, p. 32.

43. Yeḥi'el of Pisa, *Minḥat Kena'ot*, ed. D. Kaufmann (Berlin, 1898), p. 88. Gianfrancesco Pico della Mirandola, who also took a conservative position on the issue of reason and revelation, supported his position in part through the contention that Aristotle's philosophy is grounded on sense perception, whereas sense perception is not reliable. See Ch. Schmitt, *Gianfrancesco Pico della Mirandola (1469-1533) and his Critique of Aristotle* (The Hague, 1967), pp. 38-42, 75.

44. Ibid., p. 113.

45. Ibid., p. 88, citing the authority of Asher b. Yeḥi'el.

46. Ibid., p. 113.

47. Ibid., p. 9.

48. Ibid., p. 111.

49. Ibid., p. 88.

50. Ibid., pp. 113-114, citing the authority of Solomon b. Adret. See Adret, *Responsa*, §§414ff.

51. Above, at nn. 21, 23, also citing the authority of Asher b. Yeḥi'el and Solomon b. Adret.

52. J. Moscato, *Nefutzot Yehuda* (Warsaw, 1871), §4, p. 12a, quoting Baḥya ibn Pakuda.

53. Ibid., §14, p. 38b. Moscato employs a seven-fold division of the sciences; see ibid., p. 41b, and Wolfson, "The Classifications of the Sciences in Mediaeval Jewish Philosophy," pp. 513-515.

54. Ibid., §14, p. 41a, citing Naḥmanides' introduction to his commentary on the Pentateuch.

55. Ibid., §5, p. 18a, citing Ha-Levi, *Kuzari*, II, §66, and Shem Tov ibn Shem Tov, *Sefer ha-Emunot*, III, chap. 4. The notion that the Greeks borrowed their philosophy from the Jews was common; cf. H. Wolfson, *Philo* (Cambridge, 1948), I, 160-163.

56. Leone Ebreo, *Dialoghi d'Amore*, ed. S. Caramella (Bari, 1929), p. 240. Hebrew trans-

lation: *Vikkuaḥ al ha-Ahava* (Lyck, 1871), p. 56b; English translation: *The Philosophy of Love*, transl. F. Friedeberg-Seeley and J. Barnes (London, 1937), p. 282.

57. M. Almosnino, *Pirkey Moshe* (Salonica, 1563), p. 86b.

58. *Tefilla le-Moshe* (Salonica, 1563), p. 41b.

59. *Pirkey Moshe*, p. 86b.

60. Judah Loeb, *Be'er ha-Gola* (London, 1964), chap. 6, pp. 105-106.

61. *Tiferet Yisrael* (Jerusalem, 1960), chap. 6, p. 21.

62. *Netivot Olam*, I, chap. 14, p. 60. The occasion is a discussion of BT *Berakhot*, 58a.

63. *Tiferet Yisrael*, chap. 13, p. 43.

64. *Netivot Olam*, I, chap. 14, pp. 60-61. Cf. A. Kleinberger, *Ha-Maḥshava ha-Pedagogit shel ha-MaHaRaL mi-Prag* (Jerusalem, 1962), p. 61.

65. M. Isserles, *Torat ha-Ola* (Lemberg, 1858), III, p. 1b; cf. p. 9b.

66. *Responsa*, §7. Isserles does not extend his endorsement to the specific Aristotelian work entitled *Physics*, and indeed that work treats the subject of metaphysics as well as physics. In *Torat ha-Ola*, I, 13a, he supports his endorsement of the study of philosophy through the topos that Greek science was borrowed from the Jews.

67. *Shulḥan Arukh, Yore De'a*, §246.

68. O. Sforno, *Or Amim* (Bologna, 1537), pp. 4, 8.

69. See Naḥmanides, *Commentary to the Pentateuch*, Introduction; Crescas, *Or ha-Shem*, p. 52a; above, nn. 54, 57, 63.

70. *Or Amim*, p. 118.

71. Scripture guides him to philosophic solutions of the problem of creation, the nature of God, and the nature of the human soul.

72. Above, n. 57.

73. A. Ibn Migas, *Kevod Elokim* (Constantinople, 1585), p. 18b.

74. Cf. Maimonides, *Guide*, I, 33.

75. *Kevod Elokim*, pp. 15b, 16a, 16b-17a, 72a.

76. Ibid., I, chap. 16.

77. Joseph b. Isaac, *Giv'at ha-More* (Prague, 1611), III, ii, 3.

78. He does follow Isserles in incorporating an endorsement of philosophic studies into his law code. See *Levush Ateret Zahav* (=*Yore De'a*), §246.

79. J. Yavetz, *Or ha-Ḥayyim*, chap. 8.

80. Ibid., Appendix, §§12-13.

81. Ibid., Appendix, §1.

82. Ibid., Appendix, §13.

83. BT *Avoda Zara*, 17a, with reference to Proverbs 5:8.

84. Isserles, *Responsa*, §6. Luria cites the authority of Asher b. Yeḥi'el and Isaac b. Sheshet.

85. Ibid. A truly uncompromising opposition to philosophy is found in Joseph Ashkenazi and in an anonymous text that Scholem conjectures was written by Joseph Ashkenazi. See Ph. Bloch, "Der Steit um den Moreh . . . ," *MGWJ*, XXXXVII (1903), pp. 157-158, 276; G. Scholem, "Yedi'ot Ḥadashot . . . ," pp. 66-67, 80-83. Other examples of opposition to philosophy are given by I. Barzilay, *Between Reason and Faith* (The Hague–Paris, 1967), pp. 66-67.

86. The exceptions are Leone Ebreo and Moscato, who in some passages recognize—like the members of the medieval Neoplatonic school—a more or less pure Neoplatonism as their body of philosophic knowledge. See the next section, where I also point out features in Leone and Moscato which are unknown among the medieval Jews.

87. Aristotle, *Metaphysics*, XII, 7.

88. Yeḥi'el of Pisa, *Minḥat Kena'ot*, p. 20.

89. Ibn Migas, *Kevod Elokim*, pp. 71b-72b. The sixteenth-century writers do not seem to speak very much about providence.

90. The doctrine of *shemitot*, according to which every seventh millennium is a period of rest in the world, and every fiftieth millennium is a period of total renewal. See G. Scholem, *On the Kabbalah and its Symbolism* (New York, 1965), pp. 77-78.

91. The Hebrew translation has a different word.

92. *Dialoghi d'Amore*, pp. 248-249; Hebrew translation, pp. 58b-59a; English translation, pp. 292-294.

93. Examples are *Torat ha-Ola*, I, pp. 6b, 7a, 13b; III, pp. 4a-6a.

94. *Torat ha-Ola*, III, p. 3b. Cf. *Responsa*, §7. In both passages Isserles refers to Isaac b. Sheshet, *Responsa*, §157.

95. Cf. Maimonides, *Guide*, I, 57-59.

96. *Torat ha-Ola*, III, pp. 5a, 6a.

97. Ibn Migas, *Kevod Elokim*, p. 93a, citing Issac b. Sheshet, *Responsa*, §157.

98. For two characterizations of 'Renaissance philosophy,' see E. Cassirer, *The Individual and the Cosmos in Renaissance Philosophy* (Oxford, 1963), pp. 1-15; P. Kristeller, *Studies in Renaissance Thought and Letters* (Rome, 1956), pp. 21-30, 560-561.

99. M. Ficino, *Commentary on Plato's Symposium*, ed. and transl. S. Jayne (Columbia, Missouri, 1944), pp. 39-40, 126-129.

100. G. Benivieni, *Dell' Amore, Celeste e Divino . . . col Comento del . . . Gio. Pico Mirandolano* (Lucca, 1731), pp. 14-20. English paraphrase: *A Platonick Discourse upon Love by Pico della Mirandola*, paraphrased by T. Stanley in 1651 and republished by E. Gardner (Boston, 1914), pp. 5-8. I would classify Ficino and Pico as medieval philosophers.

101. The two latter aspects are its thought of itself as a necessary being and its thought of itself as a possible being. The subject is discussed by me more fully in "The Active Intellect in the *Cuzari* and Hallevi's Theory of Causality," *REJ*, CXXXI (1972), pp. 356-357.

102. Avicenna, *Shifā': Ilāhīyāt*, ed. G. Anawati and S. Zayed (Cairo, 1960), pp. 406-407.

103. In Ghazali's critique of Avicenna's philosophy, the *Tahāfut al-Falāsifa*, he speaks of three objects of thought in each intelligence. Alfarabi had presented the theory prior to Avicenna and he distinguished two objects of thought in each intelligence. See the article cited in n. 101.

104. In Ghazali, the two thoughts are the intelligence's consciousness of being "necessarily existent by virtue of another" and its being "possibly existent by virtue of itself." In Maimonides—as in Alfarabi—the two objects of thought are itself and "another," i.e., itself and the First Cause.

105. Ghazali, *Maqāṣid al-Falāsifa* (Cairo, n.d.), pp. 219-220; Maimonides, *Guide*, II, 22.

106. Cf. Averroes, *Tahāfut al-Tahāfut*, ed. M. Bouyges (Beirut, 1930), pp. 179-182, 184-187; English translation: *Averroes' Tahafut al-Tahafut*, transl. van den Bergh, pp. 107-109, 111-112.

107. Alfarabi, Avicenna, and their followers, enumerated nine main celestial spheres: the spheres of the seven planets, including the sun and moon, which are thought of as planets; the sphere of the fixed stars; and the outermost, 'diurnal' sphere. Leone writes that according to the Greeks there are "eight" spheres, according to the Arabs there are "nine," and according to "the ancient Hebrews and some moderns" there are "ten." Cf. Ibn Gabirol, *Keter Malkhut*, in H. Schirmann, *Ha-Shira ha-Ivrit bi-Sefarad u-ve-Provans* (Jerusalem–Tel Aviv, 1954), I, p. 271.

108. *Dialoghi d'Amore*, pp. 281-282; Hebrew translation, p. 67b; English translation, pp. 333-334. "The giver of forms" was a standard medieval designation for the active intellect so that only the connection with Plato is new.

109. *Dialoghi d'Amore*, p. 284; Hebrew translation, p. 68a; English translation, p. 336.

110. *Dialoghi d'Amore*, p. 285; Hebrew translation, p. 68b; English translation, p. 338.

111. *Dialoghi d'Amore*, p. 348; Hebrew translation, p. 85a; English translation, pp. 415-416.

112. I take the obscure passages on pp. 242 and 355—Hebrew translation, pp. 57a, 87a; English translation, pp. 285, 424—to be of a Neoplatonic character.

113. Avicenna, *Shifā': Ilāhīyāt*, pp. 405-406; Ghazali, *Maqāṣid al-Falāsifa*, p. 216; Maimonides, *Guide*, II, 4.

114. Averroes, *Long Commentary on Metaphysics*, XII, comm. 44; H. Wolfson, "Averroes' Lost Treatise on the Prime Mover," reprinted in his *Studies in the History of Philosophy and Religion*, p. 425.

115. Avicenna, *Shifā': Ilāhīyāt*, pp. 386-387, 399-401; Ghazali, *Maqāṣid al-Falāsifa*, pp. 209-210; Maimonides, *Guide*, II, 4.

116. Cf. Averroes, *De Substantia Orbis*, II; III; *Middle Commentary on De Caelo*, Vatican Hebrew ms. Urb. 40, p. 50b. See commentaries of Narboni and Shem Tov on *Guide*, II, 4; P. Duhem, *Le Système du Monde*, IV (Paris, 1916) pp. 548-551. In his *De Substantia Orbis*, VI, his *Long Commentary on Metaphysics*, XII, comm. 41, and his *Tahāfut al-Tahāfut*, pp. 184-185, Averroes recognizes both a rational soul in each sphere as well as an intelligence apart from, and paralleling the sphere.

117. Cf. above, n. 87.

118. *Dialoghi d'Amore*, pp. 159-160, 282; Hebrew translation, pp. 36b-37a, 67b; English translation, pp. 183-185, 333.

119. *Dialoghi d'Amore*, pp. 160-161; Hebrew translation, pp. 37a-b; English translation, pp. 185-186.

120. On p. 246—Hebrew translation, p. 58a; English translation, p. 290—Leone cites Ibn Gabirol's *Fons Vitae*.

121. *Nefutzot Yehuda*, §8, p. 21b.

122. As regards Plotinus, the statement that the "cosmic soul emanates the physical universe" would have to be qualified. See above, n. 3.

123. He quotes Pico's "small work . . . on heavenly and divine love," to the effect that the Platonists call the first intelligence "God's son." Moscato is struck by the expression because he understands that Proverbs 30:4 also terms the first being created by God, His "son." The reference to Pico is to his commentary on Benivieni, *Dell' Amore Celeste e Divino*, pp. 15-17; English paraphrase, pp. 5-6. Pico stresses there that the son of God, or first created being, of the Platonists—that is to say, of the Neoplatonists—is not identical with the son of God of the Christians.

124. Presumably Plato's Idea of the Good.

125. *Nefutzot Yehuda*, §8, p. 21b.

126. Above, n. 53. Moscato presumably believes that the Greeks borrowed their cosmology from the Jews. See above, nn. 54-55.

127. The well known Aggadic passage explaining how God created "the light"; *Bereshit Rabba*, III, 4, and parallels.

128. *Nefutzot Yehuda*, §9, p. 22b.

129. Ibid., p. 23a.

130. Avicenna, *Commentary on the Theology of Aristotle*, Arabic text in *Arisṭu ʿind al-ʿArab*, ed. A. Badawi (Cairo, 1947), pp. 60-61; French translation: G. Vajda, "Notes d'Avicenne sur la Théologie d'Aristote," *Revue thomiste* LI (1951), pp. 384-385; Avicenna, *Risâleleri*, II (Istanbul, 1953), p. 78.

131. See D. Rosin, "Die Religionsphilosophie Abraham ibn Esra's," *MGWJ*, XLII (1898), p. 209.

132. *Torat ha-Ola*, I, p. 6a.

133. Ibid., III, pp. 20a, 22a.

134. Ibid., III, p. 81b.

135. Ibid., I, p. 15a; III, pp. 16b, 84b.

136. Ibid., I, p. 15a.

137. Ibid., III, pp. 16b, 84b.

138. Isserles, ibid., 6a, refers to Arama and Baḥya b. Asher on Exodus. See also Ibn Ezra's commentary on Exodus, introduction to chapter 26.

139. *Mishna Middot.* For convenience Isserles uses Maimonides' restatement of the Mishna in *Mishne Tora, H. Bet ha-Beḥira.*

140. *Torat ha-Ola*, I, 6b. There may be a kabbalistic echo here.

141. Ibid. Cf. above, n. 108.

142. *Guide*, I, 72 (beginning).

143. *Guide*, II, 10. The factors are: the spherical shape of the sphere; the soul of the sphere; the rational faculty of that soul; and the incorporeal intelligence paralleling the sphere.

144. *Guide*, I, 72.
145. *Torat ha-Ola*, I, p. 7a.
146. Ibid., pp. 8a-b.
147. BT *Pesaḥim*, 94b. Cf. Twersky, "Joseph ibn Kaspi," p. 256, n. 52.
148. *Guide*, II, 8.
149. Isserles connects the rabbis' theory to Ezekiel I:24; cf. *Guide*, II, 8.
150. Isserles, *Meḥir Yayin* (Amsterdam, 1769), p. 9a.
151. *Guide*, II, 11. The thought is not original with Maimonides.
152. Cf. Maimonides, *Guide*, I, 71.
153. *Meḥir Yayin*, p. 9a; *Torat ha-Ola*, I, p. 5a.
154. *Guide*, II, 22. See H. Davidson, "Maimonides' Secret Position on Creation," *Studies in Medieval Jewish History and Literature*, pp. 30-31.
155. *Torat ha-Ola*, III, p. 41a.
156. Judah Loeb, *Derekh Ḥayyim* (London, 1960), pp. 56-57 (on *Avot* I:18).
157. *Tiferet Yisrael*, p. 39; *Derekh Ḥayyim*, p. 57.
158. *Be'er ha-Gola*, p. 109. Judah Loeb refers to BT *Bava Batra*, 74a, which he understands as meaning that the spheres do rotate.
159. Ibid., p. 110; to be harmonized with *Netivot Olam*, VIII, 2, p. 223.
160. The cosmic significance of love is a theme found in Avicenna's *R. fi'l-Ishq*, ed. M. Mehren, in *Traités Mystiques . . . d'Avicenne*, III (Leiden, 1894). English translation: E. Fackenheim, "A Treatise on Love by Ibn Sina," *Mediaeval Studies*, VII (1945), pp. 208-228.
161. Ficino and Pico had also cited and allegorized Greek mythology.
162. A list is assembled by I. Bettan, "The Sermons of Judah Moscato," *HUCA*, VI (1929), p. 305.

Aspects of Hebrew Ethical Literature in Sixteenth-Century Poland

JACOB ELBAUM

I

The centrality of Poland in sixteenth-century Jewish life is well known. The great majority of Ashkenazic Jews lived there, and Polish Jewry held a position of leadership among all Ashkenazim. This leadership role, however, was not merely a result of the numerical preponderance of its Jewish population as compared to the other Ashkenazic centers in Germany and northern Italy. Quantity that is not combined with quality cannot attain a position of leadership. The ascendancy of Polish Jewry obviously resulted from its transformation into the main center of Torah study of that generation, and in this connection it is sufficient to mention such figures as Rabbi Jacob Pollack (regarded as the founder of the Polish rabbinate), R. Shalom Shakhna, R. Solomon Luria, R. Moses Isserles and their disciples. Yet it is problematic whether Polish-Jewish leadership in spiritual matters was based solely upon such centrality as regards the Halakhah, or whether there were not also other areas in which it excelled, at least within the bounds of Ashkenazic Jewry.

It is difficult to give a clear-cut answer to this question for one simple reason: The scholarly study of the cultural *oeuvre* of Ashkenazic Jewry during the period in question is still in its infancy. This is one of the periods upon which general and cultural historians have barely touched.[1] Though I shall not attempt a general analysis of this problem here, I nevertheless wish to point out that, with the exception of MaHaRaL and his circle in Prague who constitute a distinct entity in several respects, much more unites than divides the writers who were active throughout the various regions of the Ashkenazic cultural sphere. Moreover, for all his uniqueness, even MaHaRaL is a typical representative of the Ashkenazic author of his time. Let us delineate the characteristic elements of the Ashkenazic Jewish *oeuvre* of sixteenth-century Poland.

Any answer to a general question of this sort must necessarily be a generalization, perhaps even an oversimplification. This danger is a familiar one to scholars. The risk I take, however, is not an overwhelming one. The available facts show that all the historic genres of Hebrew literature find expression, to a greater or lesser extent, in this generation. Thus, it is not surprising that these works also expressed ideologies that had been espoused by previous generations: i.e., philosophical ideas, the views of the various kabbalistic systems, and, needless to say, the independent manifestations of "traditional" Ashkenazic thought — especially the different schools of ethical (*musar*) literature. This feature is not merely an incidental or marginal phenomenon; it constitutes the mainstream of the literary output of that generation, and this fact in itself is something of a novelty.[2] These authors became receptive to many intellectual currents; in fact they displayed receptivity to all the spiritual trends in the Jewish world of the time. However, even if this itself is of interest as a cultural phenomenon, the cumulative significance of this phenomenon upon the internal structure and the historical development of the various systems must still be clarified. A solution to this last question can be achieved only through detailed and exhaustive studies of the various literary genres in which the scholars of these generations chose to express their views.

Hence, there is a two-fold difficulty: First there is the difficulty of arriving at the significant statements on the various topics; and then there is the difficulty of isolating what is new in these statements. I am referring here to a special problem that is presented by the literature of that generation. Although scholars of that period adopted the various modes of expression which earlier philosophers or kabbalists had employed, this is not the only or even the most important plane on which this literature operated, even when it was concerned with subjects treated by these intellectual systems. It is difficult therefore to discover what is new in this literature, and even more so to characterize and define it, especially in so short a study as this. Nevertheless, two things can be demonstrated without much difficulty, one regarding content and the other regarding form. I refer, first of all, to the fact that in both *musar* literature and in the speculative literature of the time we can discern an effort to unite the various intellectual approaches, even where these are contradictory. The attempt at unification may or may not prove spiritually fruitful, but in any case it testifies to an awareness of spiritual problems and an effort to grapple with them.

Secondly, I refer to the problem of the modes of expression employed by this literature. I have already remarked that the authors of the period did not necessarily choose to express their opinions by means of the traditional genres for *musar* and speculative literature. It is true that we also find systematic moralistic works, i.e., books that describe in detail the totality of spiritual stages and types of conduct through which a man must pass if he is to achieve perfection (among these works should be included some books, or rather parts of books, by R. Solomon Ephraim Luntshitz; and if we choose not to limit ourselves to Poland, we seem to have a perfect example in *Netivot Olam* of MaHaRaL [Prague, 1595–96]), moralistic monographs (such as *Brit Avraham* by R. Abraham Horowitz [Lublin, 1577; Cracow 1602]), ethical wills (such as *Yesh Noḥalin* by the same author), books of instruction for proper behavior (*hanhagot*, such as the *Hanhagot MaHaRSHaL*, which was published only in our time; *Petaḥ Enayim* by R. Moses Yakar Ashkenazi [*ed. princeps*, Cracow before 1600]; *Lema'an Telekh be-Derekh Tovim* by R. Hirsh b. R. Henokh Zundel [Cracow, 1604], as well as the *tikunim* literature of the seventeenth century, with which I shall deal below), anthologies of moralistic maxims, usually bi-lingual (such as *Mar'e Musar*, i.e. the *Tzucht Spiegel* by R. Zelikman Ulme, and similar works).[3] However, as indicated, this does not constitute the main stream of the *musar* literature of that period, which appeared principally in the form of books of "glosses" (*hagahot*) and exegesis, and especially in various types of homiletical works (*drush*). Indeed it sometimes found expression in the guise of halakhic monographs, collections of responsa and so forth. We must not forget that study of Halakhah lay at the center of the spiritual activity of those generations, and therefore it is not surprising that halakhic tomes were filled with short or lengthy remarks on matters of *musar*, or even on theoretical issues. The domains of law and morality (and to some extent certain speculative issues as well) were never unconnected, certainly not during the period under discussion.[4]

In the exegetical literature of this period, and not only in works built around the Book of Proverbs or *Pirkei Avot* that inherently lend themselves to moralistic discussion, we find an extra emphasis on allegorical moralistic interpretaions, a tendency that is most obvious in the *drush* literature of the time.[5] Moreover, even systematic ethical treatises tend to take on the appearance of homilies rather than organizing their material along the lines of the classical works of ethical literature, except that they are arranged according to a different organizing principle; i.e., not according to the order of the Torah portions, etc., but rather around certain ethical subjects. Yet why *drush* became the chief vehicle of *musar* literature must be clarified. Does this phenomenon express an inability to master the demands of the genre? Or, perhaps we should find some positive explanation for this turning to the method of *drush*. At first sight it would seem that they were in fact incapable of satisfying the demands of the genre, for which Ashkenazic literature lacks any real literary tradition,[6] and that therefore they chose to express their views through *drush*, which would appear to offer a less rigid framework, and which is intrinsically less demanding. If so, then perhaps it also indicates a degree of impotence with regard to originality, and a certain inability on the part of the authors of the period who dealt with ethics. Indeed, it still remains for us to determine whether there is in fact a solid foundation to the axiom that is presupposed by what we have said about the equation between the flimsiness of the formal framework and the lack of ability or method. I cannot treat this subject at length here, but it is sufficient to state that this assumption (which is almost taken for granted in the study of Jewish intellectual history) is a very dubious one.[7] Those who accept it assume from the first that only a systematic exposition is able to represent a system (this assumption is in itself incorrect). They overlook the fact that Hebrew literature has seldom bent itself to the demands of systematic exposition. To some extent, such systematization is the result of foreign influences which were adapted more or less completely by only one Jewish center, that of Spain and its satellites (its origins were actually in the Orient, in the works of R. Sa'adya Gaon) — and even this only in certain varieties, and only in certain literary areas. The Ashkenazic literary tradition never completely adopted systematic presentations, and certainly not as a main vehicle for expressing its views.[8]

While we are still within the realm of generalizations, we ought to review one more rule that is of relevance to traditional Hebrew literature, namely the fact that people in a traditional milieu often prefer to de-emphasize their original statements rather than to emphasize them. Writers of this period, who were exposed to all the manifestations of the spiritual traditions of previous ages, and who had to digest quickly all the various ideas with which they came in contact, imposed upon themselves a sort of modesty with regard both to their attitudes to the writings of their predecessors, and to their expression of their own views. At times this was true modesty, at times feigned. The method of *drush* was perfectly fitted for such expressions of modesty. It does not demand that its proponents commit themselves to a declaration of principles. Indeed, we must check what use the authors made of this method. Furthermore, systematic *musar* literature, especially that of the period in question, must also be examined from a similar perspective, since in it too we find at times that original ideas are being masked by quotations and ascriptions to famous authorities, so that the true nature of these works can be ascertained only through careful investigation.

If my suggestions about the character of the literature of this period are correct, it would seem that we can proceed a step further and learn an important principle regarding the particular status of *musar* literature, exegetical literature, and *drush* literature (all of which, as we have indicated, were intermingled to a point where they defy differentiation): that it is in these genres in particular that we ought to seek expression of the original thinking of those generations. In other words, within the given cultural milieu, these literatures, which in several previous cultural milieus served only as second-rate vehicles of expression for the intellectual developments of their times, became in the era under discussion the primary means of expressing such developments. And I would almost go so far as to suggest as a general rule that this is perhaps one of the characteristic elements of Ashkenazic literature in almost every age (but this is not the place to discuss this subject.)[9]

II

I have already indicated the connections that exist between the literature of this period and all the various intellectual theories that flourished in previous eras, and I have referred to the ways in which they are expressed, i.e., the attempts to harmonize the various approaches. Indeed, in several areas one can notice an emphasis on, or a leaning toward, one of the traditional approaches.

There are some elements that became inseparable parts of ethical writing, and it was difficult for a contemporary to refrain from using them. Thus, when speaking of the relations between body and soul the style is Neoplatonic (influenced, of course, by R. Baḥya, author of *The Duties of the Heart*, and his successors). On the other hand, advice on the proper norms of moral conduct often contains echoes of Aristotelean moral theory; that is, the concept of the "golden mean." Needless to say, Maimonides is cited.[10] In the description of the struggle against desire we can recognize the emphasis of medieval German pietists, *Ḥasidei Ashkenaz*. We have no maps for the subjects dealt with by *musar* literature through the ages, yet it seems possible to assert that during the period in question there was much discussion of social ethics (among other topics: the subjects of hypocrisy [*ziyuf*], quarrels, slander, charity and philanthropy, faithfulness, etc.),[11] of the ways of divine justice, the influence of the stars and the merit of the Forefathers (and hence of such subjects as faith and trust in God, simplicity, frugality, etc.). Here we find a utilization of ideological foundations that came from the writings of the *Ḥasidei Ashkenaz*.[12] Indeed, in these areas we can recognize also an element of originality which sometimes is apparent only in the conclusions — but sometimes also in the method — in the attitude to authors of earlier ages. The influence of *Ḥasidei Ashkenaz* is no less discernable in discussions of sin and repentance. Indeed in this connection we may trace the efforts to build upon the foundations of their heritage, the heritage of *Ḥasidei Ashkenaz*, a superstructure which can give expression to the other approaches: e.g., the doctrine of repentance found in the philosophical ethical literature (as it appears in the writings of Sa'adya, R. Baḥya and Maimonides) and in its rabbinic offshoot (in *Sha'arei Tshuva* and other writings of

R. Jonah Gerondi) and last, but not least, the doctrines that were formulated in the schools of the kabbalistic moralists. Furthermore, certain foundations of the doctrine of repentance that had been laid down in the literature of the *Ḥasidei Ashkenaz*, were presented in the literature of this period in forms which they had been given in the kabbalistic moralistic literature.[13] Perhaps more than in any other area, the influence of the Kabbalah on the literature of this period may be discerned in a literary genre that developed for the most part outside the period under discussion: I refer to the *tikunim* literature, which is an extension of the *hanhagot* literature. In this literature elaborations of the commandments and modes of moral-pietistic conduct that influence all facets of life were presented.

The arguments presented thus far undoubtedly need further strengthening. Moreover, it seems that we can very easily discern that, even though they were expressed in the form of declarative statements, the declarative form was merely stylistic; and in truth they contained important questions that can be answered only through many specific studies. Perhaps this is the nature of generalizations. A historian needs them but when he acts with humility (and anyone outlining aspects of the history of ethical literature should act humbly) he knows well that all generalizations are conditional. In this connection I shall take it upon myself to outline briefly two issues: (a) the question of the relationships between the *drush* literature (and to a certain extent also the exegetical literature) and the *musar* literature during the period under discussion; and (b) one detail regarding the ideological justification and background of publishing the customs of kabbalists in books of *hanhagot* and *tikunim*.

III

I have pointed out that we possess only a few examples of varieties of systematic ethical literature among the writings of the authors of this period, as opposed to a wealth of references to ethical issues in other literary genres. It should be noted, however, that this phenomenon was characteristic not only of the literary work of the Ashkenazim, much less was it limited to Poland. The appearance of systematic *musar* works became progressively less common as the philosophical method was rejected. It is true that the revival of this literary genre was influenced by the development of kabbalistic ethical literature. Nevertheless, it must be remembered that most of the latest discussions of ethical issues available to the authors of this period were included in other works. Furthermore, the scholars of that generation could also find a strong element of *drush* in several systematic *musar* and speculative books that were popular then, such as *Kad ha-Kemaḥ* by R. Baḥya b. Asher, the *Ikarim* by R. Joseph Albo, and R. Elijah de Vidas' *Reshit Ḥokhma* which had an immeasurable influence on authors who wrote at the turn of the seventeenth century. Besides, for several generations Hebrew literature had witnessed a steady increase in the importance of homiletic and exegetical literature composed in the manner of homilies, and this had had a decisive influence on the Ashkenazi authors. Arama's *Akedat Yitzḥak*, the works of Abravanel and of Joseph Yavetz and, around the beginning of the seventeenth century, the commentaries of Alsheikh were among the most frequently cited works in the literature of the period.[14]

To return to the issue of the types of exposition used in *musar* literature we note that in the introduction to the "*Homily for Passover*," in his book *Oraḥ le-Ḥayyim*, R. Solomon Luntshitz explains his reasons for resorting to the *drush* form:

> But if the servant of the Lord should speak only through moralistic reproof he will be put to mockery by the many *musar* books that lie unused in discarded corners; and since I have seen that many people have indicated a longing to read some novel homily (*drush ḥidush*), I therefore decided to supply this demand for words of moral rebuke against sin, which may be read in passing. Just as we train children in Torah by giving them sweets, so also my ethical teaching will be read by me and people of my sort who are in need of it, but the few righteous men who have been called by the Lord and who cherish the divine Torah in their hearts have no need for all this.[15]

As we see here, the whole purpose of *musar* literature lies in the fact that it leads to concrete action (and hence the reason, it seems, for his use of the phrase "moralistic reproof," *musar tokheḥa*[16]). Hence, if at any time it does not fulfill its function within certain social contexts, it is the duty of anyone who seeks to improve his contemporaries to seek ways of achieving this goal.[17] The most effective way, in the opinion of R. Solomon Ephraim, is the *drush ḥidush*—the novel homily[18]—"*drush* and *musar* combined."[19] The *drush* is merely a vehicle and the author reiterates on several occasions that he is not interested in "the homily itself, but rather in reading the moralistic teachings imbedded therein that they may be read by way of reading the homily, the homily being subordinate to them; and by accepting the moral teaching our ways shall lead us towards God for life."[20] He states that his intention is not "to offer original explanations of biblical and rabbinic passages."[21] He and others severely criticize preachers whose chief interest is in novelty rather than moral rebuke, theory rather than practical application. He also criticizes their audiences who "do not care that there is no ethical teaching" in the homilies.[22] The duty of the moralist preachers is to

be jealous for the Lord's cause and to chastise the congregation publicly for their sins, as it is written (Is. 58:1): 'As a trumpet lift your voice and call my people to account for their transgressions.' The Hebrew word, 'call to account' is *ve-haged* which is similar to *gadya*, 'sinew'—implying that you must chastise them with words as hard as sinews, and not find farfetched interpretations of Talmudic dicta or novel explanations of bibilical passages so that people should praise you saying: 'What a clever man he is who knows what is hidden in the darkness, who can transform the dictum or verse at will until it is completely altered.' What benefit is there in this?[23]

This is the way which he himself had chosen: "I have written a few books in all of which my chief aim was not various novel interpretations. Rather my sole objective was to include in them a great deal of moral teaching, which is sorely needed in this particular generation."[24] Everyone should follow this course:

It is proper to decree in every congregation that a discourse be preached on the Sabbath on moral issues and the laws of the Torah, instead of unearthing new meanings of *midrashim*, because the general public does not need this. This was the custom of our predecessors, all of whose homilies were devoted to teaching the laws of the Torah and moral teachings, to awaken those who slumber in the sleep of time and remember not their ultimate fate.[25]

For him, the *drush* is the only instrument to right what is wrong, namely "the lack of moral rebuke,"[26] to open the gates of morality that have been locked.[27]

From his unambiguous subordination of the *drush* to *musar*[28] and his bending of *musar* in the direction of "reproof," it would seem implicit that the homilies and moral teachings had been purged of all elemments of theory, of everything abstract that did not lend itself to immediate application. To a certain degree this conclusion is correct. By its own declaration *musar* literature is a literature that is addressed to the masses and not to elite cliques of *maskilim* or *mevinim* (the enlightened, cognoscenti); it must, therefore, come down from the heights of abstraction and move from the complex toward the simple.[29] Furthermore, this is accompanied by anxiety about indulging in speculations "based on conjecture," and implies as a practical principle

> reliance on the authentic tradition, searching out only the locations of the verses and dicta that testify to, and relate, the faithful testimony of the Lord regarding the existence of God, all the fundamental doctrines of our Torah and all acceptable deeds which, if a man shall do, he shall live by them eternal life, and tell of the way of life, reproofs of instruction designed to awaken those who are sleeping in the slumber of time and forget the truth because of the world.[30]

Note however that this principle is, in effect, self-contradictory. From the above quotation we learn of the existence of certain principles that lead one to deal with *drush*. It is not susceptible to every passing whim (at least not in every instance) and even if an author does not make a formal declaration of his fundamental guiding principles, this does not necessarily imply that his work is completely lacking an ideological basis.

As clarification I shall cite a few comments of MaHaRaL in the introduction to his *Netivot Olam* (a work which is obviously not divorced from very clear theoretical principles). His intention as he states it, is merely to assemble the statements in the Talmud "which chastise men in good and right ways . . . and to explain the words of the Sages, nothing else." It goes without saying that he was consciously understating the value of his work and its originality. There are authors who try to create an illusion of originalty. MaHaRaL's desire was exactly the opposite. He tried to disguise what was novel in his writing. The method of R. Solomon Ephraim Luntshitz is in some respects similar, but in others different from that of MaHaRaL. The similarity rests in the use of a medium for expressing moral matters, while the difference is (at least at first glance) in the declared relation of the respective authors to their writings. R. Solomon feels that the *drush* per se is merely subordinate, whereas MaHaRaL does not see his original contributions in this light. Apparently he regards his own remarks as the correct explanation, or at any rate as "truth." This distinction that I have drawn between the attitudes of these two authors to their own writings was too clear-cut. There still exists yet another aspect common to the two — the fact that the sources do actually fit their interpretations.[31] Moreover, in the works of both authors (as well as in those of many others) we find a desire to arrange their work in such a manner that it does not consist merely of a string of quotations with commentaries.[32]

An examination of the theoretical frameworks that underlie the sermons and homilies of R. Solomon Ephraim Luntshitz (and of his contemporaries in Poland) is desirable. I have used his words only to examine the literary means used by writers of this period to express their views on the subject under discussion; I did not enter into further detail.[33] It will suffice to find in them further support (I suggest this more as argument than as proof) for what I have already written about the flexibility of the *drush* framework. It allows for minimal reference to the earlier intellectual-literary tradition. Thus, we stand before an interesting paradox; i.e., that precisely in the places where we find signs of weakness in the *drush* framework, we also discern evidence of its strength, or at least of its breadth of spirit. Because it has no necessary allegiance to any single system, we see clearly the thread of the fabric as a whole, as well as the connecting stitches; and we can recognize the desire of the authors to relate to all the nuances of various previous theories, to weld them together and to extract from them what they needed.

This tendency is recongizable also in the *musar* literature that was composed on the eve of the seventeenth century and during its early decades. The unambiguous nature of the halakhic decisions of the period is not noticeable in the realms of ideas and *musar*. Indeed, there are clear signs of progressive strengthening of the tendency to turn to kabbalistic literature and its derivatives in the realm of *musar* literature. R. Solomon Ephraim refers to the opinions of kabbalists only rarely,[34] and then too usually with an allusion to the "enlightened" or "illuminati"[35] (these references are generally based on the Zohar, Baḥya, Recanati, the *Ḥizkuni*, *Tzror ha-Mor*, and the *Akedat Yitzḥak*.[36] This is not the case among his younger contemporaries whose references are completely explicit.

IV.

The dominant influence of the Kabbalah on the thought of the period cannot be attributed to any single element; nor is it possible to fix a single date for this change. It was the result of a process. By the end of the sixteenth century, references to kabbalistic books were becoming more and more frequent.[37] Glosses and commentaries were composed to some of the more important ones[38] and commentators and homilists would quietly insert into their works more and more kabbalistic subjects, particularly in the field of *musar*. One of the best known scholars of the age, R. Issachar b. R. Naphtali ha-Kohen of Szczebzeszyn, author of the well-known commentary on the *Midrash Raba — Matnot Kehuna*, also edited an index to the Zohar entitled *Mar'e Kohen* (Cracow, 1589), in which he deliberately assembled from the Zohar "literal explanations, allusions, exegetical comments, interpretations and terrible warnings that point with a finger saying: This is the path you shall follow in every action which a man shall do and live by them two sorts of life." In seventeen chapters, he tried to extract whatever pertained to the deepening of religious activity, both with regard to observance of the commandments and the field of ethics. This indicates a characteristic orientation. The authors of the period did not often deal in depth with the theosophical problems that distinguish the various streams of Kabbalah (at least they do not write about them), and even express hesitation as to whether one should accept the halakhic conclusions that can be derived from the detailed study of Kabbalah, insofar as these conclusions contradict the accepted law. But many referred to the kabbalistic statements regarding the nature of the Torah (the first chapter of the index mentioned above is titled "The Light of the Torah"), anthropological principles as manifested in the Zoharic literature,[39] and the fundamentals of the doctrine of repentance. They also adopted the customs that became standard among the leading proponents of Kabbalah.

It is against this background that we may find an explanation for the profusion of references to the customs of the kabbalists in the writings of the scholars of this generation which ultimately brought about an internal revival of an almost forgotten literary genre, namely the *hanhagot* or *hadrakha*. I refer principally to the *tikunim* literature.[40] The first appearance of this genre takes place in the seventeenth century, in the wake of the publication of *The Tikunim of Repentance Compiled by the 'Whelps' of the ARI in His Name* and *The Tikunim for Sabbath of R. Abraham Berukhim the Elder*, which were appended to the *Abbreviated 'Reshit Ḥokhma'* by MaHaRI Poito (Venice, 1600; Basle, 1603), and therefore we will not discuss it here. I will discuss only one issue, and that briefly, regarding the ideological justification that accompanies the activity in this field: i.e., the doctrine that there is religious significance also to the performance of actions whose theological basis is unknown to us. R. Judah ha-Kohen, author of *Tikunim for the Sabbath. . ., Order for the Outgoing of the Sabbath, Tikun for the Eve of Pentecost and the Eve of Hoshana Raba* (1613), and *Order and Tikunim of the Recitation of the "Shma" before Bedtime attributed to R. Moses Cordovero and the ARI, and Tikun for the Night Vigil according to the ARI* (Prague, 1615), asks in the latter work:

> Does everyone really know the secrets of the Torah, so that they should be able to recite with proper *kavana*? This is impossible. So what advantage is there for them in reciting this *Shma*, the words of the Living God, as if it were but a precept of men learnt by rote?

And he supplied his own answer, according to the words of the Zohar (*Pekudei*), that the prayer of those who do not know the proper *kavana* combines with that of those who do know, "and they become bound as one." His advice is therefore that "everyone, small and great, should take care in reciting the *Shma* and all its regulations, in its totality as well as in its particulars, to the extent of their ability."[41] In a similar vein writes R. Joseph Yozefa Han in *Yosef Ometz*:

> I have also written some of the teachings of kabbalists, in spite of the fact that I composed this work only for the masses, and my familiarity with that subject is minimal. In any case, since those matters allude to great and wondrous things, they should be observed even if we understand nothing of their mysteries.[42]

This shows us that there is an active force in deeds, even if the doers are not aware of the nature of their actions.

Although this argument is not expressed by all those who mention the customs of the kabbalists, we may assume that it is behind those references, whether they occur in halakhic literature (a subject that should be dealt with separately)[43] or in *musar* literature.[44]

It ultimately led to the self-assertion of this genre. It appears that the words of R. Jacob of Szczebrezszyn, in his glosses to *Yesh Noḥalin* by his father R. Abraham Horowitz, are typical. He opposed those who argue that

we need not be scrupulous about those actions which we are bidden to observe, perform and uphold, unless they are explicitly stipulated as obligatory in the Talmud; but those things and matters mentioned as not obligatory in the Talmud and matters written in the Zohar and other pious works are not binding.

In his opinion whoever does not observe them is in fact exempt from human punishment, but is deemed guilty according to divine law, and will ultimately have to face judgment.[45]

There is no doubt that two elements combined here. One was the traditional heteronomistic concepts of the commandments, an approach that is aptly expressed in the words of R. Ḥayyim b. Betzalel in his *Sefer ha-Ḥayyim*, in the "Book of Merits":

In the final account, the proper belief is that each and every commandment is suspended from a part of the divine chariot, and even though the ways of the Torah and its mysteries are concealed from us we should be careful in performing all the words of the Torah.[46]

The second element is the strengthening of the assertion that the kabbalists profess the "true wisdom." Little wonder, then, that this matter found its expression in special literary vehicles. The tendency to dress new ideas in old garments is a traditional one in *musar* literature. Only rarely does this literature adopt revolutionary changes. It prefers to rejuvenate the old. This is the case with the *tikunim* literature, and this is the nature of the "innovative *drush*," the *drush meḥudash*, which achieved expression in the plethora of works composed in the sixteenth century. It remained the method of this literature in the seventeenth century as well. Indeed, the interplay of new and old in the *musar* literature of the seventeenth century, and particularly that from before 1648–49, still awaits further clarification.

NOTES

1. See for now the studies by Ḥ. H. Ben-Sasson (infra, nn. 11–12); J. Katz, *Tradition and Crisis* (New York, 1961), especially ch. 17; and G. Scholem, "The Sabbatean Movement in Poland" (Hebrew), in I. Heilpern, ed., *Bet Yisrael be-Folin*, vol. 2 (Jerusalem, 1954), pp. 36–40.

2. On the attitude to philosophy in the 14th and 15th centuries, see E. Kupfer, "Concerning the Cultural Image of German Jewry and its Rabbis in the Fourteenth and Fifteenth Centuries" (Hebrew), *Tarbitz* 42 (1973), pp. 113–147.

3. Yiddish *musar* literature demands a separate study: for the time being, see Ch. Shmeruk, "Basic Characteristics of Yiddish Literature in Poland and Lithuania up until *Gzerot Taḥ ve-Tat*" (Hebrew), *Tarbitz* 46 (1977), pp. 258–314. On the genres of *musar* literature see I. Tishby and J. Dan, *Hebrew Ethical Literature* (Hebrew) (Jerusalem and Tel-Aviv, 1970), pp. xi–xii (of the introduction).

4. This is readily apparent if we look at *Seder Berakhot* by R. Yeḥiel Mikhel Moraptshik (Cracow, 1582) or *Emek Brakha* by R. Abraham Horowitz (Cracow, 1597). The digressions to ethical matters are very common.

5. This, e.g., in R. Moses b. R. Isaac of Biezenz, *Darash Moshe* (Cracow, 1589) a commentary on 256 Talmudic *aggadot*. The main topics dealt with therein are the questions of body and soul, the problem of the attitude to this world and material things (especially chs. 1, 2, 18, 22, 28, and 153), repentance and similar subjects. The author most frequently cited in the book seems to be "the chief spokesman in all forums, the great eagle, Maimonides" (ch. 125, p. 42d) who is cited mostly to clarify the nature of the use of moderation in moral qualities (although reference is also made to the *Guide to the Perplexed*). Kabbalistic matters are referred to in his writings only rarely, and indirectly; on this, see my "Trends and Courses in Jewish Speculative and Moralistic Literature" (Ph.D. dissertation, Hebrew University, 1977), p. 191 n. 98 (hereafter: "Trends and Courses") and my remarks on R. Solomon Ephraim Luntshitz, infra.

6. The case of *Orḥot Tzadikim* does not pose a contradiction. It demands clarification. (We have no knowledge about the identity of the author or his dates). The same goes for those halakhic works which contain somewhat systematic discussions of ethical questions. Most of these discussions concern one issue—repentance.

7. The roots of this assumption are to be traced to the researches of the "Wissenschaft des Judentums" school, which was repelled by the irrational, and for ideological reasons despised anything that was expressed awkwardly. In this matter, modern scholarship has not freed itself altogether from their conceptions. Although there has been some progress (e.g., in the study of mysticism and its offshoots), this has not yet occurred in any area that does not fit into a "recognized" ideological "system." This question deserves to be discussed separately.

8. A fine proof of this can be found in the works of MaHaRaL. Though these works are entirely exegetical-homiletical their internal integrity seems beyond all doubt; see A. F. Kleinberger, *Ha-Maḥshava ha-Pedagogit shel ha-MaHaRaL mi-Prag* (The Educational Philosophy of the MaHaRaL of Prague; Jerusalem, 1962); my article, "Rabbi Judah Loew of Prague and his attitude to Aggadah," *Scripta Hierosolymitana* 22 (1971), pp. 28–47; and "Trends and Courses," pp. 209–304, 329–340, 421–430, 472–482.

9. Cf. Tishby and Dan, *Hebrew Ethical Literature*, introduction, pp. xiv–xvii; J. Dan, *Sifrut ha-Musar ve-ha-Drush* (Hebrew Ethical and Homiletical Literature; Jerusalem, 1975), pp. 15–16.

10. R. Abraham Horowitz records, in the introduction to his commentary to Maimonides' *Eight Chapters* and Ibn Tibbon's introduction to it, a custom (in Prague?) "for some years now to listen to the *Eight Chapters* between terms." (This commentary has come down to us in two versions—Lublin, 1577 and Cracow, 1602. The differences between the two versions remain to be clarified; for the moment see "Trends and Courses" pp. 141–142.) It seems permissible to generalize and say that most scholars of that generation had no qualms about using the *Guide to the Perplexed* and the words of "the great eagle full of feathers and great wings, he shall speak—is he not the great Rabbi Moses Maimonides of blessed memory in his *Guide to the Perplexed*" (*Mizbaḥ ha-Zahav*, Basle, 1602, ch. 24, p. 34b).

Maimonides was also designated one of the "divine persons" (ibid., ch. 11, p. 18a). Glosses and annotations to the *Guide* were also composed by R. Moses Isserles (*Otzar Ḥokhma* 2 & 3) and R. Mordekhai Jaffe (*Levush Pinat Yikrat*). Isserles also wrote, following R. Yeda'ya in *Beḥinat Olam*, that Maimonides was "the last of the *Geonim* in time and the greatest in degree . . . and even though some scholars disagreed with him and burned his books, nevertheless his books have now gained acceptance among all the latter-day scholars of blessed memory, and they all have made his books a crown for their heads, to be cited as if decreed before Moses at Sinai" (*Responsa* of Isserles, no. 7). Powerful remarks in praise of Maimonides were written by R. Abraham in his polemic with R. Joseph Ashkenazi. It is in fact the attacks of R. Joseph Ashkenazi, who regards Maimonides as a "complete heretic," that are extraordinary; v. on this "Trends and Courses," pp. 123–125, 134–141. See also ibid., pp. 121–123, 136–139, on R. Solomon Luria's criticism of the tendency towards "foreign wisdom."

11. Some of these subjects were dealt with by my late teacher Ḥ. H. Ben-Sasson, *Hagut ve-Hanhaga* (Jerusalem, 1959).

12. Such as the "doctrine of the deposit"; see Ben-Sasson, *Hagut ve-Hanhaga*, pp. 73–76 and the index as well as his article "Wealth and Poverty in the Teaching of the Preacher Reb Ephraim of Lenczyca" (Hebrew), *Zion* 19 (1954), pp. 142–166.

13. Particularly noticeable is the influence of R. Elijah de Vidas' *Reshit Ḥokhma*, also published in Cracow, 1593–4.

14. *Kad ha-Kemaḥ* was published in Cracow, 1596–1597, and the *Ikarim* in Lublin, 1597. We also have a commentary on the *Ikarim* by one of the scholars of that age, R. Jacob b. R. Samuel of Brisk (*Ohel Ya'akov*, Freiburg, 1584; Cracow, 1599). The above list tells us also about the spiritual interests of authors of this period. The works named reflect much of the variety of approaches among medieval scholars. There are among them works of authors who were dubbed in contemporary writings "divine philosophers" (e.g. Arama), of opponents of philosophy (Abravanel and Yavetz), of kabbalists (de Vidas) and works belonging to rabbinic *musar* literature (e.g., *Kad ha-Kemaḥ*). Arama's *Akedat Yitzḥak* had an inestimable influence on authors of this period. Several authors used this work as an intermediary to the philosophical literature in two ways: (a) as a guide to it and (b) as a "sanction" for some of the views expressed therein (perhaps this applies also to the author of *Mizbaḥ ha-Zahav*, see supra n. 10). I have dealt in several contexts in my dissertation with the importance of checking the "libraries" of scholars of this period, and there have been some (unsatisfactory) beginnings made in this direction. This too is a preliminary study that is vitally necessary. R. David Darshan mentions, in his *Shir ha-Ma'alot* (Cracow, 1571), "over four hundred selected works" which he claims to have gathered "from the four corners of the world" (Ben-Sasson, *Hagut ve-Hanhaga*, p. 255); see infra my remarks on the works utilized by R. Solomon Ephraim Luntshitz.

15. *Oraḥ le-Ḥayyim* (Lublin, 1595), p. 41b, and similarly in the introduction to *Ir Giborim* (Basle, 1580), p. 2a–b; see also ibid., in the introduction to *Petiḥot ve-Sha'arim*, p. 5a: "Moralists also wish to know an innovative homily (*drush meḥudash*) about ethics and virtues which a man ought to acquire, and condemnation of bad qualities." In *Igeret ha-Tiyul*, (*Ḥelek ha-Pshat*, letter *dalet*) R. Ḥayyim b. Betzalel, MaHaRaL's brother, interprets the verse "But the talk of the lips only to penury" (Prov. 14:23) as meaning: "The talk of the lips is good to an attentive ear as long as there is something new that he has not heard before and is wanting; but something that is not novel is not acceptable to an attentive ear." See also R. Mordekhai Jaffe in his introduction to the *Levushim* (Venice, 1620), f. 4b, who remarks that "In *Levush ha-Simḥa ve-ha-Sasson*, the section containing homilies, I followed in the path of some preachers; i.e., I sometimes explained the intentions of the *midrashot* and the dicta and the reason for the commandments using rhetorical devices (*derekh halatza*) and farfetched interpretation, stretching the language very far." According to him, "there is nothing wrong with this, and no harm that can bring about error, God forbid, as one might fear in other matters. Quite the contrary, I regard it as a form of wisdom, because the main purpose of a public homily is to awaken the hearts of those listening, to offer guidance and to straighten their way towards ultimate perfection. And I knew that such is the nature of the masses to bend an ear and listen attentively to such matters. Furthermore, those of them who are wise and understanding, who are familiar with the *midrashot*,

wish and desire to hear something new, and they are quite right. . . ." See Ben-Sasson, *Hagut ve-Hanhaga*, p. 45, and p. 42 where he quotes from R. David Darshan in this matter.

16. Indeed his writings too display at times a terminological distinction between *musar* and *tokheḥa*. Passages of rebuke are also found in many works of *drush* and exegesis of the period. In fact, the nature of this sub-type of *musar* literature (as distinct from its manifestations in liturgical poetry) has not been clarified by modern scholarship. Moreover, the forms of influence of *pilpul* (or at least the ways of halakhic influence) on the one hand and of the Sepharadic *drush* tradition on the other, on the *drush* literature of this period have also not been examined. The traces of these systems are readily apparent in some works, for example in the above-mentioned *Mizbaḥ ha-Zahav*. The preachers of the period make much use of *gematriya* and *notarikon* according to the old Ashkenazic homiletical tradition. On the other hand they also utilize terms found in the Sepharadic *musar* and *drush* literature, such as: *hatza'a, hakdama, etzem ha-drush, ikar ha-drush* and so forth.

17. Cf. his observations in the introduction to *Olelot Efraim* (Lublin, 1590), f. 3a, that the "early authorities . . . the great stylist (Ha-Bedersi) and the authors of *Even Boḥan* and *Duties of the Heart*, as well as many other righteous men" composed books "in which can be discerned the many flaws of the generation," but they were to no avail. Bedersi's *Beḥinat Olam* was also among the books most beloved by that generation, and it was printed in Prague (1598) with the commentary of R. Yom-Tov Lipmann Heller.

18. "*Drush meḥudash*" (thus normally in *Ir Giborim*); cf. the introduction to his *Olelot Efraim*, f. 4a, where he writes that the only field in which people of his generation may take pride is "producing something new, so that he who sees will say: 'See, this is new; there was before no book like it in beauty containing homilcs for all purposes," (cf. Eccl. 1:10 and Psalms 111:2) since the fields of "codes and customs" have already been filled "by all the books that are overflowing with knowledge as the waters cover the sea" (cf. Is. 11:9), and also on the subject of "exegesis of Torah portions and the *Megilot*, the early authorities have said all there is to be said".

19. *Ir Giborim*, Introduction, f. 2b.

20. *Oraḥ le-Ḥayyim*, f. 7a. These and similar statements explain why R. Solomon Ephraim allowed himself to interrupt his homilies with rebukes.

21. Ibid., f. 5b. R. Solomon makes a clear distinction (unlike many of his contemporaries) between exegesis and *drush*. Exegesis is usually referred to in his writings as *be'urim*. The point of departure of a homilist is the present: He reads the verses, and reads into them, in the light of his own reality. The exegete, on the other hand, turns his gaze towards the past, to the historical and textual context of the object of his commentary. Though the exegete cannot free himself from his situation either, and his questions and solution must also reflect his own reality, consciously at least, he focuses his attention on the past. Indeed the complex of relations between *drush* and exegesis, those two neighboring genres, is a tangled one. R. Solomon of Mezhirech in *Mizbaḥ ha-Zahav* (ch. 5, f. 12b) points out the need to interpret according to one's own time, and comments on the verse "If a man turns a deaf ear to the law, even his prayers are an abomination" (Prov. 28:9), saying: "The commentators have explained what they wrote was fine for their generation, since they did not experience our evil, namely the neglect of the Law, as I witness the deeds and remember the Halakhah. And indeed I did see fit to explain the verse according to our own generation. The meaning of 'If a man turns a deaf ear, etc.' is: If he turns a deaf ear to hearing the Torah, then his prayer that he prays three times a day — 'Return us to your Law' — is also an abomination before the Lord." See Ben-Sasson, *Hagut ve-Hanhaga*, p. 40. This homily itself, with some minor changes, appears in *Igeret ha-Tiyul* by R. Ḥayyim b. Betzalel, "*Ḥelek ha-Peshat*," letter *mem*. (The work was composed in 1569, but was printed in Prague in 1605, so that it was one of the homilies known to the preachers of that generation from oral tradition. Such parallels are common.)

22. *Ir Giborim, Pinḥas*, f. 109a; see Ben-Sasson, *Hagut ve-Hanhaga*, pp. 46ff.

23. *Oraḥ le-Ḥayyim* f. 43 (50)b; cf. *Ir Giborim*, ibid., and Ben-Sasson p. 48 (and similar statements also at the beginning of his remarks to Deuteronomy). The quoted passage contains opposition (expressed in similar terms) to the criticisms of the unacceptable homily as cited there; see also *Ir Giborim*, Introduction, f. 2a–b. In *Olelot Efraim, ma'amar* 210, f. 67b, R. Solomon Ephraim attaches "to the shape and form of the shofar . . . a lesson about

rebuke and the conduct of the rebuker" (and the rebuked–*J.E.*), and learns that "just as the shofar draws in at one end and out the other, such are the words of *musar* that go in one ear and out the other. Furthermore a little enters and a lot goes out, just as in the case of the shofar, [where] the sound goes in through a small opening and leaves through a large one. [This is] the opposite of what the Rabbis taught: "Make your ears like funnels" (cf. *Ḥagiga*, f. 3b), meaning that you pour in through the broad end and it goes out the narrow end. And if one glues together broken pieces of *shofarot* and blows through them, it is unfit for use—this refers to the preacher who does not identify his sources and wraps himself in someone else's garment, and all his words are stolen like broken pieces from other books, some from here and some from here, to make up a complete *drush*." (This also seems to be a perfect example of a "*drush meḥudash*.") See also the introductory remarks to *ma'amar* 1, f. 7a on authors, "one of whom copies from the other statements that are taken from the other's works, which he did not work on"; and about those who "out of the haughtiness of their spirit wrap themselves up in garments that are not their own and attach greatness to themselves." "And it is not so done, and this is the reason for the delay in the time of the Redemption and the coming of our Messiah"; See *Ir Giborim*, Introduction, f. 5b, about authors who carry in their clothing "speculative books by Maimonides and others, the *Akeda*, Zohar, *Ikarim*, etc."

24. *Amudei Shesh*, Introduction.

25. *Amudei Shesh: Musar Amud ha-Avoda*, f. 39b (R. Solomon Ephraim did not escape criticism of his own homilies; cf. *Ir Giborim* to Leviticus, f. 79a and *Olelot Efraim*, Introduction, p. 4. Nevertheless he lays down a methodological rule for homilies: "Every homily must be hinted at in the meanings of the words of the verse," *Siftei Da'at, Koraḥ, ma'amar* 247 (Prague, 1610), f. 77b; see also *Ir Giborim* to Numbers, f. 109a, where he says that his words constitute "the literal meaning of the dicta . . . (and) they contain *musar* and reproof." See also the second introduction, f. 3a, and, among other things, his attack on allegorical *drush*, ibid., f. 6a, regarding homilies "that contain not one of the seventy aspects of the Torah,"—but rather, all is "rhetorical devices" and "foreign ideas."

26. *Oraḥ le-Ḥayyim*, f. 14a. And see *Olelot Efraim*, Introduction, f. 2b, in which he "quotes" the arguments of the rebuked to the rebuker: "Seeing that all the [members of the] congregation are holy, each one of them, wherefore then lift up one above the congregation, and the sharp sword of his tongue is unsheathed to chastise the land with the staff of Dan, and a double-edged sword is in his hand to tell the House of Israel words as hard as sinews. Why should he open his ass's mouth in his generation like Samuel in his generation, this despised bordered with cords of ridicule, etc."

27. *Oraḥ le-Ḥayyim* f. 7a. According to him: "I have never seen a true rebuker or chastiser," ibid., f. 41 (49)a.

28. He refers to *Ir Giborim* simply as a "*musar* book"; see *Olelot Efraim*, f. 4a.

29. The matter is especially conspicuous in the reproof passages, which retain many ingredients of the oral discourse. Indeed, not every *drush* work preserves traces of the oral homily, and we need not invariably find the source of every *drush* work in public discourses. When I speak of *drush*, I refer to the method. By the way, I may note that the distinction between *drasha* and *drush* is absent from Hebrew lexicography as well. Ben-Yehuda does not list the term *drush*, and its character is also not clarified in Even-Shoshan's dictionary.

30. *Olelot Efraim*, Introduction, ff. 3b–4a. In the latter image, R. Solomon Ephraim is alluding to Maimonides' phrase in the Laws of Repentance 3:4; see also ibid., note 25. From this quote we may also learn that their philosophical interest is internally circumscribed; see also *ma'amar* 264, p. 84b. (This issue demands a separate discussion.)

31. The assumption that the sources (biblical and Talmudic) "speak to a man according to his comprehension" (*Mekhilta*, *Yitro*, ch. 9, ed. Horowitz-Rabin, p. 235; cf. *Pesikta de-Rav Kahana*, *Ba-Ḥodesh ha-Shlishi*, ed. Mandelbaum, p. 224) was essentially shared by all scholars of that generation. Indeed the nature of the relationship between source and commentary is regarded by each commentator (and of course by each reader) in a different way. R. Solomon Ephraim writes in *Olelot Efraim, ma'amar* 177, p. 57b: "The words of Torah are a hammer that breaketh the rock in pieces, and every matter can be interpreted in 70 ways. Therefore there are many opinions, *and it is possible that all of them are* the words of the living God" (my emphasis –*J.E.*). In his opening remarks to his explanation of the tales

of Raba bar bar Ḥana, ibid., f. 5b (following the Index) he states: "Even though I am not decreeing absolutely that the stories do not tolerate any other interpretation besides mine, in any case, seeing that the words of the Torah are like a hammer breaking the rock in pieces (Jer. 23:29), and more than this they are the words of the wise and their dark saying (cf. Pr. 1:6) which have been fixed in the Talmud as parables and poetic expressions referring to some hidden matter, whether of wisdom or ethics, do they not support whatever form with which the artist may shape them? And if this is so, then all the interpretations given about them are all true, because of all the forms they intended only such as are in conformity with the Torah and its commandments, and not, God forbid, ones that contradict it." See also "Trends and Courses," pp. 287 and 318. Still another of many examples of this belief, from another author: R. Moses Mordekhai Margaliot concludes one of his discussions as follows: "This seems to be the application of the above dictum according to the difficulties we raised, and we shall follow this course as long as we don't hear a more acceptable explanation, and we say that perhaps the original intention of the author of this dictum was also our explanation. But even if, God forbid, his original intention was not this at all, in any case, our *drash* has the function of 'study and receive reward'—'for it is no vain thing for you' [Deut. 32:47]"; see *Ḥasdei ha-Shem* (Cracow, 1589), *Ha-Derekh ha-Shlishi*, f. 9a.

32. Hence the effort to concentrate discussions around topics. This is easily discernible in the works of MaHaRaL, but it is apparent also from a study of R. Solomon Ephraim's writings. He prefaced *Ir Giborim*, a product of his youth, with two introductions. In the first he collected dicta dealing with questions of the desires, while in the second he dealt with the three pillars: Torah, worship and benevolence. To these introductions he appended additional "gateways." In the first was brought a selection with commentaries on the subject of repentance; in the second, matters relating to "the conduct of the Virtues"—charity, humility, truth and peace and their opposites—pride, envy, lust and vainglory as well as to the matter of the four classes—the frivolous, the flatterers, the liars and the slanderers (cf. BT, *Sota* f. 42a). In *Olelot Efraim* the ethical (and speculative) discussions are attached to the calendar, and revolve about rabbinic quotations. In *Oraḥ le-Ḥayyim* we find two thematic homilies—a *drush* for the New Year and the Day of Atonement that deals with repentance, and one for Passover which describes "the conduct of a man and a great spiritual awakening," and more specifically the relations between the physical and the spiritual in man. Preceding these is an introduction in which the author discusses the flaws in the pillars that support the world, and a paragraph that serves as a preface to the homilies about the "foundation of faith" (dealing with love and communion, *dvekut*). Similar materials are found in other works as well. R. Solomon Ephraim's desire to link his views to the sources is discernible in the overall plan based on *Pirkei Avot* (regarding the pillars: Torah, worship and benevolence; truth, justice and peace) and also, of course, in his title, *Amudei Shesh*. In fact, he introduces new content into the classical schema and ties together, by means of homilitical connections, dozens of new subjects. Among the subjects discussed are: hypocrisy (*ziyuf*), discord, unity and peace, envy, hatred and vainglory, verbal and financial deception, vengefulness and grudge-bearing, pride, vulgarity, submissiveness and humility, tale-bearing, the power of desire, lust, sin and repentance, *kavana*, fear of God, love, *dvekut* and prophecy, and so on (see supra, n. 11). In the book there is, according to the author, only a selection from his original comments in homilies "about matters touching upon the six pillars that was retained by the memory"; see his introduction and hence an allusion to the complex relationships between a homily and a polished work. Many of the subjects were also dealt with in *Ir Giborim, Kli Yakar* and *Siftei Da'at*, his exegetical works. This occurs in two ways: (a) in passages of obvious reproof; and (b) by means of emphasizing the ethical lessons of the verses. In fact he distinguishes, as already mentioned, between the homiletic and exegetical methods; see *Kli Yakar* on Num. 16:1, Num. 33:49, and Deut. 12:30. R. Solomon Ephraim enumerates many types of sin, since "if we read carefully in all the books of the prophets according to scribes and Scripture, we find all the accusations of which our forefathers were blamed for the destructions of the first and second Temples, all are to be found in our generation, except for idolatry, sexual offenses, and murder which are not so common; but against them there has been an increase in the sin of the tongue, which is considered equal to the other three, as is well

known"; see *Oraḥ le-Ḥayyim*, p. 34 and cf. the list of sins found in the homily for the Day of Atonement in *Olelot Efraim, ma'amar* 239, pp. 75ff.

33. I have dealt with his views on several subjects in my dissertation (on his concept of Torah in chap. 12, and on the doctrine of repentance in chap. 14). As regards his social theory, see my references in nn. 11–12 to Ben-Sasson and the important discussion of I. Bettan, *Studies in Jewish Preaching* (Cincinnati, 1939), pp. 273–316.

34. E.g., in details concerning the nature of the Torah that is "entirely made up of the names of God"; the question of the mutual relationships between man and the celestial powers ("The righteous add to the celestial power"); prayer, etc.

35. He holds firmly to the principle (as expressed in *Olelot Efraim*) that "I have come to the decision not to seek in my book after great and wonderful things"; see *ma'amar* 104, f. 38b; cf. also *Kli Yakar* on the verse: "And therefore do the children of Israel eat not the sinew of the thigh-vein . . . " (Gen. 32:33). He finds in this verse "an allusion . . . for future generations to discourage Israel from delving into hidden mysteries, as it says 'You have no business in hidden things,' because we should fear lest they injure their minds and become heretics, since there are not many men who are wise enough to understand properly all the secrets since their brains pass through a dark valley . . . "; cf. *Ir Giborim* to this verse, as well as *Kli Yakar* to Ex. 25:17, and *Siftei Da'at, ma'amar* 207 regarding the blasphemer. He decides there that one should not teach "the kabbalistic study of divine Names to everyone, for he whose heart is not perfect might thereby come to harm." On his attitude to the various intellectual currents we may learn from combinations of terms such as this one, brought in his commentary to the Talmudic dictum "If he is standing in a foreign land he should direct his heart towards the Land of Israel, etc." (*Berakhot*, f. 30a). He says "that it is a wonderful allusion to the source of divine influence that comes from the celestial pool (*brekha elyona*), through the causal chain (*hishtalshelut ha-sibot*) as every cause is linked in turn to the First Cause, as explained in the *Guide*, II, 48" (*Olelot Efraim, ma'amar* 498, f. 334a; and see also ibid., *ma'amar* 508, f. 336).

36. All these are in addition to the quotes from the *Duties of the Heart*, from Maimonides (the *Book of Knowledge* and the *Guide to the Perplexed*), Naḥmanides, Ha-Bedersi, R. Jonah Gerondi, the *Rokeaḥ* (on repentance), Judah ha-Levi, the *Ikarim* (whose opinion he follows in the question of the principles of faith), *Shvilei Emuna*, *Nevei Shalom*, the commentaries of Almosnino, scientists and astronomers, *Menorat ha-Ma'or* and others. He also cited the well-known Bible commentators: Ibn Ezra, Gersonides, *Ba'al ha-Turim*, Kimḥi, Abravanel and others. The most frequently mentioned work in his writings is the *Akeda*, but kabbalistic remarks are alluded to usually through R. Baḥya's commentary to the Torah (*Sha'arei Ora* is mentioned only rarely, and Cordovero's *Pardes Rimonim* seems to be mentioned only once, *Kli Yakar* to Num. 1:1). *Kli Ḥemda* by R. Abraham Laniado (also published in Prague, 1610) and Alsheikh are referred to in the Introduction to *Siftei Da'at* (Prague, 1610–11) in a critical tone (though he did compose one of the approbations to the Prague, 1616–1617 printing of the Alsheikh). R. Solomon Ephraim designates "the authors of the *Akeda*, the *Guide* and the *Ikarim*" as "*ḥakhmei ha-emet*"(sages of the truth), *Olelot Efraim, ma'amar* 292, f. 92a, an epithet that seems to be reserved by his younger contemporaries exclusively for kabbalists.

37. Already Isserles in *Torat ha-Ola*, (Prague, 1570) III, 4, laments that "even householders who cannot distinguish between their right and their left and walk in darkness, who are incabable of explaining a Torah portion with Rashi's commentary, nevertheless are quick to study Kabbalah." This argument recurs in other authors.

38. See "Trends and Courses," pp. 78–79, 97, 116–117, 172. Many books of Kabbalah were printed in Poland during this period; on this see ibid., pp. 156–159, 178–184.

39. A perfect example of this may be found in R. Moses Mordekhai Margaliot's *Ḥasdei ha-Shem* on the 13 *midot*, mentioned above, or in *Tamim Yaḥdav*, R. Israel b. R. Moses' commentary on Psalms (Lublin, 1592). In the introduction to this book the author deals with the doctrine of psychology according to the Zohar, and severely criticized the author of the *Akeda* who, according to him, did not "check all the statements in the Zohar", and therefore made mistakes.

40. On this literature see Y. D. Wilhelm, "Sidrei Tikunim," *Alei Ayin* (Jerusalem, 1948–1952), pp. 125–146; E. D. Goldschmidt, "Prayers for the Eve of the New Moon Day"

[Hebrew], *Kiryat Sefer* 44 (1959), pp. 129–140 (*On Jewish Liturgy—Essays on Prayer and Religious Poetry* [Jerusalem, 1979], pp. 322–340); J. J. Cohen, "Tikunei Shabbat," *Kiryat Sefer* 39 (1964), pp. 539–542; M. Benayahu, "*Tikun* for the Seventh Day of Passover," *Kiryat Sefer* 52 (1977), pp. 818–833; idem, "The Special Liturgy *Tikun* for the Seventh of Adar," *Tarbitz* 48 (1979), pp. 117–145; "Trends and Courses," pp. 159–163, 185–190. The above-mentioned *tikunei tshuva* had a far-reaching influence on the repentance literature in Poland and Ashkenaz at the beginning of the seventeenth century, as did R. Elijah de Vidas' book *Reshit Ḥokhma* also printed, as we have said, in Cracow, 1593–1594) and its abridged version *Totza'ot Ḥayyim* (Cracow, 1600). This extremely interesting subject was dealt with in my dissertation, chapter 14 (pp. 430ff.), and it goes beyond the scope of this article. It too can teach us about the growing inclination toward the Kabbalah.

41. F. 22b (my own pagination–*J. E.*). The authors of the approbations to this book were R. Solomon Ephraim Luntshitz and R. Isaiah Horowitz (the *SHeLaH*). For a different approach to this problem, see I. Tishby "The Confrontation Between Lurianic Kabbalah and Cordoverian Kabbalah in the Writings and Life of Rabbi Aaron Brakhya of Modena" [Hebrew], *Zion* 39 (1974), pp. 46–47. R. Judah mentions in his *Tikunei Shabat* the statement of the scholars of Cracow, who advised him not to reveal "hidden mysteries" in his book, obviously referring to the Lurianic doctrines; see ff. 1b–2a (Among those who wrote approbations for the book were R. Moses Mordekhai Margaliot and R. Phoebus b. R. Israel Samuel, the teacher of the *SHeLaH*).

42. *Yosef Ometz* (Frankfurt, 1908), p. xv. Later, he explains this conclusion in accordance with what he found in *Sefer Ḥaredim*, but cf. ibid., I, § 180, in which he expresses the opposite approach. Apparently R. Joseph Yozefa distinguished between *asiya* (doing) and *amira* (saying). He did not recite the song "which mentions Ben-Yoḥai ("*Bar-Yoḥai nimshahta ashrekha*") because it was so profound with Kabbalah," par. 589. On the change which he underwent with regard to the Kabbalah, see ibid., II, 271, and on this whole matter, see "Trends and Courses," p. 162–163, 188–189. R. Joseph Yozefa knew the two books of *Tikunim* by R. Judah and relied on them, as well as on *Sefer ha-Kavanot* (Venice, 1620), and others of the sort.

43. See for the time being "Trends and Courses," pp. 351–353 and 362–364. There is still room for expansion on this point.

44. Such as in R. Moses Yakar Ashkenazi's book of *hadrakha*, *Petaḥ Enayim* (*ed. princeps*, Cracow, before 1600; see I. Mehlman, "Hebrew Printing Houses in Salonika" [Hebrew], in *Genuzot Sfarim, Bibliographical Essays* [Jerusalem, 1976], p. 88, no. 75) on the law not to remove the phylacteries until after the *kdusha* of *u-va le-tziyon* since "such is the view of the kabbalists, that one should recite three *kdushas* while seated and one standing, etc." (ibid., f. 4b; cf. *Levushim*; "*Levush ha-Tkhelet*," no. 28:13); or in the book of *hadrakha* by R. Tzvi Hirsch b. R. Henokh Zundel, *Lema'an Telekh be-Derekh Tovim* (Cracow, 1625), f. 7b (*ed. princeps*, Cracow, 1604), that "according to the Kabbalah one should always cut the bread at night from the bottom loaf, and on the Sabbath day from the topmost loaf," a custom mentioned by many scholars of the age. See "Trends and Courses," pp. 351, 362 and 365, n. 36. Indeed, the matter was not exhausted there. R. Tzvi Hirsch's book contains, according to the author, "each and every law necessary for each day", and it shows dependence on the "*hadrakha*" of R. Yoḥanan Luria, a scholar of the fifteenth century (appended to the *Sefer ha-Gan*, first printed in Prague, 1597); and even more, it shows traces of *Sefer ha-Yir'a* by R. Jonah Gerondi. Customs of the kabbalists are found in R. Ephraim b. R. Joseph Yavorover, *Bakashot* (Cracow, 1608), which by its nature belongs also to the *tikunim* literature. He looks for customs mentioned in the Zohar and tries to establish them as binding law, indicates customs current among the people of the Land of Israel with which he was familiar, and traces the deeds of his teacher R. David Shinena b. R. Jacob of Szczebrzeszn, "whose every word was usually correct and founded upon the basis of the Kabbalah, from the honeycomb words of R. Simeon b. Yoḥai in the Zohar and the *Tikunim* [*Tikunei Zohar*]; he was extremely erudite in them, and the pathways of those books were as familiar to him as the path of the literal interpretations of Scripture" (ibid., f. 6a–b).

45. Amsterdam, 1701, f. 269a.

46. "We need not search for the reasons for the commandments, since they are like royal decrees for us even if we are ignorant of their reasons." Such are the words of R. Mordekhai Yaffe in *Levush Ateret Zahav*, no. 181:1.

The Moral Philosophy of MaHaRaL

MARVIN FOX

Rabbi Judah Loew ben Betzalel, the MaHaRaL of Prague, was one of the most important Jewish thinkers of the sixteenth century. As Jacob Katz points out, during this period MaHaRaL was "the only Jewish author . . . to expound Judaism as a comprehensive conception."[1] His work includes contributions to most of the main branches of Jewish thought, and among them his expositions of Jewish ethics occupy a central place. While there are comments on matters of ethical interest in every one of his works, the most concentrated treatment is contained in *Netivot Olam* and in his commentary on Mishna *Avot* under the title *Derekh Ḥayyim*. In these works he deals with almost every aspect of ethics, but he does so in an unstructured and unsystematic way. No single subject is fully developed in one place, nor is there an explicit set of connections between the subjects which forms them into a coherent and comprehensive theory. The MaHaRaL did not produce a great systematic treatise on ethics on the order of the major works of Greek antiquity or of modern philosophy. Neither are his studies of the genre of the Jewish works of philosophical piety such as *Ḥovot ha-Levavot*, or of the intensive explorations of the later *musar* literature. Yet, careful study shows him to be a Jewish ethical thinker of great interest and illuminating insight.

Our task is to construct the system which is lacking in the writings of MaHaRaL and to do so without imposing upon him thought-forms and structures which are alien and which distort or misrepresent his intentions. We begin with a methodological premise, namely, that there is a latent system underlying the seemingly disconnected thoughts in the works of MaHaRaL and that this system was clearly present in his mind, although not in his form of writing. Having chosen the genre of commentary, he was largely tied to the occasions provided by his particular texts. Yet, through it all, whether he is beginning from a biblical verse, a Mishnah, an Aggadah or a halakhic passage, there are consistent lines of thought which bear witness to a clear formulation in his mind of an approach to the basic questions of ethics. The text on which he is commenting is often the occasion for an excursus which is only loosely and in the most general sense a "commentary." The attentive reader cannot help but conclude that MaHaRaL had important ideas to share with his readers and that he frequently used whatever text was before him as an opportunity to express himself on a subject of general importance. As we assemble these seemingly isolated notes and comments we can see that they constitute a comprehensive and important treatment of our subject. We shall engage in an exercise of the intellectual imagination as we try to formulate the main themes in MaHaRaL's moral philosophy as he might have done himself had he chosen to write a single systematic treatise on this subject.

Let us first consider briefly the place of MaHaRaL in the history of Jewish ethical thought and in the wider context of general religious and philosophic thought. While some writers have tried to make much of the deep roots that MaHaRaL presumably had in the culture of sixteenth-century Europe, there is no evidence that his thinking about ethics was affected by his particular time and place. His sources are in the classical Jewish works and, in considerable measure, in some of the main trends of medieval Jewish philosophy. There are also important points where he is clearly affected by Kabbalah, but for the most part this is more a matter of atmosphere than of particular doctrines. Scholem correctly includes MaHaRaL among those who attempted in some degree "to explain kabbalistic ideas without using technical language."[2] However, as we shall see, some of his doctrines which appear to be kabbalistic may well have their origins in standard rabbinic sources. Finally, with respect to ethics, there is no reason to think of MaHaRaL as a bridge between the Middle Ages and the modern world. He is primarily a Jewish thinker standing fully inside the classical Jewish tradition, one who at the same time reflects in his ideas and terminology the effects of his studies in both philosophy and Kabbalah.

The most fundamental principle that MaHaRaL sets forth with respect to human behavior is that there is an unbreakable connection between the moral and the metaphysical realms. The order of reality includes rules for human action, and human action, in turn, has significance for the entire cosmic order. The ultimate source of virtuous human behavior is more than just a code of laws. True human virtue embodies the structure and pattern of all reality. MaHaRaL begins his *Netivot Olam* with this theme. "The Torah is the order of man which directs him to the actions that he should perform, the way in which he should perform them, and how he should be ordered with respect to his actions. This is the concern of the Torah. And just as the Torah is the order of man, so is it the order of the world and ultimately the order of all that exists."[3] The manifest content of the Torah is its commandments, which are essential for the proper ordering of human life, while the deep content of the Torah includes the structural principles of all reality. So direct is the connection between human behavior and the cosmos according to MaHaRaL, that the destiny of the world rests on man. When the righteous observe the commandments they are a force helping to sustain the entire world, and when sinners violate the commandments they are a counterforce which tends to destroy the world.[4]

MaHaRaL describes the Torah in its essential nature as supernal divine wisdom which exists apart from, and independently of, the created world. Following the well-known midrash,[5] he conceives of the Torah as the pre-existent pattern which God consults as He creates the world. The Torah is pure reason unsullied by any corporeal elements. As such it would seem to be far removed from the world of man and of human concerns. Yet, in a characteristically dialectical turn, MaHaRaL simultaneously roots the essence of the Torah in its relationship to man. He affirms, on the one hand, that nothing that is created is worthy of existence in and of itself. Only insofar as its existence is connected with the Torah does anything become endowed with true value and gain conjunction with true being. Even the human intellect, sometimes spoken of by MaHaRaL as man's glory, is in this connection seen as of relatively low-grade and inconsequential status. "Although man has intellect, this is only human intellect which is tied to matter. The world is not worthy of sustained existence because of this good which is of low and inferior standing."[6] Only when the human intellect is connected to the wisdom of Torah does it become truly worthy and thus help to sustain the world. Yet, at the same time, the value of the Torah itself arises from its connection with man. All the world was created for man and he has the highest rank among all existents. The order of reality is thus a reflection of the order of man, since "God created the world in accordance with what would be appropriate for the human order."[7] This is the true meaning of the statement that God consulted the Torah when He created the world, since the Torah is *seder ha-adam*, the ordering principles for human existence and fulfillment. From one perspective the Torah is pure being, a transcendent reality whose manifest content reveals to our limited intelligence only glimmers of its perfection. At the very same time its perfection, which man never fully grasps, results from its connection with the human order to which it gives ideal form.

We have here the metaphysical basis of the moral dimension of reality. Ideal human behavior is determined by the Torah. It derives from the supernal world and helps to determine the very order of that world. What is true of the formal ideal is also the case with respect to individual human actions. Man's behavior is seen as having cosmic effects. We see in this theory, which provides the philosophical-theological foundations for morality in the thought of MaHaRaL, a cluster of influences. MaHaRaL bases himself on standard scriptural and aggadic texts. The understanding of these texts is filtered through both philosophic and kabbalistic modes emerging finally in the form which MaHaRaL makes available to us.

A second layer in the theoretical structure of MaHaRaL's moral philosophy is his understanding of the metaphysical source of evil in the world. The Torah is conceived as the intemediary power created by God to give being to the world. Good is identified with being and evil with non-being. It follows that only the good can truly exist, and since the Torah is the model of all good, it alone among created things can be said to have absolute fullness of being. The reason for this is that reason can only be directed toward the good, and a world which derives from the divine creator must be ordered in accordance with reason. One is reminded here of the passage in Plato's *Phaedo* in which Socrates argues that if *nous* is the ordering force of the world, then all things must be disposed toward the good.[8] Reason is the antithesis of non-being, and the Torah which is regularly conceived by MaHaRaL as perfect reason in its pure essence is the created ground of being, just as

God himself is the uncreated and eternal ground of being. When the world is oriented toward the Torah, it achieves the force of being standing against non-being.[9]

What then is the source of evil in the world? Evil is identified with privation or non-being, and this, in turn, is identified with matter or the corporeal. When the created world is oriented toward the Torah it overcomes its inherent non-being, which is its evil. "Because of the fact that this world is material and is far removed from the realm of reason, the Torah which is itself reason has no place in the world. But the moment the desire of the nether world for the rational Torah is aroused, the Torah answers, 'Here I am,' since all things that are rationally ordered have positive ontological status."[10] We should note in passing that familiar Zoharic ideas and terminology are used here.

This doctrine translates into a very clear picture with respect to specifically human experience and concerns. Sin is explicitly and repeatedly identified by MaHaRaL with privation or non-being.[11] The source of sin in man is his matter which is essentially privation. Human virtue is conceived as the victory of form over matter, intellect over the body, being non-being.[12] "*Tshuva* is the removal of sin. The cause of sin is matter, and if man were totally without matter, he would be like an angel and would be totally without sin."[13]

This sharp break between body and spirit is characteristic neither of biblical nor of much rabbinic thinking on this subject. The philosophic tradition, absorbing Platonic and Neoplatonic influences, introduced this theme into the center of Jewish religious thought. One hears in MaHaRaL echoes of familiar passages in Maimonides and other medieval Jewish philosophers. "All man's acts of disobedience and sins," say Maimonides in an oft-quoted passage, "are consequent upon his matter and not upon his form, whereas all his virtues are consequent upon his form. . . . His eating and drinking and copulation and his passionate desire for these things, as well as his anger and all bad habits found in him, are all of them consequent upon his matter."[15] What separates even Moses from the perfection of virtue which would come with a complete apprehension of God is the fact that "his human intellect is still resident in matter."[16] For MaHaRaL this principle is fundamental to an understanding of all human evil. It is a theme which pervades all of his works.

Yet, unlike Plato and those who follow him, MaHaRaL does not reject the body completely. The Platonic ideal is that of the philosopher who is always pursuing death. To the fullest extent possible he seeks to achieve the separation of soul from body even in this life.[17] Despite Maimonides' explicit concern with *tikun haguf*, he exhibits strong attachment to the Platonic ideal.[18] MaHaRaL works out an important compromise with the inescapable fact that human beings are corporeal and thus inevitably subject to sin. The matter out of which man is constituted can be progressively refined. Since we are not angels, but men, our task is not to reject matter or cast it off completely, but rather to transform it so that it can serve to advance rather than inhibit our achievement of the highest virtue. Some men are born with refined matter and this enhances from the first their moral-spiritual development.[19] Even those who are less fortunate are still able to concentrate their powers in such a way as to overcome the threat of non-being inherent in their material substratum and to live a life of virtue and ultimate fulfillment.

In fact, the ideal model is Abraham, who is represented by MaHaRaL as having achieved perfection of the material element and was thus fully able to rise to the highest level of spirituality. If the spirit alone is cultivated while the body is ignored, we have a perilous situation in which the "branches are stronger than the roots." What distinguished Abraham from earlier generations is that his roots, i.e., his body, were perfected, and this provided the basis for his spiritual ascent. "For when man achieves the true perfection of the body which is his foundation and root, he is then fit to receive the full perfection of form, . . . the glory of the divine *tzelem* at the highest level which is appropriate, and finally the intellect controls matter fully."[20] In this respect MaHaRaL understands each man to be unrealized potentiality seeking actualization. The soul is a pure umblemished entity housed in the human body. Man must first realize the highest potentialities of the body itself so that, in turn, the soul may be completely actualized.[21]

As a corporeal being seeking full moral-spiritual-intellectual actualization, man lives in the world of action, not only in the realm of thought and contemplation. The Torah, which is the model for ideal reality, is both supernal wisdom and a concrete guide to human behavior. MaHaRaL considers it to be a major and irredeemable error for man to concentrate on knowing to the exclusion of doing. "Wisdom without action is not proper for man, since man is not pure intelligence. What is required rather is that man's actions should follow after his intellect."[22] Similarly, actions alone that are blindly performed without relation to man's higher intellectual-spiritual nature are unworthy of human beings. To paraphrase a well-known Kantian aphorism, actions without thoughts are blind, and thoughts without actions are empty. The Torah as pure perfected wisdom is inaccessible to man. Only by way of *mitzvot* which are simultaneously directed to body and soul does man establish his connection with the true Torah. It is a mark of man's superior nature that he must concentrate deliberate effort in order to actualize his potentiality. Creatures which exist only in the order of nature achieve whatever measure of actualization is open to them in the normal course of events. Aristotle's notion of *orexis*, the striving of all things for their own proper fulfillment, does not necessarily entail struggle and labor. Only for man is there the possibility and demand for intense and conscious effort to become what he might properly be. MaHaRaL sees this uniquely human situation as evidence of man's special worth. Unlike a plant or an animal he will not automatically fulfill himself. At the end of the road, however, his active effort is rewarded when he rises to an ontological status which is shared by no other earthly beings.[23]

This leads us directly to those practical questions regarding human behavior and its values which concern every moral philosophy. Given the general metaphysical framework which we have set forth, we must now consider the criteria of good and evil according to MaHaRaL. We must determine what kinds of human action meet those criteria and also what the grounds are upon which MaHaRaL bases his judgments. The foundation of the entire system is God. All being is good, as over against privation which is evil. As necessary being, God is fully and necessarily good.[24] However, His fullness of pure being does not, in and of itself, provide us with imitable models of virtuous behavior. We require some source of moral guidance which translates the divine perfection into human terms. This is the function of the Torah, considered now as a body of commandments, not just as the model of supernal wisdom. As the concretized expression of the perfection of divine being, the Torah alone provides man with full and proper criteria for virtue and with explicit rules for good actions. It is by way of the commandments, which are wholly good, that finite man is transformed into a being who has commerce with God.[25]

This general statement now requires careful analysis and explication. Once we begin to set forth rules of behavior within an ethical system we confront all the problems of specification which are inherent in this task. Like every other moral theorist, MaHaRaL distinguishes between types of rules, grounds of obligation, orders of priority within the rules and similar matters.

With respect to the grounds of obligation within the Jewish religious ethic, his most general principle is that all the commandments are *gzerot*, divine decrees which are imposed upon man from above. At this level of the discourse he gives no consideration to the reasons for the commandments or to what might recommend them to us as desirable from a purely human perspective. The basic stance which MaHaRaL requires in his structuring of the Jewish system of obligation is pious submission to the absolute authority of the divine decree. At this stage man sees himself as unworthy of independent judgment or decision. The word of God has been transmitted to man and that is sufficient for the determination of human duties. MaHaRaL associates this with a psychological stance which he calls *busha*. In his usage this term cannot mean "shame" in any ordinary sense of that term. What it refers to is rather a state of retiring modesty arising from acute awareness of our human limitations. This is in sharp contrast to *azut*, an attitude of confident, even arrogant, self-assertion.

> One who is opposite in character from the arrogantly self-assertive (*az panim*) is not likely to sin. For all the divine commandments are *gzerot* which God imposes on man. When a man is retiring in nature (*ba'al busha*) he is prepared to accept and submit to the edicts and commandments which are ordained by God, since the definition of *busha* is a state in which one is fully open to being affected by others without asserting oneself. It follows that one who is able to submit to the divine decree will not transgress it.[26]

The virtuous life, defined by God's commandments is rooted in man's ready and unquestioning acceptance of the "yoke of the commandments."

It does not follow, however, that these commandments are arbitrary or capricious expressions of the divine power. We accept them as binding because they come from God, but a proper understanding teaches us that these divinely ordained modes of virtuous behavior are intrinsically good. When he considers the virtues in this light MaHaRaL rejects categorically any claim that they are good because of their instrumental or utilitarian value, although he is fully aware of the extent to which the commandments have social utility. However, when he considers them from a purely axiological perspective, it is not their usefulness which he sees as the ground of their binding value. Neither are they binding on us becaue they reflect a *consensus gentium*. "Vices are intrinsically bad and virtues are intrinsically good."[27] No direct philosophical argument or analysis is offered in defense or explication of this claim. It is clear, however, that MaHaRaL derives it from the general principle that the Torah is perfect wisdom and that, as such, there can be nothing arbitrary in it. As MaHaRaL explains, everything in the Torah is pure rational necessity which derives directly from the absolute truth of God. It follows that "there cannot be a single thing, not even a single dot, in the Torah which might be other than as it is."[28] We can conclude from this that whatever is divinely commanded through the Torah is intrinsically good. The social utility or wide-spread general acceptance of particular commandments may add to their attractiveness from our limited human perspective. Their ultimate ground, however, is their intrinsic value. Since we are incapable of grasping this fully through our own resources, we submit in modest awareness of our creaturely finitude to the divine wisdom. MaHaRaL takes it to be added evidence of the intrinsic value of some of the virtues that they are also practiced by certain animals.[29] The fact that they seem to have been built into the order of nature gives added support, in his opinion, to the claim that they are divinely ordained values.[30] We have here two poles of a dialectical exposition. On the one hand, virtues are conceived as divine decrees to which man can only submit in faithful self-suppression. On the other hand, virtues are conceived as intrinsically valuable and thus commanding the freely given assent of any intelligent person. Thesis and antithesis are synthesized in the actual situation of man. The very process of submission grants him the illumination which in turn leaves no doubt about the intrinsic worth of the commandments. Thus, the man of true piety will observe the commandments with a combination of loyalty to God's word and intelligent apprehension of the supreme wisdom implicit in that word.

A similar dialectical pattern is present in the way in which MaHaRaL structures the specific modes of human behavior. He identifies three types of good. At one extreme is the absolutely obligatory, that which is fully and unequivocally mandated in the law. At the opposite extreme is good action which is purely voluntary and gracious, action which lies beyond the line of the law. Midway between them is a less clear category which consists of actions which are neither fully mandated nor fully acts of grace, but are a combination of the two.[31] The extreme categories are *mishpat* over against *ḥesed, din* over against *lifnim mi-shurat ha-din*.

The extreme of *mishpat* consists of the strict rule of justice as commanded in the Torah. This is represented by MaHaRaL as a particularly prized moral ideal. Considered by itself strict justice is a model of moral perfection. For in justice there is nothing arbitrary, nothing unclear or uncertain. Its terms can be defined precisely, and in principle it is possible to apply justice strictly and to perfection. Justice is thought in this respect to be a paradigm of the action of God in the world. Like God Himself, justice is rationally necessary. For Israel to have received from God a rule of justice is a mark of His special favor, since it provides a rational connection between human society and the divine realm. "Justice, more than anything else, is directly associated with God, and therefore God is present whenever true justice is rendered."[32] Moreover, while the basic principles of justice are set forth in the Torah, human intelligence is sufficient for understanding and applying them properly. Unlike the ritual prescriptions whose rules and applications can only be known to us when they are divine commands, justice can be rendered in society completely through human insight and understanding.[33] Other commandments demand of us acceptance in faith since we do not fully understand them, but the rule of justice recommends itself directly to human intelligence. Not only do we recognize it as God's command, but we also see its intrinsic worth. Justice evokes our acceptance at all levels.

Having set forth this one extreme of the ethical, MaHaRaL is driven both by psychological reality and an inner logic to reject it, even while he affirms it. An unremitting commitment to strict justice carries its own seeds of destruction within itself. Such an unyielding commitment tends to harden the human character to the point of harshness, and drives man almost inexorably to a perversion of justice itself. In the words of MaHaRaL, "How great is the sin of one who rests everything on strict justice alone!" He becomes so determined to yield nothing, so insistent on receiving his due, that before long justice turns into the worst of injustice, ending up as robbery and self-serving.[34] The divine ideal of justice is readily corrupted when it is in imperfect human hands. Righteousness turns into self-righteousness and then into self-seeking under the guise of justice. Human society demands something beyond justice, as is evident in the aggadic statements which teach that God had to abandon his original intention to create the world in accordance with justice alone.[35] Without the addition of grace and compassion the world could not have survived. Inescapably, human imperfection and limitation will always tend to corrupt perfect justice.

It is this that forces the dialectical movement to the opposite extreme. Within the ethical system there must be a counterbalance to strict justice. As MaHaRaL sets forth Jewish moral teaching, justice is tempered by *ḥesed*. The most general definition of *ḥesed* is that it is action in behalf of another which goes beyond the requirements of the law.[36] It is not justice which is the primary criterion here, but love and compassion. To go beyond justice in the direction of injustice is sinful corruption. To go beyond justice in the opposite direction of loving concern is the highest virtue. *Ḥesed* is now construed as the essence of the Torah, the most virtuous human behavior and the true human good. "The Torah is the absolute good, and for this reason it is know as *torat ḥesed* since that is what constitutes the absolute good."[37] The introduction of a rule of justice into the world is seen by MaHaRaL as a concession to human imperfection. If men were not inclined to sin, if they were not subject to those corporeal drives which are the ground of human corruption, there would have been no need for the imposition of rules of justice. In a perfect state of affairs *ḥesed* would prevail naturally. In our imperfect condition we live by the minimum decencies which justice requires, but our full humanity is expressed only through *ḥesed*. This is the meaning of the rabbinic statement that the Torah begins and ends with *ḥesed*.[38] For that is the essence of Torah, and it is only when we live with *ḥesed* as our guide that we become what we ought properly to be, beings who are fully formed by, and exemplify, the values of Torah. MaHaRaL notes that symbolic support for this contention is found in the fact that the numerical value of *Torah* and of *gemilut ḥasadim* is identical. *Ḥesed* is thus man's true virtue.[39]

Above all *ḥesed* is considered by MaHaRaL to be the one true way of *imitatio dei*. We walk in God's ways only if, like God, we behave in total freedom and with absolute independence of choice. Since justice is both commanded by God and imposed upon us as a rule of reason, we observe its demands as duty rather than as free choice. We behave justly, or at least recognize the demands of justice, because we must. In this case our reason necessitates our will. We may, in our corruption, violate principles of just behavior, but even then our reason forces us to acknowledge that there is a rule of justice. In contrast, every act of *ḥesed* is completely free. We behave lovingly and graciously because we choose to do so, not because we are required to do so. In this way we truly imitate God, who acts only of His own volition and is never subject to external powers. For "only when one performs *ḥesed* which is beyond the demands of the law do we behave fully in accordance with our own personal decision and choice. It is such behavior that can properly be termed walking in the ways of God."[40]

Mishpat and *ḥesed* live in man in dialectical tension. MaHaRaL speaks in enthusiastic support of each of these virtues when he is expounding them. He also recognizes the limitations of each. A world of pure *ḥesed* is not possible in the context of human history. We cannot rely exclusively on man's generosity and love to establish a good society. For, as we noted earlier, men are not angels. Lacking the rigorous controls of justice, human society would be exposed to the unrestrained self-seeking assertiveness which is present in some measure in every man and in intolerable measure in those who are coarse and tend toward the beastly. A rule of justice functions to restrain such impulses. Justice alone, however, is also unsatisfactory, for it contains the seeds of its own corruption. *Ḥesed* is its necessary counterbalance. In the Jewish moral system, as set forth by MaHaRaL, these opposed modes of human behavior live in a continuous and mutually corrective relationship.

The objective virtues come into human practice as a result of basic attitudes and orientations. Most fundamental are the motivating forces which are classified under the headings of love of God and fear of God. Here again MaHaRaL sets out a dialectical relationship between two opposed tendencies, each of which has a significant role in the formation of the life of virtue and piety. Taken separately, love and fear are polar opposites which have distinct functions and serve distinct ends. Love of God is held by MaHaRaL to be positive and constructive, while fear is negative and destructive. The former is judged to be particularly good and pleasing to God, while the latter "sows ruin because of the terror which it brings into the world."[41] Love moves us to the fulfillment of the positive commandments, while fear causes us to avoid transgressing the negative commandments. The one concentrates on the pursuit of the good and the right, the other on avoidance of the evil and the wrong.[42] Fear stems from our painful awareness of our own finitude and our creaturely limitations. We are acutely conscious of the fact that we are nothing but effects of the divine causation, and that, as such, we are utterly dependent beings. We stand in awe of the divine Majesty and of His transcendent power.[43] Our fear rests on our recognition that God is the wholly other whom we can never approach in intimate relationship. Rather, like the Israelites at Sinai, we must keep our distance lest we be destroyed when drawing excessively near to God.[44] We should not underestimate the significance of this approach to God and to His commandments, since it is not mere emotion, but the result of sound intellectual apprehension. Only one who understands the role of God in the order of reality will draw the contrast between God's greatness and man's unworthiness. Only one who recognizes God as the commanding presence will be filled with anxiety at the thought of transgressing His commandments. Fear of God is valuable and necessary for the virtuous life. Yet it has its destructive elements, as we noted, and these can be balanced only by love.

Identical facts are seen in radically different colors when they are refracted through the prism of the love of God. MaHaRaL uses almost the same expressions when he speaks of the ground of our love of God that he used in expounding our fear of God. He points out that love of God is generated in man when he recognizes that "he is nothing in his own right, but that all he is comes from God and that all will return to Him. Furthermore, man knows that nothing exists apart from God."[45] Given a shift in attitude and perspective, what initially generated fear now evokes love. We love God because He is the ground of our being, because what we are and what we can become in the process of self-perfection all derives from Him. The very knowledge which caused us to feel awesome distance now fills us with a sense of intimate connection. We now think of ourselves not as the impersonal effects of a remote and overpowering cause, but rather as the children of God, attached in love and intimacy to their father.

The extremes introduce differing moments into the same set of perceptions, responses which color in distinctive ways all of our striving for lives which are virtuous. But as MaHaRaL's thought develops on this subject the extremes come together in a synthesis which interpenetrates their seemingly separate domains. In the final analysis, fear of God is not only tempered by love, but derives directly from love. Love fills us with an intense desire to do whatever is pleasing to our beloved, and this, in turn, causes us to be anxious, even fearful, concerning any act which might violate the desires of our beloved. One who loves God truly also fears any transgression of His commandments.[46] This is no longer the destructive fear which we discussed earlier, but a fear informed by love and therefore a fear which is sound and constructive both as emotion and as a guide to action.

Having set forth the foundations and structure of the main elements in MaHaRaL's moral philosophy, we must give some consideration to one further type of virtuous behavior which is often misunderstood. I refer to that extensive constellation of recommended actions which goes under the name of *derekh eretz*. Some writers claim to find in rabbinic rules concerning *derekh eretz* an independent natural morality. It is their view that the rabbis were teaching us about a realm of moral principle which is based on unaided human reason and is not derived from divine commandment. They go on to construe this as a natural moral law which has full status with the divine commandments within the Jewish moral system. At least so far as MaHaRaL is concerned this view has no foundation. *Derekh eretz* is a kind of natural virtue within MaHaRaL's system, and it is known independently. It is not, however, part of morality as such, nor does it in any way exist as an independent body of obligation parallel to the commandments of the Torah.

Of the various elements that are included by MaHaRaL under the heading of *derekh eretz*, the least interesting for our purposes is that which is purely etiquette or propriety. MaHaRaL follows the rabbinic sources in recognizing the worth of such behavior, but he certainly does not confuse it with morality. In its key meaning *derekh eretz* refers to that whole body of practice which is required for human life to be sustained and for man to be able to function within society. It is *derekh eretz* in this sense which preceded the Torah, as we are repeatedly told, and which made life possible on earth before the Torah was revealed. This *derekh eretz* is nothing more than behavior which is based on good sense, on what we learn from human experience, and on a healthy concern for our own welfare and that of our society. "*Derekh eretz* is the practical ordering of human life in this world (*hanhagat ha-olam ha-ze*). A person who does not behave with *derekh eretz* has no place in this world and is not considered part of our reality."[47] Under the rubric of *derekh eretz* MaHaRaL includes "the work that a man does in order to support himself and everything else that is required for maintaining oneself in this world."[48] We are not dealing here with commandments of the Torah, nor with some sort of law of reason, but simply with the fact that every human being must do certain things in order to survive. Specific prescriptions and rules of behavior, in accordance with *derekh eretz*, derive from the general principle that one should use one's intelligence for appropriate practical ends. MaHaRaL sometimes includes under *derekh eretz* basic rules of morality, but he explicitly labels these as commandments which are binding on us and whose violation is a sin.[49] This is an extended usage which neither affects the root meaning of *derekh eretz* nor adds to the basic concept.

Having set forth the structure of the moral system in MaHaRaL's thought, we must now turn to the place of man within that system. We cannot here attempt a full account of MaHaRaL's theory of human nature, but shall concentrate our attention only on those aspects which are immediately related to man as a being who is commanded to do the good. In his analysis of this aspect of human nature, MaHaRaL again follows a dialectical pattern. Viewed from one perspective, man is conceived of as thoroughly good in his essential nature. God created man perfectly so that man has no natural tendency toward evil. Uncorrupted, man's whole being is directed exclusively to the good. "Man was originally created without sin."[50] This is both a moral assessment and a metaphysical judgment. Having been created directly by God, man shares the divine purity and perfection. Given his divine source, man is not only created without sin, but by his very nature loves and pursues the good and the wise.[51] Righteousness is natural to man, so much so that he becomes wicked only when he violates his own natural way by a deliberate decision.[52] It should follow from this that if man would only allow his natural tendencies to prevail he would be perfectly virtuous.

There is, however, an opposed picture of man set forth by MaHaRaL. In this version man is beset by strong natural tendencies to evil. The most extreme portrait of this aspect of man's nature represents man as desiring evil for its own sake. There is a force in man which attracts him to evil not because of the pleasure that evil may offer or any other benefit that it may confer, but simply because it finds evil attractive in itself.[53] In fact, "if man were to follow his natural inclinations, he would perform no good deeds whatsoever."[54] Considered from this perspective man is a creature from whom no good or virtuous action should ever be expected.

The polar tensions are reflections of contradictory aspects of human nature. Man is constituted out of fundamentally opposed elements which cause him to live in a constant state of tension between forces which pull in contrary directions. He is created "in the image of God" and, as such, shares in the divine perfection. This is man's ultimate ground of value, that which confers upon him his unique status in the world of created things.[55] However, this quasi-divine being is housed in a physical body, and, as we saw earlier, that body is conceived by MaHaRaL as the source of evil. When he describes man as having strong natural tendencies toward evil, MaHaRaL is always speaking in the context of man's material corporeality. "So long as man is encased in his body he cannot follow the path of righteousness . . . because the body in its very nature tends toward that which is a privation of righteousness."[56]

From this it follows that virtue is not automatic for man but must be acquired with much effort and struggle. All other creatures are whatever they are in the fullness of their nature from the time that they come into existence. Man alone is created with the open possibility of becoming more or less than he initially is.

Should he allow the material element to dominate him, he will be less than a man, even less than the beasts, for he will have corrupted his higher nature. If the intellectual-spiritual element prevails then man becomes more than he initially is. He actualizes his highest potentiality and belongs to the realm of the divine.[57] The mediating power between the two extremes is the Torah. This is the force which alone addresses itself successfully to the material dimension and gives man the capactity to overcome it. It is at the same time the force which embodies the supernal wisdom that transforms man into a higher being.[58]

This brings us back to our starting point. We have seen how the various elements in MaHaRaL's thought are articulated into a systematic moral philosophy. It is essential to restate at this point our initial premise. Although there is in the works of MaHaRaL no single extended systematic discussion of these themes, it seems clear that he has offered us far more than isolated and unconnected thoughts. Careful reading makes it possible to discover the system which is implicit in the works of MaHaRaL and to construct a faithful account of his moral philosophy. What we have attempted here is an initial sketch of the main features of that system. Each of these themes needs to be further elaborated and the moral philosophy of MaHaRaL must then be considered within the larger context of his thought.

Nothing in the ethical theory that has been presented here would serve to identify MaHaRaL unmistakably as a sixteenth-century figure. His sources are traditional and his style of thought fits far better with the rabbinic tradition, with medieval Jewish philosophy, and with Kabbalah than with any emerging modernism. One has only to contrast MaHaRaL's moral theory with that of Moses Mendelssohn in the eighteenth century or with Jewish Kantians of the nineteenth century to see how traditional he was. However, modernism is not by itself an absolute value, and we can find in the traditional thinking of MaHaRaL an illuminating and permanently valuable Jewish understanding of the moral life.

NOTES

All references to the works of MaHaRaL are to the Jerusalem, 1971 reprint of the London edition by Honig. The following abbreviations have been adopted:

D.Ḥ. = *Derekh Ḥayyim*
N.O. I = *Netivot Olam*, Vol. I
*N.O.*II = *Netivot Olam*, Vol. II

1. Jacob Katz, *Exclusiveness and Tolerance* (New York, 1962), p. 138.
2. Gershom Scholem, *Kabbalah* (Jerusalem, 1974), p. 77.
3. *N.O.* I, p. 4a; cf. ibid., pp. 4b, 6b.
4. *N.O.* I, p. 4a.
5. *Gen. Rabbah* I, 1.
6. *D.Ḥ.*, p. 25b.
7. *D.Ḥ.*, p. 275a.
8. *Phaedo*, 97B.
9. *D.Ḥ.*, p. 172b.
10. Ibid.
11. *N.O.* I, p. 43a.
12. *D.Ḥ.*, p. 197a.
13. *D.Ḥ.*, p. 192b.
14. Cf. E.E. Urbach, *Ḥazal: Pirkei Emunot ve-De'ot* (Jerusalem, 1969), pp. 190ff.
15. Maimonides, *Guide of the Perplexed*, tr. S. Pines, III, 8, p. 431.
16. Maimonides, *Eight Chapters*, ed. Gorfinkle, VII, pp. 82–83.
17. *Phaedo*, 64c–67a.
18. Cf. for example, *Guide*, III, 51.
19. *D.Ḥ.*, p. 91a–b.
20. *D.Ḥ.*, p. 220b.
21. *N.O.* I, p. 63ab.
22. *N.O.* II, p. 185b.
23. *N.O.* I, p. 72b.
24. *N.O.* II, p. 123b.
25. *D.Ḥ.*, p. 182a.
26. *N.O.* II, p. 199b.
27. *N.O.* II, p. 104a–b.
28. *D.Ḥ.*, p. 117a–b.
29. *N.O.* II, p. 104a–b.
30. Ibid.
31. *N.O.* I, p. 153b.
32. *N.O.* I, p. 156a.
33. *D.Ḥ.*, p. 21a.
34. *N.O.*, I, pp. 164bff.
35. *Gen. Rabbah* XII, 15.
36. *N.O.* I, p. 146a.
37. *N.O.* I, p. 16a.
38. *N.O.* I, p. 150a.
39. *N.O.* I, p. 152a.
40. *N.O.* I, p. 148b.
41. *N.O.* II, p. 44b.
42. *N.O.* II, p. 45a.
43. *N.O.* II, p. 23ab.
44. *N.O.* I, p. 120a.
45. *N.O.* II, p. 39a.
46. *N.O.* I, p. 22b.
47. *N.O.* II, p. 250b.
48. *D.Ḥ.*, p. 153b.

49. *N.O.* II, p. 249a.
50. *N.O.* I, p. 152a.
51. *N.O.* I, pp. 31b, 33a.
52. *N.O.* II, pp. 138ab, 141a.
53. *N.O.* II, p. 40a.
54. *D.Ḥ.*, p. 141a.
55. *N.O.* II, p. 52b.
56. *N.O.* I, p. 7a.
57. *D.Ḥ.*, p. 138ab.
58. *D.Ḥ.*, p. 25ab.

The Magical and Neoplatonic Interpretations of the Kabbalah in the Renaissance*

MOSHE IDEL

In Italy of the Renaissance period, Jewish thought developed in a manner unprecedented in earlier stages of Jewish intellectual history. Several of the most creative personalities in Jewish culture were in communication with leading spokesmen of Renaissance thought. This phenomenon is unique: Greek, Arabic and Christian philosophy developed in the absence of any significant oral connection with Jewish culture. Before the Renaissance, Jewish thought exercised no decisive influence upon the major representatives of gentile thought. In those instances where a certain Jewish influence may be detected, that influence originated from a written rather than an oral source.[1] In the Renaissance period, on the other hand, a considerable number of Christian thinkers took instruction from Jews. Among them were the Italians Pico della Mirandola and Egidio da Viterbo, the German Reuchlin, and Tissard, a Frenchman.[2] In addition, Christian scholars had frequent contacts with the numerous Jewish apostates of the time. The new meeting of Christian and Jew was part of the Christian culture's search for ancient wisdom. The Christians themselves initiated these contacts and the following source serves as an illustration of the vigor of this activity:[3]

> In the last twenty years, knowledge has increased, and people have been seeking everywhere for instruction in Hebrew. Especially after the rise of the sect of Luther,[4] many of the nobles and scholars of the land sought to have thorough knowledge of this glorious science (Kabbalah). They have exhausted themselves in this search, because among our people there are but a small number of men learned in this wisdom, for after the great number of troubles and expulsions, but a few remain. So seven

* The author would like to thank Ms. Martelle Gavarin for translating this article.

learned men grasp a Jewish man by the hem of his garment and say: 'Be our master in this science!'

Here Rabbi Elijah Menaḥem Ḥalfan alludes to another aspect of gentile eagerness to learn from the Jews. Not only did the gentiles want instruction in Hebrew; they also wanted to gain access to wider areas of Jewish thought, and particularly to the Kabbalah.[5] In other words Jewish thought became an important subject of discussion among Christian thinkers. This significant change affected the intellectual climate in which Jewish Renaissance culture developed.

Jewish activity in the area of translation is clear evidence of the new Christian attitude to Jewish culture and to the reciprocal Jewish willingness to become involved in Christian culture. Until the end of the fourteenth century, Jews translated many important philosophical works into Hebrew. From the fifteenth century onwards however, Jews and apostates began to translate Jewish books into Latin and Italian or to write part of their own compositions in these languages. In contrast, there are scarcely any translations of philosophical works into Hebrew at this time. The few Hebrew translations were of books authored by Jews: for example, the translation of Judah Abravanel's *Dialoghi d'Amore* and the translation of Rabbi Abraham Herrera's book, *Puerto del Cielo*. Platonic, Neoplatonic and Hermetic writings were translated into Latin and other European languages, but they are not to be found in a Hebrew version. This fact is a clear indication of the change in the direction of translation.

This new development, a lively intellectual meeting of Christian and Jew, had interesting implications for Jewish thought. The outstanding works of medieval Jewish philosophy, *The Book of Beliefs and Opinions, The Kuzari, The Guide for the Perplexed*, and *The Light of God (Or ha-Shem)* were created in response to problems arising from the influence of general intellectual developments upon Jews.[6] Jewish thought in the Renaissance was not reactive in the same way. Here the identification of stimulus and response are not always clear. To determine who was the teacher and who the pupil is not always easy. It is often difficult, therefore, to determine whether a statement of a Jewish author derives ultimately from a Christian source or whether it represents an original development of Jewish thought. The phenomenon was one of mutual openness which began with a Christian desire to learn from Jews and continued with Jewish willingness to absorb ideas developed by the Christian Renaissance. The nature and content of this exchange is well represented in the similarity of views on magic and Kabbalah found in the writings of Pico della Mirandola and Rabbi Yoḥanan Alemanno.

The central topic of this paper concerns the Neoplatonic and magical interpretations of Kabbalah in the Renaissance period and the way in which such ideas in Jewish sources could have influenced the development of Renaissance culture in general. Before treating the subject in detail, however, it is necessary to consider the general character of Jewish Kabbalah in Italy.

Kabbalah as it developed in Italy differed from that of Spain. In Spain, the primary classical formulation of Kabbalah was cast in terms of myth. This mythical sensibility placed great emphasis upon the theosophical and theurgic meaning of the commandments of Jewish law. Italian kabbalistic theosophy on the other hand, emphasized the unity and simplicity of the divine emanation and its apprehension by man's intellection, while the theurgic nature of the Kabbalah was correspondingly de-emphasized.

Three kabbalists, Rabbi Abraham Abulafia who composed most of his works in Italy, Rabbi Menaḥem Recanati. and the author of the book *Ma'arekhet ha-Elohut*, are the central pillars of Italian Kabbalah from its early stage until the beginning of the sixteenth century. Despite the tremendous differences in the thought systems of these figures, I discern in their writing a common conceptual characteristic: the mythical conception of the Divinity which characterized the Zohar and the later works of Gikatilla was either unknown to them or incompatible with their way of thought. In the opinion of Abraham Abulafia, belief in the existence of the ten *Sefirot* is worse than the Christian belief in the Trinity.[7] To Recanati, the *Sefirot* are the instruments, not the essence, of God. The author of the *Ma'arekhet* demonstrates a clearly nominalist trend of thought.[8] It follows that a certain similarity exists between the thought of these writers and the philosophical conception of God. After the expulsion, Spanish kabbalists reached Italy and found the Italian school of Kabbalah to be unfamiliar. In the mid-1490s, Rabbi Judah Ḥayat wrote that in the province of Mantua he had seen "books of the Kabbalah that confuse the unsullied mind," and warned against reading such works.[9] In his two letters to Rabbi Isaac of Pisa, Rabbi Isaac Mar Ḥayyim gave the following advice:[10]

Do not follow the path of those scholars who base themselves upon reason and interpret the words of the Kabbalah so as to agree with philosophy. Rather make Kabbalah the foundation and try to make reason agree with it.

These descriptions underline a similarity between Italian Kabbalah and philosophy which exceeds that found in the writings of Rabbi Menaḥem Recanati and the author of the *Ma'arekhet.*[11] This affinity between Kabbalah and philosophy has an important corollary in the interpretation of the practical commandments of Jewish Law. The Kabbalah emphasizes the theocentric significance of the commandments. The kabbalists assume that observance of the commandments with kabbalistic awareness enables man to restore the harmony of the Divinity. This concept is fundamental to the Kabbalah of Spain and Safed. Proper evaluation of these kabbalistic schools depends upon recognition of the significance of this principle. It follows that, in this view, a kabbalist is one who above all else lives his life in accordance with the dictates of processes occuring within the system of the *Sefirot.*

Abulafia and the author of the *Ma'arekhet* ignore this notion, and in their teachings Kabbalah loses its theurgic value.[12] The non-theurgic nature of Italian Kabbalah until the sixteenth century facilitated Christian acculturation and acceptance of Kabbalah as a science. The Neoplatonic circles of Florence had an unabrasive encounter with the quasi-philosophical theology of Abulafia, with the kabbalistic theory of the *Ma'arekhet* and even with the teaching of Recanati.[13] Furthermore Abulafia's mystical and exegetical system of thought did not depend in essence upon any particular theology. His mystical way was an instrument for all those who sought to narrow the distance between man and the Torah or the Divinity. As H. Wirszubski demonstrated, early in his career Pico had access to Abulafia's thought.[14]

The mutual influence of Jewish and Christian Kabbalah is attested to by a change in the style of Jewish kabbalistic works during the Renaissance. Until the mid-fifteenth century Jewish kabbalistic writings did not contain digressions on other subjects while works of Christian Kabbalah, on the other hand, devoted a considerable, if not a preponderant amount of space to non-kabbalistic material.

Pico's *Theses*, his most important kabbalistic composition, contains a very heterogeneous selection of subject matter and a relatively small amount of Kabbalah. Reuchlin set down a weighty amount of Pythagorean and Platonic material alongside his kabbalistic topics. Such is also the case in the writings of Egidio da Viterbo and Francesco Giorgio. From the end of the fifteenth century however, one finds many Jewish authors who utilized the Kabbalah in an eclectic fashion and wrote works incorporating Kabbalah alongside material drawn from other systems of thought. Yoḥanan Alemanno was an outstanding representative of this change as were Isaac and Judah Abravanel, Judah Moscato and Abraham Yagel.

The identification of the lines of influence between the thought of Rabbi Yoḥanan Alemanno and that of his student, Pico della Mirandola, should be attempted within the framework of the general trends described above. It is known that the two scholars met in Florence in the year 1488.[15] If this was their first meeting then several of the ideas which Pico committed to writing between the years 1486 and 1488 were the result of an independent attempt to synthesize various systems of thought. Moreover, similar views appearing in Alemanno's writings were the result of Pico's influence on his teacher. However, if Pico and Alemanno met earlier than 1488, then it is possible that Alemanno's views on the Kabbalah and magic influenced the formulation of Christian Kabbalah as did the writings of Flavius Mithridates.

When treating the question of the direction of influence one should bear in mind also that Alemanno was some twenty years older than Pico and had begun to record his thoughts as early as the year 1470. (It is likely that some of Alemanno's earlier writings have survived in a manuscript collection of his work now at Oxford.[16]) For this reason, I tend to think that Alemanno's thought should be seen as influenced by the general Neoplatonic trend current in Florence. The Florentine interest in magic also left its mark on Alemanno. Alemanno's contribution to his cultural surroundings is represented by his Neoplatonic and magical interpretations of the Kabbalah, interpretations which influenced Pico as well as Jewish writers of the sixteenth century. My discussion is limited to the similarity of their thought and this parellism permits us to consider Alemanno a Renaissance personality in every respect.[17]

The similarity between the material found in the Christian Kabbalah and that found in Alemanno's writings also deserves attention. In neither case can these works be categorized as kabbalistic in the common sense of the term. For these writers, Kabbalah is but one of several systems of speculation. This accounts for my earlier observation that in every one of Alemanno's compositions one can find much material drawn from non-kabbalistic sources. As a result of this eclecticism, Kabbalah as presented in Alemanno's writings underwent certain metamorphoses, changes which will be discussed in the following pages.

II

One of the most significant contributions of recent Renaissance scholarship has been the recognition of the considerable impact of magic on Renaissance thought.[18] Scholarship has gradually uncovered the influence of doctrines of magic contained in the Hermetic corpus translated by Marsilio Ficino. The literary traces of *Picatrix* are discernible in the writings of several central thinkers such as Giordano Bruno and Tomasso Campanella.[19] Several authors mention another work on magic, the *Sefer Razi'el* attributed to King Solomon.[20] Solomon was also mentioned as the author of other books read by the circle of Lorenzo de' Medici in Florence.[21]

At first, Renaissance magic assumed a philosophical garb woven of Hermetic, Neoplatonic and kabbalistic strands. The demonic elements of magic were rejected by authors such as Ficino and Pico, but these elements came to the fore later and occupied a place of increasing importance in magical literature. The most outstanding representative of this development was Agrippa of Nettesheim.

The study of magic by Jewish scholars also flourished during the same period.[22] Jewish interest was sparked in no small measure by the preoccupation with the subject in Christian intellectual circles. Conceptions of magic known to, and rejected by, Judaism long before the Renaissance now returned to Jewish thought, partially or completely legitimized. Moreover, non-Jewish works on magic which, though they had been translated into Hebrew earlier, had received little attention now enjoyed wider distribution and more frequent mention. New works were also translated from Latin and Italian, and there are references to contacts between Christian and Jewish magicians. All of these provide tangible evidence of the contemporary mutual interest in magic.

The Jewish study of magic was a response to Christianity's new regard for the subject. Nevertheless, Jewish authors had greater freedom of thought than Christian writers who worked under the watchful eye of the Church. As a result, magic could become, for the Jews, a new and comprehensive perspective from which to view all aspects of their tradition.

My general discussion will be preceded by a bibliographical description which charts the increased interest in the study of magic among Jews during the Italian Renaissance.

There are two Hebrew versions of the most important composition on magic, the *Ghayat al-Ḥakim* or *Picatrix.* Both renditions contain abridgments of the larger work.

1) The most important abridgment of the work was made from the Arabic[23] and is entered here under the title, *Takhlit he-Ḥakham.*[24] This version of the work is to be found in two manuscripts, Munich MS 214 f. 46r–101v and Brit. Lib. MS Or. 9861 f. lr–38v. These two manuscripts were copied in Italy at the end of the fifteenth century. During this period, the work was mentioned in Alemanno's curriculum as one of the books on magic which must be perused by anyone who wishes to attain perfection.[25]

2) A fragment of the second abridgemnt of the *Picatrix* is also relevant to our discussion. This was preserved in two manuscripts which were part of the same codex, New York MS 2470 (ENA 2439) f. lr–10v and New York MS 2465 (ENA 1920) f. lr–5r. These two manuscripts were also copied in Italy. In the first manuscript on page 10r, we read:

> This book was translated from Aramaic into Arabic and from Arabic into Hebrew, but this translation is not the first Hebrew translation. From Hebrew it was translated into Latin and from Latin this translation was made, praise to God.

At the end of the second manuscript, we find this (on f. 5r):

> The translation of the first chapter of the book *Ghayat al-Ḥakim*, has been completed, thank God, and was translated from a Christian translation, most of which is incorrect, as their translation is in no way clear.

This evidence of the translation of the composition from the Latin (*la'az*) seems to refer to a translation made during the Renaissance period. In any case, the Hebrew translation was made after the first Arabic translation and certainly after the Latin whose approximate date is unknown.[26]

3) A small portion of the Hebrew text of *Picatrix* has been preserved in Oxford MS 1352 (Mic. 228) f. 177r. Neubauer published a section of this text in his catalogue of Oxford manuscripts. This manuscript was also written in Italy.

Three Hebrew translations of *Picatrix* have been preserved in Italian manuscripts written at the end of the fifteenth and the beginning of the sixteenth centuries. At the same time the Latin translation of *Picatrix* was widely disseminated among scholars of the Renaissance. Rabbi Yoḥanan Alemanno, who was involved in the intellectual activities of the type pursued at the Academy of Florence, is one of the few to mention the Hebrew version of the *Picatrix*.

Another work on magic which enjoyed widespread distibution among Christians in the Renaissance is the above mentioned *Sefer Razi'el*. In many respects, this composition differs from the better known *Sefer Razi'el ha-Malakh*. F. Secret has given a detailed description of the content of *Sefer Razi'el*, and I will supplement his remarks by reference to the Hebrew translation which was unknown to him. The composition is found in two manuscripts, the more complete of which is New York JTS MS 8117 f. 59–100. In Oxford MS 1959 f. 98v–131v, a large section of the composition appears in a different and less felicitous version than that of New York MS 8117. Study of the composition indicates that the translation was also made in Italy. Clear evidence of this fact appears on the first page of MS 8117, f. 1r.

In the name of the God of Israel, I shall begin to copy *Sefer Razi'el*. Pay close attention and know that I found this book in two versions, the first in Hebrew and the second in Latin [*latino*]. The names of angels and intelligences [*intientzii*(!)] are different in each work but in practical terms there is no difference (*varietati*) in any respect. Since no one who practices may succeed in any of these actions without knowing this book, I have chosen to copy it using each one of the names of the intelligences [*intelientzii*] so that the practitioner will not have to consult other books which have no value whatsoever.

The translator's remarks bear close examination. According to the above quotation, it would seem that the translator had before him two identical compositions whose textual variation concerned only the names of angels. Comparison of this composition (New York JTS MS 8117) with parts of those translations cited by F. Secret indicates that here (MS 8117) we have an actual translation and not merely an integration of different versions. Support for this conclusion may be drawn from the presence in the work itself of Italian words, the product of some individual linguistic imagination, which bear no resemblance to the terminology found in earlier works on Jewish magic. There is proof that this translation was included in Alemanno's curriculum where it is described as a "translation from Latin." Since Alemanno mentions this composition in other places in his writing it is reasonable to assume that the latest date of the translation was the beginning of the 1480s. I have found no other mention of this work by a Jewish source before Alemanno. In the middle of the sixteenth century however, two works named *Sefer Razi'el*, "the long" and "the short," are mentioned in the correspondence of two scholars. It seems that the *Sefer Razi'el* to which I have referred in this paper was known by the name *Sefer Razi'el ha-Gadol.*[27]

Jews were familiar with the *Liber Clavicula Salomonis (Sefer Mafte'aḥ Shlomo)*, a famous book on magic well known to Christian intellectuals.[28] The *Clavicula* appears to have been mentioned for the first time by Rabbi Asher Lemlin, a German Jewish Kabbalist who lived in northern Italy at the beginning of the sixteenth century.[29] "Solomon, peace be with him, wrote an esoteric book *Sefer ha-Mafteaḥ*, about secret practices. The Christians call that book *Clavicula*."[30] After Lemlin, the book *Sefer Mafte'aḥ Shlomo* is mentioned by Rabbi Gedalya ibn Yaḥya, the author of *Shalshelet ha-Kabbalah.* Of King Solomon he writes: "He composed books and incantations against the devils and they are named *Mafteaḥ Shlomo.*"[31] Close study of the version of *Sefer Mafteaḥ Shlomo* that has reached us[32] reveals that its major part is a translation of material on magic from Christian sources. The translation seems to have been made in Italy between the time of Rabbi Asher Lemlin and the period of writing of *Sefer Shalshelet ha-Kabbalah.* Alemanno, who had great interest in works on magic, especially those ascribed to Solomon,[33] does not mention the book while Rabbi Asher Lemlin does not refer to it by its usual name, *Mafte'aḥ Shlomo*, but calls it *Ha-Mafte'aḥ ha-Nistar.* It follows that Lemlin was also unfamiliar with the Hebrew version of the work.

In addition to these popular works in the literature of magic, Rabbi Yoḥanan Alemanno also mentions other books which have been preserved thanks to Alemanno's interest in them. For example, in one work, Alemanno copied out an unknown translation of the *Sefer ha-Levana*,[34] an important book on magic. In *Ḥeshek*

Shlomo, Alemanno quotes several times from the *Sefer Mlekhet Muskelet*, attributed to Appolonius.[35] I found fragments of this book in two Italian manuscripts written in the sixteenth century.[36] In Alemanno's writings, the *Sefer ha-Atzamin*[37] attributed to Rabbi Abraham ibn Ezra, and the *Sefer ha-Tamar*[38] are mentioned. Both compositions were translated from the Arabic a long time before the Renaissance. The *Sefer Pil'ot Olam* (*The Wonders of the World*) of Albertus Magnus, one of the most important books on magic in Latin in the Middle Ages, was also known to Alemanno.[39] It is no less significant that Alemanno himself devoted considerable attention to the topic of magic in one of his works.[40] He asserts that he has contacts with gentiles who studied similar subjects. In Alemanno's *Collectanaea* we read: "A master of incantations told me that he had tried to find hidden treasure."[41] In the book *Shir ha-Ma'alot* Alemanno makes a second reference to a conversation with a gentile on the subject of magic and reports "what a craftsman told me."[42] The story concerned the ancient practice of killing a man and turning him into a spirit to guard a treasure. On another occasion, Alemanno relates that he met a gentile in Bologna who discerned Alemanno's character by the art of physiognomy and that his accurate description had greatly impressed Alemanno.[43] Dealing with demonic magic, Alemanno stated: "I heard many things of this type from Jews and Christians."[44]

In Judaism as a whole, there were two important conceptions of the possibility of human influence upon the extra-human realms. According to the first, it is man's duty to bring about a unification of the *Sefirot* which constitute, in general kabbalistic theory, the revealed aspect of the Divinity. This view[45] is singularly theurgic, for man's performance of religious commandments has God as its object. The commandments symbolically represent the dynamic activities and processes of the *Sefirot*. Performance of these actions is accomplished by the prescribed esoteric meditation. In this view, the realm of extra-divine forces is rarely affected by such practices. The resulting divine harmony, however, is beneficial to the world; this is a side effect which depends upon the achievement of the primary goal. One must particularly emphasize the fact that the observance of the commandments is no less a divine than a human necessity. This is expressed in the kabbalistic saying, "Service of God fulfills a divine need" (*avoda tzorekh gavo'ah*).

In contrast, magic in general acts upon the extra-divine world: the cosmic soul, the world of angels and the forces guiding the constellations and planets. Magic achieves its objectives in various ways. At times, the individual soul cleaves to the cosmic soul; thereby, man may change nature at will, for the cosmic soul directs nature. Other magical texts prescribe actions which cause astral forces to descend into the world and operate in accordance with the magician's will. This type of magic also includes demonic magic. The magician may also utilize talismans, certain materials or things having secret properties which absorb the emanations of higher powers or protect the bearer of the object. These types of magic have one common characteristic: no divine influence is present in the various processes. Generally speaking, magic is neither directed at, nor addressed to, God, nor does God benefit from the magician's activities. In kabbalistic terms these practices are "rituals that serve man" (*avoda tzorekh hedyot*).

Despite the differences between the kabbalistic and the magical understanding of human activity, the two systems share certain common features. In both conceptions, man has a central role and exercises considerable influence upon processes in many areas. By prayer or incantation, man exerts this influence in an appeal to the *Sefirot* or angels, forces outside himself. Although they are ontologically distinct, the *Sefirot* and the realm of "spirits" contain multiple powers and each of these powers has a unique character and capacity to exert an influence in a particular direction. The kabbalist must first ensure the flow of spiritual emanation from the *Ein Sof* (the Infinite Godhead) to the *Sefirot.* This efflux creates harmony in the divine structure as a whole, and only then may the kabbalist direct his prayers and meditations to any particular *Sefira* in order to achieve a desired effect. This selective employment of sefirotic power is analogous to that of angels who each supervise a certain area. These angels respond to incantations and answer human requests. This similarity between Kabbalah and magic is probably the result of the influence of ancient Jewish magic which was concerned with the incantations of angels. It is reasonable to assume that this doctrine of magic became integrated in the Kabbalah with gnostic and Neoplatonic traditions. Magic was transformed into theurgy once the object of the spiritual efflux became the *Sefira 'Malkhut'* rather than the kabbalist or magician himself.

Renaissance thinkers were aware of the analogy between magic and Kabbalah. In Pico's writings magic and Kabbalah are so often paired that the term "Kabbalah" becomes a synonym for magic. According to Pico, *magia naturalis*,[46] that is natural magic, is an initial and less potent level of Kabbalah which in its entirety is the quintessence of magic.[47] He emphasized that *magia naturalis* shares a common principle with Kabbalah; both are conceived as instruments for the reception of the efflux drawn from higher powers.[48] For Pico, Kabbalah is magic. This interpretation has altered the nature of Kabbalah by transfering its major focus from the realm of the Divinity to that of man. For Pico, the *magia naturalis* described by Marsilio Ficino is simply an initial and less potent level of Kabbalah, although Pico did not leave a detailed explanation of exactly why Kabbalah, the quintessence of magic and the highest achievement attained in the course of human development, is superior.

Pico classified the Kabbalah into "speculative" and "practical" branches, and from various statements in his writings we can identify the content of these branches. "Speculative" Kabbalah included the technique of letter permutation and the doctrine of the interrelation of the three worlds.[49] In another place, Pico offered a division of Kabbalah parallel to that of speculative and practical—namely into the sciences of the *Sefirot* and of the divine names.[50] In yet a third remark, Pico distinguished between letter permutations as one type of Kabbalah and the reception of divine powers as a second type, still superior to *magia naturalis*.[51] From these three statements we see that for Pico, the permutation of letters and the study of the divine names are separate branches of Kabbalah, while the recitation of the divine names and the reception of higher forces are both part of the practical Kabbalah. The exact nature of the latter relationship is not clarified.

There are significant parallels between Pico's classification and that offered by Alemanno and other Jewish kabbalists. For instance, a definition of speculative Kabbalah very similar to Pico's appears in a letter written in Alemanno's intellectual circle:[52]

> The speculative part of the Kabbalah concerns knowledge of the interconnection of the three worlds by means of the ten *Sefirot*, and the allusions and secrets of the Torah and the hierarchy of these three worlds and their area of influence.

Scholem[53] has already noted the resemblance between Pico's classification and Abulafia's division of the Kabbalah, in a letter to Rabbi Judah Salomon, into the study of the *Sefirot* and the study of the divine names.[54]

As for Alemanno himself, we can gain some insight into his distinction between magic and Kabbalah by analyzing his proposed curriculum of kabbalistic study. Alemanno advised one to begin the study of the Kabbalah by reading tracts on the doctrine of the *Sefirot.* For example, he recommended the works of Recanati and the book *Ma'arekhet ha-Elohut.*[55] As a further step, Alemanno suggested the writings of Abraham Abulafia and the commentaries on the *Sefer Yetzira.* The study of the corpus of Abraham Abulafia's writings was to be followed by the reading of books on magic, some of which treat the subject of divine names, and most of which discuss techniques for spiritual receptivity.[56]

A two-step technique for the working of miracles found in Alemanno's *Collectanaea* provides us with an excellent approach to that scholar's concept of the relation between Kabbalah and magic.[57] At first the kabbalist recites divine names which he reads to himself from a Torah scroll.

After the external cleansing[58] of the body and an inner change and spiritual purification from all taint, one becomes as clear and pure as the heavens. Once one has divested oneself of all material thoughts, let him read only the Torah and the divine names written there. There shall be revealed awesome secrets and such divine visions as may be emanated upon pure clear souls who are prepared to receive them as the verse said:[59] 'Make ready for three days and wash your clothing.' For there are three preparations: of the exterior (the body), of the interior, and of the imagination.

By reading the Torah as a series of divine names, man receives an initial infusion of power. This reading is preceded by a series of "preparations" which repeat the purifications performed by the Jews before the giving of the Torah at Sinai.

The second stage of the process is described in the continuation of the above quotation. In this, the Torah scroll itself becomes imbued with the spiritual force. At this time, "the writing of God, the spirit of the living God, shall descend upon the written scroll." By the expression, "the writing of God," Alemanno is referring directly to the giving of the Torah at Sinai as described in Exodus. A personal experience of the revelation of the law is a conventional thought in the Kabbalah. What is new and striking in the process described by Alemanno is the similarity of the ceremony to the ritual of dedication found in books of magic.

When a man devotes a great amount of time the intermittent becomes habitual. When he immerses himself in these things, then such a great efflux will come to him that he will be able to cause the spirit of God to descend upon him and hover above him and flutter about him all the day. Not only that, but 'the writing of God, the spirit of the living God' will descend upon the scroll to such a degree that the scroll will give him power to work signs and wonders in the world. And such are the books called '*segretti*' and all the incantations are the secret words [*segretti*] which come from evil spirits . Therefore the Torah forbade these practices. The Torah of Moses, however is entirely sealed and closed by the name of the Holy One, blessed be He. Therefore its powers are many and such is the Book of Psalms. This is a great secret, hidden from the eye of the blind and the cunning.

In Alemanno's *Collectanaea*, therefore, we find both elements of Pico's definition of the practical Kabbalah—first the reading of divine names in the Torah, and second, the reception of efflux. The connection between the use of divine names and the reception of emanation is also mentioned in the book, *Takhlit he-Ḥakham*,[60] a work known to Pico and Alemanno.

Aristotle said . . . in ancient times, divine names had a certain ability to bring spiritual power to earth. At times, these powers descended below. At others, they killed the man who used them.

Neither in Alemanno, nor in the above quotation from *Sefer Takhlit he-Ḥakham* is there any mention of practical Kabbalah. Careful study of Alemanno's statements indicates that the practices he suggests relate to the Torah scroll. The words of the Torah are, in Alemanno's view, a series of names from which meaning may be derived by reference to another source.[61] "The ancient sages said that all the Torah is but one name, and all its words are powerful names and each and every verse is an additional name."

This view originated in the books entitled *Sefer Shimushei Torah* and *Sefer Shimushei Tehilim* and in similar traditions which reached the kaballists Rabbi Ezra and Rabbi Moses ben Naḥman in Gerona. But the doctrines are now given an unequivocally magical interpretation by Alemanno. The Torah read as a series of names is transformed into an instrument of magic.[62]

Anyone who knows the science of the stars and constellations that emanate upon the creatures on earth may interpret the entire Torah according to the signs and rules of astrology. This is true of the masters of both theoretical, as well as practical, astrology. Any man, either good or evil, who knows the work of the pure and impure angels who are superior to the stars may draw their fragrance upon our heads, for he has given a kabbalistic interpretation to the entire Torah. This matter includes the masters of both the speculative and the practical sciences of the *Sefirot.*[63]

The Torah may be read in two ways, astrologically and kabbalisticaly. Each way has a speculative and a practical part. It seems to me that through the practical interpretation of the Torah (the reading of the divine names), one "may draw their fragrance upon our heads."

If my analysis of Alemanno's view is correct, then his understanding of practical Kabbalah is similar to that of Pico. Both consider the practical Kabbalah to include the use of divine names which are connected to the descent and activation of spiritual forces in the world.

The definitions of practical Kabbalah found in the writings of Pico and Alemanno share another common point. Pico considered as forbidden those kabbalistic practices which employ divine names to charm devils.[64] This distinction between pure and impure forms of practical Kabbalah is suggested by the previous quotation from Alemanno about pure and impure forces above the stars. At the end of the quote cited above from the *Collectanaea*, Alemanno speaks of incantations which are forbidden by the Torah. These are separate from the reading of the Torah in a magical way which is permitted.[65]

Alemanno's remarks appear to contain a thought parallel to material found in *Sefer Takhlit he-Ḥakham.* Immediately after the above quotation we find: "He [i.e. Aristotle] said magical incantations descend upon the globe[?]." Incantations derived from magic are forbiden but not the use of divine names.[66]

For Alemanno then, we have seen that the reading of a Torah scroll became a process for the acquisition of magical powers originating in the emanation of higher forces, and that this process had two stages. The person received an initial pulsation of the divine efflux and only then, after he had become habituated, could he receive the additional efflux, "the spirit of the living God." Alemanno describes this second stage as "bringing down into oneself the spirit of God" (the phrase is from the *Sefer Yetzira*) thus enabling oneself to perform signs and wonders[67]—in my opinion an adaptation of the famous magical formula, *horadat ha-ruḥaniyut*, which appears in many of the texts that Alemanno had before him.[68] The assumption that these are cognate idioms is supported by the fact that the expression occurs within the context of a discussion on magic.

Mention by Alemanno of interpretation of the Torah by the method of practical Kabbalah appears in Paris MS 849. This manuscript was written at the beginning of the sixteenth century. However, it is likely that Alemanno formed his opinion on the matter earlier than that. In the *Beḥinat ha-Dat*, Rabbi Elijah del Medigo opposed those who viewed the Torah and commandments as a means to cause the descent of spiritual forces.

> It is impossible to bring spiritual forces into the world in this way as do the magicians who employ forms and talismans. When we examine the words of the Torah, we find that the Torah strenuously opposes this practice for these are idolatrous practices.[69]

One may assume that Del Medigo's remarks are a criticism of Alemanno. Del Medigo was a member of Pico's intellectual circle until about 1490 and probably heard Alemanno's view expressed by intellectual colleagues.

The analogous structure of magic and a kabbalistic reading of the Torah described in Paris MS 849 has an interesting parallel in Alemanno's *Collectanaea*.[70]

> The astrologer studies every one of the creatures in relation to one of the seven planets. In the same manner, the kabbalist studies every word of the Torah, as stated before in connection with the commandments of the Torah. That is, he studies the *Sefira* to which it is related. The astrologer studies the movements and governance of the stars. In the same way the kabbalist knows what will happen to people in the future by reference to the influence and efflux of the *Sefirot*. This is in accordance with the activities and movements of those who perform the commandments and divine service. This method is superior to that of the astrologer.[71]

Thus kabbalistic study of the Torah is no longer seen as leading to preoccupation with the hidden processes of divinity. The kabbalist has become a "super-astrologer" who utilizes his knowledge to foresee the future.

A similar conception is again found in Pico's *Theses*.[72] "Sicut vera

Astrologia docet nos legere in libro Dei, ita Cabbala docet nos legere in libro legis." (Just as true astrology teaches us to read the books of God, so too does the Kabbalah teach us to read the books of the law.) This statement seems to be analogous to that of Alemanno. The practical side of astrology can be identified with *magia naturalis* for it teaches the way to receive the influx of higher powers. Kabbalah is a higher form of magic because its speculative foundation is, as Pico emphasized here, superior to that of astrology.

In his book, *Shir ha-Ma'alot*, Alemanno declares practical Kabbalah to be superior to astrology, but dismisses astral magic based upon the science of the stars.

> The kabbalists say that every limb of a man's body has a spiritual power corresponding to it in the *Sefira Malkhut*. . . . When a man performs one of the commandments by means of one of his corporeal limbs, that limb is readied to become a seat and home for the supernal power which is its likeness. . . . Our patriarch Abraham was the first to discover this wondrous science . . . as proven by his book, *Sefer Yetzira*, which was composed in accordance with this principle. It demonstrates how the likeness of each and every limb is to be found in the celestial spheres and stars and how matters stand in the spiritual world which he terms the world of letters[73]. . . . And study how this ancient science resembles the ancient science of astrology which found that every limb and form and corporeal body that exists in the world of change has a likeness in the world of celestial motion[74] in the stars and their forms. The astrologers prepared every thing in a way as to receive the efflux proper to it. However, this is a material craft which is forbidden, flawed and impure. But the wisdom of Abraham is a spiritual craft which is perfect and pure and permitted and his sons,[75] Isaac and Jacob, followed in his path.[76]

Alemanno's words indicate the nature of the new interpretation of the Torah. In his view, the kabbalists learn about future events from the Torah. This method is superior to that of the astrologers who learn from the stars. As demonstrated, practical Kabbalah teaches man how to make contact with magic forces. Thus, Kabbalah was transformed from speculation upon the mysteries of the divinity as an end in itself into a sophisticated means of exerting human influence superior to astrology or magic.

This change in the essence of Kabbalah appeared in both the writings of Alemanno and Pico, his student, but I believe that Alemanno was its source. This opinion is supported not only by the chronological data as given above, but also by the fact that

Alemanno's view of Kabbalah as magic belongs to his broader conception, while in Pico's writings the subject received only limited treatment in a few sentences.

As stated before, for Alemanno the Torah had unique properties, and the Kabbalah amounted to instruction in their application. To Alemanno, Moses was a magician who knew how to make use of kabbalistic principles.

The kabbalists believe that Moses, peace be with him, had precise knowledge of the spiritual world which is called the world of *Sefirot* and divine names or the world of letters. Moses knew how to direct his thoughts and prayers so as to improve the divine efflux which the kabbalists call 'channels.'[77] Moses' action caused the channels to emanate upon the lower world in accordance with his will. By means of that efflux, he created anything he wished, just as God created the world by means of various emanations. Whenever he wanted to perform signs and wonders, Moses would pray and utter divine names, words and meditations until he had intensified those emanations. The emanations then descended into the world and created new supra-natural things. With that Moses split the sea, opened up the earth and the like.[78]

Alemanno's view of Moses was not a new one. The idea was an old one found also in many non-Jewish sources.[79] The magic power of the word is described in a kabbalistic context, and here Moses becomes a kabbalistic magician.

Alemanno also used this approach in evaluating prophecy.

A prophet has the power to cause the emanation of divine efflux from *Ein Sof* upon the *hyle* (hylic matter) by the intermediary of the *Sefira Malkhut.* In this way the prophet performs wondrous deeds, impossible in nature.[80]

The Tabernacle and Temple also had a clearly magical function. Alemanno described them as a sort of great talisman which enabled the Jews to receive the divine emanations of the *Sefirot.* In his *Collectanaea*, Alemanno offered four explanations of the nature of the Tabernacle and its vessels of which the third and fourth are relevant.[81]

For the people were educated to believe in the possibility of causing spiritual forces and emanations to descend from above by means of preparations made by man for that purpose, such as talismans, garments, foods and special objects intended to cause the descent of spiritual forces, just as when Moses our master, peace be with him,[82] prepared the golden calf. The intention was only to cause the spiritual forces to descend by means of a physical body. In Ibn Ezra's opinion,[83] they made a figure of Aquarius in mid-sky and Taurus rising, for that had the power necessary to ease their way in the wilderness, a desolate place. In Naḥmanides' opinion,[84] they directed their meditation to the figure of the ox on the left hand side of the *Merkava* in order to be protected from the attribute of strict judgment. Therefore, they had to make an ark and vessels capable of receiving those emanations. The fourth reason was to increase those actions such as the offering of sacrifices, which give protection and cause good emanations to descend and forestall the bad emanations, which descend from the stars and their heavenly courses.[85] The purpose of most of the commandments is to safeguard the prophetic efflux which issues above and descends upon the human intellect. Therefore, it was necessary to have various heavy large vessels and a Tabernacle to contain them.[86]

The Tabernacle is described as a complex talisman which "guards" and "causes the descent" of spiritual forces.

The idea that the Tabernacle "guards" the descent of spiritual forces requires some clarification. From the context it is clear that this is not simply protection against 'evil events.' The term is elucidated by reference to a quotation from one of Alemanno's literary sources, *Sefer Mekor Ḥayyim*[87] of Ibn Zarza.

In the *Book of the Religions of the Prophets*, it is written that Enoch was a great saint and sage who brought nations to the worship of God, blessed be He. At first, he publicized the science of the stars,[88] and he gave each of the inhabitants of the seven climes a religion which conformed to the nature of that climate.[89] He commanded them to observe festivals and offer sacrifices at particular times in accordance with the position of the stars and in keeping with the dominant star in the sky so that the star would guard the efflux of that particular climate. He commanded that some of them should not eat certain foods, but permitted others to eat them.

A similar thought about the purpose of the Torah appears in a responsum of Profet Duran to Rabbi Meir Crescas.[90]

All agree that the glory of God fills the entire world and that His power extends and emanates upon the creatures in general although they differ in their receptive capacities; thus the vegetative and animal have greater receptivity to divine efflux than the mineral. Man has greater receptivity than all of them. The extent of preparation for, and receptivity to, divine emanation accounts for the hierarchy of beings. Also in the human species, men possess differing degrees of receptivity. The Torah set down the commandments for the purpose of developing this receptivity insofar as possible.

In the case of sacrifices, Duran expresses an opinion similar to that of Alemanno.

The commandment ordained that the sacrifices be seven in number for the first season . . . for the offerant will receive a new spirit of understanding and will be ready to receive prophetic emanation. . . . For by the virtue of the burnt offering future events are revealed insofar as the celebrant intends to receive prophetic emanation.[91]

A similar conception appears in Alemanno's *Collectanaea.* Describing Moses' activity he writes:[92]

I said, I shall ascend to the Lord to receive detailed instruction about the commandments concerning two institutions—one institution safeguards the receptive power and that is the matter of the Tabernacle and its vessels. . . .

Alemanno thought that the Temple service was a preparation for the reception of divine emanation. In the expression, "preserving the receptive power,"[93] the term "receptive power" refers to the innate capability of a certain object to receive divine emanation, while, "to preserve the receptive power" is to ensure the continued reception of that power by the object in question. This is but a general definition of the purpose of the Tabernacle. Alemanno's book, *Shir ha-Ma'alot*, contains another description of the Tabernacle which emphasizes the magical character of the Temple institution.[94]

Astrologers, necromancers, chiromancers and masters of pagan crafts have rituals, rules, special places, incense, garments and set times and preparations in order to receive those impure spiritual forces. These descend upon those who manipulate them by means of the relation of those objects to those forces, as the masters of these crafts know. So too, there are activities, foods, garments, preparations and sacrifices, incense and places and times which enable one to receive and cleave to the pure spiritual forces which descend from the world of the *Sefirot.* These actions concern the esoteric knowledge of the Torah and the particulars of the commandments which cause Hebrew souls to cleave to *Malkhut. Malkhut* is the source of oral law which explains all the secrets of the Torah and details of the commandments.

Magic and Kabbalah share a common technique for causing the descent of spiritual forces to earth.[95] They differ, however, in their goal. The magician directs his efforts at the stars from whom he hopes to receive beneficial emanation. The Jews seek to receive, and cleave to, the emanations of the *Sefirot.* In the book, *Sefer Ḥeshek Shlomo*, Alemanno declared the descent of spiritual forces to be the principal goal of the endeavors of King Solomon:[96]

Both Solomon's good, and his unseemly, actions indicate that his lifelong goal was to cause the descent of spiritual forces to earth. He did all this by offering thousands and tens of thousands of sacrifices in order to cause the Holy Spirit to descend upon him[97] . . . and he made a great dwelling for the Lord his God, in order to bring the *Shekhina* to earth.[98]

Alemanno's words fell upon attentive ears and his ideas were echoed by other writers. For instance, Rabbi Isaac ben Yeḥi'el of Pisa,[99] whom Alemanno mentioned in the introduction to his *Shir ha-Ma'alot*,[100] expressed a view of the purpose of the Temple quite similar to Alemanno's in a letter:

To cause a supernal power to descend and perform a certain action, one must minister to that power by means of rituals proper to it. These rituals prepare it [the power] to perform the desired action. . . . The greatest Providence concerns the perfection of the soul and its becoming godly. The noblest service possible is that instructed by the Torah. For after He gave the command concerning the Tabernacle, God said this: 'And I shall dwell in the midst of the Israelites' [Ex. 29:45]. That is to say, it is necessary to safeguard the receptive power so that the supernal powers descend. For the receptive power safeguards the relation [of the upper and lower worlds] by means of particular garments, sacrifices, places and actions, performed at certain times. When one of those particulars is missing, the desired goal will not be achieved. Moreover, harm will replace the hoped-for gain.[101]

This quotation appears with certain changes in two additional versions of the same letter and was included both in the *Commentary on the Ten Sefirot* of Rabbi Yeḥi'el Nissim of Pisa and in the book, *Sha'arei Ḥayyim* of the kabbalist Rabbi Mordekhai Raphael Rossillo. This bibliographical note is tangible evidence of the influence of Alemanno's view of Kabbalah and magic. The repetition of his view by three writers—all Italians—proves that Alemanno's opinions were influential.

As demonstrated above, the phrase "to guard the receptive power" originated in the terminology of magic. In the sources cited above from Alemanno's writings this phrase does not have a kabbalistic connotation. However, in several other discussions, Alemanno explicitly connected "the preservation of the receptive power" to the activity of the *Sefirot*. For example, one finds the following statement:[102]

For our master Moses, peace be with him, demanded only that one safeguard the power of receiving the emanation of the *Sefira Tiferet* which is the purpose of the narratives of the entire Torah and its commandments. For our master Moses, peace be with him, was empowered in this matter, as the verse says, 'That caused his glorious arm [*zroa' tif'arto*—literally, the arm of His Beauty and here the *Sefira Tiferet*] to go at the right hand of Moses' [Isaiah 63:12]. However, he [Moses] did not seek to inquire of the alien women who go around *Tiferet* in what way may the power of receptivity be used to cause the light of the Powers to dwell below. Solomon, on the other hand, was led astray by the alien women because he desired to know how they were able to sustain the adherence of a power to them[103] but he [Solomon] did not safeguard the power of receptivity, for he should not have followed their way.[104]

Solomon repeated this transgression while in the company of the Queen of Sheba, "for he did not safeguard the power of receptivity in thought or deed."[105] This was also the sin of Adam "who did not safeguard the power of receptivity of the *Sefirot* Love, Compassion and Life."[106] Here, the term 'Love' refers to the *Sefira Ḥesed*.[107] According to the following quotation man's duty is to become a receptacle for the emanation of the *Sefira Malkhut*:

The House of the King: This refers to man's preparation of himself so that each and every one of his limbs will be worthy to receive emanation, so that each [limb] might be a receptacle and contain the efflux proper to itself in a constant manner, just as a man lives in his home permanently and not temporarily. So shall a man prepare all the residences of human habitation—the apartments, upper stories and chambers to receive the efflux which descends constantly upon us. So shall man prepare his intellect, soul and Torah[108] in such a way as to receive wisdom, knowledge and enlightenment from it.[109]

What is the fundamental preparation a man must make in order to receive a constant influx of emanation? Alemanno's answer is based upon the opinion of the "sages of the *Sefira*": the purpose of all commandments is to make a place below for the powers of Love and Compassion, to awaken them and cause them to descend into the lower realms even to "the depth of the grave, and to cause the power of impurity and strict judgment to pass away from the earth."[110]

There are other expressions in Alemanno's writings of this basic idea that the commandments of the Torah enable man to receive the efflux from the *Sefirot*. Alemanno's explanation of prayer will serve as an example of these:[111]

The prayer of those versed in esoteric wisdom is superior to that of the first group for the latter's knowledge of the paths of emanation exceeded that of the former. Therefore they know which prayer suits which particular emanation. Because of the superiority of their knowledge of the character of the emanations and of the manner of preparation for that emanation in a direct manner, they know how to prepare all those things such as human souls which may receive those emanations in accordance with their deeds and their relation to the intelligible.[112]

A more general description appears in the book, *Shir ha-Ma'alot*: "When a man performs one of the commandments by means of one of his corporeal limbs, that limb is prepared to be a seat and home for the supernal spiritual power."[113] This statement bears a close resemblance to that of Rabbi Joseph Gikatilla in his introduction to the book, *Sha'arei Ora.*[114] Alemanno's formulation differs from that of Gikatilla by substitution of the word *bayit* 'home,' for the word *merkava*, a substitution probably intended to stress the fact that man may be filled by the supernal powers. In the continuation of this quotation, Alemanno observes that "all the laws of the Oral Torah" issue from the *Sefira Malkhut*, and are "modeled after its spiritual powers and prepare one to receive wisdom from it." King Solomon learned[115]

to prepare himself and his royal household, and [to order] his wisdom and all his deeds, so as to become an abode for the reception of the glory of *Malkhut* [majesty] by means of it [*Malkhut*]. He established courtyard boundaries for it, this being one of the laws of the Oral Torah. . . . By means of his preparations in the construction of the House of the King, he received blessing and perfection in all benefits [both] material [and] spiritual, [as well as in] all the sciences.

According to Alemanno, the Oral Law is also intended to cause the descent of efflux and its reception by the men who are prepared for it. Alemanno's particular esteem of the Oral Torah is also evident in a statement in his book, *Shir ha-Ma'alot*:[116]

Spiritual matters do not descend where there is addition or detraction. The matter resembles the ancient worship of spirits which visited only those who followed the rituals precisely. If the worship of such is bound by restrictions, how much more so must the worship of God be bound by restrictions so that the worshipper neither add nor detract from it. As the verse said: 'You shall not add and you shall not detract' [Deut. 4:2].

This statement amounts to a magical interpretation of the Oral Law which parallels the magical interpretation given to the Written Torah, the phenomenon of prophecy and the institution of the Temple.

This magical interpretation of the fundamental practices of Judaism underlies Alemanno's remarks on the *Sefira Bina* in his untitled composition in Paris MS 849.[117]

The sphere of Saturn is the first sphere beneath the constellations. . . . And they say that Saturn is the true judge and the master of Moses, peace be with him. The angel of Saturn is Michael, the great minister, so called because of his great power in divine matters. He is the ministering angel of Israel[118] as the verse said: 'But only Michael is your minister' [Daniel 10:21]. Because of his exceptional grandeur he was called Michael, as if to say about his great works: 'Mi kha-el' [Who is this one who is as God?] because of his extreme grandeur and spirituality. . . . And the astrologers who described Saturn say that it endows man with profound thought, law and the spirtual sciences, prophecy, sorcery and prognostication and dictates the *shmitot* [the sabbatical years] and *yovlot* [the jubilee years]. The Jewish people and the Hebrew language and the Temple are under its jurisdiction. Saturn's major conjunction is with Libra in Pisces and this occurs to assist the nation and the Torah and its prophets.[119] This planet endows the people with perfection in the sciences and divine matters such as the Torah and its commandments. This is because of its great exaltedness, for it is spiritual and loves what is spiritual, but hates what is corporeal. It is concerned only with thought, understanding and design, esoteric knowledge and divine worship and His Torah. The Sabbath day is in its sway for Saturn causes material existence to cease.

This paragraph is better understood by comparison with a statement of Rabbi Samuel ibn Zarza in his book, *Mekor Ḥayyim.*[120]

Know that the astrologers say that Jupiter who keeps watch over the seventh day has the power to renew the vigor of the corporeal bodies in nature. In truth, the Sabbath day possesses great excellence. To it fall the powers of thought, of understanding and of the maintenance of things. [To it also belong] design, knowledge of the secrets and the service of God, blessed be He. It is the star of Israel, and all the astrologers and Rabbi Joseph ibn Wakar, blessed be his memory, said that Saturn rules over the rational soul, thought and understanding and the existence of things. The Ethiopian, the Sandian [?], the Tabian [?] and the Berber nations and the Jews are under its influence. Of all the parts and the depths of the earth the Temple pertains to Saturn, as does the Hebrew language, the Scriptures and the Torah of Israel.

Alemanno was undoubtedly familiar with the book, *Mekor Ḥayyim*,[121] and he may also have seen a composition of Ibn Wakar dealing with the topic of astrology and spiritual forces. It seems however, that Alemanno did not copy his sources *verbatim.* In Ibn Wakar's account, the influence of Saturn is restricted to the Jews alone, and he omits mention of the other peoples. More important is the addition he makes to the statements of his predecessors, a modification in keeping with his personal views. To Alemanno, Saturn is appointed not only over the Torah of Israel, the Temple in Jerusalem and the Hebrew language, but also over the "spiritual sciences,"[122] magic,[123] sorcery, and prognostication. These additions to the list of Saturn's subjects conform to Alemanno's conception of the magical nature of the Torah, the Oral Law and the Temple.

As demonstrated, Alemanno based his discussions of magic and its relation to Jewish tradition upon writers such as Ibn Wakar, Solomon al-Constantini, Ibn Motot and Samuel Zarza. These authors share certain common assumptions, and this identity of views is the result of mutual influence rather than accident. Ibn Wakar's ideas influenced both Ibn Motot[124] and Zarza,[125] and the latter author knew al-Constantini's work.[126] The intellectual relationship of Ibn Motot and Zarza still needs close examination.[127]

It is useful to briefly characterize the views of this group of writers. First, all these writers attempt to combine philosophical and kabbalistic concepts into a broader system of thought. Second, in all of these attempts at synthesis, the influence of Neoplatonic streams of thought can be discerned in varying degrees. This is particularly true of these authors' renewed interest in, and reliance upon, the thought of Ibn Ezra and Avicenna. Third, these authors refer to several principles present in the Neoplatonic conceptions of Ibn Ezra and Avicenna which deal with the possibility of working miracles. Acceptance of these principles created a receptive ground for the absorption of books on magic by these writers. In this respect, the most important text on magic was *Sefer ha-Atzamim.*[128] Finally, the writings of these authors contain many discussions of the importance of astrology[129] and even of the relationship between magic and astrology.[130]

These writers exercised no major influence upon the development of Jewish thought. The pre-eminence of Ḥasdai Crescas and Joseph Albo in the area of theology and the predominance of the Kabbalah in the second half of the fifteenth century eclipsed the doctrines of most of the authors mentioned. Alemanno's extensive use of these writings, especially those of Ibn Motot and Ibn Wakar, is an exception to the general trend of thought among his Italian Jewish contemporaries. Alemanno's particular interest in these fourteenth-century works was rooted in his search for discussions of magic by Jewish sources. As I have attempted to prove in my article on his curriculum, Alemanno recommended readings on the subject of magic which were connected in one way or another to King Solomon or to the Jews in general. Alemanno utilized these sources on magic in order to construct a comprehensive system of thought which would substantiate the perfection of Judaism in theoretical and practical terms. To Alemanno "praxis" concerns man's ability to receive and command those powers which are emanations of the Divinity.

Alemanno's system of thought is not based upon a simplistic over-evaluation of magic in relation to other areas of thought and action. While the Kabbalah itself was for Alemanno the supreme speculative science, he emphasized elements in the Kabbalah which had only secondary importance in the development of that doctrine as a whole. This interpretation of the Kabbalah gave magic a pre-eminent position. Curiously enough Alemanno selected for this purpose parts of kabbalistic doctrine in which the element of magic had no function. His development of the concept of "guarding the power of receptivity" in kabbalistic contexts is one example of this tendency.

On the other hand, Alemanno adopted without qualm certain conceptions that had been strenuously opposed by the most important Jewish philosophers of the past. Judah ha-Levi stated that:

> One who seeks to receive instruction on divine matters [theology] by speculation, reasoning and syllogisms based upon the procedure of causing the descent of spirits and the manufacture of images and talismans is a heretic.[131]

Alemanno's characterization of Solomon's principal activity as "causing the descent of spiritual forces" is an open contradiction of Ha-Levi's view. The denial of the effectiveness of talismanic magic was certainly known to Alemanno from two sources which were familiar to him: Moses Narboni's citation of Averroes' negative attitude to this kind of magic in his *Commentary on the Guide*, I, 63, and Rabbi Nissim of Marseille's attacks on talismanic magic in his *Ma'ase Nissim.* Alemanno had even transcribed this latter passage in his *Collectanaea.*[132] In Florence "causing the descent of spiritual forces" was harshly condemned by Rabbi Moses ben Yo'av who considered this practice to be idolatry in every respect.[133] At the same time, Rabbi Elijah del Medigo dismissed magical interpretation of the Torah of any kind.[134]

Alemanno's revaluation of the element of magic seems to be not only the result of an internal development of Jewish tradition but also the product of outside influence which prompted Alemanno to emphasize the positive attitude to magic in Jewish sources. That influence was, in my opinion, the Neoplatonic school in Florence.[135] The meager biographical information we have about Alemanno does not permit meaningful discussion of the connections Alemanno had with this circle of scholars. It is clear that Alemanno was acquainted with Pico della Mirandola and also possibly with Lorenzo de' Medici; he mentions them in his book, *Shir ha-Ma'alot*, begun in 1488, but it is possible that Alemanno met them or at least had heard about their thought even before that time. In any case, magic occupied no place of particular importance in Alemanno's first composition, the first version of his *Ḥai ha-Olamim*, which was then entitled *Pekaḥ Ko'aḥ*.[136] The introduction and increasing prevalence of Neoplatonic elements in Alemanno's thought can be traced to the inspiration he received from the Neoplatonic school of Florence as we shall see in the continuation of this article. I have already mentioned that Alemanno sought out practitioners of magic and quasi-magic and did not restrict himself to the information he received from Hebrew sources. He also appears to have consulted Christian compositions on magic that had not been translated into Hebrew, and it seems that he was familiar with the work *Pil'ot Olam* of Albertus Magnus.

Alemanno had a noteworthy interest in the various manifestations of paganism. This is confirmed by a quotation from his *Collectanaea*:[137]

> The books of the ancient *gentili* . . . describe their various idolatrous practices and may the gods confirm everything that our Rabbis of blessed memory say concerning devils and various types of pagan worship. . . . All the idolatrous religions will come together in Rome and they will worship all of them until the coming of the Christian redeemer.

A possible explanation of the identity of the *gentili* and the nature of the "various idolatrous practices" is to be found in a lengthy comment in the *Collectanaea*.[138]

> The Chaldeans and Babylonians instituted the science of the heavenly forms[139] and star worship and astrology. Nimrod was chief among them

in the "tower which they made." Upon that tower he fashioned a form of Mars to serve as an idol as has been explained. After him, there remained Bel and Nebo of whom Ibn Ezra said that Nebo is the form of a star. Prophecy began with Abraham who disputed with them and cast down their opinions. Isaiah completed this work in his days when he said 'Let now the astrologers, the star-gazers, the monthly prognosticators stand up and save thee from the things that shall come upon thee' [Isaiah 47:13]. The latter reference [i.e., from Isaiah] is to Egypt and its wise men who were entirely preoccupied with the activities of the spirits between heaven and earth,[140] which have a strange effect upon nature. Divine prophecy disagreed with them, and our master Moses, peace be with him, cast them to the ground[141] and proved their lie. Isaiah also said: 'How can ye say unto Pharoah: I am the son of the wise, the son of the ancient Kings?' [Isaiah 19:11] and all that chapter.

This statement of Alemanno contains no clear reference to the books on paganism which he might have read.[142] In my opinion a statement which appears in Paris MS 849, Alemanno's untitled composition, contains a reference to the Hermetic literature, a corpus which greatly influenced the magic of the Renaissance.[143]

The ancient wisdom[144] was so vast that they boasted of it in their books which they attributed to Enoch 'whom the Lord has taken' [Genesis 6:4] and to Solomon who was wiser than any man and to many perfect men who performed actions by intermingling various things and comparing qualities in order to create new forms in gold, silver, vegetable, mineral and animal [matter] which had never before existed and in order to create divine forms which tell the future, the laws and the *nomoi*, as well as [to create], spirits of angels, stars and devils.[145]

I think that this is a description of the Hermetic technique of alchemy and of images and statues made of precious metals and other vegetable and animal components which capture the spirits of the gods.[146] Alemanno's statement about divine forms which speak of laws and *nomoi* also has a parallel in an Arabic source. In his writings, Jabir ibn Ḥayyan describes the preparation of an artificial man called "*asḥab al-nawamis*," that is, the lawgiver.[147]

Alemanno's view of magic did not remain an isolated individual opinion but can be traced in the compositions of other writers. Alemanno's conception of the Temple and sacrifices was repeated by three other works.[148] Traces of Alemanno's thought are also to be found in the writings of Rabbi Isaac Abravanel.[149] In his commentary to Exodus 7:8 Abravanel describes the lowest form of spirit life as demons "whose habitation is beneath the lunar sphere." Use of these demons characterized the activity of the

Egyptian magicians. This magic technique is noteworthy: "Those who engage in sorcery prepare the lower bodies to receive the emanations of demons."[150] Abravanel's commentary on Exodus was written in the year 1506 when Alemanno had completed all his writings. However, Abravanel had already expressed views similar to those of Alemanno in his *Commentary on Kings* written in Naples in the year 1493. There, Abravanel describes the Temple in terms reminiscent of Alemanno and of the letter of Rabbi Isaac of Pisa. Abravanel states that Solomon knew the science of talismans hidden from the philosophers and that this was the guarantee of Solomon's success:

> The philosophers agree that this lower world of generation and corruption is conducted by the powers which issue from the celestial spheres. As our rabbis, blessed be their memory, said: 'There is not a blade of grass below that does not have a celestial constellation above that strikes it and tells it to grow.' Behold the men of speculation are unable to apprehend the powers of the stars and the powers of each one of them in particular, its manner of activity in the lower world and the way its emanation is drawn into them . . . for the books written by astrologers on this subject are worthless and a fabrication. When the time of reckoning comes the writers of those books are lost. Men have exerted themselves already to learn how to make talismans which are forms made at particular times in order to cause the descent of efflux from the stars upon particular things. However they did not succeed. It is right that it be so; since they did not apprehend the nature and properties of the celestial bodies, it is impossible that they discern their power or the actions derived from them. Nevertheless since Solomon attained the truth of that science in a wondrous manner and knew its causes, he apprehended what is above and what is below concerning the nature of the celestial beings, their number and disposition as well as the order of their motion. By this he apprehended their true powers which conduct the lowly beings. In matters of practical kingship he made the throne and suceeded as our sages, blessed be their memory, said concerning the works he fashioned in the throne and the forms he made of lions and leopards and other forms which he fashioned to accomplish particular activities.[151]

In another place, Abravanel connected knowledge of the nature of the stars and celestial spheres and their influence to Solomon's knowledge about making talismans and also to the knowledge of "the ways of conduct of each and every one of the spheres and stars, [and] the manner of their service and worship, in order to cause emanation to descend from them upon the earth."[152] In contrast, the prophets knew how to cause "emanation to descend from Him, blessed be He, upon the nation by means of the holy *Sefirot* and the knowledge proper to them in the separate intelligences."[153] King Solomon was also conceived of as one who knew how to cause the emanation of the ministering angels to descend by means of the songs he composed.[154]

By the science of the separate intelligences Solomon composed many poems as the verse said:[155] 'And his songs were 1005.' This has been interpreted as five thousand because it was the custom of the ancients to speak about divine matters in the form of poetry.[156] It seems that he composed a great number of songs for the supernal ministering angels for each one by himself in accordance with the way the angel guided one of the nations in accordance with the ministry and service unique to him. He composed the book of the Song of Songs for God alone who exercises His providence over Israel[157] and for this reason they said:[158] 'All the songs are holy but the Song of Songs is the holy of holies' because all the other songs he made were dedicated to the holy angels but the Song of Songs was uniquely dedicated to Him, blessed be He, for He is the most holy of all. As Solomon's knowledge comprehended spiritual matters and their manner of conduct he achieved knowledge of the ways and means and preparations necessary to cause emanations to descend for each and every one of the ministering angels over the nations and lands proper to him.

In another context, he states:[159]

All the other songs he composed concern the conduct of the nations by their supernal ministering angels, but they are not included in the Scriptures and are not to be found today. It seems that King Hezekiah and the members of his generation hid them away,[160] so that man should not err and do a like deed, to worship in an alien manner.

The magical capacity of music and its intergration in magic ritual is one of the characteristic qualities of the systems of Ficino and Pico,[161] and in a certain measure of Alemanno's as well.[162] His description of Solomon as a composer of songs likely to cause the descent of emanation places Abravanel squarely within the framework of thought which crystallized about the circle of scholars in Florence.

III

In the above, I have attempted to demonstrate how Alemanno employed magical and astrological elements scattered throughout the Judaeo-Arabic tradition in order to give the Kabbalah a new interpretation. This interpretation was the result of intellectual currents in Florence, an atmosphere that lead to a similar interpretation in the writings of Pico. It seems to me that the influence of members of the Italian Renaissance also prompted Alemanno's interest in Neoplatonic literature and his use of it for a new understanding of the Kabbalah.

Although Alemanno cannot be considered a Neoplatonist in the precise sense of the term there is a striking predominance of the Neoplatonic element in his writings. A clear indication of the predominance of this element is the great number of references to Neoplatonic authors and compositions found in Alemanno's writings. Alemanno was familiar with the greater part of Jewish Neoplatonic literature. This included the works of Isaac Israeli,[163] Ibn Gabirol's *Mekor Ḥayyim*,[164] *Arugat ha-Bosem* of Moses ibn Ezra,[165] as well as the writings of Abraham ibn Ezra[166] and Rabbi Isaac ibn Latif.[167] Alemanno was greatly interested in the Neoplatonic literature that had been translated from the Arabic into Hebrew; his writings contain many references to the work *Ha-Agulot ha-Ra'ayoniyot* of Al-Batalyusi,[168] a book that exercised a weighty influence on his thought. The book, *Moznei ha-Iyunim*, an elaboration of many of the ideas which appear in *Ha-Agulot ha-Ra'ayoniyot*,[169] is frequently mentioned by Alemanno. From time to time in Alemanno's writings[170] references appear to Al-Ghazali's book, *Mishkat al-Anwar*, a work formulated in a Neoplatonic cast of thought. Alemanno was also acquainted with more specifically Neoplatonic works, such as *Sefer Ha-Atzamim ha-Ḥamisha* attributed to Empedocles; parts of this work have been preserved because Alemanno copied them into his own writings.[171] Alemanno was especially interested in *Sefer ha-Sibot* (*Liber de Causis*). He was familiar with various translations of this work and copied a passage from it into his book, *Ḥai ha-Olamim*,[172] and into his remarks upon *Ḥai ben Yoktan.*[173] This same section from *Liber de Causis* appears in Alemanno's book, *Ḥeshek Shlomo.*[174] It is interesting to note that Pico was also familiar with the *Liber de Causis*, and in his writing quoted a portion of the first paragraph of that work without attribution.[175] That same paragraph appears several times in Alemanno's works. This parallelism is a possible indication of Alemanno's influence on Pico, for Pico studied the work *Ḥai ben Yoktan*[176] with Alemanno. Another selection from *Liber de Causis* (section VI) which is to be found in the book *Imrei Shefer* of Rabbi

Abraham Abulafia, is repeated several times in the writings of Alemanno [177] and subsequently various authors copied it from Alemanno. He was intrigued by material from the *Theology of Aristotle*, which he found in the book, *Sefer ha-Ma'alot* of Rabbi Shem Tov ibn Falaquera[178] and in the *Arugat ha-Bosem* of Moses ibn Ezra.[179] Plato's works were known to Alemanno only by name from a list Falaquera had included in the work, *Reshit Ḥokhma*.[180] However, Alemanno made much use of Plato's *Republic* with the *Commentary* of Averroes.[181]

The most important Platonic and Neoplatonic works were available to Alemanno from the Judaeo-Arabic philosophical tradition. Alemanno exceeded all his Jewish predecessors in the utilization and absorption of Neoplatonic material. Alemanno was unique among his Jewish intellectual contemporaries in his interest in Neoplatonism. His contemporaries, for example Judah Messer Leon, Elijah del Medigo, Obadiah Sforno and David Messer Leon were all Aristotelians. In this respect, Alemanno represents a new trend in the intellectual life of Italian Jewry. The subsequent development of this new interest will be treated in the continuation of this paper.

Before directing our attention to the Neoplatonic bent of Alemanno's thought, mention should be made of the fact that Alemanno's writings contain references to Neoplatonic compositions which were not translated into Hebrew. It is reasonable to assume that Alemanno knew of these works from his contacts with Renaissance personalities in Florence. In the *Collectanaea*,[182] we read,

> Senior Yrhw [!] told me that he found it said in the name of Porphyry that there was a Jewish sect who were holy and ate in such weight and measure that they had no need to relieve themselves.

Further evidence of such Neoplatonic literature is to be found in Alemanno's *Collectanaea*.[183]

> The sect of Platonists said that the heavens possess only a rational soul, not an imaginative or vital soul . . . and the imaginative faculty causes man to love government and dominion, for man imagines himself great when he is honored. In this respect, the human mind is drawn to that work, and is drawn away from the path of reason so that men do not apprehend the rational truths, for then men would not serve them [i.e. the rulers]. The rulers establish pagan practices to kill people or perform acts of sexual immorality or other completely alien practices. This is so that men will not realize the truth, and will thus serve the rulers in

perpetuity by means of those alien forms of worship and not serve God. All the world erred in this except the Jews. Prophyry was one of this [idolatrous] sect, and he unashamedly confessed that at one time he wished to kill himself, and said that ever since the nations had stopped worshipping idols all good had ceased. On one occasion, he told his master, named Plotinus,[184] to accompany him to offer a sacrifice. Plotinus answered him that it was more fitting that a god come to offer a sacrifice to him than he to the god because Plotinus belittled this practice, and Porphyry was greatly astounded by this.

Obviously, Alemanno had read Porphyry's *Life of Plotinus*, of which article 10, 34–35 is summarized here. It is even more interesting that the same selection from Porphyry's book appears in an entirely different context in Pico's famous *Oration on the Glory of Man.*[185] Although Alemanno had a negative opinion of Porphyry,[186] his quotation from Porphyry proves that Alemanno had access to Neoplatonic texts which were in circulation among his contemporaries in Florence.

Two of Alemanno's contemporaries commented on the similarity of Kabbalah and Platonism. Alemanno's teacher Judah Messer Loen said of Kabbalah:[187]

There is to be found among the early exponents of that science in some small measure an approximation in principle of Platonic opinions of an agreeable kind such as would be accessible to an intellectually capable person.

His son, Rabbi David Messer Leon,[188] held the opinion that

Plato is called the divine philosopher, for one who studies his books closely will find there great and tremendous secrets and all their opinions are those of the masters of true Kabbalah.

Although he has a hostile attitude to the Kabbalah, Elijah del Medigo reached the same conclusion as Judah and David Messer Leon. Del Medigo, an Aristotelian, rejected both Platonism and the Kabbalah which followed in its path. The best known discussion of this issue is to be found in Del Medigo's *Beḥinat ha-Dat*,[189] where he comments on the statements of the kabbalists:

Most of them agree with the statements of the early philosophers, the negligibility of whose opinions are well understood by learned people. Whoever has seen the statements of the Platonists and these [kabbalistic] statements will know that such is the truth. I have already discussed this in another place and therefore I do not wish at this time to discuss the matter.[190]

Del Medigo did, however, elaborate on this matter in his commentary on Averroes' *De Substantia Orbis.*[191]

These beings which are called *Sefirot* in accordance with their degree of reality, act by virtue of the power of the tenth one which they call *Ein Sof,*[192] and by virtue of the emanation reaching the *Sefirot* from It. Therefore all exists by virtue of the power of *Ein Sof*, for the *Sefirot* are emanated from It and depend upon It. Therefore, in their opinion, the world order is derived from them. These opinions were taken from the propositions of the early philosophers, particularly from Plato. In their books, you will find these matters discussed at length. They construct proofs for these ideas in accordance with their own method. They say that one cannot ascribe any name to *Ein Sof*, but *Ein Sof* may be apprehended by the intellect as mentioned by Averroes in the *Incoherence of the Incoherence.*[193] This is known to one who has seen the books of these Platonists and the propositions of the early philosophers. In those books, you will also find statements concerning the *Shmitot* (cosmic sabbaticals), the destruction of the world and its reconstruction as well as the transmigration of souls, so that you can find scarcely any difference between these philosophers and these kabbalists insofar as terms and allusions are concerned. . . . In conclusion, they are nearly identical in principles and topics and in the matter of sacrifices. These statements are very far removed from the words of the peripatetics and their principles.

The above comparison of Kabbalah and Platonism was of a most general kind and did not concern a precise textual comparison of Kabbalah, Platonism and Neoplatonism. Even so, this general characterization is important for an understanding of the way in which the Kabbalah was able to enter into Renaissance intellectual culture. The concurrence of the Kabbalah with certain aspects of ancient philosophy[194] endowed it with the aura of an ancient theology whose vestiges were eagerly sought by Renaissance thinkers. The conceptual proximity of the Kabbalah and Pico's thought in particular enabled the Kabbalah to become part of the efflorescence of Renaissance Platonism. The relationship of Platonism and Kabbalah had no theoretical significance for Jewish philosophers of an Aristotelian bent.[195] Alemanno, who was interested in both Kabbalah and Platonism tried to find points common to both. Understandably, this search for agreement was not pursued in a critical fashion; in some instances, there was no real connection between the kabbalistic and Platonic conceptions. Furthermore, there was a clear tendency to superimpose Platonic or Neoplatonic formulations upon the Kabbalah. In the process of interpreting the Kabbalah, Alemanno ignored one of its most essential characteristics: the doctrine of *Sefirot* includes a conception of the inner dynamism of the divinity together with the tensions and inner crises that this dynamism entails and man's role in the enhancement and restoration of the system of the *Sefirot.*

Alemanno's attempt to reconcile Kabbalah and Platonism was preceded by the attempts of Rabbi Joseph ibn Wakar and Rabbi Samuel ibn Motot to synthesize Kabbalah and Aristotelian philosophy. In both writers, the system of *Sefirot* was identified with the separate intelligences of Arabic and Jewish Aristotelianism,[196] and their system had influenced Alemanno.

To exemplify Alemanno's attempt to equate Kabbalah and Platonism, I shall review Alemanno's comparison of kabbalistic concepts with the ideas that he found in the writings of one of the most important Neoplatonic philosophers, Proclus. Pico, Alemanno's student and colleague, accorded Proclus an honored place in his *Theses.* Fifty-five of the theses, the *Secundum Proclum*, were based upon the system of Proclus. These fifty-five theses, exceeded in number all the theses derived from all the other Neoplatonic philosophers taken together. In addition, Pico also formulated ten theses based upon Abucatem Avenam, whom Pico thought to be the author of *Liber de Causis.*[197] In effect, Proclus appears in another guise in Pico's *Theses.* E. Wind has pointed out the connection between the *Oration of the Honor of Man* and the thought of Proclus.[198] H. Wirszubski, on the other hand, emphasized the influence of Proclus' thought upon a kabbalistic thesis,[199] and so is supported by Alemanno's comparison of certain kabbalistic concepts to ideas which had their origin in Proclus. In his untitled composition in Paris MS 849, Alemanno copied a portion of the second introduction to the book, *Tikunei Zohar*, together with a discussion found in the *Minḥat Yehuda* of Rabbi Judah Ḥayyat,[200] which concerns our inability to describe the Supreme Cause. I shall quote but a few lines of this text.

The Supreme Crown (the *Sefira Keter*) has the attribute of oneness because it is the root of all the *Sefirot* and they are within it *in potentia* and it is within them *in actu.* It is not one of their number by virtue of its superiority to them, so that the effect does not resemble the cause. Therefore, it is not mentioned in Genesis in the chapter of the ten sayings by which the world was created[201] which are the *Sefirot.* However, the word *breshit* [Gen. 1:1] contains an allusion to the Supreme Crown. The beginning—*breshit*—of the numbers is *Ḥokhma*—Wisdom. However, nothing was said of the Master of the Worlds and of His essence; not a single name. This is because He participates in every number, for He is within each number *in actu*. In this aspect is He counted within number and contained within number in a general way. Because of this, it states in the *Book of Creation* (*Sefer Yetzira*): 'And before one what do you count.'[202] For there is no number at all, even the name One, that applies to what is before the Supreme Crown which is the Master of the Worlds. In Plato's book, *Ha-Atzamim ha-Elyonim*, it says: 'The first cause exceeds number.' However, all language is insufficient to reckon It because of Its unity. However the causes whose light is derived from the light of the First Cause may be numbered.[203]

Alemanno treats the subject of the ineffability of *Ein Sof* on several pages preceeding the above quotation. First, he cites the section of *Liber de Causis* whose beginning was mentioned before. After that, he concludes as follows:

Many of the descendents of Shem and Eber saw a vision and many gazed at the *Merkava* and regarded the entire Torah and found neither name, nor word nor any one letter which signifies the Source of everything in existence, but they found only a reference to the Primary Effect and Simplest Being.[204]

This is an allusion to a remark in the book, *Ma'arekhet ha-Elohut*, which determined that[205]

there is no allusion to *Ein Sof* in the Torah, the prophets, the hagiographa, or in the words of the sages blessed be their memory, although the 'masters of divine worship' received a brief hint about it.

Here, Alemanno gave a specific example of the correspondence between a negative kabbalistic theology concerning *Ein Sof* and the negative theology of *Liber de Causis*, a similarity which Elijah del Medigo had already sensed.[206]

Another reference to *Liber de Causis* appears in Alemanno's restatement and elaboration of a discussion found in the book, *Minḥat Yehuda*.[207] In this instance, Alemanno speaks of the relationship of *Ein Sof* and *Keter*, the first *Sefira*, the Supreme Crown. For purposes of his discussion, Alemanno draws upon a lengthy discourse of Judah Ḥayyat on this question. In opposition to Rabbi Joseph Gikatilla and Rabbi Elijah di Genazzano,[208] Ḥayyat maintained that *Ein Sof* is not identical with the Supreme Crown, but is to be found above it. Alemanno was interested in Ḥayyat's argumentation but not in the conclusion of the discussion. Alemanno utilized Ḥayyat's proofs in order to prove that the relation of the

Sefira Keter to the *Sefira Ḥokhma* (Wisdom, the second *Sefira*) is identical to the relation of *Ein Sof* to the Supreme Crown. *Ein Sof*, however, is the source of the efflux which sustains the system of the *Sefirot*:

The Supreme Crown emanated Wisdom and shines above it [Wisdom] just as *Ein Sof* radiates above the Supreme Crown. In accordance with the principle that everything that exists within the cause exists within the effect, the Supreme Crown relative to *Ḥokhma* has the same value as *Ein Sof* relative to the Supreme Crown: as we have said 'contingent yet not contingent.' *Ein Sof* is the cause of the connection of the *Sefirot* to one another for all of them are joined one to the other by the efflux emanating from *Ein Sof* to all of them, and it joins and unifies and gives existence to all as the philosophers said in the *Liber de Causis* that anything which is the cause of the existence of something else in such a manner that the other thing has no existence other than that coming to it from its cause—if that effect is the cause of something else outside itself in the same way as in the case of the first cause, then the first cause is a truer, more unique and important cause for the existence of the second effect than is the second cause in causing the second effect.[209]

I think that this statement is a clear indication of the significant contribution of *Liber de Causis* and of Kabbalah to Alemanno's thought. As stated before, this passage from *Liber de Causis* was repeated in other parts of Alemanno's writings which were written in the years before the above quotation. The book, *Minḥat Yehuda*, was written between the years 1495–7. Alemanno did not understand Ḥayyat's statement according to its original, literal meaning. Rather, he interpreted Ḥayyat according to the formula of *Liber de Causis*, which he knew well. However, this was not a complete misrepresentation of kabbalistic doctrine but a rechanneling of certain conceptions in a direction unintended by the original author. Alemanno simply restated Ḥayyat's remarks in a philosophical way which removed the mythical element.[210] This is doubly ironic. In his introduction to *Ma'arekhet ha-Elohut*, Ḥayyat warned against the interpretation of Kabbalah in a philosophical manner such as was done by Rabbi Reuben Tzarfati in his commentary on *Ma'arekhet ha-Elohut.*[211] I have already suggested that this statement in Ḥayyat's "Introduction" was directed against a trend of thought similar to Alemanno's. Alemanno took a particular interest in the very books censured by Ḥayyat,[212] and Alemanno restated Ḥayyat's words so as to suit his philosophical conceptions. Alemanno found the quotation from *Sefer Ha-Atzamim ha-Elyonim* in the book, *Imrei Shefer*, of Abraham Abulafia,[213] a kabbalist whom Ḥayyat condemned in the most explicit terms.[214] Unwittingly Alemanno made certain to reconcile the statement of Ḥayyat with material found in a composition by Abulafia.

Now let us turn to a consideration of Alemanno's use of that quotation from *Liber de Causis* which he found in Abulafia. In the work *Ḥeshek Shlomo*, Alemanno endeavored to prove the existence of the ten *Sefirot.* After citation of appropriate scriptural verses and mention of Rabbi Neḥunya ben ha-Kaneh and R. Simon bar Yoḥai as adherents of the belief in the existence of the *Sefirot*, Alemanno writes:[215]

> But the philosophers among our people did not believe in them and if they mentioned them at all it was to say that they move the heavens[216]. . . . And so too among the gentile sages, there were those who believed in their existence and others who denied them. . . . It follows that the ancients believed in the existence of ten spiritual numbers[217] but the latter day scholars denied it because there is no proof of this. It seems that Plato thought that there are ten spiritual numbers of which one may speak but one may not speak of the first cause due to its great concealment. However they [the numbers] approximate its existence to such an extent that you may call these effects by a name that cannot be ascribed to the movers of corporeal bodies. However, in the opinion of the kabbalists, one may say so of the *Sefirot*, as shall be explained in this our discourse. This is what Plato wrote in the work *Ha-Atzamim Ha-Elyonim* as quoted by Zacharias in the Book *Imrei Shefer.*[218] From this it follows that in Plato's view, the first effects are called *Sefirot* because they may be numbered, unlike the first cause, and therefore he did not call them movers.

Here Plato's theory of ten ideal numbers, as represented in Aristotle, was combined with the opinion of Proclus in the *Liber de Causis* to create the impression that Plato thought that there are ten numbers, separate from matter which may be described, unlike the first cause. These numbers which cannot be described have a relationship to one another of cause and effect. This integration of concepts substantiated Alemanno's claim that the ancients, especially Plato, held a view similar to the kabbalistic conception of the *Sefirot*, as opposed to the opinion of the prophets.[219]

I have proved that Alemanno read the words of Proclus as presented in the various redactions of *Liber de Causis* and understood them to refer to the conception of *Ein Sof* and its relation to the *Sefirot* and their number. This determination was further applied to a discussion of the worlds. An association of this kind is to be found in the book *Shir ha-Ma'alot.* There it is stated that everything that exists in the world of change can be found in some form in all the worlds, the world of motion and in the *Sefirot.*[220]

> Everything which is to be found in the world of change has an analogy in the world of motion and everything that is in the world of motion is in the world of the *Sefirot* . . . for just so the transient beings in the world of change are the image and likeness of the spiritual forms in the world of motion. It is as Alfarabi [221] wrote concerning all the forms which the Indians say are nothing other than spiritual forms known by means of the knowledge of natural phenomena which occur to the men who receive from those forms. The forms found in the world of motion such as the forty-eight forms and the twenty-eight encampments of the moon, point to the spiritual forms existent in the world of the *Sefira*—for example the twenty-eight encampments of the *Shekhina.*

It seems that Alemanno's scheme of the several worlds is based upon a principle formulated by Proclus which was repeated in various ways in the *Liber de Causis.* There it was said that all things are to be found in every world in conformity with the essence of that world.[222]

The kabbalist who, more than any other, followed in the new directions indicated by Alemanno—namely, Abraham Yagel—gave an even more detailed discussion of the topic of the worlds than did Alemanno himself. In his work *Beit Ya'ar ha-Levanon* Yagel took a Neoplatonic conception which he found in the book *De Occulta Philosophia* as the basis for his treatment of the different states of the four primary elements in accordance with the essence of the worlds. Yagel's dependence upon Agrippa becomes obvious if a linear comparison is made of Yagel's remarks with a parallel text in *De Occulta Philosophia.*

Oxford MS 1304 (Reggio 9) fol. 6r-6v.	*De Occulta Philosophia I, ch. VIII (Hildesheim and N.Y., 1970) p.18.*
This was the statement of the philosopher Plato.[223]	Est Platonicorum omnium unanimis sententia
Just as in the archetype of the world	quemadmodum in archetypo mundo
all is in all,	omnia sunt in omnibus
so also in this corporeal world, all is in all, albeit	ita etiam in hoc corporeo mundo, omnia in omnibus esse
in a distinct manner because of the nature of the separable	modis tamen diversis pro natura videlicet suscipientium.

things. Therefore the four elements[224] are not to be found in isolated form in this lower world, but also exist in the celestial bodies and stars, the angels and the separate intelligences and in what is above them in the archetype of the world, the Cause of all Causes and the Principle of all Principles. . . .	Sic et elementa nonsolum sunt in istis inferioribus sed in coelis in stellis in daemonibus in angelis in ipso demique; omnium opifice et archetypo.
However in this world they are found as dross and matter.	Sed in istis inferioribus elementa sunt crassae quaedam formae immensae materiae et materialia elementa.
In the heavens [they are] as the powers we have stated[225] and in the angels [they are] more perfect and superior powers than in the heavens.	In coelis autem sunt elementa per eorum naturas et vires: modo videlicet coelesti et multo excellentiori quam infra lunam.

Above them [the angels] there are powers more perfect than, and superior to, the powers in the angels. The world above the angels is called in the language of the kabbalists, the Throne of Glory which is the world of *Beri'a*—creation. The world of *Beri'a* is the shadow of, and the seat for, the supernal *Sefirot* which they [the kabbalists] call the 'World of Emanation'. In the World of *Beri'a* these four powers exist in a more subtle and hidden manner, and it is all the more so in the supernal world of *Atzilut*—emanation, where the powers are most subtle of all. There they [the *Sefirot*] are the root and principle for all of them. From them, all draw sustenance. In that world these four powers are called Grandeur—*Gedula*, which is the element of water; Might—*Gevura*, which is the element of fire; Beauty—*Tiferet*, which is the element of air; and Kingdom—*Malkhut* which is the element of earth. See what the author of *Ma'arekhet ha-Elohut* wrote in the chapter "On the World" [*Sha'ar ha-Olam*].[226] He said:

> "I have said in the beginning of the book[227] that there are elements in the lower earth which are three in general and four in particular, because those elements have a great and wondrous root in this. For it is known that everything in existence has a source until the beginning of every thing which is the cause of every effect. The last effect is caused by the one preceeding it and that aspect is caused by the aspect which is further beyond it until the aspect of the First Cause, blessed be His name, who is the cause of all."

It is evident that Yagel interpreted the statement which he found in Agrippa to refer to the four worlds of emanation, creation, formation, and construction. Of these he mentioned the worlds of emanation and creation. During the course of comparing kabbalistic and Neoplatonic conceptions a change was made in the definition of the essence of the *Sefirot*. They are understood to be the Neoplatonic ideas which descend and become materialized.

For all issues from the Lord of Hosts. He spoke and it was, He commanded and it stood [Ps. 33:9] but the creatures and formations above and below exist by the spirit of His mouth. . . . And the power that is in the lower beings is to be found in the upper worlds in a more subtle, exalted and sublime manner. It is to be found [also] in great purity and clarity in the holy, pure *Sefirot* which are in truth the *Ideii* for all things. They are the beginning of God's way and all His acts course through the four degrees which are the mystery of the four worlds of emanation, creation, formation and construction.[228]

These *Sefirot*—Ideas—are said to exist in the divine mind:[229]

The meaning of the word *Ideii*: that is to say a simple form, superior to bodies, souls and intelligences.[230] It is absolutely simple, invisible, indivisible and incorporeal; nor is it potentiality within a body. It is eternal and abides in the mind of the Creator and Maker of all, blessed be He. Before a man makes anything, he traces in his mind the form of that thing in quality. So too the form, quality and quanitity of the heavens and the earth and their generations were figured within the mind of the Most High before He created them. . . . And in the terminology of the Platonists that first figuration is called *Ideii*, but they do not mean to ascribe multiplicity to a simple substance, God forbid, in any way, nor to imply any change of will at all.

In effect, Yagel set aside the gnostic and dynamic character of the *Sefirot* which constituted one of the principle characteristics of the Kabbalah. He returned to a completely philosophical approach, reminiscent of the formulation of Philo.[231] It is important to emphasize that this shift in theory was not restricted to Yagel alone. It can be found in texts written in Italy in the time period betweem Alemanno and Yagel. This evidence appears in the *Responsum* of Rabbi Isaac Abravanel to Rabbi Saul ha-Cohen. Abravanel wrote:[232]

For of necessity things exist as a figuration in the mind of the active agent before that thing comes into being. Undoubtedly this image is the world of the *Sefirot* mentioned by the sages of the kabbalists of the true wisdom [who said] that the *Sefirot* are the divine images with which the world was created. Therefore they said that the *Sefirot* are not created but are emanated, and that all of them unite together in Him, blessed be His name, for they are the figuration of His loving-kindness and His willing what He created. In truth, Plato set down the knowledge of the separate general forms.

A similar thought appears in the book *Sha'arei Ḥayyim* which was written in the year 1540.[233]

The upper creatures are a model for the lower creatures. This is because every lower thing has a superior power from which it came into existence. This resembles the relationship of the shadow to the object that casts it. For the one who casts the shadow is the cause of the shadow. Even the ancient philosophers such as Pythagoras and Plato taught and made statements about this.[234] However the matter was not revealed to them in a clear way as it was to the prophets, blessed be their memory, who received it. For the principles stated by Plato resemble this for they are incorporeal forms within the divine mind and that is the cause of the existence of the individuals.

Azaria de Rossi also[235] pointed out the similarity between the terms '*Sefira*' and 'Idea'. It is reasonable to assume that these writers found and utilized a concept mentioned throughout the writings of Marsilio Ficino and Pico della Mirandola; these writers maintained that the Ideas are to be found in God Himself[236] and not only in the general Intellect of Plotinus or in the logos of Philo. From this point of view, Abravanel, the author of *Sha'arei Ḥayyim* and Abraham Yagel continued to develop these topics along lines established during the Renaissance, lines which found expression in the writings of Ficino, Pico and Agrippa.

Detailed examination of the Neoplatonic definition of the *Sefirot* by Italian kabbalists has great significance for an understanding of important developments in the Kabbalah of the sixteenth century. The Kabbalah of Rabbi Isaac Luria (ARI) reached Italy in the version of Israel Sarug. Neoplatonic interpretations of Sarug are to be found in the writings of Abraham Hererra and Yashar of Candia.[237] The principal trend of these kabbalists was to divest Lurianic Kabbalah of its mythical garb and to give it a new interpretation. In method and content their efforts resemble the text of Abraham Yagel cited above. The new treatment of Kabbalah was not a synthesis of Kabbalah and philosophy but represented an exegesis of the kabbalistic text which shifted its propositions and descriptions in a direction unanticipated by the original author.

This tendency to force Kabbalah into a Neoplatonic mold consisted in great measure of the superimposition of certain intellectual and conceptual innovations of the Renaissance upon ideas of Jewish origin. This development began in a modest way in the writings of Alemanno. My discussion of certain passages from Alemanno's writings indicates that he placed great emphasis upon the similarity of Kabbalah and Platonic[238] thought. Aided by the various versions of Proclus' teaching Alemanno went beyond emphasis of the intellectual proximity of these systems and introduced a Neoplatonic interpretation of Kabbalah, and Abraham Yagel continued this activity. The essential difference between Alemanno and the later Neoplatonic interpreters of the Kabbalah—Herrera and YaSHaR of Candia—derives from the fact that a greater amount of Neoplatonic literature was available to the latter than to Alemanno. These later writers were much more conversant with Neoplatonic sources and used them in order to explain the new school of Kabbalah of Israel Sarug. Despite these differences, the approach of all the kabbalists mentioned here to their sources was the same, for they shared the same cultural phenomenology. Consciously or not, they ignored the literal meaning of their kabbalistic sources and dressed them in garb which completely changed the originial meaning of the kabbalistic texts.

I will conclude my discussion at this point with a very concrete example of this change in interpretation. I have in mind Rabbi Judah Moscato's sermon entitled "The Divine Circle." A detailed analysis of Moscato's understanding of the Jewish sources he quoted in this sermon will have to wait for another time. It will suffice to say that his reading of the sources was dictated by a commonplace Renaissance conception which Moscato mentioned in his sermon:[239]

> In the writings of Mercurio Trimesto it is written: The Creator, blessed be He, is a perfect circle whose center is to be found at every point and whose circumference is nowhere.

In his sermon, Moscato interpreted the opinions of Ibn Ezra and the Kabbalists so as to prove the proposition of Hermes Trismegistus that God is a Divine Point or a Divine Circle.[240] These are but a few of Moscato's remarks:

> The kabbalists revealed to us a great measure of true wisdom in the matter of the circle. At times they depict it as a crown, surrounding and encompassing all the rest of the *Sefirot* from without. At times they depict

it as a point within a circle. I found the following written in the book *Sha'arei Tzedek.*[241] The Crown encompasses all the *Sefirot* and is called *soḥaret* derived from the word *seḥor-seḥor* (around and around).

Here, the homileticist combined two entirely different kabbalistic conceptions in order to construct the same proposition as the Pseudo-Hermes. There is something unique about Moscato's method. He did not express himself in a philosophical genre as did Alemanno or Yagel, but expounded his views in a sermon. Here, a conception drawn from outside sources was absorbed into a traditional Jewish literary genre while Moscato voided the Jewish sources of their original meaning in order to accomodate the ideas found by him in Renaissance theology. As proved above, Jewish thinkers had developed their systems under the direct influence of Renaissance ideas. It seems that this particular feature was the reason for their lack of enduring influence. Two main causes contributed to the weakening of the influence of these authors: the printing of the classical kabbalistic literature such as the *Zohar* and *Ma'arekhet ha-Elohut*, and the increasing impact of the Kabbalah of Safed. In both cases, there is a emphasis on the genuine unmixed Kabbalah. However, it seems to me that Alemanno's influence, directly or indirectly, can be found both in Safed and in Ashkenazi authors, but this must remain a subject for future research.

NOTES

1. This refers particularly to the influence of Maimonides' *Guide of the Perplexed* on Aquinas and the influence of Ibn Gabirol's *Fons Vitae* on Franciscan theology. A peculiar and interesting exception to this lack of cultural exchange through personal communication and instruction is to be found in Byzantine culture. It is reported that a Jew named Elisha was the instructor of Gemistos Plethon.

2. On this personality and his relations with Abraham Farissol see David Ruderman, "Abraham Farissol. An Historical study of His Life and Thought in the Context of Jewish Communal Life in Renaissance Italy," (Ph.D. diss., Hebrew University, 1974), pp. 170–185.

3. This is the end of an epistle on the history of the Kabbalah written by Rabbi Elijah Menaḥem Ḥalfan. Jewish Theological Seminary [JTS] MS 1822, f. 154v.

4. For the attitude of Jews to the Lutheran movement see H. H. Ben-Sasson, "The Reformation in Contemporary Jewish Opinion," *Proceedings of the Israel Academy of Sciences and Humanities* 4 (1970), pp. 239–326.

5. Some of the Christian Hebraists in Italy had learned Hebrew as a prerequisite for the study of Kabbalah. See also Ruderman, "Abraham Farissol," p. 173.

6. See E. Schweid, *Feeling and Speculation* [Hebrew] (Ramat Gan, 1970), pp. 17ff.

7. See M. Idel, "Abraham Abulafia's Works and Doctrine," (Ph.D. diss., Hebrew University, 1976), p. 436.

8. For an analysis of these two kabbalists' conception of the *Sefirot* see E. Gottlieb, *Studies in the Literature of the Kabbalah* [Hebrew] (Tel Aviv, 1976), pp. 293–310.

9. *Sefer Ma'arekhet ha-Elohut* (Mantua, 1558), f. 3a–b.

10. Y. Nadav, "An Epistle of the Kabbalist Rabbi Yitzḥak Mar Ḥayyim on the Doctrine of *Tzaḥtzaḥot*" [Hebrew], *Tarbitz* 26 (1962–3), p. 458. In his second letter to Rabbi Isaac of Pisa, Rabbi Isaac Mar Ḥayyim expressed a similar view. This letter was published by A. W. Greenup, "A Kabbalistic Epistle," *JQR*, n.s., 21 (1931), p. 370.

11. Rabbi Reuben Tzarfati's commentary on *Sefer Ma'arekhet ha-Elohut* is particularly representative of this trend. In his commentary, Tzarfati integrates the theology of the *Ma'arekhet* author with the conceptions of Abraham Abulafia. See Gottlieb, *Studies*, pp. 357–69; Idel, "Abraham Abulafia," pp. 12 and 43, n. 48.

12. The term "theurgic" employed here and below refers to the kabbalist's belief in his ability to influence the process and condition of the *Sefirot*.

13. Flavius Mithridates translated several of Abulafia's works as well as Menaḥem Recanati's commentary on the Torah from Hebrew into Latin. These translations served as one of the most important sources of kabbalistic teaching for Pico. See H. Wirszubski, *Mekubal Notzri Kore ba-Tora* [Hebrew: *A Christian Kabbalist Reads the Law*] (Jerusalem, 1977), pp. 23 and 30. On an unknown translation of the *Ma'arekhet ha-Elohut* and *Sefer Ḥayyei ha-Olam ha-Ba* of Abulafia which was made in the circle of Egidio da Viterbo see Idel, "Egidio da Viterbo and Abulafia's Works," *Italia* 3 (1980), pp. 48–50.

14. Wirszubski, *A Christian Kabbalist*, pp. 11 and 17ff.

15. See *Sefer Shir ha-Ma'alot*, Oxford MS 1535, ff. 18r and 20r.

16. This refers to a considerable amount of the material found in Alemanno's *Novellae and Collectanaea*, Oxford MS 2234 (Reggio 23). I intend to make a separate study and analysis of the material in this manuscript. Here it suffices to note that Alemanno collected material during the last third of the fifteenth century, but on the whole made use of it in compositions written between the years 1499 and 1505. For that reason one should not always assume that opinions written in his later works were the result of deliberations made at the time of writing.

17. Rosenthal had a different opinion of Alemanno. In his view, Alemanno was intellectually a medieval figure even though he lived during the Renaissance period. See E.J.F. Rosenthal, "Yohanan Alemanno and Occult Science," *Prismata: Naturwissenschaftgeschichtliche Studien. Festschrift für Willy Hartner* (Wiesbaden, 1977), p. 356.

18. See in particular D.P. Walker's pioneering study, *Spiritual and Demonic Magic from Ficino to Campanella* (London, 1975).

19. Walker has already made this point. See s.v. "Picatrix" in the index to his *Spiritual and Demonic Magic*. F. Yates added much to Walker's treatment in confirming the literary importance of *Picatrix* during the Renaissance period in her book *Giordano Bruno and the Hermetic Tradition* (London, 1964). See also the important studies of E. Garin, "La diffusione di un manuale di magia," *La Cultura filosofica del rinascimento italiano* (Firenze, 1961), pp. 159–165; "Astrologia e magia: Picatrix," *Lo Zodiaco della vita* (Laterza, 1976), pp. 33–60; and "Postille sull'Ermetismo del rinascimento," *Rinascimento* 16 (1976), pp. 245–6. On the influence of paganism on *Picatrix* see J. Seznec, *The Survival of the Pagan Gods* (Princeton, N.J., 1972). On the Hermetic sources of *Picatrix* see H. and R. Kahane and Angela Pietrangle, "Picatrix and the Talismans," *Romance Philology* 19 (1965–6), pp. 574–93, and D. Pingree, "Some Sources of the Ghāyat al-Ḥakim," *JWCI* 43 (1980), 1–15.

20. F. Secret collected a great deal of material on this work in "Sur quelques traductions du Sefer Raziel," *REJ* 128 (1969), pp. 223–45.

21. R.A. Pack, "Almadel Auctor Pseudonimus de Firmitate Sex Scientiarum," *Archives d'Histoire Doctrinale et Littéraire du Moyen Ages* [*AHDLMA*] 42 (1976), pp. 147ff, esp. 177f.

22. This particular subject has not been discussed in the scholarly literature. Studies of the topic have dealt for the most part with popular superstitions and magical practices but have not considered the place of magic in the intellectual framework of the Renaissance. See M.A. Shulwass *The Jews in the World of the Renaissance* (Leiden, 1973), pp. 328–32; C. Roth, *The Jews in the Renaissance* (Philadelphia, 1959), pp. 59–63.

23. A detailed description of Munich MS 124 is to be found in M. Steinschneider, *Zur pseudoepigraphischen Literatur* (Berlin, 1862), pp. 28–51. This translation contains certain varia when compared with the original Arabic text and one of these was discussed by M. Plessner, "A Medieval Definition of a Scientific Experiment in the Hebrew Picatrix," *Journal of the Warburg and Courtauld Institutes* [*JWCI*] 36 (1973), pp. 358–9.

24. In his book *Ma'ase Efod*, Profet Duran refers to this work by this name. Alemanno knew Duran's book. See Idel, "The Curriculum of Yoḥanan Alemanno" [Hebrew], *Tarbitz* 48 (1980), p. 304, n. 6.

25. See Idel, "Curriculum," p. 311. In his *Collectanaea*, Oxford MS 2234, f. 121r, Alemanno includes a passage from the book *Sefer Megale Amukot* of Rabbi Shlomo ben Ḥanokh al-Constantini who had seen the work in the Arabic original. This reference parallels what is said in *Sefer Megale Amukot*, Vatican MS 59, f. 6r.

26. All the manuscripts of the Latin translation of *Picatrix* date from the fifteenth or sixteenth centuries. See Yates, *Giordano Bruno*, p. 15, n. 3.

27. See I. Sonne, *From Paul the Fourth to Pius the Fifth* [Hebrew] (Jerusalem, 1954), p. 108.

28. L. Thorndike, *History of Magic and Experimental Science* (New York: 1958), II, p. 280.

29. For more information about this kabbalist, see A. Kupfer, "The Visions of Rabbi Asher ben Rav Meir also named Lemlin Reutlingen"(Hebrew), *Kovetz al Yad* 8 (Jersalem, 1976), pp. 389–423.

30. Budapest, Kaufmann MS 179, p. 134.

31. *Shalshelet ha-Kabbalah* (Jerusalem, 1962), p. 231.

32. See the edition of Gollancz (Jerusalem, 1940). It is noteworthy that an abridgment of *Sefer Mafteaḥ Shlomo* is listed as follows in Coronel's catalogue of manuscripts (London, 1871) p. 12, no. 123: " '*Sefer Mafteaḥ ha-Zahav*': an abridgment of '*Mafteaḥ Shlomo*': an introduction on the writing of amulets with several unusual figures (pictures) and letters." This description does correspond to the content of *Sefer Mafteaḥ Shlomo*. Abraham Colorni translated the Hebrew version of the book into Italian.

33. See Idel, "Curriculum," p. 321ff.

34. See Paris MS 849, f. 64r–v. G. Scholem first noted this in his article "An Untitled Book of Rabbi Yoḥanan Alemanno" [Hebrew], *Kiryat Sefer* 5 (1929), p. 276. Greenup published another translation: *Sefer ha-Levana* (London, 1912). A fragment of a third translation appears in *Sefer Yesod Olam* of Rabbi Abraham Eskira, Moscow–Ginsburg MS 607, f. 72v. This work is also to be found in Arabic and Latin manuscripts.

35. *Sefer Ḥeshek Shlomo*, Oxford MS 1535, ff. 47v, 48r, 65v, 68r, and 118v. For a bibliography on this work see Rosenthal, "Occult Science," p. 350–351 and the accompanying notes. I will discuss the subject at another time. References to Apollonius by Alemanno's contemporaries in Italy are contained in Ruderman, "Abraham Farissol," p. 50f and in Walker, *Spiritual and Demonic Magic*, p. 147f.

36. Bar Ilan University MS 286 (formerly Vienna MS x, 25), ff. 83r–92v. At the beginning of this section the following appears: "In the book *Shir ha-Ma'alot* of Solomon it is written that about the year 150 of the sixth millenium the scholar Rabbi Shelomo ben Rav Natan translated this composition from Latin into Hebrew. The author was the very ancient Apollonius and the book is called *Mlekhet Muskelet*." Undoubtedly, this statement relates to what Alemanno said in his book *Shir ha-Ma'alot* which is an introductory work to the *Sefer Ḥeshek Shlomo*. See Oxford MS 1535, f. 47v and the printed work *Sefer Shaar ha-Ḥeshek* (Halberstadt, s.a.), pp. 8b–9a. There is an important difference between Alemanno's comments in Oxford MS 1535 and *Sefer Shaar ha-Ḥeshek* (which states: "It has been one hundred years") and the remark in Bar Ilan MS 286 ("the year 150"). It follows that the Bar Ilan MS was written fifty years after the composition of *Sefer Shir ha-Ma'alot*, that is to say at the end of the first half of the sixteenth century. About the same time, Rabbi Rephael Shlomo ben Ya'akov Prato copied Budapest Kaufman MS 246. In pp. 3–17 of the Budapest manuscript there are excerpts which are also to be found in the Bar Ilan MS. The Budapest manuscript contains a more complete and linguistically clear version of the excerpts. The translator Rephael Prato worked for Rabbi Yeḥi'el Nissim of Pisa in whose grandfather's house Alemanno was a guest. It is possible that Alemanno himself gathered these excerpts from the book *Mlekhet Muskelet* which was, according to Alemanno's own description, a composition of some two hundred folio pages, much longer than the extant version. A considerable part of the material found in these excerpts also appears in *Sefer Shir ha-Ma'alot*.

37. See Idel, "Curriculum," p. 312, n. 76.

38. Ibid., p. 312, n. 74.

39. Alemanno, *Sefer Shir ha-Ma'alot*, Oxford MS 1535, f. 116r.
40. See Scholem's remarks in the article mentioned above, n. 34.
41. Oxford MS 2234, f. 15r.
42. Oxford MS 1535, f. 126r. See also J. Dan "Teraphim: From Popular Belief to a Folktale," *Scripta Hierosolymitana* 27 (1978), pp. 100–102. Compare Alemanno's report with the marginal comment in Oxford MS 2234, f. 68r. and with a story mentioned in M. Bouisson, *La Magie* (Paris, 1958), p. 132.
43. *Collectanaea*, Oxford MS 2234, marginal comments f. 68r.
44. Paris MS 849, f. 47v. At the bottom of folio 20v Alemanno tells of his connections with Paris Ceresarius Mantuano a former physician who claimed that he knew the secret of immortality. See G. Scholem in *Kiryat Sefer* 5, p. 274.
45. See Gottlieb, *Studies*, pp. 29–37.
46. On the development of this conception see P. Zambelli, "La Problème de la magie naturelle à la Renaissance," *Astrologia e religione nel rinascimento* (Wroclaw, 1974), pp. 48–49.
47. Yates elaborated upon the relation of magic and Kabbalah in Pico's writings in *Giordano Bruno*, pp. 86–110.
48. Ibid., p. 96f.
49. Ibid., p. 95.
50. Pico, *Opera Omina*, p. 107–8; Yates, *Giordano Bruno*, p. 95.
51. Pico, *Opera Omina*, pp. 180–1; Yates, *Giordano Bruno*, p. 96.
52. Montefiore MS 316, f. 28v. I shall attempt to prove in another article that the letter was written by Rabbi Isaac ben Yeḥi'el of Pisa. A similar definition appears in the famous address of Rabbi Simone Luzzatto: "E l'altra parte più teoricale e scientifica che considera la dispendenza di questo mondo corporale dal spirituale, incorporale et architipo; tengono che vi siano alcuni principii, e orgini seminarii de tutte le cose sensibili." F. Secret "Un texte malconnu de Simone Luzzatto sur le Kabbale," *REJ* 118 (1959–60), p. 123.
53. Scholem, "Zur Geschichte der Anfange der christlichen Kabbalah" in *Essays Presented to Leo Baeck* (London, 1954), p. 164, n. 1.
54. This was published by A. Jellinek, *Auswahl kabbalisticher Mystik* (Leipzig, 1853), p. 15. Flavius Mithridates translated the letter into Latin and Pico knew of this text.
55. See Idel, "Curriculum," p. 310, nn. 65, 66.
56. See Idel, "Curriculum," p. 320ff.
57. Oxford MS 2234, f. 164r.
58. The manuscript in Hebrew reads: הנקיוי.
59. Exodus 19:15.
60. Munich MS 214, f. 51r. See also note 101 below.
61. Paris MS 849, f. 92v. Cf. also f. 6v.
62. See also Scholem's discussion of this matter in his *Pirkei Yesod be-Havanat ha-Kabala u-Smaleha* [Elements of the Kabbalah and its Symbolism] (Jerusalem: 1976), p. 14ff. In Alemanno's time, several scholars were of the opinion that the Torah had magical properties which enabled the Jewish sages to master nature. See the remarks of Rabbi Joseph Yavetz in his commentary on *Avot* (Warsaw, 1880), p. 68. See also the remarks of S. Heller-Wilenski, *The Philosophy of Isaac Arama* [Hebrew] (Jerusalem and Tel-Aviv, 1956), p. 131; *Sefer Minḥat Kena'ot* of Rabbi Yeḥi'el Nissim of Pisa, and the remarks of YaSHaR of Candia in *Sefer Matzref la-Ḥokhma*, ch. 4 and 10.
63. Paris MS 849, f. 7v.
64. *Opera Omnia* p. 181; Yates, *Giordano Bruno*, p. 97.
65. References to a classification of practical Kabbalah according to categories of pure and impure can be found in the Italian Kabbalah in the first half of the sixteenth century. Rabbi Elijah Menaḥem Ḥalfan wrote in an epistle: "First of all the science of the Kabbalah is divided into two parts called the right side and the left side. Each one of the two parts mentioned is divided into the speculative and the practical. The right side is all purity and holiness and divine and angelic names and holy matters. The left side is all[?] and demons and shells of the impure side." JTS MS 1822, f. 153v. This categorization which considers practical Kabbalah of the left side to be worship of the "other side" (*sitra aḥra*) is based upon the Zohar which contrasted magic and Kabbalah. Compare this to the Mazdaic belief which claims that magic is the ritual worship of Ahriman. See J. Bidez and F. Cumont,

Les Mages hellenisés (Paris, 1938), vol. 1, p. 143. See also Profet Duran's *Klimat ha-Goyim*, ch. 2 where Jesus is considered a practical kabbalist who worked his miracles by the impure side of practical Kabbalah. Compare this to Pico's statement that Jesus' miracles were not done by magic or by Kabbalah. See *Opera Omnia*, p. 105, and Yates, *Giordano Bruno*, p. 106.

66. Munich MS 214, f. 51r.

67. Compare this to a conception appearing in a short composition entitled *Sod Pe'ulat ha-Yetzira*. There a technique of letter combination is described for the reception of the efflux of wisdom. The composition then describes the reception of the holy spirit and the creation of a *golem*. See Idel, "Abraham Abulafia," p. 131.

68. This term appears most frequently throughout the book *Takhlit he-Ḥakham*. See for example Munich MS 214, f. 51r. The expression is also repeated on p. 14 of the work *Sefer ha-Atzamim*, attributed to Ibn Ezra which has been mentioned before. See also *Sefer Megale Amukot* of Shlomo al-Constantini, Vatican MS 59, f. 6rff, and *Sefer Mekor Ḥayyim* of Rabbi Samuel Zarza (Mantua, 1559), f. 6a. Magic based upon "causing a descent" is also known from the literature of the Midrash. See L. Ginzburg, *The Legends of the Jews*, vol. 5, p. 152, n. 56. While the Midrash concerns the descent of the sun and moon, Hermetic magic concerns the descent of the celestial emanations. In *Sefer Takhlit he-Ḥakham* the descent of the spiritual forces is a type of revelation: "For every wise man has power so that some part of the spirit may come to him and awaken him and open up to him what was hidden from him, and this power was described as the perfect nature." On the perfect nature see Scholem, *Elements*, pp. 361–4. About "drawing upon the spiritual forces of the stars" see also Rabbi Baḥya ben Asher's *Commentary on the Torah* to Deut. 18:11. There he quotes material very similar to that found in *Sefer Takhlit he-Ḥakham* from *The Epistle of Galen*. And cf. the statement of Rabbi Moses Cordovero, *Sefer Pardes Rimonim*, Gate 30, ch. 3.

69. *Beḥinat ha-Dat* (Vienna, 1833), pp. 68–9. David Geffen did not identify the person at whom Del Medigo directed his criticism in "Faith and Reason in Elijah del Medigo's Beḥinat ha-Dat and the Philosophical Backgound of the Work" (Ph.D. diss., Columbia University, 1970), pp. 454–457. See also Idel, "Curriculum," pp. 328–329.

70. Oxford MS 2234, f. 2v. Cf. Naḥmanides' *Commentary on the Torah*, Deut. 32:40. It is important to note that these words of Alemanno in his *Collectanaea* were set down at a very early date, perhaps before the year 1478 or even the year 1470, but the proofs I have for this cannot be included here. This determination is significant in view of the similarity between Alemanno's statement and Pico's theses. The problematic relation of Kabbalah to astrology was discussed in Italy before Alemanno. In the opinion of Rabbi Isaac Dieulosal, the systems of Kabbalah and astrology are compatible. See J. Hacker, "The Connections of Spanish Jewry with Eretz Israel between 1391 and 1492," *Shalem* 1 (1974), p. 145 n. 64 and p. 147.

71. The text should probably read "and the rituals" והעבודות instead of והעבדות.

72. *Opera Omnia*, p. 113. On the relationship of Kabbalah and astrology in Christian Kabbalah see F. Secret "L'Astrologie et les kabbalistes chrétiens à la Renaissance," *Le Tour Saint-Jacques* 5 (1956), pp. 45–9.

73. The term appears in the writings of the kabbalistic school of Gerona and in texts of the *iyyun* circle. For example see *Sefer Meshiv Dvarim Nekhoḥim* of Rabbi Ya'akov ben Sheshet, ed. G. Vajda (Jerusalem, 1969), p. 150 and the text published by G. Scholem in his article, "The Development of the Doctrine of the Worlds in Early Kabbalah" [Hebrew], *Tarbitz* 2 (1931), p. 430. It seems that this term is a translation of the Arabic "alam al-ḥuruf" which appears in the writings of the Ismailliya. See S. Pines, "Note sur l'Ismalijja," *Hermes* 3 (1939), p. 58.

74. The world of change is the lower world because it changes its forms. The world of motion, however, is the middle world because it is in constant motion. Alemanno uses these terms many times in all his books.

75. This appears to be an allusion to BT, *Sanhedrin*, 91a. Compare Alemanno's description of the ancient Jews, found in *Ḥai ha-Olamim*, MS Mantua 21, f. 216v.

76. Oxford MS 1535, f. 104v–105r. The quotation found in the printed version of the work *Shaar ha-Ḥeshek*, f. 33b–34a is quite corrupt.

77. This term is worthy of note. Moses does not repair the divinity but rather the vessels which transmit divine emanation. Compare this to Alemanno's statement in *Sefer Einei ha-Eda*, Jerusalem MS 598, f. 51r–v, concerning the status of man: "Were it not for Him who endows the lower world with perfection as He is perfect, the world would be void and empty, for nothing is called Godly but He. He repairs all the channels and emanations of the supernal and middle worlds, for no one receives that good in its entirety but He. When He receives it, then all the emanations descending to earth are in balance and work to perfection."

78. Oxford MS 2234, f. 8v.

79. See J. Gager, *Moses in Graeco-Roman Paganism* (Nashville, New York, 1972), pp. 134–160.

80. *Sefer Ḥeshek Shlomo*, Moscow MS 140, f. 287r.

81. Oxford MS 2234, f. 22v.

82. This attribution of the making of the Golden Calf to Moses is very strange; I have found no parallel to it in Hebrew literature. Cf. L. Smolar and M. Aberback, "The Golden Calf Episode in Postbiblical Literature," *HUCA* 39 (1968), pp. 91–116. However Giordano Bruno reports in the name of "kabbalists" that Moses made the Calf and the Brass Serpent for magical purposes. *De Imaginum, Signorum et Idearum Compositione Opera Latine Conscripta*, vol. II, *pars* III (Stuttgart, 1962) p. 102: "Cabalistarum doctrina confirmat et exemplum Mosis qui interdum, atque Jovis favorem comparandum vitulum aurem erexit ad Martis item temperandum simul atque Saturni violentem aeneum serpentem adorandum ofiecit." On the conception of the making of the Golden Calf as a technique to cause the descent of spiritual forces, see also *Shaar ha-Ḥeshek*, p. 17b and Rabbi Shlomo Franco's commentary on Ibn Ezra, Munich MS 15, f. 268r–v.

83. See Abraham ibn Ezra's prefatory comment on Exodus 32 in his *Commentary to the Torah*, Ex. 32:1.

84. See Ibn Ezra's *Commentary to the Torah*, Ex. 32:1.

85. This is one of the important rationales for sacrifices found in the writings of Ibn Ezra and his interpreters. For example, the comment of Rabbi Samuel Zarza in *Mekor Ḥayyim*, f. 9a and the statement of Rabbi Samuel ben Motot in *Sefer Megilat Starim* (Venice, 1554) ff. 10b, 11a.

86. Compare to the statement of Rabbi Samuel ibn Motot quoted by Alemanno in his *Collectanaea*, Oxford MS 2234, f. 127r: "When Israel observes the Temple service the Holy Spirit rests upon its noble men for the power of the human soul is increased and they prophesy."

87. See f. 9a. On the possible connection between this passage and Hermetic conceptions, see Georges Vajda, *Judah ben Nissim ibn Malka, Philosophe juif marocain* (Paris, 1954), p. 154, n. 1. There is a possible connection between the *Book of the Religions of the Prophets* and the book *Ilot ha-Ruḥaniyot* whose content parallels the content of this quotation from Ibn Zarza. See E. Blochet *Etudes sur le gnosticism musulman* (Rome, 1913), p. 96. Ibn Zarza's younger contemporary, Profet Duran, reported in his book *Ḥeshev ha-Efod*, ch. 15, that Hermes is the ancient Enoch who set down the various scriptures. Duran's remark on Enoch was included in the book *Kol Yehuda* of Judah Moscato on *Kuzari* I, i. See also note 89.

88. Compare to *Sefer Ḥeshev ha-Efod*, ch. 15. This is an ancient idea. See A.J. Festugière, *La Révélation d'Hermes Trismegiste* I (Paris, 1959), p. 334; Y. Marquet, "Sabéens et Ihwan al Safa," *Studia Islamica* 24 (1964), p. 58; "Liber Hermetis Mercurii Triplicis de VI Rerum Principium," ed. Th. Silverstein, *AHLDMA* 22 (1955), p. 247: "Hermes . . . astronomiam prius elucidavit."

89. In Alemanno's opinion "Enoch had sons and daughters and strong and weak descendants and a multitude of laws and religions." *Sefer Einei ha-Eda*, Paris MS 270, f. 125r. In the course of his remarks Alemanno associates astral magic with Enoch's descendants: "Methuselah studied the heavens and their power and constellations. Lemech however, reigned over the upper world so as to cause their spirit to descend to the lower world, to know the future and the spirit of the stars."

It is reasonable to assume that here the roles ascribed to Enoch in the *Book of the Religions of the Prophets*, as a lawgiver, astrologer and magician were reassigned to his descendants. This was in keeping with Alemanno's conception that every generation from Adam to Abraham engaged in the study of a different branch of knowledge. On Enoch as a lawgiver, see also *Sefer Ḥeshek Shlomo*, Berlin MS 832, f. 249r.

90. In the printed edition of *Sefer Ma'ase Efod*, p. 183, included by Alemanno in his *Collectanaea*, MS Oxford 2234, f. 105v with slight variations.

91. *Sefer Ma'ase Efod*, p. 182. Compare to the preface, p. 1.

92. Oxford MS 2234, f. 201b.

93. This expression appeared as early as Ibn Ezra's *Commentary* on Deut. 31:16.

94. *Shaar ha-Ḥeshek*, p. 41b. On magic temples and Alemanno see my note, "Magic Temples and Cities in the Middle Ages and the Renaissance," *Jerusalem Studies in Islam and Arabic* 3 (1982). For Alemanno's distinction between holy emanation originating in the world of the *Sefirot* and impure emanation emanating from the world of motion—the world of the celestial spheres—see his remarks in *Sefer Ḥeshek Shlomo*, MS Moscow 140, f. 100r. There he cites *Sefer ha-Tamar* in support of his position. Alemanno's reference seems to be found on p. 13 of Abuflaḥ's work.

95. Cf. Alemanno's comment in his *Collectanaea*, Oxford MS 2234, f. 95v: "The secret of the world of the letters is that they are forms and seals which receive supernal spiritual emanations as are the seals which receive astral emanations." Undoubtedly, this text refers to talismanic magic: "The seals which receive the emanations of the stars" is a paradigm of kabbalistic seals which function in the same way. The above comment appears at the end of the quotation of Ptolemy from *Centiloquium* (*Ha-Pri*), book 5, ch. 9 where the subject of talismans is treated. Compare to Paris MS 849, f. 77v. "How does one make a figure for the spirit of the *Sefirot*? He depicted the motion of the letters with the vocalization marks." Here the vocalization marks are an expression of the spirituality of the *Sefirot* that is the efflux of the *Sefirot* while the vocalization points are seals for the *Sefirot*.

96. Oxford MS 1535, f. 15r.

97. On causing the descent of the holy spirit, see the quotation from the *Collectanaea*, f. 164v. which was discussed above.

98. On the extension of the *Shekhina* into the lower world, see Y. Tishbi, *Mishnat ha-Zohar* II, p. 267. This occurrence, however, does not have a magical connotation.

99. Montefiore MS 316, f. 28v. The different versions of this letter include the passage quoted here and will be published in my forthcoming article in *Italia* 4 (1982?) I have also analyzed the relation between the writer of this letter and Rabbi Yeḥiel Nissim of Pisa in my "Three Versions of the Letter of R. Isaac of Pisa(?)," *Kovetz al Yad* (1982).

100. Published in J. Perles, "Les savants juifs à Florence à l'époche de Laurent de Médici," *REJ* 12 (1886), p. 256.

101. The danger involved in the practice of magical rituals without precise attention to their details is mentioned in books on magic. It is reasonable to assume that this quotation is based upon *Sefer ha-Atzamim* which states (f. 13): "If one is not expert and knowledgeable in causing the descent of forces and in the performance of rituals and sacrifices, they will kill him." See also ibid., f. 14–5. This selection also appears in Alemanno. See *Shaar ha-Ḥeshek*, p. 43a and the remarks of *Sefer Takhlit he-Ḥakham* mentioned above. Munich MS 214, f. 51a.

102. *Shaar ha-Ḥeshek*, p. 16a. Compare to *Sefer Ḥeshek Shlomo*, Oxford MS 1535, f. 146v.

103. *Shaar ha-Ḥeshek*, f. 15r.

104. Ibid., f. 44r.

105. Ibid., loc. cit.

106. Paris MS 849, f. 121v.

107. In the sixteenth century formulations similar to those of Alemanno recur in texts other than Rabbi Isaac of Pisa's letter and in the book *Shaarei Ḥayyim*. For example, see the statement of Rabbi Yeḥiel Nissim of Pisa, the nephew of Rabbi Isaac, who writes in *Sefer Minḥat Kena'ot* (Berlin, 1898), p. 49f: "All these practices are derived from the side of the forces of impurity. Therefore the gentiles made use of them, but the Jews are forbidden to practice them because they are a nation holy unto God. These practices were particularly forbidden in the holy land, for there the power of the holy heaven is revealed more than in other lands, because it is prepared to receive this light and spark." See also *Ma'arekhet ha-Elohut*, f. 6v, and *Avodat ha-Kodesh*, I, 12.

108. On the Torah as an instrument for the reception of efflux, see the passage from Alemanno's *Collectanaea*, f. 164r.

109. *Shaar ha-Ḥeshek*, f. 33b.

110. Paris MS 849, f. 137v.

111. Oxford MS 2234, f. 3v.

112. Ibid., loc. cit.

113. Edition of Joseph Ben-Shelomo (Jerusalem, 1971) I, p. 49f.

114. *Shaar ha-Ḥeshek*, p. 33b–34a. The term "laws of the Oral law" here parallels the term "the laws" found in the citation from Paris MS 849 together with a discussion of prophecy, language and the Temple. Proof of the identity of the term "the laws" with "the Oral law" is found in the statement of Alemanno which was copied into the book *Ḥai Olamim* from *Sefer Ḥalukat ha-Ḥokhmot* of Alfarabi: "The science of the law is one whereby man may learn a judgment on a matter which a statute of Scripture does not explain or when a statute of Scripture is restricted to certain matters" (Mantua MS 21, f. 195v).

115. Ibid., loc. cit. Compare to Alemanno's remarks on f. 26r–v in the same text. There, he speaks of a Chinese temple built in accordance with the structure of the middle world for the purpose of learning about the emanations of the middle world upon our own. A similar conception also appears in *Picatrix*; see Yates, *Giordano Bruno*, pp. 54–6 and pp. 367–71. On Alemanno's source for the Chinese temple passage see M. Idel, "Magic Temples and Cities in the Middle Ages and the Renaissance. A Passage of Masudi as a Possible Source for Yohanan Alemanno."

116. *Shaar ha-Ḥeshek*, f. 43b.

117. Paris MS 849, f. 94v. Parallel versions of several parts of this quotation are to be found in material from the commentaries on Ibn Ezra that Alemanno copied into his *Collectanaea.* See Oxford MS 2234, ff. 125v, 126v and 128v. This is supplemented by Ibn Zarza's statement which will be quoted in the continuation of this paper. The analogy of *Bina* to the planet Saturn appears in Ibn Wakar and following him in Rabbi Moses Narboni and Ibn Motot.

118. Cf. Georges Vajda, "Recherches sur la synthèse philosophico-kabbalistique de Samuel ibn Motot," *AHDLMA* 27 (1960), p. 59, n. 112.

119. On the origin of religions as linked to the great conjunction of Saturn and Jupiter, see Georges Vajda, *Recherches sur la philosophie et la kabbale dans la pensée juive du moyen âge* (Paris, 1962), p. 264, n.3.

120. Folio 6, col. 3–4 as compared with Leiden MS Or. 2065. E. Zafran, "Saturn and the Jews," *JWCI* 42 (1979), 16–27 explores the Christian sources.

121. See Oxford MS 1535, ff. 43r, 163v and others. It is possible that Pico had the book in his library. Compare to Kibre, *The Library of Pico della Mirandola* (New York, 1936), p. 160: "Samuel Sarsa, *De Secretis Legis.*" Page 149, no. 210 lists a commentary on the Pentateuch. *Sefer Mekor Ḥayyim* is a supercommentary on Ibn Ezra's *Commentary on the Torah.*

122. See Idel, "Curriculum," p. 311, n. 69.

123. In Alemanno's view, magic is to be distinguished from spiritual science because it pertains to pagan worship. In *Shaar ha-Ḥeshek*, f. 44a he says: "Since Saturn is the cause of magic and pagan worship . . . our master Moses blessed be his memory, had to stand in the breach and guard Israel in the matter of the Torah and commandments which issue from the *Sefira Tiferet* and from all kinds of pagan worship. All kinds of magic issue from Saturn."

124. See Vajda, "Samuel ibn Motot," pp. 31 and 35.

125. See *Sefer Mekor Ḥayyim*, ff. 6b–c.

126. Al-Constantini is mentioned in the book *Mikhlol Yofi* of Ibn Zarza. See C. Sirat, *Ḥanokh b. Salomon al-Constantini* (Jerusalem, 1976), Hebrew part, p. 5.

127. There is a great similarity between several passages of Ibn Zarza's *Mekor Ḥayyim* and Ibn Motot's *Megilat Starim.* For example, compare *Mekor Ḥayyim*, f. 129, col. 3 to *Megilat Starim*, fol. 52. col. 3.

128. See Vajda, *Recherches*, p. 152, n. 2 and *Mekor Ḥayyim*, f. 117, col. 3.

129. See Vajda, *Recherches*, 249–53. Al-Constantini's and Ibn Zarza's astrological conceptions have not yet been the subject of any scholarly study. On the subject of astrology in *Megale Amukot* see Vatican MS 59, ff. 5r–6v, 9r, 10r, and others.

130. See the passage from Rabbi Samuel ibn Motot's book *Meshovev Netivot* translated by Vajda in *Judah ben Nissim*, p. 120f.

131. *Kuzari*, I, 79; III, 23. One must remember that in Alemanno's time, the *Kuzari* of Rabbi Judah ha-Levi enjoyed widespread distribution in Italy. See R. Bonfil, *Ha-Rabanut be-Italya bi-Tkufat ha-Renesans* [The Rabbinate in Renaissance Italy] (Jerusalem, 1979), pp. 186 and 200.

132. See Paris MS 720, f. 32v. Rabbi Nissim was one of the first, perhaps even the first, to mention the book *Ma'ase Nissim*. See Oxford MS 2234, fol. 123r.

133. See his sermons in Montefiore MS 17, ff. 12r, 58r and on. For more details about this author, see Cassuto, *Ha-Yehudim be-Firentze bi-Tkufat ha-Renesans* [The Jews of Renaissance Florence] (Jerusalem, 1966), pp. 194–200.

134. See the above discussion on the subject of the magical interpretation of the Torah.

135. See Yates, *Giordano Burno*, pp. 80–2, concerning the special esteem of magic in the intellectual circles of Florence.

136. I shall devote a lengthy discussion to this composition and its relation to *Sefer Ḥai Olamim* in another article.

137. Oxford MS 2234, f. 125r.

138. Ibid., fol. 129r.

139. The Hebrew term "tzurot" (forms) has a magical meaning. In this case the word seems to refer to talismans. See M. Steinschneider, *Die hebräischen Übersetzungen des Mittelalters* (Gratz, 1956), p. 846, n. 8.

140. See also the discussion of Rabbi Isaac Abravanel in the continuation of this paper.

141. Alemanno writes in the book *Einei ha-Eda* that the demons were subdued and subjugated by the Egyptian religion. See Jerusalem MS 8° 598, f. 122. Concerning the connection between Egypt and demonic magic in Reuchlin, see H. Zika "Reuchlin's *De Verbo Mirifico* and the Magic Debate of the Late Fifteenth Century," *JWCI* 39 (1976), p. 112 n. 25 and p. 123.

142. This is possibly evidence of the influence of the Brethren of Purity who report the transmission of talismans from the Syrians to the Egyptians and from the Egyptians to the Greeks. See Marquet (above n. 88), pp. 36 and 53.

143. Paris MS 849, f. 25r–v. Cf. also Maimonides, *Guide*, III, ch. 29.

144. On the conception of ancient wisdom see note 194.

145. Compare to the thirteenth chapter of Asclepius. See *Corpus Hermeticum*, ed. A.D. Nock and A.J. Festugière (Paris, 1945), pp. 347–9; ed. Scott, I (Oxford, 1926), p. 358. These words of Asclepius were well known during the Renaissance and had a decisive influence upon the thought of Marsilio Ficino. See Walker, *Spiritual and Demonic Magic*, pp. 40–2.

146. See Asclepius, ch. 3, in *Corpus Hermeticum*, ed. Scott, I, p. 338. Concerning the influence of the Hermetic conception of the animation of images on Jabir ibn Ḥayyan, see also the important comments of P. Krauss in his "Jabir ibn Ḥayyan et la science grecque," *Mémoires présentés à l'Institute d'Egypte* 45 (1942), pp. 126–34. On page 133 in note 11, Krauss points out that Proclus in his commentary on the Timeus also considered statues of the gods to have a prophetic character. However, Alemanno's statement has a greater similarity to the conception of Jabar, and Alemanno perhaps preserved a lost Hermetic tradition which influenced the Arab author.

147. Krauss, "Jabir ibn Ḥayyan," pp. 104, 106, 133.

148. See the discussion above concerning the passage from the letter of Rabbi Isaac of Pisa.

149. Concerning the possible influence of some other of Alemanno's conceptions on Abravanel's *Commentary* on Exodus see M. Steinschneider, *Die Handschriftenverzeichnisse des königlichen Bibliotek zu Berlin* (Berlin, 1879), II, p. 6. See also Idel, "Sources of the Circle Images in the 'Dialoghi d'Amore'" [Hebrew], *Iyyun* 28 (1979), p. 160 and note 17.

150. See also B. Netanyahu, *Don Isaac Abravanel* (Philadelphia, 1953), pp. 124–5.

151. Jerusalem ed. (1955), p. 474.

152. Ibid., p. 480.

153. Ibid., loc. cit.

154. Ibid., p. 475. See also ibid., p. 478.

155. Kings I:5, 12.

156. On this subject see Walker, *The Ancient Theology*, pp. 22–41, and H. Wirszubski, *Shlosha Prakim be-Toldot ha-Kabala ha-Notzrit* [Three Chapters in the History of Christian Kabbalah] (Jerusalem, 1975), pp. 11–27.

157. It is reasonable to assume that in this context the word refers to the *Sefira Malkhut*.

158. BT, *Yadayim*, 86.

159. *Commentary* on Kings, p. 476.

160. BT *Pesaḥim*, f. 56a. Cf. the statement of Rabbi Abraham Yagel in the book *Beit Yaar ha-Levanon* which was published by Isaac Samuel Reggio in *Kerem Ḥemed* 2, pp. 51–2. Yagel was influenced by the statement of Alemanno and by Abravanel's *Commentary* on Kings.

161. See the material in note 156 above and also Walker's comments in *Spiritual and Demonic Magic*, pp. 3–24 and 62–3.

162. See the texts of Alemanno which were published in I. Adler, *Hebrew Writings Concerning Music* (Munich, 1975), pp. 41–5. A detailed discussion of the place of music in Alemanno's thought and particularly of its magic power will be the subject of my paper, "The Magic and Theurgic Interpretations of Music in Jewish Sources from the Renaissance to Ḥasidism" (Hebrew), *Yuval* 4 (1982).

163. See *Collectanaea*, Oxford 2234, f. 42v, 58r, 88v.

164. See *Einei ha-Eda*, Paris MS 270, f. 13r: "Two Axioms on the Nature of the Soul Taken from the book *Mekor Ḥayyim of* Shelomo ibn Gabirol." Alemanno proceeds to quote from the *Likutei Mekor Ḥayyim*, III, paragraph 8 (which has a parallel in *Sefer More ha-More*, p. 86) and 10. The work *Mekor Ḥayyim* was known to Rabbi David Messer Leon and Alemanno was a student of his father, Rabbi Judah Messer Leon. See *Sefer Magen David*, Montefiore MS 290, fol. 14a and *Sefer Tehila le-David* (Istanbul, 1576), fol. 42r. Rabbi Isaac Abravanel and his son Judah became acquainted with *Mekor Ḥayyim* while in Italy. Therefore the opinion of D. Kaufmann that "only the living oral tradition of Spanish Jewry" made it possible for Abravanel to know the name of the author of *Mekor Ḥayyim* is not definitive; see D. Kaufmann, *Meḥkarim ba-Sifrut ha-Ivrit shel Yemei ha-Beynayim* [Studies in Hebrew Literature of the Middle Ages] (Jerusalem, 1965), pp. 157–8.

165. See below, n. 178 on the *Theology of Aristotle.*

166. In the book *Ḥeshek Shlomo*, Oxford MS 1535, fol. 163v, he says: "And as in the words of the sage Ibn Ezra, who is worthy to be called a sage."

167. See Idel, "Curriculum," pp. 309–310, n. 64.

168. On the influence of Al-Batalyusi on Alemanno, see D. Kaufmann, *Die Spuren Albataljussis in der jüdischen Religionsphilosophie* (Leipzig, 1880), pp. 56–60. See also, M. Idel "The Sources," (above, n. 149), pp. 160ff. There are more references drawn from the work *Ha-Agulot ha-Ra'ayoniyot* in Alemanno's writings than those noted by Kaufmann.

169. See for example *Sefer Ḥai Olamim*, Mantua MS 21, fol. 14v. and 215r and others. On the different versions of this text, see A. Altmann, "The Ladder of Ascension," *Studies in Mysticism Presented to Gershom Scholem* (Jerusalem, 1967), p. 8 n. 28, and pp. 10–11.

170. For example see *Collectanaea*, Oxford MS 2234, f. 186v–187v.

171. See note 164 above. See D. Kaufmann, *Studies in Hebrew Literature*, pp. 78–125. The passage published on pp. 106–112 from Paris MS 301 is taken from the untitled work of Alemanno which is to be found in Paris MS 849 (new listing). Kaufmann did not know of Alemanno's authorship. The material in Kaufmann, *Studies*, pp. 112–8 is from Alemanno's *Collectanaea.* In the copying of the material from the *Collectanaea* several errors, at times very significant ones, were made in the text.

172. Mantua MS 21, f. 22v. See the first entry in this text.

173. Munich MS 59, f. 87v. The passage and its context parallel a discussion in the book *Ḥai Olamim*; see Steinschneider, *Alfarabi* (St. Petersburg, 1869) p. 249. Compare to Paris MS 849, fol. 124v and to my discussion below of the statement in the Paris manuscript.

174. Oxford MS 1535, f. 145v–146r.

175. On the similarity of the passage in the *Heptaplus* VI:4 to the first paragraph of *Sefer ha-Sibot*, see O. Bardenhewer, *Die pseudo-Aristotelische Schrift über das reine Gute* (Freiburg, 1882), p. 301. This fact passed unnoticed by the editors of Pico's works. It should be noted that the phrasing of Pico differs from that of the Latin translation of *Liber de Causis*.

176. See the evidence of Gianfrancesco Pico della Mirandola, *Opera Omnia* (Basel, 1573) p. 1371. *The Heptaplus* was written in 1488 in the same year that Alemanno reports that he had contacts with Pico.

177. See *Collectanaea*, Oxford MS 2234, f. 21v; Paris MS 849, ff. 91r–v and 123r; *Sefer Ḥeshek Shlomo*, Berlin MS 832, f. 83r. In Abulafia and in several of Alemanno's quotations the passage is quoted as *Sefer ha-Atzamim ha-Elyonim.* This passage was published by Steinschneider, *Alfarabi*, pp. 114f.

178. *Collectanaea*, Oxford MS 2234, f. 71v. There Alemanno copied the passages from *Sefer ha-Ma'alot* (Berlin, 1872) which were attributed to Aristotle. One passage found in *Sefer ha-Ma'alot*, p. 22f parallels the *Theology of Aristotle* I, 1–29 (=*Ennead* IV, 8, 6, 1). Alemanno also made use of this passage in the book *Einei ha-Eda*, Jerusalem MS 598, f. 98r. Another passage is to be found in *Sefer ha-Ma'alot*, p. 26f and parallels the *Theology*, VII, 41–50 (=*Ennead* IV, 8, 8, 1–23). Alemanno also integrates this material within the text of *Sefer Einei ha-Eda*, Jerusalem MS 598, f. 99v. On Alemanno's confusion of the *Sefer ha-Ma'alot* with the *Reshit Ḥokhma*, see M. Steinschneider, *Die hebraischen Übersetzungen*, p. 243 n. 973. Alemanno was also familiar with the tradition of Aristotle's repentance which was apparently connected with the attribution of the *Theology* to Aristotle. This tradition appears in Rabbi Joseph ibn Shem Tov's commentary on *Ethics*; see Oxford MS 1267, f. 171v. It is quoted in Alemanno's *Collectanaea*, f. 50r and in a note to *Sefer Ḥeshek Shlomo*, MS Moscow, f. 105r. On this tradition see S. Munk, *Mélanges de philosophie juive et arabe* (Paris, 1953), p. 249 n. 3.

179. In the *Collectanaea*, MS Oxford 2234, f. 72r a comment appears with the attribution "from a commentary on *Kuzari* . . . ." This comment concerns the ascent of the soul in a version similar to that of Moses ibn Ezra in the book *Arugat ha-Bosem* as published in *Zion* 2 (1842), p. 121. This parallels a passage in *Sefer ha-Ma'alot*, p. 22. Concerning the content and literary history of this passage, see A. Altmann and S. M. Stern, *Isaac Israeli* (Oxford, 1958) pp. 191–2.

180. See *Collectanaea*, Oxford MS 2234, f. 140r–v which parallels *Sefer Reshit Ḥokhma* (Berlin, 1902), p. 77.

181. See Idel, "Curriculum," p. 306, n. 32.

182. Oxford MS 2234, f. 22r.

183. Ibid., f. 125r.

184. In the marginal note at the bottom of f. 210r of *Sefer Ḥeshek Shlomo*, Moscow MS 140, Plotinus is described as the disciple of "Orieno," that is of Origen. It seems that this is a corruption of the authentic tradition that both Plotinus and Origen were disciples of Ammonius Saccas.

185. See Pico, *Opera Omnia* (Basel, 1557), p. 328.

186. Also compare to Alemanno's comment on the page margin of *Sefer Ḥeshek Shlomo*, Moscow MS 140, f. 105r. There he states that Mani and Porphyry desired to obliterate the Torah.

187. In his letter to the worthies of Florence published by S. Asaf, *Sefer Minḥa le-David* [Hebrew] (Jerusalem, 1935), p. 227. For the Renaissance background of this quotation and the one following it see Scholem, "Anfänge der christlichen Kabbalah," pp. 192f.

188. *Magen David*, Montefiore MS 290, f. 25 published by Schechter, "Notes sur David Messer Leon," *REJ* 24(1892), p. 122.

189. Ed. I.S. Reggio (Vienna, 1833), p. 48.

190. No serious attempt has been made to discover which work Del Medigo has in mind here. See Reggio's notes ad loc.; Ruderman, "Abraham Farissol," p. 75, and Geffen, "Faith and Reason," pp. 435f (who did not discuss the matter although he had seen the discussion of Kabbalah contained in the commentary on *etzem ha-galgal.*

191. Paris MS 968, f. 41r–v. Comp. Bohdan Kieszkowski, "Les rapports entre Elie del Medigo et Pic de la Mirandole," *Rinascimento* 4 (1964), pp. 58–61; F. Secret, *Les kabbalistes chrétiens de la Renaissance* (Paris, 1964), pp. 30–1 and 42, n. 24.

192. This passage concerns a kabbalistic conception in which *Ein Sof* is identical with the Supreme Crown (*Keter*, the first *Sefira).* The most important exponent of this idea in the Spanish school was Rabbi Joseph Gikatilla. Two kabbalistic contemporaries of Del Medigo in Italy also held this view: Rabbi Elijah ben Benjamin of Genazzano, the author of *Sefer Igeret Ḥamudot* and the Spanish kabbalist, Rabbi Isaac ben Samuel Mar Ḥayyim who lived in Naples at a period when Del Medigo was writing *Sefer Beḥinat ha-Dat.* In this composition Del Medigo demonstrates a familiarity with the dispute over the problem of the identity of *Ein Sof* with the Supreme Crown.

193. Chapter 4.

194. On the ancient theology, see D. P. Walker, *Studies in Christian Platonism from the Fifteenth to the Eighteenth Century* (Duckworth, 1972), pp. 1–131 and Ch. B. Schmitt, "Perennial Philosophy: From Agostino Steuco to Leibniz," *Journal of the History of Ideas* 27

(1966), pp. 505–31. Alemanno makes much use of this term and its place in Alemanno's writings deserves a special study.

195. This is also true of David Messer Leon whose knowledge of Kabbalah was quite limited. He tried insofar as possible to reconcile Kabbalah with reason. See Schechter's article, note 188 above, p. 125f. A portion of the kabbalistic material found in *Sefer Magen David* was copied from Rabbi Isaac Mar Ḥayyim as Gottlieb established. See his *Studies*, p. 404–22.

196. See Vajda, *Samuel ibn Motot*, p. 35.

197. Neither Bardenhewer in his edition of *Liber de Causis* nor Dodds in his edition of Proclus' *Elements of Theology* comments upon the literary history of this other version of Proclus which found its way to Pico. I do not know of another source which attributes the *Liber de Causis* to Abucatem Avenam. It is possible that this is a corruption of the name Abu Nasir Alfarabi who was thought to be the author of the work. See Bardenhewer's remarks in his edition of *Liber de Causis*, p. 309f. It is noteworthy that the third thesis based on *Liber de Causis* parallels what is quoted in the *Heptaplus* in content but not in language, see above.

198. E. Wind, *Pagan Mysteries in the Renaissance* (Penguin Books, 1967) pp. 134, 174.

199. Wirszubski, *A Christian Kabbalist*, pp. 16–8. The passage discussed by Wind is well interpreted by the thesis that Wirszubski analyzed. Both scholars however did not perceive the connection between these two discussions by Pico. I hope to elaborate on the subject in a later article.

200. *Sefer Minḥat Yehuda* in *Sefer Ma'arekhet ha-Elohut* (Mantua, 1558), f. 41b–42a. This passage is quoted without attribution of the author or work. Such is the case in Alemanno's *Collectanaea*, Oxford MS 2234, f. 158r. On Alemanno and Rabbi Judah Ḥayyat see the appendix to my article, "Curriculum," pp. 330–331.

201. BT *Rosh ha-Shana*, f. 32a.

202. *Sefer Yetzira* I:5.

203. Paris MS 849, f. 123a. On *Sefer ha-Atzamim ha-Elyonim* which is but another title of *Sefer ha-Sibot*, see note 177 above.

204. Paris MS 849, f. 91v.

205. *Sefer ha-Ma'arekhet*, f. 82b. Compare what is said in Paris MS 859, f. 29b with Vatican MS 428, f. 55r ("Not a single allusion to the First Cause is to be found in the Torah") and with the statements in a commentary on the ten *Sefirot*, Vatican MS 224, f. 121r.

206. The commentary on *etzem ha-galgal* was completed as of 1485 and it is possible that Alemanno was familiar with it. See Steinschneider, "Elia del Medigo," *H.B.* 21 (1881/2), p. 68. It is significant that the work *Beit Ya'ar ha-Levanon* of Abraham Yagel contains a broader discussion of negative theology than that found in Alemanno. Yagel compares the kabbalistic concept of *Ein Sof* with the passage from *Sefer ha-Sibot* that Alemanno cited from the work of Abulafia on the one hand, and with the Hermetic conception on the other. Alemanno's comparison of *Ein Sof* and the First Cause of *Sefer ha-Sibot* served as an inspiration for Yagel's discussion. On the subject of negative theology and its relation to the concept of *Ein Sof* see also *Sefer Sha'ar ha-Shamayim* of Abraham Herrera, part IV, ch. 4.

207. *Sefer Ma'arekhet ha-Elohut*, p. 44.

208. As to the identity of the person whom he names "the author of the tract," ff. 41r and 42v, see Gottlieb, *Studies*, p. 430, n. 25 who suggests Rabbi Elijah of Genazzano.

209. Paris MS 849, fol. 124v.

210. Alemanno tends to remove dictations from the Zohar from Ḥayyat's writings and also to replace Ḥayyat's mythical expressions with philosophical formulations. For example Ḥayyat writes: "All the *Sefirot* ascend to it (*Keter*) to receive a reward." Alemanno's version reads "that all of them ascend to the Supreme Crown and the Supreme Crown receives efflux and existence from *Ein Sof*." The replacement of the expression "to receive a reward" by "receives efflux and existence" is evidence of Alemanno's trend of thought.

211. See *Sefer Ma'arekhet ha-Elohut*, f. 114r.

212. See Idel, "Curriculum," Appendix, pp. 330–331.

213. See Munich MS 285, f. 3a–b.

214. *Sefer Ma'arekhet ha-Elohut*, f. 3b.

215. Berlin MS 832, f. 83a–b.

216. For Rabbi Moses Narboni's opinion on the subject, see A. Altmann, "Moses Narboni's Epistle on Shiur Qoma," *Jewish Medieval and Renaissance Studies* (ed. A. Altmann, Cambridge MA, 1967), pp. 243–5. Rabbi Abraham ben Eliezer ha-Levi, Alemanno's contemporary, writes that "In the opinion of several of our contemporary Spanish sages who pursue philosophical studies there are ten spiritual degrees called angels . . . and they say that these degrees are the ten *Sefirot*." *Sefer Masoret he-Ḥokhma,* ed. G. Scholem, *Kiryat Sefer* 2 (1925), p. 126.

217. In the section omitted, Alemanno quotes Aristotle's *Metaphysics* M (13) 1084, which deals with the numbers and ideas. Alemanno refers to the Platonic concept that these are corresponding ideas for only the numbers 1–10, which Aristotle mentioned in order to refute it. On the views of Plato and Aristotle on the ideal numbers, see L. Robin, *La théorie platonicienne des idées et des nombres d'après Aristote* (Hildesheim, 1963), p. 267 ff. On the comparison between Pythagorean numbers and the *Sefirot*, see also Simone Luzzatto in the reference found in n. 51 above.

218. See note 213 above.

219. On the similarity of Plato and the Prophets see *Sefer Ḥeshek Shlomo*, Oxford MS 1535, f. 162v and on, and also Idel, "Curriculum," pp. 325, 331–332, nn. 55–56.

220. See *Shir ha-Ma'alot*, Oxford MS 1535, f. 63r–v. In another part of *Ḥeshek Shlomo*, Moscow MS 140, f. 23r, Alemanno speaks of "the forms which ascend from form to form in order until they come to the First Form which is the Form of all Forms, for It is the Form of the World in entirety, for all of them (the forms) are made for Its purpose, for they have no other purpose but to imitate those abiding forms which are in Him all together in the simplest most excellent and most encompassing and eternal manner possible." On the forms in God, see Simon van den Bergh, *Averroes: Tahafut al Tahafut* (Oxford, 1954), II, pp. 88–9. On the form of the body limbs and their connection to the stars, see F. Cumont, "Astrologia," *Révue archéologique* 3(1916), pp. 7–10; A. Sharf, *The Universe of Shabbetai Donnolo* (Warminster, 1976), pp. 52ff.

221. I am not familiar with any such opinion in Alfarabi. However, in *Sefer Takhlit he-Ḥakham*, Munich MS 214, f. 46r–47v, the twenty-eight encampments of the moon are mentioned and the author notes that this is the opinion of the Indians. On the Indians and records of the twenty-eight encampments and their literary history, see M. Plessner, "Hermes Trismegistus and Arab Science," *Studia Islamica* 2 (1954), pp. 57f; Cornelius Agrippa, *De occulta philosophia*, II, ch. 33.

222. See paragraph 5 of *Sefer ha-Sibot* which is the paragraph quoted by Alemanno from *Imrei Shefer*: "For what is possessed by the effect is also possessed by the cause, but in the cause it is of a more exalted, worthy and superior way;" Paris MS 849, f. 91v. See also paragraphs 7 and 11 of *Sefer ha-Sibot* and Pico's first thesis in the "Secundum Proclum."

223. Yagel changed the wording of Agrippa who claimed that this was the opinion of all the Platonists. Among the Neoplatonist thinkers it seems that Agrippa's statement most closely resembles the conception of Proclus. The idea that in the world of archetypes "all is in all" has parallels in the *Elements of Theology* of Proclus, sentences 170, 173, 176.

224. Cf. the opinion of Pico on the elements expressed in the *Theses* and *Heptaplus*, Wirszubski's description of this passage in *A Christian Kabbalist*, pp. 35–6, and also F. H. Gomrbrich, "Icones Symbolicae: The Visual Image in Neoplatonic Thought," *JWCI* 11 (1948), pp. 167–8. The remarks of both authors mentioned above are supplemented by Pico's comment in his commentary on the *Canzone de Amore* of G. Benivieni, ch. 12. See also M. Idel, "Prometheus in Jewish Garb" [Hebrew], *Eshkolot*, n.s., 5–6 (1980–81), pp. 124–125.

225. In a section found before this discussion.

226. F. 164a.

227. F. 89b.

228. Oxford MS 1304, f. 10v. In the continuation Yagel reaches certain conclusions about the possibility of magic practices which are based upon the correspondences between the different levels of reality.

229. Ibid., f. 10r. Again the source for Yagel's statement is to be found in Agrippa, *De occulta philosophia* I, ch. 11: "Platonici omnia inferiora ferunt esse ideata a superioribus

ideis: ideam autem definiunt esse formam supra corpora animas mentes, unam simplicem puram immutabilem incorporem at aeternam; atque eandem idearum omnium esse naturam, ponunt autem ideas primo in ipso quidem bono, hoc est Deo, per causae modum solum." Compare also *De occulta philosophia* III, ch. 10.

230. The elevation of the Platonic ideas to a level higher than that of the separate intelligences also appears in the writings of Yagel's contemporary, Rabbi Judah Moscato in *Nefutzot Yehuda*, sermon 8 (Lwow, 1859), ff. 33b–34a. Moscato follows Pico and calls the place of the ideas by the name "The First Creature." However, in Moscato one does not find the identification of *Sefirot* with Ideas. On this sermon see Y. Dan, "Hebrew Homiletical Literature in Renaissance Italy" [Hebrew], *Proceedings of the Sixth World Congress of Jewish Studies* (Jerusalem, 1977), pp. 107f. The term "first creature" is common in the writings of Rabbi Isaac ibn Latif whose writings were known both to Pico and to Moscato. Yagel knew Moscato; see *Beit Ya'ar ha-Levanon*, Oxford MS 1306, f. 23r.

231. See H. A. Wolfson, "Extradeical and Intradeical Interpretations of Platonic Ideas," *Religious Philosophy* (Cambridge, MA, 1965), p. 37.

232. (Venice, 1574), f. 12d.

233. Florence, Laurenziana, Plut. II, 38, f. 91v. The passage also appears in a later version of this composition in Munich MS 49, f. 38v.

234. Compare to the statement of Rabbi Yeḥi'el Nissim of Pisa in the book *Minḥat Kena'ot* (Berlin, 1898), p. 49: "Everything possesses a power proper to itself which is the cause of its existence and being. For this reason Plato inclined to this opinion when he propounded his general principles called forms." See also ibid., p. 53 and 84. In another article I will discuss the connection between Rabbi Yeḥi'el and Rabbi Mordekhai Rossillo.

235. See *Sefer Me'or Einayim, Imrei Bina*, ch. 4. See also the statements of Simone Luzzatto in his *Ma'amar al Yehudei Venetziya* [Hebrew: *Discourse on the Jews of Venice*] (Jerusalem, 1950), p. 144–5; for the original Italian see n. 52 above.

236. On the opinion of Ficino see, E. F. Rice, *The Renaissance Idea of Wisdom* (Cambridge MA, 1958), pp. 61ff. On Pico's view see *Commento sopra Canzone de Amore composta de Girolamo Benivieni*, ch. 12.

237. See G. Scholem, "Was Israel Sarug a Disciple of the Ari?" [Hebrew] *Zion* 5 (1930), pp. 214–43. See also, Scholem's essay *Avraham Cohen Herera, Ba'al Sha'ar ha-Shamayim: Ḥayyav, Yetzirato ve-Hashpa'ata* [Abraham Cohen Herrera, Author of *Shaar ha-Shamayim:* his Life, his Works and their Influence] (Jerusalem, 1978), pp. 34–46.

238. This follows Scholem's opinion in his essay *Abraham Cohen Herrera*, pp. 35f.

239. See *Sefer Nefutzot Yehuda*, sermon 31 (Warsaw, 1871), p. 80a. The definition offered by Moscato has as its source a twelfth-century work, *Liber XXIV Philosophorum*; see C. Baumkehr, *Das pseudo-hermetische Buch der XXIV Meister* (Munster, 1937), p. 208. On the dissemination of this concept see D. Mahnke, *Unendliche Sphäre und Allmittelpunkt* (Halle, 1937). This may be supplemented by Yates, *Giordano Bruno*, p. 247; H. Wirszubski, "Francesco Giorgio's commentary on Giovanni Pico's Kabbalistic Theses," *JWCI* 27 (1974), p. 154; and G. Poulet, *The Metamorphoses of the Circle* (Baltimore, 1966), pp. 1–14.

240. The term "the divine circle" appears already in the book *Beḥinat Olam* of Rabbi Yedaya ha-Penini as David Kaufmann already noted, "Die Spuren," p. 64. However, Moscato's conception differs absolutely from that of Al-Batalyusi. The conception of the intellectual circle appears in the writings of Renaissance authors as I have shown in my article, "Sources" (note 149 above). See also I. E. Barzilay, *Between Reason and Faith* (The Hague and Paris, 1967), p. 175.

241. In *Sefer Sha'arei Tzedek* of Rabbi Joseph Gikatilla I did not find the same wording as in Moscato, although the idea is to be found in Gikatilla's writings. See Gottlieb, *Studies*, p. 152 and note 158. I do not know of any use of the word "soḥaret" as a term for *Keter*.

242. Highly significant is the fact that anti-philosophical attitudes are held by supporters of the printing of the Zohar. Cf. Y. Tishby, "The Polemic on the Book of the Zohar in the Sixteenth Century in Italy" [Hebrew], *Perakim, Yearbook of the Schocken Institute* (1966–67), pp. 180–181.

Remnants of Jewish Averroism in the Renaissance

ALFRED L. IVRY

I

It is generally agreed that there are no original works of a Jewish Averroistic sort written in the sixteenth century.[1] There are, though, some valuable books written in this genre or influenced by it which were composed in the late fifteenth century and which circulated and were first printed in the sixteenth. There is also in this period an important movement to translate Averroes, a movement in which a few Jews played a crucial role.[2] While we are dealing with a small and ever dwindling number of individuals, it should be recalled that Jewish philosophy (as most philosophy) was never a mass movement, its writers in any period a handful, their influence, such as it was — a separate and debateable topic — out of proportion to their literature. In these respects Jewish Averrroism in the Renaissance is not markedly different from that of earlier periods. It may be only in retrospect, from the vantage point of developments in the latter half of the sixteenth century, that the movement seems to be reduced to remnants of its former self. Indeed, the hundred years from 1500 to 1600 is a poor and arbitrary periodization for our topic, a more logical period being from the mid-fifteenth to mid-sixteenth century, years coterminous with the Italian High Renaissance.[3]

Jewish philosophers of this period, Averroists among them, represent a bridge between the old philosophy and the new learning. Even as they embody the physical relocation of Jewish life then underway, so these translators and philosophers represent the transition from a discipline rooted in Islamic philosophy to one familiar with, and reaching out to, European thought. Their linguistic points of contact shift from Arabic to Latin, with Hebrew the common intermediary.

Much of the Renaissance philosophy in the fifteenth and sixteenth century is tied up with the study of Averroes' writings, and

Jews played a leading role in making these works available. Working from Hebrew translations done more than two hundred years earlier, Jews in this period rendered into Latin about three-fourths of Averroes' corpus.[4]

The Jewish translator in the Renaissance was thus a person relating to two communities, familiar with two literary traditions and the cultures and religions of each. For most of the translators this dual relationship was positive, joined as it was by the bond of the "new" learning and the promise of a more open society. Paradoxical as it may seem, it was the twelfth-century Averroes who represented to many the new wave of learning in the Renaissance, and it was through the translation and study of his works that Jews as well as Christians expressed the temper of the time.

For Renaissance humanists, this new learning was to be built upon the best of what had preceded, for which the availability of lucid tests was deemed a prerequisite. These humanists desired well-written translations, an aesthetic correlate of their quest for scientific truth. The translation movement of this period is thus very much at the heart of Renaissance goals and values, and the translators were aware of the significance of their mission.[5] It is not coincidental, therefore, that some treatises were printed with two translations.[6] This is an expression of the pursuit of excellence and beauty, which is the pursuit of truth itself, the hallmark of this movement.

It is apt that the Averroian *oeuvre* was a major vehicle of expression for Renaissance philosophy, since Averroes, acknowledged by all as Artistotle's foremost commentator, was identified with him who was still considered to be "the master of those who know." It is the world which Aristotle analyzed and categorized to which many in the Renaissance turned. That world was made more comprehensible by a centuries-long tradition of commentary which Averroes, it was felt, best represented. The Aristotle so depicted was the model of a natural scientist, albeit not yet an experimentalist. Many of the scholars of the Renaissance were attracted to this "natural" world view, and with it, to the writings of Averroes.

This awareness of the significance of the Averroian commentaries for natural science is reflected in the work of the Jewish translators in various ways, in their spare but revealing comments at the beginning and end of works, and in the very choice and pattern of their labor. This pattern and its product have yet to be studied in depth. The little scholarship that has been done discloses a self-awareness on the part of the translators that renders them more than mechanical *meturgemans*. They are revealed, rather, as partners in the enterprise of learning then underway.

Thus in 1527, Calo Calonymos, alias Kalonymos ben David the Younger, alias Maestro Calo, translated Averroes, *Tahāfut al-Tahāfut*, the *Incoherence of the Incoherence*, from the fourteenth-century Hebrew translation (of Calonymos b. David), since he knew that the extant thirteenth-century Latin translation (of yet another Calonymos, this the son of Calonymos[!] b. David, first published in 1497) was a corrupt text.[7] Calo's work is a testimony to his honesty as a translator, even as his own treatise, *De mundi creatione*, shows him to be more than "merely" a translator, and more than merely a blind disciple of Averroes. For the same man who translated Averroes' *Destructio destructionum philosophiae Algazelis* and his *Epistola de connexione intellectus abstracti cum homine*, argues in his own treatise against Averroes and for creation from nothing.[8]

Calo, with his diverse accomplishments, is typical of other Jewish translators and scholars of this period who worked largely in the shadow of Averroes, men like Judah Messer Leon, Abraham De Balmes, Jacob Mantinus, and particularly Elijah Del Medigo. Most of their compositions, written in Latin or Hebrew, still await the attention of scholars trained both in philosophy and in classical and Semitic languages. It is only the scholar with this sort of equipment who is able fully to evaluate the Averroian and Averroistic texts of this period, and to point to the subtle transmission of ideas as they move from language to language, a task so brilliantly performed by the late Harry Wolfson. Research on the translators will require comparison with their sources, with whatever original studies they wrote, and with the works of their contemporaries, both Jewish and Christian. Such research will add to our knowledge of the Averroism of the period, and of the Jewish involvement in it.

II

The infusion of Averroian and Averroist thought—to distinguish between the thought of Averroes and that of his interpreters—into the philosophical writing of the Renaissance is apparent not only in the works of admitted and obvious disciples of these approaches but also in the compositions of their major intellectual adversaries, the Platonists of the period.[9] Like Jewish and Scholastic thinkers before them, these Renaissance philosophers saw the weakening of Aristotelianism in general, and of Averroism in particular, as a precondition for their subsequent assertions. This was difficult, however, since so much of the Aristotelian corpus had by then become conventional wisdom for all philosophers. The Platonic, or rather Neoplatonic, challenge to Averroism concentrated on metaphysical issues, of both an ontological and epistemological kind: the nature of the divine being and His relation to the world on the one hand, and our relation to Him, on the other. At issue was not only truth, but salvation and the attainment of immortality. The arguments advanced by the Renaissance Platonists in these crucial areas may often be seen as responses to Averroism, part of a dialogue with a not-so-silent partner, one whose voice can be heard over the protestations of the speaker.

The most famous Jewish Platonist of this period, and one of the most famous of the Renaissance, is Judah Abravanel, known also as Leone Ebreo.[10] His great work, *Dialoghi d'Amore*, called in Hebrew *Vikuaḥ al ha-Ahava*, shows much awareness of Aristotle and Averroes. For Ebreo (as we may call him to distinguish him from his well known father, Isaac Abravanel), Averroes' philosophy is not, however, only one among many to be mentioned and refuted. Rather, Averroism may be seen as the primary example of an Aristotelianism which Ebreo resists, but which persists in his thought and helps shape it. Some examples, taken from the *Dialoghi*, illustrate this fact, and attest to the strength of these "remnants" of Averroism.

Stylistically and, to some degree substantively, the basic dichotomy of this work is between love and knowledge, *Philo* and *Sophia*, where knowledge is that had by the intellect, conceived in essentially Aristotelian terms. In presenting love as a counter-principle to intellection, Ebreo takes his place with those who are anti-Aristotelian in general, and anti-Averroian in particular.[11] For it is Averroes with whom the theory of intellection common to medieval philosophy received its most extreme naturalistic expression, even as it is his theory of an impersonal conjunction which received the most attention in late medieval and Renaissance times.

Ebreo is, however, more of an Aristotelian, and more of an Averroist, than he would care to admit. Despite his insistence on the significance of love as a causal principle for the workings of the universe, he is hard-pressed to offer a definition or description of love which is essentially different from that of the intellect. "The end of goodness," he says near the opening of the book, "is the perfecting of our intellect,"[12] and it is this essentially Aristotelian mechanism which Ebreo uses throughout the work. The few attempts he makes to distinguish explicitly between love and intellect are inconclusive, though indicative of his awareness of the problem.

Thus in the First Dialogue, Ebreo has *Sophia* say, "I have at some time heard it propounded that happiness consists, not exactly in knowledge of God, but in love and blissful enjoyment of Him."[13] *Philo's* response, after presenting "equally valid" arguments for both positions, is to acknowledge that "happiness consists in an activity of the most noble and spiritual faculty of the soul — and that is the intellect." Love is seen as following upon knowledge and stimulating it to further effort. "Love and desire are means of raising us from imperfect knowledge to the perfect union, which is the true end of love and desire; and these are affects of the will, which translates dual cognition into enjoyment of perfect cognitive union."[14]

This enjoyment is thus viewed as a function, even as it is a (subsidiary) cause, of intellection. Love and knowledge have a reciprocal relation, though intellect occupies the first and last stages of a process which is, essentially, a cognitive experience.[15] "As we know His perfection," Ebreo writes, "so we love and desire to enjoy Him in the most perfect union of knowledge possible to us."[16] The phrase "possible to us" is a conventional qualification expressing the concern to maintain God's transcendence, a belief Ebreo holds in uneasy alliance with the conviction of His imminence. With regard to divine imminence, Ebreo goes further towards uniting man directly with God than do most medievals. Once he even identifies God with the Agent Intellect of our world, its formal principle with which individual intellects may conjoin.[17] As such, God is seen as the cause and goal of all essential being. "He is the first Being, and all that exists, exists through participation in Him. He is pure activity. He is the Supreme Intellect, from which all intellect, activity, form and perfection, derive."[18]

For Ebreo, these terms are equally predicable of God when He is pictured in more traditionally Platonic terms, as is done towards the end of the book.[19] Aristotle and Plato are seen as agreeing that the totality of forms is in the divine mind; the noetic principle is the same whether it is called Agent Intellect, Idea of the World, Pattern of the Universe, or Divine Mind.[20]

Aristotle and Plato do differ, Ebreo recognizes, in their conceptualization of the structures whereby God relates to the world, and Ebreo, as is known, holds ultimately for a view of Neoplatonism in which the source of all beauty and wisdom, the origin of all being, is ostensibily different from that of which it is the origin and source.[21] Like his predecessors, however, Ebreo is unable to do more than make this assertion dogmatically, for the emanative scheme adopted clearly establishes, despite his protestations, a certain commonality of being between God and His creation.[22]

For Ebreo, therefore, the dynamics of God's relation to the world is not essentially different in a Platonic or Aristotelian world view, though the structures might vary. There is even a certain structural parallelism within Aristotelianism to the Platonic view of the deity as a force extrinsic to the world and relating to it through intermediaries. In this regard, Ebreo points to the view advanced by Al-Ghazzāli [!], Avicenna and Maimonides.[23] The alternative model to this view is that which Ebreo has previously and rightly associated with Averroes,[24] *viz.*, a view in which God is the first mover of the world and in it, an intelligent being directly related to all other intelligent being and responsible for all form. Though Ebreo explicitly subscribes to the "Platonic" view, and is thus more sympathetic towards the Avicennian-Maimonidean approach of Aristotelianism, it might well be argued that it was the Averroian model which effectively influences his thought. For Averroes ultimately posited a single principle of form which pervades the universe directly, though in an infinite number of guises and degrees of perfection. It is this direct pervasiveness of the divine Intelligence to which Ebreo is attracted,[25] even as he fears its diffusion and naturalization. He thus indulges in one place in a critique of Averroes' view of the Prime Mover, seeing it a "strange" interpretation of Aristotle that the same presumably unified being should be both a final and efficient cause,[26] though his own view of God is equally that of a composite unity.

While Ebreo goes finally to the extreme of delegating God's presence in the world to intermediaries in order to preserve His unique character, he yet permits these intermediaries—the divine Wisdom and Beauty—to pervade and produce not only the formal component of our world, but also its material aspect.[27] Ebreo's immanentism receives its boldest expression, perhaps, in the view of God as creating the world by an act of self-love;[28] a notion which aptly describes Ebreo's belief in love as a purposive, constructive act directed always to a noble and ennobling end, which for God can only be Himself. Similarly, the love of any superior being for an inferior one can well be described as an instance of self-love. The perfection of the inferior being which occurs in the relation of two beings is real, but incidental, as it were, to the perfection of the superior being itself.[29]

The double perfection thus described calls to mind Averroes' view of the relation of disparately comprehensive intelligences, as described in his *Treatise on the Possibility of Conjunction.*[30] There, the lower form is said to perfect the higher, even as the higher obviously perfects the lower. The perfecting of the higher form can be understood as the result of its relation with the lower, that form presenting an opportunity for the higher form to express its own perfection, and in that sense perfecting it. "Higher" and "lower" forms are of course all related; in Averroes' thought, they are parts of a whole.[31] It is this organic unity and inter-relation of specific forms, so characteristic of Averroes' thought, which also inspires Ebreo.

Our Renaissance Neoplationist is also influenced by a version of what he probably believed to be Averroes' doctrine of the double truth, not mentioned by name but significantly used on two occasions in his work. In the first instance, Ebreo invokes this principle apropos of his acceptance of a Platonic view of creation, one which posits an eternal "chaos" or principle of matter. Recognizing that negation of Aristotle's position on the eternity of the world renders his support of Plato's position anomalous, Ebreo writes in defense of Plato's view that

Since it is sufficient that faith should not conflict with reason, we have no need of proof, for then we should have knowledge and not faith; and it is enough to believe steadfastly that which is not disproved by reason.[32]

This notion of faith as separate from reason, not opposed to it but not in agreement with it either, reflects a reaction to the approach characteristic of most Jewish philosophy until Crescas, and of Islamic philosophy through Averroes, with whom it received its classical expression—the approach harmonizing reason and faith. The identification of a "double truth" theory of separate but equal truths with Averroes is an irony reflecting the disbelief with which Averroes' teachings on this subject were received, as well as a reflection on the intractable nature of the issues involved, and the desire to maintain both one's faith and philosophical reason.[33]

The conviction that faith and reason represent two separate epistemological spheres is utilized elsewhere by Ebreo, when he distinguishes between the teachings of philosophy and revelation on man's highest perfection. "While philosophy teaches that man can approach the divine beauty or intellect only indirectly, through conjunction with the Agent Intellect, Holy Writ reveals that man can, through God's grace, be united directly with Him."[34]

Moses' experience is the paradigm for this latter experience, which Ebreo sees as not incorporated within the philosophical interpretation of prophecy. The normative experience of conjunction is thus one thing, philosophically defensible; the extraordinary experience of revelation at Sinai another, philosophically incomprehensible.

III

If we find a double-truth theory in a Platonist like Leone Ebreo, we should expect it also in the foremost Jewish Averroist of the Renaissance, Elijah Del Medigo; and indeed, leading scholars have so written.[35] Critics have differed in their assessment of the influences upon Del Medigo and have debated whether his view on this matter is a reflection of innate Jewish self-assertion or of the influence of a Christian predecessor such as John of Jandun. Still, they have largely agreed that Del Medigo's major work in this vein, his *Sefer Beḥinat ha-Dat* (usually called *The Examination of Religion*), is fundamentally different from Averroes' *Kitab Faṣl al-Maqāl, The Decisive Treatise*, with which it was originally enthusiastically compared.[36]

Reflection upon these two treatises shows that indeed there are discrepancies between them, though not necessarily those hitherto emphasized. Thus, whereas both authors defended philosophy, Averroes did so aggressively, while Del Medigo acted almost apologetically, in both senses of the word. The warranty of philosophy for Averroes was all-inclusive, but apparently it was limited for Del Medigo. Allegory on behalf of reason was practically an all-purpose tool for the Cordovan Muslim, but of much less utility for the Candian Jew. *The Faṣl al-Maqāl* is a work "On the Harmony of Religion and Philosophy," as its English translator has called it; while the *Beḥinat ha-Dat* emphasizes, or seems to emphasize, the relative autonomy of religion vis-à-vis philosophy. We might, finally, call Averroes' work more of a theoretical study of its subject, while Del Medigo wrote what appears to be an applied text. The political dimension of this subject, handled discreetly by Averroes, was treated openly by Del Medigo. His work offered his fellow Jews a model of adaptability to European society which circumstances rendered irrelevant, but which anticipated later views held in the period of the Jewish Enlightenment.

Notwithstanding the significance of the above differences, it appears to me that Elijah Del Medigo is more of an Averroist, or rather an Averroian, following the master himself, than has been usually allowed. The differences mentioned can be charged largely to his personal fortunes and to the political and religious circumstances in Italy in his day. Much had happened in the three hundred years since Averroes had written his treatise to make philosophy more defensive vis-à-vis organized religion. Jewish philosophers had been under attack periodically for their interpretation of the faith, and even blamed for the misfortunes which befell their people. Del Medigo's student and friend Pico della Mirandola had been punished by the Church for wishing to speak his mind freely, and Del Medigo himself was harassed by fellow Jews, and possibly non-Jews too, who did not share his views.[37]

These views had been expressed in a number of treatises, both commentaries and super-commentaries as well as translations of Averroes' works in areas of logic, physics, metaphysics, politics and "psychology."[38] In the last mentioned area, Del Medigo's two treatises on the intellect show a marked Averroian inclination at a time when this was officially condemned by the Church. Whether he was forced to leave Italy or chose to do so, we find Del Medigo in his native Crete in 1490, where he composed a work different from all his preceding efforts. *The Beḥinat ha-Dat* is a work of practical philosophy, in many ways a political tract which reflects the pressures Del Medigo had encountered, and which offered a kind of *apologia pro vita sua.* While appearing to be a justification for religious orthodoxy, it is nevertheless an essentially orthodox example of Averroian thought.

The treatise opens on a note both particularly Jewish and classically philosophical. According to Del Medigo, peace and a well-ordered government are, in general, essential for both political and scientific accomplishment, of which exile has deprived the Jews.[39] Del Medigo notes that the extant Rabbinic literature lacks unanimity on religious issues, and this lack of agreement, he later adds, corrupts the community.[40] Exile and internal dissension are thus, in his view, reciprocal causes for the abject state of the Jewish people, and much of the treatise is an attempt to break out of this vicious cycle. If the exile itself cannot be undone, the Jewish people are free at least to establish one of the conditions for a successful political life in exile. This condition is an agreement on the principles of the faith,[41] agreement, that is, on the nature and practice of Judaism.

That this agreement is not something which had been, or could be, elicited through rigorous logical proofs, is Del Medigo's second point. It is crucial for him that the assertions he intends to discuss be understood for what they are—namely, non-demonstrative assertions, essentially rhetorical statements. This is important because the establishing of religious principles on non-demonstrative grounds allows Del Medigo to assent to a number of propositions which he is not obliged to defend, let alone prove, logically. He allows that logical, demonstrative proofs are at the least religiously permissible, though restricted, in scope and by the audience to which they can appeal. It is the latter point which Del Medigo makes at first, but the former which justifies it.[42] For not only can relatively few people rigorously apply philosophy to religion, but only a few need to do so, since this approach has limited relevance to the subject matter. Even the philosopher, Del Medigo claims, assents to the principles of faith on more than abstract theoretical grounds, and it is these extra-logical reasons which fundamentally determine the beliefs held by all Jews.

These reasons are embodied in the reports of a written and oral tradition, and reinforced by a consensus of well-known beliefs. Now, traditionally accepted and well-known beliefs (*kabbalot* and *mefursamot*) are themselves traditional and well-known sources of knowledge, going back to Aristotle and discussed by many philosophers with whom Del Medigo was acquainted.[43] These sources are, moreover, regarded in the philosophical tradition as primary sources of knowledge, akin for purposes of reasoning to "first intelligibles." As the latter serve as premises for demonstrative arguments, the former are the basis for dialectical and rhetorical propositions and assertions. As primary, they are axiomatic for these modes of argument, and constitute assumptions which cannot be refuted historically or logically, barring self-contradictory statements. While rhetorical and dialectical arguments lack the analytic necessity of demonstrative propositions and are therefore probabilistic by nature, the unassailability of their premises grants them a status akin to certain truth.[44]

Though Del Medigo does not discuss this entire issue topically in this work, his writing here and elsewhere reveals his familiarity with it. He frequently refers to beliefs which are *mefursamot*, well-known, presumably commonly held and therefore legitimate.[45] Early on, he distinguishes between arguments based on demonstration and those which rely on tradition, rhetoric and dialectic. It is these latter kinds of assertions to which the mass of people can relate, he says, and by which the principles of the faith proclaimed by the Torah and prophets should be understood.

> Therefore the Torah and prophets postulated various principles as tradition and as a rhetorical or dialectical exposition, in accordance with the way of verification which the masses have. They alerted the elite to investigate these matters by the [type of] verification peculiar to them.[46]

It is awareness of this self-contained and non-demonstrable justification of religious beliefs that allows Del Medigo to say that "the study of philosophy [literally, 'science'] is not necessary for religion *qua* religion,"[47] an assertion which he follows by an enumeration of religious principles illustrating his point. Unlike his later conventional and more logically ordered list of such principles, the three "roots" Del Medigo chooses to highlight in this opening section of his treatise are specifically "religious" beliefs: prophecy, reward and punishment, and the possibility of miracles.[48] Del Medigo is aware that these beliefs may in fact be incorporated into a rational scheme and given a philosophical justification, and he is familiar with the assertions of Averroes and others to this effect.[49] Nevertheless, the strength and significance of these assertions lies not in their philosophical compatibility, but in their "religious" inviolability.

To say this is not, however, to claim that Del Medigo is establishing a principle of knowledge essentially foreign to Averroes' own espitemological scheme. For it is Averroes who, in the *Decisive Treatise* and elsewhere, emphasizes this very division of the sciences and discusses the varying kinds of propositions and audiences for which each is appropriate.[50] Del Medigo has simply taken Averroes' general strictures and applied them, presenting religion as having its own body of unimpeachable assertions, while passing lightly over the theoretical justification for this claim. The larger theory of cognition is not, however, repudiated, and Del Medigo soon enough introduces qualifications which show his awareness of it. For he knows that religious claims cannot be immune to basic logical criteria, and that the truth they profess should not be in contradiction with that provided by other sources of knowledge.[51] In accentuating the special qualities of religious claims, and decrying the attitude which sought through allegorical means to rationalize them, i.e., to convert them to other kinds of propositions, Del Medigo is merely following Averroes' own precepts, though not his actions in the *Decisive Treatise.* The impression of a double-truth theory in the *Beḥinat ha-Dat* is accordingly understandable, though not ultimately justified.

This becomes evident the more Del Medigo warms to his topic, for he moves from essentially strategic concessions to philosophy to substantive ones. Thus initially the most that can be said for philosophy is that it agrees with some fundamental religious claims, providing a kind of external, religiously irrelevant yet nevertheless pleasant confirmation of these principles.[52] More significantly, Del Medigo next acknowledges (without elaboration) that it is philosophy which imparts understanding of the different types of subject matter that exist, and of the nature of their respective propositions. It is philosophy, Del Medigo states, which teaches the high cognitive value of the sources of knowledge employed by religion, and which enables the believer to see through the unwarranted claims of his opponents.[53]

Philosophy is, however, more than a propaedeutic to religion for Del Medigo, as is clear from the discussion of the relationship between religion and philosophy which immediately follows. In the guise of a not-so-subtle, and subsequently censored, critique of Christian doctrine, Del Medigo asserts the supremacy of rational criteria with which to refute beliefs in the corporeality of God, the unreliability of the senses, and the essentially independent relationship of substance and accident.[54] For Del Medigo, not only does the Torah not require beliefs of this sort, self-contradictory as well as counter-factual, but the Jewish religion could not possibly profess anything which the intellect rejects!

> Our divine Torah does not at all oblige us to believe contradictory remarks [literally, 'things'], nor to deny primary intelligibles and their like, or sensible realities. Were our religion to do so, we would decide the issue by rejecting the religion. We would not be punished for disbelief even if it were established that the truth was so, since the nature of our intellect, which God has determined, can neither receive nor believe in such.[55]

The strength of Del Medigo's assertions is matched by the dogmatic nature of his reasoning.

> If, however, one is found agreeing with all these [propositions which have been seen as absurd], saying that it is not the role of the intellect, but of prophecy, to perceive them, we will not persist, not desiring to argue. For this is not something in which we are engaged, the controversy concerning it being very bizarre and most inappropriate.[56]

This remark is itself "most inappropriate" for Del Medigo, were he seriously to consider holding a double-truth theory. It is only because he subscribes to a philosophically intelligible universe, one in which nature is identifiable and accountable, that he can so cavalierly dismiss religious claims which are incompatible with such a view. Just which claims are incompatible is another matter, however, since Del Medigo does not elaborate here on his understanding of natural versus unnatural, and therefore impossible, events.

Our philosopher's few remarks are, however, more revealing than he might have wished. Apropos of his brief discussion of

God's omnipotence Del Medigo stated that it extended "[*lo*] *al ha-sotrim ve-lo al ha-ḥolfim*, neither to contradictory nor to past states of being."[57] That God does not change His own nature, the next and only other qualification of His omnipotence here mentioned, is understood, no doubt, as an instance of His inability to overrule the law of contradiction. For clearly, God cannot alter His own nature (however conceived), since He would then be what He is not. As all else, in contrast, is said to be subject to God's power, one might assume that for Del Medigo there is no internal necessity to nature as there is to the divine being. It is questionable, however, if Del Medigo believed in the radical contingency of all being beside God; or whether he considered all such being as naturally independent in effect, though dependent in principle, and ultimately in practice, upon God as first cause.

God cannot, on this reading, radically alter the nature of such beings either, presumably because He would thereby destroy the very existence He had produced, the expression of His own perfection and nature.[58] Viewed in this context, Del Medigo must believe that God's miracles, and indeed, all the principles of faith which had been declared as not given to rational proof, are yet to be understood as naturally possible, and theoretically rational in themselves.

Confirmation of this interpretation comes later in the treatise, in a rare specific mention of allegedly miraculous events. Such specific mention is rare because the major burden of the book is the literal acceptance of Bibilical miracles, avoiding the dispute that Del Medigo believed followed exegesis of the literal sense of the test, the *pshat.* This approach is limited, Del Medigo admits, by self-contradictory statements, examples of which he finds in the biblical report of what would seem to be corporeal angels and a talking snake.[59] The existence of such beings is naturally and therefore logically impossible for Del Medigo, a view which is tenable only if he has a strong sense of what is naturally possible and concomitantly, a belief in a defined, and thus limited, natural order. The miraculous for him has somehow to occur within the natural limits which God Himself has established, even though we need not, cannot, and should not attempt to understand this in detail.

Del Medigo's reluctance to philosophize Scripture and religion in general, and his disapproval of those, Maimonides barely exempted, who did, are clearly motivated by political considerations. It is the misunderstanding and divisiveness which such public philosophizing causes, he claims, that leads him to what appears to be a more dogmatic approach to religion.[60] There is, however, something ironic about his position, and his advocacy of silence and discretion for philosophers.[61] He knows that even if the philosophers behave themselves, social and religious unity would still elude the Jewish people. Much of the *Beḥinat ha-Dat* is a chronicling of the differences which existed in earlier periods and in his own day among the non-philosophical interpreters of Judaism, the rabbis and kabbalists. Both the disagreements between schools of thought as well as those within each school are mentioned.[62] So widespread is this contentiousness and disagreement among Jews, he says, that it almost appears to be a characteristic property of theirs, whatever their individual orientation.[63]

Del Medigo elsewhere retreats from this view and blames the negatively perceived nature of the Jewish people upon its lack of self-government and thus upon the exile itself.[64] Yet this implies that for him, short of the messianic advent, disagreements over the correct approach to the religion will continue. The philosophers' retreat from this issue would not, therefore, make any real difference to the body politic, though it would remove the philosophers themselves from the abuse and misinterpretation they had suffered. Philosophers would then presumably be free to pursue their own scientific investigations quietly, conveying their insights in all areas in appropriate ways, while not "meddling" in politics.

This advice is not merely self-serving. It is also justified by Del Medigo's view of the nature of the principles of religion, as we have said. These principles do not call for, and indeed they resist, philosophical investigation. Their purpose is to encourage not speculation and theoretical understanding, but social conformity and unified virtuous behavior in the service of ultimate personal and collective salvation. They are, like the commandments which derive from them, socio-political instruments, justified by the necessity for such instruments in society. Many of the principles of faith are explicitly justified on these grounds, conceded to them in effect by the very act of their being recognized and accepted just as principles of the faith.

This is not, of course, the only reason for believing in this particular set of principles. They have been shaped by a tradition the sources of which are deemed sacred in themselves. The contents of faith are not therefore essentially or necessarily political, but the act of assenting to them is. This view can be seen in the extended treatment of the principles of religion which Del Medigo offers in his treatise,[65] a treatment which is best studied in relation to those lists of principles which his predecessors, particulary Maimonides and Albo, had offered.[66] For our purposes, however, it will suffice to examine these principles briefly from one standpoint, that of *hekhreḥ ha-dat*, "religious necessity." This term is first listed as one of the components for ascertaining the principles of religion, following the teachings of the Torah and prophets, and those of the Talmudic sages.[67] Another criterion, rational comprehensibility, is in effect introduced immediately in referring to the first of the principles, God's existence, and His unitary, incorporeal and causal nature. These were features of the Divine which the "early scholars," *kdumei ha-ḥakhamim*, called "first wisdom," (*ḥokhma rishona*), Del Medigo says, using *ḥakhamim* and *ḥokhma* as synonyms for philosophers and philosophy in an obvious allusion to Aristotle's use of *protē philosophia.*[68]

Traditional religious sources are next brought to substantiate the primacy of these views, denial of which, Del Medigo mentions, was condemned in terms of excommunication and eternal damnation by the rabbis of the Talmud. "The necessity [of believing] in these principles for this religion is clear," Del Medigo adds,[69] and the connection with the foregoing threats is obvious. No further justification for the "religious necessity" of these primary principles is offered, but the immediately following discussion of the principle of God's incorporeality is helpful for the light it sheds on the perspective in which Del Medigo viewed these principles. For unlike the beliefs in God's unity and His role as a first principle and cause of all, both clearly comprehensible to the masses without causing them any loss,[70] the belief in God's incorporeality is viewed as incomprehensible to the masses, and thus potentially damaging to them, leading as it could to disbelief in the very existence of God, and thus to apostasy.

Del Medigo, by his own admission, is aware that acceptance of the principle of God's incorporeality is sufficiently widespread in his day to avoid this development, and he acknowledges Maimonides' efforts in establishing this principle — efforts, however, which had, in his view, originally caused some public damage. From this political perspective, the doctrine of God's incorporeality is therefore not a satisfactory principle of religion, and Del Medigo's ambivalence about it as such is clear.[71]

He has no such reservations about the remaining principles of religion which he proceeds to enumerate, and in each case the political dimension is significant, if not paramount. Thus the beliefs in prophecy and reward and punishment, which entail, in Del Medigo's view, belief in divine knowledge and providence, are first mentioned as clearly "necessary to members of this religion" (*hekhreḥi le-vaalei zot ha-dat*, that is, necessary conditions for belonging to this religion), and then mentioned as necessary by way of prophecy and the other sources of faith.[72] Belief in the immutability of the Torah and Moses' prophetic superiority is described only as "very necessary for members of this religion," in view particularly of the counter-claims of other faiths. There is no need to attempt to prove this, Del Medigo emphasizes, discreetly sidestepping invitations to disruptive polemics and disputations.

Belief in resurrection is explicitly laid at the Rabbis' door, Del Medigo mentioning only their insistence on it as a principle of religion, denial of which would also lead to heresy, damnation and excommunication. Finally, belief in the Messiah is even more explicitly said to be post-Biblical, but similarly insisted upon by the Rabbis. Del Medigo does not need to adduce any greater reason than this for belief, his concern being practical rather than theological. He is absolved in fact of the need to explain philosophically any of the religious principles he enumerates, for as long as they are considered as such traditionally, do not violate natural and logical limits, and express a consensus of opinion, they are legitimate and even necessary principles. They are necessary not in themselves, but within the context of that group which believes in them, which group is as it is owing to those beliefs. The identity of the Jewish people is thus tied for Del Medigo to a specific set of beliefs, and allegiance to them is the condition for social harmony and felicity in all areas, including the philosophical.

The view just explicated sweeps certain issues aside, as we have remarked. Thus, the logical possibility of some of these beliefs, and what Del Medigo specifically meant by them is never really discussed, while the consensus which legitimates them is on Del

Medigo's own account, frequently less than what one would have liked. While Averroes had used this latter fact to press for the legitimacy of a philosophical interpretation of religion,[73] Del Medigo, anxious to preserve whatever national unity there was, and also, probably, to preserve a place for philosophy and science within Judaism, minimizes the significance of the very evidence he cites.[74]

This philosophically circumspect posture at times gives Del Medigo an overly deferential bearing, leading the unwary reader to believe that he is witnessing at last the "destruction of the philosophers." Thus, Del Medigo preaches respect for the Rabbis in all their utterances, even those which are non-halakhic, and therefore admittedly non-binding. Ridiculing them for even a patently false belief is, he claims, tantamount to impugning their authority and denying the faith itself.[75] Later in the treatise (and rather inconsistently with the preceding), Del Medigo argues that should the early Rabbis (the *rishonim*) have said anything as far-fetched rationally as the rabbis of his own time hold, he would suspect his own reason and defer to their view.[76]

This concession to authority is not as great as it may seem, however, since Del Medigo qualifies it by saying he would first have to be sure an anti-rational interpretation of the original utterance was necessary, or nearly so. One can rest assured Del Medigo would not find this to be the case, even as we can be confident that his respect for rabbinical authority was genuine. Like the Rabbis, Del Medigo stresses the importance for religion not of abstract theological or philosophical issues, but of the commandments, the *mitzvot* of Judaism, its particular way of life.[77] These commandments are allegedly rational in principle, though the fundamental principle of their rationality is that they are the laws of this particular group, and as such the necessary means for its survival and wellbeing. "I mean by deeds that which includes the virtuous traits and good deeds by which man is good to himself, his family, and to all his compatriots." [78]

In making this assertion, Del Medigo was keeping faith not only with the teachings of Judaism but with those of philosophy as well, following Averroes in emphasizing the necessary, beneficial and practical aspects of religion.[79] We need not believe that Del Medigo was insincere in this attempt, that he was engaged in a species of "wily graciousness" on any more than a tactical level. His belief system may indeed have been traditional, his philosophical credo allowing for that understanding of traditional religion which leaves it intact. In his attempt to serve two masters in unison, to harmonize disparate pursuits without subverting either, Del Medigo, as those who followed in the sixteenth century, offered the Renaissance a most worthy "remnant" of Averroism.

NOTES

1. Cf. J. Guttmann, *Philosophies of Judaism*, trans. D. Silverman (New York, 1964), p. 257; and see S. Pines' entry, "Averroes," in the *Encyclopedia Judaica* (1971), 3:952. The danger of labeling a Renaissance work as Averroist, Platonist or whatever — dangerous due to the diversity within and between authors — is well brought out in descriptions of the Latin works of this period. Cf. Paul O. Kristeller, "Renaissance Aristotelianism," *Greek Roman and Byzantine Studies* 6.2 (1965), pp. 157, 160–164. It is the absorption with themes and methods of Aristotelian texts and commentaries — of the late Greek as well as Islamic tradition and, in the latter, with Averroes' commentaries particularly — that gives the Averroists their identifying characteristics; and cf. Kristeller, p. 163, and John H. Randall, Jr., "Padua Aristotelianism: An Appraisal," *Atti del XII Congresso Internazionale di Filosofia* (Firenze, 1960), p. 202. Both these foremost interpreters of the period use the term "secular" for the perspective from which the Averroists worked; a term which in my opinion, and certainly as concerns the Jewish Averroists, is not satisfactory. Note, in this regard, Randall's description of the "Padua" doctrine of man, with its transcendental dimension, ibid., and reiterated in his "Paduan Aristotelianism Reconsidered," *Philosophy and Humanism: Renaissance Essays in Honor of Paul Oskar Kristeller*, ed. Edward P. Mahoney (New York, 1976), p. 277.

2. Cf. now F. Edward Cranz, "Editions of the Latin Aristotle Accompanied by the Commentaries of Averroes," *Philosophy and Humanism*, pp. 116–128. As for the appearance of works written in this period which draw heavily upon Averroes, it is interesting to note that, for example, while Judah b. Yeḥiel's (Messer Leon) *Nofet Tzufim* appeared as an incunabulum in the fifteenth century, Elijah Del Medigo's *Beḥinat ha-Dat*, written in 1490, was not published until 1629. Cf. the relatively few philosophical works listed in the "Incunabula" entry of the *Encyclopaedia Judaica*, and see M. David Geffen, "Faith and Reason in Elijah Del Medigo's *Beḥinat Ha-Dat* and the Philosophic Backgrounds of the Work" (Columbia University doctoral dissertation, 1970), p. 34.

3. The period may be demarcated by the effects upon Italian culture of the Turkish conquest of Constantinople in 1453 on the one hand, and by the Council of Trent in 1545, or the Bull *Cum nimis absurdum* of Pope Paul IV in 1555, on the other. The effect of this period of the Renaissance upon Italian Jewry has been described by C. Roth, *The Jews in the Renaissance* (New York, 1959) pp. x, 64, 73ff.; and cf. S. Baron's wide-ranging survey of Humanism and the Renaissance, including developments in Italy, in the second edition of his *A Social and Religious History of the Jews* XIII (New York, 1969), 159–205.

4. Cf. H. Wolfson, "The Twice-Revealed Averroes," and "Plan for the Publication of a *Corpus Commentariorum Averrois in Aristotelem*," now in *Studies in the History of Philosophy and Religion*, ed. I. Twersky and G.H. Williams (Cambridge, Mass., 1973) I:384f. and 437ff. respectively. The figure of "nineteen" sixteenth-century commentary translations from the Hebrew given in the latter study may mislead the reader, twenty-six (out of thirty-four) translations, as mentioned on p. 384, being closer to the mark.

5. Cf. F. Edward Cranz, op. cit., pp. 117, 120ff. Of course the Jewish translators viewed their activity as complementary to, and certainly not in conflict with, Jewish scholarship and ideals. Cf. the remarks of Abraham de Balmes in his 1523 edition of Averroian logical commentaries, as quoted by Cranz, p. 123f. Information on translations made from the Hebrew by men like De Balmes, Elijah Del Medigo, Paul Israelita and Jacob Mantinus is

found in M. Steinschneider, *Hebraïsche Übersetzungen des Mittelalters* (Berlin, 1893; reprint, Graz, 1956), pp. 971–987 and index. A popular survey is found in Roth, op. cit., pp. 74–81, and cf. his updated though necessarily still thin bibliography, p. 345.

6. Cf. Wolfson, "Plan," op. cit., pp. 437ff. The Long *Posterior Analytics* commentary edition of 1575 even has three translations, two complete. There are also three translations of the Long Commentary Prooemium to Book XII of the *Metaphysics*, though Wolfson mentions only two. The translation omitted, that done in the late fifteenth century by Elijah Del Medigo, has been recently published. Cf. Bohdan Kieszkowski's edition in his study, "Les rapports entre Elie del Medigo et Pic de la Mirandole," *Rinascimento* 4 (Firenze, 1964), pp. 78–91 (though a Hebrew source, given on facing columns, is replete with mistaken readings of the MS).

7. Cf. *Averroes'* Destructio Destructionum Philosophiae Algazelis *in the Latin Version of Calo Calonymos*, ed. B.H. Zedler (Milwaukee, 1961), p. 57f., and see the editor's discussion on p. 26f. of these and other remarks of Calo, showing his sense of dedication to presenting an authentic Averroes. Cf. too the similar justifications of Paul Israelita and Jacob Mantinus, as quoted by Cranz, op. cit., p. 122f.

8. Cf. Zedler, op. cit., pp. 47–50.

9. Cf. Paul O. Kristeller's concise survey, "Francesco da Diacceto and Florentine Platonism in the Sixteenth Century," *Miscellanea Giovanni Mercati* (Vatican City, 1946), IV:2–9. As discussed by Kristeller, depiction of the relationship between Aristotelians and Platonists as "adversarial" is largerly inaccurate. Granted, though, that the approach of many philosophers in this period is eclectic and often deliberately synthetic, the views of Plato and Aristotle were yet understood as differing significantly. At least an initial explication was required in order to appreciate the similarities between the two views.

10. The major study of Ebreo has been that of H. Pflaum, *Die Idee der Liebe* (Heidelberg, 1926). Cf. now also S. Damiens, *Amour et Intellect chez Léon l'Hébreu* (Toulouse, 1971). E. Friedberg-Seeley and J.H. Barnes have tranlated Ebreo's work into English as *The Philosophy of Love*, London, 1937; and an anonymous early Hebrew translation, sometimes attributed to Leone Modena, was published in Lyck in 1871 as *Vikuaḥ al ha-Ahava.*

11. As, e.g., Ḥasdai Crescas in the Jewish tradition, and Marsilio Ficino in the Christian Italian. It is Ficino who is thought to have had the major influence on the entire Platonizing movement of the time.

12. Cf. *The Philosophy of Love*, p. 29, 30. On p. 324 we find the intellect divided into four or five stages in ways common to medieval Aristotelians.

13. Ibid., p. 46.

14. *La divisa cognizione* is the Italian for "dual cognition," as given in note 3, p. 49 of the translation; the Hebrew translation, op. cit., p. 9v, being *hakara nifredet.* So too "perfect cognitive union" is a translation of *cognizione perfetta e unita*, rendered in Hebrew as *hakara be-aḥdut u-devekut shalem.*

15. This is so even though the highest form of knowledge had by the intellect is seen as a uniquely intuitive grasp of the totality of truth; cf. p. 389. This last stage of perfection exceeds the normal bounds of knowledge, but is not conceived of as other than a form of cognition. Cf. too Damiens' discussion of this and of Ebreo's view of the relation of love and intellect, op. cit., pp. 52ff., 159.

16. *The Philosophy of Love*, p. 49.

17. Ibid., p. 45. This identification is not Ebreo's last word on the subject of God's nature, but neither is it a negligible part of his philosophy.

18. Ibid., p. 46.

19. Ibid., p. 401ff.

20. Ibid., p. 411.

21. Ibid., p. 415f.

22. Ibid., loc. cit., and cf. too pp. 34f., 317f.

23. Ibid., p. 415. It is clearly the Al-Ghazzāli of the *Intentions of the Philosophers* to which Ebreo is referring, in company with Avicenna and Maimonides.

24. *The Philosophy of Love*, p. 336.

25. Ibid., p. 311f., and cf. Damiens, op. cit., p. 32f.

26. *The Philosophy of Love*, p. 185f.

27. Ibid., p. 304.
28. Ibid., p. 298f.
29. Ibid., pp. 181f., 274f.
30. Cf. K. Bland's edition of *The Epistle on the Possibility of Conjunction by Ibn Rushd with the Commentary of Moses Narboni* (Brandeis University dissertation, 1972), Hebrew section, p. 29f. and English section, p. 23f. See also my article, "Averroes on Intellection and Conjunction," *Journal of the American Oriental Society*, 86.2 (1966), p. 81f.
31. Cf. *Philosophy of Love*, p. 336.
32. Ibid., p. 282. This broad sense in which Ebreo uses a double-truth theory corresponds to the majority tradition of Averroist writers who subscribe to such a notion. Cf. P. Kristeller, "Paduan Averroism and Alexandrism in the Light of Recent Studies," *Atti*, op. cit., p. 151f. While Kristeller rightly claims that many non-Averroists also held such a modified double-truth theory, his view that such a position should therefore be disassociated from Averroism appears to this writer as excessive. Differing philosophers frequently share certain views, without thereby losing their own identity or requiring the primary, conventionally accepted identification of the shared opinion to alter its identification. While it may well be true, with Kristeller, that the Averroism of the Renaissance is not Averroes' own in every respect, neither is its Aristotelianism completely that of Aristotle, or its Platonism that of Plato. Having said that, however, we may return and identify these terms, albeit carefully, with certain broad themes as well as texts.
33. Ebreo may have been influenced in this matter by Averroists like Albalag in the Jewish tradition, or John of Jandun in the Christian.
34. *The Philosophy of Love*, p. 325.
35. Cf. J. Guttmann, *Philosophies*, p. 259, and his article, "Elia del Medigos Verhältnis zu Averroës in Seinem *Bechinat Ha-Dat*," *Jewish Studies in Memory of Israel Abrahams* (New York, 1927), pp. 196ff. Cf. too, U. Cassuto, *Gli Ebrei a Firenze nell'età del Rinascimento* (Firenze, 1918); translated into Hebrew by M. Hartum (Jerusalem, 1967), pp. 229ff. See also M. David Geffen, op. cit., pp. 228ff., 250, 256f.
36. Cf. A. Hübsch, "Elia Delmedigo's: Bechinath ha-dath, und Ibn Roschd's: Façl ul-maqâl," *MGWJ* 31 (1882), pp. 555–563; 32 (1883), pp. 28–46. Comparison with *The Decisive Treatise* is facilitated now by an excellent edition and translation of that work and related pieces. Cf. *K. Faṣl al-Maqāl*, G.F. Hourani (Leiden, 1959); and Hourani's translation, called *Averroes on the Harmony of Religion and Philosophy* (London, 1967). The *Beḥinat ha-Dat* itself was edited with a commentary by I. S. Reggio (Vienna, 1833), and this edition was reprinted in Jerusalem, 1969. A critical edition of this text has not yet appeared, though the materials for it, in manuscript and printed sources, inform Geffen's (rough) translation, op. cit., pp. 389–462. The Hebrew translation of Averroes' *Faṣl al-Maqāl*, of the sort which Del Medigo used, has been edited by Norman Golb, *PAAJR*, 25(1956), pp. 91–113; 26(1957), pp. 41–64.
37. Cf. Geffen, op. cit., p. 31f., and see Kieszkowski's discussion of the close relationship which existed between Pico and Del Medigo, op. cit., pp. 43–58. Kieszkowski has also published and commented upon the theses which Pico naively wished to debate publicly; cf. Giovanni Pico Della Mirandola, *Conclusiones* (Geneva, 1973).
38. The complete works of Del Medigo, formerly discussed by Steinschneider and Cassuto, and more recently by Kieszkowski, have been reviewed by Geffen, op. cit., pp. 9–31.
39. "Accomplishment" is literally *hatzlaḥa* (ed. Reggio, p. 1), a term redolent with religious significance. It is obvious that, in this work, Del Medigo has been powerfully impressed by Averroes' *Commentary on Plato's* Republic, as well as by his *Decisive Treatise*. Geffen has tracked down these and other Averroian sources in detail in his notes to the above-mentioned translation, op. cit., pp. 389–462.
40. Cf. *Beḥinat ha-Dat*, p. 66.
41. This position assumes free will, which Del Medigo does not discuss as such here, but which is compatible with his general philosophy. His critique of the Kabbalah in this treatise is limited to its philosophical structures and ignores kabbalistic historiosophy.
42. Ibid., p. 5.
43. Del Medigo's familiarity with these views would have come from many sources. Cf., e.g., Averroes' passing remarks in the *Faṣl al-Maqāl,* op. cit., p. 7, and see the English

translation, op. cit., p. 45, and the additional sources the translator brings on p. 85, n. 25. To these may be added now for the English reader Averroes, *Short Commentary on Aristotle's "Rhetoric,"* as edited and translated by Charles Butterworth in *Averroes' Three Short Commentaries on Aristotle's "Topics," "Rhetoric," and "Poetics"* (Albany, 1977), pp. 63, 73–76 (Arabic, pp. 169, 187–195). Cf. too *Avicenna's Treatise on Logic*, translated by F. Zabeeh (The Hague, 1971), p. 40f. Maimonides discusses these issues in his treatise on logic; cf. I. Efros' edition, "Maimonides' Arabic Treatise on Logic," *PAAJR* 34(1966), p. 21, and see Efros' earlier and incomplete edition and translation, *Maimonides' Treatise on Logic* (New York, 1938), chapters seven and eight. Alfarabi, Maimonides' source in these matters, writes of them in this *Fuṣūl . . . fi sināʿat al-mantiq*, edited by M. Türker, *Revue de la Faculté de Langues, d'Histoire, et de Géographie de l'Université d'Ankara* 16 (1958), pp. 165ff.; translated by D. M. Dunlop as "Al-Farabi's Introductory Sections on Logic," *Islamic Quarterly* 2 (1955), p. 275f. The entire discussion goes back to Aristotle, and cf. in particular *Topics* I. 1. 100a, 25ff.

44. Cf., in addition to the preceding, Averroes' *Short Commentary on Aristotle's* Topics, ed. Butterworth, op. cit., pp. 47, 51 in English, pp. 152, 158 in Arabic.

45. Cf. *Beḥinat ha-Dat*, pp. 2, 8, 11 and elsewhere.

46. Ibid., p. 5: ולכן שמה התורה והנביאים שרשים מה ע״צ הקבלה והביאור ההלציי או הנצוחיי כמשפט האמות אשר אצל ההמון והעירה היחידים לחקור על האמות המיוחד להם בדברים אלה.

47. Ibid., p. 6: מבואר שלימוד החכמה אינו הכרחי בדת הזאת במה שהיא דת.

48. Ibid., pp. 8, 9.

49. Cf. Geffen's discussion of these principles in comparison with their treatment in both Averroes' work and in a considerable number of Jewish writers, beginning with Maimonides; op. cit., pp. 260–318, 397.

50. Cf., in Hourani's translation and notes, *The Decisive Treatise*, pp. 48f., 61f., 66f. See too the trenchant remarks on this topic by Alfarabi in his *Book of Religion, K. al-Milla*, ed. M. Mahdi, p. 46f., 66; and in his *Book of Letters, K. al-Ḥurūf*, ed. Mahdi (Beirut, 1970), pp. 11, 131. Compare also Avicenna's *Topics* commentary, *K. al-Shifā'*: Al-Jadal, vol. 6, ed. A. El-Ahwany (Cairo, 1965), pp. 8, 14. Finally, see Maimonides' *Guide of the Perplexed* III:27, 59b; III:51, 123b; and III:510, 618 in S. Pines' translation (Chicago, 1963).

51. Cf. *Beḥinat ha-Dat*, p. 14. This claim is a tenet of Averroes' thought, and Del Medigo's adherence to it is a decisive indication of his loyalty to Averroes.

52. Ibid., p. 11.

53. Ibid., p. 12.

54. Ibid., pp. 13–16, and see Geffen's notes, op. cit., pp. 400–403.

55. *Beḥinat ha-Dat*, p. 14.

56. Ibid., p. 16.

57. Ibid., pp. 16, 17. I am indebted to Professor Seymour Feldman for his assistance in interpreting this passage.

58. This is the thrust of Averroes' quarrel with al-Ghazzāli in the First Discussion on the Natural Sciences in the *Tahāfut al-Tahāfut*, ed. M. Bouyges (Beyrouth, 1930), p. 531; translated by S. Van den Bergh (London, 1969), pp. 325.

59. *Beḥinat ha-Dat*, p. 50.

60. Ibid., pp. 18–21, 48–53.

61. Ibid., p. 52.

62. Cf. ibid., pp. 32, 38, 45, 54.

63. Ibid., p. 54.

64. Cf. also, ibid., p. 36.

65. Ibid., pp. 23–28.

66. Cf. above, note 49, and see Geffen's notes to his translation, op. cit., pp. 410–419. Concern with the discovery and use of the appropriate "principle" in each area of scientific investigation is also a typical example of Renaissance Aristotelianism. Cf. J. Randall Jr., "The Development of Scientific Method in the School of Padua," *Journal of the History of Ideas* 1 (1940), p. 185.

67. *Beḥinat ha-Dat*, p. 23.

68. Cf., e.g., *Metaphysics* VI. 1. 1026a, 29. Del Medigo is thus expressing the widely held belief that metaphysics, following Aristotle's example, could legitimately establish certain universal propositions about God.

69. *Beḥinat ha-Dat*, p. 25.

70. Ibid.: ומבואר שאלה הענינים כולם יתכן ציורם להמון מבלתי שיקרה מזה הפסד להמון.

71. Earlier in the treatise, p. 15, Del Medigo even says that a belief in divine corporeality need not "damage" other, more essential, beliefs!

72. Ibid., p. 26.

73. Cf. *The Decisive Treatise*, trans. Hourani, p. 52; *K. Faṣl al-Maqāl*, p. 15.

74. *Beḥinat ha-Dat*, pp. 52, 55.

75. Ibid., p. 58,

76. Ibid., p. 71.

77. Ibid., p. 17.

78. Ibid., p. 66, translating *bnei ha-medina* as "compatriots." This emphasis on practical morality instead of the contemplative ideal is also part of the Renaissance perspective. Cf. P. Kristeller, "Renaissance Aristotelianism," op. cit., p. 172.

79. A point made frequently in *The Decisive Treatise* and elsewhere. Cf., e.g., *Averroes' Commentary of Plato's "Republic,"* ed. E.I.J. Rosenthal (Cambridge, 1969), pp. 47, 66 of the Hebrew text, pp. 155, 185 of the translation; and compare R. Lerner's translation, *Averroes on Plato's "Republic,"* (Ithaca, 1974), pp. 48, 81. Cf. too the *Tahāfut al-Tahāfut*, ed. Bouyges, pp. 514, 527, 581; as translated by Van den Bergh, pp. 315, 322, 359.

Rabbi Mordekhai Jaffe and the Evolution of Jewish Culture in Poland in the Sixteenth Century

LAWRENCE KAPLAN*

Among the stars in the firmament of rabbinic scholarship in Eastern Europe during the sixteenth century, the golden age of rabbinic scholarship in Poland-Lithuania, that of Rabbi Mordekhai Jaffe shines bright. In a galaxy of outstanding rabbinic giants, R. Jaffe's own position both as head of the Council of Three Lands and, more important, as the author of *Levush Malkhut*, a code which during the seventeenth century was, for a time, a serious rival to the *Shulḥan Arukh* of R. Joseph Karo and R. Moses Isserles, is firm and assured.

But exactly how are we to define the place and achievement of Jaffe within the religious, cultural, and intellectual evolution of Polish Jewry in the sixteenth century? Particularly, we wish to focus on Jaffe's literary efforts in the meta-halakhic disciplines of philosophy and Kabbalah and determine his contribution in those areas to the religious culture of his day. For if, as we shall see, these works of Jaffe both resulted from, and are an outstanding exemplification of, the openness toward and interest in religious and general culture beyond the boundaries of Talmudic study that was manifested throughout the deeply and profoundly rabbinic culture of Polish-Lithuanian Jewry, at the same time they also constituted a significant new stage in the process of Polish Jewry's assimilation of these broader religious horizons.

If we are to determine Jaffe's place within, and contribution to, the religious culture of sixteenth-century Polish Jewry, we must

* This essay is based upon my dissertation, "Rationalism and Rabbinic Culture in Sixteenth-Century Eastern Europe: Rabbi Mordecai Jaffe's *Levush Pinat Yikrat*," Harvard University, 1975. Full discussion and documentation of the theses of this essay may be found therein.

first delineate, albeit in sketchy fashion, the major features of that culture. To that task we now turn.

I

The remarkable social, economic and demographic growth of Polish-Lithuanian Jewry in the sixteenth, and first half of the seventeenth centuries has been described many times and we do not propose to recount the story here.[1] Rising above a firm economic and demographic base, Jewish cultural life in Poland-Lithuania flowered and flourished. It was, thus, during this period that rabbinic learning reached the zenith of its development.

Yet despite the new heights to which they raised the halakhic tradition, Polish Jewry, in terms of halakhic practice and custom, saw themselves as the bearers, continuers, one might even say the inheritors, of the Ashkenazic tradition. There was a strong element of traditionalism, even of conservatism, in their outlook, for they felt that the halakhic tradition, in the particular form they had received it, as it was formed and shaped by the great and recognized latter-day German authorities of the fourteenth and fifteenth centuries with all its particular laws, practices, decisions and customs, was authoritative and binding.

While Jewish culture in Poland-Lithuania was primarily rabbinic in nature it was open to, and absorbed within itself, the various meta-halakhic disciplines such as the secular sciences, philosophy, pietism and Kabbalah.

Salo Baron has recently emphasized that the philosophical interests of Polish Jewry in the sixteenth century were stimulated by the remarkable general Polish humanistic renaissance of the day.[2] This is no doubt so. However, we wish to emphasize a different reason for this philosophical interest, viz. that the rationalist current in Polish Jewry was, as R. Moses Isserles himself states, "a legacy of the fathers,"[3] i.e., an inheritance from, and continuation of, the Ashkenazic tradition. As Ephraim Kupfer has demonstrated,[4] there was a strong current of rationalist culture and interest in speculative philosophy among German Jewry at the end of the fourteenth, and through the fifteenth centuries. More important, this philosophic learning passed from German to Poland and Lithuania when the latter communities reached maturity at the end of the fifteenth and beginning of the sixteenth centuries. If, then, the "rationalist tinge" of Jewish culture in Poland and Lithuania came to them as a tradition from Germany,[5] we may conclude that the philosophical current in their culture is a manifestation of the same spirit of traditionalism and even conservatism as is manifested in the rabbinical and halakhic current. In both instances the Jews in Poland and Lithuania cultivated the various traditions, be they halakhic or philosophical, that they had received from their parent communities in Germany.

In this respect, paradoxical as it may seem, it is the mystical, kabbalistic current in the Jewish culture of Poland and Lithuania that is a comparatively new cultural development and that was not received as a tradition from their fathers. As Gershom Scholem has noted, the kabbalistic movement developed in Poland only toward the middle of the sixteenth century, and the primary country of influence was Italy. Nevertheless, despite the relatively late start of kabbalism in Poland it soon became a staple element in Jewish culture there so that a generation later the Kabbalah itself was already for such scholars as R. Moses Isserles an integral part of the Jewish culture and tradition as they knew it and as such was both studied and revered.

This spirit of a rich, variegated, creative traditionalism permeating Jewish culture in Poland is best exemplified by R. Moses Isserles, one of the two leading teachers of R. Jaffe. R. Isserles was active in a wide number of spheres, primarily Halakhah, but also astronomy, philosophy and Kabbalah. But in all areas, despite his great achievements, he builds upon the work of his predecessors, and sees himself as continuing the Ashkenazi-Polish tradition that he had inherited. This is true with regard to both his codificatory labors and his attitude towards, and use of, philosophy. R. Isserles' codes were based primarily on the principle of *halakha ke-batra'ei* (the law is in accordance with the recent authorities), and this for two reasons. First, because it was a generally accepted norm of juridical methodology and second, and more importantly, because the customs and practices prevalent in Poland were all based upon this principle; that is, R. Isserles' contemporaries accepted the views and opinions that the recent German-Polish authorities had transmitted, as being authoritative on the basis of this principle. Thus this principle served to legitimate the recently developed Ashkenazic tradition which was then flourishing in

Poland. Similarly, R. Isserles' attitude toward philosophy is permeated by the same spirit of traditionalism. Thus, in response to an attack of R. Solomon Luria upon him for relying upon philosophy, R. Isserles states: "This is an old dispute among the sages and therefore I need not reply."[7] Thus R. Isserles refuses, as a matter of principle, to be drawn into discussing the issue of the acceptability of philosophy within Judaism and merely attempts to demonstrate that his positive attitude toward philosophy is in accord with the views of a long line of sages. The thrust of R. Isserles' response is to demonstrate that philosohy has been legitimated by the rabbinic tradition and has become part of that tradition. Moreover, R. Isserles says, (1) his positive attitude extends only to Jewish and not to non-Jewish philosophy, and (2) he himself does not engage in independent philosophical speculation but simply cites the approved philosophical opinions of his notable Jewish predecessors. In his entire responsum, then, the argument for, and defense of, philosophy manifests a thoroughly conservative spirit.

This approach of creative traditionalism that characterized Jewish culture in Poland in the sixteenth century and that was exemplified by R. Moses Isserles was challenged by his most famous contemporary, R. Solomon Luria who, we may say, exemplified a spirit of critical independence. And this spirit was again manifested both in his halakhic activities and in his attitude to the place of philosophy within the Jewish tradition.

R. Solomon Luria, in his introduction to his massive torso of a code, the *Yam Shel Shlomo*, states that his code would bring together the views of all the halakhic authorities on points of law and, more important, would decide between them solely on the basis of the Talmudic sources as he understood them. Such a spirit of critical independence that did not recognize any inherent authority in the views of the post-Talmudic scholars can only be seen as a radical break with the spirit of Ashkenazic traditionalism. We would argue that this same spirit of critical independence as manifested in his bold juridical methodology is also evident in Luria's negative attitude toward philosophy. For as we have seen, the rationalist philosophical current in Jewish culture in Poland-Lithuania in the sixteenth century was a *tradition* they had received from their Ashkenazic ancestors, just as, *mutatis mutandis*, their halakhic teachings were also received as a tradition from the same ancestors. Just as R. Solomon Luria manifested intellectual independence in examining critically the received halakhic tradition and subjecting it to a searching analysis on the basis of the Talmud itself so he also manifested intellectual independence and daring—albeit, obviously, not to the same degree—in severely criticizing the received philosophic tradition, and rejecting all of the attempts, even if they had acquired a certain aura of legitimacy, to synthesize in any manner philosophy with the rabbinic tradition.

R. Solomon Luria's challenge, his attempt to change radically the accepted halakhic and cultural patterns of Polish Jewry, failed. R. Moses Isserles' literary legacy, though perhaps less intellectually impressive than that of R. Luria, proved to be more enduring and influential.

That this is the case in the realm of Halakhah is well known. It was R. Isserles' *Mapa*, his critical glosses on the *Shulḥan Arukh*, which became the authoritative code for all East-European Jewry, not Luria's *Yam Shel Shlomo.* And Isserles' code was accepted precisely because it relied on the views of his authoritative predecessors while Luria's code was rejected precisely because its bold and independent mode of decision-making was seen as violating the accepted traditionalist canons of juridical methodology.

But the failure of R. Luria is manifested in the cultural realm as well. For philosophy, despite R. Luria's severe attack on it, still maintained a firm, if secondary, place within the culture of Polish-Lithuanian Jewry into the first decades of the seventeenth century. We can not elaborate here but such diverse works as the famous anti-Christian polemic, *Ḥizuk Emuna* of Isaac of Troki, the Commentary on the *Guide, Giv'at ha-More* of R. Joseph b. Isaac, the Commentary on Maimonides' *Eight Chapters, Ḥesed Avraham* of R. Abraham b. Shabbetai Horowitz,[8] the glosses on *Giv'at ha-More* of R. Yom Tov Lippman Heller, all written at the end of the sixteenth and beginning of the seventeenth centuries, indicate the strength of philosophical currents still coursing through Polish-Lithuanian Jewry.[9]

If there was a certain trend of development in the rationalist current in Poland-Lithuania from the first half to the second half of the sixteenth century, it was that as Kabbalah became a fundamental part of the religious tradition, there was a movement away from a stance of extreme rationalism, inimical to the Kabbalah, to a more moderate rationalism that could be synthesized with the Kabbalah. Here again, it was Isserles who led the way in this new approach. For R. Isserles, both philosophy and Kabbalah were "the words of the living God," part of the rabbinic tradition. Therefore, in his major non-halakhic work, *Torat ha-Ola*, he constructed a rationale for the commandments, in particular the commandments dealing with the sanctuary and sacrifice, that wove together, in an eclestic fashion, both philosophy and Kabbalah.

But the clearest evidence of R. Isserles' success and R. Luria's failure can be seen in the activities and attitudes of their outstanding student, R. Mordekhai Jaffe. For though R. Jaffe was a student of both R. Luria and R. Isserles, and had the highest respect for the former, in the course of his long and illustrious career he followed closely in the footsteps of his teacher par excellence, R. Moses Isserles, with regard to (1) the issue of juridical methodology, (2) the trend, initiated by R. Isserles, to synthesize philosophy and Kabbalah, and (3) the question of philosophy's place in rabbinic Judaism. It is these aspects of Jaffe's activities upon which we now wish to focus.

II

R. Mordekhai Jaffe[10] was born in Bohemia, most probably in Prague, sometime between 1530 and 1535. At a young age he was sent to Poland to study Talmud and Halakhah under R. Moses Isserles and R. Solomon Luria. Jaffe refers to the well known kabbalist, R. Mattathias Delacrot as his tacher in Kabbalah and we may assume that his teacher in astronomy and philosophy was R. Isserles himself. After he completed his course of studies he returned to Prague where he married in 1553. It was at about this time that R. Joseph Karo's *Beit Yosef* appeared and R. Jaffe, in the introduction to his own great code, the *Levush Malkhut*, relates that he shared in the general elation that greeted the work and "chose to study only it" for it made it possible to "delve into the true depths of the Halakhah." However, R. Jaffe soon realized that the length, massiveness and complexity of the *Beit Yosef* was bound to make it forbidding to the average student. He therefore decided to abridge the work just citing the laws themselves and very briefly adducing the reasons for these laws. He resolved to call his code, patterned after the *Beit Yosef*, the *Levush Malkhut*. R. Jaffe's work on this project was interrupted. In 1561 the Jewish community of Prague, where he resided, was expelled and R. Jaffe went to Venice. There he heard the news that R. Karo himself was preparing his own abridgement of the *Beit Yosef* and therefore R. Jaffe ceased working on his abridgment. When R. Karo's abridgement finally appeared in 1567, R. Jaffe upon examining it realized that there was still a need for his own abridgement. First R. Karo's abridgement was terse to a fault omitting all legal reasons and principles. Second, R. Karo relied primarily on Maimonides, neglecting all the recognized Ashkenazic authorities. Therefore, there was a need for a code that would present "the laws that are current in Germany, Bohemia, Moravia, Poland and their environs" together with their reasons. He therefore resolved to start yet once again on his abridgment.

No sooner did R. Jaffe return to his work than he heard that his teacher, R. Moses Isserles, was in the process of writing critical glosses on the *Shulḥan Arukh*. Certain that R. Isserles would remedy the faults of R. Karo's code, R. Jaffe desisted from his work a second time. It was at this time that R. Jaffe began to write his meta-halakhic works, in particular his commentaries on Maimonides' *Guide of the Perplexed*, Maimonides' *Laws of the Sanctification of the New Moon* and Recanati's *Commentary on the Pentateuch*, dealing with the areas of philosophy, astronomy and Kabbalah respectively. In the year 1571, when R. Jaffe was in the midst of working on the meta-halakhic commentaries, the first edition of R. Karo's *Shulḥan Arkukh: Oraḥ Ḥayyim* appeared together with R. Isserles' glosses. Upon examining the glosses, R. Jaffe saw that while it corrected one of the faults of the *Shulḥan Arukh*, inasmuch as it forcefully and consistently presented the Ashkenazic tradition of halakhic practice, it, like the *Shulḥan Arukh*, was terse to a fault, presenting the normative conclusion, without the legal rationale. There was room for another code which would be a mean between the length and complexity of the *Beit Yosef* and the extreme brevity, bordering on obscurity, of the *Shulḥan Arukh*. R. Jaffe, therefore, once again, returned to work on his code, now patterned after the structure and organization of the *Shulḥan Arukh*, but more expansive in quantity, fusing the differing legal positions of R. Karo and R. Isserles into one harmonious and fluent whole, accompanied by a brief presentation of the accompanying legal rationales drawn primarily, though not exclusively, from the *Beit*

Yosef. In 1572, almost immediately after he began working for the final time on his code, he returned to Poland where, for the next forty years, he served in rabbinical positions in the leading cities of Eastern and Central Europe and also was head of the Council of Three Lands. During this time he worked both on his halakhic code and his meta-halakhic commentaries, which he now considered to be two parts of one work. The work as a whole appeared in sections over the years 1590–1603.

From this sketch of R. Jaffe's halakhic approach and activities we can notice the great influence that his teacher, R. Isserles, had upon him. More, it also reveals R. Jaffe's general halakhic conservatism. R. Jaffe's initial reaction of elation to the appearance of the *Beit Yosef*, followed almost immediately by the feeling that it was too lengthy and complex a work, parallels almost exactly the reaction of R. Isserles, as described in his introduction to his *Darkhei Moshe*, his glosses on the *Beit Yosef.* Moreover, R. Jaffe's juridical methodology which ascribes primacy to "the laws that are current in Germany, Bohemia, Moravia, Poland and their environs," i.e., to the views of the most recent authorities, follows exactly the approach set down by R. Isserles. Indeed R. Jaffe's introduction to the *Levush Malkhut* in many ways sounds like a reprise of R. Isserles' introductions to both the *Darkhei Moshe* and *Mapa*, except that where R. Isserles always finds his halakhic plans being anticipated by R. Karo, R. Jaffe finds his plans being anticipated by both R. Karo and Isserles.

Moreover, Jaffe's own narrative and the nature of the *Levush* itself indicate the conservative nature of R. Jaffe's own halakhic activity—even more conservative than that of R. Isserles, his teacher. For while R. Isserles always followed in the path of his great Ashkenazic predecessors, at the outset he had it in mind to compose an independent code. It was only after R. Karo composed the *Beit Yosef* and later the *Shulḥan Arukh* that R. Isserles saw his task as supplementing, and more important correcting, R. Karo's works. However, R. Jaffe from the outset never intended to compose any independent code.[11] First, he wanted to abridge the *Beit Yosef* and later to supplement the *Shulḥan Arukh* in the end, as we have noted, the *Levush* itself is a very skillful and fluent blend of R. Karo's and R. Isserles' halakhic conclusions as found in the *Shulḥan Arukh*, with legal rationales drawn primarily from the *Beit Yosef*. Moreover, from the organizational point of view, Jaffe deliberately keyed his own work to the *Shulḥan Arukh* to the extent that not only the work's general order but even the paragraph numbering followed the order of the *Shulḥan Arukh*, this despite the fact that as a result many of the *Levush*'s paragraphs, which contain a good deal more halakhic material than the corresponding paragraphs of the *Shulḥan Arukh* were, of necessity, overly long and unwieldly. Indeed we would suggest that it was ultimately the close correspondence between the *Levush* and the *Shulḥan Arukh* which proved to be the ultimate downfall of the former. For the *Levush* was not seen as being an independent code but rather as a commentary on the *Shulḥan Arukh*, except that the commentary was fused with the code. Thus the great seventeenth-century commentators, particularly R. Joshua Falk, saw the *Levush* not as a rival code to the *Shulḥan Arukh*, but as a rival to their commentaries on the *Shulḥan Arukh*. And ultimately it was not the *Shulḥan Arukh* per se that became authoritative but the *Shulḥan Arukh* together with the standard commentaries.

If, however, in the realm of Halakhah Jaffe, while following in the path of Isserles, is, if anything, even more conservative than his teacher, in the realm of philosophy and Kabbalah, Jaffe, while again following in the synthesizing path of Isserles, initiates a new stage in the assimilation of these currents on the part of the rabbinic culture of the Polish Jewish community at its height. R. Isserles includes certain philosophic and kabbalistic motifs in his work *Torat ha-Ola*, but this work is separate and distinct from his halakhic works. Jaffe includes his commentaries on classic meta-halakhic works within the *Levush Malkhut.* The *Levush Malkhut* is thus not only a code of law which sums up the halakhic scholarship of the day but rather an entire "*summa*" of rabbinic Judaism, both halakhic and non-halakhic. Jaffe clearly implies that the intended audience for his commentaries on the *Guide, Laws of the Sanctification of the New Moon* and Recanati's *Commentary on the Pentateuch* are the rabbinical students untrained in the sciences. The commentaries would thus make available to them an outstanding Jewish classic in each of the various sciences. The commentaries were therefore designed with their needs in mind and their major features were determined by this consideration.[12] In a word, R. Jaffe's commentaries were not intended to be works of original scholarship but rather works of "haute vulgarization." As a result, in one work the young rabbinical student could find an entire structured course of study, beginning with and covering the various areas of Halakhah and concluding with the meta-halakhic disciplines.[13] We have here a bold attempt on R. Jaffe's part to incorporate the meta-halakhic disciplines of astronomy, philosophy and Kabbalah into the standard rabbinic curriculum whose basic text was to be his own work, the *Levush Malkhut.* Here the trend of Jewish culture in Poland-Lithuania to include philosophy and Kabbalah as part of the rabbinic tradition reaches its climax. Thus does R. Jaffe continue and build upon the traditions, attitudes and values he received from his teacher par excellence, R. Moses Isserles.

The inclusion of philosophy and Kabbalah within the rabbinic tradition, and how much more so within a rabbinic curriculum, required that these two disciplines be synthesized with each other and with the rabbinic tradition as a whole. Jaffe, though he does not work out any synthesis in detail, raises the issue in a number of places and follows the two classic, not wholly compatible, modes for harmonizing philosophy and Kabbalah. The first mode asserts that philosophy and Kabbalah each describe a different level of reality and therefore, in principle, cannot conflict. This approach was especially adopted by kabbalists who willingly branded philosophy a true but inferior type of wisdom. Jaffe uses this approach when explaining the order of his three meta-halakhic commentaries, asserting that philosophy deals with the lower (i.e., sublunar) world,[14] astronomy with the intermediate world (i.e., the celestial spheres), and Kabbalah with the divine realm. We may see in this subordination of philosophy to Kabbalah,[15] the balance between these two disciplines tipping to the side of Kabbalah, in terms of the religious evolution of Jewish culture in Poland.

The second mode of reconciling philosophy and Kabbalah—the more popular one—was to assert that both philosophy and Kabbalah describe the same reality and that they essentially agree as to the nature of that reality merely using different symbols and terminologies in describing it. The major problem involved in this type of attempt to harmonize philosophy and Kabbalah was the question of the relationship between the kabbalistic doctrine of the *Sefirot* and the philosophical doctrine of divine attributes. However, the doctrine of the *Sefirot* posed an additional problem. For by apparently positing a plurality within God it was not only in conflict with the philosophical conception of God but also in conflict with the basic biblical and rabbinic affirmations of God's unity.

Jaffe's approach to this issue illustrates an interesting and little-noticed aspect of the problem. Jaffe adheres to the kabbalistic position that the *Sefirot* are the *atzmut* (essence) of God. Both kabbalists and scholars have argued as to whether the adherents of this view in their attempt to maintain the unity of God are not, in effect, forced to deny the ontological reality of the *Sefirot* and must conclude that they only exist from the vantage point of the recipients. And here when we examine Jaffe's position on this question we see something striking. In his commentary on the *Guide*, i.e., in a philosophic context where the kabbalistic doctrine of the *Sefirot* as *atzmut* is being harmonized with the philosophic view of attributes, Jaffe offers a strictly philosophical, nominalistic interpretation of the *Sefirot*, depriving them of real ontological existence, of real theosophical significance, and reducing them to different names whereby we may perceive the absolutely simple, divine perfection.[16] Jaffe here does not even speak of the *Sefirot* existing from the vantage point of the recipients of God's actions—so strongly does the philosophic context impose itself upon him! However, when Jaffe in a kabbalistic context, i.e., in his super-commentary on Recanati, attempts to reconcile the view of *Sefirot* as *atzmut* with the biblical-rabbinic doctrine of divine unity, we have a radically different picture. Jaffe in this context asserts that the *Sefirot* are not identical with the philosophical conception of absolute divine simplicity but rather constitute a dynamic, organic divine unity. They are not just a plurality of names indicating the divine perfection but rather a dynamic interweaving of potencies and forces within God himself.[17] Moreover, Jaffe here admits that this interpretation of divine unity will not be acceptable to the philosopher, insofar as it is not fully comprehensible rationally. Thus the interpretation of the doctrine of the *Sefirot* will differ depending on the context and more, on the corpus—whether philosophy or the rabbinic tradition in general—with which it is being harmonized.

However, the major problem in including both philosophy and Kabbalah within the rabbinic tradition is neither that of harmonizing philosophy and Kabbalah nor that of harmonizing Kabbalah and the rabbinic tradition but that of harmonizing philosophy and the rabbinic tradition. And here too, especially here, Jaffe initiates a new stage in the assimilation of philosophy within the rabbinic culture of Polish Jewry. Jaffe not only continued the tradition of moderate rationalism that he had inherited from his teacher, R. Moses Isserles, but in his commentary on Maimonides' *Guide* substantially advanced that tradition. For while R. Isserles in *Torat ha-Ola* had utilized some of the doctrines of the *Guide*, Jaffe was really the first native Polish halakhist to directly confront the *Guide*. Moreover, Jaffe, in his role as commentator, had to confront not only the naked text of the *Guide*—and the philosophy of the *Guide* was in any event bound to be problematic for a rabbinic scholar writing for a rabbinic audience; he had to confront the *Guide* as it appeared in its first printed edition (Sabbioneta, 1553)—that is, surrounded by a number of standard philosopical commentaries, particularly those of Shem Tov and Efodi which attributed to Maimonides several esoteric, radical views that were totally unacceptable to the bearers of the rabbinic tradition. Jaffe, in the introduction to the *Levush*, says that he would "supplement" the already existing commentaries to the *Guide* "in accordance with the need of the inquiring rabbinical student." However, his commentary is not only a supplement to the earlier commentaries. A close examination reveals that it is also a corrective to these commentaries. Jaffe rarely confronts the views of those commentaries head on. Nor does he state explicitly at any point that he is out to present a consistent conservative interpretation of the *Guide*. Nevertheless we find that on a number of crucial issues with regard to which Jaffe explicitly dissents from the interpretations of the standard commentaries or without explicitly dissenting offers an alternative explanation, his explanations are of a "conservative" nature, as opposed to the more "radical" interpretations of his predecessors.

"Conservative" and "radical" are vague terms but for the present purpose we may define the difference between Maimonides' "conservative" and "radical" interpreters as follows; if the opinion of the philosophers on a given issue differed from the classic, accepted, ostensible position of the rabbis, and Maimonides' own position on the issue was either unclear or problematic, Jaffe the "conservative" would offer an interpretation of the Maimonidean position that would bring it more closely into line with the ostensible rabbinic position while his "radical" predecessors would interpret Maimonides' position as closer to or identical with, the opinion of the philosophers.

This is not the place for a thorough analysis of Jaffe's commentary. However, such an analysis and more important a comparison of Jaffe's views, when pieced together, with those of his predecessors reveals the following.[18] Jaffe's interpretation of the *Guide* differs from that of his predecessors on the following crucial issues: esoterism, the authority of *midrashim*, allegory, prophecy and providence. Let us briefly take a look at their contrasting positions on each issue.

Esoterism: for earlier radical commentators, Maimonides, through a variety of esoteric devices, particularly deliberate subtle contradictions strewn throughout the *Guide* ("the seventh cause"), conceals a number of opinions from the vulgar while simultaneously revealing them to the elite. These opinions are generally the opinions of the philosophers. Jaffe, on the other hand, downplays the esoteric nature of the *Guide* and treats contradictions as a pedagogic device.

Authority of rabbinic *midrashim*: according to the earlier commentators, Maimonides, in a number of places, subtly suggests that certain rabbinic *midrashim* are of no value. Jaffe, on the other hand, attributes to Maimonides the view that all the rabbinic *midrashim* are of value and attempts to neutralize the effect of any apparently problematic statements that Maimonides made regarding the subject.

Allegory: a number of the earlier commentators claim that throughout the *Guide* Maimonides, in treating a number of biblical narratives (e.g., the existence of Adam, the birth of Cain, Abel and Seth, the story of the sons of "Elohim" and the daughters of man, and the revelation on Mt. Sinai) drops subtle hints that these narratives are to be understood allegorically and downplays their historical actuality. It is not entirely clear whether these commentators wish to claim that Maimonides went so far as to actually deny the historical actuality of these narratives, but they tend in that direction. Jaffe, on the other hand, while not denying that Maimonides understood these narratives allegorically, attempts to show that for Maimonides the allegory is always derived from the historical reality of the events themselves as narrated in the Bible.

Prophecy: for the earlier commentators Maimonides' position on prophecy does not differ from that of the philosophers; prophecy, for Maimonides, is not a source of supernatural knowledge unavailable through ordinary means of human speculation, and certain incidents in the lives of the prophets such as, for example, the binding of Isaac, took place in a vision.[19] Jaffe by contrast argues that Maimonides' view of prophecy differs from that of the philosophers,[20] that prophecy for Maimonides can give the prophet certain knowledge in matters not subject to demonstration, and that it is wrong to believe ("heaven forbid") that for Maimonides the binding of Isaac did not actually occur.

Providence, for Maimonides, according to the standard commentators, is built into the natural order. According to Jaffe, Maimonides' view is that providence suspends the natural order.

Jaffe's views on all these issues strikingly resembles the views of that great conservative interpreter of Maimonides, Isaac Abravanel, of whose commentary Jaffe was unfortunately unaware. Abravanel, the staunch spokesman of tradition, who set out to "defend" the master against those unworthy disciples who falsely attempted to attribute their corrupt doctrines to him, and Jaffe, the classical halakhist, who only intended to "supplement the commentaries a bit," from their different vantage points arrived at similar conclusions. We would argue, however, that unlike Abravanel who consciously set out to offer a conservative interpretation of the *Guide*, Jaffe was not wholly conscious of the fact that his specific interpretations of the *Guide* coalesced to form a coherent conservative interpretation of that masterpiece of Jewish rationalist philosophy. The process of assimilation of the *Guide* to the dominant rabbinic culture, on the part of Jaffe, was a complex mix of conscious and unconscious individual processes.

But this assimilation in turn was only possible precisely because moderate rationalism was already rooted in Jaffe's society and precisely because Maimonides, perhaps uncritically, was already revered as the outstanding proponent of that tradition. Only for this reason was Jaffe able in his commentary, contrary to interpretation of the earlier commentators, to present the *Guide* as a work of moderate, almost tame, rationalism, devoid of any dangerous esoteric levels that lie beneath the surface, shorn of any threatening naturalistic implications—in a word, a rationalism like the rationalism prevalent in the rabbinic culture in sixteenth-century Poland-Lithuania. Jaffe's commentary to the *Guide*, then, was one stage—an important one—in an ongoing process of cultural assimilation in which one Jewish sub-culture, i.e., Polish rabbinic culture, absorbed and integrated into itself another Jewish sub-culture, i.e., Jewish philosophic culture.

If we look at R. Jaffe's career and concerns in retrospect we may conclude that unlike his teacher, R. Moses Isserles, whose path he followed, and paradoxically like his teacher, R. Solomon Luria, whose example he ignored, R. Jaffe failed in what he set out to do. His halakhic code lost out to the *Shulḥan Arukh*, and neither philosophy nor Kabbalah, though both continued to be cultivated, ever became part of the standard rabbinic curriculum. Nevertheless, Jaffe's career is of historical significance both for its intrinsic interest and importance and for what it tells us abut the development of Jewish culture in the latter part of the sixteenth, and beginning of the seventeenth, centuries. Certainly it calls into question the popular view that there was a retreat from rationalism following upon the death of R. Moses Isserles.[21] For R. Jaffe's commentaries on the classics of philosophy, astronomy and Kabbalah included *alongside* his halakhic code as part of *one* work are perhaps the finest and most balanced expression of a general cultural pattern of Polish Jewry in the sixteenth and first decade of the seventeenth centuries, an essentially conservative rabbinic pattern characterized however by moderate, if unoriginal rationalism, a general eclectic, synthesizing tendency, and permeating all, a genuine, if uncritical, openness to, interest in, and *willingness to assimilate* the meta-halakhic disciplines as they had developed and been transmitted within the stream of Jewish tradition, a tradition not conceived of in narrow, purely halakhic terms. In the work and person of Jaffe the rabbinic culture of Poland-Lithuania, without breaking with its traditional patterns, achieves a certain breadth and integrity that even at this distance cannot fail to impress.

NOTES

1. Most recently by Bernard Weinryb, *The Jews in Poland* (Philadelphia, 1973); S. W. Baron, *A Social and Religious History of the Jews*, 2nd rev. ed., vol. 16, *Poland-Lithuania, 1500–1650* (New York, 1976).
2. Baron, *Poland-Lithuania*, pp. 52–53.
3. *Responsa* of R. Moses Isserles, No. 6.
4. Ephraim Kupfer, "Concerning the Cultural Image of German Jewry and its Rabbis in the Fourteenth and Fifteenth Centuries" (in Hebrew), *Tarbitz* 42 (1972–73), pp. 113–147.
5. This is in contrast to the view of H. H. Ben-Sasson ("Poland-Lithuania," in *Trial and Achievement: Currents in Jewish History* [Jerusalem, 1974], p. 155 and *Prakim be-Toldot ha-Yehudim bi-Ymei ha-Beynayim* [Tel-Aviv, 1962], pp. 205–206) who speaks of the rationalist, Sephardic tinge and attributes the rationalist currents to Italian influences. In the light of Kupfer's position, Ben-Sasson's position can no longer be maintained. Rather the path of rationalist influences is from Spain (13th century) to Provence (14th century) to Germany (15th century) to Poland.
6. *Sabbatai Ṣevi, The Mystical Messiah* (Princeton, 1973), p. 77.
7. *Responsa*, No. 6.
8. Much—too much in my opinion—has been made of the fact that in 1602 R. Abraham Horowitz revised his rationalist commentary of 1577 on Maimonides' *Eight Chapters* to make it more amenable to mystical thought. Baron (*Poland-Lithuania*, p. 341, note 61) goes so far as to say that R. Horowitz "retracted his [rationalist] views." Suffice it to note that all of the revisions are limited to the part of the commentary on R. Samuel ibn Tibbon's "Introduction," that there are a total of three revisions, and that although the new interpretations emphasize the unknowability of God somewhat more strongly than do the comments of the previous edition, they are all firmly based, as R. Horowitz himself explicitly states, upon passages from the *Guide* and R. Joseph Albo's *Sefer ha-Ikarim*—a strange retraction indeed!
9. This is in contrast to the popular view which speaks of a retreat from rationalism after the death of Isserles. Thus Ben-Sasson ("Poland-Lithuania," p. 156) speaks of an earlier "obliterated rationalist layer" of culture, while Baron (*Poland-Lithuania*, p. 56) speaks of "the victory of the anti-Maimunist Luria." If Luria won a victory over Isserles it was only fifty years later (in the 1620's) under very changed conditions when Polish Jewish culture came under the dominance of Lurianic Kabbalah, a development that itself might not have been to Luria's liking. In my thesis, pp. 79–82, I offer an explanation to account for what I consider to be the *failure* of Luria.
10. The following account is based primarily on Jaffe's general introduction to the *Levush Malkhut*.
11. As opposed to the view of H. Tchernowitz, *Toldot ha-Poskim*, vol. 3 (New York, 1947), pp. 101–107 who claims that even before the appearance of the *Beit Yosef*, R. Jaffe was planning to write a major code. See my thesis, p. 48, note 107.
12. Compare R. Abraham Horowitz's introduction to *Ḥesed Avraham.*
13. In this concern for structure and order in the rabbinic curriculum we may compare Jaffe with his contemporary the *MaHaRaL* who, as is well known, manifested a similar concern. However, while for the *MaHaRaL* structure referred primarily to sources, i.e., what was required was a structured, graduated series of source texts, for R. Jaffe structure referred primarily to subject matter. See my thesis, pp. 61–62 and especially note 123.
14. On how Jaffe might have defended his claim that philosophy only deals with the sub-lunar realm, see my thesis, pp. 85–88.
15. Jaffe also subordinates philosophy to Kabbalah in another sense. For Jaffe in his introduction to the *Levush* correlates each of the ten books of the *Levush* with one of the ten *Sefirot.* The royal garment in which the student of the *Levush* clothes himself is, then, not only, as Jaffe states, a garment of piety and knowledge, but also (primarily?) a divine garment. The *Levush* then, is conceived of as a ladder of ascension both to and within God and philosophy is seen as part of this mystical journey. Of course, in this respect, the halakhic part of the *Levush* also becomes part of this same mystical journey. But perhaps one should not make too much out of this essentially poetical conceit.

16. See *Levush Pinat Yikrat* on *Guide* I, 53. "They [the philosophers and the kabbalists] assert that God is one with absolute unity and there is no plurality adhering to Him at all. There is only a plurality of words to indicate His perfection."

17. See *Levush Even Yekara* on *Va-Yishlaḥ*. "Even though [the *Sefirot*] differ in their functions, they are bound to one another in the spirit of God. . . . And their unity consists in their being linked together in one link so that they join together to form one form."

18. The following is based on Chapter 3 of my thesis, "The *Levush Pinat Yikrat* II: The Commentary as Corrective."

19. The view expressed by Efodi in his commentary on the *Guide* II, 46, viz. that according to Maimonides the binding of Isaac (and the story of Jonah) took place only in a prophetic vision is to be found only in the Sabbioneta, 1553 edition of the *Guide*. The comment was deleted (censored?) from all subsequent editions. For recent discussions regarding the history of the controversy as to Maimonides' true view about the binding of Isaac, see Moshe Idel, "Abulafiya u-Mishnato" (Ph.D. dissertation, Hebrew University, 1976), vol. 1, pp. 186–190 and 212, n. 110; and Aviezer Ravitzky, "Mishnato shel Rav Zeraḥya ben (Yitzḥak ben) Shealtiel Ḥen" (Ph.D. dissertation, Hebrew University, 1977), p. 276, n. 1.

20. I discuss Jaffe's view on this question in my article "Maimonides on the Miraculous Element in Prophecy," *Harvard Theological Review* 70 (1977), pp. 249–250. I now, however, believe that my suggested revision of Jaffe's position is unnecessary.

21. See above, note 9.

Post-Zoharic Relations Between Halakhah and Kabbalah

JACOB KATZ

I

Halakhah and Kabbalah did not originally represent either complementary or contradictory concepts. The twin concept of Halakhah is Aggadah—the first embracing the legalistic corpus of Jewish religious tradition, the second, the body of doctrinal teachings in its various forms: legends, homilies, scriptural exegesis, aphoristic maxims and the like. As to intentions, Aggadah fulfilled, among other tasks, that of the spiritual exposition and interpretation of Halakhah, the religious law, in ethical, theological and at times even mystical terms.

This dichotomous classification of the literary tradition dates from Tanaitic and Talmudic times, that is from the classical period of what has come to be designated as normative Judaism. In the ensuing generations of the Middle Ages Halakhah gained immense layers of dialectical discussions and legalistic decisions which quantitatively, at least, outweighed the foundations on which they were built. Substantially, as far as methods, terms of reference and basic assumptions were concerned, these additions offered hardly any novelty. The legalistic texture of Judaism since Talmudic times remained the same. Not so its doctrinal aspect represented by Aggadah. The sporadically advanced theology and ethics of the Aggadah were now supplanted, or at least supplemented, by the systematic exposition of religious philosophy, or linked with the newly evolved lore of the theosophists and mystics, the Kabbalah.

Philosophy and Kabbalah, like their precursor, Aggadah, may be then seen as functioning alongside Halakhah—theirs being the realm of religious thought and sentiment while that of Halakhah, religious action. Such a distinction is usually applied or tacitly assumed whenever the relation between Halakhah and its counterparts is theoretically discussed or occasionally referred to. The notion that Aggadah had a distinctly different function from Halakhah is based on the dogmatic assumption that Halakhah operated from the very beginning as a system of revealed prescriptions. The role of Aggadah could then not be other than tentative explication of the divine intention in prescribing the details of the Law. Critical scholarship, however, is obliged to trace the development of religious praxis, taboos, rites, ceremonies and the like—the objects of halakhic discussions and decisions. In doing so it has to inquire into the motives of what must be regarded as religious creativeness in the field of religious praxis. The question then arises whether Aggadah is indeed a kind of post-facto interpretation of Halakhah, or rather, the residue of the spiritual motivations that lay behind the creation of Halakhah.

The relation of Halakhah and Aggadah lies beyond the scope of the present study and beyond the scholarly competence of its author. Still the problem of the relation between Halakhah and its explanatory counterparts is a continuous one. Posing it with regard to its initial stage may be the best prolegomenon to pursuing it within its medieval context, a context in which philosophy and Kabbalah supplanted Aggadah as the spiritual interpreters of Halakhah. At this stage indeed Halakhah presented itself as a given and self-sufficient entity, open to spiritual interpretation which, however, would leave it substantially unaffected.

With the emergence of the great codifiers of the Middle Ages, Isaac Alfasi and Moses Maimonides, and virtually since the final editing of the Talmud half a millenium prior to their time, Halakhah operated as a closed system. Any addition to its stock through clarification of its contents or through rendering decisions on unprecendented issues could be executed only by following its own rules and premises, excluding, in principle at least, the influence of any external source. Philosophy and Kabbalah, though admitted and even welcomed as interpretive agents were, as far as the halakhic material was concerned, perforce regarded as extrinsic factors.

Philosophy, it is safe to state, accepted this allotted role and behaved accordingly. Its spokesmen tried to expose with the cognitive means at their disposal the significance of the Law in general, at times surmising also the divine purpose behind individual precepts and commandments. Still the ritualistic details of the Law militated against any attempts at rational interpretation and Maimonides, as is well known, declared it to be a futile and foolish exercise.[1]

Where halakhic discussions and philosophic interpretation occurred in the same mind, in other words when the halakhist happened to be a philosopher, the philosophical attitude may have, consciously or not, impinged upon halakhic reasoning. It has been cogently argued that Maimonides omitted in his codification certain Talmudic precepts and exhortations incongruent with his rationalistic philosophy.[2] Saadiah Gaon in defining the fixing of the Jewish calendar as a purely scientific calculation—a definition from which followed the denial of the Palestinian scholars' prerogative to fulfilling this function—was certainly not unaffected by his rationalistic bent of mind.[3] Menaḥem ha-Me'iri's consistent exemption of Christians from the category of idolatry was not without consequence for the halakhic prescription governing the relations of Jews with them, and the fact that he, a rationalist, and no other halakhist arrived at this conclusion is certainly no coincidence.[4]

A close scrutiny of the philosophically minded halakhists' work would probably expose many other instances of philsophy's impact upon halakhic reasoning and decisions. Nevertheless, the general tenor of its influence can, I think, be circumscribed on the basis of the few examples quoted. It is always in the direction of restraining the sway of Halakhah rather than expanding it. Those who interpreted the rituals rationally did so in their attempt to reconcile the two elements to which they were equally attached. What is unheard of and improbable is that rationalism should become the fountainhead of ritualistic creation—the very idea either seems absurd or suggests the machinations of imposters who would invent artificial ceremonies and pseudo-rituals. These are the very opposite of the genuine rituals whose hallmark is spontaneity.

All this was different with Kabbalah. Far from being embarassed by the host of ritualistic details kabbalists took them in stride. On principle all ritual minutiae could be invested with kabbalistic, i.e. metaphysical, significance, the exact content of which was determined in the course of time according to the various systems of kabbalistic symbolism. Halakhically speaking, these minutiae may have differed in status according to whether they were biblical or rabbinic, moored in unqualified Talmudic tradition or supported merely by later authorities or possibly even contested by some and accepted by others. Once a detail of the Law was interpreted kabbalistically, it received a metaphysical dignity irrespective of its place in the halakhic hierarchy. If the kabbalistically endowed rite had been unequivocally established on whatever ground, its newly won dignity had only a reinforcing effect. If, however, the kabbalistic interpretation concerned a detail contested by halakhic authorities or a custom practised in one section of Jewry and neglected by, or unknown to, others, then the kabbalistic interpretation forestalled the due process of halakhic procedure. In lending the detail or the custom a metaphysical significance Kabbalah made it obligatory, assuming tacitly the role of the Halakhah without resorting to its method of decision making. At times the religious precept, rite or custom interpreted by the kabbalist seems to have been his own creation, as no obvious source of a halakhic nature is in evidence to support it.[5]

If the author of the Zohar, on the basis of kabbalistic symbolism, endowed the Intermediate Days, *ḥolo shel mo'ed*, of Passover and Tabernacles with significance similar to that of the festival days proper, concluding that on the former as on the latter the putting on of phylacteries is unnecessary and indeed forbidden, then he cut short a long-standing debate that had gone on among halakhists in their own terms of reference.[6] Talmudic Halakhah prescribed hand-washing for the *kohanim* prior to their reciting the priestly blessing. The Zohar transformed this act of ritual cleansing into a symbolically charged ceremony, obliging a *levi* to pour the water on the *kohen's* hand—*kohen* and *levi* representing in the kabbalistic system different *Sefirot*, or divine attributes.[7] The Zohar and, to a lesser extent, its imitator the *Sefer ha-Kana*, are replete with similar instances where, through the medium of kabbalistic symbolism, decisions of a halakhic nature and, at times, absolutely novel halakhic prescriptions and rituals are produced. Even if closer scrutiny will prove that many precepts accepted on the authority of the Zohar originated elsewhere and that the Zohar lent them only currency and dignity, the fact remains that it immensely expanded the religious ritual and fixed many of its previously wavering details.

The motive behind this creativeness is no doubt the quest for adequate means of symbolically expressing kabbalistic concepts and images. Imbued with the vision of the celestial process of interaction between the divine forces represented by the *Sefirot*, the enthusiastic kabbalist sought to detect their equivalents in the prayers and religious actions of the Jewish individual. In doing so he followed the impulses of his imagination, saturated as it was by the kabbalistic tradition of preceding generations. The kabbalist was, of course, acquainted not only with the minutiae of religious worship, but also with the theoretical discourses and discussions concerning them in the halakhic literature. How deep and broad this acquaintance with the halakhic tradition was, whether it could have allowed the kabbalist, if he wished, to become creative in the field of Halakhah, is difficult to say. What is certain is that the author of the Zohar made no attempt to use accepted halakhic methods in formulating any of the many points that involved a decision of a halakhic nature. His conclusion always rested on the kabbalistic propriety of the decision, obviously assuming that what seemed best to reflect kabbalistic symbolism could not be objectionable on halakhic grounds.[8]

II

What was left undone by the Zohar itself was accomplished by a host of interpreters endowed with halakhic sensitivity. There is no utterance of any consequence in the Zohar touching on religious praxis that has not been scrutinized in the course of time and measured by halakhic standards. This process of examination must have started, as we shall see presently, with the late Spanish halakhists but its literary expressions began to accumulate only in the post-expulsion period. This later process of examination differed from what it could have been at the time of the Zohar due to at least two important factors. First, many among the Zohar's ritualistic recommendations were in the meantime adopted by at least a part of the Jewish community and often it was this adoption by some and objection by others that made halakhists voice their opinion on the subject. As in many other areas of the community's religious life, the actual development preceded the pronouncements of the halakhic authorities. The fact that a custom was practiced by a community carried varying degrees of weight with halakhists of different schools of thought. It certainly had some importance even for those who, like Joseph Karo as we shall see later, wished to establish the Halakhah, so to speak, *in abstractione*. Thus, in relating that the decision of the Zohar concerning the phylacteries of *ḥol ha-moed* had been adopted by all of Spanish

Jewry, he was preparing the ground for its halakhic corroboration.[9] Elijah Mizraḥi, in Constantinople, objected to changing the performance of communal prayer by the repetition of the last words of the *Shma* concerning which we shall say more later. Still, with regard to congregations that had adopted this Zoharic precept, he waived his objection.[10] The very absorption of kabbalistic rituals lent them a measure of halakhic justification.

The second factor affecting halakhic judgments regarding kabbalistic innovations derived from the very fact that these were rooted in the Zohar, which had acquired, in the meantime, a quasi-canonical status.[11] This enhancement of status was prompted by the intrinsic quality of the Zohar as a highly impressive religious composition of mystical tendency, and by its successful self-presentation as an ancient tractate of Tanaitic origin. These two qualities tended to reinforce each other—the impressiveness of the work encouraged belief in its ancient origin, while its attribution to the *Tana* Shimon bar Yoḥai lent additional weight to whatever the book conveyed to its readers.

The esteem enjoyed by the Zohar naturally affected its halakhic components. Indeed, it was the quasi-canonical status of the Zohar that made its halakhic statements a cause of continuous concern among halakhists. Had these statements appeared in a less prestigious context, let us say in the homiletic writings of a contemporary lacking impressive halakhic credentials, those at variance with all known authorities would have been dismissed as oddities, while those mediating between them would scarcely have been taken into consideration. As things stood, the Zohar's Halakhah posed a problem as did, in fact, all Halakhah that appeared in a kabbalistic context, as we shall see presently. The problem elicited most varied reactions.

The truth and authenticity of Kabbalah in general and of the Zohar in particular, though widely accepted, were as we know, challenged by skeptics and negators. Among the arguments adduced in support of such non-conformist attitudes, the problematic nature of Zoharic Halakhah played a role of no small importance. Elijah Del Medigo put forward a twofold argument. If Rabbi Shimon bar Yoḥai had been known "as the dean [*av*] of the kabbalists, knowing the secrets of the ritual laws [*dinim*] and their intimations in the way of truth, the Halakhah ought to have been fixed according to his opinions, yet this was not the case." [12] While Del Medigo's first argument thus concerned the alleged authority of the Zohar, his second argument related to that of Kabbalah in general. "We also see many times that according to the intimation it is apposite that the law be thus and yet we observe the *poskim* [codifiers] and the great ones of the Talmud deciding to the contrary."[13] Del Medigo took the kabbalists at their word. If their interpretation was, as they predicated, metaphysical truth, the law interpreted by it ought to be uncontested truth as well. This argument was repeated a hundred and fifty years later by Joseph Del Medigo when his critical acumen had the upper hand over his mystical attraction to Kabbalah or, perhaps, when he let his innermost convictions concerning the truth of the Kabbalah be revealed.[14] His contemporary Leone de Modena, a committed critic of the Kabbalah, referred extensively to the contradictions between the Zohar and prevailing Halakhah in order to sustain his argument.[15]

III

Those who were attracted by Kabbalah would not, of course, repudiate their beliefs because of such logical inconsistencies. Higher mountains have been moved by faith. On the practical level, however, an accommodation of sorts between prevailing halakhic and kabbalistic prescriptions was urgently called for. The golden rule that evolved was that wherever halakhic rulings contradict the kabbalistic precepts, preference must be given to the former; otherwise, the kabbalistic precepts become mandatory. This rule is usually quoted in the name of David ibn Zimra (RaDBaZ)[16] and his own words gave rise to the alleged paternity. Asked by a correspondent what he thought of the innovation then widely spread to remove one's *tefilin* on *rosh ḥodesh* before the *Musaf* service, he answered that knowing the source of the new custom to be the *Sefer ha-Kana,* he himself had adopted it.

> For I follow a general rule: Every matter concerning which there is an opinion in the Talmud or in one of the *poskim* or halakhists, even if it runs contrary to what is written in the books of the Kabbalah, I defer to it and ignore what is written in these books. And for myself, if it [the kabbalistic custom] be a rigorism [*ḥumra*] I follow it; if a leniency, I ignore it, and I do not see fit to write the reason here.[17]

We shall return to this remarkable passage for a closer analysis below.

In the present context our concern is whether Ibn Zimra claimed to have himself established the golden rule, or only to have elaborated its details. Factually, it is beyond doubt that the resolution of the conflict between halakhic tradition and kabbalistic prescription in the way suggested by him had already been anticipated in pre-expulsion Spain. Isaac Karo in a context to be dealt with later, stated:

Reason dictates that if the sages of the Kabbalah decide contrary to the decision of the Talmud, the law should be determined according to the wording of the Talmud. Yet as [in the present case] there is no decision in the Talmud nor have all the *poskim* decided in one way or the other, each rather going his own way, and [on the other hand] the Kabbalah resolves the matter according to one of them, the sages of the Kabbalah are granted power of resolution, and thus I have received from my teachers.[18]

Himself an exile from Spain, Karo, in the last words of his passage, clearly testifies to the Spanish origin of the compromise.[19] This testimony is confirmed by another independent source, the well-known passage in *Sefer ha-Yuḥasim* by Abraham Zacuto concerning the status of the Zohar: "And it is agreed in Israel that in a matter in which it does not disagree with the Talmud or if it is not explicit [*meforash*] in the Talmud and we find it explicit there, that we accept it."[20] This somewhat confused sentence is yet clear enough to mean that where the Zohar is not in conflict with an uncontroversial statement of the Talmud its view has full halakhic authority. That this is what was meant is evident from the three examples given by Zacuto, all of them contested issues among halakhists on which the Zohar took a stand and, in so doing put an end, in Zacuto's view, to any further doubt on the subject. The rule is posited here as a well-established tradition. Zacuto completed his work in 1505,[21] about the same time that the Spanish exiles transmitted this rule of compromise as a part of their redoubtable scholarly legacy.

In addition to being of traditional status, the rule was characterized by Isaac Karo as "dictated by reason" (*ha-sekhel gozer ken*). This evaluation, however, was certainly not even shared by all those who in practice consented to it. The rationale of the rule could be related to the supposed antiquity of the kabbalistic tradition, but this turned out to be, at least with regard to the Zohar, a double-edged argument. For if the decisions contained in the Zohar were those of the *Tana* Shimon b. Yoḥai and were nevertheless disregarded by halakhists of later generations, they must have been found, for one reason or another, lacking in authority—thus the argument of Elijah ha-Levi, a colleague of Elijah Mizraḥi, and a proponent of his anti-kabbalistic response.[22] Even more pointed was the much-quoted verdict of Solomon Luria. "If Rabbi Shimon bar Yoḥai were standing before us calling at the top of his voice [*tzavaḥ*] to change the custom established by our forbears we would not heed him, since in most instances the Halakhah is not fixed according to him."[23] His last words mean that already in Talmudic times it had been decided whose opinion among the *Tana'im* would prevail in cases of controversy, and Rabbi Shimon bar Yoḥai was in most cases overruled. The gist of this argument must have been anticipated by Abraham Zacuto, for he gave to the Tanaitic origin of the Zohar a slant intended to counter it. Zacuto stated that though the Zohar consists of Tanaitic traditions going back to Shimon bar Yoḥai, it was edited by post-Talmudic generations. "And therefore the words of the Zohar are more veracious for they are the words of later authorities (*aḥronim*) who had seen the Mishna and the halakhic decisions and the statements of the *Amora'im*."[24] Zacuto thus subsumed the halakhic prerogative of the Zohar under the general rule of precedences, according to which later authorities overrule their predecessors.[25] The preference given to Zoharic prescription then has nothing to do with the work's special kabbalistic and mystical qualities.

This harmonizing interpretation of the Zohar's role is, no doubt, Zacuto's own and not part of the tradition transmitted by him as a *consensus omnium*. There is no hint of this interpretation in the words of Isaac Karo and it was certainly not shared by David Ibn Zimra. The theory is, in fact, highly questionable, for if it were the subsequent editing of the Zohar which lent it overriding authority, this ought to have been the case also where its decisions contradicted those of the Talmud.

Actually, the qualified authority granted to Kabbalah in general and to the Zohar in particular was not without precedent. Aggadic texts too contained halakhic statements, the relative authority of which as compared to halakhic sources proper had to be fixed. It was done by Rabenu Tam, who stated that insofar as these were not in conflict with other authorities, they would be valid.[26] This ruling may have served as a paradigm for those who formulated the principle of compromise concerning kabbalistic prescriptions.

The analogy between the two cases is, however, only a formal one. Though Aggadah was traditionally considered an integral part of the Oral Law, this was rarely understood in the strict sense of Sinaitic tradition.[27] None other than Naḥmanides declared that *midrashim* were like sermons containing opinions of individual scholars and preachers.[28] Thus halakhic statements occurring in an aggadic context could understandably not compete with halakhic literature proper.

This was altogether different in the case of Kabbalah. In its doctrinal teaching Kabbalah claimed to represent the deepest layer of metaphysical truth, accessible only through revelation. When this revelation took place, whether it was simultaneous with, prior to, or posterior to the giving of the Law on Sinai, and accordingly what measure of dignity it could claim—was not made explicit.[29] That it consisted of a scrupulously guarded tradition transmitted by means of a chosen elite, was never doubted. Consequently, statements of a halakhic nature scattered throughout this esoteric tradition also received enhanced status. Still, to grant Kabbalah priority over Halakhah where they disagreed would have been revolutionary. Thus the rule of compromise was accepted. It hardly deserved, however, the honor of being referred to as "dictated by reason".

Halakhah having been conceived of as a complete and self-sufficient system, any recourse to extra-halakhic sources, regardless of their nature, stood in need of justification. Hence the apologetic tone in David Ibn Zimra's response to his correspondents: "Don't accuse and suspect me of making decisions and giving guidance in the way of Kabbalah, for I am upholding the truth in the way of truth."[30] And on another occasion the closing sentence runs: "For I am reinforcing the custom which is the truth in the way of the truth."[31] He obviously felt that on principle Kabbalah had no legitimate role in forming judgments of a halakhic nature. His response to this scruple amounts to saying that the halakhic decision had been established by him on internal grounds, while the kabbalistic arguments had only a post-facto role of confirmation. In the two instances under consideration this was indeed the case. The first concerned the question of *yibum* as against *ḥalitza,* i.e. whether the marriage of a childless widow by her brother-in-law as prescribed in Deuteronomy 25:5 has preference over the ceremony of discharge which is, according to verses 7–10, its acceptable alternative. This was a long-standing problem discussed since Tanaitic times. Most authorities, however, leaned towards the first option, which happened also to conform to the kabbalists' position.[32] Ibn Zimra, indeed, marshalled first the halakhic authorities supporting his point while the kabbalistic dimension was included almost as an afterthought. In the second instance he had only to dismiss the innovation of an unknown who for some unexplained reason wished to double the threads of the *tzitzit.* Here the sanction of accepted custom would have constituted sufficient grounds for rejecting the change and Kabbalah certainly had no decisive role to play.

This, however, was certainly not always the case. Ibn Zimra resolved the doubt about phylacteries on *ḥolo shel mo'ed* in the negative, (as did the whole Sephardic community) on the authority of the Zohar, adding that he was delighted to see afterwards that RaSHBa held the same view on the basis of halakhic considerations.[33] In his responsum regarding phylacteries on *rosh ḥodesh* cited above, he confessed to following all kabbalistic prescriptions unsupported by halakhic authority and even those opposed to it as long as the kabbalistic view was in the nature of a stringency (*ḥumra*). Stringency here seems to refer to those details of the ritual about which Halakhah remained unconcerned, and which were fixed by Kabbalah. To this category belong the strict sequence of putting on *tzitzit* before the phylacteries.[34] Somewhat different is the case of *leḥem mishne,* the obligatory two loaves for the Sabbath meals. Kabbalah prescribed that the lower one be cut while, according to halakhic sources, different customs prevailed in different communities.[35]

Even where Halakhah was indifferent, the fixing of details on the basis of Kabbalah meant granting the latter a measure of authority concerning religious action—truly the realm of Halakhah. Ibn Zimra was no doubt aware of the weight of this implication and this seems to be why he declared his kabbalistically grounded decisions to be obligatory only for himself. Even this needed some theoretical justification, which he hinted that he had but was reluctant to divulge. ("I do not see fit to write it here.") It must have rested on kabbalistic premises and was therefore deemed unfit for circulation. In point of fact, Ibn Zimra laid down the law even for others, at least for those who appealed to him with their doubts. He did not invent the rule of the compromise but he can be said to have been highly conscious of the perplexities that it involved.

IV

Although, as we have seen, Spanish scholars were concerned with the relative status of Zoharic opinions for halakhic decisions the problem became truly intense only in the post-expulsion period. Indeed, only a few of the Zohar's ritual recommendations seem to have attracted attention in Spain such as that of phylacteries on *ḥol ha-mo'ed* or the repeating of the last words of *Shma* in order to complete the 248 words contained in it according to the Midrash, while in fact there were only 245. As was demonstrated by Israel Ta-Shema some years ago, this problem had been on the agenda of Spanish halakhists prior to the time of the Zohar, a fact that tended to facilitate the rapid assimilation of the Zoharic solution.[36] At any rate David Ibn Zimra, in defending the Zohar's version against an alteration in it by *Sefer ha-Kana* called it "the custom of our fathers."[37]

It took time before the text of the Zohar was scrutinized for indications of halakhic content. Joseph Karo quoted two great scholars of the preceding generations, Rabbi Isaac Aboab and Rabbi Jacob ben Ḥabib, who had heard about certain halakhic assertions attributed to the Zohar but had not seen them.[37a] Jacob Landau who composed his *Agur* in Italy in the 1480s is said to have been the first to include kabbalistic prescriptions in a halakhic compendium.[38] An Ashkenazi who, due to his wanderings, had become acquainted with the customs of other communities, he was disposed towards taking account of ritualistic diversity[39] and, being an enthusiastic adherent of Kabbalah, to include kabbalistic prescriptions in it as well. Still his observations in this regard amount to no more than wondering, in one case, why the *poskim* discussing a problem—the question of one or two blessings for the two phylacteries—did not pay attention to the Zohar's stand on the subject, and the enumeration, in another, of three prescriptions concerning the prayer shawl and phylacteries which were unknown except through the Zohar.[40] In fact only two of these are to be found in the Zohar, one concerning the correct sequence of putting on the prayer shawl and phylacteries, and the other regarding the right way of handling the phylacteries' thong. The third, a putative prescription to don the phylactery of the arm while sitting but that of the head while standing, was based on a misunderstanding of a passage in the Zohar. The Zohar referred to the two parts of the morning prayer, *de-meyushav* (sitting) and *de-me'umad* (standing), as conforming symbolically to the two phylacteries respectively. This did not imply different bodily postures to be observed while donning them—a misinterpretation that was pointed out already by Solomon Luria.[40a]

How haphazardly this process of scrutinization proceeded can be gathered also from the examples to which Abraham Zacuto resorted in order to illustrate the rule of compromise he transmitted. There were four such examples, but only two of these represented cases in which the Zohar had taken a clear stand on a controversial halakhic issue.[41] In the two others however, the alleged Zoharic opinion was not substantiated; in one of them the halakhic issue itself may have never existed.[42] The impact of the Zoharic Kabbalah on religious praxis began, no doubt, still in Spain, but it was able to gather momentum only in the post-expulsion period. The heightened receptivity to mystical teachings at this time strengthened this trend. The meeting in the Mediterranean countries of communities with differing ritual traditions, a process which began prior to the expulsion due to migrations of both Ashkenazim and Sephardim, gave rise to clashes between them which elicited controversies in which kabbalistic arguments were advanced. Elijah Mizraḥi and his colleagues in Constantinople defended local Romaniyot custom, which ignored the midrashic demand to complete the 248 words of the *Shma*, while simultaneously confirming the Sephardic communities' right to uphold the Zoharic version of the custom as against the innovation of the *Sefer ha-Kana.*[43] Once kabbalistic variations began to be included in halakhic manuals such as the *Agur*, these became the most effective vehicle for carrying them to distant places. The aforementioned protest of Solomon Luria, the Polish-Lithuanian scholar, was provoked by the novel practice of putting on the arm phylactery while sitting and that of the head while standing. As this variation is one of three Zoharic innovations pointed to by Landau in his *Agur*, and as it turns out, on closer scrutiny, to be a fictitious one,[44] it stands to reason that it was through this channel that it reached the East European communities.

V

A striking case of kabbalistic involvement in a halakhic issue which divided Sephardim and Ashkenazim was that of *yibum* versus *ḥalitza*. To be sure *yibum* (levirate marriage), as prescribed in Deuteronomy 25:5–6 ceased to be the customary solution to the problem of the childless widow already in Talmudic times. As monogamy was the prevailing pattern of the Jewish family, even where polygamy had not been legally proscribed the widow's marriage to her brother-in-law could not remain prevalent practice. Instead *ḥalitza*, the alternative ceremony by which according to Deuteronomy 25:7–10, the widow is released from her semi-married status, gained currency.[45] Still, the problem continued to be debated by medieval halakhists, the majority of whom gave *yibum* priority on principle. The halakhic stand on the problem could, however, have little if any bearing on practical decisions. Levirate marriage, like any other, could not be performed without mutual agreement and, if such agreement were forthcoming, it could be performed even if *ḥalitza* was theoretically preferable. The halakhic standpoint did, however, have decisive consequences for the legal position of the parties if no agreement on *yibum* or *ḥalitza* could be achieved. Giving priority to *yibum* tipped the scale in favor of the brother-in-law while strongly prejudicing the rights of the widow. To safeguard these rights, the priority of *ḥalitza* was legally established in eleventh- and twelfth-century Ashkenaz. This did not immediately exclude the occasional performance of levirate marriage, but in the course of the fourteenth and fifteenth centuries it became a veritable religious taboo, to be lifted by halakhists only in exceptional cases.[46] In Spain and other Mediterranean countries, on the other hand, the priority of *yibum* and its legal consequences remained in force, and even gathered strength through the kabbalistic interpretation of *yibum*'s significance. According to both Naḥmanides and the Zohar, levirate marriage is intended to redeem the deceased brother's soul, which transmigrates into the child born from this new matrimony.[47]

Such evaluations which diverged to the extent that what was for Sephardim a praiseworthy religious act was seen by Ashkenazim as shocking and reprehensible, would create no practical problems so long as the two communities had no physical contact. Such contact, however, became a regular occurrence from the mid-fifteenth century on in Italy, Candia, the Balkans and later also in Palestine as large numbers of immigrants began to arrive from the North and the West alike. From this point on the question of the priority of *yibum* or *ḥalitza* acquired actual importance whenever one of the couple was Ashkenazi and the other Sephardi or when the case under consideration was dealt with by courts of both communities. Such a case occurred in Candia in the 1460s when an immigrant Ashkenazi scholar, Moses Cohen Ashkenazi, sought to prevent the performance of a levirate marriage endorsed, as a matter of course, by the local halakhist, Rabbi Michael Balbo. The clash between the two halakhists elicited a controversy concerning the belief in transmigration, the ideological contents of which have been analyzed by the late Ephraim Gottlieb.[48] In the context of our inquiry, the interesting aspect of the matter is the relative weight given to kabbalistic lore by outstanding representatives of the two schools. When the issue was brought to the attention of the Jerusalem court, its head, the Spanish scholar Joseph ben Gedalya, testified concerning the prevailing practice in Spain where "sometimes *yibum* is performed, sometimes *ḥalitza*, according to the agreement of the couple concerned."[49] On the level of principle, however, the priority of levirate marriage was upheld on both halakhic and kabbalistic grounds. For the latter, the authority of Shimon bar Yoḥai and other Talmudists, with special reference to RaMBaN, was adduced.[50] Two Ashkenazi worthies on the other hand, the heads of the yeshivah in Muenster to whom Moses Cohen Ashkenazi appealed, upheld the prohibition of *yibum* and repudiated the belief in transmigration. One of them, Rabbi Judah Obernick, stated that his opponents may believe in Kabbalah if they like "but in legal matters [*dinim*] there is no reason to rely upon their fantasies and arguments."[51]

From the standpoint of the development of Halakhah it was the Ashkenazi ruling that deviated from the standard course—following no doubt the improved position of women in the Ashkenazi community. Sephardic halakhists stood on firm ground even without the support of Kabbalah. Nevertheless, both Isaac Karo and David ibn Zimra in their treatment of the subject made emphatic use of it. Karo's statement quoted above concerning the decisive authority of Kabbalah wherever halakhists are divided appears in this context—the issue of phylacteries on *ḥol ha-mo'ed* enters the discussion only as an aside—and serves, in fact, as a preliminary statement to a long-winded discussion.[52] This is an absolutely unusual procedure, the halakhist being expected to vindicate his point of view first on his own legitimate ground and to add kabbalistic corroboration only as a kind of afterthought. In reversing this order, Karo revealed his deep commitment to Kabbalah by granting it a decisive role in the halakhic context as well. Ibn Zimra, however, followed the customary procedure, inserting the kabbalistic confirmation only at the end of his responsum, and even then, as we have seen, he sought to offset the suspicion that he might have given decisive weight to kabbalistic considerations.[53] Still, appealing to his correspondent who had defended the priority of *ḥalitza*, he said: "I have heard about you, my brother . . . that you have some dealings with the secret lore. How then could you agree with the scholar who decided that the commandment of *ḥalitza* has priority?"[54] For Ibn Zimra too, the truth of Kabbalah had overriding significance.

The decisions of Karo and Ibn Zimra regarding the priority of levirate marriage over *ḥalitza* were not issued with the intention of influencing the parties concerned to live up to this principle. Actual marriage was out of the question in both instances. The decision was meant rather to have other legal consequences for the litigating parties. Nonetheless these scholars went to the core of the issue. Ibn Zimra quoted 2 Samuel 14:19 which was for kabbalists one of the main biblical sources for the belief in transmigration, adding that "*yibum* is the fundamental commandment and *ḥalitza* is merely an inferior substitute."[55] Karo expressed himself in a similar vein: "The commandment of *yibum* is a great advantage for the soul of the deceased, for the enjoyment of the soul increases if it transmigrates into someone nearer to his family."[56]

Whether such considerations ever influenced a couple who had to choose between *yibum* and *ḥalitza* is, of course, impossible to say. We know of a case in 1573 in Pesaro, where a couple sought the permission of halakhists to perform levirate marriage.[57] We learn from the eighteen learned responses on that case that though Italian practice leaned towards the Ashkenazi custom, *yibum* was not excluded as strictly as in Germany and Poland.[58] The experts were able to cite cases where such famous authorities as Obadiah Sforno and Moses Basola had consented to *yibum* [59] and they too granted permission in the present instance. A number of the respondents, all of whom decided in the affirmative added kabbalistic considerations to their halakhic arguments.[60] They praised the outstanding piety of the brother-in-law, a member of one of the first families in town, and considered him above any suspicion that he sought the marriage for motives other than fulfillment of the commandment.[61] That he himself was motivated in his request by kabbalistic considerations, as some of the halakhists were in formulating their legal decisions, is not mentioned, and to assume so would be unfounded speculation.

VI

The main impact of the Kabbalah was felt in the more common religious rites, and it was the changes in these which elicited the protests of Kabbalah's opponents. I have described elsewhere the repeated clashes between those who followed the Zoharic prohibition of donning the phylacteries on *ḥolo shel mo'ed* and their opponents, especially in the Italian communities.[62] Once a ritual, even if halakhically of little weight, had been kabbalistically interpreted, it assumed metaphysical significance vindicating its implementation. Bride and groom traditionally assumed a fixed order under the canopy—the Ashkenazi tradition placed the bride to the right of the bridegroom, while other communities placed her on his left.[63] A kabbalistically minded scholar in Rome, Yehuda ben Michael by name, maintained in 1528 that the latter was also the original Roman custom, and that those who followed the reverse order where ignorant and impudent innovators.[64] Still, his zeal for re-establishing the old custom did not stem from conservatism, but rather from his conviction that the bridegroom-right–bride-left position conformed with kabbalistic symbolism. He expatiated on this subject in a lengthy document submitted to the wardens of the community, whose solicitation of scholarly opinion had created strife in the community.[65] Our kabbalist went so far as to state that even if the other order had been traditional in the community, it ought to be changed in the manner of any custom that, on closer examination, proved to be unfounded or to run counter to accepted principles.[66]

What was said by the opponents of this kabbalistic zealot we do not know. From his introductory denouncement of those who would sneer at Kabbalah or even reject it altogether, we may conclude that beyond the controversy on this particular point loomed the major issue of the acceptance of Kabbalah as the true and genuine theology of Judaism. Rejecting kabbalistically based ritual changes gave scholars with reservations concerning Kabbalah an opportunity to voice their opinions. Their reservations did not necessarily extend to denial of Kabbalah's truth. It was sufficient for them to feel that religious worship and faith could be complete without the Kabbalah's mystical lore. Solomon Luria, in his previously quoted repudiation of the Zohar's authority in halakhic matters, rested his argument primarily on the formal ground of Shimon bar Yoḥai's low standing in the Talmudic hierarchy, but concluded his remarks with an emphatic appeal to his correspondent:[67]

> Therefore, my beloved, don't follow them along this way; don't engage in the occult. Those who boast of innovations as if they knew and understood the secrets of the Torah and its hidden meaning—would that they knew its overt meaning! How authoritative was the strength of Shimshon of Chinon who, after having studied the secrets of Kabbalah, said that he prays as an infant does.

In referring to this famous dictum by one of the medieval scholars skeptical of Kabbalah's true contribution to religious piety, Luria clearly revealed the deeper motivations behind his reluctance to accept the kabbalists' claim that their ritual innovations enriched Judaism.

A similar attitude is revealed in the utterances of Elijah Mizraḥi and his circle in Constantinople. One of the scholars, Tam Yiḥyeh, who supported Mizraḥi in his halakhic decision cited above, expressed himself in unequivocal terms. Tam designated Kabbalah as "elevated high wisdom . . . containing secrets of the Torah for those who know its meaning." He added that although possessors of such knowledge may have existed in the remote past, in our days this knowledge is absent and the secrets of the Torah are hidden from all.[68] Those who indulge in its study run the risk, according to Tam, of straying from the true religion. At most, he would be willing to accept the study of Kabbalah in seclusion by exceptional individuals who would, however, refrain from divulging its contents to others, and certainly from providing guidance to the community on its basis. The community in his view has no need for such guidance. It is well taken care of by overt tradition, the *kabbalah* in its original sense, which has nothing to do with mysticism or the occult.

Such skepticism concerning Kabbalah and especially with regard to its ritual aspects was, however, clearly on the decline over the period under consideration here. People with either slight knowledge of kabbalistic lore or none at all, were fascinated nonetheless by the idea that in conforming to the special prescriptions of the kabbalists they would attain a higher grade of religiosity or, as some critics claimed, religiously warranted social status. This is the gist of Solomon Luria's comment on "those of recent appearance, who wish to belong to the class [*kat*] of the kabbalists,"[69] and hope to demonstrate their affiliation by adopting the new variation of postures while putting on the phylacteries. A similar grasp of the historical process is conveyed by Tam Yiḥyeh when he speaks of the many ignoramuses who boastfully claim "God's secret is in our possession, not in yours, you Talmudists who wander in the dark."[70] That this was the way things were is confirmed by David ibn Zimra when he describes those who adopted the other kabbalistic variation connected with the phylacteries—removing it on *rosh ḥodesh* for the *Musaf* prayer. "Having seen some of those who study kabbalistic writings remove their phylacteries [for *Musaf*], they too do the same, as perfunctorily as any prescription that lacks a rationale."[71]

VII

The extent of the halakhist's commitment to Kabbalah was not the only factor determining his readiness to accept kabbalistic innovations. Solomon Luria's reluctance to do so was clearly related to the strictly fixed ritual tradition of the Ashkenazi community, whose standard bearer he always professed to be.[72] It was in such areas as Italy and the Balkans, where the confluence of different traditions weakened the hold of inherited customs that the kabbalistic trend had its best chance to be absorbed. If the weakness of local tradition coincided with deep attachment to mystical lore, the optimal conditions for integrating kabbalistic Halakhah into religious praxis had been achieved. Such coincidence occurred, as we have seen, in the case of Jacob Landau and repeated itself in a more significant way in the case of Joseph Karo.

Karo's attitude has been misrepresented on two counts. Rationalistically minded scholars of the nineteenth century could not imagine that Karo the "lawyer" could, at the same time, have been the author of *Magid Mesharim*, the mystical diary dictated to its author in a semi-conscious state of mind.[73] The historical as well as psychological misconceptions underlying this skepticism have been examined and the twofold mentality of Karo as "lawyer and mystic" convincingly established by Karo's modern biographer, R.J. Zwi Werblowsky. In the same context Werblowsky spoke also of "Karo's well-known unwillingness to allow kabbalistic considerations or mystical experiences to influence halakhic decisions."[74] The first half of this sentence is well taken. The half-conscious meditations of Karo's mystical diary contain also reflections on halakhic matters, and these indeed left no trace in his halakhic writings. Kabbalistic considerations based on literary sources, primarily the Zohar, on the other hand, are part and parcel of his *Beyt Yosef* and *Shulḥan Arukh*, as was shown long ago by Moshe Kunitz in his *Ben-Yoḥai.*[75] It was also rather clearly indicated by Karo himself. Enumerating the halakhic authorities to be consulted in his work, Karo concluded his list with the phrase "and in certain places, passages from the Zohar."[76]

What role these Zoharic passages were allotted we shall see presently. Yet we must first ascertain the significance of Karo's reference to the halakhic authorities on which he admittedly relies. As is well known Karo chose three of the great authorities—Isaac Alfasi, Maimonides and Rabbi Asher ben Yeḥiel—and declared that if two were in agreement their judgment would be followed. To what extent he was able to carry out this resolution is not our concern here. Attention however, should be drawn to the condition to which Karo linked his decisions, a condition which illuminates the basic intention of his codifying enterprise.[77]

> And if, in some countries, people customarily prohibited certain matters concerning which we shall decide to the contrary, they should nonetheless uphold their practice for they have already accepted upon themselves the view of the scholar favoring prohibition and are not allowed to introduce a permission.

What emerges from this statement is that Karo intended to fix the Law on the basis of the literary sources alone, unconcerned with the local tradition of this or that country or community. Readers should take their local traditions into consideration in applying his code. The codifier himself operated, so to speak, in a social vacuum which allowed him to measure the merits of the literary sources according to the accepted rites of halakhic reasoning.[78] Since the Zohar had been acknowledged by previous generations as a legitimate source for practical decisions, Karo could follow his kabbalistic inclinations as far as his keen halakhic sensitivity would permit.

Far from refraining from "kabbalistic considerations," Karo, working systematically on the basis of a comprehensive survey of the sources, absorbed Zoharic prescriptions and granted them higher status than had any halakhist before him. In Chapter 4 of the *Beyt Yosef* which deals with "hand-washing in the morning," Karo quotes a long passage from the Zohar as supporting evidence before anouncing his decision between two conflicting schools of thought. Was the Talmudically prescribed hand-washing in the morning a mere hygenic provision or was it, rather, a ritual one requiring the observance of all minutiae connected with the washing of hands before a proper meal. Karo adopted the second position for which he found support in the Zoharic passage he quoted.[79] Yet this passage also contained "novel prescriptions not found in the *poskim*."[80] Two of these were to pour the water when washing not on the earth but into a vessel and to avoid using the water for human purposes or even having any contact with it. Two other prescriptions concerned the proper handling of the vessel which was used for hand-washing (beginning with the right or left).[81]

While in the *Beyt Yosef* these prescriptions were wrapped in Zoharic symbolism which they were intended to reflect, in the *Shulḥan Arukh* they were reduced to a few laconic statements.[82] In the first of these concerning the ritual minutiae of hand-washing, where the Zohar had merely supported one of two halakhic opinions Karo's decision was presented as a recommendation only. ('It is commendable to take care.'[83]) The others, based exclusively on the Zohar's authority and uncontested by any known halakhist, were formulated authoritatively.[84] According to David ibn Zimra's principle, these prescriptions, being essentially ritual rigorisms should have been recommended for voluntary acceptance only. Karo, by including them in his *Shulḥan Arukh*, made them binding for all Israel. Karo also went beyond Ibn Zimra's position in cases where Zoharic statements conflicted with other authorities, be they the Talmud or the *poskim*. Ibn Zimra declared that in such cases the kabbalistic view should be ignored. For Karo, however, the Zoharic view would be binding as long as it was not explicitly repudiated in the Talmud.[85] If this were the case, the kabbalistic tradition would have to give way. Being a traditional halakhist, Karo had no alternative. He did believe, however, that if the apparent conflict between the two traditions could be resolved, kabbalistic tradition could be salvaged.[86]

At any rate, Karo, in his endeavor to reconcile the conflicting sources, refrained from the pilpulistic methods used by later interpreters who tried to defend all deviations of the Zohar from halakhic tradition. Accustomed as he was to close reading of texts and exact interpretation of their meaning, Karo found the path of pilpulistic dialectics closed to him. Surveying the controversial case of phylacteries on *ḥol ha-mo'ed*, he had to concede that, while the position of the Babylonian Talmud was open to interpretation, a statement of the Palestinian unequivocally regarded phylacteries as obligatory.[87] Later halakhists with a kabbalistic leaning, such as Menahem da Fano and Emanuel Ḥai Ricchi found ways of turning the *Yerushalmi*'s meaning into its contrary.[88] Karo did not and therefore faced a dilemma. He solved it by granting the Zohar unprecedented authority. Having presented the relevant sources, including the Zohar's appeal to consider the great metaphysical significance of the ritual according to its interpretation, Karo concluded: "Since in our Talmud this issue is not explicitly determined, who would dare to transgress actively what Shimon bar Yoḥai has so emphatically proscribed."[89] The emphasis is here on "our Talmud", meaning the Babylonian as opposed to the Palestinian. Though it contradicted the *Yerushalmi*, the Zoharic view was accepted. The uncertainty concerning the stand of "our Talmud" served as a sufficient loophole to let the kabbalistic view prevail. Far from being free from kabbalistic influence, then, the author of the *Shulḥan Arukh*, as we have seen, yielded to it to the utmost extent possible for a halakhist of his stature.

NOTES

1. *The Guide of the Perplexed*, III, 26. See Isaac Heinemann, *Ta'amei ha-Mitzvot be-Sifrut Yisrael* (Jerusalem, 1943) I, p. 68.

2. Isidore Epstein, "Maimonides' Conception of the Law and the Ethical Trend of his Halakhah," in I. Epstein, ed., *Moses Maimonides, 1135-1204; Anglo-Jewish Papers in Connection with the Eighth Century of his Birth* (London, 1935), pp. 71-72. How marginal the influence of philosophy on Maimonides' Halakhah was can be gathered from the fact that opponents of his philosophy found no fault with his Halakhah. See Isadore Twersky, "The Beginnings of Mishneh Torah Criticism" in Alexander Altmann, ed., *Biblical and Other Studies* (Cambridge, Mass., 1963), pp. 178-182; idem, "R. Yosef Ashkenazy ve-Sefer Mishneh Torah shel ha-Rambam," in *Salo Wittmayer Baron Jubilee Volume* (Jerusalem, 1974), Hebrew Section, pp. 183-194.

3. See Jacob Katz, "Rabbinical Authority and Authorization in the Middle Ages," in print.

4. Jacob Katz, *Exclusiveness and Tolerance, Studies in Jewish-Gentile Relations in Medieval and Modern Times* (Oxford, 1966), pp. 114-128.

5. I have dealt with this aspect of the problem in an article to be published in the Jubilee Volume in Honor of Yitzḥak Baer.

6. My paper on *tefilin shel ḥol ha-mo'ed* read at the World Conference of Jewish Studies in 1976 will be published in a collection of my essays.

7. See *Sota* 39a. Maimonides understood the passage in a negative sense, that unwashed hands prevent the *kohen* from participating in the ritual; *Nesiat kapayim* 15,5. Ashkenazic authorities required hand-washing preceding the ritual. See ad loc., *Kesef Mishne.* In *Beyt Yosef, Oraḥ Ḥayim* 128, Joseph Karo refers to the custom of the *levi* pouring the water on the *kohen*'s hands and attributes it to the Zohar (III, 146a-b). Whether he does so correctly is, in my opinion, still to be clarified.

8. This is a summary of a forthcoming article on the Zohar's dealings with matters of Halakhah.

9. *Beyt Yosef, Oraḥ Ḥayim*, 32, and see below.

10. Elijah Mizraḥi, *Responsa*, I.

11. The term 'canonical,' unqualified by 'quasi-,' concerning the Zohar is used by Gershom Scholem, *Major Trends in Jewish Mysticism* (New York, 1951), p. 156.

12. Elijah Del Medigo, *Beḥinat ha-Dat* (Vienna, 1833), pp. 44-45.

13. Ibid., p. 45.

14. See Joseph Del Medigo's letter to the Karaite Zeraḥ ben Natan, published by Abraham Geiger in his *Melo Ḥofnayim* (Berlin, 1840), p. 10. What the real attitude of Del Medigo towards Kabbalah was is still not entirely clear. See Tishby, *Mishnat ha-Zohar* (Jerusalem, 1957) I, pp. 46-47; Israel Zinberg, *Toldot Sifrut Yisrael* (Merḥavia, 1956), II, pp. 324-327.

15. Yehuda Arye Modena, *Ari Nohem* (Jerusalem, 1929), pp. 60-68.

16. See Ḥayim Benveniste, *Kneset ha-Gdola* (Leghorn, 1618), p. 161a; Malakhi ha-Cohen, *Yad Malakhi* (Leghorn, 1665), p. 173; Zvi Ashkenazi, *Ḥakham Zvi*, Responsum 36. The first two also quote Abraham Zacuto (see below, notes 20-21) but only in the second place. They may have been mistaken about the chronology or, more probably, referred first to the halakhically more important Ibn Zimra. *Entziklopedia Talmudit*, IX, p. 254 refers also to *Perush Sefer Yetzira* of Judah of Barcelona, mistaking the word 'Halakhah' which stands there for spritual teachings.

17. David ibn Zimra, *Responsa*, IV, 80. Similar formulation, ibid., 36. See Israel Goldman, *The Life and Times of Rabbi David Ibn Abi Zimra* (New York, 1970), pp. 71-72.

18. Isaac Karo's responsum is printed at the end of the responsa of his nephew, Joseph Karo, *She'elot u-Tshuvot Beyt Yosef.* The passage quoted is on p. 385 in the Jerusalem, 1960 edition.

19. On Isaac Karo see *Encyclopedia Judaica* V, 193-194; Abraham David, "Rabi Yitzḥak Karo," *Sinai* 66 (1970), pp. 367-371.

20. Abraham Zacuto, *Sefer Yuḥasim ha-Shalem* (Frankfurt, 1925) p. 45.

21. See Abraham Ḥayim Freimann's introduction to *Yuḥasim*, p. X; and Yitzḥak Baer in *Encyclopaedia Hebraica* I, pp. 318-321.

22. See note 10. Ha-Levi's observations are added to Mizraḥi's responsum.

23. Shlomo Luria, *She'elot u-Tshuvot*, 98.

24. See note 20.

25. See *Entziklopedia Talmudit*, IX, 342-346.

26. Ibid., pp. 252-253.

27. See the sources quoted in the article and referred to in the previous note, and ibid., I, p. 62.

28. See *Kitvei Rabenu Moshe ben Naḥman*, edited by Ḥayim Dov Shavel (Jerusalem, 1963), I, 308-309. The statement was made in the course of Naḥmanides' famous disputation with the apostate Pablo Christiani in Barcelona in 1263. That is why later authorities tried to explain it away as a mere apologetic device. See the editor's note. RaMBaN seems to have differentiated between Aggadot included in Talmud and Midrashim.

29. See Scholem, *Major Trends*, pp. 17-18; idem, "Religioese Autoritaet und Mystik," *Eranos Jahrbuch* XXIV (1958), pp. 262-264.

30. Ibn Zimra, *Responsa*, IV, 109.

31. Idem, Part VIII published by Yitzḥak Zvi Sofer (Bnei Brak, 1975), Responsum 3.

32. On this, below note 46.

33. Ibn Zimra, *Responsa* IV, 8.

34. Ibid., 244.
35. Ibid., III, 582. See *Sefer ha-Manhig*, edited by Yitzḥak Raphael (Jerusalem, 1978), I, p. 173 and the sources noted by the editor.
36. Israel Ta-Shema, "*El Melekh Ne'eman*; the Development of a Custom", *Tarbitz* XXXIX (1970), pp. 184-194.
37. Ibn Zimra, *Responsa*, IV, 55.
37a. Beyt Yosef, *Oraḥ Ḥayim* 25 (Ben Ḥabib) and 141 (Aboab).
38. Zinberg, *Toldot*, II, p. 308, and the introduction to the Jerusalem edition of *Agur* (1960) by Moshe Hershler, p. 12.
39. See Hershler's biographical sketch, ibid., pp. 6-11, and my article in *Zion* 35 (1970), p. 55.
40. See paragraphs 36 and 84. Landau mentioned some other kabbalistic variations of non-Zoharic provenance; see paragraphs 332 and 394.
40a. Zohar III, 120b and Luria, *Responsa*, No. 98 (cited above, n. 23). Luria further pointed out that Joseph Karo had not mentioned this law nor did Rabbi Issakhar Baer who, in his *Yesh Sakhar* (Prague, 1608/9), had listed all laws he found mentioned in the Zohar.
41. One of these was the case of *tefilin shel ḥol ha-mo'ed*, the other that of restricting the use of wine for the grace after meals to cases where three persons were present. The reference is to Zohar II 157b; see *Yesh Sakhar*, p. 30a.
42. Zacuto attributes to the Zohar the obligatory omission of amen after the last blessing of the *Shma*, as some of the *poskim* have it. But the Zohar only refers to the Talmudic precept of joining *ge'ula* and *tefila*, which did not exclude the answering of amen. See Ro'SH, *Berakhot* 7, 10. For the text of the Zohar see *Yesh Sakhar*, p. 15. *Beyt Yosef, O.Ḥ.*, 51, 66, 111 refers to the Sephardic influence of the Zohar without, however, quoting it. He obviously accepted this on the authority of Zacuto. Zacuto stated that RaMBaM, contrary to Ro'SH, requires *kidush* for the third meal on Shabbat, and that the Zohar follows the former. He had *Tur, O.Ḥ.* 291 and Zohar III 95a in mind. However, neither the text of RaMBaM nor the Zohar bears this out. See *Beyt Yosef* on *Tur* ibid. My guess is that Zacuto received the tradition of the rule of compromise, and tried both to justify it (as seen above) and to find relevant examples to substantiate it.
43. See Mizraḥi, *Responsa* 1-2.
44. See notes 23 and 40a above.
45. The sources referring to the problem can be found in Ze'ev W. Falk, *Marriage and Divorce, Reforms in the Family Law of German-French Jewry* (Jerusalem, 1961), index, s.v. *ḥaliza, yibum.* My short description of the actual process of development differs from that of Falk and, in fact, from all those who dealt with the problem before him, but I cannot go here into details in substantiating my point of view.
46. The proscription of *yibum* in Ashkenaz is attested, in addition to the sources quoted below, by Azriel Diena. See his *Responsa* published by Yacov Boksenboim (Tel Aviv, 1977) no. 157, especially p. 497.
47. RaMBaN to Genesis 38:8, Deutronomy 25:6; Zohar III, 177a. See Scholem, *Major Trends*, p. 243.
48. Efraim Gottlieb, "Vikuaḥ ha-Gilgul be-Kandia ba-Me'a ha-Tet-Vav" originally in *Sefunot* 11, now included in Joseph Hacker, ed., *Studies in the Kabbalah Literature* (Tel Aviv, 1976) pp. 370-396. Gottlieb (pp. 374-377) expressed his doubts whether the controversy was occasioned by a concrete case of *yibum.* The additional sources referred to in the following notes answer this question in the positive unequivocally.
49. Joseph Hacker, "The Connections of Spanish Jewry with Eretz Israel between 1391 and 1402," *Shalem* I (1974) p. 153.
50. Ibid., pp. 152-154.
51. Ephraim Kupfer, "Concerning the Cultural Image of German Jewry and its Rabbis in the Fourteenth and Fifteenth Centuries," *Tarbitz* 42 (1972), pp. 128-130. The quotation is on p. 129.
52. See note 18.
53. See note 30.
54. Ibid., the passage is in part 4 of the *Responsa*, p. 40a.
55. Ibid.

56. As above in note 18, p. 385.
57. The Responsa relating to the subject were printed in *Paḥad Yitzḥak* III, pp. 21a-26b.
58. Ibid., 22b, 25b. The two scholars speaking here maintain that Italy had no fixed custom in this matter at all.
59. Ibid., 21b, 25a.
60. Ibid., pp. 23a, 25a, 26b.
61. The religious intention of the brother-in-law is halakhically relevant for the permission to marry one's sister-in-law, otherwise forbidden, is according to one Talmudic view dependent upon it. *Yevamot* 39b.
62. Paper read at the World Conference of Jewish Studies in Jerusalem, 1976, not yet published.
63. The Ashkenazi custom is mentioned already by Elazar Rokeaḥ, *Sefer ha-Rokeaḥ* 353 citing Psalms 45:10 as a reference. That in other countries the reverse order was observed we learn from the Roman scholar referred to below. That this may have been the case is also indicated by the fact that it became accepted by Isaac Luria. See Aaron Alfandari, *Yad Aharon* (Izmir, 1666) 61, 4.
64. This unknown incident is reflected in a manuscript of 9 pages in the Library of the Jewish Theological Seminary (sig. R. 1466 mier. 7187) Dr. Joseph Hacker was good enough to draw my attention to it and provide me with the microfilm. The date 1528 is mentioned on the last page. Yehudah b. Michael's name appears among the *dayanim* of Rome about this time; see Vogelstein-Rieger, *Geschichte der Juden in Rom* (Berlin, 1895) II, p. 99. The original Roman custom is testified to by three other scholars (p. 9), the custom in other countries on p. 7.
65. Ibid., p. 2.
66. Ibid., pp. 6-7.
67. See note 23.
68. At the end of Mizraḥi's Responsum no. 1.
69. As note 23.
70. As note 68.
71. As note 17.
72. Well documented in the introduction to his *Yam shel Shlomo* to *Ḥulin*.
73. See R.J. Zwi Werblowsky, *Joseph Karo, Lawyer and Mystic* (Oxford, 1962), pp. 1-7.
74. Ibid., p. 184.
75. Moshe Kunitz, *Ben-Yoḥai* (Vienna, 1815), pp. 136-149.
76. The introduction is to be found in all the editions of *Beyt Yosef* published with the *Turim* of Jacob b. Asher.
77. Ibid.
78. Stressed also by Isadore Twersky, "The Shulḥan 'Aruk: Enduring Code of Jewish Law," *Judaism* 16 (1967), p. 145.
79. *Beyt Yosef, O.Ḥ.*, 4.
80. Ibid.
81. On this point Karo found a contradiction in two passages of the Zohar and had to resolve it before coming to a binding conclusion. His method of dealing with the Zohar is the same as that used with any other rabbinic source.
82. *Shulḥan Arukh, O. Ḥ.*, 4, 7-11.
83. Ibid., paragraph 7.
84. Ibid., paragraph 8-11. Kunitz in his *Ben Yoḥai*, p. 136 maintained that Karo accepted Zoharic prescriptions only as recommendations. This is contradicted by the instances under consideration here. See also *Shulḥan Arukh, O. Ḥ.*, 32, 44.
85. This is stated in *Beyt Yosef, O. Ḥ.*, 120, 141.
86. Upon reconsideration, Karo managed to find a means of reconciling the Talmudic requirement, as understood by most *poskim*, for the person called to the Torah to read the text along with the reader, with the Zohar's prescription not to do so. He noted that the Zohar referred only to reading aloud.
87. *Beyt Yosef, O. Ḥ.*, 31.
88. Menaḥem Azarya mi-Fano, *Responsa*, 108; Emanuel Ḥai Ricchi, *Aderet Eliyahu* (Leghorn, 1741/2), p. 14bf.
89. *Beyt Yosef, O. Ḥ.*, 31.

The Influence of Moses ibn Ḥabib's *Darkhei No'am*

JAMES KUGEL

"The first problem of Renaissance criticism was the justification of imaginative literature"—so begins a well-known treatment of this period[1]—and for that justification Boccaccio, Petrarch, Poliziano, Minturno and other defenders of poetry employed the same tactic: they turned to the Bible.[2] For was not the origin of poetry to be sought in man's earliest religious ceremonies? Was not the Bible itself full of poetry, the songs of Moses, and David, and Solomon? Indeed, was not theology itself a form of poetry, "poetry concerning God"?[3] With these arguments, Renaissance poets aimed not only at defusing the claims of poetry's pious detractors, but as well at raising the standing of their own art to new heights. By analogy the poet became little less than a prophet, and his works were henceforth scrutinized and interpreted with a zeal previously reserved for one book alone.

In Hebrew letters the same argument had been encountered somewhat earlier. From the beginning of the Spanish Golden Age, Hebrew poets had compared their craft with that of their biblical "counterparts" and sought the origin of poetic diction and even such institutions as meter in biblical songs.[4] Not only did the biblical analogy enhance the poet's standing—this is the burden of a great *ars poetica* of the period, Moses ibn Ezra's *Kitāb al-muḥāḍara wal-mudhākara*—but occasionally exalted the modern practitioner even above his ancient forebear: Isaac Abravanel holds that the Hebrew poems of his own day surpass the style of biblical poetry.[5]

One of the later treatises to touch on biblical poetry is the booklet *Darkhei No'am*[6] by Moses ibn Ḥabib. Born in Lisbon, Ḥabib wandered to various centers of southern Italy, where he wrote, *inter alia*, a Hebrew grammar, *Marpe Lashon*. Perhaps as a companion-piece, he composed *Darkhei No'am* in the same period, completing it (according to Ḥabib's dedicatory poem) in 1486 at Bitonto. The two were published together in Constantinople (ca. 1510) and have appeared since then.[7]

The purpose of *Darkhei No'am* was the same as that of *Derekh La'asot Ḥaruzim*,[8] *Imrei Shefer*,[9] *Shekel ha-Kodesh*,[10] and similar manuals:[11] to explain the principles of Hebrew meter and to compile examples of different metrical patterns for would-be poets to emulate. But before setting himself to this task, Ḥabib begins by classifying poetry among various types of utterances and setting out its characteristics. He distinguishes three classes of Hebrew songs corresponding to three purposes and effects of poetry. These are: 1) *tikun ha-sekhel* (improvement of the rational faculty), 2) the correction of "accidents of the soul" (*mikrim nafshiyim*) which threaten to overcome it (such as anger, pride, aggressivity, violence) and their redirection towards the good, and 3) elevation of the soul from "lesser accidents" such as fear, pain, cowardice, and the like. His source for this classification is to be found in a passage in al-Fārābī's *Fuṣūl al-madanī*.[12] Al-Fārābī asserts that there are *six* kinds of songs, but details only the first three; of the latter three he says only that they are the opposite of the first and "destroy all that they correct." This idea Ḥabib repeats, adding "Heaven forfend [that anyone think] that the slightest word of them be found in the books of prophecy and divine inspiration."

At the end of his exposition, al-Fārābī notes that "the different types of tunes and songs follow the different types of poetry and have the same divisions." Perhaps this is what led Ḥabib to further list three types of poetic structure (although he may have been influenced by other three-fold divisions of poetry elsewhere in Hebrew).[13] It is in any case clear that Ḥabib's three types of poetic lines are really only two: lines can be metrical, like much of the poetry of his own day, or they can *not* be, like, for example, the songs of the Bible. But biblical songs, or rather verses, he further subdivides into two groups: those which, like medieval Hebrew lines, divide into two equal hemistichs, possessing the same number of syllables; and those other lines—the vast majority—which are not exactly equal in syllable-count, but only approximately so. Even the first group is not, by medieval Hebrew standards, metrical, for (as Ḥabib points out) the arrangement of syllables within the line is random and instances of agreement in successive lines quite accidental. Moreover, Ḥabib points out, rhyme does not occur in biblical songs, unless by chance. Nevertheless, these lines of equal numbers of syllables constitute for him a separate category.[14] He then proceeds to give examples of each of his three classes. Bibilical verses with equal hemistiches include Ps. 119:146, 146:9; Prov. 1:8, 10:5; and Job 5:20.[15] As for the second class, whole songs may be placed within it—he cites the four *shirot*[16] of Exod. 15, Deut. 32, Judges 5, and 2 Sam. 22 (=Psalm 18). Finally, the third class, metrical poetry in the contemporary sense, he will discuss at length, for this is his true subject.

But just before embarking on his exposition, he recounts an incident bearing on the antiquity of meter in Hebrew.[17] While in the Kingdom of Valencia, in Murviedro (Sagunto),[18] Ḥabib was shown a Hebrew tombstone reputedly belonging to an army commandant of the biblical king Amaziah, on which was engraved a poetic epitaph:

שאו קינה בקול מרה   לשר גדול לקחו י–ה.

O sing lament in bitter voice   for the great prince
whom the Lord hath taken.

"We were unable to read more [than the first line]," Ḥabib wrote, "because the writing had been eroded, but the second line ended 'to Amaziah.' Then I truly believed that this metrical sort of poetry had existed since the days when our forefathers were dwelling in their own land."[19] What Ḥabib saw in this inscription was, of course, evidence of the Spanish-style Hebrew meters: the line falls into two symmetrical halves, each of which consists of two units both composed of one *yated* and two *tenu'ot.* This is the meter known as *ha-marnin*, the same scheme as that of the celebrated hymn *Adon Olam.* Moreover, he adds that the last word of the second line was "Amaziah" to show that it rhymed with the first.

Ḥabib's treatise in general is most interesting, and one might elsewhere pause longer on these and other details of his exposition. But our subject here is Ḥabib's *influence*, and specifically the role of these few lines in what was to develop into a full-blown theory of sixteenth- and seventeenth-century biblical scholarship, namely, the idea that biblical poetry was not metrical in the Greco-Latin sense, but merely counted the number of syllables per line without regard to quantity; and—quite closely related to this—the idea that biblical poetry contains rhyme, or even (in the extreme formulation) that rhyme *alone* is the structural principle on which biblical songs were composed.

Other Hebrew writers had of course addressed these questions, some more directly and in greater detail than Ḥabib. Surely this is true in regard to rhyme. A fragment attributed to R. Sa'adya Gaon, while dismissing rhyme as a regular feature of biblical style, nevertheless cited three verses where rhyme is to be found: Job 28:15, Job 21:4, and Is. 49:1.[20] Moses ibn Ezra took up this list for his *Kitāb al-muḥāḍara*, but, significantly, dropped the last and added Job 33:17 in its place. (Perhaps Ibn Ezra preferred not to attribute a poetic device to a "non-poetic" book like Isaiah, for he believed the poetry of the Bible to be confined to the books of Psalms, Proverbs and Job, with their special system of "poetic" punctuation, plus a few scattered songs in the Pentateuch and Prophets.)[21] Meanwhile, the thirteenth-century tract *Kuntrus be-Dikduk Sfat Ever* asserted that rhyme is "hinted at" in the Bible: its examples are I Kings 8:57 and Is. 63:17.[22]

After Ḥabib, the sixteenth-century poet and grammarian Samuel Archivolti took up the subject of rhyme in his *Arugat ha-Bosem* (1602). "And now," he wrote, "to demonstrate that rhyme was conceived and born in sanctity, consider the following examples . . . ." He then cites Deut. 32:6, Ju. 14:18, Ps. 115:8, Prov. 31:18, Prov. 15:15, Ps. 2:3, "and many others."[23] Abraham b. David Portaleone (1542–1612) also wrote about rhyme. After having confessed his inability to find an exact metrical system in biblical songs, he noted:

> However, I am unable to overlook the fact that in certain ancient *meshalim* which resemble poems I have found rhymes at the end of the lines. But the number of their syllables is in general not equal, as in this case (Num. 21:27ff.): *bo'u ḥeshbon*, four syllables with a rhyme-word at the end, *tibane ve-tikonen ir siḥon*, which are ten syllables with a rhyme-word almost fitting the first; *ki esh yatz'a mi-ḥeshbon*, eight syllables with a true rhyme to the first line of four syllables, *lehava mi-kiryat siḥon*, also eight syllables with a true rhyme to the rhyme word of the ten-syllable line; *akhla ar mo'av*, six syllables without a rhyme. *Ba'alei bamot arnon* is likewise six syllables if the *ayin* of *ba'alei* is muted; this line also has a similar-looking rhyme, although I am aware that *arnon* is not a true rhyme with *siḥon.*[24]

He was apparently not bothered by the fact that all the "true rhymes" of this passage consisted of actual repetitions of the same word!

Beyond these (and perhaps other) specific assertions, the widespread notion among all Jews that rhyme was a truly wonderful invention, an aid to memory and indeed the essence of poetry—fed by the confusion whereby *ḥaruz* was used not only to mean "rhyme" but also "poetry" and "line of metrical verse" in Abravanel and others—certainly would have led Jews to prize any sort of rhyme they might hit upon in the Bible, and to foster the notion that, however sparingly, this feature might be found in the "poetic" books of their sacred Scripture. Amongst all these authorities, Ḥabib's brief tale—which does not specifically mention rhyme, but only implies it in the remark about "Amaziah" at the end of the second line—seems an unlikely source on which to base a theory of biblical rhyme.

About meter, too, there had been other (some more detailed) expositions than Ḥabib's brief remarks, most notably Samuel ibn Tibbon's discussion of biblical poetics in the introduction to his commentary on Ecclesiastes (which was, in fact, a direct or indirect source of Ḥabib's words).[25] It was echoed in Moses ibn Tibbon's Song of Songs commentary and Immanuel of Rome's Song of Songs commentary. Abravanel discussed biblical poetry in his commentaries,[26] and Azariah de Rossi devoted a chapter—later to be a famous treatment—to the subject in *Me'or Enayim* (citing Ḥabib among his sources).[27] But especially among Renaissance Christian scholars of Hebrew, Ḥabib's little treatise was uniquely well-known. The words of Gilbert Genebrardus (1537–1597), bishop of Aix and an outstanding scholar and translator of Hebrew, are indicative:

> On this question [of biblical poetics] the Hebrews are silent—they say they do not know the method of scansion. . . . As far as I know, only R. Moses Ḥabib deals with this matter: The sacred songs of the ancients [he says], such as those in Psalms, Job, and Proverbs, are distichs. Some of these are measured by a specific number of syllables, so that the first verse will now be longer than the second, now shorter, as the genius of the author moved him. Others consist of equal measure, except that occasionally the first verse will differ from the second in the exact number of syllables, but not in their time. But this difference is compensated through having them sound the same to the ear and through the motions of the throat, or else the melody and allurements of the voice will absorb the inequality (as, in Latin or Greek, a tribrachus is used in place of an iamb, a dactyl or an anapest in place of a spondee, and for a dactyl, a proceleumaticus, etc.) These afterwards he illustrates with examples from Psalms 119, 146, Proverbs and Job 6.[28]

Perhaps because the ideas of some (like Abravanel) were too obscure, and those of others (like Samuel and Moses ibn Tibbon) insufficiently *systematic*, Ḥabib's remarks had a special appeal to Christian scholars. His assertion of syllabic equivalence surely pleased those who searched for the *ratio scandendi* of Hebrew poetry, yet his "second type" provided an escape clause: approximate equivalence was enough. Moreover, the imputation of syllabic equivalence *but not quantitative meters* to the Bible, and to an equal extent, the idea of biblical rhyme, were notions some Christian readers were most eager to hear. Why?

These questions were crucial to the Renaissance for one simple reason: vernacular poetry. For while there were some scattered attempts to apply classical, unrhymed prosody to the emergent poetries of French, Italian, English and other vernacular tongues, by and large poets in these languages wrote in systems decidedly *un*-classical—lines without "long" and "short" syllables but based solely on the total number of syllables, or stresses, or some combination; plus *rhyme*. Did this not doom vernacular poetry to being forever the inferior of classical verse? Perhaps not. For while the Renaissance was inclined to defer to the cultural superiority of Greece and Rome, there was one civilization with as great (or greater) a pedigree, biblical Israel. If it could be shown that the poetry of the Bible consisted not of *metrum* ("meter" in the sense of Greco-Latin quantitative systems) but, like vernacular poetry, contained merely *numerus*,[29] this would provide the vernacular systems with an important precedent and justification. Moreover, if it could be shown that the Bible occasionally *rhymed*, the presence of rhyme in vernacular poetry would be, far from a defect, an instance of its superiority to classical Greek and Latin verse.

The first Christian scholar to advance precisely this argument was the Italian Hebraist Augustinus Steuchus of Gubbio (1496–1549), who, in the preface to his commentary on the Psalter, wrote:

> Hebrew poetry is not the same as that of the Greeks and Latins, just as Italian, or Etruscan,[30] is not the same as Latin. And indeed, Hebrew has more in common with Italian than with Latin. For Latin, in imitation of Greek, takes into account the times of the syllables; Hebrew does not account times but at most the number (*numerus*) and the similarity of the ending syllables. Just as in Italian poetry there is no such thing as a spondee, or a trochee, or a dactyl, but only the counting of so many

syllables and the taking care that they end in the same way, so similarly is it in Hebrew.[31]

Steuchus does not specifically connect his statement with any Hebrew source, and certainly there were many writers who might have suggested to him that biblical poetry had *numerus* but not *metrum.* But one likely source was certainly *Darkhei No'am.*[32] In the matter of biblical rhyme in particular, perhaps the influence of Ḥabib's rhyming tombstone anecdote is to be seen; Ḥabib's presence in the Italian peninsula is suggestive in this regard.[33]

Similar sentiments were voiced by another Italian, Marianus Victorius of Rieti (d. 1572), who edited and annoted Jerome's *Letters.* In a scholion to Epistle 117, he fixed on a phrase in Jerome's distinguishing of prophetic from poetic style:

[Jerome says:] "Or think anything similar to what is the case with the Psalms or the works of Solomon": The Psalms [in Latin] have the sort of brief aphoristic utterances (*sententiae*) which are the mark of verses in Hebrew; therefore they admit neither periods [i.e. periodic sentence structure] nor any uninterrupted discourse [as, by inference, do the works of Isaiah et al., from which Jerome is distinguishing the Psalms]. They do not, however, proceed by being confined to the rules of metrical feet, as is done in Greek or Latin, but go along in the same manner as, in Etruscan, as they now call [Italian], those songs which are called "loose."[34] Such is the case in the works of Solomon, especially the Song of Songs, in which you will find not only the ideas broken up in the manner of verse, but also the ends corresponding to the middle [of the verse], as in: *apiryon asa LO ha-melekh ShloMO*,[35] "A litter did King Solomon make for himself." Of this manner are amongst us those songs which are called *leonine*,[36] such as those lines in the apse of Saint Peter's above his tomb in Rome, which read as follows: Summa Dei *sedes* haec est, sacra Principis *aedes.* Mater cuncat*arum* decus, & decor ecclesi*arum.*"[37]

If Ḥabib's influence on Steuchus and Victorius can only be inferred, it was direct and obvious in the work of the seventeenth-century Hebraist Johannes Buxtorf I. Buxtorf added a small treatise and his immense reputation to Ḥabib's ideas—or his version of them. The treatise, "Tractatus Brevis de Prosodia Metrica," was appended to Buxtorf's *Thesaurus Grammaticus*[38] and widely circulated. One interesting facet of Buxtorf's approach is that he mingles everything together—medieval Hebrew terminology (*delet, soger, bayit*) is used to describe biblical lines, and medieval Hebrew meters are described in terms of Greek metrics (thus *Adon Olam* consists of "an iamb and spondee alternately placed").

He begins by asserting that the Bible contains poetry—he cites specifically Psalms, Proverbs, Job, Exodus 15, Deuteronomy 32, the Song of Deborah, (but not David's Song [II Sam. 22], perhaps because he includes it among the Psalms [i.e. Psalm 18]), then two of the Church's long-recognized canticles, I Sam. 2 (Hannah's prayer) and the third chapter of Habakkuk. He notes that biblical poetry has long been discussed, and cites Jerome's *Preface* to Job and Josephus' remarks about Exodus 15.[39] "But although the method and skillful organization of sacred meter began to be neglected shortly after the time of the Prophets, and thence, with the ancient wisdom of the Hebrews more and more on the decline, alas finally was cast into a shameful oblivion amongst them, nevertheless we shall have a few words to say of its general characteristics, and explain in greater detail the system of metrical speech in common use."[40]

He then defines poetic *numerus* as being either *metrum* or *rhythmus. However, metrum* according to Buxtorf means not only the Greco-Latin quantitative system, but any system that counts the total number of syllables as well. What then is *rhythmus*? To Buxtorf it means rhyme,[41] either an individual rhyme or rhyme as an organizing principle of poetry:

Meter [in the Bible] consists of a certain specific number of syllables, according to R. Mosche Schem Tobh [ibn Ḥabib] and other Hebrews; the sacred poem is represented in the highest degree by the books of Job, Psalms and Proverbs, as well as several of the canticles of the sacred. Here, depending on the idea, a metrical line is completed with a single half-verse [*versus*], or by two hemistichs, or even three or four strung together so that one פסוק or verse will include a tristichon or tetrastichon.

Each hemistich has either an equal number of syllables, or else one or the other will go beyond the number. [He gives examples from Job 3:10, 5:27; Prov.1:8 10:5, and Ps. 119:146, 146:6.] Of the exceeding meter, that is when one hemistich or the other has a greater number of syllables, there are infinite examples, and almost all the sacred songs are so defined, in which either the extra number is absorbed by a speeding up of the time-measuring, or the deficiency is filled out and made complete by a smooth varying and drawing-out of the voice.

So far, this is a paraphrase of ibn Ḥabib. But now he comes to the matter of rhyme and its different classes.

Rhyming verse [*rhythmus*] was not cultivated in a manner other than what might be produced spontaneously and happen quite by chance,[42] not that it seem to be summoned up by some belabored attention; yet not infrequently, especially in the case of David, we have noticed its occurrence, of whom we have previously heard Jerome saying that a certain *rhythmus* [43] and jingling [*tinnulus*] may be heard [in the Psalms], as:

Job. 21:4 האנכי לאדם שיחי ואם מדוע לא תקצר רוחי.

Psalm 105:20-21 שלח מלך ויתירהו משל עמים ויפתחהו.
שמו אדון לביתי ומשל בכל קנינו.

Psalm 106:5 לראות בטובת בחיריך לשמח בשמחת גויך
להתהלל עם נחלתך.

Prov. 24:19 אל תתחר במרעים אל תקנא ברשעים.

If in this poetry there was any other system of ordering, as perchance the hidden arrangement of טעמים [44] would indicate, from hoary antiquity it lies buried in oblivion with the Hebrew sages. Thus was the, as it were, infancy of this sacred poetry bound solely by the number of the syllables, which popular practice then polished with the sweetness of rhyme and more exact arrangement. So may it be observed in other peoples, that early poetry was delimited solely by *rhythmus*, without any measuring of longs or shorts.

Somewhat later, Buxtorf recounts Ibn Ḥabib's tale of the rhyming tombstone:

Rhyming verse (*rhythmus*) is a poetic arrangement (*numerus*) containing a specific number of syllables and ending with specific concluding parts; this is called חרז or חירוז and thence, שיר חרוזי rhyming poetry . . . .R. Moshe Shem Tov from the celebrated Ḥabib family, which flourished at one time in Spain, wrote in the pamphlet לשון מרפא that he had seen, during his long wanderings, on a certain high mountain the tombstone of Amaziah the king of the Jews, on which he was able to read these words incised, the rest having been obliterated by age:

שאו קינה בקול מרה לשר גדול לקחו י-ה
לאמציה

He understood from the similar ending of these words, that rhyming verse was then in use at the time when the Israelites still dwelt in their own land.[45]

Here a host of possible misprisions seem to come into play. Jerome's "rhythmus," rhythmical effect, is taken here to mean "rhyming verse." Of the illustrations that follow, the first is one of Sa'adya's rhymes (a coincidence?); the illustrations from Psalm 105 are, however, certainly Buxtorf's own discovery. (The rhyme *beito-kinyano* was hardly suitable by the Judeo-Arabic standard.) Then, in the tombstone story (it was not Amaziah's grave in Ḥabib's version but that of his general) the line is apparently split into four and misread as a quatrain with the rhyme scheme: aaba.[46] Thus:

se'u kina
be-kol mara
le-sar gadol
lekaḥo yah

Ḥabib's story had originally been intended to prove that Spanish-style verse—the system of *tenu'ot* and *yetedot*—existed in biblical times. But Buxtorf apparently read it as proof that the system of vernacular poetry of his own day—based on rhyme and syllable-counting—had biblical ancestry.

In the late sixteenth and seventeenth centuries, Ḥabib's view—or, rather, the view attributed to Ḥabib by Buxtorf and others—became widely accepted: biblical poetry was not analogous to classical Latin verse, but to vernacular European poetries, based on the number of syllables and, perhaps, rhyme. Thus Immanuel Tremellius, an Italian Jewish convert to Christianity, and F. Junius, wrote in their translation of the Bible:

We shall call these books [the poetic books of the Bible] by the collective name "Psalms," for they are *rythmici*, written not in prose, as all the other books (although even in these the elegant canticles of Moses, Deborah, David, Isaiah, Ezekiel [a mistake for Hezekiah], Jeremiah and Habakkuk are interspersed) but written in verse [*numerus*] for the ease of the memory and song.[47]

Similar views were expressed by J. J. Scaliger, and later G. J. Vossius, Wasmuth, Kircher and others.[48] Louis Cappel, in his influential treatise *Arcanum Punctuationis Revelatum* (1624), cited Ḥabib's role:

Buxtorf, in his *Hebrew Prosody*, follows Rabbi Moses the son of Shem Tov in his pamphlet called *Darkhei No'am*, pages 21 and 22. He says the sacred poem of Job, Psalms and Proverbs are composed of meters which are based solely on a fixed number of syllables, such that in most a single פסוק or verse comprises two hemistichs, or more rarely, three or four.

On occasion it may occur that the first hemistich will equal in the number of syllables the second of the same verse, but if this should happen it is due to chance rather than to any effort or definite plan on the part of the writer.[49]

These ideas were of some importance to the whole undertaking of Renaissance literature. Not only was "David the shepherd poet" an important model for the Renaissance defender of poetic art, but the rather more polemical notion of Hebrew poetry's equality with, or superiority to, Greek and Latin verse (and the corresponding exaltation of vernacular systems *which were like Hebrew*) was critical. As Milton noted in the *Reason of Church Government*, "Those frequent songs throughout the law and prophets . . . not in their divine argument alone, but in the very critical art of composition, may be easily made appear over all the kinds of lyrick poesy to be incomparable."[50] And in *Paradise Regain'd* he chastened the style of ancient Greek poetry:

Remove their swelling Epithetes thick laid
As varnish on a Harlots cheek, the rest
Thin sown with aught of profit or delight
Will far be found unworthy to compare
With Sion's songs . . .

IV 343-7

On this issue was Milton's stance as a divine poet, a recipient of "the inspired gift of God, rarely bestowed, but yet to some (though most abuse) in every Nation"[51] partially predicated.

One cannot leave the theme of *Darkhei No'am*'s direct and indirect descendents without mentioning what was surely the most learned treatment of the subject of biblical rhyme—that put forth by Jean Le Clerc (Joannes Clericus), a well-known biblical critic of the late seventeenth century. It was published first in French in *La Bibliothèque universelle* in 1688, and later translated into Latin and included in Le Clerc's *Veteris Testamenti Prophetae.*

Ḥabib's ideas were certainly known to Le Clerc, if only in translation and restatement by the Buxtorfs, F. Gomarus, and Louis Cappel (all of whom he specifically mentions). In an apparent allusion to Ḥabib and Cappel, Le Clerc notes at the outset: "Certain learned men, when they found evidence of rhyming verses here and there in the poetical books of the Old Testament, believed these to owe their origin to mere chance and not to any deliberate effort on the part of Scripture. The following, however, will show the falsity of this view." For Le Clerc was convinced that rhyming in the Bible was not only deliberate, but in fact the sole structural constant of biblical poetry.

He begins by arguing that it is not in the nature of Semitic languages to create a truly metrical poetry, because they are ill-suited to distinguishing between long and short syllables. Moreover, Hebrew, because word-order is fixed by such features as noun constructs, does not have the flexibility necessary for metrical compositions. Therefore, there is no sense in looking for a Greco-Latin style metrical system. On the other hand, rhyme is extraordinarily easy in Hebrew. He points out that rhyme is favored in the poetry of other Semites, and mentions the three classes of rhyme in medieval Hebrew.[52] It is only natural to conclude that it might then have had some place in biblical poetry as well; however, the fact is that the Bible's concept of rhyme was somewhat freer than that of later poetry: thus in Psalm 1 one finds *yehegeh* rhyming with *palgei*, and *mishpat* with *adat(h)*.[53] No wonder that, as the conventions of rhyme tightened up and true *numerus*, the measuring of syllabic equivalence, entered world poetry, the more flexible and primitive system of the Bible was overlooked.

Le Clerc gives various illustrations of biblical rhyme, including the "rhyming" section of Psalm 2 mentioned by earlier commentators[54]

Eth mosrotheMO
Venaschlica mimmennou abotheMO
Joscheb baschamajim jischAK
Adonai jilAG
LaMO
Az jedabber eleMO
Baappho oubacharono jebahaleMO

The fact that the unusual suffix "MO" replaces the more normal *-HEM* indicates, Le Clerc says, that rhyme was cultivated and not accidental (here he is apparently arguing against Buxtorf's treatise); the same is proven by the use of rare words and forms elsewhere in the biblical poetry corpus.[55] He also cites Psalm 150 as a fine "brief" example of rhyme. Acknowledging Cappelus' misgivings about the accuracy of Masoretic vocalization,[56] Le Clerc says there may be many other rhymes whose existence is obscured by artificial differences in the vowel points; nevertheless, enough evidence exists to leave no doubt about the role of rhyme as the sole structural element in biblical poetry. Elsewhere, Le Clerc gave a still more impressive demonstration of biblical rhyme, dividing up Deut. 32 according to its true units;[57] here is the beginning:

1. haazinu haššamaim vaadabberah
vetišmaע
haarez imrɛ pi.
2. jaערop cammaṭar likḥi,
tizzal caṭṭal imrati;
cisעirim
עale deše, vecirbibim
עale עeseb. 3. ci šem jahavoh
ekra; habu
godel l'elohɛ̣nu.
4. hazzur tamim poעolo,
ci col deracau mišpaṭ, el
emunah veɛn עavel;
zaddik vejašar hu.

Le Clerc's theory did gain some admirers, but eventually it was noticed that any part of the Bible may be made to rhyme as well as the Psalms or Deut. 32. Thus T. Edwards' *Psalms* (1755) observed:

> If it be considered that, according to [Le Clerc's] hypothesis, the historical as well as poetical parts of the old testament may be reduced into rhyme, this most evidently shows it to be entirely visionary [i.e. illusory]: which would still farther appear, were the learned reader to consult a specimen of it, at the end of Bishop Hare's Psalms[58] in which, (not to mention that some of the verses are so far from rhyming to each other, that there is not the least similitude of sound in the last syllables) he will soon, very soon be convinced, that the rhymes are not the inspired Poet's but Le Clerc's.[59]

With that, Le Clerc's theory of rhyme in the Bible was dismissed as "evidently fantastical."

The refutation of Le Clerc quickly brought biblical rhyme into well-deserved disrepute, and so at least one aspect of *Darkhei No'am*'s extraordinary after-life came to an end. The idea of biblical meter, however, to which Ḥabib, along with the Tibbonides, Azariah de Rossi and other Hebrew writers contributed, is still with us. It is, in this writer's opinion, equally ill-founded, based on a similar attempt to "discover" later poetic systems in writing that not only did not know meter, but even had no concept corresponding to that Greek notion "poetry." If, in this respect, Ḥabib's brief words on biblical poetry have had a less than beneficial effect on the course of biblical scholarship, the loss must be weighed against the salutary results in the history of European literature. No doubt Renaissance vernacular poetry would have marched on tolerably well without Ḥabib's tale of the rhyming tombstone; but did not he, and other Renaissance Jewish writers on biblical poetry, play a significant role in legitimating the rhymes and "numbers" of European verse in the eyes of the world?

NOTES

1. Joel Spingarn, *Literary Criticism in the Renaissance* (New York, 1899, reprinted 1963), page 1.

2. See especially Boccaccio's "Genealogy of the Gods" (*Opere*, ed. G. Ricci, Milan, 1965; see pp. 946–8 and 1010) and Petrarch's *Epistolae de rebus familiaris* X, 4 and XXII, 10; the former passage is translated in J.H. Robinson, *Petrarch the First Modern Scholar* (New York, 1907) pp. 261–4. For Poliziano see his poem "Nutricia" in *Prose volgare e poesie latine e grecche* (Florence, 1867) page 384, and Minturno's *De Poeta* (Venice, 1559) page 9. All of these invoke biblical "poets" to justify the poet's craft. Later on this theme passed into other literatures, notably English; see the well known "Defenses" of poetry by Lodge, Puttenham and Sidney.

3. This statement is found in Boccaccio (loc. cit.) and, later, in Tasso; see W.K. Wimsatt and C. Brooks, *Literary Criticism: A Short History* (New York, 1957) p. 152.

4. See in general my article, "Some Medieval and Renaissance Ideas about Biblical Poetry," *Studies in Medieval Jewish History and Literature*, I. Twersky ed. (Cambridge, 1979), pp. 57–81.

5. *Commentary on the Pentateuch*, *ad* Exod. 15:1.

6. The title comes from Prov. 3:17, "Its [wisdom's] ways are ways of pleasantness, and all its paths are peace." The roots *n'm* (be pleasant) and *nğm* (make music), while still separate in Arabic, had come together in biblical Hebrew. Obviously Ḥabib is playing on this "musical" sense of the verse: his title really means, "The Ways of Poetry."

7. *Darkhei No'am* was published by Daniel Bomberg in Venice in 1564 and again by Wolf Heidenheim in Roedelheim, 1806.

8. Written by David b. Yom Tov Bilia (Villa?) in the fourteenth century. An edition of it appeared in *Kovetz al Yad* 16 (1966), 225–46, edited by N. Allony.

9. Printed in A. Neubauer, *Melekhet ha-Shir* (Frankfurt, 1865). E. Carmoli attributes it to Abshalom Mizraḥi, but see Neubauer, page iv.

10. Published in Constantinople (1506), this work has been attributed to M. Kimḥi and D. ibn Yaḥya; H. Yalon, in his critical edition of the text (Jerusalem, 1965) argues forcefully that it is the work of S. Almoli.

11. See also Yehuda ha-Levi's Arabic treatise on meter, published by H. Schirmann in *Yedi'ot ha-Makhon le-ḥeker ha-Shira* 6 (1946), pp. 319–322; Sa'adya b. Maimun ibn Danaan's "Chapter on Meter" in *al-Ḍarūri fi al-lugha al-'ibrāniyya* (1473)—see the Hebrew translation in Neubauer, *Melekhet ha-Shir* (Frankfurt, 1865) pp. 1–18; and Menaḥem Tamar's *Shir ha-Shirim*, which was apparently published in the first half of the sixteenth century in Salonika. It is cited by Carmoli and mentioned in Yalon's edition of *Shekel ha-Kodesh*, page 14n.

12. See al-Fārābī, *Fuṣūl al-madanī*, ed. D. M. Dunlop (Cambridge, Eng., 1961) pp. 135–136, English version pp. 49–50.

13. Moses ibn Tibbon's preface to his *Song of Songs Commentary* lists three classes of poetry (ed. Lyck, 1874, p. 7), as does Immanuel of Rome's commentary to the same book (Frankfurt, 1908, page 5); Immanuel's classification, which comes directly from Ibn Tibbon's, begins: "It is well known to every learned man that the classes of song are three in number." Abravanel's three-fold classification of poetry is to be found in his commentaries on Exodus 15:1 and Isaiah 5:1; a quite different three-fold classification of poetry, embracing Prophecy, words of Divine Inspiration, and medieval Hebrew verse, is to be found in Falaqera's *Book of the Seeker* (*Sefer ha-Mevakesh*), "Meeting with the Poet." The ultimate source of these three-fold classifications is Aristotle's *Poetics*; see my *The Idea of Biblical Poetry* (New Haven, 1981), p. 193 n.

14. The source of Ḥabib's classification, in my view, is Samuel ibn Tibbon's preface to his *Commentary on Ecclesiastes.* (Several manuscripts of this work are extant, but it has never been published; a brief excerpt, precisely the passage in question, was cited by Judah Moscato in his Commentary on Yehuda ha-Levi's *Kuzari* entitled *Kol Yehuda* [Venice, 1594 and subs.] *ad* Part II, 70.) Samuel ibn Tibbon argued that biblical poetry had no meter (the same view is found in the *Kuzari,* loc. cit.) but that verse-halves were roughly equivalent and that melody and vocal rendition could smooth over any slight inequalities in performance. This same statement is found in his son Moses' *Song of Songs Commentary* and subsequently; it was only a short hop from this view of things to *Darkhei No'am*, where Ḥabib, by counting syllables, found a few scattered cases of actual equivalence for which the smoothing-out of music and voice was unnecessary.

15. Dan Pagis has pointed out about this list that Ḥabib was the first to attribute to the *sheva* independent status as a syllable; see his "Hebrew Metrics in Italy and the Invention of Hebrew Accentual Iambs," *Ha-Sifrut* 4 (1973), p. 686.

16. The precise difference between *shir* and *shira* in different periods is an interesting question. Apparently in rabbinic times there was no clear technical sense to the distinction; hence the possibility of the homiletical distinction drawn in *Mekhilta de-R. Ishma'el* (Tractate *Shirta*, 1): "All these songs (*shirot*) of the past are called by the feminine form, since just as the female gives birth so were these past salvations followed by subjugation; but the salvation to come has no subjugation after it, hence it is called by the masculine form (*shir*)" (see Lauterbach ed., vol. 2, pp. 6–7). In Spain both words were understood as describing the nature of a composition (*viz.*, "poetry") rather than merely the manner of performance (something sung); this was certainly strengthened by the similar sounding but etymologically distinct Arabic *shi'r*, "poetry." The nuance implied by the term *shira*, according to *Shekel ha-Kodesh*, is length; it consists of ten lines or more. But this does not seem to reflect biblical usage, for it apparently contradicts the use of *shira* in Nu. 21:17. The four biblical *shirot* par excellence (mentioned above by Ḥabib) were commonly singled out by special stichography even when this practice began to die out for other passages, especially after the sixteenth century: see M. Breuer, "Ketivat ha-Shirot" in his *Keter Aram Tzova* (Jerusalem, 1976) pp. 149–189. Note also that Ḥabib and others use the word *shir* to mean "line of verse" as well as "song" or "poem." *Shira* meant "song" (as opposed to *shir* "poem") to Moses ibn Tibbon (op. cit.) and others.

17. In general, it had been maintained by Yehuda ha-Levi, the Tibbonides, Sa'adya ibn Danaan etc. that meter as they knew it was an Arab invention, "*ḥokhmat ha-aravim*," and so forth (see my above-cited "Some Medieval and Renaissance Ideas" for a summary). Those who implied that there was some *system* to biblical poetry felt it was quite different from the "Arabic" system. The precise import of Ḥabib's incident was to show that antiquity of Arabic-style meters in Hebrew, and to imply that the Arabs learned their system from the Jews. The same was argued by the author of *Shekel ha-Kodesh* "About this craft [of metrical poetry] we do not know of a single one of our sages who discussed it and did not conclude that its roots lay among the Ishmaelites, for [they say] from them did we take it, and [the proof is] they are most adept at it. But I myself believe that on the contrary everything the Ishmaelites know of this craft they took from the sages of our nation, just as they took their somewhat confused language from the Holy Tongue." See H. Yalon; ed., *Shekel ha-Kodesh*, pp. 52–3.

18. On Murviedro (Murvedre, etc.) see A. Chabret, *Sagunto: su historia y sus monumientos* (1880); also L. Piles Ros, "La Juderia de Sagunto," *Sefarad* 17 (1957), pp. 352–73.

19. On the inscription see F. Cantera—J.M. Millas, *Las Inscripciones hebraicas de España* (Madrid, 1956) pp. 294–303. Cantera and Millas here reproduce the text of Ḥabib's remarks (from the Venice, 1546 edition, folio 7) and then cite the further reports of later historians and travelers who were shown the supposed inscription. Cantera and Millas associate Ḥabib's story with an actual extant stone (of, however, later origin: the word read as *Amaziah* they correct to *amatzim*, or perhaps "(V)alencia") and explain the townspeople's attribution of the stone to biblical times as local legend-making, woven around the phrase *sar gadol* (great chief); cf. the "Adoniram inscription" discussed in *Inscripciones*, p. 313ff.

20. See N. Allony, ed., *Sefer ha-Egron* (Jerusalem, 1968), pp. 386–389.

21. Moses ibn Ezra, *Kitab al-muḥāḍara wal-mudhākara*, ed. Halkin (Jerusalem, 1975), pp. 46–47. Apparently, Sa'adya did not believe poetry (i.e. *shi'r*) to be a relevant category for the Bible, but had a more evolutionary view of style; see *Ha-Egron*, loc. cit. The notion that Job, Proverbs and Psalms were—by reason of their special *te'amim* (Masoretic punctuation)—the "poetic" books of the Bible was quite widespread; see, for example, S. al-Ḥarizi, "Taḥkemoni" in H. Schirmann, ed., *Ha-Shira ha-Ivrit bi-Sfarad* . . . (Jerusalem, 1955) 2: 133; Moses ibn Tibbon, *Song of Songs Commentary*, p. 7; Immanuel of Rome, *Song of Songs Commentary*, p. 5. It is still not clear why these special *te'amim* were used for these books and not others (since, in the common view, biblical "poetry" now embraces far more than these three). In any event it is significant that Christian Hebraists not only received this association of these books with poetry, but even designated them as the *libri metrici*. See J. Le Mercier (Mercerus), *Commentarii in Iobum, et Salomonis Proverbia* . . . (Lugduni Batavorum, 1551), (unnumbered) preface and p. 19; Valentinus Schindler, *Institutionum Hebraicorum*, p. 320; and many later writers.

22. S Poznanski, ed., *Kuntrus be-Dikduk Sfat Ever* (Berlin, 1894).

23. S. Archivolti, *Arugat ha-Bosem* (Amsterdam, 1729), p. 102.

24. A. Portaleone, *Shiltei ha-Giborim* (Mantua, 1612) p. 3b. Portaleone then goes on to scan Numbers 21:17 ("The Song of the Well") which, with some juggling, he manages to find "with equal numbers of syllables" though "lacking rhyme."

25. See above, note 14.

26. *Ad* Exodus 15 and Isaiah 5.

27. Azariah in fact cites the entire tombstone story, and apparently agrees "that our sacred tongue, by reason of both its nature and use, did not in ancient times abhor this metrical type of poetry; indeed, this was manifest not only in the music to which these songs were sung, as Don Isaac [Abravanel] writes, but also from the standpoint of the words themselves; in fact, some such are to be found in the Bible." See Azariah de Rossi, *Meor Enayim*, ed. Cassel (Vilnius, 1866), p. 208. This passage of *Meor Enayim*, containing the Ḥabib excerpt, was reprinted by Johannes Buxtorf II in an appendix to his translation of the *Kuzari*, thus further diffusing the tombstone anecdote.

28. G. Genebrardus, *Chronographiae libri VI* (Paris, 1600) pp. 109–110. Note how Genebrardus has broadened Ḥabib's "syllabic equivalence" class to include isochronic lines; perhaps he is reading into Ḥabib and idea from Jerome's description of biblical poetry—see below.

29. A vaguer and more general term. In some classical texts it is used as a synonym of *metrum*, but it also had the sense of *any* poetic system, and particularly one which counted the number of syllables alone without regard to vowel quantity. See on this matter I. Baroway, "The Accentual Theory of Hebrew Prosody" in *English Literary History* 17 (1950), pp. 115–35. (On this and other questions Baroway's article has been a valuable source. It is to be noted, however, that this article is deficient in its understanding of the meaning of *accentum* in the texts cited: this term clearly refers to the Masoretic *te'amim*, and the "accentual theory" Baroway discusses is in fact non-existent. Moreover, the construction of poetic lines on the principle of equal numbers of syllables does not mean that the line is therefore accentual [witness the French *alexandrin*]. This is a serious misunderstanding.)

30. Another name for Italian (i.e., the vernacular tongue).

31. A. Steuchus Eugubinus, *Ennarationum in Nonnullos Psalmos Praefatio* (Venice, 1590), unpaged. Steuchus's remarks were later cited in L. Cappelus, *Arcanum Punctuationis Revelatum* (Lyon, 1624), pp. 96–97, and F. Gomarus, *Davidis Lyra*, reprinted in his *Opera Theologica Omina* (Amsterdam, 1664), page 314.

32. Note that Gomarus, in citing him (see above note), explicitly makes this connection: "Quibus praeire videtur vir doctissimus Augustinus Steuchus, episcopus Eugubinus (Rabbi Mosche ben Chabib in libro דרכי נועם, seu prosodiae secutus) quum sua praefatione in Psalmos ait quidem: Moses omnium vetustissimus carmen Deo cecinit . . . "

33. Apart from this, two other possible influences suggest themselves. First is the force of analogy between vernacular poetry, specifically Italian (which rhymed and counted syllables), and biblical verse. Did not songs which merely counted syllables *need* something more to bind one line to the next, something like rhyme? Second is the fact that Hebrew verse written by Italian Jews at this time had begun to adopt the syllabic rhyming meters of Italian Christians. Perhaps this is what led Steuchus to think biblical Hebrew incapable of basing its meters on syllabic quantities—the language by its very nature forbade it. See on the latter subject D. Pagis, "Hebrew Metrics in Italy . . .," *Ha-Sifrut* 4, pp. 650-712.

34. *Soluta*—"oratio soluta" was the common expression for prose. These songs are *soluta* in the sense of "free from metrical constraints," that is, not quantitative.

35. Song of Songs 3:9. The text here is written in Hebrew script in the Antwerp (1573) edition; however there are several mistakes in the Hebrew.

36. Leonine verses contain an internal rhyme, sometimes at the caesura; see below.

37. Marianus Victorius Reatinus, *Epistolae D. Hieronymi* (Antwerp, 1573), page 620.

38. J. Buxtorf, *Thesaurus Grammaticus* (Basle, 1629).

39. For Josephus see his *Jewish Antiquities* II, 16:14—"Moses also composed a song to God [Exodus 15] containing his praises and thanksgiving for his kindness, in hexameter verses" (cf. *Antiquities* IV 8:44 and VII 12:3, and Philo's remarks on Hebrew meter in *The Contemplative Life* sections 3, 10, 29–30; and in *Life of Moses* I, 23). Jerome discussed meter in several places (see J.P. Migne, *Patrologia Latina* 22:547; 25:295; 26;1258 28:825, 904, as well as the detailed pronouncements in his *Preface to Job* and *Epistle 30* [to Paula]). The passage in his *Preface to Job* was crucial because there, after having asserted Hebrew poetry to be metrical, he added: "Sometimes as well a sweet, jingling rhythmical effect is achieved by the poetic arrangement being set free from the laws of meter." (*Interdum quoque rhythmus ipse dulcis et tinnulus fertur numeris lege metri solutis*—the last phrase, incidentally, is an allusion to Horace's description of Pindar's poetry in one of his *Odes* [Book IV, Ode 2]: "Verba devolvit numerisque fertur/Lege solutis . . . .") This seemed to imply that Jerome recognized biblical poetry to be freer than classical prosody, more like the "lawless" Pindar or, indeed, vernacular poetry of the Renaissance. So Steuchus concluded from Jerome's words (see loc. cit.) and, later, J. J. Scaliger and others; see I. Baroway, op. cit.

40. Buxtorf, *Thesaurus Grammaticus*, page 627.

41. As seen in Jerome above, this word was used in a general sense to mean "rhythmical effect," or indeed (it being the Greek correspondent to Latin *numerus*) as a general term for poetic arrangement. The Renaissance however also associated it with the word "rhyme," and believed the latter term to be derived from it (hence our spelling of rhyme in English). In Latin texts of the sixteenth and seventeenth centuries, *rhythmus* thus can mean "a rhyme," "poetry that rhymes," or "(non-quantitative) meter," i.e. *numerus*.

42. Now this also comes from Ḥabib's words, but he speaks of one verse "agreeing" with another by chance, that is, *in the number of syllables*.

43. Thus Buxtorf misreads Jerome's *rhythmus* as having the Renaissance meaning of "rhyme."

44. The antiquity and significance of the *te'amim* was one of the great debates in biblical criticism of the period, and Buxtorf an enthusiastic participant. See C. D. Ginsburg's translation of Elijah Levita's *Massoret hammassoret* (1867, reprinted New York, 1968), pp. 102–143, and Ginsburg's copious introduction, especially pp. 44–48; also G. Weil, *Eli Lévita* (Leiden, 1963), page 315; P. G. Schneidermann, *Die Controverse des Ludovicus Cappellus mit den Buxtorfen* (Leipzig, 1879).

45. Buxtorf, ibid., page 636.

46. In Buxtorf's printed text, "le'amaṣiyah" is centered underneath the first line; apparently, he did not even think it was part of the "poem," but the name of the man buried. Buxtorf's son (more cautious on this whole question of biblical prosody) also divides this line into four in his Latin translation, separating each unit by a colon; but this may simply be his scansion of the line.

47. Tremellius and F. Junius, *Testamenti Vet. Biblia Sacra* (Hanover, 1603), 106. The "canticles" mentioned are Deut. 32 (and perhaps also Exodus 15), Judges 5, 2 Sam. 22, Isaiah 26, Isaiah 38, Lamentations (attributed to Jeremiah), Hab. 3.

48. See J. J. Scalinger, "Animadversiones in Prologum Hieronymi" in *Thesaurus Temporum Eusebii* (Amsterdam, 1658), II, pp. 6–7; G.J. Vossius, *De Artis Poeticae Natura ac Constiutione* (Amsterdam, 1647), page 77; M. Wasmuth, *Institutio Methodica Accentuationis Hebraicae* (Lipsia, 1694), page 14; Athanasius Kircherus, *Musurgia Universalis* (Rome, 1650), page 63; see also Grotius' Commentary on the New Testament *ad* Luke 4:61, and A. Calovius (1612–1682) "Prolegomenon in Genesin" and "Ad Lamentationes Praefatio," in his *Biblia Test. Vet.* (Dresden, 1719).

49. *Arcanum Punctationis Revelatum* (edidit Th. Erpenius; Lugduni Batavorum, 1624), page 101.

50. D. M. Wolfe (ed.), *Complete Prose Works of John Milton* (New Haven, 1953–66), vol. I, page 816. Milton's words here seem to come from Francis Junius' "Oratio de Lingua Hebraica": "One book of the Psalter, a single prophecy of Isaiah, has more truth, majesty, [etc.] . . . than all the Homers and Vergils, than all the books of the Demosthenes and Ciceros. Not by their argument alone (*non argumento solum*) (for who in good faith shall compare human tales and petty trifles with God's truth?) but by their very speech (*sed oratione ipsa*), which the Holy Spirit, author and originator of all grace, has tempered more judiciously for the advancement of their arguments . . . " (*Opera Theologica*, Geneva, 1613; vol. I, col. 10). Similarly, John Donne maintained that "David is a better poet than Vergil." (*Sermons of John Donne*, ed. Simpson and Porter, Berkeley, 1953, vol. IV, 167). This claim, that biblical poetry is *aesthetically* superior to other poetry, is not to be confused with the (rather common) contention that the Bible's polysignificant form of expression is superior to that of other texts, for this argument, whether in Augustine or Thomas Aquinas, is aimed at the *sensus spiritualis.* Thus Gregory, *Moralia* 20:1, "Holy Scripture by the manner of its speech transcends every science, because in one and the same sentence while it describes a fact, it reveals a mystery."

51. *Prose Works*, loc. cit.

52. On which see Allony's edition of *Sefer ha-Egron*, pp. 114–115; E. Goldenberg in *Leshonenu* 38 (1974), 86–87.

53. Joannes Clericus, *Veteris Testamenti Prophetae* (Amsterdam, 1731), vol. II, page 624. In connection with this last rhyme, it is to be noted that Le Clerc says that the Jews consider it a license to rhyme with two words which sound the same but whose rhymemes are different letters, such as סוכה and צוקה Now this example is also cited in Archivolti's *Arugat ha-Bosem*, loc. cit. It is interesting that Archivolti's second example of this principle, :מסה—מצה, is not cited: perhaps Le Clerc did not understand that these two words were pronounced identically by Italian Jewry.

54. See M. Flacius Illyricus, *Clavis Scripturae Sacrae* (Basle, 1609), page 308.

55. This same argument was used by Abravanel and others in regard to Exodus 15 to demonstrate that its language was ordered according to some principle of poetic structure; see his *Commentary* ad loc.

56. In *Arcanum Punctuationis* . . . ; the subject of vocalization was of course related to that of the *te'amim*; see above, note 41, and works cited therein.

57. This does not appear in the Latin version of his treatise; the version cited here is reprinted from F. Hare's *Psalmorum Liber* (London, 1736), Vol. II, page 834.

58. Cited in above note.

59. T. Edwards, *Psalms* (Cambridge, 1745), page 4.

Three Sixteenth-Century Attitudes to Judaism: Reuchlin, Erasmus and Luther

HEIKO A. OBERMAN

1. Introduction: The Plight of the Historian

During the sixteenth century, Europe made a hesitant but significant transition to modern times. This generalization does not apply to all of Europe nor to all facets of life, but in northern Europe we can notice a marked step forward in the understanding of human rights and in the advocacy of tolerance.[1] Reuchlin, Erasmus and Luther contributed to this development, each in his own way. From this advance, however, the Jewish communities hardly profited; the ideal of tolerance by-passed the Jews, geared only towards the coexistence of Christian factions within the fractured unity of a basically Christian society. In point of fact the ideal of tolerance grew very much at the expense of the Jews in northern Europe, particularly in Germany—at the expense of their social role, their legal status, and their religious liberties. Reuchlin, Erasmus and Luther contributed to this development as well; and again, each in his own way. Before we turn to the questions of how such diverse roles can be assigned to the same people, or how it can be justified to mention in one breath three such dissimilar historical figures, I have to comment upon the state of research in this highly sensitive field.

If I had to rank the factors that continue to obstruct our grasp of the interaction of the history of the Jews and the history of European society in the sixteenth century, I would not start with a complaint about the lack of sources and of reliable interpretive articles. Nor would I be inclined to mention the abundance, the baffling and at times indeed disgusting number of books and articles seemingly concerned with our theme but de facto utilizing the plight of the Jews to document the priority of economic forces which are claimed to underlie or even to determine Christian-Jewish relations in early modern Europe. In these cases research in depth is replaced by research into debts and indebtedness which, however, fails to solve the riddle why, symbolically speaking, the Fuggers merely met with scattered protests but not with pogroms. To be sure, economic considerations are necessary[2] when used in the service of that kind of intellectual history which one might call motivation research. It is important to note that the lower-strata 'Flugschriften' crying out for reform of society are often rabidly anti-Jewish, whereas positive statements are found among publicists close to the Emperor or to those 'Landesherren' who exercised the right to protect and tax the Jews in their territories. Nevertheless, the many exceptions all around warn us not to regard economic factors or social status as an historical determinant for the attitude to the Jews.

There exists today a more subtle and hence more formidable obstacle to research in our period, a silent and suppressed undercurrent in the treatment of our theme. To put the matter as simply as possible: We are writing history in the wake of the Nazi massacres. Historians have forced one another to hold out for an unconfessional presentation of the past; and at least we have learned to read the danger signs of treatments by colleagues who fall short of this scholarly ideal. Yet we are still so haunted by a nightmare which continues to be daylight reality, that in our field it is hard to find a middle ground between aggressive accusations and escapist apologies. If the historian's first task be to act as the final advocate for the dead, it is nearly impossible for him to distinguish between his role and his conscience; if the historian's second task be to act as public prosecutor, it is nearly impossible for him not to judge the past in order to prevent recurrence in the future. And worst of all, if it is true that both tasks, the advocate's and prosecutor's, presuppose a careful hearing of the sources as eye witnesses, it requires a more-than-human effort not to follow the relativizing escape route of 'attenuating circumstances'—attenuating for a single man like Martin Luther or for all northern Europe's hesitant history of tolerance, said to be the finest fruit of Renaissance humanism.

Under the impact of the all-too-recent epoch in the history of the diaspora, the typecasting by enlightened historians of the beginning of this century has fashioned a new orthodoxy: Reuchlin is the hero of emancipation, Pfefferkorn the fanatic, Luther the bigoted anti-Semite and Erasmus the father of tolerance and human dignity. Historians should bear in mind that even minor revisions in this script are suspect of heresy. At this point it is high time to abandon our concern with the historian and turn to history itself.

2. The Fictitious Triumvirate

In the scholarly tradition of the nineteenth century the Renaissance and the Reformation were still understood as kindred movements which together led Europe towards the emancipation from medieval patterns in life and thought. Today it is by no means obvious to rank Reuchlin, Erasmus and Luther together. Without being blind to interaction, derivations, and alliances we are acutely aware of the difference in motives and goals of these two, perhaps even three, programs of renewal. There is admittedly a significant element of historical truth in the typology of Johann Eberlin von Günzburg's (d.1533) *15 Bundsgenossen* (1521) which presents Reuchlin and Erasmus as forerunners of Luther: They have the "ersten stain gelegt alles hails."[3] We shall have to return to this point to grasp how Eberlin could have come to this view. But seen from close quarters the three 'forerunners' prove to have far less in common than what sets them apart.

Johannes Reuchlin (1455–1522), Desiderius Erasmus (1466[9?]–1536), and Martin Luther (1483–1546) differ in a number of respects. The first and seemingly most pedestrian is the fact that they flower and reach their zenith in three successive decades. And these are decades of crucial events and shifts in Europe's intellectual climate. Furthermore, Reuchlin is a son of southern Germany whose geographical ambiance runs basically from Pforzheim to Stuttgart and Tübingen. Erasmus, on the other hand, is in touch by letter and horse with the educated all over Europe, always at once in exile and at home. As he likes to put it: "My *patria* is where my library is," but particularly along the Rhine, for him the "fruitful mother carrying news and culture." As Reuchlin explicitly indicates in his letters of recommendation on behalf of Melanchthon to the Elector Frederick dated 25th July, 1518, he is very much aware that Erasmus is not a German: "In Germany I do not know anyone better [for this Greek chair than Melanchton] except for Erasmus, and *der ist ein Holländer*."[4] Luther, too, travelled widely but except for one trek on foot over the Alps to Italy he stayed within the boundaries of the Empire preferring solid land to rivers which for him had no positive meaning; at times swollen as if at the order of the devil, rivers thwarted his missions or prevented him from returning to his family. And thirdly, on that decisive point where career and motivation coincide Reuchlin is the literate jurist and German Pico,[5] Erasmus the philological ethicist, and Luther the prophetical and professional *Doctor Sacrae Scripturae.* Even in that momentous endeavor which Eberlin of Günzburg described as their common effort, namely the interpretation of Scripture on the basis of the original texts instead of the Vulgate, they differ most. Reuchlin is the only one to be truly *trilinguis*, with command of Hebrew, Greek and classical Latin. Erasmus for a time tried his hand at Hebrew but soon gave up invoking the shortness of life and the pressures of his many scholarly projects.[6] Luther came to know and respect Hebrew: "Lingua Ebraica est omnium optima . . . ac purissima . . . ,"[7] and he pitched its non-speculative clarity against Greek[8] without ever being so much at home with the language of Aristotle and Origen as later lore has it.

All these differences in age, origin, vocation and ability, were later overlooked by Eberlin and many scholarly generations to follow because of the wartime pact uniting Reuchlin, Erasmus and Luther against the *viri obscuri*, the past masters of scholasticism (Ortvinus Gratius) in alliance with the Dominican protectors of orthodoxy (the inquisitor Jacob Hochstraten). This alliance was still so firmly entrenched in the centers of power that it achieved a common lot for all three: Reuchlin and Luther were condemned in 1520; Erasmus' works were put on the *Index librorum prohibitorum* of Pope Paul IV in 1559 and, with some alterations, in subsequent editions as well.[9] Here indeed we may well have touched upon a significant feature, not in stance but in joint common effect, since nothing furthers the cause of intellectual freedom more than the proscription of books which continue to be read and respected.

Yet Reuchlin, Erasmus and Luther cannot be remodeled into a triumvirate merely because all three met with ecclesiastical censure: their motivations were too different. Reuchlin for one stood up for Hebrew wisdom, never attained by the pedestrian techniques of scholasticism.[10] Erasmus—in contrast with his disciples, the City reformers, and after his own 'Sturm und Drang' — came to lean back from antischolastic and anticlerical satire; he feared that such would not further the cause of the *bonae litterae*. Luther early declared himself against the 'infelices Colonienses,' the calamitous Doctors of Cologne.[11] But his line of attack differed from those of both Reuchlin and Erasmus; he did not assail the *magistri nostri* for matters of classical style or uncultured simplicity but in the name of biblical doctrine.[12] In 1522 Luther even made a point of saying that his own fight against scholasticism did not concern its lack of eloquence or erudition. As far as these two were concerned, he confessed: "Sum et ego barbarus."[13]

The one sound reason for regarding the triumvirate of legend and lore as an intellectual phalanx is their shared confidence that a fresh investigation of the biblical sources would yield that wisdom which, once recovered, was to restore pristine truth and thus renew church and society. Concomitant with this audacious vision is a shared anti-Judaism which could feed upon popular conceptions but—far from being merely a medieval survival—was with significant variations an organic part of their reform program with wide-reaching consequences for what was to develop into modern anti-Semitism. It is in their attitude to Jews and Judaism, I submit, that we can discern most clearly in what respects Reuchlin, Erasmus, and Luther did, or did not, transcend their times, and how beneath what later came to be proudly looked upon as a program for religious tolerance lay sobering origins.

3. Reuchlin and the Jews: Emanicpation and the Birth of a New Anti-Semitism

We have overcome our long-time preoccupation with *The Letters of Obscure Men* which encouraged the view of two warring camps, the 'humanists' versus the 'scholastics.' Paul Oskar Kristeller[14] and Charles Trinkaus[15] have pointed to the medieval roots of Renaissance humanism in Thomism and Nominalism. We know that we have only begun to trace the indebtedness of leading humanists to the 'schoolmen.' Reuchlin himself was not in doubt about the opposition's chief motive: he expected to be attacked for jeopardizing the authority of the Vulgate. Yet recently it has been argued that the 'Obscure Men' attacked in Reuchlin not primarily his humanism but his Jewish sympathies: ". . . the anti-Reuchlinists were made up of a disparate group of anti-Semites from the many walks of life: they included some scholastics, but also a few humanists and even several kings."[16]

One implication of this anti-Semite thesis must at least be considerably qualified: Reuchlin's campaign was not pro-Jewish, let alone pro-Semite. I am well aware that we have to tread here most carefully, since there is no 'dictionary clarity' and consensus about the precise content of such terms in relation to sixteenth-century attitudes. After all, how does one grade degrees of anti-Judaism in a Christian world which is unable to decide whether it finds more self-confirmation in Jewish mass conversion or in the stubborn blindness of those stricken by God? As George Santayana put it: Fanaticism is 'redoubling your effort when you have forgotten your aim.' The dangerous fanaticism of Christian anti-Judaism is rooted in the inability to decide between these two aims of mass conversion and mass expulsion. What then *are* the characteristics of anti-Judaism: confiscation of Jewish books or a resident-alien tax? Neurotic suspicion of Jewish conspiracy, or outright slander based on the stories of host desecration or of ritual murder in order to use Christian blood for treating Jewish illness? Is the mere fact that one does not call for slaughter as in previous centuries, and allows expulsion with all movable possessions a sign of leniency?[17] Let us look at the writings of Reuchlin and his opponent Pfefferkorn with these questions in mind.

I do not intend to deal with the 'Reuchlin Case' which developed only after publication of the *Augenspiegel* in Tübingen (1511) when, instead of the Talmud, the author's orthodoxy becomes the main issue, and a fortiori not with the two volumes of the *Epistolae obscurorum virorum* published by Crotus Rubeanus in 1515 and by Ulrich of Hutten in 1517. Of Reuchlin's preceding works,[18] the *Vocabularius breviloquus* (Basel, 1478) does not yield any statement pertaining to our theme. This leaves us with the illusive but most significant *De verbo mirifico* (Basel, 1494), the *Tütsch Missive* (Pforzheim, 1505), the *De rudimentis hebraicis* (Pforzheim, 1506) with its programmatic preface, and finally the imperial *Opinion* or 'Gutachten' against the confiscation of Hebrew books (1510), published in the *Augenspiegel*[19] together with a defense in Tübingen a year later.

Reuchlin's *De verbo mirifico*[20] is the first we must take in hand.

The 'Wonder-Working Word' has been read in a number of ways: as a proof of the necessity of the study of Hebrew, as a defense of the Christian Kabbalah, as a personal expression of Reuchlin's mystical concerns, and most recently—and most convincingly[21]—as a program to recover the divine gift of the occult sciences which enables man to master the forces of nature by means of the Kabbalah. Irreverently we by-pass Reuchlin's own theme to look at his mis-en-scène repeated later in his *De arte cabalistica* (1517): a disputation between Sidon, the former Epicurean and spokesman for pagan philosophy; Baruch, the learned Jew; and Capnion speaking for Reuchlin, the Christian.

In the form of a 'sectarum controversia'[22] but much sharper than in the similar dialogue in Lessing's *Nathan der Weise*, Capnion establishes the superiority of the Christian faith, and both calls for, and achieves, the penance[23] or conversion of Sidon and Baruch, to be followed by baptismal rites of purification. Just as Sidon has to disavow his Epicurus, Baruch must renounce his Talmudic sources: "Resipiscentia vestra haec esto: A Thalmudim Baruchia, tuque Sidoni ab Epicuro . . . receditote. Lavamini, mundi estote."[24] Of course, this is not the crude conversion rite which medieval disputations between Christians and Jews had intended to achieve; rather it is the initiation into the art of the *magus.* Yet this is the art of the Christian *magus*, bound by the faith of the Christian Church. This tie has consequences since Capnion combines his respect for Hebrew and its kabbalistic interpretation with a rejection of the Talmud and, what is more, with a vehement attack on 'the' Jews:

> You [Jews] have subverted the Holy Books; therefore you rattle off your prayers in vain, in vain you invoke God, in vain because you speak to Him in self-made prayers, not in the way God wants to be worshipped. At the same time you hate us, us the true worshippers of God. You hate us with a never-ending hatred. . . .[25]

In the 'German Open Letter'[26] completed ten years later in 1504, this animosity has become thematic. Reuchlin explains the 'Elend,' i.e. the exile of the Jews, in terms of their self-invoked collective guilt punished by God with such blindness that they cannot find the way to penance, "die weg der buß, das ist ruw und leid,"[27] the way to that contrition which means conversion to the Church. But only the learned Jew will find this solution; only the scholar who is trained in the secret art of the Kabbalah will understand that the Hebrew letters for the name of the Almighty mean *Jeschuh*, Jesus. In short, this treatise is the practical application of *De verbo mirifico*,[28] except for the fact that the turnabout, Baruch's change of heart, *resipiscentia*, is here unambiguously described as conversion, a real option only for the happy few, for those Jews initiated into the mysteries of the wonder-working word.

The misery of the Jews is not the consequence of man-made injustice but of God-willed punishment, to be escaped only through conversion. He concludes by pointing to the Good Friday prayer for the *perfidi Iudaei*: "I pray God that He will illumine and convert them to the right faith so that they are liberated from captivity by the Devil. . . . Once they acknowledge Jesus as the true Messiah everything will turn to their good in this world and in the world to come. Amen."[29]

Now we turn to the revealing Preface in *De rudimentis*, dated March 7, 1506. Here we have at once a summary of his earlier views and a prophetic forecast of the events to come, those events which were to make and break his career as 'Praeceptor Germaniae'—a title and task he had to bequeath to his grandnephew Melanchthon. This Preface is easily summarized: Reuchlin expresses his readiness to stand up against all three parties concerned: the humanists, the scholastics and the Jews. His point of departure is the thoroughgoing damage done to the study of Scripture not only by the 'sophists' but also by the students of eloquence and poetry.[30] The *literati* may well think that he, Reuchlin, with his concern with grammar, deals with *puerilia*, not befitting an educated man.[31] But the study of grammar has been the very basis of his achievements in philosophy, since the knowledge of Hebrew is the precondition for initiation into the Kabbalah.[32]

While the humanists may merely laugh at him and lose their respect, the Jews will assail him and the sophists will fall upon him like growling dogs.[33] What enormity, they will cry out. This man dares to criticize the holy Vulgate, and to call into question the inspired work of such holy men as Jerome and Lyra.[34] Since Reuchlin correctly assessed these opponents—as history amply illustrates—the following statement combines the power of rhetorical rhythm with the ring of truth: "Quamquam enim Hieronymum sanctum veneror ut angelum, et Lyram colo ut magistrum, tamen adoro veritatem ut deum. (Though I admire Jerome as an angel and highly esteem Lyra as a master, I bow before the truth as before God.)"[35]

This impressive declaration of independence is indeed the basis of all truly historical research. It includes at the same time the obligation to apply Reuchlin's dictum to the great master himself. His own golden rule for the iconoclastic emancipation from reverence yields the admission that for him 'the Jews' are collectively guilty for their lasting rejection by God, with the rare elitist exemption made for the cultured Jew who abandons the Talmud to accept the Christian Kabbalah. Though Reuchlin acknowledges his indebtedness to Jacob Yeḥiel Loans, 'the learned and widely read' physician to Emperor Frederick III, who taught him the Hebrew alphabet,[36] he knows that the Jews are not going to respond favorably to his undertaking.[37] This Christian syntax, thus Reuchlin concludes his Preface to Book III, is all the more necessary "since our [German] Jews are unwilling to teach Christians their language either due to ill-will or to inability, but basically because a Talmudic saying forbids them to do so."[38] Once again the Talmud stands between the Jews and their conversion, between the Jews and their eternal salvation.

When Reuchlin in his legal 'Gutachten' or *Opinion* of 1510 advises against the proposed confiscation of the 'Jewish books' he argues—as Guido Kisch in his precious *Zasius und Reuchlin*[39] has shown—like Bartolus before him on the basis of Roman law, of the *Codex Iustinianus.* As a jurist he concludes that the Jews are not slaves but 'concives', fellow citizens, not heretics but a tolerated 'secta', and finally, for the Christian, neighbors. The Jewish books should not be burned; rather the Jews should be converted by persuasion, "durch vernünfftig disputationen, senfftmüttigklich und güttlich."[40]

The lasting significance of Reuchlin's 'Gutachten' is easily lost in the cloud of his later retractions. He heralds the two-kingdoms doctrine which Luther was to make his mainstay albeit ultimately without benefit for the political status of the Jews. The basis of Reuchlin's argument is precisely that the Jews in civil law are 'concives,' fellow citizens "inn ainem burgerrecht und burgfriden." At the same time they are "unsers glaubens fiendt," enemies from the perspective of the Christian religion.[41] Once assaulted as a heretic in the pay of the Jews, Reuchlin claims in the *Augenspiegel*

(Tübingen, 1511) to have been thoroughly misunderstood in his defense of the Jewish books, and proves amenable to the solution that 'the blasphemous parts' of the Talmud be confiscated and stored in Christian libraries.[42] In this way at once the interests of ecclesiastical inquisition and of scholarly investigation are safeguarded.[43]

Has the great spokesman for Jewish emanicipation been brought to heel by intimidation or is the *Augenspiegel* a reliable commentary upon the 'Gutachten' of the year before? It must be said that if we are prepared to trust Reuchlin himself as 'sui ipsius interpres' his sole concern remained what it had been from the beginning: not the Jews, nor the Talmud as such, but free scholarly access to the sources of the Christian Kabbalah. Reuchlin combines the plea for civil emancipation of the Jews with social discrimination and religious ostracism.

4. Pfefferkorn: A Convert's Shrill Voice

For over a century no one has made a detailed study of the tracts of Josef Pfefferkorn (1469–1522/23);[44] the frenzies of this fanatic seemed sufficiently documented. Baptized 'Johannes' Pfefferkorn in 1504 he published by 1507 in Nuremberg and Cologne his *Judenspiegel* in German and Latin.[45] A series of pamphlets reprinted in various cities followed: *Die Judenbeichte* (1508), *Wie die blinden Juden yr Ostern halten* (1509) with as a first climax the *Judenfeind*,[46] adorned by an Epigram of Ortwijn van Graes (1509), soon as anti-Reuchlinist the object of scorn in the world of learning.

It is in the *Judenspiegel* of 1507 that Pfefferkorn formulates the portentous proposal that the Talmudic books are to be confiscated and burned—the only passage noted by Reuchlin's biographer, Ludwig Geiger, and hence one of the few statements ever quoted in secondary literature.[47] The first part of the *Judenspiegel* fully suffices to explain why Pfefferkorn's readers must have lost all inclination to read any further: the convert turns on his own with the resentment of one who, having painfully broken away from his anchorage, has now fully imbibed the anti-Jewish hostility of his new environment. Based on the Vulgate which Reuchlin is about to call into question Pfefferkorn wants to convert his 'brethren according to the flesh' with that mixture of proofs and charges known from centuries of Christian 'mission.' Four points deserve our full attention.

Pfefferkorn advocates as a 'good work' for Christians, particularly for the princes and the magistrates, that the obstacles to conversion be removed by confiscation of all Hebrew books except the Scriptures.[48] "On first sight someone can object," thus Pfefferkorn anticipates Reuchlin's arguments,

that my proposal is both imprudent and morally wrong since I seem to suggest that the authorities take away possessions of the Jews against their will (*ab invitis*), illegally and contrary to law (*contra ius et fas*). Yet I insist that no one's possessions should be taken; on the contrary, something is *given* to the Jews. But let me ask first: Why are the Jews so severely persecuted by you [Christians]? As everyone knows they have to pay heavy taxes for their protection and public safety; they are burdened like packhorses, though they are, by nature, as free as birds in the air.[49] You bring hardly convincing arguments for your greed by claiming that in this way you want to achieve their conversion; you want to make believe that everything the Jews have to suffer from you is for their betterment. Why shouldn't you now for once do something you cannot profit from which really serves them, their conversion and eternal benefit?'[50]

Our first point is that Pfefferkorn combines the awesome plan which would inscribe his name in the historical record with a daring critique of the manceps-tradition,[51] the 'Reichskammerknecht' interpretation and 'Rechtsbasis' for exploitation.[52]

The second point worth noting is that Pfefferkorn not only visited Reuchlin and saw him at work in his study but basically accepted Reuchlin's views as described in *De verbo mirifico*: Not just in the words but in the very letters of the Hebrew Scriptures the occult knowledge is stored which provides dominion over the forces of nature.[53] Therefore Pfefferkorn does not subscribe to the 'Gutachten' of the University of Mainz which suggested that all Jewish books including the books of Moses should be confiscated.[54]

Thirdly, Pfefferkorn's confiscation plans stand in the context of the expectation of the imminent end of the world. At least a major revolution is at hand, injustice is growing fast and God's justice is about to strike. Before God's intervention the Jews will convert en masse—he himself is merely the beginning of a mass movement—provided they are treated properly. This includes 'of course' confiscation since this serves their betterment.[55]

As is also the case with Luther, there is here a basic ambivalence[56] and oscillation between a concerted conversion effort in view of God's eschatological timetable, and a fear-ridden hatred because the stubborn unrepenting Jews involve the Christians in a guilt-by-association soon to be horribly punished. Though the reasoning in Luther's plea for conversion by cordiality and decency in *Jesus was Born a Jew* of 1523[57] is quite different from Pfefferkorn's in 1507,[58] the same shift from conversion hope to bitter hostility is to be noted in the further development of both.[59] Generally it can be said that, so long as the conversion of Jews served Christian needs either by signifying or by forestalling the End, Christian Europe would remain a dangerous habitat for Jews, and especially so in times of heightened religious fervor.

A fourth and final observation leads us away from Cologne on the eve of the Reformation to Nuremberg and Ingolstadt in the forties when a new peak of anti-Judaism is reached. Pfefferkorn warns the Christians—and respect for his daring should not be withheld at this point—that they weaken their own case by their base credulity in circulating stories about Jewish ritual murder. With this popular belief in Jews killing children to get at the healing power of their blood, 'we make ourselves ridiculous and the Christian faith a matter of mirth and contempt.'[60]

Early in the year 1529 an anonymous treatise was published on this same risky theme: 'Whether it is true and credible that Jews secretly kill children and use their blood.'[61] It is now well established[62] that this treatise is the work of Andreas Osiander (1498–1552), a Lutheran minister in Nuremberg, one of Luther's chief strongholds in the South, which opted the next year publicly for the Reformation by signing the *Confessio Augustana*. It has not been noted that Osiander uses Pfefferkorn's warning in building his own case against the ritual murder charge. For Osiander this accusation is not based on fact or reason but more likely on greed and envy. After all, Moses not only forbids murder but also the taking of blood. Furthermore why would Jews have to commit murder in order to get at blood; and if it is to be Christian blood, what about the Jews in Turkey? Were not also the early Christians accused of ritual murder? In all known murder cases not Jews but Christians were guilty. In every future case a series of primary suspects should be investigated who all have an interest in making Jews responsible for their own crime: a poverty stricken feudal overlord or one of his civil servants; the clergy interested in a new miracle and the concomitant attraction of pilgrims; indebted citizens, witches or abusive parents—they all want to put the blame on the Jews.[63]

Osiander, one of the foremost Hebrew scholars of his day, was an enthusiastic disciple of Reuchlin and came to share Reuchlin's respect for the hidden power and secret knowledge stored in Kabbalah and Talmud. And again, as before with Reuchlin, this implied for him not a lesser effort at conversion but rather the correction of misleading Talmudic errors. Yet Osiander goes beyond Reuchlin, in that he not only respects the learned Rabbi, the Baruch-figure of *De verbo mirifico*, but also the common Jew, the collective assailed and caricatured in popular Christian stories.

It is exactly this aspect which infuriated Johannes Eck (1486–1543), for a time even host to Reuchlin in Ingolstadt (December, 1519). By way of response, Eck wrote a booklet expressly designed to lend scholarly credence to popular anti-Judaism in which he manages to surpass in crudity, fury and defamation all preceding publications of the Reformation era: *Ains Judenbüchlins Verleging* [*Widerlegung*].[64] Two Jews from Sulzbach try to aid Tittingen Jews accused of the ritual murder of young Michael Pisenharter shortly after Easter 1540.[65] They present in their defense Osiander's 'Gutachten' of 1529, which the Bishop of Eichstätt, ex officio chancellor of the University of Ingolstadt, refers to his vice-chancellor John Eck, for twenty-five years the most significant and learned spokesman for the counter-reformation. For Eck it is immediately clear that the author must be a 'Lutherischer predicant' (whom he rightly suspects to be Osiander) so blinded by his heresy that he makes the Jews out to be better than Christians—Lutherans that is.[66]

With the same repetitiousness with which Reuchlin had discredited Pfefferkorn as 'der Tauft Jud' in the *Augenspiegel* Eck calls Osiander 'Judenschützer' or 'Judenvater' who has the gall to denounce the authorities for their financial greed instead of denouncing the Jews for their guilt. Osiander must have received a good bit of the Jewish golden calf to line his pockets. After all, the Talmud explicitly commands the Jews to kill Christian children.[67] When that man argues that no baptized Jew has ever reported such a thing, Eck replies that the appeal to Pfefferkorn does not prove a thing, since Pfefferkorn can only speak for himself.[68] It is equally inadmissible to introduce Reuchlin's authority; the *Augenspiegel* makes perfectly clear that 'der ehrlich Doctor' differed from Pfefferkorn only in a matter of words: Reuchlin never denied that there are Talmudic prayers directed against the Christians.[69] Eck himself knows about a ritual murder case in Freiburg, 1503 and furthermore about many well attested published cases. Why have the Jews been thrown out of so many countries and cities? Eck goes on to relate the European history of banning Jews over 50 years from the Spanish expulsion until his own day, which serves as proof of a common Christian stance and of Christian common sense.[70]

The peak of fury is reached when Eck piles nineteen caustic characteristics of the Jews into one sentence, summarized in the designation: a blasphemous people, 'ein gotslesterlich Volck.'[71] Not in keeping with our present state of research and therefore quite unexpected is Eck's final conclusion. 'Der Judenvater' who wants to whitewash the Jews is a natural product of Wittenberg and 'the latest fruit on the Lutheran Tree':[72] the devil speaks through you, Lutherans, in order to exculpate the Jews from ritual murder.[73] The inversion of this charge had been expressed before. Josel von Rosheim reports that the Jews had been made responsible for the 'outbreak' of the Reformation.[74] Eck, however, reverses these roles by pointing to the spiritual havoc caused by Luther: 'Luthersohn' and 'Judenvater' are but two sides of one coin. One example suffices for him: Destructive insistence on the scriptural principle leads to the equally irrational and heretical respect for the Hebrew Scriptures.[75]

Eck construes here an identification of Luther's Reformation with philo-Judaism which is wholly untenable as far as Luther himself is concerned. At the same time, he rightly alerts us to the fact that it is equally impermissible to deal with 'Luther and the Jews' in terms of a *solus Lutherus*, so long pursued by a Luther scholarship which isolates Luther from the wider context of Wittenberg theology and from the social and intellectual history of his times.

5. The Surprising Intolerance of Erasmus

In the following two sections on Erasmus and Luther we can be brief, not because these two prolific authors would not provide us with ample material but because we must restrict our presentation to points where the sources require a partial or total reorientation.

Three points are to be noted in respect to Erasmus' view of the Jews. In the first place the signal contribution made by Guido Kisch in his booklet on Erasmus' view of the Jews[76] has not yet left its imprint on Erasmus scholarship.[77] Kisch's conclusion, summarized in the words "der tiefverwurzelte, maßlose Judenhaß" (a deeply rooted, boundless Jew hatred),[78] is indeed not easily reconciled with our equally deepseated respect for the *philosophia christiana* of this great Dutchman, his plea for peace and tolerance, and his vision of the *bonae litterae* as the basis of a new human dignity. Yet Kisch has not overstated his case, but rather understated it by not collecting all evidence. Erasmus saw 'the Jews' collectively at work as allies of Pfefferkorn and accused them of being the masterminds of the Peasant Revolt. France is 'the most spotless and most flourishing part of Christendom,' because France alone is 'not infected with heretics, with Bohemian schismatics, with Jews, with half-Jewish marranos.'[79] A baptized Jew remains a half-Jew; but the 'creep' Pfefferkorn is not merely a half-Jew but a Jew and a half. And when a person is disliked, as in the case of the papal nuncio Aleandera, the explanation is obvious: The man must be a Jew.

With the critique of Pfefferkorn Erasmus combines a warning against baptizing Jews: If we could look inside Pfefferkorn we would find not one but six hundred Jews;[80] we should show more caution in admitting others into the Church.[81] To contain the new upsurge of Judaism Erasmus is prepared to discard the Old Testament. In this way the New Testament and the unity of the Christians can be kept intact. "If only the Church would not attach so much importance to the Old Testament—it is a book of shadows, given just for a time (*pro tempore datum*)!"[82] We will have to redefine our concept of tolerance significantly in order to claim for Erasmus the historical respect he really deserves.

Our second observation concerns the type of tolerance in which Erasmus did believe and for which he labored. The tolerance intended by Erasmus is the freedom of the Christian scholar to publish his findings regardless of schools and party alignment. This vision explains his seemingly contradictory statements about Reuchlin made within three years of each other. In the Louvain

1519 edition of the *Colloquies* he makes a point of stating: "I am no Reuchlinist . . . never have I given him support; and he would not have wanted it."[83] To the enlarged re-edition of the same *Colloquies* (Basel, 1522), already in press, Erasmus hastens to add in the summer of 1522 his *Apotheosis Capnionis*, his glorification of Reuchlin who has just died.[84] In this 'In Memoriam' Reuchlin is honored as a second Jerome—for Erasmus the highest praise conceivable.[85] Yet, far from being presented as the protagonist of Jewish emancipation Reuchlin is depicted by Erasmus as the victim of Satan, Satan who attacks some of the most eminent contemporary men just as he once assailed Jesus Christ—through the Scribes and the Pharisees.[86] His identification is clear; his loyalty to Reuchlin is owed not to the great Christian kabbalist but to the sturdy student of the *bonae litterae*, suffering like Erasmus under the Dominican obscurantists.[87] Erasmus was indeed a protagonist of tolerance. Yet his concept of 'tolerance' was too erudite to temper his own virulent anti-Judaism. This apparently belonged for him to another world of reference. As critique Erasmus could coin the often quoted phrase: "Si christianum est odisse Iudeos, hic abunde Christiani sumus omnes."[88] But this critique never served as a criterion.

Finally, there is a strong, theological anti-Judaism[89] underlying Erasmus' very program,[90] which cannot be simply identified with racial anti-Judaism, or what we nowadays would call social or political 'anti-Semitism.' It is his anti-legalism, his campaign against formal religion and its multiplication of observances, which allows the easy alternation between 'Pharisees' and 'Scholastics,' between 'Jewish' and 'legalistic.' This anti-Judaism insists on the duality of body and soul or, in terms of reform ideology, on the tension between external religion and internal truth which would become a major theme for his younger disciples, the City reformers. Yet the very facility with which the terms 'Pharisaic,' 'Jewish,' and 'Judaistic' are used nearly interchangeably, and invariably with negative connotations, suggests that this symbolic language refers to the continuous threat of the old Israel, a life threat to the values of the Erasmian trinity of scholarship, society and religion: unpartisan scholarship, a learned society, and genuine piety.

In view of the foregoing three points it should no longer surprise us that the amalgam of peace, concord and erudition which constitutes the new tolerance as a typical Christian virtue, is restricted to a Christian society, excluding Judaism as "the most pernicious plague and bitterest enemy that one can find to the teaching of Christ."[91] When Erasmus wanted the whole world to know 'I am no Reuchlinist' he obviously was afraid of being implicated in a heresy trial. He spoke out of fear. And yet he spoke the truth: he was no Reuchlinist.[92] Erasmus feared above all that with the renaissance of literature not only paganism but also Judaism would become a new intellectual force,[93] and this 'pernicious plague' already making headway,[94] was for him the direct consequence of the revival of Hebrew studies.[95]

6. The Eve of the Reformation

It is not too harsh to say that in medieval and early modern times phases of intensified religious fervor and programs for reform of the *Corpus Christianum* always spelled doom for the Jews. In the sixteenth century there are, as far as I see, three major factors which coalesced to lead to a new peak of anti-Judaism.

1. The pamphlet war, leading up to the explosion of the so-called 'German Peasants' Revolt' of the years 1524–1526, made renewal of society through the justice of God thematic and added to the traditional gravamina against extortion of the Empire by the Church a general critique of the powers that be, particularly with regard to tithing and taxing.[96] The protection of the Jews by the emperor and the patrician faction among the city fathers who opposed the expulsion of Jews, led to the easy identification of tithing with usury. In a large number of early 'Flugschriften,' obviously intended to mobilize popular discontent against conservative territorial or city policies,[97] the Jews are depicted as an intolerable threat to life and good,[98] and usually as thirsting after the blood of young Christian children.[99] Eck's treatise on this theme is but a late and dismal climax.

2. Favored by the high authority of St. Jerome the story of the Antichrist and the history of the Jews came to be placed on converging lines. The Antichrist is expected to be circumcised in Jerusalem and to find his first worshippers among the Jews. In the beautiful picture book, 'The Antichrist' (first published in Strasbourg, 1480 and often reprinted), the Jews are the first to gather around him and cry out that "yr got sy kumen."[100] 'Gog' and 'Magog' from Ezekiel 38 and 39 signify either the fearsome

re-emergence of the ten lost tribes or of the ferocious infidels, the Mohammedans or Turks, for whom the Jews are the natural allies and undercover agents.[101] The older interpretation which regarded the story of the 'Antichrist' as the lore of the common people must be corrected: the 'Endchrist' is the product of learned exegesis, of exegetes who were less arbitrary and speculative than they would seem from a modern perspective; they are rather the *speculatores*, the watchmen on the walls of the true Jerusalem trained to interpret the signs of the times and to relate them to scriptural data.[102]

A heightened sense of the approach of the Last Times, by no means to be confused ipso facto with the pursuit of the millennium, sharpens the profile of the Antichrist and makes an immediate mobilization of all Christian forces mandatory. As we have seen in the case of Pfefferkorn this means a massive campaign for the mass conversion of the Jews described by St. Paul as the fulfillment of history (Romans 11:25–32). Yet this missionary concern is but a small step away from an equally radical dissociation, rigorous 'Apartheid'[103] and even expulsion, as propagated by sundry pamphlets of the twenties, earlier by Pfefferkorn and later by Eck.

3. Eschatological urgency incites to immediate reform. The parallelism assumed between the first and the last *adventus* of Christ, made it clear that as John the Baptist had quoted the prophet Isaiah (40:3) we are again to heed his voice crying out in the desert: "Prepare a way for the Lord; clear a straight path for him" (Matthew 3:3).[104] In so far as preparation for the Second Coming is interpreted as the need for reform of the Church, the contrast between the 'Spirit' and the 'Letter' takes on a fundamental significance, based on St. Paul's saying: "The letter kills, the spirit gives life" (II Corinthians 3:6). Though variously interpreted by Erasmus and Luther—for the first in line with Origen and Jerome an exegetical device and directed against ceremonial external laws, for the latter as with St. Augustine basic to the doctrine of justification and the contrast between the Gospel and Law as such—this new Paulinism was bound to cement the identification of 'legal' and 'external,' with 'Judaistic' and 'Jewish.'

The gusts of social and apocalyptic fervor fanning the never-extinguished medieval brushfires of anti-Judaism find in this Paulinist reform theology an ideological confirmation, lending a durability to anti-Judaism which outlasts by far the times of immediate social and eschatological duress. With this conclusion I do not join the ranks of those who regard economic factors as the basis for an ideological 'Überbau';[105] after all, the indicated social discontent and apocalyptic anxiety are themselves riddled with 'ideology.' Moreover, one glance at the timetable of expulsions from German cities reveals that after 1520 only a handful cities decreed expulsion—Prague (1541), Kaufbeuren (1543/1636), Schweinfurt (1555) and Nordhausen (1559)—whereas in the preceding period from 1388 (Strasbourg) through 1520 (Weissenburg) some ninety cities took such action against the Jews.[106] True, the imperial Diet at Augsburg required by order of September 4, 1530 that all Jewish men should wear a yellow ring on their coat or cap,[107] but this was an effort to guarantee some kind of uniformity for long existing territorial laws rather than an innovative measure of discrimination against the Jews. Hence the new 'Paulinism' with its peculiar brand of anti-Judaism follows *after* and does not precede or create the rising tide of Jewish repression. Luther's attitude towards the Jews should be considered within this larger context.

7. Luther's Voice Raised Against the Jews

When we now turn to Luther's attitude to Judaism we have been introduced to a larger context than is usual in the impressively extensive literature on the theme 'Luther and the Jews.'[108] As before in the case of Erasmus, we limit ourselves to such areas where corrective interpretation seems called for. There are three such points to be made.

1. We cannot completely by-pass the issue of changes in Luther's thought since this has dominated Luther research for over a century. In 1523 Luther is concerned about removing obstacles in order to facilitate Jewish mass conversion, whereas his harsh writings of the late thirties and forties heap invectives on the Jews for their stubborn and malicious blindness. But this change, significant both from a modern perspective and from the perspective of his Jewish contemporaries, is not indicative of a change of heart as far as those Jews are concerned who want to retain their religious identity and remain outside the Christian fold.

A key document is the revealing letter of June 11, 1537, to the ubiquitous advocate of oppressed Jewry, Josel of Rosheim.[109] Luther rejects Josel's request to intercede with the Elector on behalf of the Jews who by edict of August, 1536 had been ordered to leave Saxony. Notwithstanding Capito's plea on Josel's behalf, Luther says, politely but firmly, 'no,' because the acts of charity he had called for in 1523[110] had not only proven to be ineffective as a means of conversion but had on the contrary confirmed the Jews in their error. The fact that Jesus the Christ was a Jew, which was formulated in 1523 as a Christian self-critique with a clear edge against the papal church,[111] is now turned directly against the Jews: Pre-Christian anti-Semitism, i.e. the gentile hatred of the Jews, highlights the miracle of divine intervention so that the Christians were prepared to acknowledge a Jew as their savior.[112] Hence the Jews should give up their hopes and stop looking for the end of their captivity and dispersal over the earth. Luther announces a special treatise on this matter—de facto developing into those five final writings[113] which only Eck matches in fury. Basic to Luther's anti-Judaism[114] is therefore the conviction that since the coming of Jesus there is no future for the Jews as Jews.[115]

2. As we saw, Erasmus had good reason to deny that he was a Reuchlinist. The same applies to Luther. In his 'Gutachten' on the Reuchlin case of February, 1514,[116] Luther indeed declared Reuchlin's orthodoxy to be beyond suspicion. Yet his critique of the burning of the books was argued in quite a different way.[117] Since, as the prophets foretold, the Jews are to curse and blaspheme Christ, their very God and King, even a first-year theological student can see that to purge the Jews from blasphemy is to contradict God and to call Him a liar. Besides, if Jews are to be converted that is not a matter of men fooling around with burning, banning and such mere external doings; God converts from within.[118] Not just the middle or the late Luther, but the earliest Luther recorded, holds that there is no future for the Jews as Jews—in this 'Gutachten' supported with the contrast 'internal—external' which we encountered as a typical element of the Augustinian theme of the 'Spirit and the Letter.' Though on first sight Luther argues with Reuchlin that no external force is to be applied, Reuchlin had tried to defend the Talmud against the charge of blasphemy whereas Luther takes this blasphemy as an unshakable, divinely ordained fact.

3. Related to this is a third point. Luther is also no Reuchlinist

in view of his explicit scepticism concerning the Kabbalah.[119] Notwithstanding his great interest in Reuchlin's *De verbo mirifico* and his immediate reading of *De arte cabalistica*[120] he rejects the Kabbalah as suitable only for curious and idle scholars, 'curiosi et ociosi.'[121] Theologically he regards it as superstition to hold that the Hebrew letters contain divine power: Words only have impact when received in faith.

As far as method is concerned, Luther's nominalist training had taught him to find the *proprietas verborum*, the exact meaning of words, in their precise usage as clarified by the grammatical context. The very same reason which soon afterwards made him oppose the biblical exegesis of the Zurich and Strasbourg theologians—nearly all trained in the *via antiqua*—with respect to the eucharistic words of institution[122] underlies his rejection of the Kabbalah as a reliable exegetical device. Generally it can be said that the nominalistic interpretation of words and their conventional and contextual significance gainsays all 'word-works' of the *magus*, irrespective of whether it concerns black or white magic.[123]

4. Luther is not a Reuchlinist; neither is he a 'Lutheran.' This surprising conclusion deserves at least a short explanation. As we saw, Eck regards Osiander as a 'Luthersohn' and 'Judenvater,' a natural fruit on Luther's tree. It is clear from the foregoing that this view is untenable. Luther's prescriptions and 'remedies' may have changed—and change they did, considerably so—but his diagnosis remained the same from the beginning: the blasphemy of the Jews is punished with blindness and dispersal; they will never have a country of their own.[124]

Osiander, however, is not an isolated Nuremberg deviant from the Wittenberg party line. We have good reason to assume that Melanchthon was as embarrassed as some of the leading City reformers by the ferocious anti-Judaism of the later Luther. We know that he protected Osiander against Luther's wrath by suppressing the evidence that Osiander had sent an apology for Luther's utterances to the Venetian scholar Elias Levita.[125] It is even more important to take notice of the position of Justus Jonas (1493–1555),[126] Luther's lifelong colleague, marriage witness and, above all, the translator of Luther's treatises on Judaism. The independence of Jonas' position may well have gone unnoticed because he praises and recommends Luther's views as if his own were a mere explication of Luther's attitude to the Jews; ultimately he leaves Luther far behind and ends up with a position which nearly coincides with modern biblical exegesis. In the 1524 preface to his Latin translation of Luther's treatise of the preceding year[127] his deviation is not yet obvious and only a matter of emphasis. Jonas underscores the common lot of Jews and Christians in having been misled, the Jews by Talmudic trifles, the Christians by scholastic figments.[128] Just as Christians have been won for the Reformation by the recovery of Holy Scripture so Jews will see the light of truth by returning to the unadulterated witness of Moses and the Prophets. Christians should pray for the Jews, "particularly since also among us not all Christians deserve that name."[129] Yet Luther's chief argument is taken up when the rabbis are accused of leading the Jews astray with their fantasy of the perpetuation of the messianic kingdom: "Do they want to make us believe that this kingdom has been transferred to the moon?"[130]

In his second preface to the Latin translation of Luther's treatise against the Sabbatarians, written 15 years later (1539),[131] Jonas boldly disregards the fact that Luther's position has hardened, already presaging the vitriolics to come. As if bending over backwards to neutralize Luther's irritated impatience he develops a new, positive vision of the Jews. The papists are now presented as far more removed from the Scriptures than even the most unworthy offspring of Abraham: The recovery of the Gospel 'in our days' has opened our eyes to the fact that there were never more significant doctors of theology than among the people of Israel;[132] the opening of the Gospel has led to the discovery that we, Christians, are guests in Abraham's house, and latecomers to the promises of God, gentiles grafted on the tree of Israel, made into one body with the Jews under the one Head, Jesus Christ.[133]

The final conclusion of Jonas may not seem to be so different from the early Luther: We owe it to the Jews to save as many as possible 'as if from shipwreck.'[134] Yet a new sense of historical obligation to a common past and a new biblical vision of a common future is unmistakable. Luther confirms our conclusion when he informs Jonas on December 21, 1542 that he goes his separate way against Jonas' advice to tone down and temper his anti-Jewish utterances.[135] Luther himself had already come to despair of the mass conversion of the Jews—Christians can "mit gutem Gewissen an ihnen verzweifeln."[136] Convinced that their dispersal is the central issue, he swears that, as soon as the Jews return to Jerusalem to re-establish the Temple, priesthood and statehood, the Christians will follow them "und auch Juden werden."[137]

8. Epilogue: The Arduous Road to Peaceful Coexistence

We began this lecture with Europe's slow trek towards tolerance, a journey hesitantly commenced in the sixteenth century and pursued very much at the expense of the Jews, particularly in Germany. Is this progress due to any of the three: to Reuchlin, the 'trilinguis,' admirer of the Kabbalah and proponent of the Jews as 'concives'; or to Erasmus, the patient editor of the Fathers and propagandist for peace and concord; or perhaps to Luther, the nominalist exegete and mighty prophet of a truly 'secular' state, freed from supervision by the Church?

It seems obvious that it is the humanist line to be drawn from Reuchlin and Erasmus to Hobbes, Voltaire and Lessing, which points to modern concepts of equality and human rights. No one has presented this view more convincingly and eloquently than Peter Gay in his magnificent interpretation of the Enlightenment. One passage taken from *The Rise of Paganism* may at once illustrate and document this prevailing point of view. Amidst the deadlock of Catholicism and Protestantism a third force, thus Gay, provided Europe with a new option: "The Humanists [had] prepared the way for that solution; their realism made possible a secular view of political power and a secular, or at least no longer specifically Christian, justification for political obligation; their critical philology, combined with their admiration for antiquity, prepared educated men to read Christian documents with skeptical detachment, and pagan philosophies with sympathy; their appeal to nature laid the foundation for . . . a style of thought that ordered the world by natural law, natural morality, and natural theology."[138]

Yet it is exactly the test case of Judaism which, I submit, when seen from afar might appear to confirm Gay's findings but under closer scrutiny represents a major obstacle to them, and a chief reason to look for new answers. Gay's misconception is not singularly his own, nor is it a chink in the armor of his own wide-ranging research. Our common misunderstanding is due rather to the predominance of German Reformation research which in this century was first focused single-mindedly on Luther and during the past ten years concentrated with equal determination on the City Reformation. Not until we acknowledge the significance of what I am inclined to call—after Luther and the City Reformation—'the Third Reformation' will we be in a position to complete our story.

The City Reformation is a significant but brief episode of about ten years' duration from 1523 to 1534 which reached its climax in the late twenties and was over by 1549. The 'Third Reformation' owes its very emergence to the weakening of the political and religious status of the city, for which the Imperial Interim of 1548 spelled final doom.[139] The Third Reformation is the reformation of the refugees banished from their cities in Southern Germany, in France and soon in the Netherlands. It is a movement of much longer duration and deeper penetration than that of the cities. This refugee reformation entails a re-interpretation of government in church and state, and a re-reading of the Scriptures in the light of its own enforced exile.[140] One of its salient characteristics is a new attitude to Judaism.

City reformers like Zwingli in Zürich and Bucer in Strasbourg may not have assented to Luther's intemperate outbursts against the Jews; they did, however, agree with his basic attitude.[141] Christian Hebraists like Osiander in Nuremberg and Capito in Strasbourg accumulated exegetical knowledge of the Old Testament, and expressed a deep respect for rabbinical learning.[142] But only after this knowledge and this respect were kindled by the experience of the roaming refugees did the diaspora cease to be regarded as the deserved punishment for the 'blind stubbornness of the Jews': the traditional explanation for the dispersal of Israel had now become self-indictment. In the late French sermons of Calvin, recently edited,[143] we find the first traces[144] of a growing awareness of the parallels between the persecution of all true Christians and the diaspora of the Jews.[145]

In a two-pronged movement from Zürich and Geneva via Bullinger and Beda, the Third Reformation extends the message of the one covenant for Jews and gentiles. It proclaims the fidelity of the God of Abraham, Isaac and Jacob Who does not reverse His promises. In the course of the 17th century, first in the Netherlands, then in England and finally in a number of early settlements in the New World, the Jews are granted protection and certain civil rights. In 1657 the Dutch demanded that its Jews be recognized as full citizens abroad[146]—an act of emancipation which, in sharp contrast with the short-term effects of the French Revolution elsewhere, was never revoked.

Presentation of the precise shape of the 'Third Reformation' would require a separate lecture and, indeed, a separate monograph.[147] The one point I wish to stress is that this movement honors Luther's basic Reformation writings of 1520 as its theological charter, that its Old-Testament insights are essentially derived from the Christian Hebraists, all students of Reuchlin, and that in the seventeenth century it could absorb Erasmian ideas all the more readily because of its own origins in the City Reformation, so heavily indebted to Erasmus of Rotterdam. Interpreted by the Third Reformation, Reuchlin, Erasmus and Luther were divested of their anti-Judaism and could now function together in a positive fashion which none of them had envisioned.

In light of the preceding remarks, I dare to conclude with one thesis and one hypothesis. My thesis is: The first significant advances towards tolerance were not achieved by Gay's 'new paganism,' not by the *philosophes* of royalist France, nor by the elitist Deists of the English Enlightenment, not to mention the much overrated *Aufklärung* of Lessing in Germany. There was such a thing as the 'rise of paganism.' However, the rise of paganism meant de facto the rise of the gentiles, without benefit for the Jews.

And finally, my hypothesis: What is inculcated by centuries of religious fury in the minds of the elite and the uneducated populace alike, can only be eradicated or, indeed, exorcized by an equally powerful and fervent antidote. If this does not occur, as recent European history has proven, the flames of religious bigotry subsist under the new secular paganism, and the horrid phantoms of the past re-emerge out of the smoldering ashes of anti-Judaism to haunt us in the stubborn, mercurial and unsuppressible form of anti-Semitism.

In the very cities and regions from which the Jews had been expelled, the witch hunts started which bound Europe under their spell throughout pre-industrial times. The new paganism of the Enlightenment had its finest hour in building the dams of human dignity solid enough to contain the floods of this irrational fear of the devil.[148] It could not reach, however, beyond the phenomenon of witchcraft; it could not fathom nor control the preceding wave of anti-Judaism which, if left to agnostic indifference, would continue to inundate the inner recesses of Western man and his society.[149]

When the 'Third Reformation' turned anti-intellectual, anti-cultural and pietistic—and thus turned against the legacy of Reuchlin, Erasmus, and Luther—it lost its impact on Europe's intelligentsia and could no longer perform its early mission. But it was prophetic in insisting that without an enduring foundation for co-existence between Jews and Christians—in their words: without the recovery of the one covenant for Jews and Gentiles—there will be no future for Western society.

NOTES

1. Erich Hassinger, *Religiöse Toleranz im 16. Jahrhundert. Motive — Argumente — Formen der Verwirklichung*, Vorträge der Aeneas-Silvius-Stiftung an der Universität Basel 6 (Basel and Stuttgart, 1966); Hans R. Guggisberg, "Veranderingen in de Argumenten voor religieuze tolerantie en godsdienstvrijheid in de zestiende en zeventiende eeuw," *Bijdragen en Mededelingen betreffende de Geschiedenis der Nederlanden* 91 (1966), 177–195.

2. See the important article on the fourteenth century by Stuart Jenks, "Judenverschuldung und Verfolgung von Juden im 14. Jahrhundert: Franken bis 1349," *Vierteljahrschrift für Social- und Wirtschaftsgeschichte* 65 (1978), 309–356.

3. Published first by Pamphilus Gengenbach (Basel, 1521). Johann Eberlin von Günzburg, "Der erst bundtsgnoβ," *Ausgewählte Schriften*, 3 vols., ed. L. Enders, Neudrucke deutscher Literaturwerke des XVI. und XVII. Jahrhunderts: Flugschriften aus der Reformationszeit 11 (Halle, 1896–1902), 1:3.

4. *Corpus Reformatorum*, vol. 1: *Philippi Melan[ch]thonis Opera quae supersunt omnia* 1, ed. C. G. Bretschneider (Halle, 1834; reprint ed., New York, London and Frankfurt a.M., 1963), 34.

5. Lewis W. Spitz has coined an expression which applies as well and would have pleased Reuchlin even more: "Reuchlin: Pythagoras Reborn," *The Religious Renaissance of the German Humanists* (Cambridge, Mass., 1963), 61–80.

6. See his letter to John Colet, Paris, December 1504; *Opus Epistolarum Des. Erasmi Roterodami* [= Allen], ed. P. S. Allen, 12 vols. (Oxford, 1906–1965), 1: 405, lines 35–37. Cf. Michael Andrew Screech, *Ecstasy and the Praise of Folly* (London, 1980), 10.

7. "Lingua Ebraica est omnium optima ac in thematibus omnium copiosissima ac purissima, quia ab aliis linguis nihil prorsus mendicat. Sie hat ir eigen farb." *D. Martin Luthers Werke. Kritische Gesamtausgabe* [= *WA*] (Weimar, 1883 ff., reprint ed., Graz, 1964 ff.), *Tischreden* 1, no. 1041, p. 525, lines 42–44; September-November 1532.

8. *WA Tischreden* 2, no. 2771a; cf. no. 2779a.

9. See particularly Myron P. Gilmore, "Italian Reactions to Erasmian Humanism," in *Itinerarium Italicum. The Profile of the Italian Renaissance in the Mirror of its European Transformations, Dedicated to Paul Oskar Kristeller on the Occasion of his 70th Birthday*, ed. H. A. Oberman and Th. A. Brady, Jr., Studies in Medieval and Reformation Thought 14 (Leiden, 1975), 61–115; 84.

10. *Johann Reuchlin. Sein Leben und seine Werke* (Leipzig, 1871). Cf. James H. Overfield, "A New Look at the Reuchlin Affair," *Studies in Medieval and Renaissance History* 8 (1971), 165–207; 206; cf. 181. Of the older literature see esp. Gustav Kawerau, s.v. 'Reuchlin', in *Realencyklopädie für protestantische Theologie und Kirche*, 3. ed., vol. 16

(Leipzig, 1905), 680–688. For earlier English literature see Werner Schwarz, *Principles and Problems of Biblical Translation. Some Reformation Controversies and their Background* (Cambridge, 1955), 61–91; esp. 70, n. 2.

11. *WA Briefe* 1. 23, line 28. Letter to Georg Spalatin, February 1514; Gutachten on Reuchlin's case, probably based on Reuchlin's most recent publication, the *Defensio contra calumniatores suos Colonienses* (Tübingen, 1513).

12. In 1518 Luther called himself indeed Reuchlin's 'successor.' *WA Briefe* 1. 268, lines 9 f.; 14 December 1518. Max Brod, the most recent biographer of Reuchlin — and exceptional in that he makes explicit that he treats Luther from the perspective of centuries of persecution — praises Reuchlin for not having fallen for this 'ingratiation' and 'fake claim' of Luther. *Johannes Reuchlin und sein Kampf* (Stuttgart, 1965), 122. But on reading this letter itself it is clear that Luther means with 'successor' that he is the next on the black list of the 'sophists'; by no means, however, next in line as concerns his scholarly gifts. Nor was Luther a disciple of Reuchlin in a programmatic sense. Schwarz concludes, however, in too un-nuanced a fashion: "Yet Reuchlin was opposed to every aspect of Luther's doctrine. He died a member of the Roman Catholic Church. His aim was, to use a phrase of Erasmus, 'to restore the old,' and he did not see the danger that this implied for the Church of his time." *Principles and Problems*, 86. Another significant parallel between Reuchlin and Luther has gone unnoticed. The Elector Frederick of Saxony, who decisively protected Luther against Rome (Cajetan) and 'Reich' from 1518 is already in 1513 regarded by Reuchlin as a protector against ecclesiastical interference: "Quo ardentius ad te Saxonesque tuos confugio . . . ut me contra quorumlibet latronum in cursus semper tuearis." Letter dated 13 August, 1513, accompanying Reuchlin's translation of the 'Life of Constantine the Great'; *Johann Reuchlins Briefwechsel*, ed. L. Geiger (Stuttgart, 1875; reprint ed., Hildesheim, 1962), 190.

13. *WA* 10 II. 329, line 10; 1522.

14. See especially *Medieval Aspects of Renaissance Learning. Three Essays by Paul Oskar Kristeller*, ed. E. P. Mahoney, Duke Monographs in Medieval and Renaissance Studies 1 (Durham, NC, 1974).

15. *In Our Image and Likeness. Humanity and Divinity in Italian Humanist Thought* I (London, 1970); idem, "Erasmus, Augustine, and the Nominalists," *Archiv für Reformationsgeschichte* 67 (1976), 5–32; idem, *The Poet as Philospher. Petrarch and the Formation of Renaissance Consciousness* (New Haven and London, 1979), esp. 111.

16. J. H. Overfield, "A New Look at the Reuchlin Affair" (above, n. 10), 206. Cf. a few years later more cautiously: "A number of letters [in Gratius' *Lamentationes obscurorum virorum*, Cologne, 1519] also depicted the Reuchlinists as anti-Christian pagans who hurt the Church by aiding the Jews"; idem, "Scholastic Opposition to Humanism in Pre-Reformation Germany," *Viator* 7 (1976) 391–420; 398, 419. For Ortvinus (Ortwijn, Gratius of Deventer (c. 1480–1542) as victim of 'unjust attacks' see Jozef Ijsewijn, "The Coming of Humanism to the Low Countries," in *Itinerarium Italicum* (above, n. 9), 193–301; 277, 290.

17. See Yosef Hayim Yerushalmi, *The Lisbon Massacre of 1506 and the Royal Image in the Shebet Yehudah*, Hebrew Union College Annual Supplements 1 (Cincinnati, 1976), 2.

18. Josef Benzing, *Bibliographie der Schriften Johannes Reuchlins im 15. und 16. Jahrhundert*, Bibliotheca Bibiographica 18 (Bad Bocklet and Wien, 1955). Cf. Guido Kisch, *Zasius und Reuchlin. Eine rechtsgeschichtlich-vergleichende Studie zum Toleranzproblem im 16. Jahrhundert*, Pforzheimer Reuchlinschriften 1 (Konstanz and Stuttgart, 1961), 71.

19. J. Benzing, *Bibliographie der Schriften Reuchlins*, 26.

20. Reprint of the Amerbach edition of *De verbo mirifico* (Basel, 1494) together with *De arte cabalistica* (Hagenau, 1517; Stuttgart—Bad Cannstatt, 1964). The second edition of *De verbo mirifico* was published in the same year, 1494, by Thomas Anshelm, the patron of the so-called 'Tübingen Academy'. See my critique of this epitheton in *Werden und Wertung der Reformation. Vom Wegestreit zum Glaubenskampf*, 2nd ed. (Tübingen, 1979), 19–24.

21. It is the continuation of "Pico's attempt to subordinate the occult sciences to religion through the agency of Kabbalah." Charles Zika, "Reuchlin's *De Verbo Mirifico*

and the Magic Debate of the Late Fifteenth Century," *Journal of the Warburg and Courtauld Institutes* 49 (1976), 104–138; 138.

22. *De verbo mirifico*, fol. a 2^r. Johannes Franciscus Pico, nephew of Reuchlin's greatest Italian example, later (1512) quite appropriately summarizes this 'Dialogue' with the words: ". . . de verbo mirifico secundum tria dogmata, scilicet philosophorum, Judaeorum et Christianorum, ubi continetur nomen sacrum id est tetragrammaton ineffabile, quin potius pentragrammaton effabile." Geiger, *Reuchlins Briefwechsel*, 88.

23. The word used by Reuchlin, 'resipiscentia', does not necessarily mean 'penance'; some ten years later it will be used by Erasmus in his *Novum Instrumentum* as the Latin equivalent of the Greek word 'metanoia', conversion. In his *Breviloquus* (1494; Benzing, *Bibliographie der Schriften Reuchlins*) Reuchlin describes 'resipere' as 'iterum sapere': "proprie ille resipit, qui penitens forefacti redit ad satisfactionem. . . ." See the "Index," s.v. 'resipere'.

24. *De verbo mirifico*, fol. b 5^v; cf. c 6^r. The unique features of Reuchlin's 'three rings' may appear most clearly in comparison with the trilogue in Cusanus' *De Pace Fidei* (shortly after the fall of Constantinople in 1453). See the edition by John P. Dolan, *Unity and Reform. Selected Writings of Nicholas de Cusa* (Notre Dame, Ind., 1962), 195–237; cf. 185–194.

25. ". . . vos legitima sacra mutastis: ideoque frustra murmuratis, frustra deum invocatis quem non ut ipse vult colitis, sed inventionibus vestris blandientes etiam nos dei cultores livore immortali oditis. . . ." *De verbo mirifico*, fol. b 5^v.

26. Benzing, *Bibliographie der Schriften Reuchlins*, 25. Cf. G. Kisch, *Zasius und Reuchlin*, 16–22.

27. Cf. Kisch, ibid., 19.

28. Geiger finds in this treatise 'das Princip einer milden Duldung der Juden'. *Reuchlin. Sein Leben*, 164. He points to the 'praiseworthy' fact that Reuchlin does not call for the eviction of the Jews; ibid., 208. The same observation is made by G. Kisch, *Zasius und Reuchlin*, 20. See, however, Reuchlin: If the Jews burden society with their usury "essent per superiores nostros emendandi et reformandi seu expellendi. . . ." *Doctor Johannsen Reuchlins . . . Augenspiegel* (Tübingen, 1511), fol. H 2^v; reprint ed., Quellen zur Geschichte des Humanismus und der Reformation in Faksimile-Ausgaben 5, München, [1961]. It is to be remembered that Reuchlin's first sponsor and protector, Count Eberhard im Bart, had in his testament stipulated that the Jews be evicted from his dominions—carried through since 1492. Reuchlin was Eberhard's council and together with Gabriel Biel was a member of the Rome delegation which requested papal authorization for the University of Tübingen (1477). Eberhard's founding letter excluded Jews from this city. For the most recent data on Reuchlin's life see Hansmartin Decker-Hauff, "Bausteine zur Reuchlin-Biographie," in *Johannes Reuchlin 1455–1522. Festgabe seiner Vaterstadt Pforzheim zur 500. Wiederkehr seines Geburtstages*, ed. M. Krebs (Pforzheim, [1955]), 83–107. For Eberhard's anti-Jewish policy see Lilli Zapf, *Die Tübinger Juden. Eine Dokumentation* (Tübingen, [1974]), 15f.

29. Cf. G. Kisch, *Zasius und Reuchlin*, 20. Reuchlin has made good on his concluding offer to further the social integration of converted Jews by 'placing' them as Hebrew teachers in monasteries: They should serve the purpose of spreading the knowledge of Hebrew which in turn is the necessary basis for introduction to the Kabbalah. See the revealing autobiographical letter to Ellenbog of March 19, 1510 in *Nikolaus Ellenbog, Briefwechsel*, ed. A. Bigelmair and F. Zoepfl, Corpus Catholicorum 19/21 (Münster, 1938), 54 f.

30. "Persaepe mihi cogitanti de communi sacarum literarum jactura, Dionysi frater, quae cum multitudine sophismatum annis superioribus, tum maxime nunc propter eloquentiae studium et poretarum amoenitatem non modo negliguntur, verum etiam a quam plurimis contemptui habentur, in mentem venit tandem opportuni cujusdam remedii, ne sanctae bibliae scriptura vel aliquando tota pereat. . . ." Geiger, *Reuchlins Briefwechsel*, 88 f.

31. "Fateor itaque, circa literarum rationem puerorum esse studia, et esse me etiam eo nunc provectum, ut partim me philosophum, partim jurisconsultum arbitrentur his de causis maxime, tum quod ex Capnione nostro quem edidimus 'De verbo mirifico'

non nihil quod verae philosophiae accedat, sibi persuadeant posse exanclari, tum quod jam annos complures super fortissimis Suevis confoederatos principes dignitatem triumviratus non ambitione sed electione mera sim consecutus, eumque honorem usque in hunc diem servare me sentiant inconcussum atque sanctum"; ibid., 90. The lukewarm support of Reuchlin by a majority of the humanists in the ensuing battle can indeed be explained by their preoccupation with the Greek and Latin authors. As Hans Widmann has pointed out the great Hebrew master failed to find a market for his *De Rudimentis*. "Zu Reuchlins Rudimenta Hebraica," in *Festschrift für Josef Benzing*, ed. E. Geck, G. Pressler (Wiesbaden, 1964), 492–498. Apparently not only the scholastic 'Hochburgen' like Cologne, but also the humanist sodalities did not hail Hebrew studies at this 'early' date.

32. "Inscriptio hujus libri est: 'De rudimentis hebraicis', eo quod non jam doctis, sed rudibus ac erudiendis ea volumina composuerim, deinceps altiora deo annuente daturus, quae ad arcanae Pythagorae disciplinam et artem Cabalisticam deserviunt, a nemine prorsus intellecta, nisi Hebraice praedocto." Geiger, *Reuchlins Briefwechsel*, 93.

33. ". . . ego miseratus tam sanctas literas, indolui, mea aetate studiosos diutius hebraicae linguae scientia carere: quapropter illorum ingenio favens ausus sum, licet supra modum forsan temere, primus omnium et tam grave pondus meis humeris imponere et simul me offerre latratibus mordacium; utinam judaicis solum." Ibid., 90.

34. "At gravius insurgent, credo, invidi contra Dictionarium nostrum in quo multorum frequenter interpretationes taxantur. Proh scelus, exclamabunt, nihil indignius patrum memoria, nihil admissum crudelius, cum ille homo audacissimus tot et tam sanctos viros divino spiritu afflatos labefactare contendat. Hieronymi beatissimi scriptura, Gelasio Papa teste, recepta est in ecclesia, venerabilis pater Nicolaus de Lyra, ordinarius expositor Bibliae, omnibus Christifidelibus vir integerrimus probatur." Ibid., 97.

35. Ibid., 98.

36. Cf. ibid., 91f.

37. Ibid., 93.

38. ". . . nolui etiam huic decori tuo deesse quin hebraica, nunc sacerdos, addisceres, praesertim cum nostrates Judaei vel invidia, vel imperitia ducti Christianum neminem in eorum lingua erudire velint idque recusant cujusdam Rab[b]i Ami auctoritate, qui in Thalmud . . . ita dixit: 'Non explanantur verba legis cuiquam gentili eo quod scriptum est: Qui adnunciat verba sua Jacob, praecepta sua et judicia sua Israel non fecit similiter omni genti.' Nobis autem in statu gratiae aliter mandatur [Mt. 10:27]. . . ." Ibid., 100.

39. Kisch, (above, n. 18), 23–36.

40. *Augenspiegel*, fol. E 4^{v}., Cf. Johannes Reuchlin, *Gutachten über das jüdische Schrifttum*, ed. and trans. A. Leinz-v. Dessauer, Pforzheimer Reuchlinschriften 2 (Konstanz and Stuttgart, 1965), 106f.

41. *Augenspiegel*, fol. J 3^{r}.

42. ". . . conservandus esset saltem apud ordinarios, ut docti apud nos in lingua hebraea aliquando possent eum habere, et ubi Iudaei aliqua futuris temporibus confingerent, possent cum opus esset probati apparere in reprobatione eius et condemnatione." *Augenspiegel*, fol. F 3^{r}.

43. Not all the Jewish books are to be burned, but some are to be preserved: "Ad hoc respondeo intelligendum esse dictum meum quod non debeant comburi universaliter et omnes, sed quod aliqui essent conservandi. . . ." *Augenspiegel*, fol. H 2^{r}. I differ at this point from Wilhelm Maurer who concluded in his otherwise excellent study: "Bildungseinheit statt Judenmission — das ist im Grunde Reuchlins Programm, durch das er das Anliegen der Judenemanzipation vom Ende des 18. Jahrhunderts schon vorweg nimmt." *Kirche und Synagoge. Motive und Formen der Auseinandersetzung der Kirche mit dem Judentum im Laufe der Geschichte (Stuttgart, 1953), 38.*

44. See the bibliographical data given by G. Kisch, *Zasius und Reuchlin*, 75, n. 3.

45. Translated as *Speculum adhortationis Judaice ad Christum.* For this international forum I prefer to use the Latin edition with the explict: Editum Colonie per Iohannem pefferkorn [sic] olim Judeum modo Chirsitanum. Anno domini 1507, feria tertia post Decollationem sancti Joannis baptiste.

46. Meier Spanier has questioned the authenticity of Pfefferkorn's pamphlets. The Latin works are excluded *in toto*: "Er konnte kein Latein." "Zur Charakteristik Johannes Pfefferkorns," *Zeitschrift für die Geschichte der Juden in Deutschland* 6 (1936), 209–229; 210. But also the German pamphlets are said to betray external guidance. His Hebrew and Talmud knowledge were not a bit better: "Er wußte eben nicht mehr als irgendein anderer ungebildeter Jude der damaligen Zeit; vom Talmud verstand er gar nichts . . . ," ibid., 212, Finally, also all typically German 'folksy' colloquial sayings, "von denen einige uraltes deutsches Sprachgut," are proof of Cologne 'humanist' origin, ibid., 222. Our *Speculum adhortationis Judaice* (*Judenspiegel*, Latin and German edition, 1507) is almost completely assigned to Ortvinus: "Die erste Schrift . . . dürfte fast ganz ein Werk des Ortuin Gratius sein," ibid., 221. A collection of the German and Latin Pfefferkorn writings is being gathered at the Institut für Spätmittelalter und Reformation in Tübingen to facilitate future research. It should be noted that the Latin versions are not in keeping with late medieval scholastic Latin. Perhaps intentionally so; but in that case the riddle is unsolvable. As far as Pfefferkorn's 'Bildungsstand' is concerned, Josef was several years in Prague the houseguest of Rabbi Meir Pfefferkorn and must, in view of his successful mission to the sister of Emperor Maximilian, have possessed better credentials than assumed by Spanier. Cf. Heinrich Graetz, *Volkstümliche Geschichte der Juden*, 3 vols. (Berlin and Vienna, 1923), 3: 170–220; 175 and 185.

47. This limitation is noted, however, by Salo Wittmayer Baron, *A Social and Religious History of the Jews*, 16 vols., 2nd. ed., rev. and enlarged (New York, 1952–1976), vol. 13; *Inquisition, Renaissance, and Reformation*, 184–191; 186.

48. "Ergo omnes huiusmodi fallacias et fabulas continentes libros [Talmoth] auferte ab oculis eorum, et in ignem mittite. Ita magnum facietis opus charitatis, cum occasione errorum sublata eos inducetis in viam rectam. Postquam amiserint hos libros, tum convertent se eo promptius et facilius ad sacras literas," *Speculum adhortationis Judaice* [=*Speculum*], fol. C 4^v. Actually Pfefferkorn makes three proposals. Usury should be forbidden, since to be a usurous Jew is more attractive than to be a poor Christian; fol. C 1^r–C 2^v. Secondly, Jews should be forced to attend Christian sermons: This is merely a return favor since without the (preaching of the) Jews Christians would still be worshipping idols: "adhuc adoraretis idola"; fol. C 4^r. Thirdly, the Jewish books should be confiscated and burned: "ita magnum facietis opus charitatis"; fol. C 4^v.

49. "Notorium est quod magnis vectigalibus censibus teloneis pecunia pro tuitione et securitate onerantur, quasi servum pecus et hec prestare coguntur, quamvis sint liberi quasi avis. . . ." *Speculum*, fol. C 4^v–D 1^r.

50. Cf. *Speculum*, fol. C 4^v–D 1^r.

51. See Guido Kisch, *The Jews in Medieval Germany. A Study of their Legal and Social Status* (Chicago, 1949), 129 ff.; 145–153.

52. The principle on which Reuchlin bases his 'concives', thus according the Jews the legal status of 'fellow citizens', had by the end of the Middle Ages lost its—relatively seen—positive aspects when nobility and city magistrates vied with the Emperor for the 'protection' taxes, usually only yielding a residency permit for six years. See the documents published by Friedrich Battenberg, "Zur Rechtsstellung der Juden am Mittelrhein in Spätmittelalter und früher Neuzeit," *Zeitschrift für historische Forschung* 6 (1979), 129–183; 'Urkundenanhang', 171–183; and the transition as described by Renate Overdick, *Die rechtliche und wirtschaftliche Stellung der Juden in Südwestdeutschland im 15. und 16. Jahrhundert, dargestellt an den Reichsstädten Konstanz und Eßlingen und an der Markgrafschaft Baden*, Konstanzer Geschichts- und Rechtsquellen 15 (Konstanz, 1965), 158–164.

53. "Homo qui vetus testamentum intelligit, novum legit, ex vetere novum dilucide cognoscit, neutra parte labascens. Dum nova veteribus novis vetera componit, necesse est ut oblectetur, quoniam ex figuris spiritum videt, spiritum oculis mentis quasi corpus oculis corporis cernens. Ita Iudeis accidit, quoniam ipsi acutius et comprehensibilius ad intelligendum sua dispositi profundius plerisque ceteris inquirunt et examinant scripturas. Cum et apud eos vera sint sacrarum scripturarum fundamenta originaliaque primordia a deo tradita per servos eius, hebraica lingua perscripta et multe particule sunt et clausule in sacris literis in libris Moisis presertim secrete adhuc et obstruse, que

tamen possent prodire in lucem per eos. Ego certum puto imo nec dubito, quoniam [quin] omnis scientia, que naturali ratione comprehendi potest, veluti astronomia et cetere, in sacra maxime scriptura in litteris hebraicis mirabiliter complexa et occultata sit. Non verbis solum, sed (ut dixi) litteris, praeterea Sancta Mysteria ex singulari earum litterarum vix aliis cognoscibilium extra Judeos proprietate. Quapropter hebrei omnia hec perscrutantur funditus, et conversi ad religionem christianam conferent ea tandem ad intellectum fidei, unde dominus noster Iesus Christus laudari queat et cognosci. . . . " *Speculum*, fol. D 3^v.

54. L. Geiger, *Johannes Reuchlin. Sein Leben*, 283. Cf. H. Graetz, *Volkstümliche Geschichte* 3, 188.

55. "Vos autem fratres Judei secundum carnem et o christiani fratres spiritu auscultante, . . . aurem paulisper accommodate. Late et vulgo dicitur iudeos mansuros eorumque stirpem et religionem (cum horum multa interierint) in finem usque mundi, tum erit ovile unum, una fides, unus pastor. Ex meis nonnullis propositis et animo multa repetenti meditatis videtur prope adesse novissimus mundi dies. Dico ego ad hoc, quantum intelligo et sentio, Judeorum gens, non unus solum aut alter convertetur ad fidem Christi, si a christianis ita tractentur et habeantur, ut dixi et consului . . . an venturus sit dies novissimus brevi aut multo post conversionem iudeorum nihil certi scio . . . omnino sic fore credo, quod mutatio humanarum rerum orietur et consurget brevi in mundo, maxime in populo christiano." *Speculum*, fol. D 4^r.

56. This ambivalence is also part and parcel of the confiscation plan itself: "non quasi vi sed in emendationem Judeorum." *Speculum*, fol. D 1^r. Furthermore, it is necessary for us, for the Church: " . . . quandiu idola hec (sic enim nominare placet hos falsos et blasphemos libros) non tolluntur e medio et internitioni [sic] dantur, nunquam ecclesia christiana in quiete et pace erit aut perdurabit." Ibid.

57. For Luther see the concluding passage of his famous 1523 treatise (see below, n. 110): "For they have been led astray for so long that one must deal gently with them. . . . In this way some may be won over. Instead of this we try to drive them by force. . . . So long as we treat them like dogs how can be expect to work any good among them? Again when we will not let them work or do business or have any human fellowship with us, and so force them into practising usury, how can that do them any good? If we really want to help them, we must be guided by Christian love, not by popish legalism. We must receive them cordially and allow them to trade and work among us, hear our Christian teaching and witness our Christian life style. If some of them prove obstinate, what of that? We are not such good Christians ourselves." *WA* 11. 336, lines 19–34; translation according to *Luther's Works*, American Edition, vol. 45 (Philadelphia, 1962) 229, cited by E. Gordon Rupp, *Martin Luther and the Jews*, Robert Waley Cohen Memorial Lecture, 1972 (London, 1972), 11f. For Pfefferkorn note: "Igitur vos, o charissimi christiani, obtestor per nomen Iesu redemptoris nostri, qui cum publicanis et peccatoribus manducavit, qui a peccatrice sanctos pedes suos lachrymis eius lavari et a samaritana petere potum non dedignitus est, recipite iudeos benigne, oculos commiserationis in eos coniicite, misereminique populi dei, quem in miseriis et exilio cernitis. Adversus eos mites et moderati sitis suaviter eos doceatis instituatis non modo in fide, verum etiam illis opera misericordie et virtutum impartiamini. Ipsi enim inordinato et incomposito regimine moralis vite secundum naturam motumque sensualem potius vivunt. Hec via est quam dominus Iesus monuit et docuit, ut tandem in unum ovile [John 10:16] cum pastore nostro Iesu Christo, qui animam suam posuit pro ovibus suis, conveniamus rabidis luporum morsibus non derelicti. Quod vobis concedat pius pater et misericors dominus. Amen." *Speculum*, fol. D 3^v–4^r.

58. " . . . veniet dominus noster Jesus Christus qui non cum Iudeis fuerat temporis in carne . . . " *Speculum*, fol E 3^v. " . . . meditemur passionem domini Jesu assidue, sequamur doctrinam eius, in fide integra perseveremus, contemptum eius non feramus aut patiamur, ulciscamur pro viribus." Ibid.

59. Cf. *WA* 51. 195f.; 15 February, 1546; sermon preached three days before his death.

60. If Jews kill children at all it is out of revenge but not to get blood for medical purposes: "Fugite ergo et vitate orationem hanc ridiculam, falsam, et (si recte

conspicere vultis) nobis christianis non parum contemptui existentem." *Speculum*, fol. D 1v.

61. Gottfried Seebaß, 'Verzeichnis der Werke Andreas Osianders, 'in *Das reformatorische Werk des Andreas Osiander*, Einzelarbeiten aus der Kirchengeschichte Bayerns 44 (Nürnberg, 1967), 6–58; 17, no 80. In the *Bibliographia Osiandrica. Bibliographie der gedruckten Schriften Andreas Osianders d. Ä. (1496–1552)*, (ed. G. Seebass, Nieuwkoop, 1971) this treatise is dated as "1540?" with the comment, "Originaldruck nicht gefunden." Ibid. 124, no. 29. My Erlangen colleague, Professor Gerhard Müller, kindly provided me with a copy of the only known print which is in American 'Privatbesitz'. Moritz Stern edited this text with a preface under the title *Andreas Osianders Schrift über die Blutbeschuldigung* (Kiel, 1893).

62. Emanuel Hirsch, *Die Theologie des Andreas Osiander und ihre geschichtlichen Voraussetzungen* (Göttingen, 1919), 276–280; G. Seebaß, *Das reformatorische Werk des Andreas Osiander*, 82–85. For Osiander's attitude to Judaism see his revealing request to the town council of Nuremberg (17 February, 1529) to allow a Jewish teacher to visit and train him in Aramaic: "Dieweil nun unwidersprechlich ist, das die Juden baide, das gesetz und propheten, baß [besser] verstehn dan wir Christen, ausgenomen, das sie die person nicht fur Christum halten, die wir darfur erkennen, und sonst auch vil guts verstands und grosser gehaimnus haben, deren sie ytzo selbs nicht geprauchen, als die nichts mer studirn, sonder nur dem wucher und andern posen stucken anhangen, were es ye wol werd, das die Christen solchs zu sich prechten, nicht allain wider die Juden, sonder auch fur sich selbs zu geprauchen, welchs aber nicht geschehen kan noch mag on verstand der caldaischen sprach. Dieweil aber bißher in vil hundert jaren kain Christ dieselben konnt hat, es were dan der graff Picus von Mirandula, der zu frue gestorben, ists offenbar, das wir die von Juden mussen lernen; dan das sie ymand von im selbs solt lernen, ist unmuglich, dieweil wir weder grammatica noch vocubularien darzu haben, die gegrundt wern." *Andreas Osiander d. Ä. Gesamtausgabe*, vol. 3: *Schriften und Briefe 1528 bis April 1530*, ed. G. Müller, G. Seebaß (Gütersloh, 1979), 337, lines 14–25. This request may well have started the rumor that Osiander was a Jew. See the excursus of G. Seebaß, *Das reformatorische Werk*, 82–85.

63. "Zum zwelfften so sein die taufften Juden hin und wider an mancherley orten in mancherley weg von geschickten gelerten und weysen leuten bespracht [i.e. verleumdet] worden und hat doch keiner nie bekant das er etwas darvon wisse oder das er glaube das es war sey. Nun werden nicht allein die Juden getaufft die auß gottes gnaden die warheyt erkennen. Sonder auch ye zuzeyten die so unter den Juden jrer mißhandlung halben veracht, verstossen, und verbannet sein. Nun hat ye kein teyl ursach die sach zu verlaugnen wann etwas dran were. Dan die rechtglaubigen solten es ja Christo dem herrn zu ehren bekennen und oeffnen, damit die Christen gewarnet und weg gesucht wurden das man solchs ubel unterkeme. Die andern aber so auß haß der Juden Christen werden, solten es freylich auch nich verschweygen von jren feynden und verfolgern. Als dann der Pfefferkorn zu Coeln den Juden zu wider vil angezeygt und eroeffnet hat—obs alles war gewest oder nit, ist hie nicht not anzuzeygen. Het er aber von der kinder mord etwas gewust, wie were es jm und seinen Prediger munchen ein freud gewest das selb anzuzeygen, und aller welt bekant zu machen." *Ob es war und glaublich sey, daß die Juden der Christen kinder heymlich erwürgen und jr blut gebrauchen ein treffenliche schrifft auff eines yeden urteil gestelt* (s.a., s.l. [1540]), fol. b 1v–b 2r.

64. Ingolstadt, 1541. Durch Joh. Ecken. I used the copy of the 1542 edition at the University Library, Freiburg.

65. Johann Casper Ulrichs includes this 'event' in a survey which he concludes with the words: "Wir beschliessen nun diese Mord Geschichten mit vielem Eckel, und gestehe[n] gerne daß aus so vielen Mordthaten, die man ehedem den Juden aufgebürdet hat, die allermeisten schändliche und unverantwortliche Zulagen seyen. Es dienet auch der Christenheit nicht zur Ehre, daß man aus diesen angegebenen Martyrern Heilige gemachet hat." *Sammlung Jüdischer Geschichten, welche sich mit diesem Volk in dem XIII. und folgenden Jahrhunderten bis auf MDCCLX. in der Schweitz von Zeit zu Zeit zugetragen. Zur Beleuchtung der allgemeinen Historie dieser Nation herausgegeben* (Basel, 1768), 92, 87.

66. J. Eck, *Ains Judenbüchlins Verlegung*, fol. G 2^{v}.
67. Ibid., fol. G 3^{r}.
68. Ibid., fol. N 4^{r-v}.
69. Ibid., fol. H 3^{v}.
70. Eck alludes to well recorded events at Freiburg, "a community with a long tradition of special hostility to Jews." Steven W. Rowan, "Ulrich Zasius and the Baptism of Jewish Children," *Sixteenth Century Journal* 6, 2 (1975), 3–25; 7; German translation: "Ulrich Zasius und die Taufe jüdischer Kinder," *Zeitschrift des Breisgau-Geschichtsvereins ("Schau-ins-Land")* 97 (1978), 79–98; 82.
71. *Ains Judenbuchlins Verlegung*, fol. J 3^{r}.
72. " . . . kumt auch da ain newe frucht herfur ains luterischen, der schön machen will der juden kindermord." Ibid., fol. N 4^{r}.
73. Ibid., fol. Q 4^{r}.
74. Cf. Selma Stern, *Josel von Rosheim. Befehlshaber der Judenschaft im Heiligen Römischen Reich Deutscher Nation*, Veröffentlichung des Leo-Baeck-Instituts (Stuttgart, 1959), 83.
75. Why then, Eck shrewdly insists, did not the *Confessio Augustana* (1530) reject the Vulgate and argue on the basis of the Hebrew text! *Ains Judenbuchlins Verlegung*, fol. Q 1^{r-v}.
76. *Erasmus' Stellung zu Juden und Judentum*, Philosophie und Geschichte 83/84 (Tübingen, 1969). After the appearance of this article, Cornelis Augustijn published "Erasmus und die Juden," *Nederlands Archief voor Kerkgeschiedenis* 60 (1980), 22–38. More clearly—and most appropriately—Augustijn underscores that 'Iudaei' often refers to legalistic Christians. Yet, I cannot agree with his conclusion that Erasmus respects the individual Jew *sub specie aeternitatis*: "Das Judentum hat als Religion keine Zukunft. Die Juden schon!" Ibid., 37. Erasmus' expectation that ultimately all Jews would be converted is not a specific view on his part. The whole tragedy of toleration based on conversion is formulated by Erasmus himself: " . . . quia Paulus praedixit fore ut Judaei tandem aggregentur ad ovile Christi, toleramus impaiam ac blasphemam gentem. . . ." "Declarationes ad censuras facultatis theologiae parisiensis," *Opera omnia* (Leiden, 1703–1706, reprint ed., London, 1962), IX. pag. 909AB; quoted by C. Augustijn, "Erasmus und die Juden," 37, n. 95. Simon Markish does not go beyond Augustijn in bringing new arguments. *Erasme et les Juifs* (Lausanne, 1979).
77. In the Toronto edition of Erasmus' letters, exemplary both in its translations and in its annotations, we find an exceptionally long note to letter 541, which is addressed to Wolfgang Capito, dated 26 February, 1517. Erasmus' warning against the revival of Judaism, "the most pernicious plague . . . ," is explained in terms of "a deep Paulinism rather than any notable interest in, or concern about, the Jewish community . . . ;" *Collected Works of Erasmus. The Correspondence of Erasmus* [=*EL*], trans. R. A. B. Mynors, D. F. S. Thomson, annotated J. K. McConica (Toronto, 1974ff.), 4: 266f.; note to line 154. Though Kisch (see nn. 76, 78) is referred to in the preface to letter 694 which at the end of the same year is addressed to Pirckheimer (2 November, 1517), Erasmus' view of the Jews in connection with Pfefferkorn—here designated as a Dominican (!)—is characterized as "unprecedented as far as his earlier correspondence is concerned." Ibid., 5:164.
78. G. Kisch, *Erasmus' Stellung zu Juden und Judentum*, 29.
79. Allen, 2:501, lines 10–13; *EL* 4:279, lines 12–15; 10 March, 1517.
80. Allen, 3:127, line 24.
81. Ibid., lines 37f.
82. Allen, 3:253, lines 25f. Cf. *EL* 5:347, lines 26–28.
83. Erasmus' concern is of course to deny his complicity in the publication of the *Illustrorum virorum Epistolae* of May 1519, particularly after Hochstraten's publication in April, 1519 of the *Destructio Cabale* in which he attacked also Erasmus' *Novum Instrumentum*; see Allen, 4:120–122; 121, lines 13, 16f. Erasmus' denial contains a double untruth since Reuchlin not only asked Erasmus explicitly to champion his cause, Allen 1:556, lines 22–28; *EL* 2:285, lines 25–33 (April, 1514), but secondly, Erasmus had actually written on Reuchlin's behalf to Cardinal Riario († 1521), generally thought to be *papabilis*. Allen, 2:73, lines 135–138; *EL* 3:91, lines 145–148 (15 May, 1515).

84. In Bad Liebenzell on 30 June, 1522. See Hans Rupprich, "Johannes Reuchlin und seine Bedeutung im europäischen Humanismus," in *Johannes Reuchlin* [above, n. 28], 10–34; 33. Cf. Allen, 5:124, line 46 and corresponding note.

85. His name is to be inserted in the saints' calendar just as in the library his books "... proxime divum Hieronymum." *Desiderio Erasmo da Rotterdam: L'apoteosi di Giovanni Reuchlin*, ed. and trans. G. Vallese (Naples, 1949), 130, lines 210f.

86. "Quod olim fecit Sathanas per Scribas et Pharisaeos in Dominum Iesum, hoc et nunc facit per Pharisaicos quosdam in optimos quosque viros, ac de genere mortalium suis vigiliis bene merentes. Nunc ille metit optiman messem pro semente quam fecit. Interim nostrae partes erunt illius memoriam habere sacrosanctam; illius nomen ferre laudibus; ac subinde illum salutare verbis huiusmodi: O sancta anima, sis felix linguis sanctis, perdito malas linguas, infectas veneno gehennae." Ibid., 134, lines 247–257.

87. Cf. his letter to John Fisher dated 1 September, 1522; Allen, 5:123, lines 19f.

88. To Hochstraten, 11 August, 1519; Allen, 4:46, lines 142f.

89. For the parallel phenomenon with Jerome, Erasmus' favorite Church father, see Horst Dieter Rauh, *Das Bild des Antichrist im Mittelalter: Von Tyconius zum Deutschen Symbolismus*, 2. ed., Beiträge zur Geschichte der Philosophie und Theologie des Mittelalters, NF 9 (Münster, 1979), 132f.

90. Though a constant theme in Erasmus' writings, a most concise formulation is found in *Commentarii in Psalmum 'Beatus vir'* [Ps. 1] *finis*, often overlooked while attached to the second edition of the *Enchiridion* (Basel, 1518): "Sub lege sunt servi, in lege liberi. Iudaei . . . nihil habentes praeter insipidam litteram, legis onere gravantur. . . . Superstitio litterae contrahit animum, spiritus et caritas dilatat." *Opera omnia* [above, n. 76], V, pag. 182B. Cf. "Item, qui summo legis cortici insistit, non meditatur in lege Domini. Cortex insipidus est plerumque tum adeo non frugifer, ut pestilens etiam ac letalis, teste Paulo." Pag. 183A.

91. To Capito, 26 February, 1517; Allen, 2: 491, lines 138f.; *EL* 4: 267, lines 154f.

92. See Charles Zika, "Reuchlin and Erasmus: Humanism and Occult Philosophy," *Journal of Religious History* 9, 3 (1977), 223–246; 229.

93. "Nunc audimus apud Bohemos exoriri novum Iudaeorum genus, Sabbatarios appellant, . . . " *De amabili* [Allen: *Liber de sarcienda*] *Ecclesiae concordia*, dedicated to Julis Pflug, and dated 31 July 1533. Erasmus, *Opera Omnia* [above, n. 76] V. pag. 505D–506A. Cf. "Dicuntur et hodie repullulascere Sabbatarii, qui septimi diei otium incredibili superstitione observant." *Ecclesiastae, sive de ratione concionandi*, lib. III, dedicated to Christoph von Stadion, dated 6 August 1535. Ibid., pag. 1038B.

94. "Nuper exierunt in vulgus aliquot libelli merum Iudaismum resipientes," Allen, 2:491, lines 147f.

95. "... ne renascentibus Hebraeorum literis Iudaismus meditetur per occasionem reviviscere." Ibid., lines 137f.

96. Oberman, *Werden und Wertung*, 199f.; 263–266.

97. Cp. Johannes Teuschlein, 'Auflosung ettlicher Fragen zu lob und ere christi Jesu auch seiner lieben mutter Marie wider die verstockten plinten Juden und alle die jhenen so sie in jren landen und stetten wider recht enthalten füren und gedulden neülich geschehen,' printed by Fryderich Peypus, Nuremberg, 1520.

98. "Als es aber jetzo in der welt steet/ dz gemeinlich alle stend beladen seind mit dem teufflischen geytz/ so wil uns nützer sein/ dz wir sie von uns weysen/ dan gedulden." Ibid., fol. C 2^{r}. "Seitmal nun die juden uns sovil schaden bringen an leib/ seel/ eer und gut/ so lernet uns das natürlich gesetz/ das wir sie nach unserem vermügen sollen verweisen." Fol. C 3^{r}. "Darumb auch etwa der herr durch Titum und Vespasianum/ als seinen verwalter gerochen der juden missethat durch außtreybung von dem jren." Fol. C 3^{v}. "Sehen wir aber an die sitten der menschen geistlicher und weltlicher/ finden wir das sie sich vol gefressen haben durch juden gut das der kropff der selbigen geschenck gar schwerlichen von jn gezogen mag werden/ deßhalb die juden solcher ort nit leichtlich vertriben." Fol. C 4^{v}. Mary, answering a prayer: "Du bittest mich umb das/ so thu du auch meinen willen/ treib von dir/ mein und meynes lieben suns grosse feindt." Fol. C 5^{r}.

99. In one case the ritual murder charge is not contradicted in order to defend the

Jews but to sharpen the accusation; they do not thirst after Christian blood for 'medical' purposes but out of blank hatred: "Es ist gleublich was ich uch sag/ den ir gantzer ostertag/ allein dorumb ist uff gestifft/ das er ir find uff erd antrifft/ Wie parro der vor was ir here/ mit allem volck erdranck im mere/ . . . So sy nun kein parro haben/ des nemen sy ein christen knaben/ Dem sy vergiessen do syn blut/ alß obs ein findt dem andren dut." 'Enderung und schmach der bildung Marie von den juden bewissen. und zu ewiger gedechtniß durch Maximilian den römischen keyser zu malen verschaffet in der löblichen stat kolmer. von dannen sy ouch ewig vertriben syndt' (anonymous, s.a., s.1.; cf. Emil Weller, *Repertorium Typographicum*, Nördlingen, 1864, no. 1), fol. D 5^r. "Ich habs von einem ein verstandt/ wie das sy gsyn in hispaier landt/ do sy das under in erkandt/ In eim concilium betracht/das die iuden handt gemacht/ Das ieder fliß sich wer do mag/ das kein iud den ostertag/ Begang on christen blut do by/das alle zytt ein zeichen sy/ Allen die dar syndt gesessen/ unnd handt matz kuchen do selbst gessen/ Das sy das christen blut erman/ mit uns ein ewige findtschafft zu han." Fol. D 6^v. "Darumb in soelches blutes krafft/ bestettiget wurdt ir bruderschafft/ Der christen hatt kein groesseren findt/ den fur wor die iuden sindt/ Die unser blut all tag begeren/ das sy gern unser herren weren/ Sy durstet alle zytt und stundt/ noch unserem blut—der recht blut hundt/ Dorumb sol mans ouch mit in tryben/ das sy solch schelmen moegen blyben/ Wir ziehen ein schlangen in dem geren/ der im syn gifft nit lasset weren/ Den es sich alle stundt dut meren/ wider christum unßeren lieben herren." Fol. E 1^r.

100. *Der Antichrist und Die Fünfzehn Zeichen vor dem Jüngsten Gericht. Faksimile der ersten typographischen Ausgabe eines unbekannten Straßburger Druckers, um 1480*, 2 vols. (Textband, Kommentarband), ed. Ch. P. Burger et al. (Hamburg, 1979), Textband, 5.2. Cf. especially the commentary by Christoph Peter Burger, "Endzeiterwartung im späten Mittelalter. Der Bildertext zum Antichrist und den Fünfzehn Zeichen vor dem Jüngsten Gericht in der frühesten Druckausgabe," Kommentarband, 18–53; 36, 39, 43.

101. Ibid., 47ff.

102. See my article "Fourteenth-Century Religoius Thought: A Premature Profile," *Speculum* 53 (1978), 80–93; 90f. For rich materials see Hans Preuß, *Die Vorstellungen vom Antichrist im späteren Mittelalter, bei Luther und in der konfessionellen Polemik. Ein Beitrag zur Theologie Luthers und zur Geschichte der christlichen Frömmigkeit* (Leipzig, 1906), 12ff., and Joshua Trachtenberg, *The Devil and the Jews. The Medieval Conception of the Jew and its Relation to Modern Antisemitism*, Harper Torchbooks, The Temple Library TB 822 (New York, 1966; New Haven, 1943), 32–43.

103. George, Duke of Bavaria (1486–1529), and Bishop of Speyer (1515–1529) argues on the basis of the wrath of God in a hitherto overlooked harsh 'Mandat' (4 April 1519) against the Jews, for him 'rather dogs than human beings'. As with Pfefferkorn we find here the charge against the secular authorities of bribery by the Jews: "Quo circa officii nostri esse visum est tante hominum seu potius canum perversitati quocumque modo resistere aut obviam ire, et eo magis cum seculares prefecti quorum esset [officium] hec nephanda ob christi gloriam prohibere, non solum hec non prohibeant, sed interdum (judeorum donis corrupti) etiam tolerent et quantum in ipsis est non sine gravi peccato tutentur. . . . Cum autem verendum sit ne divinam propter hoc indignationem incurramus . . . pro contumeliam creatoris respublica ledatur, fames, terremotus et pestilentia (qua etiam nunc laboratur) fiat, dum nimis pacienter christi dei nostri opprobria sustinemus. . . . Volumus . . . sub excommunicationis pena publice moneatis et requiratis ne posthac judeis cohabitent sive cum eis manducent neque servitia aliqua illis prestare aut proles eorum mercede lactare vel nutrire aut medicinam ab eis recipere presumant aut frequentiorem cum eis conversationem habeant. . . ." *Mandat gegen die Juden* (Hagenau: Heinrich Gran, 1519), Univ. Bibliothek Tübingen, Gb 599.2°.

104. See my characterization in *Forerunners of the Reformation. The Shape of Late Medieval Thought* (New York, 1966), 4–14.

105. Cf. Peter Herde, "Probleme der christlich-jüdischen Beziehungen in Mainfranken im Mittelalter," *Würzburger Diözesan-Geschichtsblätter* 40 (1978), 79–94; esp. 88.

106. See the 'Table of Expulsions' drawn up by Phillip N. Bebb, "Jewish Policy in Sixteenth Century Nürnberg," *Occasional Papers of the American Society for Reformation Research* 1 (1977), 125–136; 132f. Mr. Bebb explicitly warns that his data and dates are only approximate. His list is to be completed—e.g. the Donauwörth expulsion in 1517—with the data presented by Helmut Veitshans, *Die Judensiedlungen der schwäbischen Reichsstädte und der württembergischen Landstädte im Mittelalter*, Arbeiten zum historischen Atlas von Südwest deutschland 5 (Stuttgart, 1970), 12–43; 38.

107. "Desgleichen sollenn die Judenn ein Gelbenn Ring an dem Rock ader kappenn allenthalb unverborgenn Zu Irer erkannthnus offenntlich tragen." *Urkundenbuch zu der Geschichte des Reichstages zu Augsburg im Jahre 1530*, ed. K. E. Förstemann, vol. 2: *Von der Übergabe der Augsburgischen Confession bis zu dem Schlusse des Reichstages* (Halle, 1835; reprint ed., Osnabrück, 1966), 347. For the efforts to enforce—and endure!—the badges in Strasbourg and Regensburg see Ḥaim Hillel Ben-Sasson, "Jewish-Christian Disputation in the Setting of Humanism and Reformation in the German Empire," *Harvard Theological Review* 59 (1966), 369–390; 372f.

Still in Augsburg Charles V confirmed on 15 October 1530 the 'privileges' of Württemberg in being 'unencumbered' by the imperial protection of the Jews. This horrifying, anti-Jewish 'Mandat'—in the literature misleadingly quoted as 'kaiserlicher Freiheitsbrief'—is published by August Ludwig Reyscher, *Vollständig historisch und kritisch bearbeitete Sammlung der württembergischen Gesetze* IV (Tübingen, 1831), 60–65.

108. See particularly the comprehensive presentation by Johannes Brosseder, *Luthers Stellung zu den Juden im Spiegel seiner Interpreten. Interpretation und Rezeption von Luthers Schriften und Äußerungen zum Judentum im 19. und 20. Jahrhundert vor allem im deutschsprachigen Raum*, Beiträge zur Ökumenischen Theologie 8 (Munich, 1972). For the most recent literature see C. Bernd Sucher, *Luthers Stellung zu den Juden. Eine Interpretation aus germanistischer Sicht*, Bibliotheca Humanistica & Reformatorica 23 (Nieuwkoop, 1977), Unreplaced and probably irreplacable is the analysis provided by Reinhold Lewin, *Luthers Stellung zu den Juden. Ein Beitrag zur Geschichte der Juden in Deutschland während des Reformationszeitalters*, Neue Studien zur Geschichte der Theologie und der Kirche 10 (Berlin, 1911, reprint ed., Aalen, 1973). Rabbi Lewin must be highly commended for his unusual degree of fairness (in my view even 'leaning over backwards') which gained for him the annual prize of the Protestant faculty of the University of Breslau. Together with his family he fell victim to the Nazi terror after "the American consulate in Berlin refused to grant him a visa. . . ." Guido Kisch, "Necrologue Reinhold Lewin 1888–1942," *Historia Judaica* 8 (1946), 217–219; 219.

109. *WA Briefe* 8. 89–91; R. Lewin, *Luthers Stellung zu den Juden*, 62ff.; S. Stern, *Josel of Rosheim* (above n. 74), 125–130; 137f.

110. Cf. *Daß Jesus Christus ein geborner Jude sei* (1523), *WA* 11. 314–336; 315, lines 14–24; 336, lines 22–37.

111. "Aber nu wyr sie nur mit gewallt treyben und gehen mit lugen teydingen umb, geben yhn schuld, sie mussen Christen blutt haben, das sie nicht stincken, und weys nicht wes des narren wercks mehr ist, das man sie gleich fur hunde hellt, was sollten wyr guttis an yhn schaffen? Item das man yhn verbeutt, untter uns tzu erbeytten, hantieren und andere menschliche gemeynschafft tzu haben, da mit man sie tzu wuchern treybt, wie sollt sie das bessern? Will man yhn helffen, so mus man nicht das Bapsts, sonder Christlicher liebe gesetz an yhn uben und sie freuntlich annehmen, mit lassen werben und erbeytten, da mit sie ursach und raum gewynnen, bey und umb uns tzu seyn, unser Christlich lere und leben tzu horen und sehen." *WA* 11. 336, lines 24–33. Cf. ibid., 314, lines 26–31 to 315, lines 1–13.

112. *WA Briefe* 8. 90, lines 21–28; as one among other arguments this is mentioned already in 1523; *WA* 11. 331, lines 3–8.

113. *Daß Jesus Christus ein geborner Jude sei* (1523), *WA* 11. 314–336; *Wider die Sabbather an einen guten Freund* (1538), *WA* 50. 312–337; *Von den Juden und ihren Lügen* (1543), *WA* 53. 417–552; *Vom Schem Hamphoras und vom Geschlecht Christi* (1543), *WA* 53. 579–648; *Von den letzten Worten Davids* (1543), *WA* 54. 28–100. The impact of Luther's 'no' on Saxonian politics is documented by the 'Ausschreiben' of the Elector Johann

Friedrich of the year 1543 confirming the 'Mandat' of 1536, published at the end of the last century: Dr. Burkhardt, "Die Judenverfolgungen im Kurfürstentum Sachsen," *Theologische Studien und Kritiken* 70 (1897), 593–598; 597.

114. Cf. the harsh judgment of Peter Maser, "Luthers Schriftauslegung im Traktat 'Von den Juden und ihren Lügen' (1543). Ein Beitrag zum 'christologischen Antisemitismus' des Reformators." *Judaica* 29 (1973), 71-84, 149–167.

115. See *WA* 42. 448, lines 25–42 to 451, lines 1–34. For future research it should be noticed that in the Genesis Commentary (1535–1545) we find the main exegetical arsenal for arguments of the aging Luther against the Jews. Cf. below, note 124.

116. *WA Briefe* 1. 23 f. It is Luther's first letter to Frederick's later confidential secretary, Georg Spalatin. Cf. Irmgard Höss, *Georg Spalatin 1484–1545. Ein Leben in der Zeit des Humanismus und der Reformation* (Weimar, 1956), 75–78.

117. I bypass Luther's first observation, that while evil *within* the Church is crying out to heaven, these Dominicans start to clean the streets *outside*, a theme which he pursued in 1523. *WA Briefe* 1. 23, lines 20–30.

118. Ibid., lines 39–42; line 41.

119. For a detailed and convincing treatment of this issue see Siegfried Raeder, *Grammatica Theologica. Studien zu Luthers Operationes in Psalmos*, Beiträge zur historischen Theologie 51 (Tübingen, 1977), 59–80.

120. *WA Briefe* 1. 149, lines 11–13 to 150, lines 14f.; 22 February, 1518.

121. *WA* 5. 384, line 12; quoted by S. Raeder, *Grammatica Theologica*, 79.

122. Cf. *Werden und Wertung*, 368f.

123. Cf. Ibid., 208f., 224.

124. Since all interest has been focused on Luther's treatises on the Jews some most revealing passages from his lectures have escaped attention. For the dispersal of the Jews as tangible evidence of God's wrath see the commentary to Genesis 12:3; *WA* 42. 448, lines 25–42 to 451, lines 1–34; esp. 448, lines 34 ff.

125. April 1545; see G. Seebaβ, *Das reformatorische Werk des Andreas Osiander* (above, n. 61), 82; cf. *Corpus Reformatorum* vol. 5: *Philippi Melan*[*ch*]*thonis Opera quae supersunt omnia*, ed. C. G. Bretschneider (Halle, 1838; reprint ed., New York, London and Frankfurt a.M., 1963), 728f.

126. See Walter Delius, *Lehre und Leben: Justus Jonas 1493–1555* (Gütersloh, 1952). Only part of the Jonas letters is available in *Der Briefwechsel des Justus Jonas*, 2 parts, ed. G. Kawerau, Geschichtsquellen der Provinz Sachsen und angrenzender Gebiete 17 (Halle 1884/85; reprint ed., Hildesheim, 1964).

127. *Libellus Martini Lutheri, Christum Ieum* [*sic*] *verum Iudaeum et semen esse Abrahae, è Germanico versus, per I. Ionam* (Wittenberg, 1524); cf. *WA* 11. 309f.

128. Jonas added a dedicatory letter to his Latin translation in which a common middleground is suggested, since the Jews have to draw away from Talmudic distortions 'like we from Scotistic and Thomistic nonsense': "Videmus plane contigisse Iudaeis, ut haud aliter a verbo Dei et simplicitate scripturae avocati sint Thalmudicis nugis ac nos Scotisticis et Thomisticis somniis." *Briefwechsel des Justus Jonas*, 1: 93, lines 4–6.

129. "Sed orandum est nobis pro hac gente, praesertim cum inter nos quoque non omnes Christiani sunt, qui titulum Christianismi gerunt." Ibid., lines 12–14.

130. "Quin in lunares urbes regnum Iudaeorum translatum comminiscuntur?" Ibid., lines 11f.

131. *WA* 50. 311.

132. "Nos autem, quibus Deus hoc seculo aperuit libros sacros, quibus contigit hoc tempore aspicere claram lucem evangelii, iam cognitum habemus, nullos unquam doctores theologiae verae praestantiores sub sole vixisse, quam in illo populo Israel, . . ." *Briefwechsel des Justus Jonas*, 1: 323, lines 19–22.

133. " . . . et ecclesiam Iudaeorum olivetum pinguissimum et uberrimum esse, imo hortum balsami generosissimi, cuius fragrantissimo odore delectatus est Deus, nos vero gentes campos illos, unde oleastri desumpti in veras olivas translati sunt, sicut et Paulus ad Romanos hac similitudine utitur. Nos gentes hospites utique sumus et peregrini, qui ad communionem tantarum opum et benedictionum in Christo Iesu vero Messia

admissi sumus, olim sine Deo in hoc mundo, nunc facti mysteriorum Dei participes et cum Abraham et patriarchis, tantis Dei viris, sub uno eodemque capite Christo unum facti sumus corpus." Ibid., lines 22–30.

134. "Ideo cum tam nobilis et sanctus populus sunt Iudaei, ex quorum plenitudine nos omnes accepimus, profecto perpetuam nos gentes eis debemus gratitudinem, ut quantum omnino fieri potest, quosdam ex eis adhuc quasi e medio naufragio servemus." Ibid., 324, lines 7–10.

135. "Hactenus in Iudeorum me mersi furias, postquam tu quiescendum esse consuluisti, dum aliam viam tentaretis." *WA Briefe* 10. 226, lines 19–21. For Jonas' complex efforts to translate also Luther's harshest tract 'Von den Juden und ihren Lügen' in March 1543, see *WA* 53. 414. I doubt that the editor J. Luther is right in assuming that Jonas did not translate 'Vom Schem Hamphoras' because of linguistic problems: *WA* 53. 573.

136. "Und summa: Weil diese Funffzehen hundert jare im Elende (da noch kein ende gewis ist noch werden kan) die Jueden nicht demuetigen noch zur erkentnis bringen, So muegt jr mit gutem gewissen an jnen verzweiveln. Denn es unmueglich ist, das Gott sein volck (wo sie es weren) so lange solt on trost und weissagung bleiben lassen." *WA* 50. 336, lines 1–6.

137. "Oder ist solches nu verseumet und nicht geschehen, So lasst sie noch hinfaren jns land und gen Jerusalem, Tempel bawen, Priesterthum, Fuerstenthum und Mosen mit seinem gesetze auffrichten und also sie selbs widerumb Jueden werden und das Land besitzen. Wenn das geschehen ist, so sollen sie uns bald auff den ferssen nach sehen daher komen und auch Jueden werden. Thun sie das nicht, So ists aus der massen lecherlich, das sie uns Heiden wollen bereden zu jrem verfallen gesetze, welches nu wol Funffzehenhundert jar verfaulet und kein gesetze mehr gewest ist. Und wir solten halten, das sie selbs nicht halten noch halten konnen, so lange sie Jerusalem und das Land nicht haben," *WA* 50. 323, lines 36–37 to 324, lines 1–8.

138. *The Enlightenment: An Interpretation. The Rise of Modern Paganism*, 2nd ed. (New York, 1977), 297.

139. Cf. Gustav Bossert, *Das Interim in Württemberg*, Schriften des Vereins für Reformationsgeschichte 46/47 (Halle, 1895), 95–105. Thomas A. Brady, Jr., *Ruling Class, Regime and Reformation at Strasbourg, 1520–1555*, Studies in Medieval and Reformation Thought 22 (Leiden, 1978), 275ff. Erdmann Weyrauch, *Konfessionelle Krise und soziale Stabilität. Das Interim in Straßburg (1548–1562)*, Spätmittelalter und Frühe Neuzeit, Tübinger Beiträge Zur Geschichtsforschung 7 (Stuttgart, 1978), 159ff.

140. After reaching a state of near-establishment in France, the Hugenots again experienced, in the aftermath of St. Bartholomew's day on August 24, 1572, a traumatic shock comparable with the Interim's effect. See for this impact particularly Robert M. Kingdon, *Geneva and the Consolidation of the French Protestant Movement 1564–1572. A Contribution to the History of Congregationalism, Presbyterianism, and Calvinist Resistance Theory*, Trauvaux d'Humanisme et Renaissance 92 (Geneva, 1967), 200f.

141. See R. Lewin, *Luthers Stellung zu den Juden* (above, n. 108), 98f.; J. Cohrs, *WA* 54. 20f. Cf. also the ample evidence presented by John W. Kleiner, "The Attitudes of the Strasbourg Reformers toward Jews and Judaism," (unpublished dissertation, Temple University, Philadelphia, 1978). For Martin Bucer see esp. Rabbi Dr. Kroner, "Die Hofpredigerpartei und die Juden unter Philipp von Hessen," *Das Jüdische Literaturblatt* 11 (1882), 165f.; 169 f.; Wilhelm Maurer, "Martin Butzer und die Judenfrage in Hessen," *Zeitschrift des Vereins für hessische Geschichte und Landeskunde* 64 (1953), 29–43.

142. For Osiander see *Andreas Osiander d.Ä. Gesamtausgabe* (above, n. 62) 3: 335–340, and literature cited in the footnotes there. For Capito see James M. Kittelson, *Wolfgang Capito. From Humanist to Reformer*, Studies in Medieval and Reformation Thought 17 (Leiden, 1975), 21f.; 25f.; 33f.; 211f.

143. Sermon d. 8 July 1549 (Jer. 16:1–7): "Quant donc nous voyons que nous sommes pareilz aux Juifz, nous avons ung mireoir pour congnoistre nostre rebellion contre Dieu. Or quant il nous chastiera bien rudement, pourrons nous dire qu'il n'a pas assez attendu et que de nostre costé nous ne nous sommes pas monstrez incorrigibles

jusques au bout? Ainsi donc, quant nous lisons ce passage, aprenons de ne point condampner les Juifz mais nous mesmes, et de congnoistre que nous ne vallons pas myeulx, et que s'il y a eu alors une telle brutalité que la parolle de Dieu n'ait de rien servy, que aujourdhuy il y en a autant ou plus." Jean Calvin, *Sermons sur les Livres de Jérémie et des Lamentations*, ed. R. Peter, Supplementa Calviniana 6 (Neukirchen-Vluyn, 1971), 59 lines 12–18. Sermon d. 10 July 1549 (Jer, 16:12–15): "Et combien que nous ne soyons pas de la race d'Abraham et de ce peuple qui a esté delivré d'Egipte, neantmoins pource que nous representons ce peuple lá, ceste delivrance ne nous doibt point sortir des aureilles." Ibid., 78, lines 27–29. Sermon d. 6 September 1550 (Lament. 1:1, Introduction): " . . . sy on faict comparaison avec ceux dont parle icy le prophete on trouverra que nous sommes beaucoup pires que ceulx lá de son temps." Ibid., 183, line 34–35 to 184, line 1.

144. For a different conclusion on the basis of earlier materials see A. J. Visser, *Calvijn en de Joden.*, Bijlage van *Kerk en Israel* 17, ('s Gravenhage, 1963), esp. 18. In a less than profound article (first published in *Judaica* 2, 1946, 203–208) Jacques Courvoisier concludes: " . . . was Calvin zu diesem Thema sagt, ist für diese Sache nicht von groβer Bedeutung." "Calvin und die Juden. Zu einem Streitgespräch," in *Christen und Juden. Ihr Gegenüber vom Apostelkonzil bis heute*, ed. W.-D. Marsch, K. Thieme (Mainz and Göttingen, 1961), 141–146; 146.

145. With this new evaluation of the phenomenon of 'diaspora' corresponds an optimistic Jewish interpretation. See the evidence compiled by Ḥayim Hillel Ben-Sasson, "The Reformation in Contemporary Jewish Eyes," in *Proceedings of the Israel Academy of Sciences and Humanities* 4 (1969–1970; Jerusalem, 1971), 239–326; 286f. From the Jewish perspective the refugee-Reformation is just another sign of the breaking apart of the *corpus christianum.* But as in the case of the Hussite movement it is not merely a negative sign: " . . . the anti-hierarchical, anti-monastic and iconoclastic tendencies characterizing the Hussite movement [is considered] to be a change in the right direction. . . . The rise of Luther in Germany occurred at a time when Jews were in particular need of encouragement." Ibid., 255.

146. See J. van den Berg, *Joden en Christenen in Nederland gedurende de zeventiende eeuw*, Verkenning en Bezinning 3, no. 2 (Kampen, 1969); cf. the elaboration "Eshatological Expectations Concerning the Conversion of the Jews in the Netherlands During the Seventeenth Century," in *Puritans, the Millennium and the Future of Israel. Puritan Eschatology 1600–1660*, ed. P. Toon (Cambridge and London, 1970), 137–153. See also Robert M. Healey, "The Jew in Seventeenth-Century Protestant Thought," *Church History* 46 (1977), 63–79; 64. On 13 December 1619 the states of Holland and Westfrisia permit the cities to make their own legislation governing their relations with 'the Hebrew nation'. The document is published by J. Meijer, *Hugo de Groot: Remonstrantie nopende de ordre dije in de landen van Hollandt ende Westvrieslandt dijent gestelt op de Joden* (Amsterdam, 1949), 101. The key document in this edition is the liberal proposal of Hugo Grotius. Most revealing is, however, the anonymous reaction (c. 1617) from the Jewish side to the proposed legislation. Ibid., Appendix C, 141–143. Cf. also W. J. M. van Eysinga, "De Groots Jodenreglement," *Mededelingen der Koninklijke Nederlandse Akademie van Wetenschappen*, Afd. Letterkunde 13 (Amsterdam, 1950), 1–8.

147. H. R. Trevor-Roper in his effort to unravel the mysterious bonds between Calvinism and the Enlightenment has pointed to a later but structurally parallel phase: "We find that each of those Calvinist societies [sixteenth-century Heidelberg, seventeenth-century Holland, Puritan England, Huguenot France, eighteenth-century Switzerland and Scotland] made its contribution to the Enlightenment at a precise moment in its history, and that this moment was the moment when it repudiated ideological orthodoxy." "The Religious Origins of the Enlightenment," *Religion, the Reformation and Social Change and other Essays* (London, Melbourne, Toronto, 1967), 193–236; 205.

148. The most powerful antidote which medieval thought itself had provided remained an untapped source—until this very day. See Oberman, *Werden und Wertung*, 211ff.

149. Cf. Alexander Bein, "Der moderne Antisemitismus und seine Bedeutung für die Judenfrage," *Vierteljahrshefte für Zeitgeschichte* 6 (1958), 340–360.

Medieval Doctrines in Renaissance Garb? Some Jewish and Arabic Sources of Leone Ebreo's Doctrines

S. PINES

I

Judah ben Isaac Abravanel, commonly known as Leone Ebreo, may have been in some ways an original philosopher. He has also the distinction of having helped to set an intellectual fashion which had some vogue in sixteenth-century Italy, Spain and France.

Leone's *Dialoghi d'Amore*,[1] in particular the last two *Dialogues*, expound some metaphysical doctrines which may have been influenced by medieval Jewish and Arabic philosophers. In the course of our enquiry we shall try to gauge the measure in which these sources may have determined Leone's views on some doctrinal points. We shall also try to evaluate the credibility of Leone's own statements concerning some of the sources in question.

The starting point of our discussion must be a few of the references to ancient and medieval philosophers occurring in the *Dialoghi*. Apart from Plato and Aristotle, only three Greek philosophers seem to have been explicitly mentioned: Empedocles (once), Themistius (once) and Plotinus (twice).[2] It may be added that these references have no great significance in the context of our investigation. Empedocles for instance, is merely reported (II, 23a) as stating that the causes of generation and corruption of all lowly things are six in all: love, discord and the four elements. This resumé of the Pre-Socratic's doctrine, may have been borrowed from some doxographer. Themistius is said (III, 104b-105a) to have maintained that the Sun, the Moon and the Stars should be called forms rather than uninformed bodies, a piece of information which Leone Ebreo may have encountered in Latin or, more probably, Hebrew texts.[3] One of the references to Plotinus (II, 39b) deals with a statement of his concerning the ether; the other (III, 44a–b) with his view that (despite the cosmogony of the *Timaeus*) Plato believed the world to be eternal. The second reference accords with the opinions of Plotinus as expressed, for instance, in *Enneads*, II, 1 and II, 9.

The references to Plato and Aristotle are much more numerous and some of them relate to central tendencies and doctrines in Leone Ebreo's thought. Leone considers (III, 125b–126a) Plato superior to Aristotle because of the farther reach of the former's knowledge of abstract things (*cose astratte*). Unlike his erstwhile student, Plato was aware of the fact that the First Wisdom and Beauty is, because of its dependence on the Supreme God (*Sommo Dio*), the Second rather than the First Principle of all things.[4] Plato's superiority in these matters Leone ascribed to Plato's greater knowledge of, and acceptance of, Mosaic theology. This explanation may be (although this is by no means certain) a variation on the widely held medieval belief that Aristotelian science was borrowed or stolen from the Jews.[5] The fact that Leone Ebreo prefers Plato to Aristotle reflects the vogue of Platonism in Italy in the fifteenth and the beginning of the sixteenth centuries.

With regard to some Aristotelian quotations occuring in the *Dialoghi*, it is impossible to determine whether Leone first encountered them in a Hebrew or in a Latin[6] text; this uncertainty exists even in cases in which Leone's terminology is obviously taken over from the Latin, as in his rendering (III, 135a–b) of the Aristotelian categories[7] *honestum, utile*, and *delectabile*, by *honesto, utile*, and *dilettabile.*[8] In other instances, however, it seems certain that Leone drew upon Latin (or Greek) texts, or texts derived from the Latin. For example, Leone records (II, 29a) Aristotle's supposed rejoinder to Alexander when the latter wrote and expressed puzzlement at his master's revelation of the secrets of philosophy in books. Aristotle is said to have answered, "The books are both published and unpublished (*editi et non editi*)," this being an allusion to Aristotle's difficult, elliptical style.[9] This exchange of letters between Alexander and Aristotle is referred to in two sources, Gellius' *Noctes Atticae*, 20, 5 and Plutarch's *Life of Alexander*, 7. Leone's use of the word *editi* is clearly modeled on *ekdedomenoi*, which is used in these two texts.[10] As far as I know the story in question is not found in Arabic texts.[11] (One of the numerous references to Aristotle may be singled out for mention. In the

Dialoghi II, 19a, Aristotle's *De Caelo* [II, 2, 284b6ff.] is quoted in connection with the question of the nature of the right-hand and the left-hand side in heaven. The quotation may be significant because the problem is discussed at some length by Leone's father.)[12]

The *Dialoghi* also contain a considerable number of references to Plato's doctrines. Some of these may be derived from Neoplatonic and Renaissance Platonistic writings, but there can be no doubt that Leone had carefully read the *Symposium* and was also acquainted with some of the other *Dialogues* of Plato. One reference to Plato (III, 74b) is of particular relevance to the main theme of the present paper:

> We have spoken about Love in the Universe in a more universal fashion [*piu universalmente*] than was done by Plato in his *Symposium*, for we treat of the principle of Love [existing] in all the created world, [whereas] he only [treats] of the principle of human Love . . . .

In this passage Leone clearly alludes to the difference, which is evident and has been often pointed out, between his theory of love and the views of Platonists such as Marsilio Ficino.[13] Various hypotheses as to the possible source of Leone's theory will be discussed in the last section of the present paper.

At this point we shall examine a reference to Plato and Aristotle which certainly derives either directly or indirectly from Maimonides' *Guide of the Perplexed.* Leone cites (III, 44b) three opinions concerning the creation of the world: the first that of Aristotle according to which the whole world was produced from all eternity (*fu produtto ab eterno*); the second that of Plato according to which only Matter or the Chaos was produced from all eternity whereas the world was produced at the beginning of Time;[14] and the third that of the faithful,[15] according to which everything was produced out of nothing at the beginning of Time.

In its essentials this opinion is indubitably derived either directly or indirectly from the *Guide of the Perplexed* II, 13 as is clear when we examine Maimonides' work:[16]

> There are three opinions of human beings, namely of all those who believe that there is an existent deity with regard to the eternity of the world or its production in time. The first opinion, which is the opinion of all who believe in the Law of Moses our Master . . .[17] is that the world as a whole . . . was brought into existence by God after having been purely and absolutely nonexistent, and that God . . . had existed alone,

and nothing else. . . . Afterwards through His will and His volition, He brought into existence out of nothing all the beings as they are, time itself being one of the created things. . . . [18]

The second opinion is that of all the philosophers of whom we have heard reports and whose discourses we have seen. . . . Hence they believe that there exists a certain matter that is eternal as the deity is eternal; and that He does not exist without it, nor does it exist without Him. They do not believe that it has the same rank in what exists as He . . . but that He is the cause of its existence. . . . This is also the belief of Plato. . . .

The third opinion is that of Aristotle, his followers and the commentators. . . . He thinks that this being as a whole, such as it is, has never ceased and will never do so; that the permanent thing not subject to generation and passing-away, namely the heaven, likewise does not cease to be; that time and motion are perpetual and everlasting and not subject to generation and passing-away; and also that the thing subject to generation and passing-away, namely that which is beneath the sphere of the moon, does not cease to be.

The three opinions concerning the creation of the world set forth in the *Guide* II, 13—that of Plato, that of Aristotle and that of the faithful—are also mentioned at the conclusion of Leone's discussion of this subject (55a–b); this fact strengthens the impression that this chapter of the *Guide* provides, as it were, a scheme of reference for the treatment of this topic in the *Dialoghi*.

The confrontation of these texts, which appears to prove that Leone derived his classification of the various opinions concerning the creation of the world from the *Guide of the Perplexed*, also shows that some of the details in his account of this opinion have no parallel in II, 13 of the *Guide*. Some references to time and eternity may be cited as examples. Another instance which is significant in the context of this inquiry occurs in the exposition of Plato's doctrine. Leone speaks in this connection of "Matter or Chaos" (*la materia, o Chaos*). It is tempting to suppose that "Chaos," identified here with Matter, is meant to correspond to the Hebrew *tohu*, which in the first chapter of Genesis is used to describe the earth as it was in the beginning. Medieval texts tended to take this Hebrew word as a synonym of *hyle*, whereas *bohu* was used as a synonym of form.[19] But this supposition seems difficult to reconcile with two other passages of the *Dialoghi* and it should accordingly be modified. In the first of these passages (III, 53a) Leone in the course of an exposition of what he apparently regards, probably correctly, as a kabbalistic interpretation[20] of the commandments concerning *shemita* speaks of the "Chaos which the Jews as well as the Chaldeans and other Gentiles usually call earth."[21] In this context Leone translates or interprets the Hebrew words "*ve-ha-aretz hayta tohu va-vohu*" as "*la terra, sive il Chaos, era inane e vacuum.*"[22] This appears to indicate that in this context the counterpart in biblical exegesis of the notion of Chaos is not the term *tohu* by itself, but *ha-aretz* in its state of *tohu va-vohu.* It follows from this terminological discussion that in using the word *Chaos* Leone probably had in mind *inter alia* a Hebrew word or expression (though he was also aware of Ficino's recourse to the word).

Furthermore, we note in his translation of the first part of the first verse of Genesis Leone remarks that the word which is usually translated "in the beginning" may also mean "prior to." Accordingly, Leone interprets the Bible as saying that before God created and separated heaven and earth, i.e. the terrestial and celestial worlds, from Chaos, the earth, i.e. the Chaos, was void and empty. In other words, Chaos existed before the creation. As Chaos may be equated with Matter, this interpretation of the first verse of Genesis implies the correctness of the Platonic opinion.

Leone's position thus emerges as quite different from Maimonides'. The latter appears to dismiss in a rather off-handed way the opinion regarded by him as Plato's. The debate that engages his attention is one that opposes the Aristotelians who affirm the eternity of the world to the believers who consider that our world, which is the only one that has ever existed, was produced by the act of creation referred to in the first chapter of Genesis. For reasons set forth in the *Guide*, II, 68, Maimonides opts for the latter opinion. In contrast, Leone holds no brief for the opinion of those whom he calls the "faithful," i.e. those who believe that there was only *one* creation of the world. He prefers a Platonistic opinion, the adherents of which are in his view (55a) more capable than the "faithful" referred to above of refuting Aristotle's arguments. This opinion is however by no means identical with the one ascribed to Plato in *Guide*, II, 13. It is rather the doctrine of a Plato transformed into a kabbalist.[23]

According to this doctrine (54b–55a) both the Intellect (which contains the Ideas[24] and is pure act and form) and Primal Matter or Chaos[25] (which is pure potentiality) participate in God's Eternity, the first being the Universal Father of all things and the second their Mother. Their Sons, however, made and formed—as is the whole and every part of it—by God through the intermediary of these two parents, have not the capacity for being eternal. For everything that has been made is composed of the Matter of Chaos (*di materia del Chaos*) and of the Form of the Intellectual Idea (*di forma della Idea intellettuale*) and must (therefore) have a temporal beginning and an end—followed by a new beginning. The process is cyclical.

There are two kinds of cylcles (III, 50aff.) already described by pre-Platonic theologians. One of them lasts seven thousand years and can be divided into two parts: (1) a six-thousand-year period during which the "lower world," i.e. the world which is beneath the heavenly sphere, passes away because one of the elements (Fire or, less often, Water) becomes predominant; and (2) a one-thousand year period which may be designated by the Hebrew appellation *shemita* (*scemita*—cf. III, 53a). During this latter period the things contained in the "lower world" return to the Primal Chaos (*nel chaos primo*), which is at rest for one thousand years. In the course of this interval of Time, it is impregnated with a view to the generation of a new world. There are also cycles which last fifty thousand years. These are divided into forty-nine thousand years comprising seven "short" cycles, and the last thousand years[26] called in Hebrew *yovel* (*iobel*). In the course of these last thousand years, the two worlds, the celestial and "the lower," are renewed (III, 53b).

Leone offers two very similar exposés of this doctrine, both of which have been referred to above, and one of which (53af.) is clearly derived from a Jewish source, as is proved by the use of the terms *shemita* and *yovel.* This exposé is followed immediately by the likewise Jewish interpretation of the beginning of Genesis dealt with above. The second exposé (50aff.) attributed to theologians who lived before Plato, contains the statement that after forty-nine thousand years of the great cycle of fifty thousand years have elapsed, the heaven and everything that is corporeal[27] will be dissolved and revert to chaos and primal Matter. It is believed—though it takes some daring to speak of unknown things that are "so sublime"—that following upon this dissolution Chaos, after being inactive for some time, is impregnated by the divinity and gives birth to the world. Thus, there has been a succession of worlds which pass away.[28]

How do the intellectual souls, the angels and the pure intellects fare at the time of universal dissolution? This question which is natural in the context of the doctrine under discussion admits, according to Leone, of two answers. The first of these is based on the premise that the entities in question are not composed of matter and form and have no part in the Chaos. Though the answer is not fully spelled out, Leone apparently feels that this premise entails the consequence that these entities will at the time of universal dissolution persist in their essences and comtemplate the deity.

The second answer is based on the theory of "our Albenzubron," i.e. Ibn Gabirol, according to which the entities in question are composed of matter and form. Their (incorporeal) matter and substance participates in Chaos, which is the universal Mother, while their forms participate in the supreme God, who is the universal Father.[29] If this theory is accepted, it may be assumed that after the passage of forty-nine thousand years of a great cycle, the matter of the incorporeal entities is given back to Chaos which at that time takes back into itself all the parts which it possesses in its "sons," whereas the intellectual forms of the entities are restituted to the Supreme God and are preserved in the sublime ideas of the divine Intellect until the new Return. At the time of this Return, i.e. the creation and generation of the universe, the Chaos impregnated by the deity gives birth to material substances informed by all the ideas. This takes place in the lowly corporeal world subject to generation and corruption, in the corporeal celestial world, and in the intellectual world of incorporeal matter.

It is in the context of this discussion that Leone apparently quotes Ibn Gabirol's *Fons Vitae.* It has, as far as I know, never been pointed out that the tenor of this quotation, which is often referred to by scholars,[30] is incompatible with the doctrine of the work from which it is supposed to be derived. The passage in question (resumed above) reads as follows (III 51a—the entities referred to being "the intellectuals souls, the angels and the pure intellects"):

. . . et se ancora sonno composti di materia e forma, cosi come participano le sue forme nel sommo Dio padre commune, cosi ancora participano sustantia, et materia incorporea dal chaos madre comune, come pone il nostro Albenzubron nel suo libro de fonte vite, che ancora loro renderanno la sua parte à ciascuno de li due parenti nel quinquagesimo millesimo anno, cioè la sustantia e materia, al chaos il quale all'hora di tutti li figliuoli le sue portioni in se raccoglie, e l'intellettuale formalità al sommo Dio padre et datore di quella, le quali lucidissamente sonno conservate ne le altissime Idee del divino intelletto fino al nuovo ritorno loro . . . .

It seems to me probable that the conclusion of this passage, starting with the words *che ancora loro renderanno*, purports to give the answer of Leone, rather than that of Ibn Gabirol, to the question as to what happens at the time of the dissolution of the world, and after, to the immaterial entities, if these are supposed to be composed of matter and form.

As regards the first part of the passage, there may be some doubt as to the words which constitute the quotation from the *Fons Vitae*. The text in question contains a statement and what may be regarded as an interpretation of the latter. The statement, which consists of the affirmation that the (incorporeal entities) are composed of matter and form, conforms to the doctrine of Ibn Gabirol's *Fons Vitae*. However, it is the "interpretation" that is explicitly ascribed to this philosopher (designated as Albenzubron): "cosi come participano le sue forme nel sommo Dio padre comune, cosi ancora participano sustantia, et materia incorporea dal chaos madre comune, come pone il nostro Albenzubron nel suo libro de fonte vite." This phrase conveys the information that, according to what is said by Ibn Gabirol in the *Fons Vitae*, the forms (of the incorporeal entities) participate in the Supreme God, who is the universal Father, whereas the substance and incorporeal matter (of these entities) participate in Chaos, which is the universal Mother. The implication is that Ibn Gabirol adhered to a dualistic theory according to which Chaos co-exists with, but is separate from, the Supreme God, the forms (of the immaterial entities) being supposed to relate to the latter, matter and substance to the former. It is evident that this theory and the passage in the *Dialoghi* based on it cannot be reconciled with the doctrine of the *Fons Vitae*, in which Ibn Gabirol not only posits the derivation of both Matter[31] and Form from God, but, at least in V, 42, appears to assume that the former has a more direct connection than the latter with the divine Essence.[32] This difference is of so radical a nature that—in spite of the many contradictions occurring in the extant text of the *Fons Vitae*—it seems highly improbable that the phrase under discussion could have been found in some version of this work.

The hypothesis that the "interpretation" contained in the phrase of Ibn Gabirol's doctrine concerning the composite nature of the immaterial entities is due to Leone himself has the disadvantage of not taking into account the latter's explicit ascription of the phrase to Ibn Gabirol. This difficulty would be avoided if we supposed that the "interpretation " adopted by Leone was derived from some unidentified author's attempt to explicate the doctrine of the *Fons Vitae.* We may also consider the possibility that the phrase in question was taken from some other, no longer extant, work of Ibn Gabirol and was mistakenly regarded by Leone as culled from the *Fons Vitae.* It has been pointed out[33] that Joseph Solomon del Medigo had commited an error of this kind: he believed, quite incorrectly, that a piece of biblical exegesis authored by Ibn Gabirol was contained in the *Fons Vitae.* In this context a terminological peculiarity of the phrase under discussion may be mentioned: the words *sustantia e materia*, which are part of it, seem to indicate that the two terms have an identical meaning—as is sometimes the case in the *Fons Vitae.*[34] In the Christian Latin philosophical vocabulary *sustantia* does not generally have this signification (though it is employed in this sense by Ficino, see above). *Jawhar*, on the other hand, which is the Arabic equivalent of this Latin term, can have the meaning "matter" in early philosophical texts antedating Ibn Gabirol.[35] It can accordingly be argued that the phrase in question was originally written in Arabic.[36] As has already been stated, its ascription to Ibn Gabirol would entail an acceptance of the hypothesis—which cannot be disproved on a priori grounds—that the poet-philosopher expounded in some of his writings views which run counter to the fundamental doctrines of the *Fons Vitae.*

To sum up this part of our enquiry, if with the sanction of the *Dialoghi* (see above) we use the scheme of reference provided by Maimonides in his account of the different views on the creation of the world, Leone is a Platonist of sorts. He also, on his own avowal, appears to be a follower of pre-Platonic theologians.[37] According to the doctrine adopted by him, the cosmos is periodically created by the interfusion of Forms which are directly related to the Divine Principle described in at least one passage (III, 48a) as the Supreme Form,[38] with matter, which is derived from or identical with the Chaos, an inferior Principle, that is coeval with the deity. Upon the dissolution of the cosmos in the concluding phase of a great cycle each of these two components returns to the Principle from which it had come forth.[39]

According to an assertion of Leone that does not wholly square with the facts as we know them but need not therefore be dismissed out of hand, this view of the two Principles was held *inter alia* by Ibn Gabirol, who is the only medieval philosopher named in this context in the *Dialoghi.* Ibn Gabirol appears to be mentioned because he believed that the immaterial entities were, like all other existents (except God), composed of Matter and Form.

The main difference between Leone's doctrine with which we are dealing and the theory of creation propounded in Isaac Abravanel's *Mif 'alot Elohim* (a treatise written at about the same time as the *Dialoghi*) may be found in the divergent views of the father and the son concerning the status of Form. As regards other questions, there are significant points of resemblance[40] between the two works. Both Leone and his father identify the Chaos or *tohu* with the Abyss (*tehom*) likewise mentioned in the first chapter of Genesis.[41] This identification is not currently found in the Jewish commentaries; it is by and large similar to Augustine's suggestion that the Abyss and the Darkness may together signify the confused state of things which is designated in Greek by the word *Chaos*.[42] There is also a certain resemblance between Isaac Abravanel's interpretation (*Mif 'alot*, III, 8, 25d) of the expression 'Spirit of God' likewise occurring in the first chapter of Genesis as referring to the Separate Intellect, and his son's explanation (III, 54a) according to which the expression signifies the Supreme Intellect (*il sommo intelletto*) which is full of ideas. Neither of these interpretations is in keeping with the line generally taken by the Jewish philosophical commentators who usually hold that the Spirit of God referred to in the passage in question is something that is corporeal; most of them believe that some sort of air is meant.[43]

Isaac (*Mif 'alot*, 51b) holds like Leone (see above) that the world is destroyed at the end of a forty-nine-thousand-year cycle and that after this return to chaos, it is renewed at the end of the year fifty thousand. Like his son he designates the great cycle lasting from the beginning till the end of a world as *yovel.*[44] Moreover, he too speaks of the lesser cycles of seven thousand years—at the end of which there is, according to him, partial destruction. It may however be noted that these beliefs or variations on them are widespread. On the other hand, the conception that the return of the world to chaos consists in the separation of Form from Matter is by no means usual, and may be peculiar, as far as philosophical speculation is concerned, to Leone (see above) and Isaac (*Mif 'alot*, 25b).

For the rest the connection between the *Dialoghi* and the *Mif 'alot* is evident not only because of the points of resemblance referred to above; it also comes out very clearly in the exposition in the two works of a problem with regard to which the father and son are not in complete agreement. Isaac poses (*Mif 'alot*, VIII, 5, 58a–b) the question whether the "spiritual angels"—apparently the Separate Intellects are meant—pass away, as do the corporeal existents, at the time of the general dissolution of the world. His answer is a negative one, his argument being that the "angels" proceed directly from God, while the corporeal beings are created out of nothing. In support of his contention Isaac quotes Ibn Gabirol's poem *Keter Malkhut.* As has been stated above, a similar question is posed in the *Dialoghi.* However Leone's approach is different; according to him two equally valid answers are possbile. One of them, which is by and large identical with his father's solution, is predicated on the assumption that the immaterial entities are not composed of matter and form. The other one, which Leone possibly prefers, is based on the contrary assumption which, as is quite correctly asserted in the *Dialoghi*, was propounded by Ibn Gabirol in the *Fons Vitae*: if the spiritual entities are composed of Matter and Form, they too must at the time of the general dissolution of the universe be resolved into these two components. The fact that the (partly spurious) quotation from Ibn Gabirol is used in the *Dialoghi* in an argumentation which is meant to prove the thesis according to which the incorporeal entities are dissolved at the time of the general destruction of the world, whereas in the *Mif 'alot* the poet-philosopher's authority is invoked in order to strengthen the opposite contention can hardly be due to mere chance.

II

Four Islamic philosophers are named in the *Dialoghi*: Averroes on the one hand, and on the other, thinkers belonging to a different school of thought. These are al-Farabi, Avicenna, and al-Ghazali. Jointly with them Leone names Maimonides. They form according to him "the First Academy of the Arabs" (*la prima academia de gl'Arabi*, II, 69b), an appellation which calls to mind the first Platonic Academy as well as the Academy of Marsilio Ficino[45] and may therefore be intended to suggest that the medieval philosophers under consideration were Platonists.[46] It may be noted in this connection that already Giovanni Pico della Mirandola employs with reference to Avicenna the adjectives *divinum et Platonicum.*[47]

The controversy discussed in *Dialoghi* II, 59bff. is often referred to in medieval philosophical writings, the moot question being whether the Supreme God may be identified with the Mover of the Universe (*muḥarrik al-kull*), i.e. the First of the Separate Intellects each of which has charge of a sphere, or whether He who is called the *First* or the *First Cause* is different from, and superior to, the Separate Intellects. According to the latter opinion, the appellation Prime Mover does not befit the Supreme God. The first opinion is that of Averroes[48] and, according to Leone Ebreo (II, 71a), also that of Aristotle. Leone remarks in this context (ibidem) that to give an opinion on the doctrinal point at issue would argue some over-boldness on his part. In the third *Dialogue* (122b–124a) he may have shed these scruples. In this *Dialogue* Aristotle is said to equate the First Intellect with the Supreme God, whereas Plato is supposed to hold that the two are distinct, the First Intellect being identical with the Divine Wisdom and the Ideal Verb (*Verbo Ideale*). It stands out clearly that Leone—without saying this in so many words—favors Plato's opinion. Some Peripatetics, namely Avicenna, al-Ghazali and Maimonides (*Rabi Moyses nostro*) are reported by him[49] to have adopted this opinion in an imperfect manner: they believed that the First Intellect was the Mover of the First Sphere, but not the First Cause. Leone considers that this view is an attempt to patch up the differences between the theologies of Plato and Aristotle, and inferior to either of these.[50]

Leone also refers (III, 75bff.) to a second point of doctrine with regard to which Averroes disagrees with Avicenna, al-Ghazali and Maimonides. The latter philosophers are said to believe that God, who is a simple unity, conjoined with love for His own great Beauty, produces the First Intellect. The latter entity contemplates, on the one hand, the Beauty of its Cause producing thereby the second intellect; on the other hand it contemplates its own beauty and produces thereby the first heavenly sphere, composed of an incorruptible body and of an intellective soul. The Second Intellect contemplates the divine Beauty in indirect fashion (apparently Leone means that it contemplates directly the beauty of the First Intellect) and also its own beauty; the first part of this contemplation produces the Third Intellect and the second the second sphere. This process goes on until finally the sphere of the Moon[51] and the Active Intellect are produced. The latter is the intellect of the Lower World. It contemplates and loves its own beauty and as a result, gives to that world all the forms subsisting in the first matter.[52] It also contemplates its own cause and as a result produces the human intellect, which is the last in the series of the intellects. In its first stage this intellect is inactive and then, being illuminated by the Active Intellect, it may be actualized, become an intellect *in habitu* and finally be conjoined with the Active Intellect and see, as in a mirror, the divine Beauty.

It may be noted that the part of this account which deals with the production of the Separate Intellects approximates only in its rough outline the doctrines expounded by Avicenna and in al-Ghazali's *Intentions of the Philosophers.* The latter work,[53] which purports to be an exposé of the Avicennian system, refers as does Leone's text to a duality in the Separate Intellects, the existence of each of them having two aspects according to al-Ghazali, a necessary and a contingent one. This duality is quite clearly different at least in formulation from that postulated in the *Dialoghi d'Amore*, but it has a similar effect, the necessary aspect producing the Separate Intellect which is next in the series, and the contingent one a heavenly sphere.

Avicenna himself in *Kitāb Shifā' al-Nafs*[54] (the *Sufficientia* of the Latins) states that three different intellections may be postulated in the first Separate Intellect (as well as in the other Intellects which are dealt with more briefly): 1) The Intellection of the First

(Principle), which produces the Second Intellect; 2) the intellection of the First Intellect's own essence (*dhāt*), which produces the soul of the first sphere; and 3) the intellection of the contingence of the existence (of the First Intellect), which produces the body of that sphere.

It may be noted that when citing the Arabic philosophers from whom the doctrine, summarized above, concerning the production of the Separate Intellects is derived, Leone rather curiously omits to mention al-Farabi who, as has been seen, is referred to elsewhere in the *Dialoghi* as belonging alongside Avicenna, al-Ghazali and Maimonides to the "First Academy of the Arabs." The fact is that al-Farabi's account, occurring in *al-Siyāsāt al-Madaniyya*,[55] of the generation of the Separate Intellects resembles the exposé found in the *Dialoghi* in one respect: it attributes to each Separate Intellect two intellections, one of the First (Principle) and one of itself. It does not however explicitly refer, as is the case in Leone's exposé, to the production of each Separate Intellect by the one that precedes it. Only the production by each of the Intellects of a heavenly sphere is mentioned in so many words.[56]

The closest parallel to the exposé in question is found in al-Farabi's *Ārā' Ahl al-Madīna al-Fāḍila*,[57] a treatise, which, as far as is known, has not been translated into Latin or (except for some excerpts) into Hebrew. According to this treatise (p. 19) each of the Separate Intellects has the two intellections ascribed to these entities in *al-Siyāsāt al-Madaniyya.* However in *al-Madīna al-Fāḍila* al-Farabi states in addition that each Intellect produces by virtue of its intellection of the First (Principle) the Intellect that immediately follows it in the hierarchy, whereas by virtue of its being substantialized (*yatajawhar*) in itself (a notion which in all probability is closely related to the entity's intellection of itself) it produces a heavenly sphere.[58] But for some terminological divergencies, this conception is strongly reminiscent of the doctrine set forth in Leone's exposé.

At this point our attention may be addressed to a detail in Leone's account: he speaks of each of the Separate Intellects contemplating its own beauty (*belleza*), and the beauty of its cause. The notion that the Separate Intellects have beauty (*jamāl* in Arabic, *yofi* in the Hebrew translation) occurs in al-Farabi's *al-Siyāsāt al-Madaniyya* (see p. 40 in the Arabic text; p. 8 in the Hebrew translation). Beauty is also attributed in that work to the intellective souls of the heavenly bodies (p. 41 in the Arabic text; p. 10 in the Hebrew translation), and to the First (Principle) (p. 46 in the Arabic text; p. 13 in the Hebrew translation; in this passage *jamāl* is rendered by *noy*).

Supreme Beauty (*jamāl*) is ascribed to the First (Principle) also by Avicenna in the *Ilāhiyyāt* of *Kitāb al-Shifā'* (II, 268) and by al-Ghazali (*Maqāṣid al-Falāsifa*, p. 171). The latter refers in the passage that is quoted also to the beauty of the "angels that are close to God" (*al-malā'ika al-muqarrabīn*). The concept of divine Beauty[59] and of beauty in general was central in the Renaissance thought to which Leone sought to adapt his Judaeo-Arabic philosophical heritage. The fact that the concept in question was referred to in medieval texts which he may have studied before his initiation into Italian Platonism may have helped him in this endeavor.

According to Leone (III, 77aff.), Averroes[60] considers, in contradistinction to the other philosophers mentioned above, that "the coordinated multitude of the essences of the universe" (and not only the First Intellect) may have an immediate dependence on God, in spite of the latter's absolute simplicity. This is possible because the essences in question are conjoined in a union similar to that formed by the various bodily parts of a human individual. Averroes is also reported to have believed that the divine Beauty is impressed in immediate fashion upon all the Intellects that move the heavenly spheres; this impress is more perfect in the First Intellect than in the Second and in the Second than in the Third and so forth down to the human intellects. The impress of the divine Beauty upon bodies is of a more imperfect kind, but can be found not only in the heavenly sphere, but also in the sublunar bodies and in the prime matter. Some of the principal conceptions set forth in this account of Averroes' doctrine occur in the latter's *Tahāfut al-Tahāfut.*[61] However the Arabic philosopher does not mention the divine Beauty in this context.

Continuing his exposition (III, 77b–78a) Leone, or his spokesman Philone, introduces a new theme: he refers to the love and desire of the divine Beauty, and to the wish to participate in it, which, according to both Averroes and to the Arabic philosophers whose opponent he is, subsists in all existents from the First Intellect to prime matter. This is an answer, albeit an incomplete one, to a question put to Philone by Sophia, who generally does not proffer opinions of her own. The passage is intercalated (III,

76b–77a) between the two accounts of Philone summarized above; the one dealing with the views of Avicenna, al-Ghazali and Maimonides on the Separate Intellects, and the other treating of Averroes' conception of these entities. Sophia is reported as saying that she had heard that "these Arabs"[62] (i.e. Arabs referred to by Philone in the conclusion of the exposé to which Sophia responds)[63] considered that love descends from the summit of the world of the angels to the last (degree) of the lower world and that thence it descends grade by grade in a circular "form" to its First Principle. The question she asks is on what points the other Arabs disagree with this (conception). Philone's answer to this question is described above as incomplete because it only refers to opinions concerning the love of the inferior for the superior; views whether positive or negative, concerning the possibility that a superior entity may bear love of some kind for an inferior one are not alluded to. Thus a part of Sophia's question remains unanswered.

Who were the Arabs that are referred to by Philone and Sophia? There can be little doubt as to the answer, unless Leone was very inaccurate indeed in his phrasing. As has already been mentioned, Philone speaks of *gl'Arabi*[64] at the end of this account of the teaching of Avicenna, al-Ghazali and Maimonides, and it seems pretty obvious that it is these philosophers who in the passage under consideration are designated as Arabs. It follows that it is likewise them (or one of them) that Sophia is supposed to have in mind when she states that, according to what she has heard, *questi Arabi* propounded a conception of cosmic love.

This brings us to one of the main themes of the present article, namely the possible relation between the *Dialoghi d'Amore* and Avicenna's *al-Risāla fi'l-'Ishq*, "The Epistle on Love," a well-known treatise, which seems to have been popular at certain periods. Y. Mahdavi's *Bibliographie d'Ibn Sina* (in Persian; Teheran, 1954, p. 180) lists thirty-two manuscripts of the work. The fact is that to the best of our knowledge the only Arabic theory of cosmic love fitting the description given in the *Dialoghi* is set forth in this treatise by Avicenna. There is, however, a difficulty with this identification. We have no information as to the treatise having been translated into Hebrew or Latin, and it seems improbable that Leone knew Arabic. To my mind this objection is not insuperable for several reasons. First, such a translation may have existed despite our ignorance of the fact. Indeed G. Bajda suggests,[65] albeit rather hesitantly,[66] that an *Epistle on Love*, *Igeret Ahava*, referred to in a treatise written by the fourtheenth-century philosopher Judah Cohen, may have had some connection with Avicenna's treatise. For the rest, this treatise may have been known to Hebrew readers under another title, and it may also have been ascribed to another author. Such a suspicion may be encouraged by the tenor of a passage on love ascribed to al-Ghazali[67] which occurs in a work of Yoḥanan Alemanno, a Renaissance author, who was considerably older than Leone.[68] *Al-Risāla fī'l-'Ishq* may well have been attributed to al-Ghazali. Yet another possibility might be that Leone might have learnt to know the doctrines of *al-Risāla fī'l-'Ishq* at second hand, from some unknown work which had summarized them.[69] A hypothesis brought forward by Moshe Idel would, if accepted, cut the ground from under these speculations. According to Idel,[70] Leone may have misinterpreted a passage of Alemanno when he ascribed the doctrine concerning the descent and ascent of love to Arabs. Some of Leone's principal conceptions were, according to this hypothesis, borrowed from the latter author.

It seems to me that a comparison between *al-Risāla fī'l-'Ishq* and the *Dialoghi d'Amore* may be a correct method for establishing with some degree of probability whether Leone was cognizant of, and influenced by, the doctrines of the Arabic treatise. Leone's adoption of some doctrines found in Ficino's *Commentary on the Symposium*[71] will also be discussed.

Some of the parallels I have come across in the course of a by no means exhaustive confrontation between the Arabic and Italian works may be listed as follows:[72]

I. *al-Risālā fī'l-'Ishq*, Ch. I, pp. 71–72:

> [God] is the extreme [degree] qua beloved and the extreme degree qua lover.[73] As Avicenna explains, God, who is the First Good, has a perfect comprehension of Himself; hence His love for Himself is the most perfect of loves.

Dialoghi, III, 55b:

> *Philone*: Thus God, [Who] cognizes and wills, is the first lover [*primo amante*], and this God, [Who is] supremely beautiful is the first beloved [*primo amato*].
> *Sophia*: Consequently the first love is that of God for Himself.
> *Philone*: Certainly.

II. *al-Risālā fī'l-'Ishq*, Ch. I, p. 69:

It is clear that each existent governed [by Providence; *al-mudabbarāt*] has a natural longing [*shawq ṭabī'ī*] and a natural love [*'ishq gharīzī*]; it follows necessarily that in these things love is the cause of their existence.

Ibid., Ch. I, p. 71:

Hence the existence of each of [the things] governed [by Providence] is in virtue of its natural love.

Dialoghi, II, 74a:

I see clearly that in the world that which has no love has no being.

III. *al-Risālā fī'l-'Ishq*, Ch. VII, p. 90:

. . .If the Absolute Good had not manifested Himself [*tajalla*] He would not have been received; and if He had not been received, there would have been no existence. Consequently His Self-manifestation is the cause of all existence. Since He, in virtue of His existence, loves the existence of the [things] caused by Him, He loves the reception of His Self-manifestation. . . . The true [object of] His love [*ma'shūq*] is the reception of His Self-manifestation. This is the true reality of its reception [*nayl*] by the souls striving to be God [or: the pious souls; *al-nufūs al-muta'alliha*]. For this [reason] they may be His beloved. . . . As Wisdom does not permit the neglect of what is excellent in some way in what exists through Him,[74] even if the supreme [degree] of excellence is not attained, the Absolute Good loves because of His Wisdom, that it[75] be received from Him, even if the perfection of its degree [as it is] in Him is not attained.

Dialoghi, III, 43a:

Sophia: What then does this term love mean with reference to God? *Philone*: It means the will to improve [the beings] created by Him [*le sue creature*] as well as the universe and to increase their perfection to the extent of which their nature is capable. The love which is in God presupposes a deficiency in the beloved, but not in the lover . . . though the Deity rejoices and joys (if the word is suitable) in the increase of the perfection of the created beings because of the love of God for them; in this supreme perfection becomes more resplendent.

Ibid., III, 147b:

The Divine Love is the tending of His most beautiful Wisdom towards His beautiful image, i.e. the universe produced by Him, and the return of this [universe] to union with His supreme beauty; and His joy [*delettatione*] is the perfect union of His image with [literally: in] Him Himself, of the universe [that is] produced with [literally: in] the producer.

IV. *al-Risālā fī'l-'Ishq*, Ch. VII, p. 87:

Every existent loves the Absolute Good with a natural [*gharīzī*] love; the Absolute Good manifests Himself to His lovers; but their reception [*qabūl*] of His Self-manifestation and their conjunction with Him[76] varies. The extreme [degree] of closeness to Him [consists in] the reception in true reality of His Self-manifestation, that is to say, in the most perfect manner that is possible, and this is the notion [*ma'nā*] named by the Sufis: Union [*ittiḥād*]. He in His generosity loves the reception [*an yunāl*] of His Self-manifestation; the existence of the [existent] things is in virtue of His Self-manifestation.

Dialoghi, III, 43a:

You know that with reference to all created [beings], even the celestial and spiritual ones, love means a deficiency for all who fall short of the supreme divine perfection; and all their actions, desires and loves [tend] towards coming closer[77] to this perfection to the extent to which they are able [to do so].

Ibid., III, 143a:

. . . The Unitive enjoyment by the intellectual created [being] of its creator . . . .

Ibid., III, 148a:

It cannot be denied that in the same way as the love of the universe is that which leads it to the delectable, blissful[78] union with the creator, the love of God for this universe is that which draws the latter to that divine union . . . .

V. *al-Risālā fī'l-'Ishq*, Ch. V,[79] p. 90:

Both the rational and the animal soul love everything that [has] beauty in [the way it is] ordered, arranged and proportioned . . . . The rational soul [loves these things] because it has been prepared to conceive [*taṣawwur*] matters [*ma'ānī*] transcending nature[80] and knows that as [a person][81] one comes closer to the First Beloved. His[82] [harmonious] arrangement becomes more beautiful and one's [bodily] proportions more excellent . . . . Whatever[83] is near Him has acquired a greater oneness and its concomitants: [harmonious] arrangement and conformity [of the parts].

Dialoghi, III, 103b:

Matter which is the foundation of all lower bodies is in itself deformed and mother of every deformity in these [bodies]; but when it is informed in all its parts through participation in the spiritual world, it is made beautiful, inasmuch as the forms radiated into it from the divine Intellect or the Soul of the World, or from the spiritual and the heavenly world remove from it its deformity and give it beauty; thus beauty comes into this lower world from the spiritual world.[84]

VI. *al-Risālā fī'l-'Ishq*, Ch. V, p. 82:

Three desires [*ḥubb*] consequent upon love [*'ishq*] for a beautiful [human] form are enumerated by Avicenna: 1) the desire to embrace it; 2) the desire to kiss it; 3) the desire for coition [*mubāḍaia*] with it. The first and the second are not reprehensible. As for the third " . . . this desire [the desire for coition] is peculiar to the animal soul, which has the greater portion in it. [This soul] has [in this desire] the status of an associate or rather of one who employs a servant [*al-mustakhdim*], not the status of an instrument, and this is exceedingly bad. Nay, rational love [*al-'ishq al-nuṭqī*] cannot be saved as long as the animal faculty is not suppressed in an extreme [manner]. For this reason it is fitting that the lover who entices his beloved with a view to this need should [stand] accused unless indeed this need is in his [case] of a rational sort; I mean his intending thereby to engender [a being] in [his] likeness. [But] in the case [of a beloved who is] a male this is impossible and in the case of a female who is forbidden to him by the religious law it is blameworthy [*qabiḥ*]. Thus a man is permitted [to do it] and approved for it only [if he does it] with his wife or his female slave.

Dialoghi, III, 133b–134a:

Philone: There may be in one matter good and evil . . . so that one thing may be good with regard to a small part of it which is visible, but bad in a more intimate and essential way with regard to its greater part. Such are the bad and intemperate pleasures [*deletattioni*] which are and seem good in so far as they give pleasure, but are bad in themselves since the good which they have and which [derives] from their form is conjoined with, and submerged in, the evil of matter. Hence they in themselves are evil, [but] have something that is seemingly good and that gives pleasure. However this is not an absolute good . . . nor does it give pleasure to everyone, but only to those that have an intemperate desire for it, those which are drawn by the desire of a minimal good without taking into account the great evil which [this good] has beneath it. However, temperate [persons] are not deceived by this little seeming good, for they know the excess of evil with which it is misused. Hence

they do not deem it pleasureable or desirable, but a real pain which should be abhorred, feared and shunned. A great many of such [matters] are within [the purview] of carnal appetite. For the greater part of the pleasures of [the sense of] taste, of venereal touch and of other emollients is bad and pernicious.
Sophia: Are there some of these carnal pleasures which are really good?
Philone: Yes, those which are temperate and necessary for human life and [human] offspring. Though these be carnal pleasures, they are, and are called, honorable [*honeste*] because they are tempered by the intellect [which is] the principle of honorability. The desire for these [pleasures] and those desirous of them are truly virtuous.

It may be noted that there exists a similarity both in content and in wording between this passage and one that occurs in Ficino's *Commentarium*, I, 4. We can see how close the likeness occasionally is from the following phrases and expressions in a part of the text of the *Dialoghi* translated above starting with the words "but a real pain": "Ma uera doglia, la quale si debbe abhorrire, temere e fuggire, e di questi si truouano assai ne l'appetio carnale, che la maggior' parte de le dilettationi del gusto, e del tatto uenereo e altre mollicie sono gattive e pernitiose." A corresponding text in Ficino reads: "Voluptates itaque gustus et tactus . . . amor mon modo noncupit, sed abominatur et fugit. . . . Rabies venerea ad intemperantiam trahit." It seems probable that when writing the text translated above Leone had some recollection of Ficino's *Commentarium*, IV, 3, and of other chapters of that work.[85]

VII. *al-Risālā fī'l-'Ishq*, Ch. II, III, and IV, pp. 72–75:

In these chapters Avicenna enumerates various kinds of love. The most significant for the purposes of this inquiry are:

1) (Ch. II, p. 73) The natural [*gharīzī*] love of matter for form. When it is stripped of one form, it hastens to replace it by another. This is due to the fact that without a form, matter is the abode [*maqarr*] of [absolute] nothingness, a state which is repugnant to it as well as to all other existents. When matter is endowed with a form, its nothingness is only relative. Matter may be likened to a woman full of blemishes,[86] who shrinks from rendering public her ugliness; whenever her veil is withdrawn she covers up her blemishes with a bonnet[?].[87]
2) The five simple bodies[88] and the compounds of four of them

(i.e. of the terrestrial elements) are attached to their own perfections and to their natural places to which their movements, due to desire [*ḥaraka shawqiyya*] are directed when they are separated from them.

3) (Ch. III, p. 73) The love with which plants or the vegetative souls are endowed is directed towards a) nutrition, b) growth, c) generation.

4) (Ch. IV, pp. 74–77) Love characteristic of irrational animals. As far as the sensitive part (of the animal souls) is concerned, natural [*gharīzī*] love is manifested by the fact that some of the objects grasped by the senses are agreeable while others are obnoxious. However love characteristic of the irrational animal is not restricted, as is thought by the great multitude, to the sensitive part; in fact it pertains in particular to the concupiscent [*shahwāniyya*] part[89] and is [determined] by choice [*ikhtiyārī*], as in the case of a donkey which, perceiving the approach of a wolf, stops munching barley and flees away. It is this element of choice which differentiates, in spite of their purposes being to a great extent identical, between the animal concupiscent faculty and the vegetative faculty. Avicenna's reference to rational [*nuṭqī*] love which is found in human beings, has been quoted above.

Dialoghi, II, 4a–b, 11a–12b:

There are some discrepancies between the two passages with which we are concerned. In the second (11a–12b) Leone refers to the love of first matter for the various forms, of the loves of the elements producing mixed substances of vegetative and animal love and of the love of human beings. In the first passage (4a–b), he speaks of natural love which is that of inanimate things, sensitive love which is that of irrational animals, and rational love (determined by) will (*amor rationale e volontario*) which is only found in man. This passage differs from the relevant passages of *al-Risālā fī'l-'Ishq* in two or three particulars. Leone omits in it any reference to vegetative love and, what is more, he classifies animal love as sensitive, a view which as we have seen is attacked by Avicenna, who regards this love as being determined by choice, whereas Leone finds an element of will only in human love. The classification propounded in this passage conforms by and large to that current among Christian scholastics, for instance the Thomists, and may have been taken over from them, perhaps through the intermediary of some Renaissance philosopher.[90]

The second passage may be, from our point of view, more interesting because it starts with a description of the love of first matter for the various forms. This description is followed by a lengthy disquisition on the "friendship" of the elements for each other in consequence of which the production of the vegetative, the animal and the intellective soul comes about. The love of matter for all the forms has, according to Leone (12a), been likened by Plato to that of woman for man. Some people, because of the insatiable appetitie for new forms that characterizes matter, have called the latter a harlot (*meretrice*). Leone, who seems to have been mistaken in attributing the simile referred to above to Plato, probably had in mind a well-known passage in Aristotle's *Physics* (I, 192a23). The likening of matter to a harlot may be found in Maimonides' interpretation (in the *Introduction* to the first part of the *Guide of the Perplexed*) of Proverbs 7:6–21.[91]

Though, unlike Maimonides, Leone admires the succession of wondrous forms generated by the appetite of matter, his explanation of Aristotle's simile is closer to that of the Jewish philosopher than to that of Avicenna who considers that matter has this appetite because of its dread of absolute nothingness. Nevertheless, the fact that this desire of matter for the forms is regarded both in the *Dialoghi* and in *al-Risālā fī'l-'Ishq* as forming a part of the cosmic hierarchy of various kinds of love does indicate a similarity of approach, which is possibly also found in Thomas Aquinas' *Commentary on the Physics* (*Liber* I, *Lectio* XV, 138) where, in an explanation of 192a23, the desire of matter for form is designated as *appetitus naturalis.* In this explanation Aquinas refers to Plato's likening matter to a mother and to a female and form to a male.[92]

There are considerable differences between the excerpts quoted above both with regard to the philosophical significance of the subject dealt with in each section, and to the degree of concordance between the opinions of Avicenna and Leone. The historical and philological importance that should be attributed to this concordance if it exists depends to a great extent on the particularities of the subject on which the two philosophers agree.

The opinions propounded in the passages of the *Dialoghi* quoted in sections V and VI could have been encountered by Leone in

Ficino's work, and perhaps in those of other Renaissance writers, as well as in *al-Risālā fī'l-'Ishq.* With respect to these passages Ficino's influence may be regarded as certain, whereas that of Avicenna is hypothetical. The matter is less clear with regard to the passages of the *Dialoghi* quoted in section VII. The classification set forth in these texts by Leone seems to be borrowed from Christian Latin authors. However no classification of the various kinds of loves which corresponds exactly to that of Leone[93] has yet been found in their writings.

The main metaphysical themes of Leone's, as well as Avicenna's theory of love are dealt with in sections I to IV. The relation of these sections to Ficino's *Commentarium* shall now be briefly examined. The use in the passage of the *Dialoghi* quoted in Section I of the correlative terms Lover and Beloved applied to God cannot, as far as I can see, be matched in the *Commentarium*, in which (II, 2) God is called *amor.* Nor do the two terms joined together occur in relation to God in Ficino's source (see below), the *De Nominibus Divinis* ascribed to Dionysius Areopagita. In this work (cf. XIV Migne, *Patrologia Graeca*, III, col. 712) the designations of God that are mentioned in connection with love are: *Erōs* and *Agapē* on the one hand and *Erastos* and *Agapetos* (Beloved) on the other.[94]

The position is similar in respect to section II. The expression employed by Leone has, as far as I can see, no parallel in Ficino's *Commentarium*, though the doctrine to which the expression refers is found in that work. The *Commentarium* may be regarded as Leone's main Christian source as far as the metaphysical theory of love is concerned.

Sections III and IV deal with the love of God for the created beings and the love of the latter for Him. The passages of the *Dialoghi* that are quoted in these sections bear a general resemblance to Ficino's *Commentarium* II, ch. 2 and III, ch. 1 and 2. In all three chapters Dionysius Areopagita is quoted. The quotation in II, 2 refers to a passage in the *De Nominibus Divinis* (c. 4, col. 712) which speaks of the circle of love (*Amor circulus est*). Given the practical certainity that Leone was familiar with the *Commentarium*, it seems probable that the expression *circulo degl'amori* occurring in the *Dialoghi*, III, 145b, has something to do with Ficino's quotation from Pseudo-Dionysius.[95]

In an attempt at summing up and stating conclusions, it may

first of all be mentioned that there does not seem to exist a decisive proof for the hypothesis that Leone took over directly or indirectly some details of his theory of love from *al-Risālā fī'l-'Ishq*; the indications that seem to support this view (such as Leone's designation of God as the First Lover and First Beloved, the place he assigns to the desire of matter for form in the hierarchy composing the various kinds of love, and so forth) carry weight, but are not conclusive. Views on these points similar to Leone's may conceivably be discovered in some medieval or Renaissance authors.

Two other considerations may, however, be brought to bear on the question under discussion. One of these has already been noted: In *Dialoghi*, III, 76b–77a there is a reference to a theory of love propounded by "these Arabs"; the doctrine of *al-Risālā fī'l-'Ishq* or of some version of it (that may have also been known to Alemanno), appears to be the only one fitting the description. An alternative solution would be to suppose that Leone had no knowledge of any such theory—that, in other words, for some reason of his own he decided to impart false information to his readers.

If the passage does refer to the views set forth in *al-Risālā fī'l-'Ishq,* it may be arguable that the words "in a circular form" (*in forma circulare*) which serve to characterize the descent and ascent of cosmic love, may not have occurred in the text summarized by Leone,[96] but have been added by him in order to explain the doctrine in question.[97] They may have been suggested by the expression "circular line of the universe" (*linea circulare de l'universo*), which is found (III, 76b) shortly before the account of the theory of love in an exposé of an Arabic doctrine which, as Idel has plausibly shown, may refer to Batalyūsī's opinions.

The second consideration is of a more general nature. In *Dialoghi*, III, 74, Leone claims[98] to have "spoken of the love of the universe in more universal fashion [*piu universalmente*] than was done by Plato in the *Symposium*, because here we treat of the principle of love in all the created world, [whereas] he only treated of the principle of human love."

The same claim could be made on behalf of Avicenna's *al-Risālā fī'l-'Ishq.* In point of fact, both the Arabic and the Italian treatises are very detailed, comprehensive, and coherent statements of the theological and metaphysical theory of cosmic love.[99] As has been shown with respect to six or seven major points of doctrine the two treatises agree either completely or in essentials, the differences being relatively minor. If we suppose for the sake of argument that Leone had no knowledge whatever, direct or indirect, of *al-Risālā fī'l-'Ishq* this accord would perhaps be even more significant than on the contrary assumption. It would, of course, also pose various problems.[100]

If Leone was acquainted with *al-Risālā fī'l-'Ishq*, it may be supposed that he combined in his theory of love elements of this treatise with conceptions belonging to Renaissance philosophy and science just as he amalgamated, within the framework of his doctrine concerning the production of worlds, in treating for instance of the notion of Chaos, some ideas which according to him were derived from Ibn Gabirol with views that appear to be borrowed from Ficino.

It may be contended that the theory concerning the production of the worlds dealt with in the first section of the present study and the theory of cosmic love which is discussed in the second may on many counts be incompatible with one another. Nevertheless the two of them together constitute much the greater part of what may be termed Leone's metaphysical system, the sources of which we have tried to indicate.

Arabic and Jewish philosophers, as well as Greek ones, are referred to more often in the context of the theory of the coming into being and passing away of the worlds than in connection with the doctrine of cosmic love, but as has been seen, Leone suggests in a passage of the *Dialoghi* that the latter doctrine may have an Arabic origin.

It is certain that Leone owes a great deal to Renaissance, and perhaps also to Christian scholastic, thought, and yet he does not mention a single Christian author in the *Dialoghi.* His consistency on this point may have been due to a personal decision or to a Judaeo-Spanish convention;[101] what is evident is that he must have had a reason for this line of conduct.

Because of Leone's omitting to name his Christian sources it may be tempting, but would be incorrect, to examine his thought exclusively in the context of the history of the Judaeo-Arabic philosophical tradition. Although he was undoubtedly a representative, one of the last, of this tradition,[102] he was also aware, as were other Jewish authors in his time, of ideas that were debated in the outside world of Renaissance Italy. This duality enabled him to write his one extant book—*habent sua fata libelli.* By a curious turn of fate, the *Dialoghi d'Amore* which, though written in Italian, is in many passages a typical product of the Judaeo-Arabic philosophical tradition in its final phase, contributed greatly to the propagation of a modish philosophy, one of the earliest European philosophies whose vogue spread far beyond university, clerical, and humanistic circles. The popularity of the work is attested by a sentence in the prologue of Don Quixote[103] and even more so by verses of Ronsard, who apparently made a present of the *Dialoghi* to Charles IX of France[104] but was strongly opposed, perhaps for personal reasons, to the doctrine of two sorts of love—the carnal and the sublime—and expressed at least in one piece of poetry his displeasure with Leone Ebreo by venting anti-Jewish feelings half in jest and half in earnest.[105]

The *Dialoghi*, a treatise that is perhaps, chronologically speaking, the last important work that was produced by the Jewish medieval philosophical tradition had become a favorite topic for polite conversation and literary composition. It is a bizzarre fact that the long history of that tradition may, in a meaningful sense, be regarded as ending upon this note.

NOTES

1. All references are to Carl Gebhardt's edition, published *Curis Societatis Spinozanae* (Heidelberg, London, Paris, Amsterdam, 1929). According to a passage in the *Dialoghi* (III, 50b), Leone was writing the 3rd Dialogue in the year 5262 (1501/1502 of the Christian era).

2. The opinions of Greek philosophical schools (the Peripatetics, the Stoics, the Academics, and the Epicureans) are also referred to.

3. Cf H. A. Wolfson, *Crescas' Critique of Aristotle* (Cambridge, Mass., 1929), pp. 596-597. It is of some interest to note that in his reference to *li Philosophi commentatori d'Aristotle* (II, 69b) Leone Ebreo appears to have meant primarily Arabic and Jewish philosophers (see also below).

4. Cf. also III, 123 a–b.

5. It may also be a variation on the well-known dictum that Plato was an Atticizing Moses.

6. Or Spanish or Italian.

7. Cf. for instance the *Nicomachean Ethics*, 1104b 31: *Kalou*, *sympherontos*, *hēdeos*.

8. Cf. for instance, Thomas Aquinas' Commentary on the *Nicomachean Ethics*, *lib.* II, sect. III, 273.

9. Leone cites Aristotle's remark in the course of an explanation for, and an historical account of, the recourse to poetry, poetic fiction and a difficult style in the exposition of various scientific disciplines. *Inter alia*, Leone remarks (28b): "The fact that those poems are the common food of all sorts of men is the cause of their being perpetuated in the mind of the multitude. For there are few [men] who have a taste for very difficult things, and the memory of these few may be rapidly lost when a time comes that makes men turn

away from the [true] doctrine [or learning], as we have seen in the case of some nations and religions, such as the Greeks and the Arabs, which after having been most learned have almost entirely lost [the knowledge of] science. This was already the case in Italy at the time of the Goths; [it was] afterwards [that] the little that exists there at present was renewed."

10. Cf. Aristotle's *Fragmenta*, collected by V. Rose, *Aristotelis Opera* published by Academia Regia Borussica, V (Berlin, 1870), p. 1581 (No. 612).

11. A parallel story occurs in al-Farabi's *Kitāb al-Jama' bayna Ra'yay al-Ḥakīmayn*, ed. A. Nader (Beirut, 1968), p. 80; its source being a *Risāla* of Aristotle to Plato. The latter is reported to have upbraided the former for having composed and published (*ikhrāy*) complete expositions of science. Aristotle's defense is that he composed his book and chose the terms used in them in such a way that they can be accessible only to people who are capable of appreciating them.

12. See Isaac Abravanel, *Shamayim Ḥadashim* II, 2 (Rodelheim, 1828; reprint, Jerusalem, 1966), 14a.

13. One of whose main works was a Commentary on the *Symposium*.

14. *La seconda di Platone che solamente la materia, o Chaos fu produtto ab eterno, ma* [*il mondo*] *in principio di tempo.* The words *il mondo*, which do not occur in the printed text have been inserted, as without them the sentence does not make sense.

15. I.e., the people who believe in the doctrines of religion: *delli fideli.*

16. See my translation of the *Guide* (Chicago, 1963), pp. 281ff.

17. The adherents of this opinion are referred to by Leone Ebreo (III, 46a) as "noi tutti che crediamo la sacra legge Mosaica."

18. Leone states (III, 65b) that according to the philosophers time is infinite and had no beginning (*principio*), although "we the faithful believe the contrary." Plato's opinion about Time is formulated as follows (III, 55a): "Time is eternal not in virtue of the motion of Heaven, but in virtue of the eternal motion in succession of Chaos, [a motion] which causes germination." This opinion relates to the theory concerning the eternal succession of worlds, each of which in its turn is generated and destroyed (see below). This opinion is accepted by Leone. The opinion according to which time is a function of the motion of Heaven is that of Aristotle. As has been seen, it is rejected in the passage quoted above.

19. This is the meaning assigned to the two terms by Naḥmanides (*Commentary* on Genesis I, 1 [Jerusalem, 5732], p. 12); Isaac Abravanel, (*Mif'alot Elohim* [Lemberg, 1863; reprint Jerusalem 5727], 25b) and others. Gersonides, on the other hand, considers that *bohu* is matter and *tohu* form. (See his *Commentary* on Genesis I, 1 [Venice, 5307], 9c.) Isaac Abravanel points out (ibidem) that there is a difference of opinion between Gersonides and Naḥmanides as to the meaning of *tohu* and *bohu.*

20. Cf. III, 52b: *li sapienti degli hebrei chiamati Cabalisti.*

21. *Il Chaos il quale gli Hebrei soglieno chiamare terra e ancora li Caldei e altri gentili.*

22. In the next sentence, the earth, i.e. the Chaos, is equated with the Abyss (the *tehom* of Genesis 1:1) of many dark waters. The Spirit of God (III, 54a) (which occurs in the verse in question) is the Supreme Intellect (*il sommo inteletto*) that is full of Ideas (a term which has in the context a Platonic connotation). This Intellect created light in the dark Chaos, whose occult substances were illumined by the ideal form (*da la formalità ideale*). The Firmament fashioned on the second day of Creation is the heaven; the Upper Waters, separated by it from the Lower, are the Intellectual Essences; while the Lower Waters are the Essences of the world of generation and corruption. The Chaos is thus divided into three worlds, the intellectual, the celestial and the corruptible. Ficino in his Commentary on the *Symposium, Commentarium in Convivium*, I, 3, also speaks of three kinds of Chaos, which correspond to those referred to by Leone.

23. Cf. *Dialoghi*, III, 54a: *Mi piace vederti fare Platone Mosaico, e del numero de Cabalisti.*

24. *Nel quale sonno le Idee.*

25. Cf. Marsilio Ficino, *Commentarium in Convivium Platonis*, I, 3: *Chaos Platonici informem mundum vocant, mundum vero formatum chaos.*

26. In the context this is certainly the meaning of *quinquagesimo anno* (III, 53a; cf. III, 50b). In connection with speculations concerning the fifty-thousand-years cycle, Leone

touches (III, 51a–b) upon the problem posed by the (independent) motion proper to the eighth sphere, which is the sphere of the fixed stars. According to the ancient astronomical or astrological calculations, this motion results in a complete revolution in no less than thirty-six thousand years; according to the verifications of the latter-day "astrologers"—"because of the longer experience (*la piu longa esperientia*)" of which they are the product—such a revolution takes place in forty thousand years. It is clear in any case that in the course of the span of existence allotted to it, between its generation and dissolution the eighth sphere accomplishes only one revolution of the kind referred to.

27. Literally "everything that is full," "*tutto il pieno*."

28. It should be noted that in the *Dialoghi* the answer given to a question with regard to this point is *forssi che si*, "perhaps yes" (III, 50b). In the context, however, the dubitative character of this answer need not be taken seriously.

29. Also Ficino seems to have professed a theory according to which mind (*mens*) is composed of matter and form. This theory is set forth in the following passage in his *Commentarium in Convivium* (I, 3) in the context of the doctrine of three kinds of Chaos:

> In his utique mundis tribus tria et chaos considerantur. Principio deus mentis illius creat substantiam, quam etiam essentiam nominamus. Haec in primo illo creationis suae momento informis est et obscura. Quoniam vero a deo nata est, ad deum sui principium ingenito quodam appetitu convertitur. Conversa in deum, ipsius radio, illustratur. Radii illius fulgore ille suus appetitus accenditur. Accensus appetitus deo totus inhaeret. Inhaerendo formatur. Nam deus, qui potest omnia, in mente sibi inhaerente creandarum rerum naturas effingit. In ea igitur spiritali quodammodo pinguntur, ut ita loquar, omnia quae in corporibus istis sentimus. Illic caelorum elementorumque globi, sidera, vaporum nature, lapidum, metallorum, plantarum, animalium formae gignuntur.

The word *substantia*, which occurs at the beginning of this passage, appears to mean: matter.

30. Cf., for instance, D. Kaufmann, *Studien über Salomon Ibn Gabirol* (Budapest, 1899), pp. 113–114. This work also lists other references in 15th-, 16th-, and 17th-century Jewish authors to Ibn Gabirol regarded as the author of the *Fons Vitae* (pp. 112–115); Isaac Abravanel is one of these authors. M. Idel in the paper entitled "The Magic and Neoplatonic Interpretation of the Kabbalah," which he contributes to the present symposium indicates additional references (by Alemanno and Messer Leon) to the *Fons Vitae*.

31. Which Leone occasionally equates with Chaos (see above).

32. Cf. *Fons Vitae*, ed. U. Baeumker (V, 42, 4–5): " . . . materia est creata ab essentia, et forma a proprietate essentiae; id est sapientia et unitate . . . "; (335, 4–5) "ergo oportet ut materia fiat ab essentia et forma a volutate, id est a sapientia."

33. Cf. Sen. Sachs, *Ha-Teḥiya* (Berlin, 5607), p. 9; D. Kaufmann, *Studien über Salomon Ibn Gabirol*, p. 75, n. 3.

34. Cf. Baeumker's edition, "Index," s.v. *materia*, pp. 47–9; s.v. *substantia*, p. 520.

It may, however, be noted that the term *substantia*, as used in the *Fons Vitae*, has a great variety of significations; inter alia it may mean: form, cf. *Index*, p. 520. *Sustantia* may have the signification *matter* in a quotation from "one of the Platonists" (*alcuno de li Platonici*), occurring in the *Dialoghi* (III, 51b). Gebhardt's suggestion (see *Dialoghi*, "Register," s.v. *Albenzubron* (p. 8), according to which the Platonist in question is Ibn Gabirol is very plausible. In Abraham Ibn Ezra's writings the meaning of the Hebrew word *etzem*, corresponding to *substantia* approximates, *pace* H. Greive (*Studien zum jüdischen Neuplatonsimus* [Berlin, 1973], p. 54), to matter.

35. In the last analysis, this meaning given to the Arabic term may be explained by the Stoic use of the word *ousia*; cf. P. Kraus, *Jābir Ibn Ḥayyān*, II (Cairo, 1943), p. 170, 3, 4.

36. The term Chaos, which occurs in the phrase under discussion, is not found in the *Fons Vitae* (on this term see above). It may be noted that Chaos is designated in this phrase as the "Universal Mother"; and that the designation mother is used to characterize corporeal matter in a commentary, attributed to Ibn Gabirol, on the account of the Paradise given in the book of Genesis; cf. D. Kaufmann, *Studien über Salomon Ibn Gabirol*, p. 69.

37. It may be added that the theory he propounds bears a pronounced resemblance to some Stoic doctrines.

38. "Dio non e formato, ne ha forma, ma e somma forma in se stessa" (thus in the printed edition; the reading *stesso* seems preferable). The conception that God is a form is reminiscent of medieval Aristotelianism which regarded God as the formal cause of the world, rather than of Neoplatonism; cf., for example, "Dieu et le Monde selon Moise Narboni," *Archives d'histoire doctrinale et littéraire du Moyen Age* (1954), p. 199. As regards Thomas Aquinas, see K. Kremer, *Die neuplatonische Seinsphilosophie und ihre Wirkung auf Thomas von Aquin* (Leiden, 1971), p. 380f.

39. This doctrine seems to have kabbalistic overtones. I cannot however go here into this aspect of the matter.

40. Some of the similarities between the two works were pointed out by M. Idel.

41. *Dialoghi* III, 53b; *Mif'alot*, III, 8 (ed. Lemberg, 1863; reprint Jerusalem, 5727), 25c.

42. Augustine, *De Genesi ad Litteram* in Migne, *Patrologia Latina*, vol. 34, Col. 224.

43. In the Christian exegesis the Spirit of God, mentioned in the first chapter of Genesis, is sometimes identified with the third Person of the Trinity.

44. *Mif'alot*, 51b.

45. According to Ficino, as quoted by Kristeller (op. cit., p. 26), "The multitude of Platonic interpreters was divided into six "academies," three in Athens and three abroad. In Athens the oldest flourished under Xenocrates . . . ."

46. The fact that they were apparently regarded by Leone as commentators of Aristotle (*Dialoghi* ibidem) does not necessarily disprove this suggestion.

47. With reference to al-Farabi and Averroes he uses somewhat less significant adjectives: the expression *grave et meditatum* applies to the former and *solidum et inconcussum* to the latter; see Pico's *De Dignitate Hominis Oratio*, 140ff.

48. In this context Leone Ebreo gives a correct exposition of the opinion of Averroes as well as of the views of the Members of the "First Academy of the Arabs." With regard to this controversy, cf. Averroes' criticism of the "latter day" (*al-muta'akhkhirūn*) philosophers—i.e. in the first place, of Avicenna and his followers—occurring in his *Great Commentary on the Metaphysics*, ed. M. Bouyges, Vol. III (Beirut, 1948), p. 1648. It may be noted that in the *Epitome of the Metaphysics* (*Talkhīs mā ba'd al-Ṭabī'a* attributed to Averroes, the doctrine adopted on the point at issue is diametrically opposed to the one expounded in the *Great Commentary*; see *Talkhis*, ed. U. Amin (Cairo, 1958), pp. 149f.

49. By and large quite correctly, if al-Ghazali is regarded as the author of the *Intentions of the Philosophers* and Maimonides as a philosopher.

50. (III, 124a) " . . . fu una compositione de le due vie theologali d'Aristotile, e Platone, piu bassa e minoretta, meno astratta che nissuna di quelle."

51. In this context Leone evidently does not wish to give a personal opinion as regards the total number of the heavenly spheres. A clause occurring on fol. 76a may be rendered as follows: " . . . whether there be eight spheres as the Greeks [believed], or nine as the Arabs [thought], or ten as [was the opinion of] the ancient Hebrews [*gl'antichi hebrei*] and of some moderns. . . ." The statement concerning the views of the Greeks and the Arabs is by and large correct. The reference to the opinion of the Hebrews may be founded on an astronomical or astrological interpretation of the doctrine concerning the ten *Sefirot.*

52. This seems to refer to an Avicennian conception.

53. See al-Ghazali, *Maqāṣid al-Falāsifa*, n. d., 1st edition, pp. 219–220.

54. See Ibn Sina, *al-Shifā', Ilāhiyyāt*, ed. M. Youssef Moussa, Solayman Dunya and Sa'id Zayed (Cairo, 1960), II, pp. 405–407.

55. *The Political Regime.* The Arabic text has been edited by F. M. Najjar (Beirut 1964). The treatise has a second title: *Mabādi' al-Mawjūdāt*, "The Principle of the Existents," which accounts for the title of its Hebrew translation: *Hatḥalot ha-Nimtza'ot.* This translation, which was done by Moses Ibn Tibbon, was published by Z. Filipowski in *Sefer ha-Asif* (Leipzig, 1849; reprinted Tel Aviv, 5730), pp. 1–64.

56. Cf. the Arabic text, pp. 52–53; the Hebrew translation, p. 18.

57. Ed. F. Dieterici (Leiden, 1895).

58. In the *Guide* II, 12, Maimonides outlines, going into particulars, a theory concerning

the Separate Intellects; he may have had in mind al-Farabi's doctrine. The theory in question is criticized in the *Guide* II, 22.

59. Cf., for instance, Marsilio Ficino's *Commentarium in Convivium Platonis*, Oratio V, caput IV, entitled: *Pulchritudo est splendor divine vultus*; see also P.O. Kristeller, *The Philsophy of Marsilio Ficino* (New York, 1943), p. 266 and passim.

60. According to Leone (III, 77a), Averroes, in spite of being an Aristotelian, contradicted some of the opinions of Aristotle, either because some of the latter's works notably in the area of philosophy and theology were not available to him or because he disagreed with them. It may be noted in connection with this remark that Averroes wrote commentaries upon all the authentic philosophical or theological texts of Aristotle that are known to us, but not upon the so-called *Theology of Aristotle* which is partly composed of excerpts from Plotinus' *Enneads.*

61. Cf. M. Bouyges' edition of this treatise (Beirut, 1930), p. 216f.; p. 219ff.; p. 237f.; cf. also S. Van den Bergh's translation, *Averroes' Tahāfut al-Tahāfut* (*The Incoherence of the Incoherence*) (London, 1954), I, pp. 129f., 136ff., and 141f. It goes without saying that Leone may have known only at second hand some of the opinions of the philosophers he refers to.

62. "Ho inteso come questi Arabi intendono che l'amore discenda dal capo del mondo angelico fin a l'ultimo del mondo inferiore, e che di lì ascenda fino al suo primo principio, tutto successiuamente di grado in grado con ordine mirablile in forma circulare con signalato principio. Io non uaglio per giudicare quanto questa oppinione habbi del uero, ma ha del ingegnoso, et apparente e molto ornata, dimmi la discrepantia de gl'altri arabi in questo."

63. I.e., at the end of Philone's account of the opinions of Avicenna, al-Ghazali and Maimonides on the Separate Intellects. This reference is dealt with by M. Idel in an article on al-Batalyusi as a source of the *Dialoghi d'Amore*; the article is discussed below.

64. Who according to him make a circular line (*linea circulare*), which starts with the Deity, descends gradually till first matter and then goes up again degree by degree to the point which is reached in the conjunction of the human intellect with the divine Beauty. M. Idel in an article entitled "The Sources of the Circle Images in *Dialoghi d'Amore*" (in Hebrew), *Iyyun* 28 (1978), pp. 156–166 makes a strong case for the circle images that occur in the *Dialoghi d'Amore* deriving from al-Batalyusi's work *The Intellectual Circles*, which was translated into Hebrew and had a considerable influence on Jewish philosophy. Idel points out that Isaac Abravanel also uses a circle image which seems to be likewise borrowed from al-Batalyusi. He considers that, in spite of apparent chronological difficulties, the son may have been influenced with respect to this point by the father; this thesis will be discussed below.

65. See G. Vajda, "La Question disputée de l'Essence et de l'Existence vue par Juda Cohen, philosophe juif de Provence," *Archives d'histoire doctrinale et littéraire du Moyen Age* 44 (1977), p. 136f., n. 58. The Hebrew text of the passage in which the title *Igeret Ahava* occurs is quoted by L. Berman in *Kiryat Sefer* 53 (5738), p. 371.

66. He states, speaking of *al-Risālā fī'l-'Ishq*, that "à notre connaissance il n'est pas été traduit en hébreu." In making his suggestion he does not refer in any way to *Dialoghi d'Amore.* The suggestion might be objected to on linguistic grounds; for according to medieval usage *al-Risālā fī'l-'Ishq* should be rendered *Igeret ha-Ḥesheq* rather than *Igeret Ahava.*

67. Abū Ḥamd, i.e. Abū Ḥāmid (al-Ghazali).

68. The passage in which Alemanno cites al-Ghazali is quoted by M. Idel ("Circle Images," p. 163).

69. It may be recalled that, according to our analysis (see above) Leone's views on the production of the Separate Intellects resemble in some points closely those expounded in *Arā' Ahl al-Madīna al-Fāḍila*, a work which, as far as we know, was not translated either into Hebrew or into Latin.

70. "Circle Images," p. 162ff.

71. *Commentarium in Convivium Platonis de Amore.* It seems certain that Leone was familiar with this work.

72. The *al-Risālā fī'l-'Ishq* is quoted from the text published in a collection of treatises entitled: *Jāmi' al-Badā'i'* (Cairo, 1917), pp. 68–91.

73. "... *huwa al-ghāya fī'l-ma'shūqiyya wa'l-ghāya fī'l-'āshiqiyya.*" *Ma'shūqiyya* means "belovedness" and *'āshiqiyya* more or less "the state of a lover."

74. *Fi wujūdihi*: literally, in His existence.

75. Apparently: the excellence.

76. Or: with His Self-manifestation.

77. *Son per approssimarsi.*

78. *Felicitante*: giving bliss.

79. The chapter treats according to the superscription with the love of beautiful faces by certain categories of peoples.

80. Or: prepared by nature to conceive transcendent matters.

81. Or: (a thing).

82. Or: (its).

83. Or: whoever.

84. Leone attacks (III, 102bff.) the conception that beauty is proportion. In criticizing this notion he probably follows Plotinus and Ficino (see *Commentarium in Convivium*, V, 3; Kristeller, op. cit. p. 265f.). Ficino's theory of beauty resembles the one propounded in *Dialoghi*, III, 103b. On beauty as something incorporeal and immaterial see Ficino's *Commentarium* V, 3, 4 and 5.

85. Ficino does not refer in I, 4, as is done by Leone to the honorability of the pleasures (*delettationi ... honeste*) that result in progeny. However a statement to this effect occurs elsewhere in the *Commentarium.* In VI, 8 the following phrase is found: "... quoniam tam sobolis procreatio quam indagatio veritatis necessaria et honesta censetur." Parallels to passages in the *Dialoghi* may of course be looked for not only in the *Commentarium*, but also in other works of Ficino. However Leone's statement (quoted above; see also below) that in one respect his *Dialoghi* are superior to Plato's symposium seems to indicate that when writing his work, he may have reflected on that dialogue and doubtless also on its *Commentary.*

86. Literally; blameworthy.

87. The printed text has *k.m. Kumma* signifies a kind of cap or bonnet; *Kumm* a sleeve. The term *kam* "quantity" would not fit into the simile.

88. I.e., the four terrestrial elements of Aristotelian physics, and the "fifth body," out of which the heavens are constituted.

89. Which in the case of some animals is assisted by the sensitive part.

90. See, for instance, E. Gilson, *Le Thomisme* (Paris, 1948), pp. 332ff. and 378ff.; J. Festugière, *La Philosophie d'amour de Marsile Ficin* (Paris, 1941), p. 56; P. O. Kristeller, op. cit., p. 171ff., especially p. 185ff. Some rather vague indications as to the Platonic and Neoplatonic antecedents of this classification are given by S. Van Den Bergh, *Averroes' Tahāfut al-Tahāfut*, II, p. 91, note to p. 138, 6. It may be noted that the classification in question does not occur in Ficino's *Commentary on the Symposium*; it is however possible that Leone borrowed it from some other work of Ficino. Robert Burton (d. 1640) states in *The Anatomy of Melancholy* (first published in 1621; see First Vintage Books edition [New York, 1977], Pr. 3, Sec. 1, mem. 1, subs. 2, pp. 15–16): "I will follow that accurate division of Leon Hebraeus, *dial.* 2, betwixt Sophia and Philo, where he speaks of natural, sensible, and rational love, and handleth each a part." The terms quoted by Burton from the *Dialoghi* are in Latin. Elsewhere (p. 11) Burton calls Leone Hebraeus "the most copious writer on this subject" (love); cf. also p. 17.

91. See Munk's edition of the Arabic text, I, 7b; my translation (Chicago, 1963), p. 13.

92. Speaking in a passage (III, 144b–145a) which will be discussed below, of the circle of love, Leone refers to the following hierarchy of desires: that of first matter for the elemental forms; that of the elemental forms for the mixed (substances); that of the mixed (substances) for the plants, that of the plants for (beings) endowed with senses; that of those beings for the intellectual forms, which ascends from the intellection of the lower intelligibles to that of the higher intelligibles and so on up to the highest of all which is divine; thus the love of the Supreme Beauty is attained. This classification too starts with the desire of first matter for a form.

93. In naming the desire of matter for form together with the other natural loves. We must however keep in mind that Aquinas called this desire *appetitus naturalis* (see above); but see also below, n. 94.

94. The point I wish to make is not a doctrinal, but a strictly terminological one. According to scholastic theology God loves Himself. Cf., for instance, Thomas Aquinas, *Summa Contra Gentiles*, I. I, cap. 91: *Deus igitur et se et alia amat.* Do scholastic texts which may have been available to Leone designate God as the *Lover*? The question calls for further investigation.

95. Idel's contention (in the "Sources of The Circle Images," see above) may nevertheless be in some measure correct. The use of the term "semicircle" (*semicirculo, Dialoghi*, III, 144b and 145a) with reference to the circular motion of love may have been influenced by his exposé concerning the circle of being (III, 143b–144a) which immediately precedes his account of the circle of love; and this exposé may owe much to al-Batalyusi's treatise. This treatise may also be the source of the reference (III, 76b) to the circular line in the universe made by Arabs. On the reference to an Arab doctrine of love, which descends and ascends in a "circular form" (III, 76b–77; the passage is quoted above) see below. S. Damiens (*Amour et intellect chez Léon l'Hébreu* [Toulouse, 1971], p. 162; quoted by Idel) suggests that the expression "circle of love" may have been taken over by Leone from Ficino who—according to Feougière, whose quotation from the Christian Platonist she cites—was influenced by Dionysius. She does not refer to the explicit quotations from the latter found in the *Commentarium*.

96. They are not found in a similar context in *al-Risālā fi'l-'Ishq*.

97. The relation pointed out by Idel between Alemanno's and Leone's theories of cosmic love requires further classification. In this connection we may note that Alemanno agrees with Leone in considering that the lowest degree of cosmic love is found in matter (*hyle*); see Idel, "The Sources of Circle Images," p. 163.

98. See also above.

99. They are superior in this respect to Ficino's *Commentarium* and to most or all other works treating of cosmic love.

100. Not all of which could be resolved by the supposition that Avicenna may have been indirectly influenced by Pseudo-Dionysius, as was Leone through the intermediary of Ficino.

101. Which, however, in the second part of the fifteenth century was more often honored in the breach than in the observance.

102. Though in many ways not of its Aristotelian mainstream. It may be significant in this respect that Isaac Abravanel reports in *She'elot Sha'ul* (quoted by H. A. Wolfson, *Crescas' Critique of Aristotle*, p. 600) that his son criticizes Averroes' view on first matter and regards the latter as identical with corporeal form. The view attributed in this passage to Leone is similar to an opinion advocated by Ḥasdai Crescas. On the other hand there are many Aristotelian elements in the *Dialoghi*, for instance the doctrine that being known precedes being loved (I, 31a). Leone's interpretations of biblical verses should be compared with those propounded by the Jewish philosophical commentators; he considers, for instance, that the Song of Songs treats of the love of the intellective soul for the divine Beauty or for God (III, 149b f.). In Maimonides' *Guide*, III, 51, verses from this biblical book are said to refer to the love of God that accompanies intellection of God, whereas according to Joseph Ibn Aqnin's Arabic commentary on the Song of Songs, it is the reciprocal love of the intellective soul and the Active Intellect that is the theme of the book. The beauty (*jamāl*) of the Active Intellect is mentioned by Ibn Aqnin in some passages (see, for instance A. S. Halkin's edition of the *Commentary*, p. 66 and p. 294). An examination of Hebrew commentaries on the Songs of Songs considered as sources upon which Leone may have drawn is called for.

103. "Si trataredes de amores con dos onzas que sepais de la lengua toscana topazreis con Leon Hebreo que os hincha las medidas." This and other references in various languages to Leone's *Dialoghi* are quoted by H. Pflaum, *Die Idee der Liebe, Leone Ebreo* (Tübingen, 1926), pp. 149–154.

104. One of his Odes is entitled: "Au Roy Charles luy donnant un Leon Hebrieu." Ronsard, *Oeuvres complètes*, ed. G. Cohen, (Paris: Editions de la Pleiade, 1950), I, p. 611.

105. Ronsard, *Oeuvres complètes*, II, p. 674: "Je n'ayme point les Juifs, ils ont mis en la croix/ Ce Christ, ce Messias, qui nos pechez efface,/ Des Prophetes occis, ensanglanté la place,/ Murmuré contre Dieu qui leur donna les loix./ Fils de Vespasian, grand Tite, tu devois,/ Destruisant leur Cité, en destruire la race,/ Sans leur donner ny temps, ny moment, ny espace/ De chercher autre part autres divers endroits./ Jamais Leon Hebrieu des Juifs n'eust prins naissance,/ Leon Hebrieu, qui donne aux Dames cognoissance/ D'un amour fabuleux, la mesme fiction;/ Faux, trompeur, mensonger, plein de fraude et d'astuce,/ Je croix qu'en luy coupant la peau de son prepuce/ On luy coupa le coeur et toute affection."

Exile and Redemption in Jewish Thought in the Sixteenth Century: Contending Conceptions

SHALOM ROSENBERG

1. Introduction

This article is devoted to clarifying certain aspects of the idea of *ge'ula* in sixteenth-century Jewish thought, within the context of a general historical-philosophical conception.[1] How did Jewish thought in this period perceive the character of Exile? How did it explain the dramatic events of the fifteenth and sixteenth centuries: the fall of Constantinople, the expulsion of the Jews from Spain, and the appearance of the Protestant Reformation? To those who formulated them, the answers to these questions served to confer meaning on the past and present; however, it seems to me that they can also contribute to understanding conceptions of *ge'ula* in this period—that is to say, conceptions of the future. In the following pages we will review the principal answers given to these questions, presenting them according to a general typological scheme. We will attempt such a scheme even though aware of the great difficulty attending any effort to find pure categories in the literature with which we will deal. As we will try to show, some of the categories in this typology have roots in medieval thought, and even in Talmudic and biblical literature. Other categories, however, appear to represent entirely new ideas.

We will first treat in a schematic way the principal historical-philosophical conceptions of Exile. These conceptions can be divided for our purposes into two categories. The first of these had a decisive place in classical Jewish thought. It includes: (1) the view of Exile (and in parallel fashion also the expulsion from Spain) as punishment; (2) a view of the sufferings of Exile as representing the "messianic birth-pangs"; and (3) a position, originating with

R. Yehuda ha-Levi and Naḥmanides, which perceives the cause for Exile not in the history of the Jewish nation but in the special status of *Eretz Yisrael*, which may repel its inhabitants for their moral transgressions.[2]

The survey of the first category would not be complete if we did not mention yet another position, one which was not without influence in medieval Jewish thought and of which traces can be discerned even in the sixteenth century. This view (4) interprets the tragic course of Jewish history as a consequence of certain astrological conditions related to the horoscope at the time of the birth of the Jewish nation.

In the sixteenth century, in contrast to the positions outlined above, Exile is characteristically regarded not as a punishment but as an end in itself, the meaning of which must be searched out.[3] Three theoretical positions can be discerned:

1) *The theory of mission*: Exile has a special goal; the dispersion of the Jewish people has enabled them to become a guide and teacher to humanity as a whole.

2) *The theory of "tikun"*: The Jewish people in its dispersion serves a mystical function in raising up the scattered sparks and thereby bringing salvation to the world.

It can perhaps be said that both of these views regard Exile as a means for altering reality and for bringing about redemption. While according to the earlier set of positions outlined above Exile is explained in categories internal to Jewish history, the later positions employ an explanation which involves more general historical processes, and indeed even makes use of cosmic categories. In such a conception the Jewish people represents the instrument of a grander program, the aim of which is to correct a catastrophe exceeding the narrow bounds of Jewish history. Israel in exile is identified with the suffering servant of the Lord, who suffers not because of his own actions but for the sake of others.

Counter to these positions, which continue to assume the catastrophic character of Exile, can be discerned a third position:

3) *The theory of alienation* explains Exile in metaphysical categories. According to this view Exile is not the result of a catastrophe. Rather it is a result of the fundamental ontological structure of the world; it can be said that Exile belongs to the "ontological"

character of the Jewish nation. In my opinion this is the heart and core of the position of the MaHaRaL of Prague. An echo is found here of ancient themes, but a fundamental change has transpired, for now it is not the soul of the individual which finds itself alienated — i.e., in Exile — but rather the collective soul of the entire nation.

4) *Exile as sin:* It should be added that a new and contrary view was to emerge later, according to which Exile represents neither punishment nor mission, but rather in itself constitutes a transgression.

This schematic survey, which will be expanded in the following pages, will in my opinion permit the formulation of a number of theses concerning the character of certain shifts in Jewish thought towards the end of the Middle Ages and in the modern period —shifts which achieved particularly strong expression in the Jewish conception of history. These trends had already appeared in fifteenth-century Spain, but only became central in the generation of the exiles.

We will first present briefly what appear to us to be the leading historical processes of the period, which will aid in understanding the above-mentioned changes.

(1) Historical events, it seems to me, compelled the abandonment of the traditional conception which viewed Exile as a punishment.[4] The emergence of new conceptions was accompanied by the rediscovery of certain ancient notions which permitted a different interpretation of the exilic condition. Even those who, like R. Moses Alsheikh, clung to the accepted conception, were forced to demonstrate that the very fact of a law of "transgression and exile," valid only for the Jewish nation, was a sign of the special mission or condition of this nation. As the MaHaRaL expressed it, if the transgression is the cause then we must search for the cause of the cause.

This change of interpretation can be explained, it seems to me, by the experience of suffering of those expelled — a suffering endured by precisely those Jews who had been faithful to the Torah, resisting conversion (even with the possibility of a double-life as a crypto-Jew) and choosing instead the wanderer's staff, along with its dangers and afflictions.

There is a second aspect to this experience of suffering, theological in character. The theological confrontation with Christianity, which in my opinion reached its height in the fifteenth century, presented Jewish thinkers with the problem that their own view of Exile as punishment was precisely that of Christian theology, a claim which the Church used in order to prove the truth of its teachings.[5] Answers to this problem which did not take into account the present situation of the Jews were not sufficient. Jewish religious life could not survive on the basis of the memory from the distant past of Revelation, but required a consciousness of God's presence in contemporary history as well. The sons were exiled from the table of their fathers, but had not been rejected in order to admit other, alien sons.

(2) The historical vicissitudes experienced by the Jews of Spain from the end of the fourteenth century made clear the need for a new perception of history. In discussions of the principles of faith in this period, a newly felt necessity for the idea of divine Providence can be discerned. The problem of divine Providence appeared increasingly central, to the point where it obscured problems which had appeared crucial to the scholars of earlier centuries.

The decline and collapse of Spanish Jewry confronted Jewish scholars with the question, "Why was Spanish Jewry lost?"[6] "And the offspring of these principles will bring forth and cause to flourish a great *mitzva* . . . [namely], to justify the verdict of our Maker, may He be blessed, concerning all of these events."[7] Or, in another formulation, the task of Jewish thought now became to console those "many and esteemed [among us] . . . who have endured the crises of exile and the waves of expulsion and suffer all of this for the Lord their God, though not with joyous countenance, in order to prove that (Ps. 30:6) 'a moment of His wrath' is itself 'the life He desired.' "[8]

The old controversy concerning the Creation became secondary. The importance of *emuna* to the Creation lies in the fact that this is the essential thing on which Providence depends. "Thus the deniers of the root [*ikar*] also denied the branches [Providence]." [9] And indeed "Aristotle, first among the Greek philosophers, was the father of them all and did not believe in divine Providence;

and this is the faith of the infidels (*kofrim*) who say [Ez. 8:12], 'The Lord hath forsaken the land.' "[10]

Such a change was needless to say also prompted by general trends which had altered the face of medieval thought. We will discuss several examples reflecting different aspects of this change.

The first is the gradual shift by which the realm of cosmology lost its centrality. Medieval thought had been anchored in a hierarchic picture of the world in which the upper levels of the ladder of existence were the celestial spheres. The boundless authority of this view was undermined at the close of the Middle Ages, and the position of man—and thus also of Israel—was thrown into a new light. This situation is expressed in certain lines of Renaissance thought, for example in Marsilio Ficino, according to whom man is the highest of the creatures, save God and the angels.[11] The cosmic dimensions of man, which the kabbalists had always emphasized, thus gained broader recognition.

Another similar shift of focus from nature to history is evident in the conception of prophecy. In order to understand this shift, we will contrast two views. A first—generally accepted in medieval thought—regarded prophecy as the revelation of the ultimate truths of science and philosophy. A second—which was paradoxically influenced by Averroes' critique of the first—held that the task of the prophet is essentially one of the precognition and interpretation of historical events and processes.[12] At the end of the medieval period, we are witness to the increasing influence of this second conception, and consequently the increased emphasis on the historical realm.

Jewish thought was forced to undergo a radical change in order to permit an understanding of historical reality. Such a change is not reflected in all the works of this period. There are indeed many sixteenth-century authors who do not deal with contemporary problems in the conception of history at all. In some cases this may be due to the fact that we know their works only partially. In others, however, the absence of such conceptions is not merely a result of an historical accident. This situation of course also existed in the fifteenth century. It throws new light on the charge that philosophy did not succeed in preparing its followers to withstand the terrible ordeal of persecution and expulsion. Rationalist philosophy could supply neither motivation for resisting persecution nor the means to understand and give meaning to the tragic events of the period.[13]

(3) The character of the Jewish nation became a focal concern of Jewish thought. The discussion of divine Providence does not center about the life of the individual, but rather about the collective "I," the existence of which had become newly evident. The awareness of this collective personality also led to an effort to deal with its uniqueness and its fate.

2. Conceptions

In this part we will broaden our discussion of the chief conceptions of Jewish history and the understanding of Exile and Redemption in this period.

(1) *Suffering as Punishment.*

According to the classical view, although Exile itself constitutes a form of punishment, its prolongation represents the mercy of God. Instead of collecting the full debt at once, He observes His covenant, and spreads payment of the debt over many generations[14]—or as Alsheikh writes, "He provides relief between one wave and another."[15] This explanation in itself requires explanation. Why is this relentless cycle of sin and punishment valid uniquely for Israel? The dominant theme in answers to this question lies in the midrashic idea that while exile is a severe punishment, the alternative is Gehenna, and God in His love for Israel therefore chose the alternative of exile.

On the verse (Gen. 15:17), "And it came to pass that when the sun went down," the Midrash remarks:

> Simeon b. Abba said in R. Yoḥanan's name: He [God] showed him four things: viz., Gehenna, the [foreign] kingdoms, Revelation, and the Temple, with the promise: As long as thy children occupy themselves with the latter two, they will be saved from the former two; if they neglect the latter two they will be punished by the former two. Wouldst thou rather that thy children descend into Gehenna or into the power of the [foreign] kingdoms?[16]

A classic view is reflected here in the idea that Exile guards Israel against inheriting Gehenna.

(2) *Suffering as the Messianic Birth Pangs.*

An additional response to contemporatry events could lead easily to a view of the expulsion from Spain as constituting the "messianic birth pangs." Thus writes one contemporary witness: "I think that the afflictions visited on the Jews in all the kingdoms of Edom from the year 250 of the sixth millenium to the year 255 [1490–95] 'a time of trouble unto Jacob, but out of it shall he be saved'—they are the messianic birth pangs.'[17] R. Isaac Aboab the Elder interprets the story in Tractate *Brakhot* as hinting at redemption: "It can be compared to a father and son who were traveling on a road. . . . He [the father] said to him, 'Let this be a sign for you: when you see a cemetery you are near to a town. . . . It is a sign [for us] when we see afflictions, that the advent of the Messiah is near."[18]

Given this view we can understand the prevalence among the first generation of exiles of calculations predicting the advent of the Messiah by virtue of the expulsion: "That the good should come to Israel in the days of the Spanish Jews who left Spain."[19] The conquest of *Eretz Yisrael* by the Turks and even the Reformation appear to be signs of the realization of the prophecy (Song of Songs 2:12): "The time of the singing bird is come, and the voice of the turtle is heard in our land."[20]

(3) *The Astrological Interpretation.*

Against the background of the classical theodicy with its two chief notions—the theory of sin and punishment and the theory of the messianic birth pangs—an essentially different position emerged which gave to Jewish history, to Exile and Redemption, an astrological interpretation. The sources of this notion can be found in the Middle Ages and even in the ancient period. It is based on the interpretation of the horoscopes by which the fates of entire nations were determined.[21]

In the works of various thinkers who were influenced by this position can be found a more radical view by which astrology constitutes not only a means to explain the history of the nation, but also the key to understanding its Torah. The commandments of the Torah were given as a means of resisting the blind and harsh decrees of fate. If the persecutions which the Jewish nation endured can be explained only as a result of the malign influence of the stars, the commandments come to be regarded as antidotes to the suffering thus produced, or even as ritual substitutes for the fulfillment of the astral decrees. It is in this spirit, for example, that the blood of circumcision was regarded as a means of evading the bloodshed ordained by the stars.[12]

In the sixteenth century such a position is represented by R. Abraham ibn Migash in his *Kvod Elohim.*[23] He avers that the Jews' patron "is Saturn, and this [heavenly body] indicates servitude, captivity, poverty and degradation."[24] In fact, however, two motives are here combined: the astrological interpretation and the theory of sin. The transgression is not the cause of punishment but rather the removal of divine Providence (*hester panim*): "And He has abandoned you to your patrons and their decrees." There are special properties to the commandments as well as to any transgression of them. "Just as there is in the commandments a property (*davar sagul*) guiding the way to the world to come, so there is in iniquity and transgression a poison 'bearing gall and wormwood' [Prov. 5:4], 'her feet go down to death' [ibid., 5:5]. . . ." The primary consequence of Israel's transgressions is that they are abandoned "to the accidents of the time."[25]

The relationship to Saturn is ambivalent. On the one hand, Saturn as patron brings about servitude and captivity. On the other, Saturn is located in the outermost orbit: "It being above everything, it is close to the Separate Intellects."[26] Thus, "there is no good thing in it [Saturn], except the [characteristics of] reflection and speculation by which wisdom is attained." It is "isolated from material things and pleasures." The influence of Saturn is responsible for the sequence of the cosmic periods and the annihilation of worlds (*shmitot*). Therefore "it destroys all human affairs and monarchies." Saturn is the agent of destruction "because it has no affinity for things of the body; therefore it destroys them and does not keep watch over them."[27] Since it is the heavenly body which bestows the wisdoms, Saturn is "appointed over the Jews, but due to this they are afflicted in this world, together with the slaves of Africa, as it is written (Amos 9:7): 'Are you not to me as the children of the Kushites?' " Saturn's influence is responsible for "the worry and the filth of [those] men in their actions, in their dress and in their utterance, and it indicates darkness and decline from [their] level of honor and greatness."

These remarks explain the fate of the Jewish nation. Thus, for example, the period of exile in Egypt was decreed at the time of Israel's birth. Moreover this decree could not have been a consequence of the behavior of the Jews, for their behavior is a matter of free choice, altogether independent of any prior decree.[28]

(4) *The Theory of Mission.*

I would like now to discuss what became known in the terminology of the nineteenth century as the "theory of Israel's mission," as it appeared in different forms in the sixteenth century. First, however, we will look at the earlier parallels to this position.

As early as the fourth century, Chrysostom of Antioch maintained that the Jews believed they had been dispersed among the nations in order to become the instructors of humanity, whereas in truth, he continues, "God has sent you forth, [you who are] worse than idol-worshippers, more cruel than beasts, and worse than the men of Sodom, in order that all the iniquities should be learned from you."

The author of an anonymous polemical treatise from the early Middle Ages repeats the notion of mission in biblical terms: "They have been dispersed (*menupatzim*) among all the nations in order that they should be (Ex. 19:6) 'a kingdom of priests'[29] to all the nations."[30] In another passage the author describes the fate of the Jewish people, namely

> to make for us a great and awesome name and to put us over all the nations which He has made, in praise, in name, and in honor; and [that we may be] a holy people, as He has spoken;[31] to teach all the nations a statute and an ordinance, to try them with signs and wonders, to know what is in their hearts, whether they will observe His commandments or not.

This author's further development of his theory has not been preserved. However, that he rejects the idea of the Dispersion as a punishment is clear:

> Not for nothing did He scatter them over the face of the entire earth. Yet not because of the evil of their deeds did He expel them from their soil, and not because of the severity of their transgressions "have I dispersed them in the gates of the land" [Jer. 15:7], but rather for this [cause].[32]

The cause mentioned here refers to the mission of Israel. In addition, the author mentions a second cause for the dispersion:

that in the future we should make known and explain carefully what the Lord our God has commanded and what our fathers who feared Him have taught us, to whom [God] revealed his secret and his Covenant, making them known.

Unfortunately, the manuscript that has come down to us does not contain the passages explaining this reason. It should be noted that the discussion is developed in the context of a polemic with those heretics who argued that the Torah is valid only for *Eretz Yisrael*. In any case the first theme—that the Jews have been dispersed to be instructors to the nations—is tied up with the second, according to which the purpose of the continued survival of the Jewish nation is "to try them [the gentiles] with signs and wonders, to know what is in their hearts, whether they will observe His commandments or not."[33]

R. Jacob Anatoli interprets the Exile in the same spirit, as a process of purification:

The will of God was thus, to scatter us among the nations in order to purify us—[and it is] not that he abandoned us entirely, for he "neither cast us away nor abhorred us". . . . Rather the lengthy exile we have endured serves to destroy the thorns in the vineyard and to leave standing the good ones, the poor and meager who take refuge in the Name of God. . . . Not that He has anywhere promised to leave remaining a great and numerous nation, so that salvation will come with great power and might, as the masses and a few among the sages, who are easily swayed and believe everything they hear, have supposed. [It is] as if [the latter] had forgotten what they have learned in Talmud and Scripture, as well as what is written in the Torah [Deut. 4:27]: "You shall be left few in number among the nations," thus teaching of the few [only who will remain].

Thus far Anatoli has interpreted Exile in its aspect of servitude. However this will not suffice, for Exile is not merely servitude, but also dispersion;[34] and this second aspect serves another purpose: that of bringing about the repentance of the nations.

As for our being dispersed among all the nations—at the time of Redemption this will serve to convert the nations to one language, worshiping Him as one, [and this will happen] when they witness the Redemption and Salvation. Then the prophecy will be fulfilled, so that none will dispute it and claim that it has already been fulfilled.[35]

This passage introduces an entirely different idea. The influence of Israel on the nations comes not as a consequence of the activity of the Jews during Exile, but rather as a response to the eschatological transition from servitude to Redemption.

The idea of Exile as a historical mission occupies a prominent place in the works of R. Judah ha-Levi and also, as a result of his influence, in Maimonides' *Hilkhot Melakhim.* Maimonides explains the appearance of Christianity and Islam as reflecting the divine cunning by which history is guided.[36] Even the idea of the Jewish nation as a "kingdom of priests" is interpreted in this context. Thus Maimonides' son R. Abraham writes in the name of his father:

> In keeping My Torah you will be leaders to the world; your relation to them will be that of a priest to his congregation. The world will follow in [your] footsteps; they will imitate your deeds and follow your ways. This is the explanation I received explicitly from Father, my teacher, may his memory be blessed.[37]

The comments of R. Judah ha-Levi and Maimonides clearly represent a reversal of the conventional traditional Christian theological view. Christianity and Islam are regarded as preparing the way for the final diffusion of Judaism to every corner of the world. Such a view ascribes importance to the direct influence of Judaism on the nations as a consequence of the Dispersion. In the medieval period we find this notion also in the *Kad ha-Kemaḥ* of R. Baḥya b. Asher:

> And in my opinion the reason for the Dispersion . . . [is] in order that Israel should spread to all the ends [of the earth] among the nations, who lack understanding [*tvuna*]. And they [Israel] will teach them concerning belief in the existence of God, may He be blessed, and in the matter of divine Providence which influences individual men.[38]

There is particular significance to the fact that this idea is reiterated in a slightly different fashion by R. Ḥasdai Crescas in the early fifteenth century. Crescas brings various reasons for the Exile—in his words: "The fruits of Exile . . . are extremely far-reaching."

> (1) As it concerns the collective being of our nation, the afflictions of this world are a great treasure and advocate [for us] in the world to come, and it may be that just as the Exile in Egypt, the . . . nature of which we did not know beforehand, turned out to be preparation for our conversion to the service . . . [and] worship of God, may He be blessed—[so] His Wisdom decreed this great Exile in order to make our hearts [?] to the greatest degree possible, or to increase His mercy towards

us in gathering us from among the peoples after this prolonged Exile, in order that we should not walk in the stubborness of our hearts, as at times [has happened], and also to encourage our love and our worship. . . .

(2) As it concerns others, (a) it may be that [by our dispersion] we will serve to draw them to the worship of God, may He be blessed, at the end of days, or (b) that by the merit of the [Jewish] people they will draw benefit, as they [the Sages], may their memory be blessed, have said: "The entire world is fed out of compassion for my son Ḥanina". . . . And this is what is meant by the prophet in the passage [Is. 52:13] "Behold, my servant shall prosper," which appears to be an appellative for Israel in this Exile. [This is so] even though [the passage] begins with a reference to the Messiah, saying as the Midrash states, that when their king is raised up, Israel will also be raised up.[39]

In the sixteenth century we find a development which had important implications for the theory of mission, traces of which can be found in various thinkers even in the modern period. I am referring to the perception of the activity of the *anusim* as influencing Christianity and altering it from within.[40] This notion can be discerned in the writings of R. Ḥayyim b. Betzalel, the MaHaRaL's brother. In his interpretation of Isaiah's prophecy concerning the Suffering Servant of the Lord he writes:

And it should be interpreted thus: It pleased the Holy One, blessed be He, to crush Israel and to disperse it among the nations for the sake of his righteousness—for the rest of the nations are also the work of His hands; and by means of Israel, who are dispersed throughout the entire world, the true faith will spread throughtout the entire world.[41]

He continues concerning the nations who seek to know the truth: "For they sense from day to day that they are in possession of falsehood, and a different spirit blows among them bringing them to the truth; for most of them are also of the seed of truth."[42]

A variant on this idea is to be found in the writings of R. Eliezer Ashkenazi. In his view the very survival of the Jewish nation in Exile, despite all of the persecutions to which they have been subjected, serves to make manifest the reality of divine Providence. This mission is at the heart of the Israelites' sojourn in Egypt and their servitude there: "The intention and desire of the Righteous One [Abraham] that the divinity of God, may He be blessed, be made known, was fulfilled by his descendants' going down to Egypt and by their being brought out 'by a mighty hand.' "[43] The Exodus from Egypt represents a unique, non-recurring event—"until the fame [*pirsum*—of the event] at that time came to be of no avail" in the course of generations. But Jewish history reveals a constant repetition of these events. The fact that "in every generation they stand up against us to destroy us, and the Holy One, blessed be He, saves us from their hand" is the continued manifestation in history, from generation to generation, of "the fame of His might, may He be blessed, and of His love for us." The survival of the Jewish people is a challenge to the laws of history and to the political aims of the nations, and the perpetuation of the Jews as a nation serves as the sign of a metahistorical factor. Jewish life represents a continuous delivery from danger, and it depends constantly on the protection of divine Providence. It is only through the understanding of this that "His tremendous love for us" is manifest; this love will be verified "to the point where there can be no doubt." Such a delivery from danger is not brought about through war or violence. This is expressed in the story of Laban the Aramean who seeks to extirpate Israel entirely, but who yet survives. Salvation which proceeds from love of the victim does not require the destruction of the aggressor.[44]

The fact of Exile is thus a consequence of a historical plan which was already determined and revealed in the first visions of the patriarchs and which has been played out over the course of all the generations. This idea is to be found in the thought of R. Eliezer Ashkenazi, in his commentary on Genesis 15. His interpretation was developed in explicit refutation of Naḥmanides' assertion that the Exile in Egypt was brought about because of transgression. In the Covenant of the Pieces, Abraham was promised that he would have seed. Abraham's desire was to have "many sons in order to realize his aim of proclaiming [his monotheistic] faith," and the response of God was thus that "his seed would succeed in proclaiming and making known and providing light, like the stars, for all mankind."[45]

The recurring idea of the powerlessness of philosophy to prove divine Providence is apparently what provokes R. Eliezer's idea that the proof of Providence is to be found in Jewish history. Melchizedek, who symbolizes the nations, did not believe in Creation or in Providence "until he witnessed God's providential protection of Abraham, in delivering Nimrod [i.e. Amrafel] into his hands."[46]

A theory of mission expressed in modern terms appears in the sixteenth century in the writings of R. Mordekhai Dato, particularly in his Italian sermons.[47] In a sermon on *parshat lekh lekha*, he explains that the practice of circumcision was intended to make known among the nations the teachings of the Torah. This was Abraham's mission which he carried out at grave risk to his life and which was passed on to his descendants. The exile of Israel under successive empires was intended to atone for its sins, yet also to spread word of the Torah among the peoples.[48] This view clearly expresses the situation of Italian Jews vis-à-vis their Christian neighbors in the sixteenth century. Unlike earlier positions which regard repentance of the nations as an event which will occur in the messianic period, Dato sees the Jews as exerting a direct influence already during the period of Exile.[49]

The classical scheme—the origin of which can be traced, as mentioned above, to R. Judah ha-Levi and Maimonides—views the spread of Christianity as part of a divine plan leading eventually to the repentance of all mankind, and thus to Redemption. It should be noted that a contrary view was also expressed in the medieval period, one which did not view the rise of Christianity to Israel's credit, but rather as an evil "which has sprung forth, owing to our iniquities, from members of our own people, bringing the [other] nations to err after it." By bringing forth Christianity, Israel had thus caused the nations to sin. This is the view of R. Nathan b. Samuel ibn Tibbon.[50] Ibn Tibbon concludes that it is therefore incumbent on the Jewish nation to correct this sin. He prays "that we will return to God in perfect repentance, and that He will give us strength and might and wisdom and understanding to bring those who err back to the true faith."

According to this perspective, the Dispersion itself has an appointed purpose:

> For it would not be fitting that by God's decree, may He be blessed, [foreign] kingdoms and rule should be imposed on the holy nation forever, until "the spread [!] of the Holy people" [Daniel 12:7] is completed in their being expelled and defeated. And we do not see any nation that is spread and dispersed, except the holy congregation of Israel.[51]

We will conclude the discussion of this point with the ideas of R. Azariah Figo, despite the fact that he belongs to the borderline of this period. R. Azariah asserts that "there is not even one among those who suffer in exile" who would not admit "that even if we had been afflicted, God forbid, many times beyond what we have suffered, we would still not have endured even a small part of what is deserved [by us] in view of the extremity of [our] great iniquities."[52] Nevertheless he feels obliged to offer an additional explanation for Exile:

We cannot restrain our great grief at the decree of His Wisdom, may He be blessed, [namely] that the punishment for [our] many transgressions should be the wandering of this bitter exile, and our being expelled from our beloved holy land and dispersed among [other] lands amid numerous peoples in all corners of the world. We have been compared to the evil generation of the Tower of Babel, whom God scattered over the face of the entire earth. For God could have left us in our land and there increased[53] our troubles and made heavy the yoke of our afflictions.

Exile means not only suffering and humiliation, but also the domination of the enemy, and

there is in this a desecration of His Honor, may He be blessed; for when they see that they rule over us, they attribute this to their power and the might of their hands, and [think] that He, God forbid, has either been struck by weakness or has withdrawn His providential protection from Israel, and no longer has anything to do with them.

In addition, there is the danger

that in their [Israel's] being subjected to the rule of the nations they are put in a position to break the Covenant, God forbid, and to violate the Torah, whether becasue of the anger of the oppressor and the duress of Exile, or because of the temptations of those who incite them and seduce them with their fallacious claims.

R. Azariah cites three different possible reasons for the Exile: 1) because of the nature of the Holy Land "which cannot bear within it the transgressing nation"; 2) as a means to disperse the Jews so that they cannot commit transgressions as a group, for "a sin of the multitude will be accounted more severe than a sin of the individual"; and 3) as a means to influence the nations, "to bring many from among the gentiles [*amei ha-aretz*] under the wings of the *Shekhina*." R. Azariah does not regard these explanations as sufficient to justify Exile, for in Exile the Jewish nation is subject to serious dangers from every point of view.

The problem of why Israel is exposed to these dangers has a different solution. The condition of the Jewish nation, R. Azariah explains, resembles that of the soul, which is also in exile:

The answer to this problem is the same as the answer to the problem of [why] the soul is sent into this dangerous world . . . [i.e.] to increase its perfection, which lies in its freedom. The strengthening[54] of the power of intellect will overcome all burdens [originating] in materiality and will thereby increase its reward greatly; and for the sake of such great gain we will not have misgivings concerning [the possible] harm [caused by] this danger.

Exile is not a punishment, but rather an opportunity for repentance, a constant trial, "and they [the Jews] by their righteousness will overcome everything . . . and moreover if need be they will sacrifice themselves for the sake of His Holy Name."

This is the essential aspect of Exile; however, Exile also entails a mission to the nations:

And moreover by means of the ingathering of the exiles many gentiles will adhere to the Lord and will recognize His divinity and will establish the words of the prophet, may he rest in peace [Zeph. 3:9]: "For then I will convert the peoples to a purer language, that they may all call upon the name of the Lord, to serve him with one consent."

This will not be brought about by direct influence or instruction of the nations during exile, but rather will occur at the time of final redemption.[55] "For . . . the ingathering of the exiles will make all this known, and all the inhabitants of the earth will recognize and know 'that to Me every knee shall bow' [Is. 45:23]."

(5) *Exile as Alienation.*

Azariah Figo's remarks on the analogy between the exile of Israel and the incarnation of the soul introduce us to an additional view, which we will refer to as the theory of alienation. We will begin by examining a passage from R. Joseph ibn Yaḥya.

One must not hold the Almighty responsible for the length of the Exile in this world and for the short period of the benefits of redemption after the resurrection of the dead. For this present world of generation and corruption belongs to the corrupt idol-worshippers, while the eternal world is for Israel, who possess eternal godly souls.[56]

The messianic period possesses symbolic meaning; it does not serve merely to reward the righteous. Here we have an almost gnostic division of worlds, according to which the present world cannot be perfected. This division corresponds to the distinction between Israel and the nations. The nations do not enjoy divine

Providence, "and the cause for the evil or the good [that befalls them] . . . is according to [how] the stars of the heavens decree."[57] Unlike them, Israel enjoys divine Providence, and thus is subject to punishments and afflictions.

These ideas explain in my opinion the system of thought presented in the MaHaRaL's works. Perhaps the most important apologetic claim in the MaHaRaL's approach is the contention that Israel's election is independent of its righteousness.

God who took Israel to Himself did not do so because of the righteousness and deeds of Israel . . . . Even if their deeds were a factor for good or for evil . . . still the fact of their being chosen was not the result of any deed.[58]

And elsewhere:

This present world was created in the seven days of Creation, and this present world belongs to the evil-doers. The righteous scarcely have a share in this world, for He did not create it except for Ahab and his cohorts (*Berakhot* 61b).[59] From this [we learn] that the righteous man is taken to God, may He be blessed, on the seventh [day], which belongs to God, may He be blessed, and this you should understand from what is written [Ex. 21:2]: "Six years he shall serve, and in the seventh he shall go out free."

It appears that this view is tied to the MaHaRaL's conviction "that the death of a man does not signify a fall in dignity, but rather adds to the dignity of the righteous man."[60] By this explanation impurity (*tum'a*) does not signify the failure inherent in transgression, but rather the characteristic of remoteness, either because of a decline—as in the case of the leper, who is far below us—or because of a rise, as in the case of the dead, who are far beyond us.

The MaHaRaL develops a philosophy of history within a cosmic framework.[61] This framework, however, is entirely different from the parallel medieval one, which was a field of action for the laws of astronomy and physics. The MaHaRaL's scheme is an ontological one, one of the principles of which is the duality which we have mentioned above between Israel and the nations, and correspondingly between the world to come and this world. This ontological duality produces two different systems, each with its own laws.

The present world has no existence by itself. This is the lesson to be drawn from the comparison between the world and the cycle of the year:

> The world has a cycle and a harvest; for after achieving the end of all, the world is gathered unto its Sustainer, for the world has no self-subsistence, and is gathered unto its Sustainer on Whom it depends, and so it is with the year . . . .[62]

This "gathering"—i.e., the Redemption—is hinted at in the Festival of the Ingathering (Tabernacles), a festival which symbolizes by means of the image of the "Clouds of Honor" the fact "that Israel is gathered into Him, may He be blessed, and takes refuge under His wings."[63] While the Festival of *Matzot* (Passover) signifies the Days of Creation, the Festival of Ingathering signifies Redemption—"since the world returns to Him and is not established except by Him."[64]

In the dimension of time, the ontological conflict is realized on the plane of history. The images of the Messiah who sits at the gates of Rome and of Jacob seizing the heel of Esau at birth hint at the power of privation (*he'eder*) eventually bringing about annihilation, which is present in the Kingdom of Edom at its zenith—a power which was to destroy it, at which time the Kingdom of the Messiah was to emerge from its ruins.[65] The appearance of a new existence after its destruction is an onotological principle from which we cannot escape.[66] This existence is not of this world.

According to the analysis we have presented, the MaHaRaL's remarks can be understood as an elaboration of a fundamental intuition concerning the character of the Jewish nation and its existence in exile, within the context of a conception which views the world as limited from a temporal point of view. This view is quite close to the theory of *shmitot*, or to a theory of cosmic cycles in general, except that instead of proposing many worlds the MaHaRaL proposes only two, one following on the heels of the other.[67] His basic intuition can in my opinion be stated in this way: that the Jewish nation, despite its existence in the present world, belongs to another world which has not yet been realized, and from this situation results the fundamental alienation characteristic of Israel's condition.[68] This alienation is expressed in the ontological hostility between Israel and the nations, as well as in the combination of sociological and political facts which we refer to as "Exile."[69]

The general scheme which sees the difference between Israel and the nations as reflecting a metaphysical difference already appears in the works of R. Abraham Bibago. Bibago offers two basic models for this difference: the first, corresponding to the ontological distinction between substance and accident—a notion found frequently in the MaHaRaL; and the second, a psychological model seeing this difference as analogous to the difference between intellect and other mental faculties.[70] Such an analogy is perceived in the periods of Exile.

> It is because of this [distinction] that this nation has been exiled thrice in succession. The first time in Egypt—[a nation] which pursues the senses, [Israel being in exile here] just as the intellect is "in exile" among the senses. From there she [the nation] went up and was redeeemed. The second time [was] in the midst of the unreliable imagination, i.e. in confused Babylon. And afterwards she was redeemed. Then she was taken up amid the reasoning sense where she remains until now, in Edom. Since this reasoning power is esteemed to the point that it is almost thought to be identical to the intellect, this Exile will be prolonged until the . . . misleading similarity [between Edom and Israel] will come to an end.[71]

R. Joseph Yavetz also regarded the struggle between Israel and the nations as the function of an inherent contradiction in nature.[72] On the verse "which the Lord thy God has allotted to all the nations" (Deut. 4:19), he writes:

> For the kingdom of heaven and idol-worship represent two contraries; when one prevails, the other is brought low. This is hinted [in the verse Ex.17:11]: "And it came to pass, when Moses held up his hand, that Israel prevailed." All of the nations have sought to eliminate Israel from the world. . . . This was the idea of the generation of the Tower of Babel . . . for they intended with this Tower that the handmaid should inherit her mistress. . . .[73]

(6) *Exile as "Tikun."*

Gershom Scholem sees as a characteristic of post-expulsion Kabbalah—especially of Lurianic Kabbalah—"its novel attitude toward the messianic tradition,"[74] an attitude that was not discernible in earlier kabbalistic thought. The redemption which these former mystics sought, "that is, redemption of the soul," differed in that it was "a private, individual matter, and therefore independent of the sphere of national redemption with which traditional messianism was concerned."[75] The new approach gave rise to an interpretation which was "unparalleled in breadth and in depth of vision. The kabbalistic answer illuminated the significance of exile and redemption and accounted for the unique historical situation of Israel within the wider, in fact cosmic, context of creation itself.[76] These new relationships were expressed, according to Scholem, in a changed understanding of the concept of *tikun*. Purification and *tikun* do not constitute "a utopian event dependent on supernatural intervention."[77] On the contrary, *tikun* is a precondition for the advent of the redeemer.

This development can be examined from another point of view. The Zohar speaks of the *Shekhina* going into exile[78] like a mother who accompanies her children, as a guarantee that God will not abandon Israel, or even as a result of the fact that the *Shekhina* has been subjugated by evil forces.[79] That is to say, it is suggested here that cosmic changes have been brought about by historical events. In contrast, we are witness in this period to a view by which historical events are regarded as the means for correcting cosmic catastrophies which preceded them. In other words, although a transgression was committed, Exile is not its consequence, but rather represents a task imposed on the Jewish nation from its beginning.

R. Moses Cordovero describes the first exile, in Egypt, as part of a divine plan. Until "the light of Abraham shone forth" divine souls were dispersed "among the chosen few of humanity." With the appearance of Abraham, God allotted the different lands to the peoples, "each according to the place that suits it." These are the source of the "coats of skin (כתנות עור)" as against the "coats of light (כתנות אור)" which Abraham fashioned (*tiken*). Yet at this point Abraham's *tikun* was not complete, "for dross (*sigim*) is still mixed with silver and silver with dross." Further purification will be achieved by two processes: first by family selection, by which Ishmael and Esau were excluded, a selection which continued up to the generation of Jacob "whose couch was perfect (*she-mitato shlema*), pure and clean." The completion of this process enabled a second:

> Afterwards He desired to purify and to collect the banished sparks, because he desired "that he that is banished be not an outcast from Him"

(II Samuel 14:14), and He introduced silver into the melting-pot of servitude in Egypt in the midst of the powerful *klipa*, and there all the sparks were gathered to the pure silver.[80]

This process is possible as a result of the return of earlier generations by means of *gilgul*:

Therefore all of the generations transmigrated there: the generation of the Deluge, of whom it was said [Ex.1:22], "Every son that is born you shall cast into the river"; and the generation of the Tower of Babel of whom it was said [Gen. 11:3], "Let us make bricks," while in Egypt it was said [Ex. 5:18], "Yet shall you deliver the quantity of bricks."

With Redemption, at the end of this process, the silver must all be "refined, cleansed of all dross"; the sparks must all be gathered, as it is to be at the end of days.[81] "For at this point [the Exodus] there were no sparks, just as there will be none at the coming of the Messiah, as it is said, 'Proselytes will not be accepted in the days of the Messiah.' "[82] Such a position sees the dispersion in a positive light. In the words of R. Ḥayyim Vital: "Concerning this all of Israel has been directed to disperse with the four winds of the earth in order to raise up all."[83]

What is the attitude to Redemption that corresponds to this view? It appears to me necessary to point out the possibility of two contrary positions proceeding from such a view, in relation not only to the two critical moments, Exile and Redemption, but also to the transition processes that link them. Much has been written of the messianic activism based on Lurianic teachings. Below we shall bring a contrary example reflecting the acceptance of a fundamental scheme which entails the total rejection of possible messianic activity. This position is found, in my opinion, in the works of R. Menaḥem Azariah da Fano. R. Menaḥem Azariah accepts the conception which sees in Exile a cosmic mission. However, in his interpretation an entirely different conclusion from that which we have seen is drawn concerning the relationship between Exile and sin. While the classical view regards Exile as a punishment, R. Menaḥem Azariah offers the notion that the cosmic task is imposed, paradoxically, on those who have repented:

Happy are the penitents (*ba'alei tshuva*), for it was in order to preserve life that God sent them to purify the places to which they have been scattered. And beloved were Israel who have guarded the Torah and the commandments while great princes[84] did not stand the test to which they were put, and this [reflects the Talmudic dictum that Exile is] "the place where the penitents [Israel] stand" the test without doubt [and where the righteous do not stand the test].[85]

Thus we find, paradoxically, that sin is not the cause of the expulsion, but rather a condition of their mission. Similarly, Adam was expelled from the Garden of Eden "in order to bring about *tikun* of the air outside [Paradise] with the breath of his mouth, and to prepare the throne of honor for the dwelling of the *Shekhina* everywhere." This too enables us to explain why the Israelites repeatedly wandered in the wilderness of the peoples (*midbar ha-amim*)[86]—"and God led them not through the way of the land of the Philistines" [Ex. 13:17]. The very closeness of *Eretz Yisrael* is the reason for avoiding the direct route. For without their wanderings, "the wilderness of the peoples would not be sanctified." This idea is carried further in the assertion that if Edom, Amon and Moab had permitted the Israelites to pass through their territories, these countries too would have achieved perfection.

The exile following the destruction of the First Temple must also be understood in these terms: "For among the exiles of Samaria there were enough students of Torah to sanctify only one corner of the world—'Halah and Habor, by the river of Gozan, and in the cities of Media' [II Kings 17:6]—but with the exile from Jerusalem, they [the Jews] were scattered to the four winds of the earth in order that their fountains should spout forth for the benefit of the whole, and this is certainly the correction of repentant sinners ['of' and not 'for,' as in Talmudic sources—*takanat ha-shavim*]." For R. Menaḥem Azaria, *takanat ha-shavim* provides the appropriate symbol. The law stipulates that "if one steals a beam, and [afterwards repents], he must destroy the building [constructed with that beam] and restore the beam to its owner. This is the law of the Torah." However, the Sages established as *takanat ha-shavim* that "[those who stole a beam] need only restore the price of the beam to the owner; its equivalent is sufficient."

On a symbolic plane, halakhic distinctions correspond to different conditions. The destruction of the building corresponds to the removal of the sparks of holiness (the beam) on which impurity thrives. The restoration of the price of the beam corresponds to the reception of proselytes: "And if there is hope of taking out from there one good seed, like Ruth and Na'aman and Obadiah the proselyte of Edom, for the sake of these they ordained that one need only restore to the owner the price of the beam; the equivalent is sufficient for *tikun Shekhina*, for a proselyte who converted is like a new-born child."

This positive view of Exile is accompanied by a rejection of messianic politics, even in its most fundamental aspect—namely the return to *Eretz Yisrael.*

"And to visit His Temple" [Ps. 27:4]—this [refers to] the population (*yishuv*) of *Eretz Yisrael*, in their frequent visits to the Temple. Know that he who lives in *Eretz Yisrael* during its destruction resembles one who has no God. But with its rebuilding, he resembles one who has a God, in the sense of "because our God is not among us these evils come upon us" [Deut. 31:17]. But outside the Land [of Israel] he resembles at this or any other time one who has no God.[87]

The special importance of living in *Eretz Yisrael* when the Temple does not stand is here rejected.

It may be that another passage from *Ma'amar Ḥikur ha-Din*[88] can be understood on the basis of R. Menaḥem Azariah's anti-messianic position:

This is the nature of the calculators of the end (*meḥashvei kitzim*), that in fact they delay redemption, as happened with the Ephraimites following the Exodus. Because there is no full redemption "if they should be dispersed in the uttermost part of the heaven," therefore the Sages rightly said that they [i.e., the calculators] delay redemption.

According to *Yo'el Moshe*, a seventeenth-century commentary on R. Menaḥem Azariah, those who hasten the end serve to postpone redemption. This is due to the fact that these offenders have been punished by death, "and their souls have been gathered to impurity (*tum'a*)"; consequently sparks have been added to the shells. This interpretation is in my opinion difficult to accept because of its circularity. No reason is given why hastening the end is a serious transgression—unless we should assume that the attempt to collect the Jews together prevents their dispersion, and thus the eventual ingathering of their sparks. In what follows it is stated that the Messiah son of Ephraim "will be stabbed for this," apparently referring to the offense of hastening the end. Nadab and Abihu were also "calculators of the end," a sin that was corrected (*tukan*) by Elijah who said, "For I am not better than my fathers" [I Kings 19:4], a verse which was explained by R. Zera as meaning that "the land Moses and Aaron did not merit to enter—who would say I merit this?" The effort of Nadab and Abihu to hasten the end is connected with a seizure of power: "And probably they expected to exercise dominion over *Eretz Yisrael.*" In contrast to them, "Elijah rose in a storm to heaven at the other side of the Jordan"—and not in *Eretz Yisrael*!

3. Epilogue

Having reviewed the various positions adopted in the sixteenth century concerning Exile, we may now suggest briefly the relationship these positions imply concerning the present, from the perspective of messianic hopes.

It appears to me that there exists no univocal correspondence between the historical-philosophical view and what may be called messianic politics. In order to understand the overall picture, it appears necessary to me to define four different aspects, which have not always been sufficiently distinguished by scholars. Briefly, they are the following:

1) The general historical-philosophical view concerning the character of Exile and Redemption.

2) Messianic expectations, from a chronological point of view—i.e., the hope of the realization of the messianic vision in the near future.

3) Messianic activism—that is, the faith in the effectiveness of human activity (in the wide sense of the term) in bringing nearer, or in actually bringing about, the messianic era.

4) The naturalistic and rationalistic conception of messianic activism. Here is determined for us the character, contents and method of actual messianic politics.

Our discussion to this point will aid us in clarifying these aspects.

(1) *The influence of the historical-philosophical perspective*: This perspective is expressed in the conception of Jewish and general history, and of its future. The theory of alienation produced an identification of the condition of Exile with the present world. This meant a renunciation of the arena of history and the transfer of Redemption to a realm beyond the present world, the messianic

era being conceived as a mere process of transition between worlds. This greatly differs, in my opinion, from the theory of *tikun*.

(2) *Messianic expectations*: This expectation became prominent in two different areas which can be distinguished in the sixteenth century. The first is tied to astrological views, especially in light of the near conjunction between Jupiter and Saturn. The second attained expression in the works of various thinkers who perceived in the events of the fifteenth and sixteenth centuries processes leading to Redemption. Especially important among these events were the fall of Constantinople and the appearance of the Reformation.[89]

(3) *Messianic politics*: a function of the third and fourth areas sketched above. It may take the form of mystical activism, as that originating in R. Isaac Luria's thought. On the other hand, it may take the form of non-active, but rationalistic, messianic expectations. A case of the latter is found in the conviction that redemption would be realized through military activity initiated by the Ten Tribes, by which "the scattered of Judah" would be redeemed. Such a conception lay behind the mysterious activity of David Reubeni.

The most interesting example of messianic politics is one which unites all of the areas we have distinguished—namely, that which provokes rationalistic and realistic activism as a response to messianic expectations. An example of the latter can apparently be found in R. Jacob Berav,[90] according to whom the words of Maimonides concerning the renewal of *smikha* were intended "for the period close to [the advent of] the Messiah, that is, our own time."[91]

Against the background of these positions we can perhaps better understand the opposing view of R. Menaḥem Azariah da Fano. Not without reason were his writings an important source for the opponents of Zionism in the last centuries. In my opinion the MaHaRaL, in relying on the idea of the "three oaths," presents an anti-political approach similar to that of R. Menaḥem Azariah. What appears to me unique to the approach of the realistic activism of the sixteenth century is that it combines three directions of thought. The messianic expectations which developed in kabbalistic circles were united with the views of Maimonides, who maintained that the passage to the messianic era was subordinate to rational, human processes. Into this mixture were blended the ideas of R. Judah ha-Levi who without doubt regarded *aliya* as an act that would bring about Redemption, and of Naḥmanides who converted this act into a commandment.[92] The view of *aliya* as a commandment, it seems to me, made it possible to arrive at the new conception which we have mentioned above, according to which Exile in itself constitutes a sin.[93] This conception was to assume decisive importance in the following centuries.

FOOTNOTES

1. In writing this article I am indebted to the work of a number of scholars in this area: the late Ḥ. H. Ben-Sasson as well as Professors Gershom Scholem, Isaiah Tishbi, Jacob Katz, and their students. The references cited in the footnotes reflect this debt only in part.

2. This assumption possibly provides the key for understanding the paradoxical stress Naḥmanides places on the flourishing of Jewish life in Exile, in contrast to the desolation associated with the destruction of the Temple and with the "expulsion" from *Eretz Yisrael*: "But once we entered Exile in the lands of our enemies, the work of our hands was not cursed. . . . In [these] lands we are like or better than the rest of the peoples, inhabitants of the land, because of His mercy on us, for our dwelling in Exile is the promise which [God] made us [Lev. 26:44]: 'And yet for all that, when they are in the land of their enemies, I will not cast them away, nor will I abhor them, to destroy them utterly, and to break my covenant with them, for I am the Lord their God.' "

3. To the above notions should be added one which views the afflictions of Exile as a trial (*nisayon*). This view is found combined with others, especially with that regarding the sufferings of Exile as the messianic birth-pangs. Still another approach is found in this period which attempts to answer the question of the suffering of Exile by severing the connection between *ge'ula* and the behavior of Jews in clinging to their faith and observing the commandments. The Jew chooses the way of faith and the commandments even if his anticipation of *ge'ula* is a vain hope. Such an effort to sever the connection between the observance of the *mitzvot* and the idea of *ge'ula* is found frequently in the literature of the period. Thus R. Joel ibn Shuaib writes: "For the necessity of affirming (*'imut*) our *emuna* is not tied to any condition" (*Drashot* of R. Joel ibn Shuaib [Venice, 1577], *Parshat Shlakh Lekha*, f. 112b). On the lack of connection between observance of *mitzvot* and messianic belief see Naḥmanides in *Sefer ha-Ge'ula* II, ed. D. Chavel [Jerusalem, 1963], pp. 279–280. Important in this context are the words of R. Ḥasdai Crescas that even excluding the coming of the Messiah as an article of faith, the binding nature of the Torah can be established (*Light of the Lord* III, 8, 3 [Vienna, 1860], f. 826). R. Joseph Albo follows this line of thought in *Ikarim* IV, 47, ed. Husik, vol. IV, p. 460; and cf. chapter 42, pp. 413–414). And similarly, R. Solomon le-Beit ha-Levi of Salonika: "And when it enters his mind [literally, "heart"], seeing himself in danger, that perhaps there is hope . . . his heart will say to him: Dust in your mouth! Close your mouth and say not, 'Perhaps there is hope,' for even if there is not hope I will act with self-sacrifice and seek the honor of His Name, may He be blessed. . . . He will freely offer his cheek. . . ." See J. Hacker, "Despair of Redemption and Messianic Hope in the Writings of Rabbi Solomon le-Beit ha-Levi" (Hebrew), *Tarbitz* 39 (1970), pp. 201–202: "For even if it should be imagined that the Messiah would not come, Moses is truth and his Torah is truth." And see there note 39, concerning similar remarks by R. Moses Ḥagiz in *Sefer Magen David*.

4. The conflict between these views and the classical views regarding Exile as punishment is expressed in the works of sixteenth-century—and later—thinkers. It appears that the

MaHaRaL regards transgression as a cause, while regarding his explanation as the cause of causes (*Netzaḥ Yisrael*, chap. 2, p. 11). We will deal below with the contradiction between kabbalistic positions. An interesting example in which various views are brought together indiscriminately is provided by the discussion of R. Ḥayyim ben Betzalel, the MaHaRaL's brother (*Sefer ha-Ḥayyim*, Part V: "Sefer Ge'ula ve-Yeshua," Lemberg edition, f. 36aff.). R. Ḥayyim cites five reasons for the Exile and the Dispersion (we have retained R. Ḥayyim's original numeration). Three belong to the classical tradition: 1) neglect of study of the Torah (*bitul tora*); 2) "delay in repentance, which postpones the footsteps of the Messiah"; and 5) "the hatred and the envy which have been renewed among them [Israel] to the point where they have become corrupted with one another." A further reason views the Exile as a trial: 4) "in order that He should be recognized in His Kingship by his servants . . . who perform His will." By yet another, Exile is seen as resulting from the sin of *reconciliation with the condition of Exile*: 3) "in that they have despaired of *ge'ula* and regard themselves as inhabitants of the land of the enemy, and build themselves nice, spacious houses—and not in the Holy Land, which the Lord has sworn to us . . . and defile themselves (*mitgo'alim*) with the wine of their feasts, and think that they become pleasing thereby in the eyes of the gentiles." And see R. Ḥayyim's further remarks there.

5. For one example of the numerous responses to theological proofs based on the Exile of Israel, see R. Menaḥem b. Zeraḥ, *Tzeda la-Derekh* I, 1, chap. 32 [Ferrara, 1554], f. 27b–28b. R. Judah ha-Levi's answer, that Israel resembles dry bones which will one day come to life, refers to the distant past and the messianic future, without explaining the present condition (*Kuzari* III, 11). An interpretation of the sufferings of Exile can however be found elsewhere in the *Kuzari* (see further, on the theory of mission).

6. *Or ha-Ḥayyim* (Amsterdam, 1781), f. 2a.

7. Ibid., f. 1b.

8. *Ḥasdei ha-Shem* (New York, 1934, based on Constantinople ed., 1533), p. 12.

9. Ibid, *Or ha-Ḥayyim*, f. 1b.

10. Ibid., f. 28b.

11. Thus for example R. Moses Isserles views the Israelites and the Levites as symbolizing the sublunar and intermediate worlds of the stars, respectively. The Israelites' laying on of hands (*smikha*) on the Levites symbolizes the fact that "the aim of the creation of the intermediate world lies in our sublunar world." This is not so concerning the uppermost world of the angels or Separate Intellects which is symbolized by the priests, who did not require *smikha*. In this fashion Isserles produces a synthesis of the view of Maimonides and the philosophers on the one hand, and of R. Isaac Arama on the other. This position resembles that of Ficino.

12. It will suffice to compare Abravanel's historical interpretation of the *ma'asei ha-merkava* with the rationalist interpretations of the thirteenth and fourteenth centuries, in order to illustrate this difference.

13. R. Jacob Yavetz wrote: "Of those who prided themselves on their wisdom, almost all converted their honor (*hemiru et kvodam*) on that bitter day, while women and the ignorant sacrificed their lives and their belongings for the sake of the Sanctification of their Creator" (*Or ha-Ḥayyim*, f. 5a).

14. Ibid., p. 114. The nation is seen as organically bound to *Eretz Yisrael*, and therefore the suffering of *Eretz Yisrael* is regarded as the suffering of Israel itself, "for everything He has done in Jerusalem and in Zion is thought to be as if He had done it to us, wiping out iniquity and making an end to sin."

15. See R. Moses Alsheikh's commentary on the Book of Daniel, *Ḥavatzelet ha-Sharon*, p. 5 and see Naḥmanides and R. Baḥya on Genesis 32:17.

16. *Bereshit Raba*, *Parsha* 44 (English translation, *Midrash Genesis*, I, p. 375). Cf. Zohar, II, f. 83b which speaks of the fire of Gehenna and the darkness of slavery. And cf. the comment of R. Solomon ha-Levi Alkabetz: "The *galuyot* were not, God forbid, revenge on His part, may He be blessed, but rather mercy and forgiveness, as are blood-letting and purgation for the patient at the hands of the physician . . . and the pain which comes from them is not intended" (*Beit ha-Levi*, I, 1). And see Bracha Sack, "The Mystical Theology of S. Alkabez," Ph.D. diss., Brandeis University, 1977.

17. These lines were added by R. Joseph She'altiel b. Moses ha-Kohen to a manuscript

of the *Book Peli'a* (Rhodes, 1495). See G. Scholem, *Sabbatai Ṣevi, the Mystical Messiah* (Princeton, N.J., 1973), p. 18, n. 13.

18. *Nehar Pishon, Parshat Bereshit* (Constantinople, 1538), f. 11a. And see Ḥ. H. Ben-Sasson, "Exile and Redemption through the Eyes of the Spanish Exiles" (Hebrew), *Yitzḥak F. Baer Jubilee Volume* (Jerusalem, 1960), pp. 216–227.

19. R. Abraham b. Eliezer, cited in Ben-Sasson, "Exile and Redemption," p. 226.

20. R. Elijah Capsali, cited ibid., p. 227.

21. "Just as when a certain man is born, the events of his life are [already] necessitated, and the expert knows what they are before their time . . . so the entire nation at the time of its origin is determined by its horoscope; and according to it will be the many events [of its existence]."

22. Since Abraham saw by the power of his wisdom that catastrophes would occur to the nation and that the stars had ordained "that we should continually be killed and [there should be] much blood shed for our nation," he ordained the commandment of circumcision in order that there should not be "a single one of us whose blood has not been shed within eight days [after birth]." See Colette Sirat, "Moses Narboni's *Pirkei Moshe*" (Hebrew), *Tarbitz*, 39, p. 306.

23. Constantinople, 1585, reprinted Jerusalem, 1977.

24. Ibid., I, chap. 37, f. 74a. The source for these remarks is undoubtedly the following passage from Abraham ibn Ezra's *Reshit Ḥokhma*: "Saturn is cold and dry and its consequences are evil and harmful. It indicates corruption, destruction, death, sorrow, mourning, weeping and moaning. . . . Its part in the human soul is the power of thought, its part in the nations are Africans and Jews." See *The Beginning of Wisdom*, ed R. Levi and F. Cantera (Burgos) (Baltimore, 1939) Hebrew text, p. 43, as well as p. 193f. Ibn Ezra's remarks require investigation, for as Altmann points out (*Encyclopaedia Judaica*, "Astrology," p. 792), he maintains in his commentary on Deut. 4:19 that Israel has no astral patron, but is above them. An interesting variation of this position regards Saturn as the ruler of *Eretz Yisrael* and not of the nation. This idea is a composite of astrological notions and geographical-climatological theories of the sort represented by R. Judah ha-Levi. This approach is prominent in the fourteenth century, especially in the works of Moses Narboni and Ibn Shaprut. It is the character of the place which explains the reasons for the prohibitions of incest and prostitution, "for they are contrary to the nature of the ruler of the land."

25. *Kvod Elohim*, f. 77b. This idea is based on an interpretation of the verses: "And if you walk contrary to Me . . . then I will walk contrary to you also in fury" (Lev. 26:21, 28). This idea is also found in *Shevet Yehuda* of Judah ibn Verga. Its source, however, is found in Maimonides.

26. There is no similarity , in my view, between this idea and the opinion of R. Abraham Bibago that "Israel among the nations is as intellect among the powers of man" (*Derekh Emuna* [Constantinople, 1522], III, f. 22a). For another view see Ḥ. H. Ben Sasson in his introduction to *Kvod Elohim*, p. 14.

27. *Kvod Elohim*, Second Treatise, chap. 17, f. 111a.

28. See his discussion, Third Treatise, chap. 2–3, f. 122bff.

29. According to Ex. 19:6 (*mamlekhet kohanim*) although the original reads (*mi-mlekhet* [מִמְּלֶאכֶת] *Kohanim*).

30. *HUCA* 12–13 (1937–8), p. 437.

31. Following Deut. 26:19.

32. Ibid., p. 453.

33. Ibid., p. 443.

34. On the distinction between servitude and dispersion see the analysis below of the MaHaRaL's remarks. Various thinkers have pointed out the weakness that results from Israel's dispersal: "And we remain a few among each nation, even though together we are many." Naḥmanides, "Ma'amar ha-Ge'ula," I, p. 263.

35. *Malmad ha-Talmidim, Parshat Tzav*, f. 96–97. The distinction between Exile and Dispersion had already been made by Ibn Ezra in his *Commentary* to the Song of Songs (attributed to Naḥmanides; *Kitvei ha-RaMBaN*, ed. D. Chavel [Jerusalem, 1964], II, p. 515. " 'And He will assemble the expelled (*nidḥei*) of Israel' [Is. 11:12]—he calls the Ten Tribes 'expelled' because they reside together but have been expelled from their place, while he

calls the exile of Judah 'scattered' [in the continuation of the verse]: 'And gather together the scattered (*nefutzot*) of Judah.' " The legendary exile of the Ten Tribes constituted a sort of alternative condition, in which exile was not accompanied by dispersion. It was not Judah's fate "to be exiled to another land, to be there 'a people that shall dwell alone' [Numbers 23:9]. Rather, she [Judah] 'sat among the nations' who shamed her and dwelt among them, and they cause her distress from all sides" (R. Isaac Arama, *Commentary* to Lamentations, f. 286b), and cf. *Akedat Yitzḥak, Ki Tavo*, Ch. 98 [Venice, 1573], f. 262a: "She dwelt among the nations . . . therefore she found no rest, for all of her persecutors overtook her . . . from every side." Ḥ. H. Ben-Sasson pointed this out in "Exile and Redemption," p. 223. The comparison with the Ten Tribes who have been "expelled but not dispersed" is found in R. Isaac Karo, *Toldot Yitzḥak, Parshat Nitzavim* (Mantua, 1558), f. 77b; Ben-Sasson, ibid., p. 223, n. 40). According to R. Joseph ibn Yaḥya the dispersion and the weakness which results from it explain why the Jews of Spain did not resist their expulsion. See Ben-Sasson, ibid., n. 42. It should be remembered that in the Middle Ages it had been asserted that in Exile the Jews would be particularly careful to observe the commandments of the Torah: "And He has hinted that when Israel is in Exile . . . they will hold to their faith and opinions more than in the time when they were at ease" (R. Joshua ibn Shuaib, *Sermons on the Torah, Parshat Noaḥ*, f. 4b).

36. *Mishne Tora, Hilkhot Melakhim*, chap. 11.

37. R. Abraham b. ha-RaMBaM, *Commentary* on Genesis and Exodus, edited and translated by Wiesenberg (London, 1958), p. 302. See Ḥ. H. Ben-Sasson, "The Reformation in Contemporary Jewish Eyes," *Proceedings of the Israel Academy of Sciences and Humanities* 4 (1971), p. 241ff., especially concerning the view of R. Nathan b. Samuel ibn Tibbon.

38. *Kad ha-Kemaḥ, Ge'ula*, f. 25b. R. Baḥya also cites a second reason, according to which the Dispersion is a punishment for Israel's transgression "[while] in the Holy Land, for this is the focal-point of the world." Since Israel withdrew themselves from the "uppermost point, (*ha-nekuda ha-elyona*)" Exile was decreed "in order that they should be exiled to the ends of the earth, i.e., the nethermost point."

39. On the influence of these remarks on R. Solomon le-Beit ha-Levi of Salonika, see J. Hacker, "Israel Among the Nations as Described by Solomon le-Beit ha-Levi of Salonika" (Hebrew), *Zion* 34 (1969), p. 45.

40. Thus Ḥ. H. Ben-Sasson understands this passage in "Reformation," pp. 249–250. This interpretation is not free of difficulties.

41. *Sefer ha-Ḥayyim*, "Sefer Geula ve-Yeshua," (Cracow, 1593), chap. 7, f. 46a.

42. Ibid.

43. *Commentary* on the *Haggada* in *Ma'ase ha-Shem*, "Ma'ase Mitzrayim," (The Hague, 1777), chap. 24, f. 106a.

44. Cf. *Ma'ase Avot*, VII, p. 2. Nevertheless salvation occasionally occurs by means of the death of the aggressor, since "delivery by means of defense has a certain deficiency, for the persecuted is not avenged; therefore God, may He be blessed, sometimes saves the righteous by defense, and sometimes by means of the death and destruction of the enemy." This assertion anticipates the position of R. Simḥa Luzzatto, who sees in Jewish passivity one of the fundamental traits of the nation. Those hundreds of thousands of Jews, "noble of mind" in his words, did not act to prevent the expulsion from Spain, "but rather dispersed themselves and scattered throughout the entire world. And herein is the conclusive proof that the Jews, in keeping with [the spirit of] the laws and customs accepted among them, are inclined to submit to, and obey, those who rule over them." *Ma'amar al Yehudei Venetziya* (Jerusalem, 1951), pp. 122–123. This issue is also of interest as it bears on reactions to the Expulsion. A different view is expressed by R. Joseph ibn Yaḥya, who maintains that the extreme dispersion was responsible for Jewish passivity. See Ben-Sasson, "Exile and Redemption," p. 223, n. 42.

45. *Ma'ase ha-Shem*, "Ma'ase Avot", chap. 9, f. 56a.

46. Ibid., chap. 7, f. 54b.

47. See Reuben Bonfil, "Expressions of the Uniqueness of the Jewish People in Italy during the Renaissance" (Hebrew), *Sinai* 76 (1975), 36–46.

48. Ibid., p. 7, n. 23, where he contrasts Dato's view of Abraham's wanderings as essential to his mission with Rabbeinu Nissim's interpretation of them as flight.

49. Cf. also Isaac Abravanel's commentary to Zechariah 8:23 and Isaiah 49:23, and the comments of R. Samuel Judah Katzenellenbogen cited in Bonfil, "Expressions of Uniqueness," p. 7, n. 23. This theme is reiterated in a later period by R. Samuel Eidels (MaHaRSHa).

50. In the sixteenth century his ideas influenced R. Abraham ibn Migash (*Kvod Elohim*, III). They have been analyzed by Ḥ. H. Ben-Sasson, "Reformation," pp. 322ff., who sees in them the spirit of Provence, "the land of heresy." Ibn Migash relies on legends concerning the origins of Christianity under Jewish influence, in order to emphasize the Jews' responsibility for its foundation and spread.

51. Even at an early period the total dispersion of Israel was regarded as a condition for Redemption. Thus, for example, R. Nathan ibn Tibbon writes: "And Scripture has already stated: 'If your outcasts are in the uttermost parts of heaven' [Deut. 30:4]. And undoubtedly this has not yet been fulfilled. Accordingly, anyone believing in the Torah of Moses must necessarily believe that our Exile is to be followed by our deliverance." See Ben-Sasson, "Reformation," p. 318.

52. *Bina le-Itim* (Venice, 1653), "Et Ketz," Sermon 54, f. 39bff.

53. I have read ירבה according to the Venice edition. The Warsaw edition of 1882–83 has ידבר.

54. "*Tigboret*"; in the Warsaw edition–"*kigvurat*."

55. Redemption (*ge'ula*) corresponds to Creation. At the time of Redemption God will act according to His attribute of mercy, "and not according to strict justice, as it was with the creation of the heavens and the earth" (f. 40b).

56. Joseph ibn Yaḥya, *Commentary* on Daniel (Bologna, 1617), f. 110a.

57. Ibid., f. 108b.

58. *Netzaḥ Yisrael*, chap. 11. Cf. *Ner Mitzva* (Warsaw, 1798), f. 82b. Israel's chosenness is explained on the basis of the special cause-and-effect relationship between God and Israel's soul.

59. That is to say, the time of the righteous is the seventh day. "Eulogy for R. Akiba Ginzburg," published as an appendix to *Gur Arye* on Numbers (Prague, 1598), p. 185ff.

60. Ibid., p. 182.

61. In a number of places the MaHaRaL mentions three historical and sociological components of Israel's Exile: the state of Exile itself, servitude, and dispersion. See above n. 35.

62. *Gvurot ha-Shem* (Jerusalem, 1971), chap. 46, p. 175.

63. Ibid., p. 176.

64. Ibid., p. 178.

65. Ibid., chap. 18, p. 81ff.

66. Ibid., chap. 34, p. 126ff.

67. A similar opinion was suggested by Dr. Benjamin Gross, *Netzaḥ Yisrael* (Tel Aviv, 1974), p. 227. The MaHaRaL developed these ideas in *Sefer Ha-Geula*, which was never published. It appears to me that in view of the different parallels we have cited above, this hypothesis can be confirmed. Certainly the theory underlying the MaHaRaL's ideas is not as far from Nietzsche's theory of eternal recurrence as Gross contends (see ibid., p. 228, note 15).

68. In the theory of *shmitot* a position is frequently adopted which holds that there exist people who belong to a previous *shmita* but who nevertheless have lived in our *shmita*. It seems to me that the position of the MaHaRaL should be characterized in a contrary fashion. That is, there are souls which belong to a world that has not yet materialized.

69. The MaHaRaL's position finds expression in the significance attributed to different eschatological epochs. The principal epoch is the world to come, which is not regarded by the MaHaRaL as identical with the world of souls after death, but rather constitutes an altogether new cosmic reality which comes at the annihilation of this world.

70. On Bibago see Avraham Nuriel, "The Philosophic Teachings of R. Abraham b. Shem Tov Bibago," Ph.D. diss., Hebrew University, Jerusalem, 1975.

71. *Derekh Emuna*, f. 94a. On the expression "reasoning intellect" (*sekhel tvuni*), see ibid., p. 123.

72. On the influence of R. Joseph Yavetz on the thought of German and Polish Jewry

cf. J. Elbaum, "Trends and Courses in Jewish Speculative and Moralistic Literature in Germanic Lands and Poland during the Sixteenth Century," Ph.D. dissertation, Hebrew University, Jerusalem, 1977.

73. This is the reason given by R. Joseph Yavetz for composing his book *Ḥasdei ha-Shem.* See Yavetz's *Commentary* to Psalms, (London, 1952), chap. 2, p. 7.

74. Gershom Scholem, *Sabbatai Ṣevi*, p. 15.

75. Ibid. 76. Ibid., p. 20.

77. Ibid., p. 47, and cf. pp. 37–38.

78. On this idea in Talmudic literature see Urbach, *The Sages* (Jerusalem, 1975), p. 59.

79. See I. Tishbi, *Mishnat ha-Zohar.*

80. R. Moses Cordevero, *Sha'ar ha-She'arim* (Koretz, 1780), chap. 3, f. 73b.

81. On the idea of the refinement of dross (*tzeruf sigim*) in R. Solomon Alkabetz, see Sack, "Mystical Theology," p. 159, accroding to *Beit ha-Levi*, f. 4b. On the comparison of final Redemption with the deliverance from Egypt see R. Baḥya, *Kad ha-Kemaḥ*, f. 66b. Concerning the differences between the Exile of Edom and the Exile in Egypt as elucidated by the kabbalists in the sixteenth century see Sack, op. cit., p. 160ff. In his writings R. Isaac Luria emphasizes the fact that in Egypt the refinement was completed and therefore redemption was complete—a fact which is hinted at by Scripture in the words [Ex. 12:36], "and they despoiled Egypt." This did not occur in the subsequent periods of Exile; therefore Jews remained in Babylonia after the return to Zion in the days of Nehemiah and Ezra.

82. See *Yevamot*, 24b.

83. An excerpt from this passage can be found in Scholem, *Devarim be-Go* (Tel Aviv, 1975), pp. 215–216.

84. The patriarchs, according to the interpretation of R. Moses b. Solomon ha-Levi, *Yo'el Moshe* (Amsterdam, 1649).

85. *Ma'amar Ḥikur ha-Din*, IV, chap. 13. This approach regards the transgression itself as part of the original cosmic design. We find a contrary view expressed in a later period, in the commentary by R. Ḥayyim ibn Atar. In his commentary on the verse [Lev. 25:35], "And if thy brother grow poor," he writes: "For if Israel had not transgressed they would have had the power, [even had they remained] where they were [*Eretz Yisrael*], to collect the sparks of holiness from wherever they might be. This is not so after they have transgressed, because their strength has been sapped, and would it be that they should achieve this [*she-tasig yadam*] [now that they are] in the very place where the sparks are."

86. Many of the exiles from Spain used this expression to refer to their sufferings. See Ben-Sasson, "Exile and Redemption," p. 219, n. 21.

87. R. Menaḥem Azariah da Fano, *Kanfei Yona, IV*, 12, and see also the passage that follows concerning the exile of David. The significance of this text was recognized by R. Isaac Meir Alter of Gur and discussed in his letter to R. Zvi Hirsch Kalischer. See the remarks of his grandson in M. Selzer, ed., *Zionsim Reconsidered* (London, 1970), p. 20.

88. IV, 16.

89. Cf. Gershom Scholem's article on "The Kabbalist R. Abraham ben Eliezer ha-Levi," *Kiryat Sefer* 2 (1925), pp. 101–141; 269–273, and Ben-Sasson, "Reformation in Jewish Eyes."

90. See Jacob Katz, "The Debate over *Smikha* between R. Jacob Berav and RaLBaḤ" (Hebrew), *Zion* 16 (1951), pp. 28–45, and especially p. 37ff.

91. Ibid., p. 39, *Responsa* of the RaLBaḤ (Venice, 1565), f. 286 b. Concerning the heart of the problem Jacob Katz is of the opinion that extra-halakhic, messianic factors played a role in R. Berav's ruling, while R. Levi's decision represented "a purely halakhic position," free of messianic considerations, and was made on the basis of the imminent canons of Halakhah and ethics. Katz writes that "the RaLBaḤ's view of the 'ordinances [*takanot*] of *ge'ula*' is one of passive expectation which does not require any special act to hasten it, but rather serves to encourage virtuous actions, which ought to be done in any case," while according to the innovators, "the renewal of *smikha* is not an act of charity which deserves the reward of *ge'ula*, but is rather 'the starting point of the redemption of our soul,' that is to say, the first of the stages of *ge'ula*" (Katz, op. cit., p. 40).

92. See on this my article, "The Link with *Eretz Yisrael* in Jewish Philosophy," *Cathedra* 4 (1977), pp. 148–166.

93. The forgetting of *Eretz Yisrael* as a reason for the continuation of Exile occasionally

appears in the literature of the period. Thus, for example, writes R. Abraham Saba: "For the pride and the dominion which were [to be found] among Israel—as if they dwelled in their land—brought this [continued Exile] about," (*Tzror ha-Mor, Parshat Ba-Har*, f. 104b). And cf. R. Ḥayyim b. R. Betzalel, above n. 4.

For my beloved grandson
Meshulam Zusha, נ״י
Born 12 Sivan, 5742.

Talmudists, Philosophers, Kabbalists: The Quest for Spirituality in the Sixteenth Century

ISADORE TWERSKY

I

This paper is a brief chapter in the dialectical history revolving around the relationship between study of the Talmud and study of philosophy, Kabbalah or other meta-halakhic disciplines[1]—a relationship which is sometimes smooth or mutually supportive, sometimes caustic, critical or competitive, sometimes openly hostile and ultimately rather sharply exclusivist in conception and value judgment.

It is necessary to emphasize that the pivot of the paper—and of the entire history which I am trying to reconstruct—is the importance of study and the concomitant relation between the cognitive effort, however directed, and the attainment of spirituality, however defined; study as an indispensable prerequisite, catalyst, and preservative for spirituality is our topic. Hence, "Talmudist" does not designate one observant of the Halakhah in contradistinction to one who makes light of normative-halakhic obligations and gives his allegiance instead to a cognitive or ecstatic antinomianism. We are not dealing with a mystic tendency which trivializes external ceremonies and revels in a purely spiritual mode of religious identification or with a philosophic tendency which claims that ritual observance may be by-passed by the intellectual elite as a result of a philosophic-teleological understanding of the laws and a rationalized view of tradition. Rather, the term "Talmudist" refers to one whose primary, sometimes exclusive, intellectual commitment is to study of the Talmud and its ever-growing corpus of cognate works rather than to philosophy or Kabbalah and who insists that this type of study is not only the ideal supplement to, and sustaining force of, religious practice but also the means to spirituality. In terms of practice, they are *all* Talmudists or halakhists—from this vantage point, all are halakhocentric. The differentiation emerges with regard to the perception of spirituality and its individual realization—from this vantage point *not all* are Talmudo-centric.

Actually, Talmudists, philosophers, and kabbalists are well-known, clearly identifiable types (even though in reality they often cross lines and assimilate certain traits of each other) with carefully formulated programs and aspirations. One of the most detailed, fecund, and suggestive typologies was sketched at the end of the fourteenth century by Profiat Duran (Efodi) in the extensive introduction to his original study of Hebrew grammar, the *Ma'ase Efod.*[2] The premise of his spiritual typology is that exponents of all three types, committed as they are to halakhic observance, accept one common axiom: the need to anchor the religious *vita activa*, the life of *mitzvot*, in some form of intellectual-contemplative-spiritualizing activity. They differ concerning the methodology and morphology—i.e., the identification of the proper subject, scope, value and goal of study, each group contending unqualifiedly, tenaciously, and passionately that its field, with the concomitant premises, objectives and repercussions, is the indispensable one and its approach unimpeachable, that its scholarly concern provides the ultimate complement to the halakhic act. Within this framework Duran is able to present a full and informative, sometimes tendentious and provocative, delineation of the intellectual preoccupations as well as spiritual presuppositions and projections of Talmudists, philosophers and kabbalists; as a matter of fact, he uses this typology as a pretext for introducing a fourth school whose advocate and theorist he becomes: the biblicists, who affirmed that the study of the Bible is the most noble and important complement to Halakhah. This Biblo-centrism is indeed a notable position; its roots and offshoots need to be carefully examined.[3] We may add here parenthetically, for the sake of completeness, that we also find protagonists of Aggadah or *musar* who present these areas of study as the most important in terms of spirituality.[4]

Many typological formulations of this sort, not all so detailed or extensive (some involve only two types—i.e. Talmudism and one kind of extra-Talmudism, but are nevertheless of great interest and importance) are forthcoming in various sources. They are found, for example, in R. Baḥya ibn Pakuda,[5] Moses ibn Ezra,[6] Abraham ibn Ezra,[7] Moses Maimonides,[8] Abraham Abulafia,[9] *Sefer Ḥasidim*,[10] Abraham Maimonides,[11] Isaac Polgar,[12] Isaac ibn Latif,[13] Shem Tov Falaqera,[14] Kalonymus ben Kalonymus,[15] Joseph Kaspi,[16] R. Menaḥem ben Zeraḥ,[17] R. Isaac Aboab,[18] R. Joshua ibn Shu'eib, [19] R. Solomon Alami,[20] *Sefer Alilot Devarim*,[21] R. Isaac Abravanel,[22] or later in R. Simḥa Luzzatto,[23] R. Yair Ḥayyim Bachrach,[24] R. Moses Ḥayyim Luzzatto,[25] R. Shlomo Ḥelma (*Mirkevet ha-Mishne*),[26] and in early Haskalah works as well.[27] They provide rich material for a history of Judaism, particulary its quest for spirituality by means of a proper alignment of ritual punctiliousness and religious experience. The upshot of these typologies is that philosophy and mysticism are alike in their demand that a secure, honored place be guaranteed for some meta-halakhic discipline. Whatever the bi-lateral relations between philosophy and mysticism, our focus is their attitude to Talmudism and vice versa.

Particularly important for our purposes is the type of Talmudist that emerges from both positive as well as negative portrayals (i.e. the self-perception as well as the image and reality as perceived by others)—the monolithic Talmudist who rejects the value or necessity of complementary disciplines and argues for the exclusivity of halakhic study, in some case even vis-à-vis Bible study or aggadah and certainly vis-à-vis philosophy, Kabbalah, or other forms of meta-Halakhah. While the spiritual-intellectual chronicle which we are investigating is so very rich in protagonists who push back the frontiers of study by *adding* subjects to Talmud (or at least to codificatory summations of law), here the movement is not accretionary but restrictive.[28]

The monolithic Talmudist just referred to is, quite clearly, not the prevalent type of Talmudist who, through the ages, ordinarily and rather naturally combined halakhic study with some meta-halakhic discipline: Maimonides, RaBaD, R. Eleazar Rokeaḥ, R. Jonah Gerondi, R. Abraham Maimonides, Naḥmanides, RaSHBa, RiTBa, R. Nissim Gerondi, R. David ibn abi-Zimra, R. Joseph Karo, R. Eleazar Azikri, R. Moses Isserles, R. Mordekhai Jaffe, R. Samuel Eidels (MaHaRSHa), R. Moshe Metz, and countless others. As I have indicated, they acknowledged and nurtured the reciprocity and complementarity of the disciplines with full awareness that this was the appropriate way to maintain punctilious observance of the Halakhah while avoiding externalization and routinization. The values and aspirations of religious experience and spiritual adventure are firmly mounted upon the norms of positive law. The problem of historical reconstruction becomes more acute when we confront thinkers who do not possess credentials in Talmudic studies, criticizing Talmudists for their scholastic exclusivism and religious parochialism.[29] The same is true when some writers reproduce either a rationale or a critique of Talmudism which also focuses on this monolithic preoccupation.[30] Sometimes, this Talmudist profile emerges in what seems to be an objective typology or historical account of intellectual classes.[31] For the most part, however, while Talmudists may argue for axiological superiority of their discipline, they do not argue for narrow exclusivism. Even those—e.g., R. Yair Ḥayyim Bachrach[32]—whose ostensible aim is to curtail study of extra-Talmudic subjects and foster a de facto Talmudism do it prudently and strategically; they initially acknowledge the uncontested significance of meta-Halakhah and then contend that since the subject matter is beyond our grasp it is wise to concentrate on Talmud. Their position is that the difficulties and dangers are so great that one had best forego these esoteric studies—intrinsically elevating and edifying—and devote one's energies to exoteric Halakhah. In sum, although not the major or representative species of Talmudism, our monolithic variant is historically significant, and the impact of this position needs to be carefully assessed; its nineteenth- and twentieth-century recrudescence warrants close study, for it was particularly influential.

Again, it is important to underscore at the outset that the conceptual center-point in this history is the issue of spirituality and religious-metaphysical perfection, not orthodoxy or heterodoxy,[33] not the respective claims of Kabbalah versus philosophy but their relation to the study of Talmud and the ways in which Talmudists welcomed, rejected, or were suspicious of them.

II

The sixteenth century provides us with a fair share of significant typologies, which sketchily or elaborately depict Talmudists, philosophers, kabbalists—their profiles and attitudes, the certainties and tensions of their programs. We may extract from the literature of this period, from a wide array of different genres, highly informative material which illustrates some of the stock features of the dialectical history—what subjects to study, the hierarchy of subjects, reasons for this hierarchy, the degree of inter-connectedness or independence and the metaphysical priorities—while simultaneously underscoring some special emphases, nuances, and novel constellations. These mutually re-enforcing extracts enable us to define with a great measure of precision what the terms mean; any possible vagueness or ambiguity is diminished not only by pointed description but also by context and contrast, inference and innuendo. In emphasizing the timelessness of certain positions or constellations of practices, values and beliefs, we must, of course, be attentive to unprecedented events and special developments of this period which have repercussions for our theme and its mutations:[34] e.g., widespread demographic shifts, emergence of new centers and confrontation between communities of divergent background or dissimilar intellectual commitment, personal and literary contacts between Italy, central Europe, Poland, and Turkey, opening of universities to Jews, intensification of Christian Hebraism, influence and challenge of the Renaissance and the counter-Reformation, the Marrano attack on the Oral Law, and a new skepticism toward the credentials of the rabbinic tradition, implications of the eschatological value assigned to study of Mishna on one hand or Kabbalah on the other, burning of the Talmud in Italy and augmented Christian criticism of the Talmud, intensive and heterogeneous halakhic creativity (particularly in the areas of codification and methodology [*klalim*] as well as the controversial development of *pilpul*), the *apparent* waning of medieval philosophy (together with the emergence of new philosophic currents and a new philosophic orthodoxy) and the triumphant spread of Kabbalah spearheaded by the publication of the Zohar and other key kabbalistic texts. In short, the sixteenth century is in many respects a continuation of earlier trends and in other respects we may find in it new postures and possibilities, new structures and confrontations. Only by being acquainted with the former will we be able to appreciate the latter. This perspective is precisely the value of history of ideas.

Indeed, our sixteenth-century authors concretize this historical-conceptual duality or bi-focal view by addressing themselves to, and debating with, thirteenth- or fourteenth-century figures on the one hand (e.g., R. Joseph Yavetz versus R. Joseph ibn Kaspi[35] or R. Yeḥiel of Pisa versus R. Yedaya ha-Penini) and on the other by turning directly to their contemporaries (e.g. R. Abraham ibn Migas singling out "ketzat bnei amenu *be-dorenu ze*"[36] or R. Moses Cordovero referring "le-hamon ha-am ve-la-ḥakhamim ha-talmudiyim *she-bi-zmanenu*"[37] or R. Joseph b. Isaac ha-Levi's characterization of "rov anshei *dorenu ze*."[38] It is obvious that the intellectual-spiritual phenomena they refer to are well-established positions—clear alternatives, with venerable pedigrees, which one could readily opt for—but the polemicizing authors here choose, with patent rhetorical skill, to emphasize their contemporaneity rather than their place in a historical typology. This dialogic feature (i.e. direct confrontation with the antagonist) of much of the literary presentation is noteworthy and effective, for it does not allow the virulence of the debate to be dampened or to be treated as a footnote to earlier developments. The issues remain live and timely; their resonance is great and their impact is immediate. Moreover, while guarding against the pitfalls of precursorism, this bi-focal view enables us also to look ahead and to see the seeds of various seventeenth- and eighteenth-century developments in the sixteenth century as well as in earlier centuries.

To spell out these substantive and methodological generalizations with somewhat greater specificity, we may note that the sixteenth century serves as a microcosm of the entire entangled issue in the following ways. (1) There is the rising crescendo of voices proclaiming the absolute axiological supremacy of meta-Halakhah—and here the kabbalists are more aggresive and sophisticated and apparently more influential. The entrenchment and dissemination of Kabbalah add a novel dimension and considerable immediacy to the dissatisfaction with an exclusivist-imperious Talmudism or even to a timid Talmudism which apologetically and respectfully shies away from the "secrets of the Torah" and meta-halakhic investigations. The philosophic contention has already been well rehearsed[39] and, even though it is repeated (e.g. by Abraham ibn Migas or indirectly by Meir ibn Gabbai),[40] the kabbalistic voice is stronger and more resonant. Thus, as we shall see, R. Moses Cordovero is engaged in an unrelenting attack on those Talmudists who thought and taught that there was no supra-literal dimension to the authoritative texts of Judaism or that even if it did exist it was dispensable. (2) On occasion it appears that the question is not only one of hierarchical supremacy, of demanding that Kabbalah be recognized as the "queen" of all sciences. Rather Talmud study per se seems to be under fire and its intrinsic worth is being questioned or qualified, demeaned or dismissed. While we may find antecedents or paradigms (e.g. Joseph ibn Kaspi, Asher Lemlein)[42] for the denial of intellectual-spiritual value to pure Talmud study and the reduction of the latter to behavioral importance, there is a certain acuity to the issue in sixteenth-century literature (as reflected, e.g., in the impassioned defense of Talmudic study provided by Yavetz and MaHaRaL).[43] The critical refrain gets sharper. Jacob Provençal urges David (son of Judah) Messer Leon not to follow the local rabbis who do not "value the Talmud at all."[44] R. Abraham ibn Migas advises his reader not to communicate with one who has spent all his life only studying Talmud.[45] In studying the sources, we must try to detect this occasional transition from the unrelenting demand that Talmud study be supplemented and enhanced to a demeaning attitude to this very study. Moreover, we must also note the differences between the latter and specific arraignment of excesses or distortions or motivational aberrations by practitioners, by "unrepresentative" unsensitive Talmudists who lose sight of the real goal and purposes of study (Alami, Yavetz . . .). The various attacks on methodological flabbiness—symbolized in our period by *pilpul shel hevel*[46]—should also be seen in the light of ad hoc and ad hominem rather than essential or phenomenological criticism. The anti-*pilpul* harangues of this century are by no stretch of the imagination to be included in the anti-Talmudic genre; they are specific methodological criticisms. (3) The protagonists of monolithic Talmudism, to the exclusion of *everything* else, never become very numerous, but they appear more strident for a variety of reasons, defensive as well as aggressive. The intriguing documents concerning the famous Posen controversy of 1559 are to be read in this light and I would suggest that the MaHaRaL's "Talmudism" should be reexamined in this context.[47]

The methodological assumption of this analysis—i.e. the history of ideas approach—should also be amplified at this point. As we shall see, the range of relevant sources is so wide from every point of view—geographically, ideologically, generically—that oversimplified socio-historical explanations are clearly untenable. While scholars are frequently—and justly—apprehensive about dissociating ideas from realities, there is also need for reverse checks and balances. "The danger that cultural analysis will lose touch with the hard surfaces of life—with the political, economic, stratificatory realities within which men are everywhere contained—and with the biological and physical necessities on which those surfaces rest, is an ever present one. The only defense against it, and against, thus, turning cultural analysis into a kind of sociological aestheticism, is to train such analysis on such realities and such necessities in the first place."[48] While this danger is certainly real and serious, we must be equally careful of the parallel danger of mechanical reductionism: not to reduce every intellectual development to extraneous influences or correlate every spiritual constellation with historical realities in the general scene. Sociological determinism is as unacceptable as sociological aestheticism. Allowing horizontal and vertical perspectives to intersect or being mindful of the similarity of conclusions and convictions crystallizing against dissimilar social-cultural-historical backgrounds provides a corrective for facile one-dimensional explanations (e.g. hastily characterizing an attitude, pro-Biblicism let us say, which has precise antecedents or definite parallels, as a "Renaissance phenomenon").[49] While being fully attentive to contemporary historical stimuli or changing historical conditions, we see more clearly the immanent tension, recurrent dialectical shifts or universality of certain positions and espousal of varying metaphysical options. Incommensurability between the spotty spiritual reality and a sublime spiritual ideal is a common occurrence and cannot simply be related to, or correlated with, a specific historic contingency. Moreover, if we are inclined to correlate external crises with inner developments, we should note that there is here a crisis not only of historical consciousness but of religious *Anschauung* and sensibility; the latter, widespread as it is, requires judicious investigation.

In our case, facts, descriptions, insights, arguments, indictments, pleas, or programmatic formulations concerning sixteenth-century relations between Talmudists, philosophers, and kabbalists are drawn from the writings of such disparate figures as Abraham ibn Migas,[50] Moses Almosnino,[51] Yoḥanan Alemanno,[52] Isaac Arama,[53] Abraham Shalom,[54] Meir ibn Gabbai,[55] Immanuel Benevento,[56] Yosef Shlomo Del Medigo,[57] Eliezer Ashkenazi,[58] R.

Joseph Ashkenazi,[59] R. Moses Isserles,[60] R. Solomon Luria,[61] R. Abraham Horowitz,[62] R. Judah Loew ben Betzalel (MaHaRaL),[63] R. Ḥayyim ben Betzalel,[64] R. Mordekhai Jaffe,[65] R. David Ganz,[66] R. Ephraim Luntshitz,[67] R. Joseph ben Isaac ha-Levi,[68] R. Ḥayyim Vital,[69] R. Moses Cordovero,[70] R. Elijah de Vidas,[71] R. Solomon Alkabetz,[72] R. Joseph Karo,[73] R. Joseph Taitatzak,[74] R. Yeḥiel of Pisa,[75] R. Abraham ben Meshullam of Asti,[76] R. Obadiah Sforno,[77] Azariah de Rossi,[78] R. Azariah Figo,[79] R. Abraham Portaleone,[80] R. Joseph Yavetz,[81] Abraham Farissol[82] and R. Leone da Modena.[83] We have here an intriguing, polychromatic array of authors who appear as learned expositors, skillful controversialists, erudite and versatile commentators, polemicists defending Judaism against external defamation while presenting their own vision of religious vitality and virtuosity, forceful proponents of a rabbinic culture free of adventitious elements, assiduous students of Bible and Aggadah, ethicists, determined defenders of a waning philosophy or optimistic proponents of a revitalized philosophy, inspired protagonists of Kabbalah, indeed of varieties of Kabbalah, or zealous devotees of Talmudism. They are writing in Italy , Bohemia, Poland, Turkey and Palestine. Some never leave their birthplace while others travel extensively from center to center. Some are living with the trauma of the Spanish expulsion while others are ensconced in the humanistic and/or counter-Reformation centers of Italy or the burgeoning communities of Poland. Their literary media vary: exegetical works (especially on Psalms and *Avot*, with increasing attention to the *Megilot*), halakhic codes and commentaries, supercommentaries on earlier works which had already become classics, technical philosophic or kabbalistic books, ethical-inspirational tracts, homilies, historical opera, polemical-propagandistic compositions and introductions to newly printed works (the Zohar is the best example). They are professionally, economically, temperamentally, scholastically and intellectually different and yet are confronting similar problems and grappling alike with the issues of religious existence and spirituality. The diversity speaks for itself and forcefully supports the history-of-ideas approach which utilizes all sources, cuts across artificial boundaries, spans centuries and countries, and in the process underscores continuities while identifying special features and novelties. The varieties of response to the same issue are significant, as are the similarities of attitude emerging from quite different quarters.

The issue in the heated dialogue or trialogue between Talmudists, philosophers and kabbalists is attainment of spirituality, deepening of ideological sensitivity, religious vitality and understanding—the interlocking of "duties of the limb" with "duties of the heart." The key term in the vocabulary of spirituality and religiosity is perfection (*shlemut* or *hashlamat ha-nefesh*). Within the framework of accepted views or on the basis of shared traditional premises, the debate revolves around how these disciplines interact, which is superior and which is subordinate and which is most conducive to *shlemut*. Whatever terms we use—axiological premises, hierarchical ratings, theological values, metaphysical priorities, or religious objectives—the relation of the disciplines is the crucial issue, and the importance of study from the vantage point of *shlemut* is being appraised continually. The curricular aspect is the practical expression while the phenomenological aspect is the theoretical motive.[83a]

When discussing philosophy, in other words, we are not concerned primarily with questions of orthodoxy or heterodoxy, with the legitimacy of philosophy and its place within the Oral Tradition, with the alleged naturalism of its views on prophecy, miracles, immortality and eschatology or its endemic antinomianism; our concern is rather with the efficacy and appositeness of rationalism as a means to spirituality. Should one strive to exert oneself intellectually and absorb the natural science and metaphysics of the philosophers in order to rise to higher levels of religious understanding and, hence, spiritual intensity? For philosophers—and their opponents heatedly contest this claim—the only road to spirituality is rationalism, the exercise of reason in the service of religion. Rationalism as a means to spirituality, to *shlemut*, is a topos of philosophic writing and at the same time a target of its critics.

By the same token, when discussing mysticism we are not concerned primarily with the question of putative heterodoxy; indeed we find during this period apodictic repudiation of Kabbalah by opponents of publication of the Zohar who contend that its study is studded with danger and actually leads to apostasy. Kabbalah is seen by these acidulous critics as a threat to traditional Judaism. This extreme charge is reminiscent of Farissol's description[84] of converts who had espoused a "spiritualized," antinomian view of Judaism—a view which made the road to desertion of Judaism easy to traverse. However, as indicated, in both cases the charge of heresy or heterodoxy is not the relevant issue. Nor, in the case of the Kabbalah of this period, are we concerned with contemplative-ecstatic procedures per se, with the practical mystical life of individuals or conventicles, the striving for *ruaḥ ha-kodesh*, with what is sometimes summarily called "mystical and magical contemplation." While this is clearly relevant, our concern is primarily with the intellectual-curricular relationship of Talmud and Kabbalah and the contemplative-spiritual "fallout" from the study of Kabbalah. We are concerned with the kabbalistic claim that an unreflective observance of commandments, not plugged in to kabbalistic concepts and intentions, misses the mark and that a merely "literalist" approach to Talmud is deficient. For kabbalists, the only road to spirituality is their system of *sitrei Tora* which perfects one's understanding and purifies one's visions. Philosophy for them is an alien, fruitless endeavor. Obviously, in the case of Kabbalah, it is not always possible to sustain such a sharp demarcation between the two converging aspects of contemplation but the attempt is phenomenologically necessary. (R. Eleazar Azikri's mystical diary is a good case in point.)[84a]

The attempted differentiation between these two related and complementary aspects is as necessary and as delicate—in some respects analogous—as the attempted disentanglement of the purely spiritualistic thrust of philosophy (which may be traced from R. Saadiah Gaon through the letter of R. Sheshet ha-Nasi on to R. Moses Ḥayyim Luzzatto who talk about the spiritualizing impact of philosophy on practice [e.g. prayer] and belief [e.g. immortality]) from its apologetic-rationalist impetus, i.e. to project "in the eyes of the nations" the image of the Jews as "a wise and understanding people."[85] We may note that this outer-directed apologetic is discernible rather strikingly in the various interpretations of the Talmudic crux in *Pesaḥim* 94b *(nitzḥu ḥakhmei ha-umot)*[86] or even in R. Ḥayyim ben Betzalel's plea that the study of grammar be revived inasmuch as the nations of the world value this discipline very much and, therefore, the Jews should not be deficient in it.[87] Although the line between them is often blurred and they are in fact historically interconnected—R. Obadiah Sforno, e.g., reports that Christians condemn Jews for lack of rationality and lack of spirituality and candidly acknowledges the link between them[88]—they are phenomenologically separate. The apologetic motive is not coterminous with the spiritualistic objective and modality; the latter usually develops its own momentum.

Now, while we are not in this context turning our attention to the philosophy-Kabbalah debate per se—i.e., to the mutual recriminations that philosophy is alien and corrosive (e.g., R. Meir ibn Gabbai and earlier R. Shem Tov b. Shem Tov) or that Kabbalah is superstitious and unworthy (e.g., R. Abraham ibn Migas and earlier the *Alilot Devarim*), we should note that there was a real *live* confrontation, the much-touted decline of philosophy notwithstanding. This means that although R. Meir ibn Gabbai selected Maimonides as his major adversary (with Ibn Ezra a respectable second) and his *Avodat ha-Kodesh* is constructed as a comprehensive rebuttal of philosophy (i.e., Maimonideanism), his argument is not antiquarian but is clearly lubricated by contemporary conditions, considerations and cultural realities. Much to their chagrin, kabbalists witnessed the continued study and cultivation of philosophy in this period. There was a substantial philosophic legacy in Italy, eastern Europe and the East as reflected in different ways, directly or obliquely, for example in R. Solomon Luria, R. Moses Isserles, MaHaRaL, R. Mordekhai Jaffe, R. Joseph b. Isaac Ha-Levi, R. Eliezer Ashkenazi, Judah Abravanel, R. Obadiah Sforno, R. Azariah Figo, R. Judah Moscato, Elijah and Joseph Solomon Del Medigo, R. Abraham Horowitz, R. Hendel Manoaḥ, R. Abraham ibn Migas, R. Joseph Taitatzak, R. Moses Almosnino, and others.[89] Awareness of this fact is important not only for the proper assessment of this confrontation but also for the correct understanding of an antithetical, yet cognate phenomenon: the degree of conscious harmonization of philosophy and Kabbalah by many of these authors. I refer not only to the well-known cases of MaHaRaL in his diverse works and of R. Moses Isserles, especially in part three of the *Torat ha-Ola,* but also to the cases of Josel of Rosheim *(Sefer ha-Mikne),* R. Joseph Taitatzak *(Porat Yosef),* and, partially, R. Abraham ibn Migas *(Kevod Elokim),* or the intriguing statement reported by Leone da Modena in the name of the Lurianic disciple R. Israel Sarug that he could explain all kabbalistic teachings philosophically.[90] The point is that meta-halakhic elements, even of diverse provenance, could be merged in the attempt to provide positive law with a spiritualistic leaven. Moreover, if not merged, they could be used successively—i.e., one disenchanted with philosophy could rapidly replace the latter with a form of Kabbalah.

The important point is that Halakhah was regularly setting itself in a meta-halakhic framework. As I have observed elsewhere, this spiritual-ideological movement, this meta-halakhic restlessness, illustrates most clearly that Kabbalah and philosophy are *phenomenologically* alike in their tense relation to Halakhah.[91] Many writers of the earlier centuries chart their spiritual odyssey, describing how they move out of one meta-halakhic spiritual ambiance into another, all along feeling the need for something to supplement positive law and invigorate it. Just as erstwhile ardent Maimonideans—R. Isaac ibn Latif, R. Joseph Gikatilia, R. Abraham Abulafia, R. Moses de Leon—became fervent kabbalists, there is a similar phenomenon in the sixteenth century (witness the intellectual itinerary of R. Yeḥiel Nissim of Pisa).

III

A few compressed case studies which reflect the tensions, criticisms, and proposals—for the relevant texts invariably combine critical-contentious components with vigorous programmatic formulations—will enable us easily and quickly to concretize the range and intensity of the problems.

R. Yeḥiel Nissim of Pisa chose a special, imaginative form for his work *Minḥat Kena'ot*: it was planned and structured as a detailed rebuttal of Yedaya ha-Penini's *Iggeret ha-Hitnatzlut,* an enthusiastic, meticulous, and pungent apology for philosophy written at the beginning of the fourteenth century in answer to R. Solomon ibn Adret's well-known, forceful, and authoritative criticisms and denunciations of the philosophic movement in Judaism. R. Yeḥiel's book consciously spans the centuries and picks up the religious debate concerning the general value of philosophy and the merits of specific philosophic doctrines which was left in abeyance at the beginning of the fourteenth century. It thus illustrates incidentally that little was changed by the ban and counter-ban: the desirability or objectionability of rationalized religion remained in dispute. The *Minḥat Kena'ot,* which places itself in a clear, repercussive historical context, is therefore a document of prime importance not only for sixteenth-century history but also for the overarching history of ideas: a good example is the quintessential definition of the two irreconcilable positions, intellectualism versus the life of *mitzvot,* which is clearly relevant to contemporary tensions but also reflects a timeless issue.[92] It is a carefully argued work in which his polemical-conceptual strategy is to fully present the philosophic view (in order to demolish it), contrast it in broad strokes with the superior view of the kabbalists and, almost as an extra dividend, also to provide an articulate defense and unequivocally positive appraisal of pure Talmud study. This defense commands our attention because of its intrinsic importance and because such paeans to Talmudism are not too common. While on many occasions he combines Halakhah and Aggadah (or metahalakhic speculation) as twin components of Talmud, the key passage concerning the indispensability of Talmud study relates exclusively to the halakhic component.[93] Skillfully and effectively, he refers to "some contemporaries" (reminiscent of the earlier Jacob Anatoli and Joseph ibn Kaspi) who question the value of traditional Talmud study—"why waste our days studying variants of the Talmud and the controversies of the *Amora'im,*" when knowledge of the normative-practical result is sufficient.[94] His rebuttal is striking, for it proceeds on a practical rather than metaphysical plane. It does not resort to the abstract, pathos-laden notion (found already in Maimonides and R. Moses of Coucy) of "study of God's word" or study for study's sake *(tora li-shmah)* even if this study be devoid of practical benefits and immediate relevance. It does not argue that divine study is its own justification, but it operates with a pragmatic-judicial argument reminiscent of the opposition to Maimonides' *Mishne Tora* and parallel to, or anticipatory of, the opposition to the *Shulḥan Arukh*: without study of the Talmudic controversy, its dialectical amplification, its multiplicity and diversity of views and interpretations, proper understanding, adjudication and application of the law will be impossible. Full-orbed study is necessary for correct practice; diversity is a boon for Talmudism and not its bane. He argues that Talmudic debate and deliberation, *plugta di-gemara, maḥloket ha-amora'im,* is the very hallmark of the Oral Law and the linchpin of the halakhic system. This strong judicial argument is then bolstered by a curt interpolation of a converging kabbalistic motif alluded to by R. Menaḥem Recanati: the essence of the Oral Law is the debate and controversy—*masa u-matan*—of the Talmud. Now, this whole trend (in which the practical and the metaphysical are finally merged) may be assessed as a veiled anti-Maimonidean polemic, for Maimonides invariably emphasized that *masa u-matan* should be seen as an undesirable and unproductive feature, an unavoidable by-product of the Talmud, rather than a premeditated or indispensable feature. The Maimonidean code was intended to restore the original state of the Oral Law which was free of "multiplicity of opinions, variety of schools . . . and the production of confusion with regard to actions"; it would provide relief from exhausting and unrewarding study. It has already been observed that the Maimonidean concept is similar to the Platonic view which exalted oral culture and underscored the superiority of the oral word over the written word.[95] The expansive-judicial argument is thus allied in the *Minḥat Kena'ot* with a kabbalistic notion and pitted against the pragmatic-codificatory argument as nurtured by a philosophic notion. This defense is all the more noteworthy inasmuch as ultimately, after the judicial argument is settled, Kabbalah emerges at the top of the hierarchy and this is seen as his major curricular-spiritual concern. It should be remembered that some contemporaries (e.g., R. Immanuel Benevento, *Livyat Ḥen*) asserted that Kabbalah was needed to stem the tide of philosophic views *after* the disappearance of the Talmud. R. Yeḥiel of Pisa himself, writing before the burning of the Talmud, cited at the very beginning of his work (page 2) the role of in-depth Talmud study as a corrective for "deviant" views. How would he have phrased his arguments some twenty years later when such study was more difficult and scholars willy-nilly turned to codes for Talmudic material?[96]

We should note an additional component of his Talmudist-kabbalist position. He insists (taking his cue from a responsum of R. Asher ben Yeḥiel) that no alien methods borrowed from logic and philosophy need to be utilized in Talmud study. Indeed, such methodological hybridization is a violation of "tamim tihyeh," of inner religious integrity and conceptual consistency. It is a sign of a "disintegrated consciousness" (Hegel). Of course, the argument that logic and dialectic are necessary tools for study is an old one as is the counter-argument that they are undesirable intrusions into a self-sufficient system. The entire issue was to be resurrected in the Posen controversy of 1559 when R. Abraham Horowitz vehemently repudiated "the fool" who advocated monolithic Talmudism by affirming that "something extra" (i.e., logic) is needed even for the proper explication of the Talmud.[97] The sixteenth century thus provides a sharp focus for this pivotal issue.

In this context, finally, R. Yeḥiel introduces the concept of *shlemut,* spiritual perfection, which he defines not in metaphysical or intellectual terms but *in relation to the body.* Only body and soul in tandem achieve perfection and this is the purpose of religious wisdom being coupled with, and expressed in, *mitzvot.* The conjunction of the soul with the body and their unification pave the way for perfection; inasmuch as we are dealing with a finite material entity, perfection must reside in bodily action rather than in pure intellectual attainment. Otherwise, man in toto would not have a chance to serve God; study would not involve the whole person. We have here another perspective on integrity and integration. The idea that the religious *vita activa* rather than the *vita contemplativa* is the channel to and for perfection—an idea which dramatically upgrades *mitzvot* while substantially constricting intellectualism of all sorts—may be found in such varied writers of the period as Farissol, Yavetz, MaHaRaL, and R. Elijah de Vidas. It is a substantive variation of Duran's fundamental thesis concerning the relation of practice and study (although Duran's long characterization of the Talmudists alludes to it) with far-reaching repercussions for the importance of the life of *mitzvot.*[98]

This brief analysis of the position of R. Yeḥiel Nissim of Pisa provides a good microcosm of the period and its central religious problem. It is all the more significant because of its literary setting: the anti-Talmudic sentiment reported and rebutted by R. Yeḥiel is contained in a work devoted to a critical review of philosophy. Now, this is not an isolated instance. We may here turn to the MaHaRaL, a colorful, intriguing figure who is certainly not a monolithic Talmudist; his extensive exegetical-homiletical writings impinge on many areas and genres (Bible, Halakhah, Aggadah, ethics, polemics). Indeed, his fame does not rest primarily on his achievements as a Talmudist. It is therefore noteworthy that (particularly in *Tiferet Yisrael* and *Netivot Olam*) he parries the anti-Talmudic thrust of the philosophers—Kaspi may well have been the irritant, for he argued with great zeal that the truly universal, imperative subject of study is philosophy and not Talmud—by insisting that *Talmud study* leads to religious perfection and attainment of spirituality. The insistence is not buttressed theologically, is not rooted in scriptural arguments, but is formulated directly in terms of spirituality and perfection— the same concepts taken from the common intellectual-religious-metaphysical argumentarium. Using his own idioms and metaphors, he reaches the same conclusion as R. Yeḥiel Nissim: perfection does not follow from contemplative achievement but rather from practical performance. Man, combining body and soul, achieves perfection through religiously-defined action which relies upon antecedent study. Of course, the latter is important but it is not the crowning achievement. Only performance of the *mitzva* engages *all* of the human resources. Now, within the sprawling realm of study, he emphatically gives priority to Halakah over Aggadah, even though Aggadah is recognized as a treasure trove of profound wisdom and theological insight.[99] From this vantage point, he may be characterized as representing Duran's school of Talmudists.

Actually, while R. Yeḥiel Nissim and MaHaRaL are shielding Talmudism from the shafts and barbs of the philosophers, the kabbalists, who with remarkable consistency and tenacity exalt their discipline as axiologically superior, seem to present the most strident and sturdy criticisms and it is they who are in the forefront of the attack upon exclusive preoccupation with Talmud. Such Talmudism is a deterrent to theological insight and sensitivity. A very pungent formulation comes from the pen of the influential R. Moses Cordovero, the great architect of pre-Lurianic Kabbalah. In the *Or Ne'erav,* a sententious handbook of Kabbalah which contains a ringing affirmation of the supremacy of the latter over "plain" or purely literal Talmud study, R. Moses Cordovero condemns (as do R. Solomon Alkabetz in *Ayelet Ahavim,* R. Moses Alsheikh in his commentaries and R. Immanuel Benevento in *Livyat Ḥen*), those Talmudists who posit with apparent equanimity and satisfaction that the Torah has only a surface literal meaning and who deny an esoteric content.[100] In the eyes of R. Moses Cordovero and his fellow kabbalists, the masses and the Talmudists of this sort are linked together as simple literalists: *kol elu ha-inyanim hevi'u la-hamon ha-am ve-la-ḥakhamim ha-talmudiyim she-bi-zmanenu leha'amin ba-inyan ki-fshuto.* This rather stinging reduction of contemporary Talmudists and masses to one category is reminiscent of Abraham Bibago who, from his philosophic vantage point, compared those who study Mishna and Talmud with the masses who walk in their innocence and are removed from knowledge of *sitrei tora;* both lack profundity, in-depth knowledge.[101] Cordovero sees this pale commitment to literalism as the most serious and pernicious source of opposition to Kabbalah and is unrelenting in his criticism of its advocates; his resounding repudiation of the literalists, the *ba'alei ha-peshat,* is obviously not connected with, or aimed at, Karaism. Halakhah is "safe"; the spiritual-intellectual strife concerns meta-Halakhah and, more specifically, the teachings of Kabbalah. We should add, however, that, while the position of R. Moses Cordovero is powerful and aggressive, it is not nearly so caustic as that of R. Asher Lemlein who refers to Talmudists as "servants" or "artisans" far removed from the King. Nor does it have too much affinity with the contemporary kabbalistic view (presented by R. Abraham of Asti) that the abundance of halakhic works has negative consequences eschatologically; excessive Talmudism is a deterrent to the realization of the messianic goals.[102] Cordovero's position, insisting upon the absolute supremacy and indispensability of Kabbalah without berating Talmud study, is the classical kabbalistic one, found in many earlier sources and to be repeated later, for example, by R. Isaiah Horowitz. Talmud study is important but it must be supplemented and sustained by Kabbalah.[103] The only possible complication or inconsistency in this classical, absolutely clear, position concerning the relation of Halakhah and Kabbalah is for one to espouse Kabbalah's superiority but to back away from the practical educational consequences, which would demand that a certain amount of time, perhaps the major part of one's study-time, be devoted to the superior discipline; we would then have a situation in which the postulates of religious axiology and phenomenology do not determine curricular practice.[104] R. Moses Cordovero contends that all difficulties and dangers notwithstanding, Kabbalah's superiority must not only be recognized in principle but its systematic study should be pursued with zeal and discipline. Timidity is inadmissible.

We may note at this point R. Meir ibn Gabbai's unequivocal assertion that full-time Talmud study actually excludes theological insight and knowledge. In a similar vein the activists who fought for the publication of the Zohar and other kabbalistic texts declared forcefully that Talmudists are incapable of achieving perfection and must have the meta-Halakhah provided by kabbalistic doctrine. Without it their religious behavior is perfunctory and uninspired and they will never deserve to be described as "a wise and understanding people"—a skillful appropriation of a philosophic motif given wide currency by Maimonides.[105]

While Yavetz and MaHaRaL defend Talmud study against its philosophic detractors who question the ultimate value of such study and deny its relevance to the quest for spirituality and perfection, they in theory recognize the ideal type as the Talmudist armed with meta-halakhic knowledge; suffice it to note MaHaRaL's polymath interests and the divergent emphasis in Yavetz' polemic *(Or ha-Ḥayyim)* where the prime focus is the importance of Talmud as distinct from his commentaries where he clearly charts the intellectual course from laws of *nezikin* to kabbalistic doctrines and *ta'amei mizvot.*[106] However, the literature of the period which has already been referred to attests to the existence of the monolithic Talmudist as well. The famous Posen incident provides a stark example *(ein mutar lilmod rak ha-talmud levad).* A forceful presentation is given by the little known but interesting *Giv'at ha-More* of R. Joseph b. Isaac ha-Levi (a work which earned the written approbation of R. Ephraim Luntshitz) which describes four classes of opponents to the *More Nevukhim*. The third consists of those who study Talmud exclusively ("samu kol megamatam la'asok ba-talmud u-be-ma she-yityaḥes elav"). They say unequivocally—and they constitute the *majority* of contemporary students—that perfection is attainable only as a result of Talmud ("it is impossible for a person to reach *shlemuto ha-nitzḥi be-ma she-hu zulat ha-talmud va-asher gadlu alav mi-ne'ureihem ve-hen hem rov anshei dorenu ze.*") Del Medigo (*Novlot Ḥokhma),* R. Ḥayyim ben Betzalel and many other kabbalists all describe for us the exclusive Talmudist syndrome. Finally, in the course of an eloquent, impassioned plea for rationalization and a concomitant arraignment of unreflective acceptance and repetition of beliefs, Abraham ibn Migas counsels his reader: "she-lo tedaber . . . im mi she-lo asak kol yamav ki im be-talmud levad ve-lo ra'a me'orot mi-yamav."[107] This warning against one who has studied only Talmud is a classical critique of the unexamined life, an exposition of reason as a means to spirituality and the radical insistence that lack of this prevents spiritual illumination. This phrase *(lo ra'a me'orot),* used in the same way by R. Meir ibn Gabbai, again underscores the mutuality of the philosophic and kabbalistic critiques.

NOTES

1. The following three terminological observations were introduced in response to questions and comments concerning the paper as presented to the colloquium participants:

(a) I use meta-Halakhah in its dual sense to connote both that area of study which comes after Halakhah as well as that which is the appropriate, indispensable culmination of the learning process by virtue of its revealing the infrastructure and superstructure, the foundations and goals, of religious law and life. For "meta-history," see C. Dawson, *The Dynamics of World History* (New York, 1956), p. 281.

(b) This conceptualization does not eclipse or curtail the autonomous significance of each discipline per se but does help us focus on their interrelationship. Inasmuch as kabbalists and philosophers recognize that their areas of study have a special relation to Halakhah, it is neither restrictive nor imperialistic to speak of Halakhah and meta-Halakhah. Indeed, the latter, whatever it be (philosophy, Kabbalah, Ḥasidism), remains sovereign in all respects and scholars continue to investigate these fields in their totality. Moreover, we are not interested in the in-house rivalries and competition between them concerning the formulation of the practical norms of Halakhah, in attempts to intrude into the halakhic process; for Kabbalah and Halakhah, see the Hebrew article of Meir Benayahu, "Vikuaḥ ha-Kabbala im ha-Halakha," *Da'at* 5 (1980), 61–115, and the article of Jacob Katz in this collection. As I was belatedly reviewing my article for publication, I came across the article of Rachel Elior in *Meḥkerei Yerushahyim be-Maḥshevet Yisrael* 1 (1981), which contains some new material on this theme—see below n. 100. Whether philosophy was also involved in such a competition needs to be clarified independently.

(c) "Dialectic" is to be understood not in the Hegelian sense of an antithetical process which reaches a placid solution which subsequently breaks down and generates a new antithesis, but in the Heraclitean sense of ongoing, tempestuous struggle. Cf. the introduction of E. R. Leach to *Dialectic in Practical Religion* (Cambridge, 1968), pp. 1–2.

I have retained the original form of this essay, in which some themes, summarily noted at the beginning, are then elaborated more fully.

2. See I. Twersky, "Religion and Law," *Religion in a Religious Age,* ed. S. D. Goitein (Cambridge, 1973), pp. 69–82, and most recently the introduction of Frank Talmage to his edition of Duran's polemical works, *Kitvei Pulmos le-Profiat Duran* (Jerusalem, 1981).

Profiat Duran's work is relatively well known in subsequent generations and his typology is used by various writers, as I show in my forthcoming Hebrew monograph on him. Many authors of our period—e.g. I. Abravanel, Menaḥem Tamar, Abraham Bakrat, Yoḥanan Alemanno, Ḥayyim ben Betzalel and somewhat later, Menaḥem Lonzano and A. Sar Shalom Basilea—mention Duran and his *Ma'ase Efod,* particularly the introduction. For our purposes, see M. Lonzano, *Sefer Derekh Ḥayyim* (Lemberg, 1931) who quotes Duran and thereby marshalls support for an uncompromising anti-philosophic position.

3. It is noteworthy that in addition to citation of verses extolling the "word of God" as the overriding subject of study, he also bolsters his position by kabbalistic arguments. For the special intrinsic quality *(segula)* of the Bible, see my "Religion and Law," p. 82, n. 35. See F. Talmage, *Kitvei Pulmos,* pp. 17ff., on contemporary Christian approaches to Bible. Part ten of Duran's *Kelimat ha-Goyim* reviews critically Christian use of biblical passages. Note that in the sixteenth century while R. Ephraim Luntshitz appreciates the significance of Bible study for ethical purposes, MaHaRaL emphasizes the importance of Bible study for halakhic purposes.

4. See, e.g., R. Isaac Aboab, *Menorat ha-Ma'or* (Jerusalem, 1961), introduction, p. 10; Eliakim Getz, *Rapduni ba-Tapuḥim* (Cracow, 1896), introduction, p. 1 and p. 15.

5. *Ḥovot ha-Levavot,* tr. M. Hyamson: *Duties of the Heart* (Jerusalem, 1962), vol. I, pp. 27, 29, 35, 221. On Ibn Pakuda's indictment of the courtier class and its cultural-spiritual values, see Betzalel Safran, "Baḥya ibn Paquda's Attitude toward the Courtier Class," *Studies in Medieval Jewish History and Literature,* ed. I. Twersky (Cambridge, 1979), pp. 154–96, esp. 161–62.

6. For Moses ibn Ezra, see P. Kokowzoff, "The Date of Life of Baḥya ibn Pakuda," *S. Poznanski Memorial Volume* (Warsaw, 1927), esp. pp. 19–20. Moses ibn Ezra's coupling of Ibn Janaḥ and Ibn Pakuda is not exact.

7. *Yesod Mora* (Prague, 1833), ch. I (p.12).

8. *More Nevukhim,* III, 51; *Mishne Tora, Yesodei ha-Tora,* IV, 13; *Talmud Tora,* I, 11, 12; *Teshuva,* X, 6. See I. Twersky, *Introduction to the Code of Maimonides* (New Haven, 1980), esp. ch. VI. Note also, for example, the brief remark of Abraham ibn Daud, *Emuna Rama,* ed. S. Weil (Frankfurt, 1862), introduction, p. 2.

9. See A. Jellinek, *Philosophie und Kabbalah* (Leipzig, 1854), pp. 33–38; idem, *Ginzei Ḥokhmat ha-Kabbalah,* p. 15 *(Igeret R. Avraham Abulafia).*

10. For *Sefer Ḥasidim,* see H. Soloveitchik, "Three Themes in the Sefer Ḥasidim," *AJS Review* 1 (1976), 311–357, esp. 339ff.; I. Ta-Shema, "Mitzvat Talmud Tora . . . be-Sefer Ḥasidim," *Bar-Ilan Annual* 14–15 (1977), 98-113. More generally, see I. Marcus, *Piety and Society: The Jewish Pietists of Medieval Germany* (Leiden, 1981).

11. *The High Ways to Perfection* of Abraham Maimonides, ed. and trans. S. Rosenblatt, v. I (New York, 1927), pp. 13–17; v. II (Baltimore, 1928), pp. 128–34; see also *Milḥamot ha-Shem,* ed. R. Margaliyot (Jerusalem, 1953), pp. 52, 59, 74. For his excoriation of "dry externalism," see *High Ways,* II, p. 227. G. Cohen claims that this work of R. Abraham Maimonides is "apologetic-defensive"; see "The Soteriology of R. Abraham Maimon," *PAAJR* 35 (1967), 75–98; 36 (1968), 33–56, and note especially 78–9. As noted further, the apologetic impetus in the quest for spirituality is important but not the exclusive factor.

12. *Ezer ha-Dat* (Jerusalem, 1970), pp. 1–2.

13. *Sha'ar ha-Shamayim,* introduction, in *He-Ḥalutz* 12 (1887), 121.

14. *Sefer ha-Mevakesh,* in *Kitvei Shem Tov Falakera* (Jerusalem, 1969); see the selection in Ḥayyim (J.) Schirmann, *Ha-Shira ha-Ivrit bi-Sfarad u-ve-Provantz* (Jerusalem, 1956), vol. 2, pp. 329–342.

15. *Even Boḥan* (Tel Aviv, 1956), p. 56.

16. *Hebrew Ethical Wills,* ed. I. Abrahams (Philadelphia, 1926), vol. I, esp. pp. 128–138, 151; also, e.g., *Asara Klei Kesef,* vol. I, Proverbs, pp. 16–17; Job, pp. 171–74; see I. Twersky, "Joseph ibn Kaspi: Portrait of a Medieval Jewish Intellectual," *Studies in Medieval Jewish History and Literature,* ed. I. Twersky (Cambridge, 1979), pp. 243ff.

17. *Tzeda la-Derekh* (Warsaw, 1880), introduction, p. 8; see also *Ma'amar* 4, *Klal* 6 (p. 131).

18. *Menorat ha-Ma'or,* introduction, p. 10.

19. *Drashot* (Jerusalem, 1969), p. 370c; also, 38a, 39a, 54b, 66b.

20. *Igeret Musar,* ed. A.M. Haberman (Jerusalem, 1946), esp. pp. 40–1. Unlike Efodi or Shem Tov, Alami does not present an intrinsic-substantive critique of Talmud per se but only of certain types of students and certain prevalent distortions of motive and behavior (e.g., ostentation, materialism, quest for power). The demand that leaders possess not only intellectual distinction but moral impeccability and integrity of character is recurrent; for our period, see now R. Bonfils, *Ha-Rabanut be- Italya* (Jerusalem, 1980), p. 40.

21. Published in *Otzar Neḥmad* 4 (1864), 176–214. See the most recent study by R. Bonfils, "Sefer Alilot Devarim," *Eshel Be'er Sheva* 2 (1980), 229–65, who speculates about the author's time and place, suggests the second half of the fourteenth century and surmises that the author may be the Spanish R. Joseph Tov Elem, author of *Tzafnat Pa'aneaḥ.*

22. *Naḥalat Avot* on *Pirkei Avot* (New York, 1953), pp. 45, 48, 74, 98, 131, 159, 212, 232. See also *Yeshu'ot Meshiḥo* (Konigsberg, 1865), introd., p. 5.

23. *Ma'amar al Yehudei Venetziya* (Jerusalem, 1951), pp. 139–46.

24. *Teshuvot Ḥavot Ya'ir,* nn. 123, 210. See D. Kaufmann in *JQR* 3 (1891), 292–313.

25. *Mesilat Yesharim* (Philadelphia, 1948), pp. 1–4; see below n. 83a. It is noteworthy that while in the *Mesilat Yesharim* RaMḤaL addresses himself to the need to study principles of piety, in his *Milḥemet Moshe,* he argues for the superiority of Kabbalah as a discipline, in intellectual-theoretical terms.

26. *Mirkevet ha-Mishne* (Frankfurt, 1751), introduction (p. 6).

27. E.g. Aaron Gumperz, *Ma'amar ha-Mada;* N. H. Wessely, *Divrei Shalom ve-Emet;* I. B. Levinson, *Te'uda be-Yisrael;* I. Reggio, *Ha-Tora ve-ha-Filosofiya.* The *Ḥeshek Shlomo* of Solomon Maimon contains a very interesting passage where the three-fold typology of Talmudists, philosophers and kabbalists is reproduced. I thank Dr. Moshe Idel, who is preparing a study of Maimon's work, for sending me a copy of this passage. See, also, S. Dresner, *The Zaddik* (New York, 1960) ch. V; M. Wilensky, *Ḥasidim u-Mitnagdim* (Jerusalem, 1970), v.

I, pp. 18, 66, 224; J. Weiss, "Talmud Tora . . . Besht," *Tiferet Yisrael* (Jubilee Volume for Israel Brodie; London, 1967), 151-69. See also the introduction of R. Israel Salanter to the journal *Ha-Tevuna* and E. Etkas, "Tevuna: Ktav Et Torani Rishon," *Kiryat Sefer* 54 (1979), 371–83.

28. This type emerges, e.g., from Ibn Kaspi's *Will,* Ibn Latif's *Sha'ar ha-Shamayim,* Duran's *Ma'ase Efod,* R. Menaḥem b. Zeraḥ's *Tzeda la-Derekh,* S. Alami's *Igeret Musar,* and others (see below, n. 107). See the important passage in J. Albo, *Ikarim,* III, ch. 28 (p. 262), and R. Meir ibn Gabbai, *Avodat ha-Kodesh* (Jerusalem, 1973), p. 86. For what follows, see I. Twersky, "The Shulḥan 'Aruk," *Judaism* 16 (1967), pp. 141–59, esp. p. 155. Note the parenthetic, but important, observation of D. Tamar, "Dmuto ha-Ruḥanit shel R. Israel Isserlein," *Meḥkarim* (Jerusalem, 1970), p. 55, that practically all the great Ashkenazi Talmudists of the 15th century—e.g., R. Shalom of Neustadt, R. Jacob of Igra, R. Nathan of Igra, MaHaRIL, R. Yom Tov Lipman Mulhausen, R. Avigdor Kara, R. Menaḥem Tziyoni, R. Naftali Treves, R. Jacob Bruna, R. Isaac Kolon, and R. Meir Mintz were engaged in the study of Kabbalah and, in some cases, of philosophy as well. E. Kupfer has greatly illumined the spiritual-cultural character of the period in "Li-Dmutah ha-Tarbutit shel Yahadut Ashkenaz . . .," *Tarbitz* 42 (1972), 113–147. M. Nehorai, in his unpublished dissertation (Jerusalem, 1978) has made available the *More Nevukhim* commentary of the Ashkenazi scholar R. Solomon ben Judah ha-Nasi. Concerning Shem Tov b. Gaon's insistence that a kabbalist must be a good Talmudist, see D. S. Lowinger, *Sfunot* 7 (1962), p. 23 (from *Sefer Badei ha-Aron*). See also the unpublished dissertation (Jerusalem, 1968) of Dr. I Dinari on "Ḥakhmei ha-Halakha be-Ashkenaz."

29. E.g., R. Abraham ibn Migas, *Kevod Elokim* (reprinted Jerusalem, 1977), 119a. Of course we need to study those de facto monolithic Talmudists who did not leave us any non-Talmudic works. For example, how should we characterize R. Solomon b. Joseph Sirillo, the great sixteenth-century commentator on the Palestinian Talmud (*Zera'im* and *Shkalim*)?

30. R. Menaḥem ben Zeraḥ, *Tzeda la-Derekh,* p. 8.

31. E.g., R. Abraham ibn Ezra, *Yesod Mora,* p. 12; R. Joseph b. Isaac ha-Levi, *Givat ha-More* (Prague, 1612).

32. *Ḥavot Ya'ir,* n. 210; see earlier the statement of R. Abba Mari, *Minḥat Kena'ot* (Pressburg, 1838), ch. 3, p. 6; אבל בזמננו זה שאנו מצפים לישועה, די לנו...כשנזכה להשיג האסור והמותר, הכשר והפסול הטמא והטהור... ודי לנו להתעסק בחבורו של רבנו הקדוש. Note also R. Isaac ben Sheshet, *Teshuvot,* n. 157; also nn. 25, 45, 394, 438–9, 447. See also R. Ezekiel Landau, *Noda bi-Yehuda, Oraḥ Ḥayyim,* n. 109; *Yore De'a,* n. 96. R. Solomon Ḥelma refers to *Ḥavot Ya'ir,* n. 210, in his introduction to *Mirkevet ha-Mishne.*

33. See, e.g., R. Asher ben Yeḥiel, *Teshuvot,* n. 55; Isaac Albalag, *Sefer Tikun ha-De'ot,* p. 2.

34. See general bibliography. The following books are especially relevant: S. W. Baron, *A Social and Religious History of the Jews,* vol. XVI (Poland-Lithuania, 1500–1650; New York, 1976), I. Barzilai, *Between Reason and Faith* (The Hague, 1967) and the review by J. Sermonetta, *Kiryat Sefer* 45 (1970), 539–46; H. H. Ben-Sasson, *Hagut ve-Hanhaga* (Jerusalem, 1959); R. Bonfils, *Ha-Rabanut be-Italya bi-Tekufat ha-Renesans* (Jerusalem, 1980); J. Elbaum, "Zeramim u-Megamot be-Sifrut ha-Maḥashava ve-ha-Musar be-Ashkenaz u-ve-Polin ba-Me'a ha-16" (Ph.D. dissertation, Hebrew University, 1977); M. A. Shulvas, *The Jews in the World of the Renaissance* (Leiden, 1973); *Sfunot* 11–13 (=*Sefer Yavan*) (Jerusalem, 1971–78). S. Asaf, *Mekorot le-Toldot ha-Ḥinukh,* 3 vols. (Tel Aviv, 1925–36) remains valuable.

35. Indeed, Yavetz identified an entire school of past "villains"; in addition to Kaspi, he mentions Narboni and Albalag. Furthermore, he identifies the ideological school to which he belongs and names some of his esteemed predecessors: Crescas, Ha-Levi, Rabenu Yona and Abravanel. We may add that there is also a literary school of commentators on *Avot* from whose members—e.g. Ibn Shoshan, Yosef Ḥayyun—he derived many insights. Consequently, in studying Yavetz and other sixteenth-century commentators, we need to be attentive to the selection of arguments and themes from earlier literature as well as their deployment in new contexts—for very often, therein lies the novelty. For Yavetz'

influence see G. Nigal, "Hashpa'ato ha-Sifrutit shel R. Yosef Yavetz," *Kiryat Sefer* 51 (1976), 289–99. R. Yeḥiel of Pisa's answer to Ha-Penini is treated below. Note also, on the other side of the fence, the small 16th-century poem in defense of philosophy against RaSHBa' published by H. Hirschfeld, *JQR* 12 (1899–90), 138–42.

36. *Kevod Elokim,* p. 119a.

37. *Elima Rabati,* ch. II, p.18.

38. *Giv'at ha-More* (Prague, 1611); Abraham Bibago, *Derekh Emuna*, 43a, 94a, also turns his criticism to "anshei zmanenu." This is also the strategem of the MaHaRaL who condemns the neglect of Mishna study and adds והן הן מעשה הדור הזה; see S. Asaf, *Mekorot* I, p. 46. Actually, Mishna had not been a subject of study for a long time and he was in truth condemning a centuries-old practice. R. Isaiah Horowitz, *Shnei Luḥot ha-Brit, Masekhet Shevu'ot;* MaHaRaL, *Tiferet Yisrael,* ch. LVI; *Derush le-Shabat ha-Gadol;* Elijah de Vidas, *Reshit Ḥokhma, Sha'ar ha-Kedusha,* ch. II.

On the neglect of Mishna, see most recently, J. Zussman in *Proceedings of the Sixth World Congress of Jewish Studies*, p. 226.

39. Note, e.g., the views cited by R. Menaḥem b. Zeraḥ and R. Joseph Albo, n. 20 above. See also appendix, below.

40. *Avodat ha-Kodesh* (Jerusalem, 1973), ch. XXIII (p. 86).

41. See below, n. 100.

42. For Kaspi, see n. 16 above; for Lemlein, see E. Kupfer, *Kovetz al Yad* 8 (18) (1975), 402–05, 416. He also (p. 404) focuses attention on "ḥakhmei elu ha-dorot."

43. See their statements cited in I. Twersky, "Joseph ibn Kaspi," p. 257.

44. See S. Asaf, *Mekorot,* I, pp. 99ff., especially p. 101.

45. *Kevod Elokim,* 119a.

46. See most recently, Dov Rappel, *Ha-Vikuaḥ al ha-Pilpul* (Tel Aviv, 1979); also R. Bonfils, *Ha-Rabanut,* pp. 40, 167.

47. See S. P. Rabinowitz, *Ikvot shel Ḥofesh De'ot ba-Rabanut shel Polin* (Jerusalem, 1959). The texts are readily available in H. Beinart and H. Ben-Sasson, eds., *Mekorot le-Toldot ha-Yehudim bi-Ymei ha-Beinayim* (Jerusalem, 1958). Also, *Beit Yisrael be-Polin,* vol. II, pp. 239–41. Note A. P. Kleinberger, *Ha-Maḥshava ha-Pedagogit shel ha-MaHaRaL mi-Prag* (Jerusalem, 1962), p. 112.

48. C. Geertz, *The Interpretation of Cultures* (New York, 1973), p. 30.

49. Cf. now D. Ruderman, *The World of a Renaissance Jew* (Cincinnati, 1981), p. 18.

50. *Kevod Elokim* (Jerusalem, 1977), passim. See the introductory essay by H. H. Ben-Sasson. For ibn Migas' comment on R. Isaac Campanton, see *Sfunot* 7 (1962), 83.

51. *Pirkei Moshe (Masekhet Avot)* (Jerusalem, 1970), passim.

52. See now M. Idel, "Seder ha-Limud shel R. Yoḥanan Alemanno," *Tarbitz* 48 (1979), 303–331.

53. See S. Heller-Wilensky, *R. Yitzḥak Arama u-Mishnato* (Jerusalem, 1956).

54. See H. Davidson, *The Philosophy of Abraham Shalom* (Berkeley, 1964).

55. *Tola'at Ya'akov* (Warsaw, 1876), p. 94 (epilogue) and *Avodat ha-Kodesh,* passim, esp., e.g., pp. 86, 109.

56. *Livyat Ḥen* (Jerusalem, 1967), introduction, p. 2.

57. *Novelot Ḥokhma,* introduction; *Mikhtav Aḥuz* (in A. Geiger, *Melo Ḥofnayim* [Berlin, 1840]) is very instructive. Also, his ancestor Elijah Del Medigo, *Beḥinat ha-Dat* (Vienna, 1833). See I. Barzilay, *Yoseph Shlomo Delmedigo* (Leiden, 1974). Prof. Jacob Ross is preparing a new edition of *Beḥinat ha-Dat* (Tel Aviv University Press) which enlarges the text by about one-third, particularly with material on anti-Christian polemics.

58. *Ma'ase ha-Shem* II (Jerusalem, 1972), pp. 75b–76b.

59. See G. Scholem, "Yedi'ot Ḥadashot al R. Yosef Ashkenazi," *Tarbitz* 28 (1958), 59–90, 201–35; I. Twersky, "R. Yosef Ashkenazi ve-Sefer Mishne Tora," *Salo Baron Jubilee Volume* (Jerusalem, 1975), pp. 183–94.

60. *Teshuvot,* nn. 6–7; *Torat ha-Ola,* introduction; *Yore De'a,* 246. See A. Ziv, *Ha-RaMa'* (New York, 1972) and the forthcoming study of *Torat ha-Ola* by Dr. Jonah Ben-Sasson to be published by the Israeli Academy of Arts.

61. See above, n. 60; also *Teshuvot ha-MaHarSHaL,* nos. 64, 73 and 98.

62. See his *Ḥesed le-Avraham* (introduction to Maimonides' *Eight Chapters*) and above, n. 47. J. Elbaum is analyzing the *Ḥesed le-Avraham* in an article to appear in the festschrift for Professor I. Tishby.

63. See, e.g., the selections in Asaf, *Mekorot,* I, pp. 46ff.; also *Tiferet Israel,* Ch. 18; *Netzaḥ Yisrael,* ch. 30; *Gevurot ha-Shem,* chs. 34, 36; *Netivot Olam, netiv* 9 (antithesis of Abraham ibn Migas). My son Mayer called my attention to the classic statement about the hazards of intellectualization in the MaHaRaL's introduction to *Tiferet Yisrael:* the love of learning may eclipse the love of God, the religious experience may be obscured by the scholastic achievement. Cf. the beautiful study of monastic culture by Jean Leclerq, *The Love of Learning and the Desire for God* (New York, 1961).

64. *Sefer ha-Ḥayyim; Etz Ḥayyim;* also *Vikuaḥ Mayyim Ḥayyim.* For bibliography, see B. Sherwin, "In the Shadow of Greatness: R. Hayyim ben Betzalel of Friedburg," *JSS* 37 (1975), 35–60.

65. *Levush Malkhut.* See the contribution of L. Kaplan to this volume and references to his unpublished dissertation on R. Mordekhai Jaffe.

66. *Neḥmad ve-Na'im* (Dessnitz, 1743); *Tzemaḥ David.* See M. Breuer, cited below, n. 87. Also, A. Neher, "Ḥomer Ḥadash al D. Ganz," *Tarbitz* 45 (1976), 138–47.

67. *Olelot Efraim* (Tel Aviv, 1964). See J. Elbaum's dissertation, pp. 132–34.

68. *Giv'at ha-More* (Prague, 1611).

69. *Etz Ḥayyim,* introduction.

70. *Or Ne'erav* (Tel Aviv, 1965).

71. *Reshit Ḥokhma* (Tel Aviv, n.d.), introduction (pp. 2a–5b) and *Perek ha-Mitzvot,* pp. 239bff. Dr. Mordecai Pechter's study will appear in volume two of *Harvard Studies in Medieval Jewish History and Literature.*

72. *Ayelet Ahavim* (Venice, 1552), 43b. Dr. Beracha Sack's doctoral dissertation at Brandeis University deals with the mystical teachings of R. Solomon Alkabetz.

73. See R. J. Z. Werblowsky, *R. Joseph Karo* (Philadelphia, 1977).

74. See G. Sermonetta, "Ha-Sifrut ha-Pilosofit ha-Skolastit be-*Sefer Porat Yosef* le-R. Yosef Taitatzak," *Sfunot* 11 (1971–78), 135–187.

75. *Minḥat Kena'ot,* ed. D. Kaufmann (Berlin, 1898).

76. *Teshuvot Matanot ba-Adam,* n. 39 (quoting R. Elijah Gennazano); see I. Sonne, *Mi-Paulus ha-Revi'i ad Pius ha-Ḥamishi* (Jerusalem, 1954), pp. 122–6, for a list of the authors who endorse this position about the superiority of Kabbalah and its scholarly-juridical consequences concerning the reliance upon a simple code; R. Bonfils, *Ha-Rabanut,* p. 169.

77. R. Bonfils, "Torat ha-Nefesh . . . be-Mishnat R. Ovadya Sforno," *Eshel Be'er Sheva* 1 (1976), pp. 200–256.

78. *Me'or Enayim,* ed. D. Cassel (Vilna, 1866). Prof. Betzalel Safran is preparing a new study of Azariah de Rossi, a greatly expanded version of his dissertation.

79. *Gidulei Truma* (on *Sefer ha-Trumot*), introduction; *Bina la-Ittim.* See I. Bettan, *Studies in Jewish Preaching* (Cincinnati, 1939).

80. *Shiltei Giborim* (Mantua, 1622).

81. *Or ha-Ḥayyim,* pp. 7–8 and passim, *Perush Avot,* III:13 and passim. See the references collected in G. Nigal, "De'otav shel R. Joseph Yavetz," *Eshel Be'er Sheva* (1976), 258–87.

82. *Perush Avot* (Jerusalem, 1969), p. 97, and see now David Ruderman's book on Farissol (above, n. 49).

83. *Ari Nohem* (Jerusalem, 1929). This list is by no means exhaustive. Important material may also be culled from the writings of R. Jacob ibn Naḥmias, R. David Messer Leon, R. David ibn abi Zimra (RaDBaZ), R. Eleazar Azikri, R. Levi ibn Ḥabib, R. Samuel Eidels (MaHaRSHa), R. Yom Tov Lipman Heller, R. Moses Alsheikh, R. Elijah Mizraḥi, R. Judah Moscato; R. Issac Luria and his disciples obviously require intensive investigation as does R. Isaiah Horowitz (*Shnei Luḥot ha-Brit*). See meanwhile Eugene Newman, *Life and Teachings of Isaiah Horowitz* (London, 1972). David Provençal (see S. Asaf, *Mekorot,* vol. II, pp. 116–119), in announcing his proposal to establish a Jewish University, also illumines the types with which we are concerned. For David Messer Leon, see the unpublished doctoral dissertation of H. T. Rothschild, "Mishnato ha-Filosofit shel R. David Messer Leon" (Jerusalem, 1978) and her article in *Meḥkerei Yerushalayim be-Maḥshevet Yisrael* 2 (1982), pp. 94–117.

83a. A classic formulation was provided by R. Moses Ḥayyim Luzzatto, *Mesilat Yesharim* (where "saintliness" and "spiritual perfection" are to be taken as interchangeable): "If you will observe the present state of affairs, you will note that most of those who possess quick mental grasp and keen intellect, concentrate all their study and thought upon the subtleties of the sciences, each according to the bent of his mind and natural taste. Some devote themselves to the physical sciences; others turn all their thoughts to astronomy and mathematics; others, again, to the arts. Finally, there are those who penetrate into the innermost sanctuary of knowledge, which is the study of the holy Torah. Of these latter, some pursue the study of dialectics, some study Midrash, and others study the Codes. There are but few who study the nature of the love and the fear of God, or communion, or any other phase of saintliness."

84. See D. Ruderman, *The World of a Renaissance Jew,* p. 43. After the burning of the Talmud in Italy, the opposition to Kabbalah was fueled to some extent by the apprehension that it might play into the hands of the Christians. On the other hand, the loss of the Talmud spurred the publication of the classical texts of Kabbalah (e.g., Zohar, *Ma'arekhet Elokut, Sha'arei Ora*). See J. Elbaum, "Zeramim," pp. 515–519, and the references to the articles of D. Tamar, I. Tishby, M. Benayahu, and E. Kupfer. See I. Sonne, *Mi-Paulus,* p. 128. There was, of course, an independent, self-propelling interest in Kabbalah.

84a. See M. Pechter, "Ḥayyav ve-Ishiyuto shel R. Eleazar Azikri bi-Re'i Yomano ha-Misti ve-Sefer Ḥaredim," *Shalem* 3 (1981), pp. 127–47; note also I. Sonne, *Mi-Paulus,* pp. 124, 133.

85. See I. Twersky, "Aspects of Social and Cultural History of Provençal Jewry," *Journal of World History* 11 (1968), 190, 204–05. The outer-directed apologetic motif—the need to maintain an intellectually impressive profile in the eyes of others—surfaces also in the context of the Posen debate concerning Talmud study. Whereas it was originally introduced as a justification for *ta'amei mitzvot,* it is here extended to cover all Halakhah and Aggadah *(svarot ha-Talmud u-drashotav);* see the text cited in n. 47 above and n. 105 below. The upshot is clear: centrality of Talmud study does not result automatically in its exclusivity, for it needs the cognate insights and methodology of universal disciplines to make it attractive and intelligible.

86. See I. Twersky, "Joseph ibn Kaspi," p. 256, n. 52, for a partial history of interpretation; note especially the references found there to authors of this period—R. Moses Alashkar, R. Elijah Mizraḥi, R. Moses Isserles, R. David Ganz, R. Joseph Ashkenazi. See S. Rosenberg, "Parshanut ha-Tora be-*More Nevukhim,*" *Meḥkerei Yerushalayim be-Maḥshevet Yisrael* 1 (1981), p. 146, n. 98.

87. See S. Asaf, *Mekorot,* I, pp. 43–44. Asher Lemlein (see above n. 42) had noted, in his virulently polemical way, that Jews turned to the two disciplines of philosophy and grammar for apologetic reasons. R. Isaac b. Samuel Ha-Levi, older brother of David ha-Levi (the TaZ—*Turei Zahav*) also complains about the neglect of the study of grammar in his little work *Siaḥ Yitzḥak* (Basl, 1627), which was printed with an approbatory letter from R. Yom Tov Lipman Heller. R. Immanuel Benevento, author of *Livyat Ḥen* (a grammar book which, in its introduction, extols the supremacy of Kabbalah) also records contemporary ridicule of grammar as a field of study (introd., *Sha'ar* I, ch. 2 [p. 3a]). Abraham Lonzano, author of *Kinyan Avraham* (1723), disputed the ability of Talmudists to study Torah without knowledge of Hebrew. The argument of David Ganz in behalf of the study of history is analogous—i.e., the nations of the world are engaged in it. See generally, M. Breuer, "Kavim li-Demuto shel R. David Ganz," *Shnaton Bar Ilan* 11 (1973), 97–118.

David Provençal relies on the same motive in pressing his case for the establishment of a Jewish university. לָמָה נגרע מכל האומות אשר יש להם אוהל מועד בשבת תחכמוני ומקום מוכן ללמוד החכמות והנמוסים.

88. *Or Amim,* introduction, p. 3.

89. H. Davidson notes correctly, in his brief introduction to the 1971 reprint of Almosnino's *Tefila le-Moshe,* how significant is the fact that large amounts of medieval philosophy could be integrated into popular works (homilies and commentaries) and presented to the general public. Presumably an author wants to be read and to be understood.

General historians of the sixteenth century have revised the conventional view concerning the nearly total eclipse of Aristotle in this period. For a good example from the beginning of the century (in the writings of Jacques Lefèvre d'Etaples), see Eugene F. Rice Jr., *The Prefatory Epistles of Jacques Lefèvre* (New York, 1972), pp. xv ff. Rice comments: "Lefèvre's enthusiasm for Aristotle reminds us how misguided is the facile distinction between an Aristotelian Middle Ages and a Platonic Renaissance . . . . A count of editions of Aristotle's works published between the beginning of printing and 1600 would run to many thousands; ample evidence that Lefèvre's esteem for the philosopher was not eccentric." See now Breuer's review of Bonfils' *Ha-Rabanut, Kiryat Sefer* 55 (1980), p. 367. On lingering rationalism in eastern Europe, see also H. H. Ben-Sasson, *Trial and Achievement: Currents in Jewish History* (Jerusalem, 1974). Also, J. Elbaum in *Sinai* 76 (1975), p. 287. Elijah Gennazano complains that kabbalists were a minority and philosophy was still in the ascendancy.

90. Modena, *Ari Nohem*, pp. 52–53. Note also R. Hendel Manoaḥ, author of a commentary on the *Ḥovot ha-Levavot*, where he mentions his commentaries on such recently published works as the *Ma'arekhet Elokut, Sha'arei Ora* as well as the recently composed *Pardes Rimonim*. The inclusion or intrusion of Kabbalah in Halakhah is, as noted (above n. 1), a separate issue treated by M. Benayahu and J. Katz, even though in this context one may choose to view it also as a form of harmonization.

91. See my "Religion and Law," p. 74.

92. *Minḥat Kena'ot*, p. 72. Note his *Ḥayyei Olam*, ed. S. Rosenthal (New York, 1962), p. 7, where he lodges a double complaint about (a) religious laxity and perfunctoriness (*mitzvat anashim melumada*); (b) the lack of Talmud study (*be-havayot de-Abayei ve-Rava lo higi'a yadam*). The *Ḥayyei Olam* is thus of interest not only for economic history—the theory and practice of banking and moneylending—but for rabbinic literature as well. See also the material edited by Rosenthal in *Kovetz al Yad* 8 (1976). For R. Yoḥanan Treves, the addressee of the *Minḥat Kena'ot*, see A. Marx, *Kovetz Mada' i le-Zekher M. Shor* (New York, 1945), pp. 189 ff. The excellent monograph of R. Bonfils, which appeared after my paper had been written, contains a perceptive analysis of R. Yeḥiel; see *Ha-Rabanut*, ch. VI (pp. 173ff.). See also J. Hacker, "Kevutzat Igrot," *Prakim be-Toldot ha-Ḥevra ha-Yehudit* (Jerusalem, 1980), 69, and J. Nadav, *Tarbitz* 26 (1957), 440–52.

93. *Minḥat Kena'ot*, pp. 2, 5, 7, 10–12, 88 (on Talmud), 109. In light of n. 89 above, R. Yeḥiel's reference (p. 11) to contemporary philosophic controversy concerning human freedom is significant. It was, of course, a prominent theme of the philosophic literature of the period.

94. See I. Twersky, *Introduction to the Code of Maimonides*, p. 104, n. 15.

95. Twersky, op. cit., pp. 97ff., esp. p. 99; also p. 72, n. 129. The Maimonidean position is reflected in Modena, *Ari Nohem*, p. 50.

96. For the cultural repercussions of the burning of the Talmud, see now J. Elbaum, "Zeramim," pp. 515ff. Reuben Bonfils, *Ha-Rabanut*, pp. 22–3, 180–82, submits that Talmud study was not diminished after the burning. E. Gennazano (*Igeret*, p. 6) endorses the reliance on codes.

97. See nn. 47 and 85 above. See the recent discussion of M. Breuer, "Min'u Beneikhem min ha-Higayon," *Sefer Zikhron Ha-Rav D. Oks* (Ramat Gan, 1978), 242–62, and the supplement by M. Idel in *AJS Review* 5 (1980), 15–20. There is an additional passage, not noted by either author, in the *Moznei Iyun* of R. Joseph ben Shem Tov, which Saul Regev is preparing for publication. Concerning the responsum of R. Asher ben Yeḥiel, see J. L. Teicher, "Laws of Reason and Laws of Religion: A Conflict in Toledo Jewry in the Fourteenth Century," *Essays and Studies Presented to S. A. Cook*, ed. D. W. Thomas (London, 1950), 83–94. The responsum is also cited by Leone da Modena, as D. Kaufmann noted in *Minḥat Kena'ot*, p. 88, n. 4.

98. Yavetz, *Perush Avot*, p. 77 (on *Avot* III:21): והטעם כי אנו בעלי חומר עיקר שלמותנו במעשה. See also his *Or ha-Ḥayyim*, p. 61, where he polemicizes with those who ignore *mitzvot* because they contend that their link to God is intellectual and by apprehension of intelligibles they resemble angels; consequently, "corporeal commandments are superfluous." MaHaRaL, *Netivot Olam*, *Netiv ha-Tora*, ch. I, p. 4b: כי המצוה שהיא על ידי מעשה האדם שנעשה על ידי גופו הגשמי היא קרובה יותר אל האדם הגשמי. E. de Vidas, *Reshit Ḥokhma*,

introduction, p. 3ff.: His whole book, he asserts (p. 4b), revolves around the superiority of action. See also, Abravanel, *Naḥalat Avot*, p. 84: המעשה עיקר ולא התלמוד בשלמות האדם השגת אושר הצלחת הנפש בקיום משפטיו. ; A. Figo, *Gidulei Teruma*, introduction: בשגם הוא בשר!

99. See P. Kleinberger, *MaHaRaL*, p. 112.

100. *Or Ne'erav* (Jerusalem, 1965), pp. 5a, 12a, 23b; *Elima Rabati*, p. 18; Alkabetz, *Ayelet Ahavim*, p. 43b. See S. Shalem, *R. Moses Alsheikh*, ed. M. Benayahu (Jerusalem, 1966), p. 73 (יש אומר די בתלמוד הפשטי). The attack on "ḥakhemi ha-pshat" continues; see M. Benayahu, "R. Abraham ibn Mussah," *Michael* 5 (1978), appendix 15 (pp. 116–121). Note inter alia, p. 117: כי אין בן דוד בא אלא בעסקי חכמת האמת, and the quotation (p. 118) from the printer's introduction to *Zohar Ḥadash* (Amsterdam, 1702). This is the thrust of the *Sefer ha-Kana* and *Sefer ha-Plia*; see now the systematic study of M. Oron, "*Ha-Pelia ve-ha-Kana*, Yesodot ha-Kabala she-Bahem. . . ," (Ph.D. dissertation, Hebrew University, 1980). There are some very relevant and revealing passages in the fragments of *Galya Raza* just published by R. Elior, "Ha-Ma'avak al Ma'amadah shel Ha-Kabala," *Meḥkere Yerushalayim be-Maḥshevet Yisrael*, 1 (1981), 177–90, esp. 186–87 (ואינם עוסקים אלא בפשטים) See also A. Sar Shalom Basilea, *Emunat Ḥakhamim*, introduction, p. 3b: והוא שם בלתי ידוע לבעלי הפשט, כי אינם מכירים רק העשרה שמות. The purpose of *Shomer Emunim* by Joseph Ergas is to convince the reader to believe that the Torah is not limited to its *pshat*, and has an esoteric as well as exoteric meaning.

101. A. Bibago, *Derekh Emuna*, *sha'ar* III, esp. p. 45b. Bibago, whose work was read in the following generations, is quoted by R. Levi ibn Ḥabib in the *Ein Yaakov*, *Berakhot*, end ויהיו בעיניו כל הלומדים בספרי המשנה והתלמוד ככל המון ישראל ההולכים לתומם ומידיעת סתרי תורה קצתם נעדרים. The parallelism between the philosophic and kabbalistic attitudes is noteworthy. For Bibago, see J. Hacker, "Mekomo shel R. Avraham Bibago ba-Maḥloket al Limud ha-Pilosofiya," *Proceedings of Fifth World Congress for Jewish Studies*, v. III (1972), 151–58.

102. For Lemlein, see above, n. 42; for the eschatological argument, see I. Sonne, *Mi-Paulus*, p. 133: ריבוי הספרים מעכבים את הקץ; and above n. 100. Study of Mishna, which also benefited from eschatological associations, was high on the list. See D. Tamar, *Meḥkarim be-Toldot ha-Yehudim* (Jerusalem, 1970), pp. 96–97, who notes that in the Safed conventicles (*ḥavurot*) Mishna was emphasized more than Kabbalah, even though Kabbalah must have had superiority.

103. "Will" of R. S. Horowitz, in I. Abrahams, *Hebrew Ethical Wills* (Philadelphia, 1948), vol. II, p. 256: אחר שתמלאו כריסכם בתלמוד ובפוסקים הנני מצווכם שתלמדו חכמת הקבלה, כי אין אדם ירא שמים מי שאינו לומד חכמה זו.

104. This is the position described in *Ḥavot Yair*, n. 210, which I hope to analyze in a separate article; see above n. 32.

105. See above n. 85. Note the statement of R. Abraham Horowitz in the Posen controversy: כי מה שאמר החמור שאין מותר ללמוד רק התלמוד לבד, זהו סותר באמת למה שאמר הכתוב: ושמרתם ועשיתם, כי היא חכמתכם ובינתכם לעיני העמים. אדרבא כל סברות התלמוד ודרשותיו ודרכיו הם לעג והיתול בעיני העמים אם לא נלמוד יותר מזה, כדי שנדע לבאר ג"כ סברות התלמוד והדרשות באופן שיוכשרו בעיני העמים.

106. Yavetz, *Perush Avot*, III:12 (p. 60). See appendix.
107. *Kevod Elokim*, 119a. See appendix.

Appendix: Selected Texts

1. R. Menaḥem ben Zeraḥ, *Tzeda la-Derekh*, p. 8.

כי שמעתי דבת רבים מהמתפלספים אומרים למתלונן בצל ש-די ולשוקד על דלתותיו יום יום מה יתן לך ומה יוסיף לך אם חכמת במשפט דין יתום ואלמנה . . . וידעת משפט שור תם ושור מועד . . . ולא הצלת נפשך מפח הפתיות והסכלות.

2. R. Joseph Albo, *'Ikkarim*, III, ch. 28.

יהי' אם כן השתדלות רוב חכמי ישראל ועסקם בתלמוד ובדיני השאלות התלמודיות דבר בלתי מועיל להקנאת השלמות, ויהי' יגיעתם לריק חלילה.

3. Joseph ben Shem Tov, *Moznei Iyun*.

לועגים על דברי חכמים ואומרים מה לנו בידיעת דיני שור ובור ודיני נזק צרורות וד' שומרין . . . .

4. R. Abraham Farissol, *Perush Avot*, p. 97.

ושנאתי השומרים הבלי שוא המונעים בניהם מן המקרא, כי בטרם ידע הנער כמעט לקרות מקרא ופסוק, יכניסוהו לתלמוד בבלי.

מה שלא הי' יודע לפרוס על שמע, ולא לברך ברכת חתנים ולרדת לפני התיבה, לרוב עיונו בפלפול ענינים אלו התלמודיים . . . וגם מצאנו תועלת אחר מדברי החכם הלז, אשר למד אותנו דרך ה' לעלות בהר ה' דרך סדר הלמוד, להיות בתחלה מתעסק בהוי' דאביי ורבא ואח"כ יתעסק בחכמות ממדרגה למדרגה, ולא יהרסו לעלות.

5. R. Meir ibn Gabbai, *Tola'at Ya'akov*, epilogue.

דלא פסק פומי מגירסא באישון לילה ואפילה בהוויות אביי ורבא, ואמרינן בסנהדרין במחשכים הושיבני — בבלי ובמדרש העם ההולכים בחושך אלו העוסקים בתלמוד ראו אור גדול לעולם הבא.

6. R. Abraham ibn Migas, *Kevod Elokim*, p. 119a.

ולא כקצת בני עמנו בדורנו זה בפיהם יכזבו לו ויחפיאו עליו כזבים, ולבם לא נכון עמו. כי יאמינו בלא ציור מה שיאמינו. והם מאבדים עצמם לדעת המאמרים ולא יקפידו לדעת ענין הדברים . . . ואשכילך בדרך זו תלך שלא תדבר עם מי שלא עסק כל ימיו כי אם בתלמוד לבד ולא ראה מאורות מימיו.

7. R. Joseph Yavetz, *Perush Avot*, p. 60.

גם יתכן לפרש כי החכמה הנזכרת בזו המשנה אינה חכמת עשיית המצות, כי אם החכמה העליונה חכמת הקבלה, והיא ידיעת טעמי המצות, ועלי' אנו מתפללים בכל יום והאר עינינו בתורתך, כי מה חסרנו באומרנו ותן בלבנו בינה להבין להשכיל לשמוע ללמוד. שאמרנו אח"כ והאר עינינו. א"ו אנו מכוונים לחכמה המפוארה הזאת, שעלי' אמר גל עיני ואביטה נפלאות מתורתך, ולא אמר דוד כן על דיני שור מועד ושור תם, ואף לא על דיני איסור והיתר שהיו נשי ישראל בקיאות בהם, אלא על זו ההכמה שאין לה סוף . . . .

8. MaHaRaL, *Tiferet Yisrael*, ch. 10.

אנשים שואלים על למוד התורה במצותיה ובדקדוקיה ובנזק השור והבור וכיוצא בזה שהיה נראה בדעתם כי יותר יצליח כאשר ישיג בענין היסודות ובמהות הגלגלים ובשכלים

הנפרדים. לכך דעתם כי הצלחת האדם בהשגת הדברים האלו ודעתם בהשארת הנפש שנשאר השכל אשר קנה האדם בחייו וזהו שנשאר אחר המות . . . כפירה גמורה.

יותר ראוי שתהי ההצלחה על ידי התורה ממה שתהי בזולת זה ואל יחשוב כאשר קונה הידיעה בארבעה אבות נזיקין שהוא קונה הידיעה בשור ובבור . . . כי כאשר יקנה האדם הידיעה בהזיק ד' אבות נזיקין וכיוצא בו ממשפטי התורה נחשב זה שקנה הידיעה בגזרת השם ית'.

Netivot Olam, Netiv ha-Tora, p. 46

כי מי שחשב כי עקר הלימוד לאדם בחכמה שישיג בנמצאים ובגלגלים ובמלאכים ולא נתנה מדרגה זאת לתורה, לנזיקין, ולטמאה ולטהרה, דבר זה הוא מכשלה גדולה מאד.

9. R. Ḥayyim ben Betzalel, *Etz Ḥayyim*, introduction.

כל העם הזה מקצה הכו בסנורים נלאו למצא את הפת"ח, עשו זאת חוק ומשפט מן היום שלא ללמד נערי ישראל דקדוק לה"ק לפי שידעו שהורס את מצב משפט התלמוד שלהם, וכהנה דברי חרופים וגדופים רבים . . . ואשיבה את חורפי לאמר . . . הלא אין לכם מחכמה זו רק מה שגנבתם מספרי העברים הקדמונים, כמו החכם ר' אברהם בן עזרא והקמחי, וספרי ר' יודא המדקדק הראשון הגדול וספרי רב יונה והאפודי וכיוצא בהם, והם ידעו קדושת התלמוד שהוא מיוסד על אדני פז משפט דקדוק לה"ק, עד שאמרו כי הרב הקדוש איש אלהי רבנא אשי ובני ישיבתו כאשר חתמו את התלמוד בחותם הקודש חתמו עמו עוד ספר אחד על חכמת הנקוד ודקדוק לה"ק. וכל זה להודיע שמשולבות הנה אשה אל אחותה . . . רק כי בהיות שהגלות המר והארוך הזה גבר עלינו מיום אל יום נתמעטו הלבבות, שלא היה בידם יכלת ללמד את בניהם את כל החכמות, ע"כ ראו אבותינו הקדושים, ובפרט חסידי אשכנז, למשוך את בניהם אחר התלמוד בלבד ולהרגילם ולחנכם אחר הספר הקדוש הזה, כי בו חכמה ויראת ה' במקום אחד, והוא הלחם והמזון האמתי אשר בצלו נחיה בגויים, ועם כל זאת יחידי סגולה אשר בכל דור ודור שמלאו כרסם מלחם התלמוד למדו גם חכמת הלשון בכלל שאר החכמות, גם חברו ספרים על זה . . .

ואחר הימים הרבים האלה קם הדור השפל הזה, יתמי דיתמי, נשתכחה חכמה זו לגמרי, ובפרט במדינת אשכנז, ודברי הספרים האלו כחתומים ואין עמנו היודע להימי"ן או להשמא"ל, לפעו"ל פעול"ה או לבנו"ת בנין, והדבר הזה כדי בזיון וקצף נגד השרים והעמים, על כן . . . קנא קנאתי לה' צבאות ואמרתי עת לעשות ולהפר מעט זמן מלמודי ולהתבונן מפי הספרים שחברו הראשונים וגם האחרונים. גם שקדתי על דלתי הגויים המחרפים עצמם . . . והנני קמתי לפתוח ג' שערים ולהיות מקצר ועולה ולכתוב רק כלל החכמה הזו בדרך משא ומתן ובלשון שהורגלו בה נערי בני ישראל, כי לא טוב היות האדם ערירי מחכמה זו מפני לעג האומות.

10. R. Joseph ben Isaac ha-Levi, *Giv'at ha-More*.

הכת הג' הם התלמודי', כלומר אותם אשר שמו כל מגמתם לעסוק בתלמוד ובמה שיתיחס אליו והם אפשר שיודו שלמות זה הספר מצד החמר והצורה, אבל לא ירצוהו לחשבם שא"א אדם שיגיע לשלמותו הנצחי במה שהוא זולת התלמוד ואשר גדלו עליו מנעוריהם וכן הם רוב אנשי דורנו זה לא יביטו לחכמת המורה כי ידמה להם שהעסק בו הוא ללא תועלת. וקצתם יאמרו כי מלבד שהחכמה החיצונית בלתי נותנת שום שלימות אל העוסק בה עוד היא סבה להעדר השלמות המגיע מעסק התורה.

Messianic Impulses in Joseph ha-Kohen*

YOSEF HAYIM YERUSHALMI

If Jewish historical writing in the Middle Ages was sparse and sporadic, there was even less interest in recording the histories of other peoples. The writing by Jews of non-Jewish history should therefore be considered a genuine novelty within the innovative context of sixteenth-century Jewish historiography as a whole.[1] Significantly, Abraham Zacuto finds it necessary to offer profuse apologies even for his rather skimpy and haphazard excursus into gentile chronology, and toward the end of the century David Gans feels constrained to do the same for his more elaborate undertaking.[2] In between, Elijah Capsali's Venetian chronicle finds its intrinsic rationale in the fact that much of it is devoted to Jewish matters anyway (as is his chronicle of the Ottoman Turks), and that the whole of it was ostensibly written in praise of God for Capsali's own deliverance when he was in Padua during the Italian wars.[3] Moses Almosnino's Judaeo-Spanish *Extemos y grandezas de Constantinopla*, which contains a sketch of the reign of Suleiman the Magnificent, is essentially travel literature, written in 1567 while the author was on a mission from the Jewish community of Salonika to the Turkish capital.[4] The last part of Gedaliah ibn Yaḥya's *Shalshelet ha-Kabala* is merely meant to complement the chain of rabbinic tradition which forms the core of the work, by presenting a mélange of gentile history, especially of gentile savants, along with persecutions of the Jews, all loosely synchronized with the Jewish literary personalities of each age.[5]

Only one Jewish historical work of the sixteenth century proclaims by its very title that its primary focus is the history of gentile

*In the preparation of this paper I am indebted to Dr. Menahem Schmeltzer, Librarian of the Jewish Theological Seminary of America, for providing me with a photostat of the *editio princeps* of Joseph ha-Kohen's *Divrey ha-Yamim*, and to Prof. Benjamin Braude of Boston College for some helpful bibliographical references concerning the Ottoman Turks in the sixteenth century.

nations, treats its non-Jewish materials consistently and amply, and offers no apology whatever: Joseph ha-Kohen's *Divrey ha-Yamim le-Malkhey Zarefat u-Malkhey Beyt Ottoman ha-Togar.*[6] If for no other reason, it invites our special attention.

Hitherto, however, Joseph ha-Kohen has not received the close and comprehensive study he merits. Much of what he wrote is still in manuscript.[7] The letters described by Loeb in 1888 were never published.[8] We still lack satisfactory critical editions of both *Divrey ha-Yamim*[9] and *Emek ha-Bakha*.[10] The former work has been neglected in favor of its more frequently cited successor, and its sources have not even begun to be elucidated. Above all, as is so often the case with other Hebrew chronicles, those of Joseph ha-Kohen have been utilized largely as repositories of historical facts. There has been no sustained effort to view his work in imminent terms, within its own organic context, nor to try to elicit his motives, methods and attitudes. What I shall set forth here represents a tentative probe in that direction, and this paper prepared under the benign pressure of a conference deadline, should be considered as no more than an interim report of work in progress. It is concerned exclusively with *Divrey ha-Yamim*, a work as problematic as it is intriguing.

1. Question Marks and Ambiguities

Joseph ha-Kohen's *History of the Kings of France and of the Ottoman Turkish Sultans* is, on the face of it, a *sefer milḥamot*, presumably of the type whose reading Joseph Karo was soon to declare forbidden on the Sabbath, while Moses Isserles would permit it because the work was written in the holy tongue.[11] Its theme is almost exclusively conflict and war among nations. Yet the book is presented to the reader with no hesitation or attempt at self-justification. Instead of the kind of introduction we would expect in light of what we have from other sixteenth-century Jewish historians, one which would defend a concern with the history of other nations or the use of non-Jewish historical sources, we have only a short one-page preamble which is worth pondering on other grounds.[12] It divides itself easily into two parts. In the first, paraphrasing the Song of Deborah, Joseph ha-Kohen announces himself loudly as the first Jewish historian since Josephus:

All the gate of my people knows that no author has arisen in Israel like

Yosippon the priest,[13] who recorded the wars of the land of Judea and Jerusalem. The writers of chronicles ceased, they ceased, until I, Joseph, did arise, I arose a writer of chronicles in Israel!

The second part speaks of the work itself:

So I set my heart to write, as a memorial in a book, most of the misfortunes that have befallen us in the lands of the gentiles, from the day that Judah was exiled from its land unto this very day, and the wars of the kings of the nations that were fought in the land of Judea and in Jerusalem, and the expulsion from France and Spain, so that the Children of Israel may know. And I gleaned among the sheaves after the reapers, whatever my hand could find, a bit here and there. Therefore I bestirred myself [14] to write a history of the kings of France and of the Ottoman dynasty, and to record their times in a book, [and] the way in which the Egyptians have afflicted us and our forefathers, so that it should not fail from among the Jews, nor the memorial of them pass from their seed, until the lame shall leap like a hart and the tongue of the dumb shall sing: Sing unto the Lord, for He hath done gloriously, this is made known in all the earth.

A close reading of these lines should arch the brow of anyone familiar with the book that follows. "Most of the misfortunes" (*rov ha-tla'ot*) that have befallen the Jewish people since going into exile do not find their way into the book, certainly not when we compare it with Ibn Verga's *Shevet Yehuda*, Usque's *Consolaçam as tribulaçoens de Israel*, or even Joseph ha-Kohen's own *Emek ha-Bakha*. Except for the ample space devoted to persecutions during the Crusades, Jewish sufferings are dealt with briefly and interspersed only occasionally into the main flow of the narrative, which concerns gentile rather than Jewish history.

"The wars of the kings of the nations that were fought in the land of Judea and in Jerusalem" are indeed dealt with, and in considerable detail, especially in the Crusade sections. By contrast, one is more than mildly astonished to discover that "the expulsions from France and Spain" are given such meager coverage in the book. We shall return to this point shortly.

"*Therefore* I bestirred myself to write a history of the kings of France and of the Ottoman dynasty" seems, at the point in which it comes, a *non-sequitur*. The decision to concentrate specifically on France and Turkey is not really explained by the preceding lines, and the matter is only obfuscated further by the renewed reference to Jewish sufferings ("the evil which the 'Egyptians' have done unto us and our forefathers").

What, then, was the motive for writing such a book? "So that the Children of Israel may know" is too obvious and, at the same time, too unsatisfactory to constitute an adequate explanation. Twice in the book this phrase is amplified into the statement: "So that the Children of Israel may know that the Lord is a zealous God and avenges the blood of His servants that has been shed." [15] But while the notion of divine retribution crops up on occasion, it is not carried through consistently. A commonplace in sixteenth-century Jewish historiography (cf. Ibn Verga and Usque), it does not further our understanding of the choice of subject and structure in *Divrey ha-Yamim*.

Only at one point in the book does Joseph ha-Kohen pause to make what seems an unequivocal statement of his motives. Immediately after describing the Spanish expulsion, he writes:

> Joseph ha-Kohen declares: The expulsion from France and this expulsion roused me to compile this book, so that the Children of Israel may know what they did to us in their lands, their courts and their castles, for behold, the days approach.[16]

Here at last, then, the ground appears firm. That the catastrophe of expulsion, especially the exile from Spain, should have "roused" him to compose an historical work seems reasonable. Indeed, it has been adduced by modern scholars as the primary impetus for the rise of sixteenth-century Jewish historiography generally. Yet once more we are confronted with a significant discrepancy between professed intention and actual execution. If the French and Spanish expulsions played so crucial role in the genesis of the book, why do we find so little about them?

The fact is that in *Divrey ha-Yamim* there is no awareness of the greatest of all the French expulsions, that of 1306. All that is mentioned, and that in one paragraph, is the expulsion under Philip II Augustus in 1182 (the date is given erroneously as 1186). Later on, after noting the recall of the Jews in 1198, we hear only that "they had not been there long, when he expelled them again to another land, unto this day." [17]

Now, if Joseph ha-Kohen was faced with a paucity of information concerning the French expulsions, surely this could not have been the case with regard to the expulsion from Spain. Joseph's own parents had apparently been caught up in the tragedy. Italy was a haven for Iberian Jewish refugees who brought their tales with them, and the Jewish literature of the age was replete with accounts of what had occurred. It is therefore doubly disconcerting to find his own account of the expulsion of 1492, however passionate, to be so laconic,[18] especially in comparison to those of Ibn Verga, Capsali or Usque. Indeed, there is altogether little on Spanish history prior to the expulsion, be it Jewish or general, in *Divrey ha-Yamim*. All that Joseph chooses to mention are the assassination of Yehosef ha-Nagid and the destruction of the Jewish community of Granada, the Almohade persecution and the shift of Jewish life to Christian Spain (both accounts are based on Ibn Daud), and the troubles unleashed in the fifteenth century by Vicente Ferrer.

In short, while we may well take Joseph ha-Kohen at his word by viewing the Spanish expulsion as a catalyst in bringing him to write his history (one suspects that the French expulsion is ancillary and thrown in for good measure), it never emerges as the dominant theme of the book, which is tantamount to saying that it does not explain it. Clearly, some additional and vital factor must have been involved in forging the very conception of a "Franco-Turkish" history in the mind of a Jew living in sixteenth-century Italy, and perhaps the real clue lies not so much in the explicit mention of the French and Spanish expulsions as in the concluding phrase of the passage: *ki hine yamim ba'im*—"for behold the days approach. . . ."

However, we should not attempt to evaluate that phrase prematurely. We must first approach the central issue around which revolve the other problems we have raised. The question is: Why *France* and *Turkey*?

2. The "French" and the "Turks"

As the structure of its opening sections reveals and any reader must readily discover, *Divrey ha-Yamim* is actually far more than a history of the French and of the Ottoman Turks proper. Opening with a ritual obeissance to the biblical genealogy of the nations and a sketch of the Franks and of the Merovingian dynasty until Dagobert, Joseph ha-Kohen goes on to survey the rise of Islam, the wars between the Persians and the Byzantines, the defeat of both by the Arabs, and the Arab conquest of Palestine. (The centrality of the latter event is underscored when the author pauses to summarize the duration of Arab rule in Palestine up to the First Crusade.) The history of France is then resumed, from the death of Dagobert until Henry I in the eleventh century, followed by a paragraph on the origin of the Turks (not the Ottomans) and the Seljuk conquest of Jerusalem, and another on the Granada massacre of 1066.

At this point Joseph ha-Kohen launches into an elaborate history of the Crusades, into which he also incorporates a history of Jewish sufferings based on the old Hebrew Crusade chronicles. This history of the Crusades, from 1096 to the beginning of the thirteenth century, is the longest and most sustained single segment in the first of the two parts into which the Sabbionetta edition of *Divrey ha-Yamim* is divided.[19] It occupies no less than 68 out of its 152 folios. And yet, although the book is ostensibly a "history of the kings of France and of the Ottoman Turkish sultans," throughout all the foregoing narrative the latter have not yet even come upon the scene. It is only midway through Part I that the Ottoman Turks appear, in a short paragraph on their origins in the fourteenth century.[20]

The framework of *Divrey ha-Yamim* is thus patently broader than its title alone might suggest. To attribute this to the strictly chronological arrangement of the book and the banal fact that French history began long before that of the Ottoman Turks is to sidestep the issue. Had Joseph ha-Kohen been concerned merely with a history of the two peoples, he could have begun just as easily with the rise of the Ottomans in the fourteenth century, prefixing a schematic summary of French history up to that time, and from thence continued along parallel lines. Instead we find, prior to the appearance of the Ottomans, a mass of material whose overriding theme is the conflict of great powers, and its fulcrum the struggle over Palestine. Not the history of any particular nation, not even that of France, but the *interaction* between nations, is the leitmotiv that runs through the history Joseph chooses to recount before he actually touches upon the Ottomans: Byzantium and Persia, the Arabs and the Byzantines, above all—the Crusades. The components are readily transferable into other terms: Europe vs. Asia, East and West, above all—Christendom and Islam. For it is with the rise of Islam and its conflict with Christian Byzantium that the opening section of the book really achieves its momentum (significantly, the establishment by Muhammad of a new religion is described even before the account of the Persian-Byzantine wars). From this perspective we can understand the inordinate attention lavished upon the Crusades themselves, for these epitomized the enduring global confrontation of the two faiths. This pattern of international conflict is the very matrix out of which the book as a whole emerges, and it provides an important clue toward an understanding of what the author had in mind. "France" and "Turkey" are what they are, their histories are treated soberly and concretely, and yet they are also more than they seem at first glance. Within the context of *Divrey ha-Yamim* they are perceived, respectively, as the most important contemporary representatives of Christendom and Islam.

That Joseph ha-Kohen should have focused upon the Ottoman Turks once he decided to venture forth into the history of the nations requires little comment. By the sixteenth century the Turkish menace to Europe was sufficient to constitute a pan-European obsession, and myriad books and pamphlets were devoted to them in a variety of languages.[21]

On the other hand, his reasons for choosing France as the preeminent Christian nation are not at all clear, at least initially. His personal background does not explain it. Though born in Avignon in 1496, this was not French, but papal territory. At the age of five he moved with his parents to Italy where, in Genoa and its environs, he spent the rest of his life. He himself invariably referred to his Spanish lineage.[22] Whence his preoccupation with France?

One could simply reply, of course, that France in the first half of the sixteenth century was indeed a dominant European power. But then, so was its arch-rival, the Empire. If France had the edge and loomed larger in the mind of Joseph ha-Kohen, I would suggest that it was because it seemed to him historically the crusading nation par excellence. This was not entirely a matter of caprice on his part. As his own account in *Divrey ha-Yamim* reveals, he saw that it was Frenchmen who had established and sustained the Latin Kingdom of Jerusalem and that it was France alone that had participated consistently in all the first four Crusades. He even records the crusades of Louis IX (the 7th and 8th Crusades) which ended with his death in Tunis.[23] Although, by the sixteenth century, the notion of a crusade against Islam was becoming less a reality than an excuse for despoiling other Christian states, the crusading idea and its rhetoric continued to exercise a powerful influence in Europe, especially as the Ottoman peril increased. Joseph ha-Kohen would not have been alone in casting France into the role of defender of Christendom. Appeals to France to lead an actual crusade against the Turk were not wanting nor, as we shall see, were there no French gestures in that direction.

Yet there is something about the very conception of *Divrey ha-Yamim* that still remains elusive. Even if I am correct in positing that the book is at its core a history of the conflict between Christendom and Islam, epitomized in the Crusades, and dwelling upon France and Turkey as the prime contemporary heirs of an age-old struggle, the question with which we began may still be pressed. Why should a Jew be so interested in such matters as to write a book about them? While there was no dearth of works devoted exclusively either to Turkish history or to that of individual European nations, I know of no precedent in the whole of sixteenth-century historigraphy, whether Jewish or non-Jewish, for a work that explicitly *combines* the history of the Ottoman Turks with that of any other state. This is to say that Joseph ha-Kohen could not have been imitating any other historical work directly when he conceived his dual history. He may have had, however, an important and vital source of inspiration in certain aspects of Jewish messianic tradition.

3. Gog and Magog

"If thou seest empires contending with one another — expect the footsteps of the king-messiah."[24] With a slight twist, Rabbi Eleazar b. Avina's ancient admonition may be of relevance to modern historians as well. When we find Jews in bygone ages expressing a sudden and keen interest in the conflict of nations, we may well expect that the interest is primarily messianic. Only in one Jewish genre do we find reflected periodically an intense alertness to global conflicts, and that is in apocalyptic literature. With the authority of the tradition of the "wars of Gog and Magog" behind them there have always been Jews who, ordinarily indifferent to world events, have been roused by a major international struggle to heightened expectations of an imminent messianic advent.

While some apocalyptic texts express their concerns on a wholly mythical level, others betray a careful scrutiny of historical events and incorporate them either directly or obliquely.[25] Of course, the form which even this type of apocalyptic literature assumes is, at least on the surface, an inversion of historiography. Instead of recording historical events as having taken place, the apocalyptic *vaticinium ex eventu* is ostensibly predictive of them. But form aside, it is the preoccupation with wars between nations that is of moment for our inquiry. Whatever else may separate them, it is striking that *Divrey ha-Yamim* has this in common with the apocalyptic tradition, and that in turn suggests some sort of direct relationship.

Certainly the period in which Joseph ha-Kohen lived was one of particularly vigorous messianic speculation and activity among Jews.[26] The cataclysmic events that had begun with the Turkish conquest of Constantinople, and had climaxed for Jewry with the Iberian expulsions at the end of the fifteenth century, had also set the stage for an accelerated messianic fervor in the sixteenth. Much of it expressed itself in a classically apocalyptic vein which, though validating itself through a messianic exegesis of biblical and other texts, took full cognizance of contemporary world events and scanned the political horizon for intimations of the wars of Gog and Magog. Limiting ourselves to the first half of the century, and without spelling out details that are well known, it will suffice to mention the astrological prognostications of Abraham Zacuto,[27] the remarkable apocalyptic works of his brother-in-law Abraham ben Eliezer ha-Levi,[28] and the David Reuveni–Shlomo Molkho episode which, as far as Reuveni's role was concerned, unfolded against an attempt to bring about a Christian crusade against the Turks and thus a final collision between Christendom and Islam.[29] Italian Jewry was particularly susceptible to every messianic tiding and, perhaps because of its geographic location, often served as an eschatological news-agency for other parts of the Jewish world. Messianic and apocalyptic texts originating elsewhere were copied here and disseminated further. Despite the repeated collapse of messianic dates, new ones were always forthcoming, and as late as 1575 messianic enthusiasm in Italy was sufficiently widespread to evoke a call for restraint from Azariah de' Rossi.[30]

That Joseph ha-Kohen should have been aware of the apocalyptic currents of his time is plausible to begin with. Can traces of such an awareness be found in *Divrey ha-Yamim*? The Ottoman

Turks consistently play a major role in the Jewish messianism of the age. But what of France? While we have already found warrant for Joseph's choice of France as foil to Turkey by virtue of its historical crusader role, it would be especially interesting to see if France figured in messianic speculation as well.

In fact, a messianic role was already forecast for France in 1494, at the very outset of the French invasions of Italy which figure so prominently in *Divrey ha-Yamim*. "There has seldom been in Western European history," writes Marjorie Reeves, "a series of events so widely viewed within the framework of prophetic drama as the Italian expedition of Charles VIII."[31] Whether Charles was seen as the Second Charlemagne of Joachite prophecy, or as the new champion of the Christian crusade, there was an almost universal popular belief that Naples was to be only a stepping stone on the way to an eventual reconquest of Greece and Jerusalem.[32]

Remarkably, such expectations were not without their parallel in certain Jewish quarters as well. In a text published by Samuel Krauss from the colophon of a Vatican manuscript of *Sefer ha-Peliah* we read that the troubles unleashed for the Jews between 1490 and 1495 are the birthpangs of the messianic age, and that in the year 1503 the salvation of Israel will be achieved. In between, the Italian expedition of Charles VIII is seen as the fulfillment of Daniel's prophecy concerning the King of the North.[33]

It is not necessary to assume that Joseph ha-Kohen was aware of this specific prophecy, which has survived merely by chance.[34] The very existence of such expectations attached to France among both Christians and Jews is significant. From the Christian side the hopes associated with Charles VIII did not disappear after his death in 1498, but continued to devolve in some measure upon his successors, Louis XII and Francis I. For their part, the French monarchs found it advantageous to continue the pose of Crusaders against the Turks even when they did little to live up to the expectations they aroused. The same pronouncements and promises of a Turkish crusade were repeated in 1507–08 when the Ottomans defeated the Mameluks.[35] Indeed, the notion of France as the spearhead of Christendom against the Turks did not die out entirely even when it was challenged on this very score by the Empire. Needless to say, in the sixteenth century as in the past, the idea of a Crusade was never quite free of messianic overtones. Joseph ha-Kohen's own concern with the conflict of nations thus appears to us now within a broader configuration than before. Structurally and thematically related to Jewish apocalyptic tradition, the concrete focus on France and Turkey also mirrors certain contemporary eschatological perceptions.

4. Internal Evidence

To be sure, *Divrey ha-Yamim* is not an apocalyptic tract but a work of history. Most of its narratives are presented in a straightforward manner and with considerable attention to historical detail. Nonetheless, there are a number of messianic elements in the book, and they are neither casual nor fortuitous. While some may be subjected to varying interpretations, two, at least, are fairly explicit and even revelatory.

The first of these is of capital importance. It crops up in the passage, already quoted, in which Joseph ha-Kohen comes closest to a clear statement of purpose, and we are now perhaps in a better position to appreciate its significance. *Ki hine yamim ba'im* is, biblically and in subsequent Jewish tradition, an almost archetypal messianic phrase. Roused, as he says, by the French and Spanish expulsions, Joseph wants his fellow-Jews to know "what they did to us in their lands, their courts and their castles" (these word are an echo from Kalonymos ben Kalonymos' *Even Boḥan*),[36] "for behold the days approach." The latter phrase is Joseph's own addition, and it would not be there if it were not meant seriously. Always laden with a sense of messianic imminence, here it must surely establish a connection between that which is related in the book and a messianic dénouement. Yet if so, then something of a sleight-of-hand has taken place. As I have stressed, the bulk of what is contained in *Divrey ha-Yamim* does not deal with Jewish afflictions but with the history of the "French" and the "Turks" to which the title alludes. We must perforce juxtapose to "behold the days approach," not what Joseph states here to be the primary content of the book, but its real content, and conclude that herein lies the vital connection that motivated him in the first place. The dawning of the messianic era was to be discerned, not only out of the length and intensity of Jewish suffering, as in Usque's *Consolaçam*, but out of a contemplation of the pattern of international conflict throughout history and now again in his own time.

Lest it appear that I am placing too great a burden on a single phrase (though it occurs in the most central context imaginable), let us turn to the second messianic clue in the book — the extensive account of David Reuveni and Shlomo Molkho in Part II.[37] This displays a number of singular features, not the least of which is the incorporation of the full text of a letter written by Molkho in 1531 to a group of rabbis. While the purpose of the letter was to inform his correspondents of what had happened to him since his arrival in Italy from Turkey, the nature of its contents makes it almost a messianic tract, for in addition to recounting his tribulations at the hands of informers, and especially of his nemesis, the physician Jacob Mantino, Molkho describes events charged with messianic resonance. He tells how he came to Rome and prayed for its destruction and for the redemption of Israel. In the midst of the *Amida* prayer his "Rabbi" [heavenly *Maggid*?] periodically spoke messianic verses into his ear. In an act of supreme messianic symbolism Molkho dressed himself in filthy rags and sat for thirty days among the beggars and lepers on the outskirts of the city. There he was finally vouchsafed a truly apocalyptic dream, set in Palestine and itself filled with symbols, in which a flood of the Tiber in Rome and an earthquake in Portugal were predicted, to be followed by a Turkish conquest of the West leading to the dawn of the messianic age for Jewry. Toward the end of the letter Molkho offers a messianic schema of twenty-eight "ages" in history leading to the ultimate redemption, based upon a homiletic exegesis of the third chapter of Ecclesiastes. "And now," he writes, "we are in the Time of Love, in which the Lord will fulfill for us the verse (Jer. 31:3): *I have loved thee with everlasting love, therefore with affection have I drawn thee*."

A copy of this letter came into Joseph ha-Kohen's possession.[38] That he saw fit to reproduce the whole of it in *Divrey ha-Yamim* (where it occupies no less than 11 folios) is already indicative of the importance he attached to it. The fact that it is the *only* contemporary document to be published *verbatim* in the book gives its inclusion added weight, and the absence of any negative comment shows that he wholeheartedly endorsed its contents.

It is clear that Joseph believed in the authenticity of Molkho's messianic mission. While he was ambivalent, at least *post factum*, about Reuveni (he calls him a "stumbling block" to the Portuguese Marranos and states that his claim to have been sent by a brother who was king of the Lost Tribes was finally exposed as false), he viewed Molkho in truly messianic terms. The very manner in which he introduces Molkho into his narrative leaves no doubt on this score: "*And there came forth a shoot from Portuagal (ve-yatza ḥoter mi-portugal)*, Shlomo Molkho was his name." His life, as Joseph describes it, was tinged with the miraculous. Though at first he knew no Torah in Portugal, after he circumcised himself "the Lord granted wisdom to Solomon, and almost in an instant he became wiser than any man, and many were amazed at him." In expounding the arcana of the Kabbalah "the spirit of the Lord spoke through him."

Even Molkho's death at the stake in Mantua in 1532 did not cause Joseph ha-Kohen to lose faith in him. He sees him as wrapped in the halo of martyrdom ("And God smelled the sweet savor and gathered his pure soul"). He even goes so far as to report the rumor that Molkho somehow escaped death and was seen for eight days in the house of a Jew before he finally disappeared. Though he admits to some doubt about this, he does not rule it out, and years later, in *Emek ha-Bakha*, he repeats the tale again.[39]

The prominence accorded the Molkho episode in *Divrey ha-Yamim*, coupled with "behold the days approach," serves also to alert us to other, more subtle elements in the book, that might otherwise be glossed over. Turning back to the preamble, we realize that it closes with two eminently messianic verses (Is. 35:6 and 12:5),[40] and that at the very end of the book Joseph states that he completed it in the year *ve-ḥash* (וח"ש) *atidot lamo* (Deut. 32:35) with its reverberations of an imminent messianic retribution against the nations ("Vengeance is Mine and recompense against the time when their foot shall slip, for the day of their calamity is at hand, *and the things that are to come upon them make haste*"). In a similar way the passage immediately following the account of the Spanish expulsion, with its otherwise conventional mosaic of fragments from the Psalms, achieves a fresh sense of urgency: "Yet have we not forgotten Thee, neither have we been false to Thy covenant; now, O God, be not far, O God, make haste to help us; for Thy sake have we been killed all the day, we have been accounted sheep for the slaughter; make haste to help us, O Lord of our salvation; and fight our cause and redeem us!" (See Psalms 44:18, 71:12, 44:23, 38:23).

It is also important that we garner whatever glimpses we can of the mentality at work in the book. This is not an easy task, for Joseph ha-Kohen generally effaces himself behind the narrative. Yet although *Divrey ha-Yamim* stands out, on one level, for its calm and methodical recital of historical events, there is occasionally great passion as well, and much besides. At certain points statements break through the narrative surface that point to deeper preoccupations. Thus, after describing the sufferings of German Jewry during the First Crusade, he introduces his account of the journey of the crusaders to the East as follows:[41]

> Joseph ha-Kohen declares: You have seen the great anguish that befell our people in those days. . . . And now I have undertaken to write what befell our enemies along all the road they travelled, so that the Children of Israel may know that the Lord is zealous and avenges the blood of His people that has been shed . . . and also, because they captured the Land of Israel and Judah and defiled it with their uncleanness and abominations for eighty-eight years, in the end the verse was fulfilled for them: *and your enemies shall be astonished at it* [Lev. 26:32]. . . .

When Saladin entered Jerusalem "he gave orders and they broke the bells of the high-places [i.e. the churches] . . . and they are still broken, to the disgrace of the uncircumcised unto this day, *and all this was from the Lord, it is marvelous in our eyes*"[42] (cf. Ps. 118:23). When the last of the Crusader kingdoms fell, the event was presaged by an earthquake, "and the uncircumcised could no longer maintain themselves in that province, for from heaven did they wage war against them in order to drive them out of the Land of Israel."[43]

Divine intervention is also directly involved at two crucial stages in the history of the Ottoman Turks. Concerning their emergence, Joseph writes: "In those days the Lord raised up Ottoman ben Ziah and his young dynasty."[44] When he describes the Turkish conquest of Constantinople, he concludes: "At that time the Lord fulfilled the word that he spoke through the prophet Jeremiah, saying — [*Rejoice and be glad, O daughter of Edom* . . .,] *the cup shall pass over unto thee also, thou shalt be drunken and shalt make thyself naked* [Lam. 4:21]."[45]

In one place Joseph shows, at least, that he is not at all averse to the use of *gematria*. Describing an attack against the Jews of Aix-en-Provence in 1430, he writes that this calamity was foretold in Psalm 69:2 — "Save me, O God, for the waters are come in even unto the soul" (כ"י בא"ן מי"ם ע"ד נפ"ש).[46] Though it is possible that he found his computation in his source, the fact that the numerical value of the final word yields him the *Christian* date of the event makes it far more likely that it was his own. The rendering of dates according to the Christian era is one of the striking features of *Divrey ha-Yamim* itself.

Illuminating, too, is the lengthy description of Charles V's abortive expedition to conquer Algiers in October, 1541, an attempt that ended in disaster when most of his huge armada was wrecked in a tremendous storm off the African coast.[47] Joseph's narrative is here almost entirely dominated by supernatural elements. The Jews of Algiers, he writes, were terrified at the approach of the Spanish fleet, and the Lord answered their prayers:

On that night the Lord of Hosts could not sleep, and He found it written: *And yet for all that, when they are in the land of their enemies, I will not reject them* . . . and the Lord descended in a cloud and warred against the nations . . . and they did not understand one another's speech, for the Lord confused their thoughts, and they ceased to do battle against the city. . . .

The storm at sea is described similarly, as due to the direct action of God, for "from heaven did they wage war against the Emperor's men." There was a great earthquake in Genoa and the borders of Milan, and people said "it is a sign from the Lord." The Emperor's retreat was dogged by further catastrophes. The Jews of Algiers, rejoicing at their deliverance, "sang, saying — *I will sing unto the Lord, for He is highly exalted, the horse and his rider hath He thrown into the sea* [Exod. 15:1], *for the Lord is a God of knowledge, and by Him actions are weighed* [I Sam. 2:3]."

The most revelatory statement, however, occurs toward the end of this account:

During those many days nothing was known in Italy concerning the Emperor's ships, for travelers had ceased to cross the sea. But in a dream I saw, and behold — a sailing ship, plated with gold and very beautiful, came to the shore, and at its top was an image of gold, and from within the sound of blasting trumpets, and many people ran to me so that they might also see and hear what would be said. But when [the ship] arrived there was no sound, except for one sick man like a seething pot stretched out upon it, and another man steering it, and I awoke and lo — it was a dream, and there was no one to interpret it for me. Then I thought: *Do not interpretations belong to God* [Gen. 40:8]? That which the Lord is doing far away he has told to His servant. So I said to my friends at that time: This can only be a sign that the Emperor will return empty-handed, and just as his sword made women childless, so will his ships be bereaved, and the remnant of his men will return here wasted by hunger and devoured by the fiery bolt, and ye are my witnesses that the Lord hath spoken, I forewarn you this day! And so it came to pass.[48]

This anecdote, unique in the book, is all the more valuable for the insight it yields. For once a corner of the veil is lifted and we catch a brief glimpse of an aspect of Joseph ha-Kohen that we would not otherwise have known, but which complements certain impressions we have derived on other grounds. If, in the preamble to the book, he has presented himself as a second Josephus, here he is identified with the biblical Joseph. Taken together, these two "Josephs" are perhaps a perfect metaphoric expression of what he combined within himself, for he was indeed both Joseph the historian and Joseph the dreamer and interpreter of dreams. By his own explicit admission we see here that the sources of his inspiration were not merely historical. He is susceptible to predictive divinatory dreams, and it is interesting to note that in the one recorded here there is a symbol that harks back to the Book of Daniel — the "image of gold" (*tzalma de-dahava*: cf. Daniel, Ch. 3). Furthermore, he does not keep the dream to himself, but relates and interprets it to certain close friends (*va-omar el ma'ahavai*). Although, regrettably, these are not named, there is obviously a circle with whom to share such a dream, and who are willing to listen. The ending — *va'atem eydai ki ha-shem diber; ha'idoti bakhem ha-yom* — also merits attention. Such a sonorous exhortation to his "friends," all the more solemn, indeed, for being made up of phrases spoken in the Bible only by God, indicates that more is at stake than this particular dream. One senses, rather, that this is only a special instance through which a more general divinatory power of Joseph's is to find its validation, and if so, one cannot help wondering what other forecasts he may have been offering his friends over the years.

As far as the book itself is concerned, we remain tantalized but not satisfied. Though I have argued from a number of different angles that Joseph ha-Kohen's "Franco-Turkish" history, which has no precedent in historiography, must necessarily be related to Jewish apocalyptic — it is to be reiterated emphatically that the book as it stands is not an apocalypse but an historical work. The apocalyptic element is latent, embedded in the structure, but all that transpires is recorded as *past*, as *history*. Despite the hints and clues we have gathered, we seem to reach a kind of impasse. What must be accounted for is, in effect, a book whose inspiration and aim may have been apocalyptic, but whose final character is pre-eminently historical.

5. The Evolution of the Book

The dilemma, however, may be illusory. I would propose that the way to resolve it lies in considering the possible manner in which *Divrey ha-Yamim* came into being. By Joseph ha-Kohen's own statement at the end, the book was "completed" by him at the end of Ḥeshvan, [5]314, that is — in October of 1553, not long before its publication in Sabbionetta. But that, of course, tells us nothing about how long it took to compile or to write, let alone when the idea of it was first conceived. In 1553 Joseph was some fifty-seven years old, an age which, though not impossible, is rather late for a first book. Of his life until then only certain external events are known, but nothing of his inner development. His extant earlier writings consist of some youthful occasional poems, and various letters, some of which deal with the ransom of captives, and others revolving around a family quarrel with his sister Clara.[49]

Fortunately, as Loeb demonstrated, we do have some important evidence as to his methods of working. For example, he was in the habit of requesting information from his correspondents and recording them in notebooks — for this purpose he asks his brother Meir, probably then in Salonika, to send him authentic news of what is happening in the East.[50] Further, he was constantly revising and adding to his work. This is clearly manifest in the composition of *Emek ha-Bakha* where, perhaps because he did not print the work, various strata are even *dated* (1557/8; August 23, 1560; November 22, 1564; June 29, 1575).[51]

There is every reason to assume that it was no different with *Divrey ha-Yamim*. Indeed, the very existence of a third part to the book, written after the publication of the first two and bringing the recital of events up to 1563, confirms it. Loeb was quite correct in stating: "Il complétait constamment sa première rédaction, et ajoutait des notes et des faits nouveaux, mais oubliait quelquefois de mettre ces additions d'accord avec l'ancien texte."

The question really concerns the Sabbionetta edition of *Divrey ha-Yamin*. What we know of its later amplification, as well as the mode in which *Emek ha-Bakha* was composed, must be applicable here as well. We can safely posit, by analogy, that *Divrey ha-Yamim* came into being through a gradual evolution rather than a single spurt, and by this I have in mind not only the process of compiling the materials, but the actual writing.

There is, in fact, yet another reason for such an assumption. It has to do once more with Joseph ha-Kohen's choice of France as one of his two primary subjects. But whereas earlier we were content to ask *why* he chose to focus on France, now we may well ask *when* he might have done so.

Such a choice would be hard to comprehend if *Divrey ha-Yamim* was first planned and written in the few years immediately prior to 1553, for by the mid-sixteenth century the image of France as the spearhead of Christendom against the Turks had become tarnished. That position had been increasingly usurped by the Empire. Beginning in 1519 with his defeat in the imperial election by Charles V, Francis I felt obliged to reverse the earlier course of his reign. Though he still desired to be the defender of Christendom against the Turks and continued to pose as such, he realized that he must actually begin to use the Turks to defend France against the Empire.[52] The first French overtures to the Turks were made already in 1523, during the captivity of Francis I in Madrid, and were followed by various diplomatic probes in subsequent years. Naturally, it took some time until the public at large became fully aware of the drift of French policy, and French propaganda was geared to keep up appearances as long as possible. But in 1536, when a French-Turkish treaty was signed, the collusion with the Infidel was plain for all to see, and beyond the borders of France the treaty stirred up a general clamor.[53] In the next year there was an abortive joint attempt by the French and the Turks to seize southern Italy. In 1543, to the scandal of the whole of Christian Europe, a Turkish fleet wintered at Toulon.[54]

By contrast, it was Charles V who gradually inherited the crusader mantle from France, not merely by default, but because parts of his vast empire were in direct confrontation with the Turks and he himself was capable of genuine crusading acts.[55] In

1529 Vienna repulsed a Turkish assault. In 1535 Charles V took Tunis. In 1541, as we have seen, he tried to take Algiers.

If, against the background of these developments, Joseph's plan for a dual history of the French and the Turks would be somewhat anachronistic if it had originated with him at mid-century or even a decade before, we are led to surmise that it must have matured much earlier, at a time when the real power of France had not yet been seriously threatened by the Empire, when its crusader-pose was still fully credible, and when, in consequence, the eschatological hopes centered around it by both Christians and Jews (though from opposite vantage-points) might still retain a strong element of plausibility.

Precisely when the plan of the work first crystallized is impossible to determine. The only aspect that can be specified with a modicum of certainty is a *terminus post quem* for the beginning of the actual writing. I have been able to ascertain that Joseph's information on the Ottoman Turks up to 1530 is taken, sometimes word for word, from Paolo Giovio's *Comentario de le cose de' Turchi*, first published in Rome in 1531.[56] If Joseph must therefore have written these sections after that year, by the same token we have learned that this important source was already available to him as early as that.

In trying to grasp the evolving character of the book we may also be helped by considering its formal arrangement. As published in 1553, *Divrey ha-Yamin* is divided into two discrete parts, the first running from the seventh century to 1520, the second from 1521 to 1553 and prefaced by a somewhat garbled account of the Portuguese and Spanish explorations. Once again, had the book been written in one concentrated and continuous effort, it would be hard to see the need for such a division, for it adds nothing to the whole and merely seems to interrupt its flow arbitrarily.

There is, however, a simple alternative explanation. We have but to entertain the possibility that what now constitutes Part I was at first the entire book, an independent entity, and that Part II was added subsequently (just as was the third part later on). Regarded as a separate work originally meant to stand on its own, Part I of *Divrey ha-Yamim* shows itself to be self-contained and, in fact, more tightly structured and coherent than what follows afterward. The pattern of conflict between Christendom and Islam stands out more clearly and consistently than in Part II, where Joseph is increasingly involved in relating the details of the continuing wars in Italy between the French and imperial forces. This conjecture can also be supported by internal evidence (for example, the Spanish and Portuguese discoveries really belong chronologically in Part I, yet they appear in Part II).

But what of Part I itself? Pursuing the same line of reasoning a step further, we must conclude that it too could not have emerged full-blown, but may rather have grown by stages. Something of the sort was already noted by Loeb in trying to account for inconsistencies in the accounts of the French expulsions.[57] Yet although Joseph did not succeed (or did not care) to smooth out every discrepancy in his evolving text, and though a closer examination of the extant manuscripts must surely shed more light on its development, in the end it is not the text that is at issue. For the text itself was the result, not only of revision and editing, but of a significant inner spiritual and intellectual development that anteceded it. To recapture the details of the process may be impossible, given the materials at hand, but its vital core — the metamorphosis of apocalyptic into historiography — can at least be understood on both theoretical and contextual grounds.

6. From Messianism to History

Based on considerations that have been amply discussed thus far, we may well conjure up something akin to the following model:

1. Like many other Jews in the early sixteenth century, the young Joseph ha-Kohen was caught up in the messianic-apocalyptic currents of the age.
2. In addition to the Ottoman Turks, who figured heavily in all apocalyptic speculation at the time, he fixed upon France as the primary Christian factor on the other side of the apocalyptic equation.
3. "France" and "Turkey" were perceived by him, not only in their concrete contemporary reality, but as the final actors in an age-old drama of world conflict between Christendom and Islam that was now heading rapidly toward an apocalyptic conclusion.
4. *It was such active messianic concerns that awakened his interest*

in world history, and especially in the history of the two paradigmatic nations.

5. Once embarked upon the study of history, however, he became absorbed with the past for its intrinsic interest as well, and while his apocalyptic hopes were not thereby displaced, they were tempered and modified in the process. To this a variety of additional factors may have contributed — the passing, without result, of a succession of predicted messianic dates; the tragic end of Shlomo Molkho; a growing awareness, perhaps, that while history exhibits meaningful configurations, it does not easily yield specific conclusions.

6. Whatever his original intentions, at some point, possibly in the early 1530s, Joseph ha-Kohen set his materials in order and wrote a "History of the Kings of France and of the Ottoman Turkish Sultans" that proceeded chronologically to 1520 (the loss of the imperial election by Francis I and the death of Sultan Selim I). This would later become Part I of the book as we know it.

7. That he did not publish this immediately, but continued to add to it until 1553, is significant as well. The continual "updating" of history by the periodic addition of new strata is yet another hallmark of much of apocalyptic literature, and points once more to a common ground. With each successive delay in a predicted messianic advent the apocalyptic visionary is forced to account for it by grafting on the intervening events and making it seem as though they too had been foretold. While Joseph was not under so severe a constraint, it was perhaps in the very nature of his undertaking that he too could leave no "gap" so long as the messianic age had not dawned. Indeed, his apparent life-long hesitation to have his works printed (the first two parts of *Divrey ha-Yamim* are the one exception) may well reflect a reluctance to commit himself prematurely, before ongoing events might clarify retroactively what was still blurred in the past, and thus point more definitively to the future.

8. By 1553, when Part II was completed, he was certainly aware of the shifts that had occurred in the European constellation, yet apparently he did not see in this a sufficient reason to change his fundamental emphasis. Perhaps because he had conceived his work long before and had invested too

much in "France" to begin all over again, perhaps because it was for him as much symbol as reality, France retained its centrality in the book and in the very title. As for the contemporary situation in Europe, he took due note of the major changes. In Part II, superimposed upon the continuing history of the wars between Christendom and the Turks, there are extensive accounts of the conflicts between the two great European powers whose outcome, even at mid-century, was still in doubt.

9. The book that was published in Sabbionetta reveals its apocalyptic origins, but is no longer coextensive with them. By the time Joseph had completed it, perhaps even by the time he came to write, the apocalyptic element, though never abandoned, was sublimated. It is there in the title and structure, and a sense of messianic urgency peeps repeatedly through the crevices in the narrative. But the result, despite the inevitable ambiguities, is indeed "history." No explicit messianic conclusions are drawn, no dates proclaimed. In marked contrast to the pristine apocalyptic vision, which chains historical events to a rigid scheme and, as it were, predetermines their outcome, in *Divrey ha-Yamim* history is open-ended and fluid. There is room for as full an account of events as possible, and an eagerness to relate them. The book carries no esoteric "message," no fixed and hidden code to be deciphered; it has become its own message. The salvation of Israel is to emerge, by divine providence, out of the chaos of global conflict among its enemies. No more than this is suggested, no less.

Much of this particular reconstruction is, of course, necessarily speculative, though I trust not arbitrary. The one point to be insisted upon is the potential inherent in an apocalyptic interest in history, once aroused, to be transmuted into a genuine absorption with history itself.

In general it may be observed that the relation of Jewish messianism to history is a dialectical one. While messianic belief in any form is nothing if not a supreme "historical" hope, it may engender radically different attitudes and perceptions. Messiansim has the capacity both to vitiate history and to validate it. Thus, if the enormous emphasis on a fulfillment that can be attained only in the future often distracted Jews from the mundane details of the historical past or present,[58] there were also times when messianic hopes had the opposite effect. The difference seems to be contingent on the temporal dimensions of messianic belief at any given juncture. So long as the time of the coming of the Messiah, however inevitable, is felt to be indeterminate, or far off in a distant future, the unfolding of historical events elicits little interest among Jews. History appears profane, repetitious, inscrutable, and to be concerned with it is, literally and figuratively, a "waste of time." It is otherwise, however, in times of acute messianic tension, when the end of exile and the messianic advent are perceived, not as distant, but as closely approaching. At such times, for some Jews at least, events that would normally be ignored are now seen as portentous. History, hitherto bland and tedious, now seems dynamic, charged with meaning. Nowhere is this process seen to better advantage than in certain forms of apocalyptic where, as I have adumbrated earlier, there is a sudden surge of interest, not merely in Jewish history, but in that of the nations of the world.

To be sure, such an interest in history does not yet lead necessarily to historiography. But it can provide a bridge toward it. As far as antiquity and the Middle Ages are concerned, the question still awaits a more extensive exploration than is possible here.[59] For our more specific purpose it will suffice to confine the discussion to the sixteenth century. A glance at the age in which Joseph ha-Kohen lived and created will indicate that the nexus between messianism and history which I have argued for *Divrey ha-Yamim* is by no means isolated, but finds its reflection, and perhaps its further confirmation, within a discernible pattern.

The extent to which messianism, apocalyptic and historiography either commingle or coexist in the sixteenth century is sufficiently striking to deserve more attention than it has hitherto received. It is most obvious in Elijah Capsali's *Seder Eliyahu Zuta*, with its blatantly messianic reading of Ottoman Turkish history, and in Samuel Usque's *Consolaçam*, which scans the whole of Jewish history as the fulfillment of biblical prophecy and proclaims that the dawn of the messianic era is at hand, subject only to the return of the Portuguese Marranos to Judaism. The convergence of messianism and history is also present in other sixteenth-century Jewish historians even when it does not find full expression in their historical works. Let us recall that Abraham Zacuto was not only the author of *Sefer Yuḥasin*, but of astrological prognostications for the unfolding of redemption in 1531, and that he spent his last years at the Jerusalem yeshiva of R. Isaac Sholal, a hotbed of apocalyptic activity.[60] Gedaliah ibn Yaḥya, in his *Shalshelet ha-Kabala*, places considerable stress on messianic calculations, and offers 1598 as the messianic year.[61] Conversely, it is noteworthy that Isaac Abravanel, whose messianic trilogy is both a summation and re-affirmation of Jewish messianism at the end of the fifteenth century, and who looked to 1503 for the messianic advent, proposed also to write a *history*, to be entitled *Yemot Olam*.[62] If the pattern does not seem to hold for David Gans and Azariah de' Rossi that is because, unlike the others, they do not emerge out of the spiritual milieu of post-expulsion Sephardic Jewry, and their works, for other reasons as well, must be considered apart. Of the historians within the Sephardic ambiance (and it is they who were largely responsible for creating the bulk of the historiographical corpus), Solomon ibn Verga is the only one who displays no manifest attraction for messianism, and he may be the exception to prove the rule. But then, we have only his *Shevet Yehuda* to go by, and we know next to nothing about his life. (For the record, let it be noted that Azariah de' Rossi copied out, in his youth, several astrological and apocalyptic treatises of both Abraham Zacuto and Abraham ben Eliezer ha-Levi.[63] This was in 1531, and one may at least wonder whether, at this phase of his life, he was merely copying such texts as a dispassionate exercise.)

The correspondences we have briefly sketched here are not without moment for a fresh look at sixteenth-century Jewish historiography as a whole. In effect, the common explanation which attributes the phenomenon to the impact of the expulsion from Spain may well be, for all its merits, somewhat simplistic. That messianism, apocalyptic, and historiography go hand in hand and interpenetrate at so many points, indicates that an important mediating factor may have been overlooked. I mean to suggest by this that Jewish historiography arose in the sixteenth century, not so much because the trauma of the Spanish expulsion brought Jews into a direct confrontation with history in which they sought causes and explanations (this might be true only of Ibn Verga), but because the expulsion brought Jewish messianism to a new pitch of intensity which, in turn, conferred upon history a renewed eschatological significance. Not merely a preoccupation with the troubled present, but a powerful and widespread intuition of an impending, radically altered future, would thus prove to have been decisive in stimulating a new interest in the past. Some, like Abraham ha-Levi, and like Zacuto in his astrological treatises, were content to remain entirely within the parameters of traditional apocalyptic, albeit with more recent historical materials to nourish their vision. Others, notably Capsali, Usque and Joseph ha-Kohen, turned toward a detailed study of the past and channeled their messianic vision into historical works.

Of the three, it was Joseph ha-Kohen who moved farthest along the path from apocalyptic to historiography, and not without reason is he the only one to style himself an historian. Even so, his work, like those of the others, cannot be severed from its messianic context and purpose. *Divrey ha-Yamim* was not written, as is sometimes suggested, because of Renaissance influences (these remain superficial and incidental), nor out of a sudden curiosity about the history of non-Jews. The implicit justification for *Divrey ha-Yamim* remained precisely this — that the history of the gentile nations, and especially the record of the wars they have fought and are fighting, is of eschatological relevance for Jews, and that it would be well to study and ponder such matters even if the specific details of the coming redemption still reside with God alone.

NOTES

1. For these and other general aspects, see my "Clio and the Jews: Reflections on Jewish Historiography in the Sixteenth Century," *Jubilee Volume of the American Academy for Jewish Research* (Jerusalem, 1980), II, 607-638.

2. Abraham Zacuto, *Sefer Yuḥasin*, ed. H. Filipowski, 2nd ed. with an introduction by A. H. Freimann (Frankfurt a.M., 1925), pp. 231ff. David Gans, *Tzemaḥ David* (Prague, 1592), Introduction to Part II.

3. Elijah Capsali, *Seder Eliyahu Zuta*, ed. A. Shmuelevitz, S. Simonsohn and M. Benayahu, 2 vols. (Jerusalem, 1975-77). The Venetian chronicle ("Sipurei Venetziya") occupies pp. 215-327 of Vol. II.

4. The original Ladino text is still in manuscript. An abridgement, transliterated into Latin characters, was published in Madrid in 1638. See Y. H. Yerushalmi, *From Spanish Court to Italian Ghetto* (New York-London, 1971), pp. 167f.

5. Gedaliah ibn Yaḥya, *Shalshelet ha-Kabala* (Venice, 1587), fols. 90v-118r.

6. All forthcoming references to *Divrey ha-Yamim* are to the first edition, Sabbionetta, 1554 (henceforth abbreviated as *DH*). The book is numbered recto only, and in the JTSA copy the numbers only begin to appear with fol. 41. References to earlier pages in the notes that follow are therefore in accordance with my own consecutive pagination.

7. These include not only poems, letters, and a grammatical work, but also his Hebrew translations (with insertions of his own) of Francisco López de Gómara's *Historia general de las Indias* ("Ha-India ha-Ḥadasha") and *La conquista de México* ("Sefer Fernando Cortes").

8. See Isidore Loeb, *Josef Haccohen et les chroniqueurs juifs* (Paris, 1888), pp. 7-15.

9. Both the Sabbionetta and Amsterdam (1733) editions of parts I and II are filled with typographical and other errors. More surprisingly, the edition of Part III by D. Gross (Jerusalem, 1955) is defective, leaving out entire passages from the British Museum manuscript. See H. H. Ben-Sasson, *The Reformation in Contemporary Jewish Eyes* (Proceedings of the Israel Academy of Sciences and Humanities, IV, no. 12), separate preprint (Jerusalem, 1970), p. 44, n. 127.

10. M. Letteris' edition, largely indebted to S. D. Luzzatto (Vienna, 1852; reprinted Cracow, 1896), must be regarded as unsatisfactory. See, for example, the significant corrections and variants (from an Alliance MS) by Loeb, *Josef Haccohen*, pp. 26-31. Cf. also *REJ*, X, 248ff.

11. *Shulḥan Arukh, Oraḥ Ḥayyim*, no. 307:16, and Isserles' gloss.

12. *DH*, verso of the title-page.

13. In common with all Jews prior to modern times, Joseph ha-Kohen regarded *Sefer Yosipon* as a Hebrew work of Josephus Flavius.

14. **נערתי חצני** literally — "I shook out my lap" (Neh. 5:13). As used here the phrase is somewhat ambiguous, and may refer to that which he had "gleaned among the sheaves after the reapers," i.e., the sparse materials he found among his predecessors.

15. *DH*, fols. 18v, 45v.

16. *DH*, fol. 113v.

17. *DH*, fol. 77. the expulsion of "1186": fol. 67r.

18. The entire account occupies one page (fol. 112r-v).

19. *DH*, fols. 11v-68v.

20. *DH*, fol. 81v.

21. See the valuable bibliography (numbering almost 2500 separately printed items) compiled by Carl Göllner, *Turcica: Die europäischen Türkendrucke des XVI Jahrhunderts*, Vol. I (Bucarest-Berlin, 1961), Vol. II (Bucarest-Baden Baden), 1968.

22. *DH*, preamble; ibid., fol. 118v; *Emek ha-Bakha*, p. 109.

23. *DH*, fol. 80r.

24. *Bereshit Raba*, ed. J. Theodor-Ch. Albeck (reprint, Jerusalem, 1965), Ch. 42, p. 409.

25. Such, for example, are some of the apocalypses assembled in Y. Even-Shemuel's *Midreshei Ge'ula*, 2nd ed. (Jerusalem, 1954), especially "Nistarot de-R. Shim'on ben Yoḥai" (pp. 187-98), "Ma'aseh Daniel" (pp. 209-28), and "Tefilat R. Shim'on ben Yoḥai" (pp. 268-86). On the latter cf. also the analysis of Bernard Lewis, "An Apocalyptic Vision of Islamic History," *Bulletin of the School of Oriental and African Studies*, XIII (1949-51), 308-38.

26. On 16th-century Jewish messianism in general, see A. H. Silver, *A History of Messianic Speculation in Israel* (Boston, 1959), ch. VI, pp. 110-50, and the anthology of A. Z. Aescoly, *Ha-Tenu'ot ha-Meshiḥiot be-Yisrael* (Jerusalem, 1956), pp. 231-417.

27. See the texts published by C. Roth, "The Last Years of Abraham Zacut," *Sefarad*, IX (1949), 445-54, and M. Beit-Arié and M. Idel, "Ma'amar al ha-Ketz ve-ha-Itztagninut Me'et R. Abraham Zacut," *Kiryat Sefer* 54 (1979), pp. 174-92.

28. G. Scholem, "Ha-Mekubal R. Abraham b. Eliezer ha-Levi," *Kiryat Sefer*, II (1925/26), 101-41, 269-73; VI (1930/31), 149-65, as well as his bibliographically updated introduction (ed. M. Beit-Arié) to a partial facsimile of ha-Levi's *Ma'amar Meshare Qitrin, Constantinople, 1510* (Jerusalem, 1977). See also M. Beit-Arié, "Igeret me-Inyan Aseret ha-Shevatim Me'et R. Abraham b. Eliezer ha-Levi ha-Mekubal mi-Shenat [5]288," *Kovetz al Yad*, New Series, VI (XVI) (1966); Ben-Sasson, *Reformation*, pp. 22ff.

29. *Sipur David ha-Reuveni*, ed. A. Z. Aescoly (Jerusalem, 1940). See, in particular, Reuveni's account of his interview with Clement VII (p. 35 of the text) in which he urges the pope to bring about a truce between France and the Empire, obviously in order that they join forces against the Turks, a common plea among Christian advocates of a crusade at that time. Cf. A. Shoḥat, "Le-Parashat David ha-Reuveni," *Zion* 35 (1970), 96-116, who argues that Reuveni primarily had the Portuguese in mind when he came to the pope. In either case, of course, the result would be the same, a Christian attack against the Turks

and a head-on confrontation. The desire to provoke such a world conflict is the only clear element in Reuveni's otherwise obscure mission. Indeed, it is entirely possible that in the first phase, which took place in Eqypt, Reuveni's plan lay in the opposite dirrection, and that he wanted the Turks to take the initiative. This may have been the "secret" he revealed to Abraham de Castro, i.e.. that he, as head of the Eqyptian mint, use his influence at the Sultan's court in Constantinople to urge a Turkish onslaught against Europe. De Castro, however, firmly rebuffed him, and this may well have led to a change of strategy, though not of ultimate goals, in which the conflict would be opened by a Christian power.

30. For a summary of the various messianic and apocalyptic currents in 16th-century Italy, see D. Tamar, "Ha-Tzipiya be-Italya li-Shenat ha-Ge'ula [5]335," *Sefunot* 2 (1958), 61-88.

31. M. Reeves, *Joachim of Fiore and the Prophetic Future* (New York, 1977), p. 85. and the discussion, ibid., pp. 85-87, as well as her more comprehensive study of *The Influence of Prophecy in the Later Middle Ages* (Oxford, 1969), pp. 354-58. Cf. also H. F. Delaborde, *L'expédition de Charles VIII en Italie* (Paris, 1888), pp. 313ff.

32. C. D. Rouillard, *The Turk in French History, Thought and Literature (1520-1660)* (Paris, n.d.), pp. 29f.

33. S. Krauss, "Le roi de France Charles VIII et les espérances messianiques," *REJ* LI (1906), 95:

אני חושב שהצרות שמצאו היהודים בכל ממלכות אדום משנת הר"ן לאלף הששי עד שנת הרנ"ה הן הם חבלי משיח, והמלחמות שהיו באיטליאה כשבא מלך צרפת קארלו שמו הם מה שנבא דניאל על מלך הצפון כדי לכלות האומות ....

34. Though I do not insist upon it, a faint echo of such prophecies may possibly be discerned in the very manner in which Joseph describes Charles VIII's Italian expedition. After laying out the historic French claim to the Kingdom of Naples, he writes of Charles' initial successes (*DH*, fol. 116v): ויהיו בעוזריו ככבי השמים וכסיליהם. Later, after describing the French retreat, he states (fol. 118v):

ויאמר קארלו המלך לשוב שנית לאיטליה ביד חזקה ולא יכול, כי נסוגו אחור כוכבי שמיו, ועצת ה' היא תקום.

35. R. Schwoebel, *The Shadow of the Crescent: The Renaissance Image of the Turk (1453-1517)* (Nieuwkoop, 1967), p. 202.

36. See *Even Boḥan*, ed. A. M. Habermann (Tel-Aviv, 1956), p. 113.

37. *DH*, fols, 206v-219v.

38. In the Alliance MS described by Loeb (*Josef Haccohen*, no. 1, pp. 7f.), which bears the famous reproduction of Molkho's elaborate signature.

39. *DH*, fol. 219r-v; *Emek ha-Bakha*, p. 117.

40. My student Abraham Gross has drawn my attention to the significant comment of David Kimhi on the latter verse, associating it explicitly with the wars of Gog and Magog. Isaiah 12:5 reads: זמרו ה' כי גאות עשה מודעת זאת בכל הארץ. Kimhi writes:

כמו שאמר על ים סוף כי גאה גאה, וזאת הגאות תהיה מודעת בכל הארץ, שיוציא עם דל מבין עמים הרבים והעצומים. ומגפת גוג ומגוג גם כן תהיה מודעת בכל הארץ. ועל זה ראוי לכם לזמר לה'.

41. *DH*, fol. 18v.
42. *DH*, fol. 65r.
43. *DH*, fol. 78v.
44. *DH*, fol. 81v.
45. *DH*, fol. 97r.
46. *DH*, fol. 91v-92r.
47. *DH*, fols. 263r-267r.
48. *DH*, fol. 266v.
49. Loeb, *Josef Haccohen*, pp. 1-15, itemizes the various materials.
50. Ibid., p. 20.
51. See Loeb's chronology of Joseph's life (op. cit., pp. 18f.), and D. Gross's introduction to his edition of Part III of *Divrey ha-Yamim*, p. 10.
52. Rouillard, *The Turk in French History*, pp. 34-37.

53. The treaty is noted in *DH*, fol. 235r. On the reaction in Europe see C. Göllner, "Der Einfluss der öffentlichen Meinung auf das Türkenbündnis Franz I. von Frankreich," *Revue historique du sud-est européen* 20 (1943), 208-27.

54. Rouillard, op. cit., 113-23.

55. See F. C. Spooner in *The New Cambridge History*, II (Cambridge, 1958), p. 336.

56. Göllner, *Turcica*, I, no. 413, who also lists all the editions and translations of the work. I shall give examples of Joseph's use of Giovio in a separate article devoted to the sources of *Divrey ha-Yamim*.

57. Loeb, *Josef Haccohen*, p. 20. Idem, "Les expulsions des juifs de France au XIVe siècle," in the Graetz *Jubelschrift* (Breslau, 1887), 39-56.

58. See G. Scholem, "Toward an Understanding of the Messianic Idea in Judaism," in: *The Messianic Idea in Judaism and Other Essays on Jewish Spirtuality* (New York, 1971), p. 35 (on the "price" paid by the Jewish people for its messianism).

59. But see, for the moment, the suggestive remarks of Yeḥezkel Kaufmann on the correlations, in the centuries from the destruction of the First Temple to the end of the Second Temple, between periods of prophetic activvity and of historiography (*Toldot ha-Emuna ha-Yisraelit*, VII [Jerusalem, 1956], pp. 392ff., 451ff.), and Gerson D. Cohen's interpretation of the messianic roots and aims of Abraham Ibn Daud (*Sefer Ha-Qabbalah: The Book of Tradition* [Philadelphia, 1967]).

60. See A. Shoḥat, "R. Abraham Zacut bi-Yeshivato shel R. Yitzḥak Sholal," *Zion* 13-14 (1948/49), 43.

61. *Shalshelet ha-Kabala*, fol. 47v. According to Ibn Yaḥya's account, the insight first came to him spontaneously in 1556, upon awakening from a sleep preceded by restless questioning as to the time of the Redemption. The discussion of messianic calculation occupies fols. 44v-47v in the book.

62. He apparently began the work in Monopoli in 1495/96 but never completed it. See B. Netanyahu, *Don Isaac Abravanel* (Philadelphia, 1953), p. 75.

63. Jerusalem, National and University Library MS Heb. 8° 3935. See Beit-Arié and Idel, "Ma'amar al ha-Ketz," 174.

Some Recent Research

BERNARD D. COOPERMAN

Baron, S. W. *History and Jewish Historians.* Philadelphia: 1964.

———. "Humanism and the Renaissance," *A Social and Religious History of the Jews, 2nd ed., XIII.* New York: 1969. Pp. 159–205.

Barzilay, I. E. *Between Reason and Faith.* The Hague — Paris: 1967. See also the review by Joseph Sermonetta in *Kiryat Sefer* 45 (1969/70), pp. 539–46.

Beit-Arié, M. "An Epistle Concerning the Ten Tribes by R. Abraham b. Eliezer ha-Levi, 5288," [Hebrew]. *Kovetz al Yad*, n.s. 6 (1966), pp. 369–378.

——— and Idel, M. "An Essay Concerning the End and Astrology by R. Abraham Zacut," [Hebrew]. *Kiryat Sefer* 54 (1979), pp. 174–92.

Ben-Sasson, H. H. "Exile and Redemption through the Eyes of the Spanish Exiles," [Hebrew]. *Yitzḥak F. Baer Jubilee Volume.* Jerusalem: 1960. Pp. 216–227.

———. *Hagut ve-Hanhaga* [Philosophy and Leadership]. Jerusalem: 1959.

———. "The Reformation in Contemporary Jewish Eyes." *Proceedings of the Israel Academy of Sciences and Humanities* 4 (1971).

———. "Wealth and Poverty in the Teaching of the Preacher Reb Ephraim of Lenczyca," [Hebrew]. *Zion* 19 (1954), pp. 142–166.

Ben-Shlomi, J. *The Mystical Theology of Moses Cordovero* [Hebrew]. Jerusalem: 1965.

Bernstein, S. "New Poems of R. Samuel Archevolti," [Hebrew]. *Tarbitz* 8 (1936/37), pp. 55–68 and 237.

Bettan, Israel, *Studies in Jewish Preaching.* Cincinnati: 1939.

Bonfil, Reuben. "Expressions of the Uniqueness of the Jewish People in Italy during the Renaissance," [Hebrew]. *Sinai* 76 (1975), pp. 36–46.

———. *Ha-Rabanut be-Italya bi-Tkufat ha-Renesans* [The Italian Rabbinate during the Renaissance]. Jerusalem: 1979.

Breuer, Mordekhai, "Rabbi David Gans, Author of the *Tzemaḥ David* — an Outline," [Hebrew]. *Bar-Ilan* 11 (1972/73), pp. 97–118.

———. "The Aims of the *Tzemaḥ David* by Rabbi David Gans," [Hebrew]. *Ha-Ma'ayan* 5, no. 2 (Tevet, 5725 [1964]), pp. 15–27.
David, Abraham. "The Historiographic Accomplishment of Gedaliah ibn Yaḥya, Author of *Shalshelet ha-Kabbala*," [Hebrew]. Ph.D. dissertation, Hebrew University. Jerusalem: 1976.
Damiens, S. *Amour et intellect chez Léon l'Hébreu.* Toulouse: 1971.
Dan, J. "Hebrew Homiletical Literature in Renaissance Italy," [Hebrew]. *Proceedings of the Sixth World Congress of Jewish Studies.* Jerusalem: 1977.
———. "The Sermon 'Tfila ve-Dim'a' by R. Judah Moscato," [Hebrew]. *Sinai* 76 (1975), pp. 209–32.
Elbaum, Jacob. "Rabbi Judah Loew of Prague and his Attitude to Aggadah." *Scripta Hierosolymitana* 22 (1971), pp. 28–47.
———. "Trends and Courses in Jewish Speculative and Moralistic Literature in Germanic Lands and Poland during the Sixteenth Century," [Hebrew]. Ph.D. dissertation, Hebrew University. Jerusalem: 1977.
Fraenkel-Goldschmidt, H. "Introduction to *Sefer ha-Makne* of Joseph ben Gershom of Rossheim," [Hebrew]. Ph.D. dissertation, Hebrew University. Jerusalem: 1969/70.
Geffen, M. David. "Faith and Reason in Elijah del Medigo's *Beḥinat ha-Dat* and the Philosophic Background of the Work." Ph.D. dissertation, Columbia University. New York: 1970.
Guttmann. J. "Elia del Medigos Verhältnis zu Averroës in seinem *Bechinat Ha-Dat.*" *Jewish Studies in Memory of Israel Abrahams.* New York: 1927. Pp. 196ff.
Hacker, Joseph. "Despair of Redemption and Messianic Hope in the Writings of Rabbi Solomon le-Beit ha-Levi," [Hebrew]. *Tarbitz* 39 (1970), pp. 195–213.
———. "Israel Among the Nations as Described by Solomon le-Beit Ha-Levi of Salonika," [Hebrew]. *Zion* 34 (1965), pp. 43–89.
Idel, Moshe. "The Curriculum of Yoḥanan Alemanno," [Hebrew]. *Tarbitz* 48 (1980), pp. 303–331.
———. "Magic Temples and Cities in the Middle Ages and the Renaissance," [Hebrew]. *Jerusalem Studies in Islam and Arabic* 3 (1982).

———. "The Sources of the Circle Images in the *Dialoghi d'Amore*," [Hebrew]. *Iyun* 28 (1978), pp. 156–166.

———. "Three Versions of the Letter of R. Isaac of Pisa[?]," [Hebrew]. *Kovetz al Yad*, n. s. (1982).

Kaplan, Lawrence. "Rationalism and Rabbinic Culture in Sixteenth-Century Eastern Europe: Rabbi Mordecai Jaffe's *Levush Pinat Yikrat*." Ph.D. dissertation, Harvard University. Cambridge, MA: 1975.

Katz, Jacob. "The Debate over *Smikha* between R. Jacob Berav and RaLBaḤ," [Hebrew]. *Zion* 16 (1951), pp. 28–45.

———. *Tradition and Crisis.* New York: 1961.

Kieszkowski, Bohdan. "Les rapports entre Elie del Medigo et Pic de la Mirandole." *Rinascimento* 4 (1964), pp. 78–91.

Kleinberger, A. F. *Ha-Maḥsava ha-Pedagogit shel ha-MaHaRaL mi-Prag* [The Educational Philosophy of the MaHaRaL of Prague]. Jerusalem: 1962.

Kupfer, E. "The Visions of R. Asher b. Meir of Lemlein Reutlingen," [Hebrew]. *Kovetz al Yad* n.s., 8 (1975/76), pp. 385–423.

Nadav, Y. "An Epistle of the Kabbalist R. Isaac Mar Ḥayyim on the Doctrine of *Tzaḥtzaḥot*," [Hebrew]. *Tarbitz* 26 (1962/63).

Neher, A. *David Gans.* Paris: 1974.

———. "The MaHaRaL of Prague as Humanist," [Hebrew]. *Hagut Ivrit be-Eyropa.* Tel-Aviv: 1969. Pp. 107–117.

———. "L'exégèse biblique juive face à Copernic." *Studies Presented to M. A. Beek.* Amsterdam: 1974. Pp. 190–96.

———. "New Material on David Gans as Astronomer," [Hebrew]. *Tarbitz* 45 (1976), pp. 138–147.

Netanyahu, B. *Don Isaac Abravanel.* Philadelphia: 1953.

Neuman, A. A. "Abraham Zacuto, Historiographer." *H. A. Wolfson Jubilee Volume*, II. Jerusalem: 1965. Pp. 597–629.

Pflaum, H. *Die Idee der Liebe.* Heidelberg, 1926.

Rosenthal, E. J. F. "Yohanan Alemanno and Occult Science." *Prismata: Naturwissenschaftgeschichtliche Studien. Festschrift für Willy Hartner* (Wiesbaden: 1977).

Rosenthal, G. "R. Yehiel Nissim da Pisa's 'Ma'amar al ha-Adam ha-Tzadik ve-Takhlit ha-Olam,'" [Hebrew]. *Kovetz al Yad* n.s., 9 (1975/76), pp. 451–478.

Roth, Cecil. *The Jews in the Renaissance.* Philadelphia: 1959.

———. "The Last Years of Abraham Zacut." *Sefarad* 9 (1949), pp. 445–454.

Ruderman, David. "The 'Igeret Orhot Olam' by Abraham Farissol in its Historical Context," [Hebrew]. *Proceedings of the Sixth World Congress for Jewish Studies.* Jerusalem: 1976. Pp. 169–178.

———. *The World of a Renaissance Jew: The Life and Thought of Abraham ben Mordecai Farissol.* Cincinnati: Hebrew Union College Press, 1981.

Sack, Bracha. "The Mystical Theology of S. Alkabez." Ph.D. dissertation, Brandeis University. Waltham, MA: 1977.

Scholem, Gershom. *Avraham Cohen Herera, Ba'al Sha'ar ha-Shamayim: Ḥayyav Yetzirato ve-Hashpa'ata* [Abraham Cohen Herrera, Author of *Shaar ha-Shamayim*: His Life, His Works and Their Influence]. Jerusalem: 1978.

———. "Zur Geschichte der Anfange der christlichen Kabbalah." *Essays Presented to Leo Baeck.* London: 1954.

Secret, F. *Les kabbalistes chrétiens de la Renaissance.* Paris: 1964.

Shmeruk, Ch. "Basic Characteristics of Yiddish Literature in Poland and Lithuania up until 1648/49," [Hebrew]. *Tarbitz* 46 (1977), pp. 258–314.

Shoḥat, Azriel. "Concerning David Reubeni," [Hebrew]. *Zion* 35 (1970), pp. 96–116.

———. "R. Abraham Zacut in the Yeshiva of R. Issac Sholal," [Hebrew]. *Zion* 13–14 (1948/49), pp. 43–46.

Shulwass, Moses A. *The Jews in the World of the Renaissance.* Leiden: Brill, 1973.

Sonne. Isaiah. "Expurgation of Hebrew Books — The Work of Jewish Scholars." *Bulletin of the New York Public Library* 46 (1942), pp. 975–1015.

———. *From Paul the Fourth to Pius the Fifth* [Hebrew]. Jerusalem: 1954.

Tamar, David. "The Messianic Expectations in Italy Concerning the Year 5335," [Hebrew]. *Sfunot* 2 (1958), pp. 61–88.

Tishby, Y. "The Polemic on the Book of the Zohar in the Sixteenth Century in Italy," [Hebrew]. *Prakim: Yearbook of the Schocken Institute (1966/67).*

———. *Torat ha-Ra ve-ha-Klipa be-Kabalat ha-ARI* [The Theory of Evil and of the "Shells" in the Kabbalah of R. Isaac Luria]. Jerusalem: 1942.

———. *Netivey Emuna u-Minut* [Byways of Faith and Heresy]. Ramat-Gan: 1964.

Twersky, Isadore, "R. Joseph Ashkenazi and Maimonides' *Mishne Tora*," [Hebrew]. *Salo Wittmayer Baron Jubilee Volume*, Hebrew section. Jerusalem: 1974. Pp. 183–194.

Werblowsky, R. J. Zwi. *Joseph Karo, Lawyer and Mystic.* 2nd ed. Philadelphia: 1977.

Wirszubski, H. *Mekubal Notzri Kore ba-Tora* [A Christian Kabbalist Reads the Law]. Jerusalem: 1977.

———. *Shlosha Prakim be-Toldot ha-Kabala ha-Notzrit* [Three Chapters in the History of Christian Kabbalah]. Jerusalem: 1975.

Yerushalmi, Y. H. "Clio and the Jews: Reflections on Jewish Historiography in the Sixteenth Century." *Jubilee Volume of the American Academy for Jewish Research.* Jerusalem: 1980. Vol. II, pp. 607–638.

———. *The Lisbon Massacre of 1506 and the Royal Image in the 'Shebet Yehudah.'* Cincinnati: 1976.

CENTER FOR JEWISH STUDIES

HARVARD JUDAIC MONOGRAPHS

1. *David Kimhi: The Man and the Commentaries*, by Frank Talmage

2. *Studies in Medieval Jewish History and Literature*, edited by Isadore Twersky

3. *Decoding the Rabbis: A Thirteenth-Century Commentary on the Aggadah*, by Marc Saperstein

4. *Hispano-Jewish Culture in Transition: The Career and Controversies of Ramah*, by Bernard Septimus

HARVARD JUDAIC TEXTS AND STUDIES

1. *Rabbi Moses Naḥmanides (Ramban): Explorations in His Religious and Literary Virtuosity* edited by Isadore Twersky

2. *Jewish Thought in the Sixteenth-Century*, edited by Bernard Dov Cooperman